Immigration and the Constitution

Volume 2
Discrimination and Equality in Contemporary Immigration Law

Edited with introductions by

Gabriel J. Chin
University of Cincinnati College of Law

Victor C. Romero
Pennsylvania State University, Dickinson School of Law

Michael A. Scaperlanda
University of Oklahoma College of Law

GARLAND PUBLISHING, INC.
A MEMBER OF THE TAYLOR & FRANCIS GROUP
New York & London
2000

Published in 2001 by
Garland Publishing, Inc.
29 West 35th Street
New York, NY 10001

Published in Great Britain by
Garland Publishing, Inc.
11 New Fetter Lane
London EC4 4EE

Garland is an imprint of the Taylor & Francis Group

10 9 8 7 6 5 4 3 2 1

The Library of Congress Cataloging-in-Publication Data

Immigration and the constitution / edited with introductions by
Gabriel J. Chin, Victor C. Romero, Michael A. Scaperlanda.
p. cm. — (Controversies in constitutional law)
Includes bibliographical references.
Contents: v. 1. The origins of constitutional immigration law — v. 2. Discrimination and equality in contemporary immigration law — v. 3. Shark infested waters : procedural due process in constitutional immigration law.
ISBN 0-8153-3346-3 (alk. paper)
1. Emigration and immigration law—United States. 2. Constitutional law—United States. 3. United States—Emigration and immigration—Government policy. I. Chin, Gabriel J. (Gabriel Jackson), 1964-. II. Romero, Victor C. III. Scaperlanda, Michael A. IV. Series
KF4819.A2 I4265 2000
342.73'082—dc21 00-064646
CIP

3 volume set ISBN:	**0-8153-3346-3**
Volume 1	0-8153-4059-1
Volume 2	0-8153-4060-5
Volume 3	0-8153-4061-3

Contents

Introduction

In four distinct parts, this volume introduces the current debate surrounding the constitutional rights of noncitizens in the United States. Much of the contemporary discussion on immigrants' rights focuses on the inherent tension between the claims by individual noncitizens to constitutional protection and Congress's plenary power to make immigration law as it sees fit.

The four articles in Part A provide different perspectives on this tension. Linda Kelly's piece, *Preserving the Fundamental Right to Family Unity: Championing Notions of Social Contrast and Community Ties in the Battle of Plenary Power Versus Aliens' Rights*, introduces the reader to three oft-cited theories advanced by other professors to properly balance noncitizens' rights claims against governmental interests in controlling immigration. David Martin's "membership" theory asserts that noncitizens are entitled to due process commensurate with their "membership in the national community."[1] Instead of classifying cases as involving plenary power or noncitizens' rights, Martin proposes evaluating claims based on the degree to which a person is a member of the American community.

In contrast, Alex Aleinikoff shifts the focus away from "membership" and onto "community ties." Aleinikoff relies not so much on a noncitizen's membership status to determine the process due her, but rather on the different relationships the noncitizen has developed with American society. Thus, according to Aleinikoff, a noncitizen's interest in entering or remaining within a community depends in part on her ability to "maintain established ties with the community."[2] Kelly then applies these two theories to different alienage categories, concluding that while both models would likely provide substantial due process protections to citizens and legal permanent residents, neither would adequately safeguard the rights of undocumented immigrants because they presumably have neither the membership status nor the requisite ties to the community to afford them protection.

This is where the third theory — Gerald Neuman's version of the "mutuality" concept — fills the gap in protection for certain noncitizens left open by the two other theories.[3] Neuman contends that even undocumented noncitizens should be protected by a nation's laws to the same extent that such nation requires compliance with its laws.[4]

Because it is less bounded by notions of social contract than either Martin's or Aleinikoff's theories, Neuman's approach appeals to Kelly in her search for a paradigm applicable to family unification issues in the immigration context. Pursuant to Kelly's amalgam of the three theories, a court would evaluate the noncitizen's rights claim by first asking the "mutuality" question: "Is the noncitizen subject to U.S. law? If so, she must be afforded some protection of our laws. The extent of that protection is determined by a balancing of the individual's interests compared with the government's."[5]

While he also advocates greater constitutional protection for noncitizens, Frank Wu takes a slightly different tack in his article, *The Limits of Borders: A Moderate Proposal for Immigration Reform*. Wu argues that the federal constitution should apply to immigration laws in the same way it applies to other federal, state, and local statutes. And while he does not enumerate when and how many rights — say, the First Amendment right to free association[6] — would apply at the border, Wu concerns himself specifically with racial bias in the admission and expulsion of immigrants. He asserts that the plenary power doctrine should have no force when invoked by noncitizens claiming they have been denied admission to the United States on the basis of race or some other suspect classification.

Wu's model justifies his method of applying constitutional doctrine to immigration law by appeals to the text and structure of the federal constitution. Textually, most of the document's rights provisions apply not just to citizens, but to generic persons as well, signifying the Framers' intent to protect more than American citizens. Therefore, affording constitutional protection to immigrants at the border comports with the text's command that both citizen and noncitizen be free from government overreaching.

As a second point, Wu contends that the structure of the federal constitution would be diminished by exempting immigration law from its purview. Conversely, the constitution and civic culture would be enhanced by subjecting immigration law to constitutional scrutiny by fully preserving the egalitarian tenets captured by the document. Wu's concern about the perceived foreignness of Asians and Latinos is not some paranoid delusion but rather a reflection of racial politics in America today. By not sparing immigration law from constitutional scrutiny, courts would ensure that citizens of color receive the full protection of the laws already granted them outside immigration.

Instead of subscribing to the dichotomy of the "plenary power versus immigrants' rights" paradigm developed in the Kelly and Wu pieces, Michael Scaperlanda attempts instead to create a unified theory for explaining the Supreme Court's alienage jurisprudence in his contribution titled, *Partial Membership: Aliens and the Constitutional Community*. Scaperlanda asserts that the Supreme Court approaches constitutional challenges brought by noncitizens by following this two-part process: The Court first asks whether "membership" issues are relevant to the government action at issue. Unlike David Martin's use of the term, "membership" to Scaperlanda refers to the Court's deferral to the political branches with respect to issues of communal formation. Thus, if the challenged legislation goes to the heart of executive or legislative privilege, then the Court is reluctant to review the law. And second, if no membership issues are present, the Court is more likely to strictly scrutinize the law at issue.

Scaperlanda derives his theory by first noting that, as both Kelly[7] and Wu[8] mention, the current legislative milieu is decidedly anti-immigrant. However, while acknowledging historical precedent for this anti-immigrant mood, Scaperlanda uses the current immigration debate as a backdrop for a renewed analysis of the Court's alienage jurisprudence. Citing the work of Linda Bosniak,[9] Scaperlanda agrees with her that the defining question should be whether the government's treatment of noncitizens beyond admission and exclusion is an extension or incident of Congress's plenary power over immigration.

After noting the primacy of the membership paradigm, Scaperlanda then goes on to question whether federal membership issues, which include the formation of non-political as well as political communities, is a superior model to the state membership ideal in which deference is only given to state legislation designed at political communal formation. Scaperlanda posits that the state membership model is more persuasive than the federal one because political communal formation by the state's members logically necessitates the deliberation of those who are citizens of the state only, even if it excludes nonresidents.

Despite highlighting the unpersuasive nature of the federal model of plenary power, Scaperlanda does not foresee the Court embracing immigrants' rights claims in the wake of discriminatory Congressional action. In Scaperlanda's eyes, the Court often refuses to protect noncitizens' rights, leaving the body politic with the responsibility of ensuring protection for immigrants. While he is justifiably cautious in his assessment of whether the political branches will respond favorably to a dialogue about noncitizens' constitutional rights, Scaperlanda believes that establishing a viable political discourse should be the paramount concern. Given the Court's abdication of its guardianship role, Scaperlanda asserts that valuing the dialogue over noncitizens' rights by incorporating it into the general political process will likely lead to the best balance between legitimate national interests and the inherent personhood of immigrants.[10]

Victor Romero's piece titled, *Expanding the Circle of Membership by Reconstructing the 'Alien': Lessons From Social Psychology and the 'Promise Enforcement' Cases*, adopts Scaperlanda's two-tier approach and accepts his premise that the Supreme Court privileges notions of membership over the personhood of noncitizens. After tracing the genesis of this tension in both the historical and legal traditions of the United States, Romero applies Scaperlanda's theory to three recent "promise enforcement" cases to show how notions of membership and personhood come in conflict. The third case, *Ramallo v. Reno*,[11] is a compelling illustration of this tension. In *Ramallo*, the Immigration and Naturalization Service ("INS") promised the noncitizen criminal defendant that it would not initiate removal proceedings if he cooperated with the U.S. Attorney's Office. The INS then reneged and began to deport the noncitizen. Adopting the personhood paradigm, the trial court ruled that the INS could not breach its own promise not to deport the cooperating noncitizen. This victory was short-lived. On appeal, the Court of Appeals for the D.C. Circuit held that the then-recently enacted Illegal Immigration Reform and Immigrant Responsibility Act of 1996 ("IIRAIRA")[12] stripped the federal courts of their jurisdiction over removal proceedings initiated by the Attorney General. The *Ramallo* case is a perfect illustration of the primacy of Scaperlanda's membership paradigm; the district court's decision to protect Ramallo's personhood was overturned by an appeals court deferring to the plenary power of Congress to decide jurisdictional issues unessential to the concept of political formation.

Romero then asks whether there might be some political solution, as Scaperlanda suggests, to counteract the ill effects of *Ramallo* and decisions like it. He suggests that the answer might lie in the work of critical race theorist Jody Armour[13] and social psychologists Gregory Maio et al.[14] on insider group perceptions of the out-group in society. Drawing from Armour's and Maio et al.'s research, Romero argues that citizens engaged in Scaperlanda's constitutional dialogue might use positive, non-stereotypical messages about the noncitizen to help overcome societal biases and facilitate an honest evaluation of the court-stripping provisions of the IIRAIRA. He concludes that such an evaluation will lead to a repeal of these laws once society realizes that they can be used to grant government the power to renege on its promises to individuals, citizen and noncitizen alike.[15]

The three remaining parts of this volume examine individual rights claims which have been shielded by the Constitution when asserted by citizens, but have not enjoyed nearly the same amount of protection when brought forth by noncitizens.

Part B focuses on issues of race and national origin as they influence the national debate over immigration and immigrants' rights. Kevin Johnson's article titled, *Race, The Immigration Laws, and Domestic Race Relations: A "Magic Mirror" Into The Heart of Darkness*, examines the intersection of racial and alienage discrimination in United States history to support his thesis: "[T]he differential treatment of citizens and noncitizens serves as a 'magic mirror' revealing how dominant society might treat domestic minorities if legal constraints were abrogated."[16] Johnson systematically reviews the history of race-based exclusionary policies in U.S. immigration laws, contrasting them with some of the gains secured by African-Americans during similar time periods. He notes, for example, how the Asian Exclusion Laws followed closely on the heels of the enactment of the Fourteenth Amendment and other benefits of Reconstruction.[17]

Johnson explains the apparent contradiction in these events by referencing psychological theories of transference and displacement. He asserts that the negative treatment of noncitizens reveals what the majority society would do to citizens of color if racial discrimination was constitutionally permissible. Because many current laws ban overt racial discrimination, the majority society thus transfers its outsider hostility from racial minorities and displaces it to noncitizens, which is permissible under the plenary power doctrine.

Johnson admonishes citizens of color to pay heed to the warnings implicit in his analysis of the anti-immigrant movement. Careful attention to the historical links between alienage and racial discrimination will serve those well who would hope to change immigration and social policy by making them more egalitarian in ways that transcend racial discrimination.

In contrast to Johnson's article, which focuses on race and immigration issues, *Legal Assistance for Vietnamese Asylum Seekers v. Department of State*[18] deals with the issue of national origin discrimination in the context of immigration law. The consolidated cases involved claims against the U.S. State Department's policy requiring Hong Kong-based Vietnamese and Laotian exiles seeking U.S. immigrant visas to return to their home countries for processing instead of applying to the U.S. consulate in Hong Kong.

The plaintiffs claimed that this policy violated the nondiscrimination clause of the Immigration and Nationality Act ("INA"), was arbitrary and capricious under the Administrative Procedure Act ("APA"), and infringed their equal protection rights guaranteed under the Fifth Amendment's due process clause.

In the first case, *LAVAS I*, the court of appeals panel split 2-1 in favor of the plaintiffs, holding that the clear language of the INA's anti-discrimination clause forbade the State Department from forcing the visa applicants to return to their home country solely on the basis of their national origin. The court never reached the constitutional issue.

In the second case, *LAVAS II*, the D.C. Circuit had the opportunity to consider these issues again in light of Congress's promulgation of the IIRAIRA, Section 633 of which amended the INA's anti-discrimination clause to exempt from its purview the Secretary of State's authority to determine the locations where immigrant visa applications would be processed. Finding that Section 633 raised no retroactivity concerns, the court concluded that plaintiffs' INA and APA claims failed by direct application of Section 633. Addressing the constitutional claim, the court first accepted plaintiffs' concession that the noncitizen migrants were barred from stating a claim under the Fifth Amendment challenging the procedures for granting immigrant visas. With the primarily injured plaintiffs barred, the court quickly dispatched of the citizen sponsors' claims by stating that the State Department's venue policy did not discriminate against them on the basis of national origin. Even assuming that Vietnamese- and Laotian-born familial citizen sponsors might legitimately claim national origin discrimination, the court concluded that this ethnic link was not a necessary condition. Nor could the citizen-sponsors have any rights greater than those of the claim-barred immigrants. Like the *Ramallo* case described in Romero's article,[19] the *LAVAS* cases illustrate the courts' total abdication of the duty to protect noncitizen rights when faced with a Congress that has decided to curtail such rights through legislative action.

Part C explores gender and illegitimacy in the immigration context. Joan Fitzpatrick's piece, *The Gender Dimension of U.S. Immigration Policy*, advocates greater scrutiny of gender issues in developing a coherent U.S. immigration policy. Despite the fact that women constitute a majority of the legal immigrants to the United States each year, federal policymakers have never consistently considered the disparate adverse impact immigration laws have on women. It is only when concerned citizens engage in a concerted lobbying effort does positive change occur. As an example, Fitzpatrick cites amendments to the "marriage fraud" provisions of the immigration code that allow for battered wives to self-petition for lawful permanent residency rather than be captive to the whims of an abusive citizen husband.

Fitzpatrick cites other areas of U.S. immigration policy where gender-specific effects should be considered. The 1986 amnesty programs for undocumented immigrants, for instance, were decidedly pro-male, especially the provisions granting legal status to certain agricultural workers, 82% of whom were men.[20] More recently, the 1996 "welfare reform" law denying public benefits to lawful permanent residents will disproportionately affect elderly immigrant mothers and divorced immigrant housewives. Even within the area of asylum law, Fitzpatrick notes that the U.S. government's reluctance to consider gender-specific circumstances in a refugee applicant's nation distorts reality and produces unfair results. The INS's insistence that a persecuted woman seek a safe haven within her country as a first alternative to migration ignores the fact that girls seeking to escape from tribal genital mutilation, for example, might not find support among members of a patriarchal society who view such behavior from women as subversive. By identifying these different immigration policies, Fitzpatrick takes a first step towards mobilizing other successful efforts to create a more gender-balanced immigration policy.

The last two pieces in this section are the Supreme Court's recent decision in *Miller v. Albright*[21] and an ensuing student note in the *Harvard Law Review*,[22] commenting on the case. In *Miller*, the Court ruled that 8 U.S.C. § 1409(a)(4)'s requirement that a citizen father take affirmative steps to confer U.S. citizenship upon his "illegitimate" child when a citizen mother was not required to do so, did not violate the Constitution's equal protection guarantees.

Despite the 6-to-3 vote in favor of upholding the statute, there were three different opinions concurring in the judgment, and two dissenting ones; needless to say, not one opinion garnered majority support: Stevens, O'Connor, and Scalia each drafted opinions concurring in the judgment, and each in turn was joined by a single Justice — Rehnquist joined Stevens, Kennedy sided with O'Connor, and Thomas followed Scalia. The two dissenting opinions were drafted by Ginsburg and Breyer, and each joined the other's opinion; Souter joined both dissenting opinions.

As the student note suggests, if *Miller v. Albright* stands for the idea that citizens' rights challenges may be made even within the plenary power-bounded confines of immigration law, then the Supreme Court might be amenable to other similar challenges to purportedly unconstitutional immigration laws. However, because it is the Court's latest statement on equal protection guarantees inherent in the immigration code, only time will tell whether *Miller* turns out to be the vehicle for greater immigrants' rights protection.

Part D rounds out this volume by examining the question of sexual orientation and immigration. While homosexuality is no longer considered a psychological disease, and therefore, not a ground for exclusion, homosexuals are not given the same rights as heterosexuals under immigration law.

The selections in this part highlight but two dilemmas faced by immigrant homosexuals. Brian McGoldrick's piece, *United States Immigration Policy and Sexual Orientation: Is Asylum For Homosexuals A Possibility?*, focuses on the practical problems facing homosexual immigrants, despite their recent successful attempts to claim asylum in the United States based on their sexual orientation. Indeed, since 1996, the INS has taken the position that homosexuals persecuted based on their status alone qualify for asylum as a particular social group.[23] While this appears to be a clear victory for homosexuals, an open question remains as to those homosexuals persecuted not because of their status, but because of their participation in illegal homosexual conduct.[24] Given the Supreme Court's pronouncement upholding the criminalization of homosexual sodomy,[25] it is unclear whether immigration judges would welcome an asylum claim based on participation in illegal homosexual *activity* as opposed to homosexual *status*.

The second dilemma faced by gay and lesbian noncitizens is implied in the *Adams v. Howerton*[26] case included in this section. In *Adams*, the Ninth Circuit affirmed the Board of Immigration Appeals' decision denying "immediate relative" status to the homosexual noncitizen spouse of an American married in Boulder, Colorado. The circuit panel held that the term "citizen's spouse" in Section 201(b) of the INA means someone of the opposite sex and that such an interpretation was constitutional. Citing Congress's plenary power over immigration, the court held that Congress's apparent decision to facilitate family unity through the statute also reflects the rational decision to afford preferential treatment to some marital relationships but not others. This decision probably comes as no surprise because homosexual marriages are generally not recognized in the United States.

It is perhaps fitting that *Adams v. Howerton* rounds out the material for this volume on contemporary substantive issues in constitutional immigration law. As noted above, any constitutional claims asserted by noncitizens must overcome the deference accorded the federal legislature under the guise of plenary power. With the *Adams* court's emphasis on the plenary power of Congress, the volume comes full circle, capturing the tension between individual rights and Congressional power starkly.

Further reading

A. Constitutional Immigration Law: Immigrants' Rights v. the Plenary Power Doctrine

T. Alexander Aleinikoff, "The Tightening Circle of Membership," 22 *Hastings Const. L.Q.* 915 (1995).

T. Alexander Aleinikoff, "Citizens, Aliens, Membership and the Constitution," 7 *Const. Comm.* 9 (1990).

T. Alexander Aleinikoff, "Strangers to the Constitution: Immigrations in American Law: Aliens, Due Process, and 'Community Ties:' A Response to Martin," 44 *U. Pitt. L. Rev.* 237 (1983).

Linda S. Bosniak, "Membership, Equality and the Difference that Alienage Makes," 69 *N.Y.U. L. Rev.* 1047 (1994).

Stephen H. Legomsky, "Immigration Law and the Principle of Plenary Congressional Power," 1984 *Supreme Ct. Rev.* 255 (1984).

David A. Martin, "Due Process and Membership in the National Community: Political Asylum and Beyond," 44 *U. Pitt. L. Rev.* 165 (1983).

Gerald L. Neuman, *Strangers to the Constitution: Immigrants, Borders, and Fundamental Law* (1996).

Victor C. Romero, "The Congruence Principle Applied: Rethinking Equal Protection Review of Federal Alienage Classifications After *Adarand Constructors, Inc. v. Peña*," 76 *Or. L. Rev.* 425 (1997).

John A. Scanlan, "Aliens in the Marketplace of Ideas: The Government, the Academy, and the McCarran-Walter Act," 66 *Tex. L. Rev.* 1481 (1988).

B. Race, National Origin, and Immigration

Robert S. Chang, *Disoriented* (1999).

Stephen Shie-Wei Fan, Comment, "Immigration Law and the Promise of Critical Race Theory: Opening the Academy to the Voices of Aliens and Immigrants," 97 *Colum. L. Rev.* 1202 (1997).

Ruben J. Garcia, Comment, "Critical Race Theory and Proposition 187: The Racial Politics of Immigration Law," 17 *Chicano-Latino L. Rev.* 118 (1995).

Neil Gotanda, "Race, Citizenship, and the Search for Political Community Among 'We the People,'" 76 *Or. L. Rev.* 233 (1997).

Neil Gotanda, "Towards Repeal of Asian Exclusion: The Magnuson Act of 1943, the Act of July 2, 1946, the Presidential Proclamation of July 4, 1946, the Act of August 9, 1946 and the Act of August 19, 1950," in *Asian Americans and Congress: A Documentary History* 309, 311–23 (Hyung-Chan Kim, ed. 1995).

Neil Gotanda, "Asian American Rights and the 'Miss Saigon Syndrome.'" In *Asian Americans and the Supreme Court: A Documentary History* 1087 (Hyung Chan Kim ed., 1982).

Ian Fidencio Haney Lopez, White By Law: The Legal Construction of Race (1996).

Bill Ong Hing, "Beyond the Rhetoric of Assimilation and Cultural Pluralism: Addressing the Tension of Separatism and Conflict in an Immigration-Driven Multiracial Society," 81 *Calif. L. Rev.* 863 (1993).

Immigrants Out! (Juan Perea ed. 1997).

Kevin R. Johnson, "An Essay on Immigration Politics, Popular Democracy, and California's Proposition 187: The Political Relevance and Legal Irrelevance of Race," 70 *Wash. L. Rev.* 629 (1995).

Kevin R. Johnson, "Fear of an "Alien Nation": Race, Immigration, and Immigrants," 7 *Stan. L. & Pol'y Rev.* 111 (1996).

Kevin R. Johnson, "Racial Hierarchy, Asian Americans and Latinos as 'Foreigners,' and Social Change: Is Law the Way to Go?," 76 *Or. L. Rev.* 347 (1997).

Kevin R. Johnson, "Immigration and Latino Identity," 19 *Chicano-Latino L. Rev.* 197 (1998).

Kenzo S. Kawanabe, Note, "American Anti-Immigrant Rhetoric Against Asian Pacific Immigrants: The Present Repeats the Past," 10 *Geo. Immigr. L.J.* 681 (1996).

Anna O. Law, "Race, Ethnicity, and National Origins in Public Policy — When Should It Matter?," 10 *Geo. Immigr. L.J.* 71 (1996).

Zig Layton-Henry, The Politics of Immigration: Immigration, "Race" and "Race" Relations in Post-War Britain (1992).

Rachel F. Moran, "Foreword — Demography and Distrust: The Latino Challenge to Civil Rights and Immigration Policy in the 1990s and Beyond," 8 *La Raza L.J.* 1 (1995).

Michael A. Olivas, "Storytelling Out of School: Undocumented College Residency, Race and Reaction," 22 *Hastings Const. L.Q.* 1019 (1995).

Victor C. Romero, "Broadening Our World: Citizens and Immigrants of Color in America," 27 *Cap. U. L. Rev.* 13 (1998).

Natsu Taylor Saito, "Alien and Non-Alien Alike: Citizenship, "Foreignness," and Racial Hierarchy in American Law," 76 *Or. L. Rev.* 261 (1997).

Enid Trucios-Haynes, "The Legacy of Racially Restrictive Immigration Laws and Policies and the Construction of the American National Identity," 76 *Or. L. Rev.* 369 (1997).

C. Gender, Illegitimacy, and Immigration

T. Alexander Aleinikoff and Cornelia T. L. Pillard, "Skeptical Scrutiny of Plenary Power: Judicial And Executive Branch Decision Making in *Miller* v. *Albright*," 1998 *Sup. Ct. Rev.* 1 (1998).

Deborah E. Anker, "Women Refugees: Forgotten No Longer?," 32 *San Diego L. Rev.* 771 (1995).

Deborah E. Anker, Nancy Kelly, and John Wilshire-Carrera, "The BIA's New Asylum Jurisprudence and its Relevance for Women's Claims," 73 *Interpreter Releases* 1173 (Sept. 9, 1996).

Collin O'Connor Udell, "*Miller* v. *Albright*: Plenary Power, Equal Protection, and the Rights of an Alien Love Child," 12 *Geo. Immigr. L.J.* 621 (1998).

Debra L. Satinoff, Comment, " Sex-Based Discrimination in U.S. Immigration Law: The High Court's Lost Opportunity to Bridge the Gap Between What We Say and What We Do," 47 *Am. U. L. Rev.* 1353 (1998).

Lee Teran, "Barriers to Protection at Home and Abroad: Mexican Victims of Domestic Violence and the Violence Against Women Act," 17 *B.U. Int'l L. J.* 1 (1999).

D. Sexual Orientation and Immigration

Laurie Martha Cochran, "The Changing Tide of Immigration Law: Equality for All?," 26 *Ga. J. Int'l and Comp. L.* 673 (1997).

Robert Foss, "The Demise of the Homosexual Exclusion: New Possibilities for Gay and Lesbian Immigration," 29 *Harv. C.R.-C.L. L. Rev.* 439 (1994).

Brian F. Henes, Comment, "The Origin and Consequences of Recognizing Homosexuals as a 'Particular Social Group' for Refugee Purposes," 8 *Temp. Int'l & Comp. L.J.* 377 (1994).

Shannon Minter, "Sodomy and Public Morality Offenses Under U.S. Immigration Law: Penalizing Lesbian and Gay Identity," 26 *Cornell Int'l L.J.* 771 (1993).

Jin S. Park, "Pink Asylum: Political Asylum Eligibility of Gay Men and Lesbians Under U.S. Immigration Policy," 42 *UCLA L. Rev.* 1115 (1995).

Samuel M. Silvers, "The Exclusion and Expulsion of Homosexual Aliens," 15 *Colum. Hum. Rts. L. Rev.* 295 (1984).

Notes

1 Linda Kelly, "Preserving the Fundamental Right to Family Unity: Championing Notions of Social Contrast and Community Ties in the Battle of Plenary Power Versus Aliens' Rights," 41 *Vill. L. Rev.* 725, 731–32 (1996). Reprinted in Volume 2 (citing David Martin, "Due Process and Membership in the National Community: Political Asylum and Beyond," 44 *U. Pitt. L. Rev.* 165 (1983)).

2 *Id.* at 751 (citing T. Alexander Aleinikoff, "Strangers to the Constitution: Immigrants in American Law: Aliens, Due Process, and 'Community Ties': A Response to Martin," 44 *U. Pitt. L. Rev.* 237, 245 (1983)). At bottom, it is not clear to us that Martin and Aleinikoff are that far apart in their theories. Indeed, our sense is that, as applied, there would be a substantial amount of common ground between the two approaches, specifically with respect to the rights of citizens and legal permanent residents. *See id.* at 752-56. Nonetheless, Aleinikoff's position appears to be more than just an elucidation of Martin's because Aleinikoff uses as his yardstick a person's efforts at developing community ties, whereas Martin begins with a person's immigration status, while her community ties are obligations arising out of her membership in the community. Put another way, Aleinikoff sees one's community ties as the source of one's due process rights, while Martin sees them as consequences of one's membership in the community.

3 *Id.* at 765 (citing Gerald Neuman, "Whose Constitution?" 100 *Yale L. J.* 909, 981 (1991)).

4 Kelly qualifies that Neuman refers to this theory as the "municipal law" approach, although Kelly prefers the term "mutuality." *See id.* at 765-66 n.206.

5 *Id.* at 772.

6 Last year, the Supreme Court stated in dicta that otherwise deportable noncitizens could not generally avail themselves of the defense that they had been selected for removal solely because of their First Amendment associations. *See Reno* v. *American-Arab Anti-Discrimination Committee*, 525 U.S. 471, 119 S. Ct. 936, 142 L.Ed. 2d 940 (1999).

7 Kelly, *supra* note 1, at 725 (describing immigration law as the "unwanted child of constitutional jurisprudence" and noting the legislative attacks on family unity within recent and pending immigration legislation).

8 Frank Wu, "The Limits of Borders: A Moderate Proposal for Immigration Reform," 7 *Stan. L. and Pol'y Rev.* 35, 37–38 (1996). Reprinted in Volume 2 (analyzing the anti- immigrant political and legislative trend in the 1990s).

9 Linda S. Bosniak, "Membership, Equality, and the Difference Alienage Makes," 69 *N.Y.U. L. Rev.* 1047 (1994).

10 Michael Scaperlanda, "Partial Membership: Aliens and the Constitutional Community," 81 *Iowa L. Rev.* 707, 772–73 (1996). Reprinted in Volume 2.

11 *Ramallo* v. *Reno*, 931 F. Supp. 884, 887 (D.D.C. 1996).

12 Section 306(a) of IIRAIRA provides, in pertinent part:

EXCLUSIVE JURISDICTION. — Except as provided in this section and notwithstanding any other provision of the law, no court shall have any jurisdiction to hear any cause or claim by or on behalf of any alien arising from the decision or action by the Attorney General to commence proceedings, adjudicate cases, or execute removal orders against the alien under the [Immigration and Nationality Act].

8 U.S.C. § 1252(g) (1996).

13 *See, e.g.*, Jody Armour, "Stereotypes and Prejudice: Helping Legal Decisionmakers Break the Prejudice Habit," 83 *Cal. L. Rev.* 733 (1995); Jody David Armour, *Negrophobia and Reasonable Racism: The Hidden Costs of Being Black in America* (1997).

14 *See, e.g.*, Gregory R. Maio, et al., "The Formation of Attitudes Toward New Immigrant Groups," 1994 *J. Applied Psych.* 1762 (1994); Gregory R. Maio, et al., "Ambivalence and Persuasion: The Processing of Messages About Immigrant Groups," 32 *J. Experimental Psych.* 513 (1996).

15 Victor C. Romero, "Expanding the Circle of Membership by Reconstructing the 'Alien': Lessons from Social Psychology and the 'Promise Enforcement' Cases," 32 *U. Mich. J.L. Ref.* 1, 45-46 (1998). Reprinted in Volume 2.

16 Kevin R. Johnson, "Race, The Immigration Laws, and Domestic Race Relations: A 'Magic Mirror' Into The Heart of Darkness," 73 *Ind. L.J.* 1111, 1114 (1998). Reprinted in Volume 2.

17 *Id.* at 1122-24.

18 45 F.3d 469 (D.C. Cir. 1995) [*LAVAS I*]. Reprinted in Volume 2; 104 F.3d 1349 (D.C. Cir. 1997) [*LAVAS II*]. Reprinted in Volume 2.

19 *See* Romero, *supra* note 15, at 30–34.

[20] Joan Fitzpatrick, "The Gender Dimension of U.S. Immigration Policy," 23 *Yale J. L. and Feminism* 23, 28 (1997). Reprinted in Volume 2.

[21] 523 U.S. 420, 118 S. Ct. 1428, 140 L.Ed. 2d 575 (1998. Reprinted in Volume 2.

[22] Note, "The Supreme Court 1997 Term – Leading Cases – I. Constitutional Law – D. Equal Protection – Gender Discrimination – The Immigration and Nationality Act," 112 *Harv. L. Rev.* 202 (1998). Reprinted in Volume 2.

[23] *See* Stephen H. Legomsky, *Immigration and Refugee Law and Policy* 816 (2d ed. 1997).

[24] Citing the Ninth Circuit's test of "voluntary association" to determine membership in a "particular social group" for asylum purposes, McGoldrick notes, "It is arguable that the common characteristic [of the association] is the commission of illegal acts. What creates the voluntary association is the willingness to engage in criminal activity." Brian J. McGoldrick, "United States Immigration Policy and Sexual Orientation: Is Asylum For Homosexuals A Possibility?" 8 *Geo. Immigr. L.J.* 201 (1994). Reprinted in Volume 2.

[25] *See Bowers* v. *Hardwick*, 478 U.S. 186, 106 S. Ct. 2841, 92 L.Ed. 2d 140 (1986).

[26] 673 F.2d 1036 (9th Cir. 1982). Reprinted in Volume 2.

PRESERVING THE FUNDAMENTAL RIGHT TO FAMILY UNITY: CHAMPIONING NOTIONS OF SOCIAL CONTRACT AND COMMUNITY TIES IN THE BATTLE OF PLENARY POWER VERSUS ALIENS' RIGHTS

LINDA KELLY*

But the fact of the matter is the Constitution of the United States obligates—it doesn't ask—it obligates the President and Congress to defend the states of the American union from foreign invasion. And when you have one, two, three million people walking across your border a year, breaking your laws, you have an invasion.[1]

Our progress in degeneracy appears to me pretty rapid. As a nation, we began by declaring that "all men are created equal." We now practically read it "all men are created equal, except negroes." When the Know-Nothings get control, it will read "all men are created equal, except negroes, and foreigners, and Catholics." When it comes to this I should prefer emigrating to some country where they make no pretence of loving liberty—to Russia, for instance, where despotism can be taken pure, and without the base alloy of hypocrisy.[2]

I. INTRODUCTION

IMMIGRATION law, always the unwanted child of constitutional jurisprudence, has survived renewed efforts to further her estrangement. In the summer of 1995, Representative Lamar Smith (R-TX), the Chairman of the House Subcommittee on Immigra-

* Assistant Professor, Saint Thomas University School of Law; B.A., University of Virginia; J.D., University of Virginia. I benefitted greatly from the 1996 Immigration Law Conference in Boulder, Colorado and the valuable insights of Gilbert Carrasco, Fernando Chang-Muy, Maryellen Fullerton, Kevin Johnson, Daniel Kanstroom, Gerald Neuman, Michael Scaperlanda and Margaret Taylor. Special thanks to the participants of the St. Thomas Faculty Forum and the thoughtful comments of Peter Bayer, Dan Gordon, Beverly Horsburgh, Lenora Ledwon, Richard Maloy, Peter Margulies, Jennifer O'Hare, Ediberto Roman and Siegfried Wiessner. Thanks also to Daniel C. Thomas for his technologically progressive research assistance.

1. Pat Buchanan, *Statement at Arizona Republican Presidential Debate*, Feb. 23, 1996, *available in* LEXIS, Cmpgn Library, Elct 96 File.

2. Letter from Abraham Lincoln to Joshua Speed (Aug. 24, 1855), *reprinted in* 2 THE COLLECTED WORK OF ABRAHAM LINCOLN 320, 323 (R. Basler ed., 1953).

tion, introduced House Bill 2202.[3] The original version of the bill proposed radical and sweeping changes in the current immigration system. House Bill 2202 would have reduced legal immigration by over thirty percent, reducing family sponsored visas from 480,000 to 330,000.[4] This reduction would have restricted certain family categories while eliminating other categories.[5] The proposed bill would have placed greater restrictions on the rights of lawful permanent residents to be with their spouses or children, placed restrictions on the rights of United States citizens to be with their parents where no restrictions currently exist, eliminated the rights of United States citizens and lawful permanent residents to be with their adult children and eliminated the right of United States citizens to be with their brothers or sisters.[6]

Despite the fact that the provisions restricting legal immigration were stripped from House Bill 2202[7] and efforts in the Senate to limit legal immigration were rejected,[8] the current wave of anti-immigrant sentiment did not subside. On April 24, 1996, in signing

3. H.R. 2202, 104th Cong. (1995).

4. Immigration and Nationality Act of 1952 (INA) §§ 201-204, 8 U.S.C. §§ 1151-1154 (1994). *See also* T. ALEXANDER ALEINIKOFF ET AL., IMMIGRATION: PROCESS AND POLICY 125-28, 150-92 (3d ed. 1995) (discussing cases and problems involving admission and exclusion of immigrants); IRA J. KURZBAN, IMMIGRATION LAW SOURCEBOOK 448-86 (5th ed. 1995) (outlining issues raised by family based immigration); STEPHEN H. LEGOMSKY, IMMIGRATION LAW AND POLICY 129-80 (1992) (discussing problems arising in INA with regard to quotas).

5. H.R. 2202.

6. *See House Committee Approves Major Reform Bill, Floor Action Next*, 72 INTERPRETER RELEASES 1503 (1995) (discussing House amendments and future of bill); *House Judiciary Committee Continues Work on Major Reform Bill*, 72 INTERPRETER RELEASES 1371 (1995) (discussing mark-up of House bill); *House Judiciary Committee Begins Considering Major Reform Bill*, 72 INTERPRETER RELEASES 1303 (1996) (same); Stephen A. Holmes, *Congress Plans Stiff New Curb on Immigration*, N.Y. TIMES, Sept. 25, 1995, at A1 (noting Congress's plans to limit immigration); Lamar Smith, *Immigration Reform Urgency*, WASH. TIMES, Sept. 25, 1995, at A16 (stating "[n]ow is the time to pass comprehensive immigration reform"); *Immigration Legislation 1995: Information and Analysis* (American Immigration Lawyer's Assoc.) (undated material) (discussing H.R. 2202's effect on families).

7. The version of House Bill 2202 which the House passed on March 21, 1996 by a 333-87 vote mostly focuses on efforts to limit illegal immigration. *House Approves Immigration Bill After Removing Legal Immigration Restrictions*, 73 INTERPRETER RELEASES 349 (1996); Carolyn Skorneck, *House Passes Immigration Bill*, BOSTON GLOBE, Mar. 22, 1996, at 3.

8. By a vote of 20-80, the Senate rejected Senator Simpson's amendment to Senate Bill 1664 which would have set an annual cap of 480,000 on family based immigration. *Senate Approves Omnibus Immigration Bill After Removing Exclusion Provisions*, 73 INTERPRETER RELEASES 601, 602 (1996). While no current family preference categories would have been eliminated, the practical effect of such a cap would have been to make visas unavailable in certain preference categories. *Id.*; *Immigration: Senate Judiciary Approves Immigration Reform Legislation*, Daily Lab. Rep. (BNA), Mar. 22, 1996, at 56, D4; *Senate Committee Splits Immigration Reform Bill*,

the Antiterrorism and Effective Death Penalty Act of 1996 (AEDPA),[9] President Bill Clinton acknowledged that the bill "makes a number of major, ill-advised changes to our immigration laws having nothing to do with fighting terrorism."[10] Yet as the 1996 presidential election drew closer, two other pieces of legislation further curtailing immigrant rights were enacted—the Illegal Immigration Reform and Immigrant Responsibility Act (IIRAIRA)[11] and the Personal Responsibility and Work Opportu-

House Floor Action Is Next, 73 INTERPRETER RELEASES 313, 315-16 (1996); *Senate Rejects Amendment to Cut Legal Immigration,* 73 INTERPRETER RELEASES 570 (1996).

9. Pub. L. No. 104-132, 110 Stat. 1214 (1996).

10. *See President Signs Terrorism Bill into Law, Congress Passes Correction Measures,* 73 INTERPRETER RELEASES 568 (1996) [hereinafter *President Signs Terrorism Bill*]. One of the most troubling provisions of the anti-terrorism legislation was § 414 which subjects any individual who has entered the United States without inspection ("EWI") to exclusion, rather than deportation proceedings, no matter how long such individual has been in the United States. AEDPA § 414(a). While Illegal Immigration Reform and Immigrant Responsibility Act (IIRAIRA), Pub. L. No. 104-208, § 308(d)(2)(D), 110 Stat. 3009 (1996) (to be codified in scattered sections of 8 U.S.C.), repealed AEDPA § 414, IIRAIRA § 301 declares aliens who arrived in the United States without inspection to be inadmissable and subject to removal. IIRAIRA § 301 (to be codified at INA § 212 (a)(6)(A), 8 U.S.C.).

AEDPA § 422 also created "expedited exclusion" proceedings for individuals who at the point of entry do not have the appropriate entry documents. *President Signs Terrorism Bill, supra* at 569. Again consistent with AEDPA's intent, while IIRAIRA § 308(d)(5) repealed AEDPA § 422, IIRAIRA § 302 allows for the "expedited removal" of most aliens who are determined to be inadmissable at the port of arrival. IIRAIRA § 302 (to be codified at INA § 235, 8 U.S.C.). Such summary processing may also apply to aliens who have not been legally admitted or paroled and cannot affirmatively show that they have been continuously, physically present in the United States for more than two years. *Id.*

These types of changes point out some of the semantics changed through IIRAIRA. Individuals previously considered "excludable" pursuant to INA § 212 are now considered "inadmissable" and subject to "cancellation of removal proceedings" rather than "exclusion proceedings." IIRAIRA §§ 301(b), 304 (to be codified at INA §§ 212(a)(9), 240A, in scattered sections of 8 U.S.C.). For a further discussion of IIRAIRA, see *infra* note 11 and accompanying text.

As this Article relies on theories published prior to the passage of this significant legislation, in order to "bridge the gap" between the old and new terms, I will use such old terms as "excludable" somewhat interchangeably with its new term "inadmissable" and "entry without inspection" somewhat interchangeably with its new term "arrival without inspection."

11. Pub. L. No. 104-208, 110 Stat. 3009 (1996) (to be codified in scattered sections of 8 U.S.C.). On September 30, 1996, President Clinton signed the IIRAIRA. Among the most severe measures is a provision replacing suspension of deportation under INA § 244(a) and INA § 212(c) relief with "cancellation of removal," a new form of relief which bears a higher burden of proof. IIRAIRA § 304 (to be codified at INA § 240A, 8 U.S.C.). For example, cancellation of removal creates a higher standard than required for the most typical suspension of deportation claims which were advanced pursuant to INA § 244(a)(1) as (a) cancellation of removal requires ten years of continuous physical presence; (b) a showing of "exceptional and extremely unusual hardship" to a United States citizen or lawful permanent resident spouse, parent or child; and (c) a showing of good moral character for ten years. IIRAIRA § 304 (to be codified at INA § 240A(b)(1), 8

nity Reconciliation Act of 1996 ("Welfare Act").[12] Supporters of severe immigration restrictions, such as those contained in the AEDPA, the IIRAIRA and the Welfare Act, will be sure to return to their efforts to limit legal immigration through family unification.[13]

U.S.C.); *see also* IIRAIRA § 308(a)(7) (repealing INA § 244). By contrast, suspension of deportation had required only (a) seven years good moral character; (b) seven years continuous physical presence; and (c) a showing of extreme hardship to the qualifying family member or to the alien himself. INA § 244(a)(1), 8 U.S.C. § 1254(a)(1). While suspension of deportation has only been available to those who are deportable, cancellation of removal is, however, stated to be available both to those who are inadmissable or deportable. IIRAIRA § 304, (to be codified as INA § 240A, 8 U.S.C.).

With the enactment of IIRAIRA § 304(b), relief under INA § 212(c) has also been repealed and replaced with "cancellation of removal." IIRAIRA § 304 (to be codified at INA § 240A(a), 8 U.S.C.). This relief is more restrictive than INA § 212(c) as it is not available to anyone convicted of any aggravated felony, and it requires that five of the seven years of continuous residence be spent as a lawful permanent resident. As this form of cancellation of removal is available, however, to lawful permanent residents who are either inadmissable or deportable, this change appears to solve the disparity revealed by *Matter of Hernandez-Casillas*. 20 Int. Dec. 262 (BIA 1990, A.G. 1991), *aff'd*, Hernandez-Casillas v. INS, 983 F.2d 231 (5th Cir. 1993) (stating INA § 212(c) relief only available in deportation proceedings when there is comparable ground of exclusion).

Another troubling measure of IIRAIRA creates a 10 year ban on admission to certain individuals unlawfully present for one year or more and a three year bar on admission to certain individuals unlawfully present for more than 180 days. IIRAIRA § 301 (to be codified at INA § 212(a)(9)(B), 8 U.S.C.). No similar bars have previously existed within the INA. There has been much discussion surrounding the passage of IIRAIRA. *See Bill to Block Illegal Immigration Passed, Signed: Controversial Education Measure Cut*, FACTS ON FILE, Oct. 3, 1996, *available in* LEXIS, News File (discussing passage of new legislation); William Branigin, *Congress Finishes Major Legislation; Immigration; Focus Is Borders, Not Benefits*, WASH. POST, Oct. 1, 1996, at A1 (same); *House OKs Bills Targeting Illegal Immigrants*, CHICAGO TRIB., Sept. 26, 1996, at 6 (same); Eric Pianin & Helen Dewar, *Immigration, Budget Agreement Reached*, WASH. POST, Sept. 29, 1996, at A1 (same); Eric Schmitt, *Bill Tries to Balance Concerns on Immigration*, N.Y. TIMES, Sept. 29, 1996, § 1, at 28 (same); *Text on President Clinton's Statement on Omnibus Appropriations and Immigration Reform Bill*, U.S. NEWSWIRE, Oct. 2, 1996, *available in* LEXIS, News File (same).

12. Pub. L. No. 104-193, 110 Stat. 2105 (1996). On August 22, 1996, the Welfare Act was signed into law. Amongst other provisions, the Welfare Act severely curtails the public benefits which have been available to lawful permanent residents. Such public benefits include not only the traditional welfare programs, but also restrictions on access to professional and commercial licenses and the earned income tax credit. Charles Wheeler, *The New Alien Restrictions on Public Benefits: The Full Impact Remains Uncertain*, 73 INTERPRETER RELEASES 1245 (1996) (discussing welfare provisions); *see also* Deborah Billings, *Welfare Reform: Clinton Signs Welfare Reform Measure; Says It Creates Second Chance System*, Daily Lab. Rep. (BNA), Aug. 23, 1996, 164, at D11 (discussing welfare benefits); Francis X. Clines, *Clinton Signs Bill Cutting Welfare*, N.Y. TIMES, Aug. 23, 1996, at A1 (same); John F. Harris & John E. Yang, *Clinton to Sign Bill Overhauling Welfare*, WASH. POST, Aug. 1, 1996, at A1 (same).

13. Some limitation was made on family unification through IIRAIRA. Beginning in the fiscal year 1999, the number of family-sponsored immigrant visas subjected to numerical limitation will include a reduction for certain parolees. IIRAIRA § 603 (amending INA § 201(c), 8 U.S.C. § 1151(c)). Another IIRAIRA

These attempts to curtail family unity reveal troubling questions about America's true commitment to the family, even within its existing immigration law. Historically, the federal government has claimed to base U.S. immigration policy upon a commitment to family unification.[14] Society's emphasis upon family makes family values such an important ideal that public figures across the political spectrum fight to identify themselves with this notion.[15] Forget the economy. "It's values, stupid."[16]

The United States Supreme Court also recognizes the importance of family. In *Moore v. City of East Cleveland*,[17] the Supreme Court determined that an extended family's desire to live together involved a fundamental liberty interest protected under the Due Process Clause of the Fourteenth Amendment.[18] The *Moore* Court's

---

provision demands that the affidavit of support provided by an individual sponsoring an alien's request for residency be executed as a contract, be legally enforceable against the sponsor and that such sponsor demonstrates an annual income 125% above the federal poverty lines. IIRAIRA § 551 (to be codified at INA § 213A, 8 U.S.C.).

14. *See generally* ALEINIKOFF ET AL., *supra* note 4, at 40-63 (giving brief history of immigration to United States); John Guendelsberger, *The Right to Family Unification in French and United States Immigration Law*, 21 CORNELL INT'L L.J. 1, 7-25 (1988) (explaining basis and history of U.S. immigration) [hereinafter Guendelsberger, *Family Unification*].

15. *See, e.g.*, Susan Baer, *Pace of Congress Tests Family Values*, BALTIMORE SUN, Dec. 11, 1995, at 1A (noting recent divorce trend with new members of Congress); Sandi Dolbee, *Family Values to Dominate Presidential Election, Black Baptists Told*, SAN DIEGO UNION-TRIB., June 22, 1995, at A14 (stating that presidential campaign will include struggle over meaning of "family values"); *Family Values Still More Hypocrisy*, CHARLESTON GAZETTE, Dec. 5, 1995, at 4A (criticizing Republican Party's use of "family values" slogan as political weapon); Marianne Means, *House GOP Finds "Family Values" Are Easier to Preach than to Practice*, SACRAMENTO BEE, Dec. 8, 1995, at B11 (stating that politicians "love to rhapsodize about the virtues of traditional family"); Alison Mitchell, *On Issue of Family Values, Clinton Unveils an Agenda of His Own*, N.Y. TIMES, July 29, 1995, § 1, at 6 (noting that President Clinton will not allow Republicans alone to define family values).

Regarding the Christian Coalition's contract, Ralph Reed, executive director, remarked, "[i]t is a pro-family agenda, and it is supported by the vast majority of the American people, Republican and Democrat, Christian and Jew, black and white, Protestant and Catholic." *Family Values II: The Christian Coalition Signs on the Dotted Line*, BOSTON GLOBE, May 21, 1995, at 45. Discussing the Christian Coalition's contract, House of Representatives Speaker Newt Gingrich declared: "Here are some key values that matter the most to most Americans. We are committed to keeping our faith with the people who helped the Contract With America." Adelle M. Banks, *Coalition's 'Contract' Focuses on Families*, TIMES-PICAYUNE, May 20, 1995, at A21.

16. David Clark Scott, *'It's Values, Stupid,' Political Essayist Argues*, CHRISTIAN SCI. MONITOR, Dec. 6, 1995, at 14 (noting that most important touch tone for today's voters is values).

17. 431 U.S. 494 (1977) (plurality opinion).

18. *Id.* at 499 (invalidating zoning ordinance which defined family through limited categories of related individuals); *see also* Frederick E. Dashiell, *The Right to*

recognition of family rights is consistent with previous decisions recognizing the right of individuals related by "blood, adoption or marriage" to live together.[19] Through a host of cases, the Court acknowledges that a "'private realm of family life [exists] which the state can not enter.'"[20] The Constitution "protects the sanctity of the family precisely because the institution of the family is deeply rooted in this Nation's history and tradition."[21] With family a foundation of civilization,[22] the Court's protection of family promotes "family needs" and "family values."[23]

Yet, when examining family-based immigration law in light of the constitutional protection awarded family unity in *Moore* and other cases, it is not clear that the right to family unity withstands attack by U.S. immigration law. In the immigration arena, the goal of family unity is not always awarded the "preferred position" it enjoys in other areas of the law.[24] Considering this apparent inconsistency between the fundamental right of family unity and the restrictions placed on this right within existing and proposed family immigration policies, the question becomes whether the federal government can constitutionally limit family unity through laws regulating immigration.

The federal political branches traditionally have enjoyed "plenary power" over U.S. immigration law, thereby allowing this area of law to develop outside of constitutional boundaries.[25] Notwith-

Family Life: Moore v. City of East Cleveland, 6 BLACK L.J. 288 (1980) (addressing reasoning and significance of *Moore*).

19. Village of Belle Terre v. Boraas, 416 U.S. 1 (1974) (upholding village zoning ordinance as valid land use regulation).

20. *Moore*, 431 U.S. at 499 (quoting Prince v. Massachusetts, 321 U.S. 158, 166 (1944)); *see, e.g.*, Zablocki v. Redhail, 434 U.S. 374, 399-400 (1978) (discussing protection of rights of family); Cleveland Bd. of Educ. v. LaFleur, 414 U.S. 632, 639-40 (1974) (same); Roe v. Wade, 410 U.S. 113, 152-53 (1973) (same); Stanley v. Illinois, 405 U.S. 645, 651-52 (1972) (same); Eisenstadt v. Baird, 405 U.S. 438, 446-47 (1972) (same); Wisconsin v. Yoder, 406 U.S. 205, 231 (1972) (same); Ginsberg v. New York, 390 U.S. 629, 639 (1968) (same); Loving v. Virginia, 388 U.S. 1, 7 (1967) (same); Griswold v. Connecticut, 381 U.S. 479, 485-86 (1965) (same); Poe v. Ullman, 367 U.S. 497, 542-44, 549-55 (1961) (Harlan, J., dissenting) (same); May v. Anderson, 345 U.S. 528, 533 (1953) (same); Skinner v. Oklahoma *ex rel.* Williamson, 316 U.S. 535, 541 (1942) (same); Pierce v. Society of Sisters, 268 U.S. 510, 534-35 (1925) (same); Meyer v. Nebraska, 262 U.S. 390, 399-400 (1923) (same).

21. *Moore*, 431 U.S. at 503.

22. *Griswold*, 381 U.S. at 496 (Goldberg, J., concurring).

23. *Belle Terre*, 416 U.S. at 9.

24. *See Moore*, 431 U.S. at 511 (Brennan, J., concurring) (quoting Appellant's Brief at 26, Village of Belle Terre v. Boraas, 416 U.S. 1 (1974) (No. 73-191)) (discussing preference for family unity).

25. *See* Shaughnessy v. United States *ex rel.* Mezei, 345 U.S. 206 (1953) (holding alien's right to enter United States depends on congressional will); United States *ex rel.* Knauff v. Shaughnessy, 338 U.S. 537 (1950) (explaining that aliens

standing the immigration law arena, aliens enjoy the protection of certain rights through what is known as the aliens' rights tradition.[26] Cracks, however, have developed in both the plenary power doctrine and the aliens' rights tradition.[27] Critics of the plenary power doctrine versus aliens' rights distinction offer alternative theories to explain the foundation of U.S. immigration policy and its treatment of aliens. Professor David Martin focuses on member-

---

have vested right of entry into United States); Fong Yue Ting v. United States, 149 U.S. 698 (1893) (holding right to exclude or expel all aliens within congressional power); Chae Chan Ping v. United States (Chinese Exclusion Case), 130 U.S. 581 (1889) (holding immigration act excluding Chinese laborers constitutional). *See generally* ALEINIKOFF ET AL., *supra* note 4, at 1-40 (explaining sources of federal immigration power through Chinese Exclusion Case); Stephen H. Legomsky, *Immigration Law and the Principle of the Plenary Congressional Power*, 1984 SUP. CT. REV. 255 (discussing plenary power doctrine and theories on which it is based) [hereinafter Legomsky, *Immigration Law and Plenary Power*]; Michael Scaperlanda, *The Life and Jurisprudence of Justice Thurgood Marshall: Justice Thurgood Marshall and the Legacy of Dissent in Federal Alienage Case*, 47 OKLA. L. REV. 55, 69 (1994) (recognizing majorities in plenary power cases consistently conclude that political branches are totally free to set whatever immigration rules they choose) [hereinafter Scaperlanda, *Marshall's Jurisprudence*]. For a further discussion of the federal political branches' plenary power, see *infra* notes 38-68 and accompanying text.

26. *See* Yick Wo v. Hopkins, 118 U.S. 356 (1886) (holding that temporary U.S. residents are entitled to constitutional protection); *see also* T. Alexander Aleinikoff, *The United States Constitution in its Third Century: Foreign Affairs: Rights—Here and There: Federal Regulation of Aliens and the Constitution*, 83 AM. J. INT'L L. 862, 865-66 (1989) (stating that resident aliens, refugees and asylees are accorded nearly all federal benefits) [hereinafter Aleinikoff, *Federal Regulation of Aliens*]; Louis Henkin, *The Constitution as Compact and as Conscience: Individual Rights Abroad and at Our Gates*, 27 WM. & MARY L. REV. 11, 14-18 (1985) (discussing extension of due process rights and protections to resident aliens) [hereinafter Henkin, *Constitution as Compact and Conscience*]. For a further discussion of the aliens' rights tradition, see *infra* notes 69-87 and accompanying text.

27. *See generally* United States v. Verdugo-Urquidez, 494 U.S. 259 (1990) (holding that Fourth Amendment protection against search and seizure does not extend to nonresident aliens); Landon v. Plasencia, 459 U.S. 21 (1982) (holding that resident alien is entitled to due process at exclusionary hearing); Linda S. Bosniak, *Membership, Equality and the Difference that Alienage Makes*, 69 N.Y.U. L. REV. 1047, 1059-65 (1994) (discussing difference in rights accorded to aliens inside and outside of immigration law); Stephen H. Legomsky, *Ten More Years of Plenary Power: Immigration, Congress, and the Courts*, 22 HASTINGS CONST. L.Q. 925, 930-37 (1995) (discussing expansion of exceptions to plenary power in lower courts) [hereinafter Legomsky, *Ten More Years*]; Hiroshi Motomura, *Immigration Law After a Century of Plenary Power: Phantom Constitutional Norms and Statutory Interpretation*, 100 YALE L.J. 545 (1990) (examining decline of plenary power doctrine) [hereinafter Motomura, *Phantom Norms*]; Hiroshi Motomura, *The Curious Evolution of Immigration Law: Procedural Surrogates for Substantive Constitutional Rights*, 92 COLUM. L. REV. 1625 (1992) (examining difference between substantive and procedural rights afforded aliens) [hereinafter Motomura, *Procedural Surrogates*]; Margaret H. Taylor, *Detained Aliens Challenging Conditions of Confinement and the Porous Border of the Plenary Power Doctrine*, 22 HASTINGS CONST. L.Q. 1087, 1135-39 (1995) (discussing conflict between plenary power doctrine and aliens' rights tradition). For a further discussion of the conflict between the plenary power doctrine and aliens' right tradition, see *infra* notes 88-120 and accompanying text.

ship in the national community to answer questions regarding due process.[28] Responding to Martin, Professor Alexander Aleinikoff widens the focus to include an evaluation of community ties.[29] While Martin and Aleinikoff predominantly discuss the constitutional rights of aliens in the United States, Professor Gerald Neuman advances mutuality notions in looking at the rights of aliens "outside the United States who have never been inside the United States."[30] This Article relies on these theories in developing a "constitutionally humane" approach toward creating policies which affect aliens. Applying this theory to the question of family-sponsored immigration will allow for a proper evaluation of the rights of all individuals who may be influenced by our immigration laws.

In Part II, this Article will address the plenary power doctrine and its evolution.[31] Part III will discuss the history of the aliens' rights tradition.[32] After highlighting the difficulties in applying these approaches through a discussion of recent cases and criticisms in Part IV, the alternative theories suggested by David Martin and Alexander Aleinikoff will be discussed in Part V.[33] Cases indicating the courts' attention to these doctrines will be reviewed in Part VI.[34] To remedy a flaw in the approaches of Martin and Aleinikoff which is noted in this discussion, Gerald Neuman's theory will be evaluated in Part VII.[35] Part VIII will suggest how aspects

28. David A. Martin, *Due Process and Membership in the National Community: Political Asylum and Beyond*, 44 U. PITT. L. REV. 165 (1983) (Professor Martin, currently on leave from academia, now serves as Immigration and Naturalization Service (INS) General Counsel). For a further discussion of Professor Martin's focus on membership in the national community, see *infra* notes 121-26 and accompanying text.

29. T. Alexander Aleinikoff, *Strangers to the Constitution: Immigrants in American Law: Aliens, Due Process, and "Community Ties:" A Response to Martin*, 44 U. PITT. L. REV. 237, 244 (1983) [hereinafter Aleinikoff, *Community Ties*]. For a further discussion of Professor Aleinikoff, see *infra* notes 127-33 and accompanying text.

30. Gerald L. Neuman, *Whose Constitution?*, 100 YALE L.J. 909, 981 (1991). For a further discussion of Professor Neuman's mutuality approach, see *infra* notes 203-214 and accompanying text.

31. For a further discussion of the plenary power doctrine and its evolution, see *infra* notes 38-68 and accompanying text.

32. For a further discussion of the history of the aliens' rights tradition, see *infra* notes 69-87 and accompanying text.

33. For a further discussion of recent cases and criticisms, see *infra* notes 88-120 and accompanying text. For a further discussion of the alternative theories suggested by David Martin and Alexander Aleinikoff, see *infra* notes 121-33 and accompanying text.

34. For a further discussion of cases indicating the courts' attention to these doctrines, see *infra* notes 134-201 and accompanying text.

35. For a further discussion of Professor Neuman's theory, see *infra* notes 203-14 and accompanying text.

of each of these theories can combine to create a "constitutionally humane" approach for the United States to follow in exercising its authority over aliens.[36] Finally, Part IX will apply this "constitutionally humane" approach to the question of family unity through immigration law in an attempt to illustrate how U.S. immigration law can be fairly established.[37]

II. THE PLENARY POWER DOCTRINE

The federal government's power to regulate immigration began with *Chae Chan Ping v. United States* (*Chinese Exclusion Case*).[38] In confirming Congress's absolute authority to prevent aliens from entering the United States, the *Chinese Exclusion Case* set the stage for an area of law exempt from constitutional scrutiny and protection.[39]

This "plenary power" the federal government enjoys in immigration matters is extracted from the federal government's recognized right to sovereignty—the right to possess full control over U.S. territory and foreign affairs.[40] In the *Chinese Exclusion Case*, the Supreme Court rationalized that because the United States certainly had the right to protect itself from invading armies, it naturally followed that it also had the right to protect itself from "vast hordes of [a foreign] people crowding in upon us."[41] Thus, despite

36. For a further discussion of the "constitutionally humane" approach for the United States to follow in exercising its authority over aliens, see *infra* notes 240-42 and accompanying text.

37. For a further discussion of applying the "constitutionally humane" approach to the question of family unity through immigration law, see *infra* notes 243-85 and accompanying text.

38. 130 U.S. 581 (1889). Petitioner had been a lawful permanent resident of the United States for 12 years. *Id.* at 582. After leaving the United States with a certificate to re-enter, petitioner was denied re-entry when Congress amended the Chinese Exclusion Act declaring these certificates "void and of no effect." *Id.* at 599.

39. Aleinikoff, *Federal Regulation of Aliens*, *supra* note 26, at 862; Taylor, *supra* note 27, at 1128.

40. *Chinese Exclusion Case*, 130 U.S. at 603-04; *see also* T. Alexander Aleinikoff, *Citizens, Aliens, Membership and the Constitution*, 7 CONST. COMMENTARY 9, 10-12 (1990) (discussing inherent power of Congress to expel or exclude aliens) [hereinafter Aleinikoff, *Citizens, Aliens, Membership*]; Henkin, *Constitution as Compact and Conscience*, *supra* note 26, at 25 (discussing holding of *Chinese Exclusion Case*). For a discussion of the transformation of the notion of sovereignty, suggesting a diminution in the government's right to absolute sovereignty since the *Chinese Exclusion Case* and thereby a weakening in the plenary power doctrine as a result of U.S. adherence to customary and conventional international law, see Michael Scaperlanda, *Polishing the Tarnished Golden Door*, 1993 WISC. L. REV. 965 [hereinafter Scaperlanda, *Polishing the Golden Door*].

41. *Chinese Exclusion Case*, 130 U.S. at 606; *see also* Aleinikoff, *Federal Regulation of Aliens*, *supra* note 26, at 863 (discussing Supreme Court's analogy between invad-

the constitutional principle that the federal government be limited to its enumerated powers,[42] the Supreme Court found Congress's power to control immigration inherent within its sovereign right to control U.S. territory and to protect its borders.[43] The Supreme Court held that the "power of exclusion of foreigners [is] an incident of sovereignty belonging to the government of the United States, as a part of those sovereign powers delegated by the Constitution."[44]

In creating the federal political branches' plenary power over immigration from the sovereignty perspective, the Constitution and the rights of the people essentially are ignored.[45] Since the *Chinese Exclusion Case*, immigration law has continued to fester, with a disregard for fundamental rights and values. Four years after the *Chinese Exclusion Case*, in *Fong Yue Ting v. United States*,[46] the Court approved Congress's power to deport resident aliens.[47] Thus, the Court awarded the federal government not only the authority to prevent people from entering, but also the full discretion to demand an individual's departure.[48] According to the Court, the right to deport foreigners, like the right to exclude them, was "an inherent and inalienable right of every sovereign and independent nation, essential to its safety, its independence and its welfare."[49] The only softening, which came early in the development of the severe principles of the plenary power doctrine, resulted from *Yamataya v. Fischer* (*Japanese Immigrant Case*).[50] As a result of the *Japa-*

ing armies and aliens in *Chinese Exclusion Case*); Taylor, *supra* note 27, at 1128-29 (discussing Supreme Court's rationale in *Chinese Exclusion Case*).

42. *See* U.S. CONST. amend. X ("The powers not delegated to the United States by the Constitution, nor prohibited by it to the States, are reserved to the States respectively, or to the people."); *see also* Henkin, *Constitution as Compact and Conscience*, *supra* note 26, at 25 (noting that "[t]he power to control immigration is not one of the enumerated powers of Congress").

43. *Chinese Exclusion Case*, 130 U.S. at 609.

44. *Id.*

45. Aleinikoff, *Federal Regulation of Aliens*, *supra* note 26, at 863.

46. 149 U.S. 698 (1893).

47. *Id.* at 713. In *Fong Yue Ting*, as a result of an amendment to the Chinese Exclusion Act, a Chinese resident could be deported if he or she had not obtained a certificate of residence or could not show "through testimony of one credible white witness" that he or she was a lawful U.S. resident. *Id.* at 727.

48. *See id.* at 731 (holding that question of whether aliens are permitted to remain in United States is determined by Congress).

49. *Id.* at 711; *see also* Aleinikoff, *Federal Regulation of Aliens*, *supra* note 26, at 863 (noting Supreme Court's use of dire terms in reaching its conclusion); Taylor, *supra* note 27, at 1128-29 (discussing Supreme Court's extension of Congress's plenary power to deport resident aliens in *Fong Yue Ting*).

50. 189 U.S. 86 (1903).

nese Immigration Case, procedural due process has been required in deportation proceedings.[51]

While the laws challenged in the *Chinese Exclusion Case* and *Fong Yue Ting* reflect the country's racist motivations at the turn of the century, these types of laws, if passed today, could arguably be upheld through the plenary power doctrine.[52] Over the past 100 years, the Court has pronounced significant individual rights which include what are currently considered basic constitutional rights of due process and equal protection.[53] This respect for individual rights is not, however, reflected within the Court's review of immigration law. The Court continues to show great deference to Congress's plenary power to control immigration.[54]

Less than fifty years ago, the Supreme Court upheld the United States Attorney General's power to exclude the wife of a United States citizen without a hearing in *United States ex rel. Knauff v. Shaughnessy*.[55] Three years later, in *Shaughnessy v. United States ex rel. Mezei*,[56] the Court "accomplished the improbable feat of render-

51. *Id.* at 101; *see also* Aleinikoff, *Community Ties*, *supra* note 29, at 238 (discussing sharp scrutiny Supreme Court gives procedure in deportation cases).

52. Taylor, *supra* note 27, at 1128-29. In *Fong Yue Ting*, the testimony of a white witness was required because it was believed that a Chinese witness was more likely to possess "loose notions" regarding the obligation of an oath. 149 U.S. at 729-30 (citing Chinese Exclusion Case, 130 U.S. 581, 598 (1889)).

53. *See* Aleinikoff, *Federal Regulation of Aliens*, *supra* note 26, at 864 (noting that Supreme Court recognized important rights in late nineteenth century); Henkin, *Constitution as Compact and Conscience*, *supra* note 26, at 15 (discussing Supreme Court's recognition of important individual rights).

54. *See* Taylor, *supra* note 27, at 1129-33 (noting that Supreme Court's recognition of plenary powers doctrine continued throughout Cold War era).

55. 338 U.S. 537 (1950). The Attorney General's power to exclude Knauff, based solely upon the Attorney General's statement that her admission "would be prejudicial to the interests of the United States," was beyond review by the Court. *Id.* at 539-40, 543. Knauff was paroled from Ellis Island only after a public outcry of support. Charles D. Weisselberg, *The Exclusion and Detention of Aliens: Lessons from the Lives of Ellen Knauff and Ignatz Mezei*, 143 U. PA. L. REV. 933, 955-64 (1995). After being afforded a hearing before the Board of Special Inquiry which found her excludable as a threat to national security, the Board of Immigration Appeals (BIA) reversed, holding that uncorroborated hearsay evidence without more, was not sufficient to support an order of exclusion. *See generally* ELLEN KNAUFF, THE ELLEN KNAUFF STORY (1952) (relating injustice inflicted on Ellen Knauff).

56. 345 U.S. 206 (1953). In *Mezei*, the husband of a U.S. citizen who had lawfully resided in the United States for 25 years was excluded and detained without a hearing after leaving the United States and returning 19 months later from visiting his dying mother in Rumania, where he had trouble securing an exit permit. *Id.* at 208. The Attorney General declared Mezei to be a threat to national security and could have been "detained indefinitely, perhaps for life, for a cause known only to the Attorney General." *Id.* at 220 (Jackson, J., dissenting). The Supreme Court reversed the lower court's grant of habeas corpus, finding that, in reviewing Mezei's due process claim, he should be "treated as if stopped at the border." *Id.* at 215. The Court found his detention did not constitute an entry

ing the *Knauff* outcome even more severe."[57] In an unrivaled demonstration of timidity, the Court in *Mezei* extended the holding in *Knauff* by finding that a returning lawful permanent resident's rights were as minimal as the rights of first time entrants, like Knauff.[58] Affirming the language in *Knauff*, the *Mezei* Court held that for a returning resident, "'[w]hatever the procedure authorized by Congress is, it is due process as far as an alien denied entry is concerned.'"[59] More recently, the Court indicated that it has some "limited judicial responsibility" with respect to Congress's power to regulate the admission and exclusion of aliens.[60] Yet, its application of this principle has been criticized as "toothless."[61] For many commentators, the *Knauff-Mezei* doctrine still forms the basis

---

into the United States and therefore, exclusion proceedings were proper and he was not entitled to procedural due process rights. *Id.* at 213-15. Moreover, his 25 years of residency in the United States did not entitle him to greater due process protection. *Id.* at 213-14. This aspect of the *Mezei* holding was modified by *Landon v. Plasencia*, 459 U.S. 21 (1982), which held that a returning resident, while placed in exclusion proceedings, is entitled to procedural due process protection. *Landon*, 459 U.S. at 34. Mezei was ultimately afforded a hearing after the Supreme Court upheld his exclusion. Weisselberg, *supra* note 55, at 964-84. While the Board of Special Inquiry upheld the charges of his membership in the Communist party, it made an off the record recommendation for his release and he was paroled after four years of detention. *Id.* at 982.

57. ALEINIKOFF ET AL., *supra* note 4, at 385 (discussing *Knauff* decision).

58. *Mezei*, 345 U.S. at 212.

59. *Id.* (quoting United States *ex rel.* Knauff v. Shaughnessy, 338 U.S. 537, 544 (1950)). Courts have criticized the reasoning used in *Knauff* and *Mezei*, which suggests excludable aliens may never invoke constitutional due process protections. *See* Jean v. Nelson, 472 U.S. 846, 874 (1985) (Marshall, J., dissenting). At an extreme, this would allow the Attorney General to invoke legitimate immigration goals to stop feeding excludable aliens in detention. *Id.* For a discussion of cases criticizing the use of the plenary power doctrine to allow for abysmal detention conditions, see Taylor, *supra* note 27, at 1132 n.232.

One year after *Mezei*, in 1954 the Court decided *Brown v. Board of Education*, 347 U.S. 483 (1954). Despite the boldness the Court demonstrated in *Brown*, that same year the Court maintained that in regards to immigration policies, "we are not prepared to deem ourselves wiser or more sensitive to human rights than our predecessors," indicating it would continue to defer to Congress. Galvan v. Press, 347 U.S. 522, 531 (1954); *see also* Louis Henkin, *The Constitution and United States Sovereignty: A Century of Chinese Exclusion and Its Progeny*, 100 HARV. L. REV. 853, 860-61 (1987) (noting Court's deference to Congress in *Galvan* is confusing in lieu of *Brown*); Kikuyo Matsumoto-Power, *Aliens, Resident Aliens, and U.S. Citizens in the Never-Never Land of the Immigration and Nationality Act*, 15 U. HAW. L. REV. 61, 77 (1993) (noting discussion by Louis Henkin regarding *Chinese Exclusion Case*).

60. *See, e.g.*, Fiallo v. Bell, 430 U.S. 787, 793 n.5 (1977) (noting acceptance of limited judicial responsibility in regulating admission and exclusion of aliens); Kleindienst v. Mandel, 408 U.S. 753, 766 (1972) (suggesting that due process places some restrictions on congressional power).

61. *Fiallo*, 430 U.S. at 805 (Marshall, J., dissenting).

for judicial deference to Congress's plenary power over immigration.[62]

Thus, while the language of the Fourteenth Amendment clearly states that the "due process" and "equal protection" provisions apply to "all persons," the development of the *Knauff-Mezei* doctrine draws distinctions among different classes of persons.[63] The suggestion that excludable aliens are "nonpersons" within the meaning of the Constitution, and thus not deserving of constitutional protection was explicit in the case of *Kwong Hai Chew v. Colding*,[64] decided one month before *Mezei*. The Court starkly framed the issue in *Kwong Hai Chew* to be whether Kwong could be stripped of "[h]is status as a person within the meaning and protection of the Fifth Amendment."[65] Although finding that Kwong himself could be recognized as a "person," the Court seemed to imply that "genuine excludable aliens" could be treated as nonpersons who are not entitled to the same constitutional protections provided to "persons."[66]

The prior discussion suggests that the political branches have nearly complete control over aliens.[67] Not all laws affecting aliens are, however, limited to such minimal judicial scrutiny. It is generally recognized that the plenary power doctrine governs cases chal-

62. *See* ALEINIKOFF ET AL., *supra* note 4, at 402-05 (noting numerous analyses and interpretations of *Mezei* doctrine); Aleinikoff, *Federal Regulation of Aliens*, *supra* note 26, at 866 (arguing that immigration regulators should be subject to judicial scrutiny accorded to other exercises of federal power); Henkin, *Constitution as Compact and Conscience*, *supra* note 26, at 25-27 (noting that flourish of individual rights has not shaken legacy of *Chinese Exclusion Case*). The "expedited removal" procedures which became law through IIRAIRA § 302 perhaps signify the demand for even greater deference to the *Knauff-Mezei* doctrine and the political branch's absolute control over immigration. *See* IIRAIRA § 302, Pub. L. No. 104-208 (1996) (to be codified at INA § 235, 8 U.S.C.) (discussing expedited removal procedures). For a further discussion of these procedures, see *supra* note 11.

For a further discussion of whether the plenary power belongs to Congress or to both the Congress and the Executive, and a criticism of the plenary power doctrine's resurfacing in the detention cases of the 1980s, see Taylor, *supra* note 27, at 1140-43, 1146 n.301.

63. *See* Martin, *supra* note 28, at 176 (noting that *Knauff-Mezei* doctrine implies excludable aliens are not persons for constitutional purposes).

64. 344 U.S. 590 (1953).

65. *Id.* at 601.

66. *Id.* The *Kwong* decision made a limited exception to *Knauff* in requiring that a lawful permanent resident, who had been gone from the United States for four months as a crewmen, be entitled to a true hearing before the INS with full disclosure of adverse information. *Id.* at 600-01. *But see* Martin, *supra* note 28, at 176 (noting that excludable aliens have the status of nonpersons). For a further discussion of *Kwong*, see *infra* notes 102-03 and accompanying text.

67. For a further discussion of the political branches' control over immigration, see *supra* notes 38-66 and accompanying text.

lenging immigration law, that is "the body of law governing the admission and expulsion of aliens."[68] Yet, this doctrine does not fully reveal the courts' treatment of aliens. In other cases, aliens have successfully asserted their individual rights. Developing concurrently with cases governed by the plenary power doctrine was a line of cases which would define the doctrine of the aliens' rights tradition.

III. THE ALIENS' RIGHTS TRADITION

Prior to the Civil War, the Supreme Court had not addressed questions regarding who was protected by the Bill of Rights and the other limited individual rights within the body of the original Constitution.[69] Yet, the ratification of the Fourteenth Amendment in 1868, brought a significant change in focus.[70] This amendment established the requirements of citizenship and sought to protect those privileges from state intrusion through the Privileges and Immunities Clause.[71] The Fourteenth Amendment also suggested that all persons, be they citizens or not, would enjoy the protections provided in the Due Process and Equal Protection Clauses.[72] This reading of the Fourteenth Amendment is consistent with the plain language of the Fifth Amendment which also suggests that due process should be afforded to all individuals, not just citizens.[73]

68. Aleinikoff, *Federal Regulation of Aliens*, *supra* note 26, at 864-65. For Aleinikoff, at the end of the nineteenth century the power over aliens was divided into two parts: (1) cases of expulsion and admission, where Congress possessed "plenary" power "virtually unfettered" by the Constitution (with the exception of due process in deportation proceedings) and (2) situations where U.S. citizens could invoke constitutional protections and where resident aliens were entitled to the same. *Id.* at 864-66; *see also* Legomsky, *Immigration Law and Plenary Power*, *supra* note 25, at 305 (discussing future of plenary power doctrine); Motomura, *Phantom Norms*, *supra* note 27, at 547 (defining immigration law); Taylor, *supra* note 27, at 1134 (noting that plenary power doctrine governs admission, exclusion and deportation of aliens).

69. Henkin, *Constitution as Compact and Conscience*, *supra* note 26, at 14-15.

70. U.S. CONST. amend XIV. The Fourteenth Amendment provides:

> No State shall make or enforce any law which shall abridge the privileges or immunities of citizens of the United States; nor shall any State deprive any person of life, liberty, or property, without due process of law; nor deny to any person within its jurisdiction the equal protection of the laws.

Id.

71. Henkin, *Constitution as Compact and Conscience*, *supra* note 26, at 15.

72. *Id.*; *see also* Matsumoto-Power, *supra* note 59, at 81-82 (noting that language of Fourteenth Amendment is not limited to U.S. citizens).

73. *See* U.S. CONST. amend. V (stating "[nor] shall any person . . . be deprived of life, liberty, or property, without due process of law"); *see also* Henkin, *Constitution as Compact and Conscience*, *supra* note 26, at 14-15 (stating that Fourteenth Amendment established criteria for protection of individual rights).

Shortly after the enactment of the Fourteenth Amendment, it was embraced by an alien living in the United States to strike down a state law denying equal protection to persons of Chinese descent in *Yick Wo v. Hopkins.*[74] The *Yick Wo* Court found:

> The Fourteenth Amendment to the Constitution is not confined to the protection of citizens . . . . These provisions are universal in their application, to all persons within the territorial jurisdiction, without regard to any differences in race, or color, or of nationality; and the equal protection of the laws is a pledge of the protection of equal laws.[75]

Yick Wo became the foundation of the aliens' rights tradition.[76] This case led a line of cases which held that when a legal challenge involving aliens' rights does not intrude upon the realm of immigration law, courts would review the claim with the same degree of judicial scrutiny afforded a U.S. citizen.[77] With the Fourteenth Amendment phrase "any person" found to include aliens, shortly after the *Yick Wo* decision the Supreme Court found that aliens are included within the meaning of "person" as identified in the Due Process Clause of the Fifth Amendment, which safeguards a person's life, liberty or property against deprivation by the federal government.[78] Aliens also fall within the definition of "people" in the

74. 118 U.S. 356, 373-74 (1886); *see also* Henkin, *Constitution as Compact and Conscience, supra* note 26, at 15-16 (discussing procedural background of *Yick Wo*); Taylor, *supra* note 27, at 1133 (discussing Supreme Court's holding in *Yick Wo*).

75. *Yick Wo,* 118 U.S. at 369.

76. Henkin, *Constitution as Compact and Conscience, supra* note 26, at 16.

77. *See, e.g.*, Aleinikoff, *Federal Regulation of Aliens, supra* note 26, at 865-66 (noting cases outside of immigration law which have afforded aliens constitutional protections); Henkin, *Constitution as Compact and Conscience, supra* note 26, at 16-18 (noting that state discrimination against aliens is subject to sharp judicial scrutiny); Taylor, *supra* note 27, at 1133-35 (noting that cases have extended Fourth and Fifth Amendment protection to aliens).

78. *See, e.g.*, Wong Wing v. United States, 163 U.S. 228 (1896) (holding that Constitution precludes punishment of aliens for being in United States unlawfully except pursuant to trial in accordance with Fifth and Sixth Amendments). In *Wong Wing*, the Court invalidated a section of the 1892 immigration statute which provided for "infamous punishment at hard labor" or the confiscation of property of any Chinese national found by executive authorities to be here illegally. *Id.* at 237. The statute's deportation provisions had been approved in *Fong Yue Ting v. United States*, 149 U.S. 698 (1893). In *Wong Wing*, the Court reaffirmed these individuals could be deported, but it found the imprisonment or confiscation of property to be punitive and that it was invalid without "a judicial trial to establish the guilt of the accused." *Wong Wing*, 163 U.S. at 237. The *Wong Wing* decision heralded the beginning of a line of aliens' rights cases which were successfully argued as outside the realm of immigration law and in the realm of criminal law, thus entitling aliens to assert Fifth and Sixth Amendment protection in criminal pro-

Fourth Amendment, and therefore, are allowed "to be secure in their persons, houses, papers, and effects, against unreasonable searches and seizures."[79] Additionally, aliens are guaranteed the protection of the First Amendment[80] and are provided the procedural safeguards and immunities of other amendments.[81]

Yet, even within the aliens' rights tradition, the courts make a distinction between a state's limitation on individual rights and the

---

ceedings. *See* Russian Volunteer Fleet v. United States, 282 U.S. 481, 492 (1931) (holding that property of alien friends may not be taken for public purposes without just compensation); United States v. Henry, 604 F.2d 908, 914 (5th Cir. 1979) (holding that aliens are entitled to *Miranda* warnings during custodial interrogation); United States v. Casimiro-Benitez, 533 F.2d 1121, 1124-25 (9th Cir. 1976) (holding that defendant's Fifth Amendment right to counsel was not violated during police interrogation); *see also* DAVID M. O'BRIEN, CONSTITUTIONAL LAW AND POLITICS: CIVIL RIGHTS AND CIVIL LIBERTIES 1503-05 (2d ed. 1995) (discussing Supreme Court's classification of aliens); Aleinikoff, *Federal Regulation of Aliens*, *supra* note 26, at 864-65 (noting that "legacy of *Yick Wo* has . . . survived and flourished in the 20th century"); Bosniak, *supra* note 27, at 1094-1101 (discussing *Wong Wing* and alien rights tradition); Michael Scaperlanda, *Partial Membership: Aliens and the Constitutional Community*, 81 IOWA L. REV. 707, 742-43 (1996) [hereinafter Scaperlanda, *Partial Membership*]; Taylor, *supra* note 27, at 134 n.240 (noting that cases following *Wong Wing* tradition extend Fifth and Sixth Amendment protections to aliens in criminal proceedings). The equal protection derived from the notion of due process as stated in the Fifth Amendment is also provided to aliens. *See* Hampton v. Mow Sun Wong, 426 U.S. 88, 116 (1976) (holding Civil Service Commission's denial of employment to resident aliens amounted to deprivation of due process); *see also* Henkin, *Constitution as Compact and Conscience*, *supra* note 26, at 16 (noting that after *Yick Wo*, Supreme Court considered aliens persons for purposes of due process). For a further discussion of the phrase "any person," see *supra* note 72-73 and accompanying text.

79. *See* Almeida-Sanchez v. United States, 413 U.S. 266 (1973) (applying Fourth Amendment protection against searches and seizures where alien was defendant); *see also* Henkin, *Constitution as Compact and Conscience*, *supra* note 26, at 16 (noting that court decisions following *Yick Wo* have held aliens among "people" entitled to Fourth Amendment protections). *But see* United States v. Verdugo-Urquidez, 494 U.S. 259 (1990) (holding that Fourth Amendment does not apply to seizure of nonresident alien's property in foreign country). For a further discussion of aliens' Fourth Amendment rights, see *infra* notes 108-13 and accompanying text.

80. *See* Bridges v. Wixon, 326 U.S. 135, 148 (1945) (discussing First Amendment); *see also* Aleinikoff, *Federal Regulation of Aliens*, *supra* note 26, at 868 (discussing the protection of First Amendment rights in immigration context); Henkin, *Constitution as Compact and Conscience*, *supra* note 26, at 16 n.42 (discussing protection under Fourth, Fifth and Fourteenth Amendments). *But see* Kleindienst v. Mandel, 408 U.S. 753 (1972) (protecting citizen's First Amendment right to personally communicate with alien); American Arab Anti-Discrimination Comm. v. Meese ("ADC"), 714 F. Supp. 1060 (C.D. Cal. 1989), *aff'd in part and rev'd in part on other grounds*, 940 F.2d 445 (9th Cir.), *vacated* 970 F.2d 501 (9th Cir. 1991) (stating aliens enjoyed full First Amendment rights in deportation context). For a further discussion of *Mandell*, see *infra* notes 198-200 and accompanying text. For a discussion of *ADC*, see *infra* note 153.

81. Henkin, *Constitution as Compact and Conscience*, *supra* note 26, at 16.

federal government's limitation on identical rights.[82] Historically, the states are held to a higher level of judicial scrutiny than the federal government, therefore entitling aliens to greater protection against discriminatory state and local practices.[83] State discrimination against aliens creates "suspect classifications."[84] Such discrimination is sharply scrutinized and is upheld only if it serves a "compelling state interest."[85] By contrast, Congress is held to the

---

82. Aleinikoff, *Federal Regulation of Aliens*, *supra* note 26, at 864; Taylor, *supra* note 27, at 1133 n.235.

83. Aleinikoff, *Federal Regulation of Aliens*, *supra* note 26, at 865 n.20-22; Taylor, *supra* note 27, at 1133 n.235.

84. Graham v. Richardson, 403 U.S. 365, 372 (1971); *see also* Henkin, *Constitution as Compact and Conscience*, *supra* note 26, at 17 (noting that discriminating against aliens creates suspect classifications which will be scrutinized).

85. *See, e.g.*, Plyler v. Doe, 457 U.S. 202, 203 (1982) (stating right of undocumented children to go to public school); Graham v. Richardson, 403 U.S. 365 (1971) (invalidating state law excluding aliens from public program). Other cases have invalidated provisions which prevented aliens from receiving economic opportunities in the private sector. *See, e.g.*, Bernal v. Fainter, 467 U.S. 216, 227-28 (1984) (ruling state statute requiring U.S. citizenship to be notary unconstitutional); Toll v. Moreno, 458 U.S. 1, 16-17 (1982) (invalidating state university policy prohibiting G-4 aliens and dependents from acquiring in-state status); Examining Bd. of Eng'rs v. Flores DeOtero, 426 U.S. 572, 605 (1976) (holding Puerto Rico's statute prohibiting aliens from engaging in private practice of engineering deprived aliens of rights); *In re* Griffiths, 413 U.S. 717, 729 (1973) (denying citizenship requirement to take bar exam); Sugarman v. Dougall, 413 U.S. 634, 645-46 (1973) (ruling unconstitutional state statute requiring U.S. citizenship to be part of state civil service).

States can, however, still use alienage classifications to deny employment and political rights if related to the exercise of an important government function. The *Sugarman* Court held that this exception was the result of a state's obligation "to preserve the basic conception of a political community." *Sugarman*, 413 U.S. at 647 (citing Dunn v. Blumstein, 405 U.S. 330, 344 (1972)). The Court has noted that citizenship "denotes an association with the polity," and that it creates a "bond" of "special significance." Ambach v. Norwick, 441 U.S. 68, 75 (1979) (upholding exclusion of aliens from employment as teachers). Furthermore, the Court stated that "[t]he exclusion of aliens from basic governmental processes is not a deficiency in the democratic system but a necessary consequence of the community's process of political self-definition." Cabell v. Chavez-Salido, 454 U.S. 432, 439 (1982) (upholding exclusion of aliens from employment as parole officers); *see also Moreno*, 458 U.S. at 12 n.17 (limiting participation of noncitizens in states' political and governmental functions); Foley v. Connelie, 435 U.S. 291 (1978) (upholding exclusion of aliens from employment as police officers). Yet, it has been noted that "laws excluding permanent resident aliens from political participation or government benefits are dramatically over- and under-inclusive if they are justified in terms of loyalty, competence, or identification with 'American values.'" Aleinikoff, *Citizens, Aliens, Membership*, *supra* note 40, at 14; *see also* Aleinikoff, *Federal Regulation of Aliens*, *supra* note 26, at 865 n.21 (discussing excluding aliens from employment as parole officers); Henkin, *Constitution as Compact and Conscience*, *supra* note 26, at 17 (arguing discrimination is not suspect discrimination when it substantially affects community members); Martin, *supra* note 28, at 196-99 (allowing states to disqualify noncitizens from jobs as police officers, teachers and deputy probation officers). For a discussion of the similarities between the states' "political function" exception and the federal government's generally low standard

lower standard of requiring only a "facially legitimate and bona fide reason" for discriminating against aliens.[86] This allows Congress to successfully use the arguments of national sovereignty, war and peace, and international relations to justify disparate treatment in areas where the states are prohibited from making similar distinctions.[87]

IV. THE PLENARY POWER DOCTRINE VERSUS THE ALIENS' RIGHTS TRADITION: A CRITICISM OF THE BATTLE

With the concurrent development of the plenary power doctrine and the aliens' rights tradition, legal challenges by aliens have been decided after forcibly being characterized as involving "immigration law" or "nonimmigration law."[88] Victim to this *Fong Yue Ting* versus *Yick Wo* phenomenon, the special equities of a case are virtually ignored.[89] Critics of this "inside/outside" immigration law characterization argue that it does not properly emphasize distinctions between the status of aliens in cases "outside" of immigration law and between the status of aliens in cases "inside" immigration

---

of scrutiny which impacts on both membership and the definition of the political community, see Bosniak, *supra* note 27, at 1110-15.

86. *See* Fiallo v. Bell, 430 U.S. 787, 799 (1977) (holding it is not judiciary's role in cases of this sort to probe and test justifications for legislative decisions); Hampton v. Mow Sun Wong, 426 U.S. 88, 99-105 (1976) (requiring legitimate basis for preserving federal rule was that it intended to serve interest); Mathews v. Diaz, 426 U.S. 67, 81-83 (1976) (stating that those who qualify under Congress's test may reasonably be presumed to have greater affinity to the United States); Kleindienst v. Mandel, 408 U.S. 753, 770 (1972) (allowing lesser standard of scrutiny when Congress delegates power to Executive); *see also* O'BRIEN, *supra* note 78, at 1503-05 (noting state and federal laws have discriminated against aliens); Mitchell Kurfis, *The Constitutionality of California's Proposition 187: An Equal Protection Analysis*, 32 CAL. W. L. REV. 129, 137 (1995) (noting "a statutory discrimination will not be set aside if any state of facts reasonably may be conceived to justify it").

87. *Compare Diaz*, 426 U.S. at 67 (ruling federal government is able to distinguish between lawful permanent residents and citizen in allocating federal welfare), *with Richardson*, 403 U.S. at 365 (prohibiting Pennsylvania and Arizona from denying aliens welfare benefits). An analogy of *Diaz* and *Graham* "is so powerful that the Court's heavy reliance on the unique nature of federal authority over immigration sounds wholly irrational." Matsumoto-Power, *supra* note 59, at 90; *see also* Henkin, *Constitution as Compact and Conscience*, *supra* note 26, at 17 (arguing that Supreme Court never held that congressional act discriminated against aliens in violation of equal protection).

88. Shaughnessy v. United States *ex rel.* Mezei, 345 U.S. 206 (1953); United States *ex rel.* Knauff v. Shaughnessy, 338 U.S. 537 (1953).

89. *See Mezei*, 345 U.S. at 216 (failing to take into account special equities); *Knauff*, 338 U.S. at 547 (same). For example, Knauff's marriage to a U.S. soldier and Mezei's lengthy residence in the United States were completely discounted once the Court characterized these cases as challenges to immigration law and therefore, beyond judicial review. For a discussion of *Knauff* and *Mezei*, see *supra* notes 55-63 and accompanying text.

law.[90] Apart from these criticisms, difficulties with this distinction arise because it does not explain recent "immigration law" cases in which the federal government's plenary power was challenged successfully.[91] It also does not explain cases seemingly outside the realm of immigration law in which aliens' rights, while expected to be protected, were ultimately not protected.[92] Some commentators offer theories for the "blur" between the plenary power doctrine and the aliens' rights tradition.[93] By virtually ignoring the plenary power versus aliens' rights distinction, however, alternative theories can be offered to explain a developing pattern. These theories are illustrated best in the cases of *Landon v. Plasencia*[94] and *United States v. Verdugo-Urquidez*.[95]

A. Landon v. Plasencia: *Defeating the Plenary Power Doctrine*

The Supreme Court in *Plasencia* held that a lawful permanent resident returning to the United States is entitled to the same due process protections as a resident who never left.[96] In so modifying

90. Bosniak, *supra* note 27, at 1063-65; Scaperlanda, *Partial Membership*, *supra* note 78; Scaperlanda, *Polishing the Golden Door*, *supra* note 40, at 991-1002.

91. *See* Landon v. Plasencia, 459 U.S. 21, 41 (1982) (holding government cannot present case without opposition when permanent resident alien's substantial interest in remaining in country is at stake); Rosenberg v. Fleuti, 374 U.S. 449 (1963) (preventing government from saying alien intended to depart after taking brief trip); Kwong Hai Chew v. Colding, 344 U.S. 590 (1953) (holding Attorney General has no authority to deny entry to permanent resident alien of United States). For a further discussion of *Plasencia*, see *infra* notes 94-100 and accompanying text.

92. *See* United States v. Verdugo-Urquidez, 494 U.S. 259, 275 (1990) (holding no Fourth Amendment warrantless "search and seizure" protection for nonresident alien's foreign property); Mathews v. Diaz, 426 U.S 67, 80 (1976) (limiting Social Security benefits to permanent residents living in United States for at least five years); Kleindienst v. Mandel, 408 U.S. 753, 769 (1972) (limiting First Amendment rights of U.S. citizens who want to bring known Marxist to United States to speak); Flemming v. Nestor, 363 U.S. 603, 608 (1960) (ruling deportee is not entitled to Social Security benefits).

93. *See* Motomura, *Phantom Norms*, *supra* note 27, at 607 (noting misdirected judicial review as problem for unpredictable solutions); Motomura, *Procedural Surrogates*, *supra* note 27, at 1646 (noting Court's readiness to recognize procedural due process as formal exception to plenary power doctrine stood in tension with its unwillingness to give procedural due process requirement any real content); Taylor, *supra* note 27, at 1134-35 (noting boundary between plenary power doctrine and aliens' rights is not easily marked).

94. 459 U.S. 21 (1982).

95. 494 U.S. 259 (1990).

96. *Plasencia*, 459 U.S. at 21. In *Plasencia*, the Court modified part of the holding in *Shaughnessy v. United States ex rel. Mezei*, 345 U.S. 206 (1953) and extended procedural due process protection in exclusion proceedings to returning lawful permanent residents who had only been gone for a few days. *Plasencia*, 459 U.S. at 34. For a further discussion of *Mezei*, see *supra* notes 56-63 and accompanying text. *Plasencia* did, however, reverse the understanding of *Rosenberg v. Fleuti*, 374 U.S.

the *Mezei* holding, the *Plasencia* Court reasoned that "once an alien gains admission to our country and begins to develop the ties that go with permanent residence his constitutional status changes accordingly."[97] In determining that an individual like Plasencia is entitled to due process protection, the Court remanded the case for a determination of what process was due as an initial matter consistent with the considerations set forth in *Mathews v. Eldridge*.[98]

The *Plasencia* decision marked the firm establishment of the notions of community ties and membership in determining what due process was owed to aliens.[99] According to *Plasencia*, if an individual challenging an immigration law can demonstrate ties binding him or her to the national polity, that individual will receive greater protection.[100] This development was the culmination of a line of cases which began with the minority voices of *Fong Yue Ting v. United States*.[101] Although more restrictive than *Plasencia*, the plaintiff's special equities were also taken into consideration in *Kwong Hai Chew v. Colding*.[102] Kwong Hai Chew's brief departure from the United States did not trigger a statutory entry upon his

---

449 (1963), that returning residents be placed in deportation proceedings and instead found that proper determination of the due process question should be in exclusion proceedings. *Plasencia*, 459 U.S. at 32.

97. *Plasencia*, 459 U.S. at 32.

98. 424 U.S. 319 (1976).

99. *Plasencia*, 459 U.S. at 32-37. The *Plasencia* Court stated:

> In evaluating the procedures in any case, the courts must consider the interest at stake for the individual, the risk of an erroneous deprivation of the interest through the procedures used as well as the probable value of additional or different procedural safeguards, and the interest of the government in using the current procedures rather than additional or different procedures.

Id. at 34 (relying on Mathews v. Eldridge, 424 U.S. 319, 334-35 (1976)). For a further discussion of the *Eldridge* test, see *infra* note 132 and accompanying text.

100. *Plasencia*, 459 U.S. at 34-35. The Court in *Plasencia* further stated:

> Plasencia's interest here is, without question, a weighty one. She stands to lose the right "to stay and live and work in this land of freedom." Further, she may lose the right to rejoin her immediate family, a right that ranks high among the interests of the individual . . . . [T]he courts must evaluate the particular circumstances and determine what procedures would satisfy the minimum requirements of due process on the reentry of a permanent resident alien.

Id. (citation omitted).

101. 149 U.S. 698 (1893). According to observers, the dissenters in *Fong Yue Ting* suggested that resident aliens should be entitled to some constitutional protection because they have significant ties to the community. Taylor, *supra* note 27, at 1136 n.251 (citing Fong Yue Ting v. United States, 149 U.S. 698, 737-38 (1893) (Brewer, J., dissenting); *id.* at 746 (Field, J., dissenting); *id.* at 762 (Fuller, J., dissenting)). This notion also influenced the *Japanese Immigrant Case*, which entitles aliens in deportation proceedings to procedural due process. *Id.* (citing Japanese Immigrant Case, 189 U.S. 86, 100-01 (1903)).

102. 344 U.S. 590 (1953).

return, as this seaman, sailing for only four months on an American ship with American security clearance, was "assimilated" to the status of a resident alien who never left for purposes of procedural due process safeguards.[103] This type of reasoning also was responsible for the development of the *Rosenberg v. Fleuti*[104] doctrine which prevents a permanent resident's brief, casual and innocent trip out of the United States from creating a statutory entry upon return because there is no meaningful interruptive departure.[105]

Despite the fact that these cases clearly impacted upon sovereignty, the plenary power doctrine did not prevail.[106] Yet, while aliens were making strides in cases challenging immigration law, victory was not to be found in the nonimmigration arena.[107] The recent decision of *Verdugo-Urquidez* illustrates the losing battle of the aliens' rights theory and reflects the Court's consideration of an individual's membership and ties to the United States in determining what protections are due.

B. United States v. Verdugo-Urquidez: *Defeating the Aliens' Rights Tradition*

Writing for the Court in *Verdugo-Urquidez*, Chief Justice Rhenquist found that the Fourth Amendment had no application to the search and seizure by United States agents of property owned by a

103. *Id.* at 596.

104. 374 U.S. 449 (1963).

105. The *Fleuti* Court held that a permanent resident's few hour trip to Mexico was "innocent, casual and brief," and therefore, not meaningfully interruptive departure that would trigger statutory "entry" upon return. *Id.* at 462-63. It appears that INA § 101(a)(13), which has traditionally provided the statutory basis for the *Fleuti* doctrine, has been narrowed to allow only for specific instances in which a lawful permanent resident's departure and return will not be considered a "meaningfully interruptive departure." IIRAIRA § 301(a), Pub. L. No. 104-208 (1996) (amending INA § 101(a)(13), 8 U.S.C.). For a further discussion of IIRAIRA, see *supra* note 11 and accompanying text.

106. Courts have also indicated that they are less inclined to give absolute deference to the federal political branches in those cases which can be characterized as "inside" immigration law. *See, e.g.*, Jean v. Nelson, 472 U.S. 846, 857 (1985) (noting INS officials must exercise their discretion under nondiscriminatory parole provisions without regard to race or national origin); Fiallo v. Bell, 430 U.S. 787, 793 n.5 (1977) (stating "[o]ur cases reflect acceptance of a limited judicial responsibility under the Constitution even with respect to the power of Congress to regulate the admission and exclusion of aliens"); Japanese Immigrant Case, 189 U.S. 86, 99-100 (1903) (noting administrative officer may not disregard fundamental principles of due process of law); *see also* Bosniak, *supra* note 27, at 1092-94 (noting courts have not absolutely foreclosed use of judicial review of government's substantive immigration decisions).

107. *See* Bosniak, *supra* note 27, at 1095-98 (discussing rights that attach as result of "territorial presence" in case of Wong Wing v. United States, 163 U.S. 228, 239 (1896)).

nonresident alien and located in a foreign country.[108] The Court held that Verdugo-Urquidez was not a person within the meaning of the Fourth Amendment.[109] According to Chief Justice Rhenquist, "the people" referred to in the Fourth Amendment are "a class of persons who are part of a national community or who have otherwise developed sufficient connection with this country to be considered part of that community."[110] In Chief Justice Rehnquist's opinion, the respondent did not exemplify these traits.[111] While the *Verdugo-Urquidez* decision may arguably have been meant to impact only the rights of nonresident aliens without ties to the United States, the decision already has affected lawful permanent residents of the United States.[112] The United States Court of Appeals for the Ninth Circuit recently suggested that lawful permanent residents may not have sufficient ties to the United States to

108. United States v. Verdugo-Urquidez, 494 U.S. 259, 261, 264-75 (1990). This case involved an alleged Mexican drug lord and murderer of Drug Enforcement Agency (DEA) agent Enrique Camarena Salazar. *Id.* at 262. Verdugo-Urquidez had been seized by Mexican police and delivered to a California border station. *Id.* The next day, while incarcerated in San Diego, DEA agents, along with Mexican police, searched his home in Mexicali, Mexico and found evidence of his narcotics smuggling. *Id.* While the United States Court of Appeals for the Ninth Circuit suppressed the evidence as a violation of the Fourth Amendment warrant clause, the Supreme Court reversed. *Id.* at 263, 275. Additionally, by the time this case reached the Supreme Court, Verdugo-Urquidez, in a separate prosecution, had been convicted for his involvement in the torture-murder of DEA agent Salazar. *Id.* at 262.

Six Justices, in three different opinions, held that the search was not a violation of the Fourth Amendment because the Fourth Amendment had no application to the search of a nonresident alien's property in a foreign country. *Id.* at 275-78. Three Justices dissented. *Id.* at 261. Justice Kennedy, while joining the majority, wrote a concurring opinion which observers suggest so drastically diverges from the majority that the opinion may only speak for a plurality of four. *Id.* at 275; *see* Neuman, *Whose Constitution, supra* note 30, at 972, 974 n.378 (discussing *Verdugo-Urquidez* opinion). The decision in *Verdugo-Urquidez* has resulted in discussion of Fourth Amendment protections and aliens. *See id.* at 912, 971-76 (discussing Fourth Amendment rights and aliens); Michael Scaperlanda, *The Domestic Fourth Amendment Rights of Aliens: To What Extent Do They Survive* United States v. Verdugo-Urquidez?, 56 Mo. L. REV. 213, 217-27 (1991) (questioning applicability of Fourth Amendment to aliens lawfully in United States) [hereinafter Scaperlanda, *Domestice Fourth Amendment Rights*].

109. *Verdugo-Urguidez*, 494 U.S. at 264-66.

110. *Id.* at 265. According to Chief Justice Rehnquist, the First, Second, Ninth and Tenth Amendments would also be inapplicable to the defendant because "[t]he language of these Amendments contrasts with the words 'person' and 'accused' used in the Fifth and Sixth Amendments regulating procedure in criminal cases." *Id.* at 265-66.

111. *Id.* at 274.

112. *See* United States v. Barona, 56 F.3d 1087, 1094 (9th Cir. 1995) (noting it is unclear whether noncitizen defendants are entitled to Fourth Amendment protection after *Verdugo-Urquidez*), *cert. denied*, 116 S. Ct. 813 (1996).

invoke the protections of the Fourth Amendment outside of the U.S. territorial boundaries.[113]

Other weaknesses in the aliens' rights doctrine are revealed in cases where the litigants had limited ties to the United States.[114] For example, an alien previously deported for past Communist membership was denied Social Security benefits in *Flemming v. Nestor.*[115] In addition, the Court restricted a permanent resident's ability to qualify for Social Security, holding that the awarding of benefits applies only to individuals who had been permanent residents for more than five years and therefore, could be considered the "most like citizens," in *Mathews v. Diaz.*[116]

113. *Id.* The Ninth Circuit noted that even if the Fourth Amendment, as interpreted in *Verdugo-Urquidez*, applies to nonresident aliens, wiretaps of telephone conversations in foreign country, that were conducted as joint operation of both United States and foreign law enforcement officials, satisfied Fourth Amendment's reasonableness requirement, regardless of whether there was probable cause because they were conducted in compliance with law of country in which they took place. *Id.*; *see also Supreme Court Declines Review of Alien's Fourth Amendment Rights in Foreign Seizure*, 73 INTERPRETER RELEASES 138 (1996) (discussing *Verdugo-Urguidez*). *But see* Wang Zong Xiao v. Reno, 81 F.3d 808, 816 (9th Cir. 1996) (noting Fifth Amendment due process rights available to undocumented alien brought to United States as prosecution witness); *Recent Immigration Decisions in the Federal Courts*, 73 INTERPRETER RELEASES 726, 730-31 (1996) (discussing *Wong Zong Xiao*).

114. *See* Mathews v. Diaz, 426 U.S. 67 (1967) (requiring permanent residence of five years to qualify for social security benefits); Flemming v. Nestor, 363 U.S. 603 (1960) (denying social security benefits to alien who was formerly communist).

115. 363 U.S. 603 (1960). The Court found that a rational justification existed for the denial of Social Security benefits, and therefore, did not violate the Due Process Clause of the Fifth Amendment. *Id.* at 611. For the Court, a deportee's residence abroad is of "obvious relevance" to justifying the denial of benefits. *Id.* at 612. The deportee's place of residence prevents the benefit of "increased over-all national purchasing power" as he or she cannot spend his or her Social Security check in the United States as can recipients living in the United States. *Id.* Additionally, it cannot "be deemed irrational for Congress to have concluded that the public purse should not be utilized to contribute to the support of those deported." *Id.*; *see also* Taylor, *supra* note 27, at 1137 (noting *Flemming* Court's rationale).

116. *Diaz*, 426 U.S. at 83-84 (discussing resident alien's unsuccessful challenge to Social Security Act provision that imposed five year residence requirement on aliens). Perhaps not so coincidentally, an individual generally needs to be a permanent resident for five years before he or she is entitled to citizenship. INA § 316(a), 8 U.S.C. § 427(a) (1994). Bosniak finds *Diaz* to be one of the "clearest examples" of the suggestion that membership concerns impact upon issues seemingly "outside" immigration law. Bosniak, *supra* note 27, at 1065-67. *But see* Graham v. Richardson, 403 U.S. 365, 372 (1971) (noting ability of states to apply their immigration laws to their alien inhabitants is confined by narrow limits). Contrasting *Graham* and *Diaz*, Bosniak recognizes that the *Graham* decision is based on the "irrelevance" of immigration principles for the states, while the *Diaz* Court found the case involved an extension of the federal government's immigration power through the challenged provisions of the Social Security Act. Bosniak, *supra* note 27, at 1101-10; *see also* Taylor, *supra* note 27, at 1137-38 (discussing *Graham* and *Diaz*).

C. *Commenting on the Battle*

Concern over the rights of individuals arising from cases such as *Verdugo-Urquidez*, *Nestor* and *Diaz* exemplifies a struggle between the aliens' rights tradition and the plenary power doctrine in which the plenary power doctrine prevails.[117] It has been suggested that these cases curb the strides of the aliens' rights tradition by allowing judicial deference to any federal action affecting aliens.[118] Consequently, attempts are made to fight Congress's plenary power intruding into the aliens' rights arena. Yet, simultaneously a battle is waged to encourage the Court's concern for fundamental rights to cross the border into the immigration arena. These efforts conflict as they encourage maintaining the plenary power versus aliens' rights distinction in cases outside the immigration arena, while arguing for the abolishment of the distinction when presented with challenges to immigration law.

Difficulty in maintaining the plenary power versus aliens' rights boundary suggests that the proper distinction in deciding whether an alien is entitled to constitutional protection is not whether his or her case falls "inside" or "outside" of immigration law.[119] Rather, the cases which contradict the premises of the plenary power doctrine and the aliens' rights tradition may be understood more easily if one considers an alien's "ties" or "membership" in the U.S. national community.[120]

For a discussion of the legislative restrictions placed on a lawful permanent resident's right to welfare through the recent Welfare Act, see *supra* notes 12-13 and accompanying text.

117. *See* United States v. Verdugo-Urquidez, 494 U.S. 259 (1990) (holding Fourth Amendment does not apply to search and seizure of alien resident's property); Mathews v. Diaz, 426 U.S. 67 (1976) (holding alien cannot receive social security benefits); Flemming v. Nestor, 363 U.S. 603 (1960) (same).

118. *See* Motomura, *Phantom Norms*, *supra* note 27, at 585 (noting that Congress makes rules that would be unacceptable if applied to citizens); Motomura, *Procedural Surrogates*, supra note 27, at 1693 (suggesting that Congress's immigration decisions "are largely immune from judicial inquiry or interference"); Neuman, *Whose Constitution*, *supra* note 30, at 972 (discussing Chief Justice Rehnquist's opinion in *Verdugo-Urquidez* which gave three conclusions as to why aliens do not have constitutional rights); Scaperlanda, *Domestic Fourth Amendment Rights*, *supra* note 108, at 231-42 (noting Congress has broad discretion in controlling immigration law); Scaperlanda, *Marshall's Jurisprudence*, *supra* note 25, at 68-69 n.83 (discussing *Verdugo-Urquidez* and its break from exception that aliens are entitled to protection from Bill of Rights); Taylor, *supra* note 27, at 1135-39 (discussing cases giving judicial deference to congressional statutes).

119. For a criticism of the preoccupation with the immigration law versus nonimmigration law distinction, see Bosniak, *supra* note 27, at 1066-67.

120. *See* Aleinikoff, *Federal Regulation of Aliens*, *supra* note 26, at 922 (rejecting plenary power); Aleinikoff, *Community Ties*, *supra* note 29 (noting living with family members is substantial interest); Martin, *supra* note 28, at 172 (noting Due Process

V. NATIONAL MEMBERSHIP AND COMMUNITY TIES

A. *Professor David Martin: Membership in the National Community*

For Professor Martin, due process determinations are a function of one's "membership in the national community."[121] Martin suggests rectifying the disparate treatment of aliens by basing treatment upon degrees of membership, rather than categorizing cases as plenary power or aliens' rights.[122] For Martin:

> [W]e, as a national community, somehow *owe less* in the coin of procedural assurances to the first-time applicant for admission than we do to our fellow citizens or to permanent resident aliens, or even to regular nonimmigrants who have been among us for awhile. This is not necessarily to say that we owe nothing; that would be to repeat the mistakes of *Knauff* and *Mezei.* Instead it is simply to assert that established community ties, which exist to varying degrees with respect to different categories of aliens, ought to count in deciding what process is due. Or perhaps the intuition is more accurately stated the other way around. We *owe more* procedural guarantees—a greater assurance of scrupulous factual accuracy—to citizens and permanent resident aliens than we do to aliens at the threshold of entry into the national community.[123]

Clause requires as constitutional minimum that aliens establish links to this country). In finding the inside/outside distinction to be an overstated generalization, Bosniak recognizes that even in outside immigration law, alienage is used to accord aliens less "constitutional and subconstitutional" rights and benefits. Bosniak, *supra* note 27, at 1063-65. Discussing Michael Walzer, a political theorist concerned with the political community's "sphere of membership," Bosniak recognizes that there is an increasing convergence of what he refers to as the admissions (or membership) sphere and the political (or equal personhood) sphere. (The spheres mentioned in this article relate to the immigration and nonimmigration arenas, respectively). *Id.* at 1069-87; *see also* MICHAEL WALZER, SPHERES OF JUSTICE: A DEFENSE OF PLURALISM AND EQUALITY (1985) (discussing spheres of justice for aliens). "[A]lienage legitimately matters not merely at the border but for the allocation of rights and benefits in the interior as well." Bosniak, *supra* note 27, at 1086; *see also* Scaperlanda, *Polishing the Golden Door, supra* note 40, at 996 (discussing Court's decision allowing aliens to get civil service employment); Taylor, *supra* note 27, at 1136 (discussing *Wing Wong* progeny which extended constitutional protection to aliens in criminal proceedings).

121. Martin, *supra* note 28, at 235; *see also* Aleinikoff, *Federal Regulation of Aliens, supra* note 26, at 868 (discussing notions of "membership"); Aleinikoff, *Community Ties, supra* note 29, at 242 (same); T. Alexander Aleinikoff, *The Tightening Circle of Membership*, 22 HASTINGS CONST. L.Q. 915, 920-21 (1995) (same); Bosniak, *supra* note 27, at 1068 (same); Matsumoto-Power, *supra* note 59, at 78 (same).

122. Martin, *supra* note 28, at 191.

123. *Id.* at 191-92 (emphasis added).

Martin points out that a large part of what is meant by community, including national community, is that relational obligations exist.[124] It is not a novel idea to suggest that "special, heightened obligations" attach as a result of special relationships.[125] Our obligations to the national community are compared by analogy to the obligations which result by being a member of a family or a neighbor in a community.[126]

B. *Professor Alexander Aleinikoff: Community Ties*

While Martin relies on consideration of community ties in his discussion of membership in the national community, Professor Aleinikoff distinguishes these terms.[127] In distinguishing the terms, Aleinikoff relies not on the premise of membership in the national community, but solely on the notion of community ties. To Aleinikoff:

> It seems that the problem is not so much in accepting Professor Martin's intuition that we "owe less in the coin of procedural assurances of the first-time applicant for admission than we do to our fellow citizens or to permanent resident aliens." Rather, it is trying to elaborate on that intuition in terms of membership in a national community. It is my belief that our intuition does not depend upon inchoate notions of membership. I think it is more easily explained as a generalization about the stake that certain groups of aliens have in entering or residing in the United States or in not being returned to their country of origin. In short, whereas Professor Martin would examine the notion of *community*, I would look at *community ties*.[128]

---

124. *Id.* at 193. This characteristic of community exists for Martin whether one believes that a community has developed for practical reasons (*i.e.*, shared purposes) or if it has developed naturally, through shared history. *Id.* at 195.

125. *Id.* at 193 & n.101. Martin finds support for this idea from various sources. *See id.* (relying on JAMES FISHKIN, THE LIMITS OF OBLIGATION 25-38 (1982); JOHN RAWLS, A THEORY OF JUSTICE 111-16, 342-50, 375-77 (1971); A. John Simmons, Moral Principles and Political Obligations 16-23 (1981); Gorovitz, *Bigotry, Loyalty, and Malnutrition, in* FOOD POLICY: THE RESPONSIBILITY OF THE UNITED STATES IN LIFE AND DEATH CHOICES 129, 132-36 (P. Brown & H. Shue eds., 1977); H.L.A. Hart, *Are There Any Natural Rights?*, 64 PHILA. REV. 175 (1955); William N. Nelson, *Special Rights, General Rights, and Social Justice*, 3 Phil. & Pub. Aff. 410 (1974)).

126. *Id.* at 193. *But see* Aleinikoff, *Community Ties*, *supra* note 29, at 240-41 (criticizing this analogy).

127. Aleinikoff, *Community Ties*, *supra* note 29, at 244-45.

128. *Id.* at 244 (emphasis added).

For Aleinikoff, community ties indicate "the actual relationships the individual has developed with a society: a family, friends, a job, association memberships, professional acquaintances, opportunities."[129] In rejecting Martin's notion, Aleinikoff compares consideration of community ties with community and finds:

> "Community" is a more amorphous concept. It connotes a sense of identification with others as a group, a sense of common enterprise, a belief in the value of shared experiences and a shared future. Community ties are almost tangible; we can see interactions among people and membership in complex social and financial arrangements. But to see "community," we must catch a glimpse of the *Zeitgeist*, we must peer into people's hearts.[130]

Aleinikoff sees part of an alien's interest "in entering or remaining within the United States [to be] his or her ability to maintain established ties with the community."[131] Having characterized these ties as the "private interest" component of the *Matthews v. Eldridge* framework, Aleinikoff suggests that one can only proceed to fully satisfy all due process concerns after analyzing the remaining *Eldridge* components.[132] Aleinikoff acknowledges that even in using the community ties approach, reasonable people might disagree as to the level of ties of each group and whether there are actual differences between them.[133] Left is the implication that evaluating all of the interests at stake will not always lead to the alien's interests prevailing over the government's interest.

VI. REVEALING THE COURTS' USE OF MEMBERSHIP AND COMMUNITY TIES

A. *Applying the Theories*

Despite the plenary power doctrine, numerous challenges to immigration law are successful as the courts consider such equities

129. *Id.*

130. *Id.* at 244-45.

131. *Id.* at 245.

132. *Id.* at 247. In *Mathews v. Eldridge*, 424 U.S. 319 (1976), the Court clearly set out the three elements to be balanced in determining the appropriate due process conferred. *Id.* at 335 These elements include: (1) the private interest at stake; (2) the value of improved procedures to prevent "erroneous deprivation" of the private interest through existing procedures; and (3) the governmental interest involved (including "fiscal and administrative burdens" imposed by any added procedure). *Id.*

133. Aleinikoff, *Community Ties*, *supra* note 29, at 245-46.

as membership in the national community and community ties.[134] Conversely, aliens, perhaps anticipating victory when challenging a law seemingly within the aliens' rights tradition, do not always succeed when the requisite community ties or national membership are lacking.[135] The greater a court's reliance upon notions of membership or community ties, the more irrelevant the plenary power versus aliens' rights distinction becomes. Beginning with a discussion of the rights of U.S. citizens, this next section will attempt to demonstrate that the weaker an individual's claim to membership or community ties, the less rights are provided within both the immigration and nonimmigration law arenas.

B. *Citizens and Lawful Permanent Residents*

In applying the premise of either Martin's membership or Aleinikoff's community ties theory to U.S. citizens, one would conclude that citizens deserve the greatest constitutional protection because they occupy the innermost ring of the community and arguably possess the strongest community ties.[136] Not surprisingly, in cases involving the denaturalization or expatriation of citizens, the courts impose many procedural and substantive safeguards.[137]

134. For a discussion of those cases challenging immigration laws, see *supra* notes 74-80 and accompanying text.

135. For a discussion of the success of challenges under the aliens' rights tradition, see *supra* notes 76-78 and accompanying text.

136. Martin, *supra* note 28, at 208-10. Aleinikoff borrows Martin's concentric circles of membership as "proxies" for the amount and kinds of ties each group has developed and concludes that, "citizens, in the innermost circle, are likely to have the greatest stake in remaining in the United States." Aleinikoff, *Community Ties*, *supra* note 29, at 245. In measuring commitment to national community, Aleinikoff points out that it is not clear that citizens, simply by virtue of their birth, are more committed to the United States than aliens who have overcome great obstacles to reach our shores. *Id.* at 241. Martin recognizes that while it may not seem fair to accord citizens greater due process rights simply by virtue of their birth, persons have to accept some of life's natural injustices. Martin, *supra* note 28, at 216-18 (relying on ALEXANDER BICKEL, THE MORALITY OF CONSENT 134 (1975); Anthony Kronman, *Talent Pooling*, *in* XXII NOMOS: HUMAN RIGHTS 58, 77 (1981)).

It should be noted that Martin and Aleinikoff, in the strictest sense, are discussing only the procedural rights of individuals based upon notions of membership or community ties. I am, however, applying their theories more liberally to explain differentiations in both substantive and procedural rights of citizens, lawful permanent residents and others based on their notions of membership and community ties.

137. *See* Afroyim v. Rusk, 387 U.S. 253, 260 (1967). In expatriating proceedings, intent (voluntary renunciation) is required. *Id.* at 265-66; *see* Vance v. Terrazas, 444 U.S. 252, 268 (1980) (noting party claiming expatriation must show intent to relinquish U.S. citizenship). The *Afroyim* Court relied not on the Due Process Clause, but on the citizenship provisions of the Fourteenth Amendment. *Afroyim*, 387 U.S. at 268. The Court in *Rogers v. Bellei*, 401 U.S. 815 (1971), created

Consistent with either Martin's or Aleinikoff's theory, in cases which involve the stripping of a lawful permanent resident's right to membership, the resident is given less protection than the U.S. citizen.[138] Unlike a U.S. citizen, the government does not need to prove a lawful permanent resident's intent to abandon his status.[139]

an exception to *Afroyim*'s holding that citizenship must be voluntarily renounced or relinquished. *Id.* at 835. Subsequent legislation, however, essentially invalidated this exception. *See* 4 CHARLES GORDON & STANLEY MAILMAN, IMMIGRATION LAW AND PROCEDURE § 100.03[2][a][vi]-[b][i] (1990) (discussing legislation invalidating exception). In expatriating proceedings, the government must meet its burden of proof by a preponderance of the evidence. *Terrazas*, 444 U.S. at 268. Historically, however, this standard was not enforced. For example, in a case later overruled, the Court held that voting in a foreign election qualified as an expatriating act without even assessing the proof of intent to surrender citizenship. Perez v. Brownell, 356 U.S. 44 (1958), *overruled by* Afroyim, 387 U.S. at 268. Also, a U.S. citizen, lost her citizenship after marrying a foreigner. Mackenzie v. Hare, 239 U.S. 299, 311 (1915). The woman could only regain her citizenship upon termination of the marriage. *Id.* at 307. The Court found that Congress, through its sovereign power, could deem marriage to be an expatriating act. *Id.* at 311-12. This statute, the Citizenship Act of 1907, was later repealed. *See* Martin, *supra* note 28, at 208-09 (discussing overruling of Citizenship Act by requiring intent to give up citizenship); Matsumoto-Power, *supra* note 59, at 71 (discussing how Congress had power to expatriate).

Denaturalization proceedings also hold the government to a high standard. *See* Schneiderman v. United States, 320 U.S. 118, 125 (1943) (stating "clear, unequivocal and convincing" standard). Naturalized citizens are not more vulnerable to losing their citizenship than born citizens. Schneider v. Rusk, 377 U.S. 163, 165-69 (1964). Before a denaturalization decree is issued, there must be a finding of fraud or illegality in the original naturalization process. *See generally* Fedorenko v. United States, 449 U.S. 490, 505-06 (1981) (noting government has heavy burden of proof to divest naturalized citizen of his or her citizenship). The government must prove its allegations by "clear, unequivocal, and convincing evidence." *Schneiderman*, 320 U.S. at 125; *see also* Martin, *supra* note 28, at 208-10 (discussing government's burden).

138. Martin, *supra* note 28, at 210-15. Aleinikoff, however, suggests that, with the exception of voting and political rights, lawful permanent residents should be accorded membership in society equal to that of citizens. Aleinikoff, *Citizens, Aliens, Membership*, *supra* note 40, at 23. Aleinikoff, therefore, questions whether it is defensible to deport residents when the United States would not consider deporting a citizen for a similar offense. *Id.* at 26.

139. *See* INA § 241, 8 U.S.C. § 1251 (1994) (IIRAIRA § 305 has recodified grounds of deportation so that they will be referred to as (INA § 237)) (providing that lawful permanent residents can be deported for committing certain acts or by failing to commit others against their wishes); Galvan v. Press, 347 U.S. 522, 530-32 (1954) (deporting long time permanent residents for earlier Communist membership); Harisiades v. Shaughnessy, 342 U.S. 580, 587 (1952) (noting aliens remain vulnerable to expulsion even after long residence); KURZBAN, *supra* note 4, at 81-99. Recognizing the length of one's membership in U.S. society, Martin suggests that these cases yielded bad results because of an unquestioning deference to sovereignty and the political question issue. Martin, *supra* note 28, at 211-12. Martin argues that the protection of lawful permanent residents could have been achieved in these cases without any negative impact on Congress's political power over substantive deportation standards. *Id.* Aliens who have a "lawful unrelinquished domicile of seven consecutive years" or more, however, have traditionally been able to have certain grounds for deportation waived. INA § 212(c), 8 U.S.C. § 1182(c).

Yet, even in these cases, procedural due process is protected.[140] Deportation must be based upon "clear, unequivocal, and convincing evidence."[141] Despite all of its failings, even the *Knauff-Mezei* doctrine recognizes that certain rights attach if an alien has "passed through our gates, even illegally."[142]

Likewise, in what might be considered nonimmigration law/aliens' rights cases, constitutional rights are contingent upon demonstrating national membership or community ties.[143] Again, as in the immigration context, the U.S. citizen occupying the innermost circle of membership is accorded the greatest protection in the nonimmigration arena.[144] For example, the right to vote or hold certain public offices is awarded only to citizens upon a recognition of their status.[145]

While there is disagreement regarding the amount of rights which should be accorded lawful permanent residents, the disa-

For a discussion of the "cancellation of removal" relief that will replace INA § 212(c) relief pursuant to IIRAIRA, see *supra* note 11 and accompanying text.

140. *See* Martin, *supra* note 28, at 212 (discussing protection of lawful permanent residents).

141. Woodby v. INS, 385 U.S. 276, 286 (1966); *see also* IIRAIRA § 304, Pub. L. No. 104-208 (1996) (to be codified at INA § 240(c)(3)(A), 8 U.S.C.) (discussing deportation). For a further discussion of IIRAIRA, see *supra* note 11 and accompanying text.

142. Shaughnessy v. United States *ex rel.* Mezei, 345 U.S. 206, 212 (1953). Ignoring this widely accepted and long held principal that those who entered without inspection are deportable and can avail themselves of greater procedural protection, the 1996 changes to the INA limit the procedural rights to those here who entered without inspection (EWI) by rendering them inadmissable. *Compare* IIRAIRA § 301 (to be codified at INA § 212(a)(6)(A)(i), 8 U.S.C.) (stating new ground of admissability), *with* INA § 241(a)(1)(B) (stating previous ground of deportability). For a further discussion of EWIs and their rights, and the critiques of Aleinikoff and Martin, see *infra* notes 154-61 and accompanying text.

143. *See* Mathews v. Diaz, 426 U.S. 67, 80 (1976) (limiting social security benefits to permanent residents living in United States for at least five years); Flemming v. Nestor, 363 U.S. 603, 608 (1960) (ruling deportee is not entitled to social security benefits).

144. *See* Aleinikoff, *Community Ties*, *supra* note 29, at 245. Aleinikoff argues that "[c]itizens in the innermost circle are likely to have the greatest stake in remaining in the United States." *Id.*

145. Martin, *supra* note 28, at 197. For a further discussion of an alien citizen's political rights, see *supra* note 80 and accompanying text. Martin asserts that the voting exception continues because of the intuitive notion that voting is intimately associated with the idea of a national community. Martin, *supra* note 28, at 198. He notes:

> Even Gerald Rosberg, after patiently dissecting all the instrumental reasons (such as concerns about fraud, bloc voting, lack of knowledge, or disloyalty) that states might advance to justify excluding resident aliens from the polls, admitted to a lingering intuition about a hard-to-pin-down justification for this exclusion, somehow connected to the notion of membership.

Id. at 198 n.119.

greement simply reflects differing opinions regarding the strength of lawful permanent residents' community ties and membership.[146] Although some courts and commentators suggest that lawful permanent residents should be accorded constitutional protection on par to that accorded citizens,[147] the opposing camp argues that a resident is a lesser member of the community than the citizen and accordingly, should be afforded less protection.[148] For example, the Court in *Mathews v. Diaz* suggested that all permanent residents may not be accorded the same rights as citizens.[149] The Court suggested that only individuals who have been permanent residents for more than five years can be considered the "most like citizens."[150] Serving as Justice, Rehnquist has also suggested that providing protection to noncitizen residents diminishes those rights which should be safeguarded as the rewards of citizenship.[151] Only naturalized citizens should be accorded certain rights for demonstrating "the willingness and ability to integrate into our social system . . . [and prove they have] become 'like' a native-born citizen in ways that aliens, as a class, could be presumed not to be."[152] This sentiment, that all aliens, regardless of their residency status, are not entitled to certain rights as they do not fully belong to the national

146. *See* Martin, *supra* note 28, at 193-204 (discussing arguments surrounding strength of lawful permanent resident's community ties and membership).

147. *See* Dixon v. Love, 431 U.S. 105 (1977) (noting that due process applies to deprivation of license); Goss v. Lopez, 419 U.S. 565 (1975) (noting school discipline must comply with due process). Justice Blackmun suggested "for most legislative purposes there simply are no meaningful differences between resident aliens and citizens." Toll v. Moreno, 458 U.S. 1, 20 (Blackmun, J., concurring). The dissent in *Harisiades v. Shaughnessy*, 342 U.S. 580 (1952), noted that "[a]n alien, who is assimilated in our society, is treated as a citizen so far as his property and his liberty are concerned." *Id.* at 599 (Douglas, J., dissenting). While recognizing that the greatest due process is reserved for citizens, Martin accepts that in legal matters which do not bear on the resident's membership, lawful permanent residents should be accorded the same due process as citizens. Martin, *supra* note 28, at 210. Aleinikoff suggests supporting equal rights for citizens and lawful permanent residents in all nonfranchise matters. Aleinikoff, *Community Ties*, *supra* note 29, at 244-47; Aleinikoff, *Citizens, Aliens, Membership*, *supra* note 40, at 19-20.

148. *See Diaz*, 426 U.S. at 67 (discussing differences afforded residents and citizens); Sugarman v. Dougall, 413 U.S. 634, 649-64 (1973) (Rehnquist, J., dissenting) (same); Martin, *supra* note 28, at 208-34 (discussing various amounts of due process afforded to different members of national community). Similarly, the restrictions imposed on the right to federal benefits through the recent Welfare Act reflect the 104th Congress's belief that lawful permanent residents should be accorded less rights than citizens. For a further discussion of the recent Welfare Act and its restrictions, see *supra* note 12 and accompanying text.

149. *Diaz*, 426 U.S. at 83-84.

150. *Id.* at 83. For a further discussion of *Diaz*, see *supra* note 114 and accompanying text.

151. *Sugarman*, 413 U.S. at 658-61 (Rehnquist, J., dissenting).

152. *Id.* at 661 (Rehnquist, J., dissenting).

community, has been reflected on occasion in other Supreme Court cases.[153]

C. *Undocumented Aliens in the United States*

In terms of the rights of United States citizens and lawful permanent residents, Martin and Aleinikoff seem in general agreement.[154] Their theories, however, begin to diverge when applied to the next outlying circle, undocumented aliens living in the United States who either evaded inspection by the Immigration and Naturalization Service (INS) upon entering the country or who arrived as nonimmigrants or parolees.[155]

153. *See* United States *ex rel.* Turner v. Williams, 194 U.S. 279, 292 (1904) (noting "those who are excluded cannot assert the rights in general obtained in a land to which they do not belong as citizens or otherwise"); United States v. Barona, 56 F.3d. 1087, 1094 (9th Cir. 1995) (holding that nonresidents failed to show they were "people of the United States" entitled to all constitutional rights), *cert. denied,* 116 S. Ct. 813 (1996); *see also* Matsumoto-Power, *supra* note 59, at 77-79 (discussing Supreme Court's concept that aliens are outsiders to U.S. society). Membership concerns have also crossed the immigration/nonimmigration line by limiting a permanent resident's ability to exercise his or her First Amendment rights. *See* American Arab Anti-Discrimination Comm. v. Meese ("ADC"), 714 F. Supp. 1060, 1078-81 (C.D. Cal. 1989), *aff'd in part, rev'd in part on other grounds,* 940 F.2d 445 (9th Cir.), *vacated* 970 F.2d 501 (9th Cir. 1991). In ADC, the district court found that it could not tolerate alienage-citizen distinctions which would limit an alien's First Amendment rights. *Id.* at 1078-79. The court struck down the challenged McCarran-Walter provisions, which proscribed various forms of advocating communist or dictatorship theories, as facially overbroad. *Id.* at 1078-84. The district court's constitutional holding was reversed and vacated on appeal because the case was not ripe. American-Arab Anti-Discrimination Comm. v. Thornburgh, 970 F.2d 501, 506, 510 (9th Cir. 1991). The McCarran-Walter provisions at issue were ultimately repealed and replaced with other provisions which allowed the deportation of aliens who engaged in terrorist activity. *See* American-Arab Anti Discrimination Comm. v. Reno, 70 F.3d 1045, 1054 (1995) (challenging deportation under terrorism provisions). For a thorough discussion of the American-Arab Anti-Discrimination cases, see Bosniak, *supra* note 27, at 1130-37.

154. *See* Aleinikoff, *Community Ties, supra* note 29, at 245 (discussing state of U.S. citizens and lawful permanent residents); Martin, *supra* note 28, at 208-15 (addressing due process for citizens and lawful permanent residents).

155. Aleinikoff, *Community Ties, supra* note 29, at 245-47; Martin, *supra* note 28, at 166, 230-34. At the time of Aleinikoff's and Martin's writing, the INA defined entry to include EWI. INA § 101(a)(13), 8 U.S.C. § 1101(a)(13) (1990); *see also* Matter of Z, Int. Dec. No. 3208 (BIA 1993) (discussing entry); Matter of Patel, Int. Dec. No. 3157 (BIA 1991) (same). Martin focuses on individuals that he refers to as "clandestine entrants," but he does not discuss with great specificity the rights of other aliens in the United States who are not permanent residents such as parolees and aliens who have entered the country legally on a valid tourist or other nonimmigrant visa. Martin, *supra* note 28, at 166, 230-34. His thoughts regarding clandestine entrants would likely apply generally to anyone not formally admitted as a permanent resident. Aleinikoff criticizes Martin for not adequately addressing differences within both the circle referred to as first time entrants and undocumented aliens living in the country. Aleinikoff, *Community Ties, supra* note 29, at 245-47. The INA has given a legal definition of "entry" stating that entry:

Under Aleinikoff's community ties theory, the undocumented alien who resides in the United States after an entry without inspection would be accorded due process in relation to the community ties he or she has developed.[156] These ties define his or her stake in the community.[157] In relying upon this theory of community ties, as opposed to Martin's notion of membership, one values the stake an individual has made here in determining the amount of due process owed.[158]

Martin suggests these "clandestine entrants" should not be given greater constitutional rights than the first time applicant for admission, despite the length of time or other ties they may have in the United States.[159] For Martin, because these individuals did not enter the national community with its permission, the national community was prevented from exercising the right to determine

---

> [M]eans any coming of an alien into the United States, from a foreign part or place or from an outlying possession, whether voluntarily or otherwise, except that an alien having lawful permanent residence in the United States shall not be regarded as making an entry . . . if the alien proves . . . that his departure . . . [from the United States] was not intended or reasonably expected by him or his presence [outside the United States] . . . was not voluntary: Provided, that no person whose departure . . . was occasioned by deportation proceedings, extradition, or other legal process shall be held to be entitled to such exception.

INA § 101(a)(13), 8 U.S.C. § 1101(a)(13). Entry has also been defined as: (1) crossing into the territorial limits of the United States, i.e., physical presence; (2) an inspection and admission by an immigration officer; (3) actual and intentional evasion of inspection at the nearest inspection point coupled with; (4) freedom from restraint. *See* KURZBAN, *supra* note 4, at 25 (citing Matter of Z, Int. Dec. No. 3208 (BIA 1993) (finding entry when person came within federal jurisdiction for reasons unrelated to immigration processing); Matter of Patel, Int. Dec. No. 3157 (BIA 1991) (finding no entry on account of lack of freedom from restraint where permanent resident alien was deferred for customs inspection after passing primary immigration inspection)). Now, pursuant to the INA as amended by IIRAIRA in 1996, an individual has only entered if it has been a lawful admission, requiring an inspection and authorization by an immigration officer. IIRAIRA § 301, Pub. L. No. 104-208 (1996) (amending INA § 101(a)(13), 8 U.S.C.). For a further discussion of IIRAIRA, see *supra* note 11 and accompanying text.

156. Aleinikoff, *Community Ties*, *supra* note 29, at 245-46. Under provisions of the 1996 immigration legislation, those individuals who Aleinikoff discusses as having "entered" without inspection and subject to deportation will now be characterized as having "arrived" without being admitted or paroled and will be inadmissable rather than deportable. IIRAIRA §§ 301(c), 302, 304 (to be codified at INA §§ 212(a)(6)(A)(i), 235, 240, in scattered sections of 8 U.S.C.). Even with the enactment of IIRAIRA, Aleinikoff's theory, as discussed in this Article, would still allow one to conclude that inadmissable individuals who arrive without legal admission or parole are entitled to greater rights than the first time applicant for admission. Aleinikoff, *Community Ties*, *supra* note 29, at 245-46.

157. Aleinikoff, *Community Ties*, *supra* note 29, at 245-46.

158. *Id.*

159. Martin, *supra* note 28, at 230-31.

its members at a critical decision-making point.[160] Consequently, this group of undocumented individuals should be treated as first time admission applicants when determining the amount of due process they should be afforded.[161]

Yet, as undocumented aliens living in the United States have generally been accorded more protections than applicants for admission, there appears to be a greater regard for the individual's community ties than his or her formal admission as a member in the national community.[162] Traditionally, undocumented aliens discovered after entering the United States either with or without inspection are afforded more substantive relief if they can demonstrate a long residency in the United States and strong community ties.[163] Additionally, individuals discovered by the INS have tradi-

---

160. *Id.*

161. *Id.* at 231. Martin believes that to allow greater due process protections to a "clandestine entrant" than those afforded to a first time applicant for entry would continue one of the most anomalous lessons learned from *Knauff-Mezei*. *Id.* at 230 n.231. The lesson involved the realization that an individual who successfully evaded immigration and secretly entered the country is entitled to more protection than individuals who honestly present themselves to immigration at the border. *Id.* This theory, which Martin advanced in 1983, charged that "the most glaring anomaly of the *Knauff-Mezei* doctrine" is that it entitles individuals who arrive clandestinely to be entitled to greater procedural protection than those legally applying for admission at the border. *Id.* at 230; *see also id.* at 212-13, 230-34 (criticizing rights provided for those who evade inspection). Thus, Martin's theory seems to be consistent with the 1996 immigration legislation charging individuals who "arrive without inspection" as being inadmissable and thus entitled to less protection. IIRAIRA §§ 301(c)(1), 302, 304 (to be codified at INA §§ 212(a)(6)(A)(i), 235, 240, in scattered sections of 8 U.S.C.).

Yet, while asserting that the due process afforded to a clandestine entrant should be limited, Martin believes that the entrant's length of stay and the ties which he or she has developed should have a positive effect. *Id.* at 232-33. For example, Martin recognizes suspension of deportation as a positive ameliorative legislative measure. *Id.*; *see also* INA § 244(a), 8 U.S.C. § 1254(a) (discussing suspension of deportation). With the recent repeal of suspension of deportation and the heightened criteria enacted for "cancellation of removal," it becomes apparent, however, that it may be unwise to fully rely on legislative protection for individuals who are here without proper inspection and admission. *Compare* INA § 244(a), 8 U.S.C. § 1254(a) (discussing suspension of deportation), *with* IIRAIRA § 304 (to be codified at INA § 240A(b), 8 U.S.C.) (discussing cancellation of removal).

162. For a further discussion of membership and community ties, see *supra* notes 121-33 and accompanying text.

163. *See* INA § 244(a), 8 U.S.C. § 1254(a) (suspension of deportation); IIRAIRA § 304 (to be codified at INA § 240A, 8 U.S.C.) (replacing suspension of deportation with cancellation of removal); INA § 249, 8 U.S.C. § 1259 (registry); IIRAIRA § 308(g)(10)(B) (amending registry); AEDPA § 413(e) (amending registry); INA § 242(b), 8 U.S.C. § 1252(b) (voluntary departure); INA § 244(e), 8 U.S.C. § 1254(e) (voluntary departure); IIRAIRA § 304 (to be codified at INA § 240B, 8 U.S.C.) (replacing previous forms of voluntary departure); *see also* IIRAIRA §§ 308(a)(7), (g)(5)(D) (repealing former provisions for suspension of

tionally been assured more protection than individuals who are apprehended upon attempting their first entry.[164]

In an attempt to restrict "illegal immigration," however, recent legislative measures limit the procedural and substantive rights of aliens who enter without inspection.[165] These measures reveal Congress stepping back from its previous position, demonstrating Congress's willingness to ignore an alien's ties to the community.[166] Congress has previously recognized the significance of community membership by preventing the potential deportation of thousands of undocumented aliens through such legalization programs as the "amnesty."[167] Presenting these programs to Congress, Attorney General Smith stated: "We have neither the resources, the capability, nor the motivation to uproot and deport millions of illegal aliens, many of whom have become, in effect, members of the community."[168]

Outside of the immigration context, for undocumented aliens who have not formally become members of the national community, Martin's or Aleinikoff's theory seem to reach the same result. These individuals have established ties and have been recognized as members of the community to the degree that they are subject to our criminal laws, participate in their local community, etc.[169]

---

deportation and voluntary departure). For further discussion of IIRAIRA, see *supra* note 11.

164. For example, *compare* INA § 241, 8 U.S.C. § 1251, *with* INA § 212(a)(1), 8 U.S.C. § 1182(a)(1) (reflecting grounds of deportation are less encompassing than grounds of exclusion as there is no comparable ground of deportation for carrying of communicable disease). Moreover, in the case of deportable aliens, the burden of proof is on the government to support a finding of deportability by "clear, unequivocal, and convincing evidence." Woodby v. INS, 385 U.S. 276, 286 (1976); *see also* Martin, *supra* note 28, at 212-13 (discussing Court's requirement of due process in deportation proceedings).

165. For a discussion of the recent changes in the immigration law, see *supra* note 11-12 and accompanying text.

166. For a discussion of the recent immigration legislation, see *supra* notes 11 and 12 and accompanying text.

167. *See* IRCA § 201, 8 U.S.C. § 1255(A) (1994) (stating amnesty provision); GORDON ET AL., *supra* note 137, at § 52.01 (discussing amnesty provision of 8 U.S.C. § 1255(A)).

168. Plyler v. Doe, 457 U.S. 202, 218 n.17 (1982); *see also* Martin, *supra* note 28, at 202 n.136 (discussing reasoning for amnesty programs).

169. *See* Aleinikoff, *Community Ties*, *supra* note 29, at 245-46 (discussing stake persons have in their community); Martin, *supra* note 28, at 202, 230-34 (arguing against Court's recognition of greater procedural protections for clandestine entrants as opposed to less protections for first time applicants for admission). Gerald Neuman finds that the constitutional rights of aliens present in the United States correspond to their "pervasive subjection" to American law. Neuman, *Whose Constitution*, *supra* note 30, at 977. *But see* Bosniak, *supra* note 27, at 1126-31 (sug-

The courts historically have recognized the rights of these individuals based upon a respect for the ties they have developed.[170] For example, the Court suggests that even illegal aliens have ties to the community which entitle them to certain rights in *Plyler v. Doe.*[171] Like *Plyler*, the Court rejected the notion that one's status as an unlawful immigrant signifies that the individual is not entitled to constitutional protection in *Wong Wing v. United States.*[172] As the Court held in *Wong Wing*, undocumented aliens living in the United States generally enjoy full constitutional protection.[173] Yet, the protection of these rights is, however, being challenged and at risk of being undone by recent efforts both nationally and locally.[174]

---

gesting that undocumented alien's ability to exercise his or her civil and political rights is limited by omnipresent shadow of federal immigration authorities).

170. For a discussion of the cases recognizing the ties of an alien, see *supra* notes 146-53 and accompanying text.

171. 457 U.S. 202 (1982) (discussing right of illegal aliens to go to school); *see also* Aleinikoff, *Citizens, Aliens, Membership*, *supra* note 40, at 25 (recognizing that undocumented children were likely to be permanent members of American society); Bosniak, *supra* note 27, at 1098-99, 1115-17 (discussing provision for constitutional protection regardless of undocumented alien status). Bosniak recognizes that *Plyler* may be limited to a finding that an unlawful status is an irrelevant factor for children, but not necessarily for adults. *Id.* at 1125 (noting "*Pyler* is not likely to be very helpful in a case in which . . . rights are denied to undocumented aliens over the age of eighteen"). Bosniak concludes that the law is divided over the difference undocumented alienage makes in an analysis. *Id.* at 1117-26. Another commentator has also been suggested that *Plyler* was decided under the federal preemption principle, and thus, is not a broad recognition of alien rights by the Court. Matsumoto-Power, *supra* note 59, at 79. For a discussion of recent federal legislative efforts to prevent undocumented children from attending public school, see *infra* note 174 and accompanying text.

172. 163 U.S. 228, 238 (1896); *see also* Bosniak, *supra* note 27, at 1095-98, 1115-17 (discussing Court's extension of constitutional protections to aliens in cases outside sphere of immigration). For a further discussion of *Wong Wing*, see *supra* note 78 and accompanying text.

173. *Wong Wing*, 163 U.S. at 238; *see also* Mathews v. Diaz, 426 U.S. 67, 77 (1976) (noting "[e]ven one whose presence in this country is unlawful, involuntary, or transitory, is entitled to [Fifth and Fourteenth Amendment] protection"). *But see* United States v. Verdugo-Urquidez, 494 U.S. 259, 261-62, 272, 274-75 (1990) (holding Verdugo-Urquidez, who was brought involuntarily to United States, was not entitled to Fourth Amendment protection); Neuman, *Whose Constitution*, *supra* note 30, at 972 (discussing *Verdugo-Urquidez*). For a further discussion of *Verdugo-Urquidez*, see *supra* notes 108-13 and *infra* notes 193-94 and accompanying text.

174. Efforts to bar undocumented children from public school failed only after the hotly debated provision sponsored by Representative Elton Gallegly (R-Cal.) was dropped from the IIRAIRA and was sponsored by Gallegly as a separate immigration bill. H.R. 4134, 104th Cong. (1996). After passing the House by a 254-175 vote, the bill was not taken up by the Senate. *Bill to Block Illegal Immigration Passed, Signed: Controversial Education Measure Cut*, FACTS ON FILE, Oct. 3, 1996, *available in* LEXIS, News File; William Branigin, *Congress Finishes Major Legislation; Immigration; Focus Is Borders, Not Benefits*, WASH. POST, Oct. 1, 1996, at A1 (discussing new legislation); Eric Schmitt, *Bill Tries to Balance Concerns on Immigration*, N.Y. TIMES,

D. *Applicants for Admission*

For Martin, the first time applicants for admission occupy the outermost ring of membership in the national community.[175] But, unlike the *Knauff* Court, Martin recognizes these individuals' "common humanity" and acknowledges that they are entitled to the due process protections applied in *Yick Wo* and found in the language of the Due Process Clause referring to "all persons."[176] Martin believes

Sept. 29, 1996, § 1, at 28 (same); *Text on President Clinton's Statement on Omnibus Appropriations and Immigration Reform Bill*, U.S. NEWSWIRE, Oct. 2, 1996, *available in* LEXIS, News File; *see also Immigration Bills Head to House-Senate Conference; Battles Over Particulars Loom*, 73 INTERPRETER RELEASES 678, 680 (1996) (discussing Gallegly amendment to House Bill 2202 allowing states to bar public education benefits to undocumented aliens, including children); *Conferees Agree on Immigration Bill; Hill Negotiators Delete Schooling Ban; Clinton Undecided on Veto*, WASH. POST, Sept. 25, 1996, at A14 (discussing alien children and school rights); David Hess, *Senate OKs Tightening the Border*, MIAMI HERALD, May 3, 1996, at A1 (discussing Senate vote to tighten border); *Immigration Bill Attracts Broader Range of Opponents*, WASH. POST, Sept. 28, 1996, at A7 (discussing proposed bill); Eric Schmitt, *Conferees Approve a Tough Immigration Bill*, N.Y. TIMES, Sept. 25, 1996, A15 (discussing proposed bill).

California's Proposition 187 also demonstrates an attempt to restrict the rights of undocumented aliens living in the United States. *See* Bosniak, supra note 27, at 1143-47 (discussing Proposition 187's denial of basic public services to aliens); Kevin R. Johnson, *An Essay on Immigration Politics, Popular Democracy, and California's Proposition 187*, 70 WASH. L. REV. 629 (1995) (discussing Proposition 187); Kevin R. Johnson, *Public Benefits and Immigration: The Intersection of Immigration Status, Ethnicity, Gender and Class*, 42 UCLA L. REV. 1509 (1995) (same); Kurfis, *supra* note 86, at 165 (arguing that portions of Proposition 187 deny equal protection to undocumented alien children); Gerald L. Neuman, *Aliens as Outlaws: Government Services, Proposition 187, and the Structure of Equal Protection Doctrine*, 42 UCLA L. REV. 1425, 1448-52 (1995) (arguing that Proposition 187 violates Equal Protection).

Initiatives similar to California's Proposition 187 are gaining the support of voters in Florida. *See* Rick Barry, *Amendment Backers Pen Hopes on Voters*, TAMPA TRIBUNE, Jan. 17, 1996, at 1 (describing attempts to put anti-immigration initiatives on Florida ballot); James G. Driscoll, *Venom Aimed at Immigrants Destroys Their Precious Dream of America*, SUN-SENTINEL, May 18, 1996, at 15A (discussing anti-immigrant sentiment); *Prop. 187 Clones Advance*, SUN-SENTINEL, May 16, 1996, at 3B (describing Florida petition driving voter initiative similar to Proposition 187); Reena Shah Stamets, *Benefits for Illegal Aliens Defended*, ST. PETERSBURG TIMES, Mar. 23, 1996, at 3B (describing local meeting defending benefits for illegal aliens); Andres Viglucci, *Immigration Hot Topic for Voters, Not Candidates*, ST. PETERSBURG TIMES, Feb. 12, 1996, at 1A (describing presidential candidate's lack of comment on immigration).

175. Martin, *supra* note 28, at 216.

176. *Id.* For Martin, "[t]he excludable alien is not a constitutional stranger, but he is not quite intimate family . . . . Thus, the character of the excludable alien's—as yet tenuous—relationship to the national polity may be used in deciding what process is owed as a constitutional minimum." *Id.* Recognizing our universal common humanity, Justice Field in *Fong Yue Ting v. United States*, 149 U.S. 698 (1893) stated:

> The moment any human being from a country at peace with us comes within the jurisdiction of the United States . . . he becomes subject to all their laws, is amenable to their punishment and entitled to their protection. Arbitrary and despotic power can no more be exercised over them with reference to their persons and property, than over the persons and

that an alien at entry should insist on minimum constitutional protections, including "an unbiased decision-maker, notice of the proceedings and of the general grounds asserted by the government for denial of admission; a meaningful opportunity to dispute or overcome those grounds, orally or in writing; and a statement of reasons, even if oral and summary, for any adverse decision."[177] Martin, justifying different procedural protections for individuals depending on their relative location to the border, argues that such an approach serves as an essential and practical tool for courts.[178] Martin agrees with the United States Court of Appeals for the Fifth Circuit which acknowledged that "constitutional protections cannot be afforded to the entire population of the world, and some distinction is necessary."[179]

Aleinikoff takes a more humanitarian approach to determining what rights should be afforded to each individual.[180] For Aleinikoff, more than the minimal due process suggested by Martin may exist for an individual, even a first time entrant at the border.[181] The fact that an individual is an applicant for admission does not definitively determine that he or she should be afforded only the most minimal due process.[182] There are "relevant differences" between individuals seeking entry.[183] While recognizing that an applicant for admission is likely to have fewer ties to the United States than a U.S. citizen or permanent resident, an appli-

> property of native-born citizens. They differ only from citizens in that they cannot vote or hold any public office. As men having our common humanity, they are protected by all the guaranties of the Constitution.

Id. at 754 (1893) (Field, J., dissenting); *see also Wong Wing*, 163 U.S. at 242-43 (Field, J., concurring in part and dissenting in part) (claiming that all persons are entitled to equal protection of laws); Yick Wo v. Hopkins 118 U.S. 356, 369 (1886) (stating that Fourteenth Amendment "is not confined to the protection of citizens"). For a further discussion of an individual alien's due process rights, see *supra* notes 53-62 and accompanying text.

177. Martin, *supra* note 28, at 218. Martin cautions, however, that it is "hazardous" to set out any procedural standards. *Id.*; *see also* INS v. Stanisic, 395 U.S. 62, 79 & n.22 (1969) (refusing to consider Director's bias because case remanded for new hearing); Henry M. Friendly, *Some Kind of Hearing*, 123 U. PA. L. REV. 1267, 1278-81 (1975) (noting danger of setting procedural standards).

178. Aleinikoff, *Community Ties*, *supra* note 29, at 239 (discussing Martin's view).

179. Martin, *supra* note 28, at 233 (citing Pierre v. United States, 547 F.2d 1281, 1290 (5th Cir.), *vacated*, 434 U.S. 962 (1977) (remanding for consideration of mootness)).

180. Aleinikoff, *Community Ties*, *supra* note 29, at 239 (questioning "why should not all [citizens and aliens alike] be entitled to the same constitutional guarantees before being ordered out of the country?").

181. *Id.* at 239, 245-47.

182. *Id.* at 245-47.

183. *Id.*

cant may have a personal stake in the United States that needs to be assessed.[184]

Because the notion of community ties allows for an assessment of "the actual relationships the individual has developed with a society: *a family*, friends, a job, association memberships, professional acquaintances, opportunities," individuals outside of the United States may have varying stakes in the United States and therefore, be entitled to varying degrees of due process.[185] For example, Aleinikoff recognizes a first time entrant may have established a "pre-existing" stake in the community, coming to the United States after being granted an immigrant visa through family or an employer located in the United States.[186] On the other hand, first time entrants on a nonimmigrant visa may have less of an interest at stake.[187] By contrast, they are not planning to make the United States their permanent home and probably have demonstrated that they will return to their country in order even to be issued the visa.[188] The restriction of due process, which could lead to the exclusion of the intended immigrant, would disrupt his or her entire future life.[189] Restricting due process in the case of the individual coming to the United States for a brief stay, however, would create less of a disruption.[190] Considering the differing interests, greater due process should be accorded to an intending immigrant who potentially has more at stake.[191]

For individuals living outside of the United States, the courts generally have taken a limited view of the rights which should be awarded to them both in the immigration and nonimmigration context.[192] In *United States v. Verdugo-Urquidez*, the Supreme Court denied Fourth Amendment protection to an individual after classi-

184. *Id.*

185. *Id.* at 244-47 (emphasis added).

186. *Id.* at 246.

187. *Id.* at 246-47.

188. *Id.* Various sections of the INA provide for obtaining a nonimmigrant visa. *See, e.g.*, INA § 101(a)(15)(B), 8 U.S.C. § 1101(a)(15)(B) (1994) (providing for temporary visitors); INA § 101(a)(15)(F), 8 U.S.C. § 1101(a)(15)(F) (providing for bona fide students); INA § 101(a)(15)(H), 8 U.S.C. § 1101(a)(15)(H) (providing for certain occupations); INA § 101(a)(15)(J), 8 U.S.C. § 1101(a)(15)(J) (providing for participants in United States Information Agency programs).

189. Aleinikoff, *Community Ties*, *supra* note 29, at 247.

190. *Id.* at 246-47.

191. *Id.* at 245-47.

192. *See* Flemming v. Nestor, 363 U.S. 603, 608, 616-21 (1960) (upholding statute which deprived deported persons of social security benefits). For a further discussion of *Flemming*, see *supra* note 114-15 and accompanying text.

fying the respondent as having no ties or membership in the United States, despite physically awaiting criminal prosecution in the United States.[193] The *Verdugo-Urquidez* Court found that *Yick Wo*, *Wong Wing* and the aliens' rights cases which developed in their wake, "establish only that aliens receive constitutional protections when they have come within the territory of the Untied States and developed substantial connections with this country."[194] Following this rationale, the Court's decision in *Russian Volunteer Fleet v. United States*[195] can be justified.[196] In *Russian Volunteer Fleet*, the Court found that the appellant, while a nonresident of the United States, had property here and therefore, was entitled to protection.[197]

In the immigration context, rights of aliens seeking entry also receive minimal attention. For example, the Court easily dismissed the challenge before proceeding to examine more closely the claims of the United States citizens involved in the suit in *Kleindienst v. Mandel*.[198] The Court noted that "[i]t is clear that Mandel personally, as an unadmitted and nonresident alien, had no constitutional right of entry to this country as a nonimmigrant or otherwise."[199] Even Justice Marshall, dissenting so as to recognize the rights of the United States citizen appellees, did not openly disagree with the holding of the majority regarding the rights of Mandel.[200] Similarly, the majority and the dissent agreed that the Court had limited judicial responsibility with respect to Congress's power to regulate the admission of undocumented children living abroad in *Fiallo v. Bell*.[201] The key to all of these cases does not

193. United States v. Verdugo-Urquidez, 494 U.S. 259 (1990). For a further discussion of *Verdugo-Urquidez*, see *supra* notes 108-13 and accompanying text.

194. *Verdugo-Urquidez*, 494 U.S. at 271.

195. 282 U.S. 481 (1931).

196. *Id.* (holding that alien petitioner had Fifth Amendment right to just compensation for property taken by United States).

197. *Id.* at 489-92. The Court found that the Fifth Amendment duty of just compensation for the taking of property applied fully to the property of nonresident aliens. *Id.*

198. 408 U.S. 753, 762 (1972).

199. *Id.*; *see also* Galvan v. Press, 347 U.S. 522, 530-32 (1954) (describing congressional power with respect to admission of aliens as "very broad"); United States *ex rel.* Knauff v. Shaughnessy, 338 U.S. 537, 542 (1950) (noting "[a]dmission of aliens to the United States is a privilege granted by the sovereign United States Government"); United States *ex rel.* Turner v. Williams, 194 U.S. 279, 292 (1904) (stating that "those who are excluded cannot assert the rights . . . in a land to which they do not belong as citizens or otherwise").

200. *Kleindienst*, 408 U.S. at 782 (Marshall, J., dissenting).

201. 430 U.S. 787, 792-95 (1977); *id.* at 805 (Marshall, J., dissenting). Fiallo involved the challenge of three sets of unwed natural fathers and their illegitimate offspring. *Id.* at 790.

seem to be whether the case involves a challenge to an immigration or a nonimmigration law, but whether the individual demonstrated an attachment to the national community or community ties.

VII. THE MUTUALITY APPROACH

Relying on either Martin's or Aleinikoff's theory, withholding constitutional rights from aliens similarly situated to Verdugo-Urquidez could be justified. An individual with neither a claim to membership nor any discernible ties to the United States is arguably not entitled to the protection of the Fourth Amendment or any other significant substantive or procedural constitutional rights.[202] Yet, despite the ostensible lack of connection to the United States, such an individual should still be entitled to protection.

A. *Gerald Neuman: The Mutuality Approach*

Gerald Neuman directly addresses the application of constitutional protections to aliens living outside the United States who have never resided or visited the United States.[203] Interestingly, Martin and Neuman begin from the same premise: that any consideration of the Constitution's application should be in keeping with the social contract tradition.[204] Yet, from this point, the theories of Martin and Neuman drastically diverge. Neuman recognizes that aliens abroad essentially have been invited to enter into a nation's social contract whenever they are subject to its law.[205] Thus, the rationale of his mutuality approach is that "American constitutional rights and the obligation of obedience to American law go together . . . the rights and the obligations are coextensive."[206]

202. For a further discussion of Martin's and Aleinikoff's theories, see *supra* notes 121-33 and accompanying text.

203. Neuman, *Whose Constitution, supra* note 30, at 981.

204. *See* Martin, *supra* note 28, at 193-204 (discussing relationship between membership and due process); Neuman, *Whose Constitution, supra* note 30, at 976-77 (discussing social contract tradition). Neuman, reflecting on the social contract tradition, asserts:

> The United States Constitution has long been understood as a fundamental law within the meaning of the social contract tradition — a design for government and limitations on government that protect the interests of the governed sufficiently to form part of a justification of their obligation of obedience to it. Establishing a legitimate government empowers that government to generate obligations that would not exist in anarchy or a state of nature.

Id. at 976-77.

205. Neuman, *Whose Constitution, supra* note 30, at 923-25 (discussing aliens and social contract).

206. *Id.* at 977. Neuman refers to the "mutuality approach" as the "municipal law approach." *Id.* In a forthcoming book, however, Neuman renames the theory,

Following this rationale, "when the United States asserts an alien's obligation to comply with American law, the alien is presumptively entitled *pro hac vice* to all constitutional rights."[207] The mutuality approach once applied only to a nation's own territory as the territory defined the sphere in which a nation's municipal law operated.[208] The United States has, however, increasingly subjected individuals abroad to U.S. law when either the United States as a country or its citizens are affected.[209] Now that the United States is living in an era of extraterritorial legislation, the mutuality approach and the protections it offers should be extended beyond the nation's territory when situations arise in which either U.S. citizens or foreigners abroad are compelled to obey U.S. law.[210] Such an approach properly addresses how the Constitution can fairly, but in a limited scope, apply abroad. The mutuality approach clearly limits the extraterritorial application of the Constitution and its protections to the case of an individual abroad being subjected to U.S. law either voluntarily or involuntarily.[211] In so doing, this approach is less encompassing than a universalist's approach.[212] Most

calling it the "mutuality approach." GERALD NEUMAN, STRANGERS TO THE CONSTITUTION 97-100 (1996). The term "mutuality" used throughout this discussion refers to what Neuman previously referred to as the "municipal law approach." For a further discussion of the mutuality doctrine, see Scaperlanda, *Marshall's Jurisprudence*, *supra* note 25, at 69 n.83.

207. Neuman, *Whose Constitution*, *supra* note 30, at 978.

208. *Id.* at 977-78.

209. *Id.* at 978-81.

210. *Id.* at 977-78. The mutuality approach considers the need for "an appropriate evolutionary response to changes in the technology of transportation and communication, background international practices, and American self-assertion." *Id.* at 980.

211. *Id.* at 984 (discussing application of Constitution to individuals abroad). Neuman argues:

> [C]onstitutional rights should not be interpreted as restricting all government action against all persons in all places, even when the government does not assert its sovereignty over the individual. This does not mean that such uses of force or wealth are immune from demands for justification, but simply that the standards of justification are not to be sought in the United States Constitution.

Id.

212. *See id.* at 983-84 (discussing application of universalist/mutuality approach). A universalist applying the mutuality approach consistent with the social contract theory would argue that the proper sphere is planet Earth and that U.S. federal statutes which demand universal obedience (reflected in prohibitions on international drug smuggling, counterfeiting) make all humans subjects of the American social contract. *Id.* at 982-83. Such an approach "would transcend the concerns of a single social contract and bind the government to the rules of a just world order." *Id.* at 983. Neuman finds that a universalist approach would dilute the protections the Constitution offers in the United States by applying it in a broader, global context, rather than the more limited, national context for which it was drafted. *Id.* at 984.

importantly, this approach is in keeping with the spirit of *Reid v. Covert*,[213] which recognizes correlation of rights and obligations for U.S. citizens abroad, and protects their constitutional rights when subjected to U.S. legislation.[214]

B. *A Mutualist's Criticism of the Membership Approach*

Following the mutuality approach, the flaws of a traditional Hobbesian "members only" approach, as reflected in Chief Justice Rhenquist's *Verdugo-Urquidez* decision and Martin's membership theory, become apparent.[215] One of the inherent difficulties of the membership approach is the illegitimacy of a nation exercising extraterritorial power without entitling those subjected to the power to any individual rights. Such a Hobbesian argument "would enable the government to withhold constitutional rights, but only at the price of delegitimating its claim to obedience."[216] A Hobbesian could try to justify this approach as a necessary means of survival.[217] Additionally, a Hobbesian might characterize this use of power as an exception to the restraints of the social contract theory.[218] Yet,

213. 354 U.S. 1 (1957).

214. *Id.* Neuman recognizes at the outset that *Reid* does not definitively apply to noncitizens, but argues that its holding should apply. Neuman, *Whose Constitution*, *supra* note 30, at 915-16, 986-87. Other commentators also question the extent of the Constitution's application abroad. *See* Martin, *supra* note 28, at 179 n.51 (discussing Supreme Court cases regarding application of Constitution abroad). Since *Reid*, commentators have discussed the lower courts' recognition of the constitutional rights of aliens abroad and one commentator, Louis Henkin, suggests that the Court has overruled previous dicta suggesting that "[t]he Constitution [can have] no operation in another country." Henkin, *Constitution as Compact and Conscience*, *supra* note 26, at 22-24; *see also* United States v. Demanett, 629 F.2d 862, 866 (3d Cir. 1980) (stating Fourth Amendment applies to alien aboard foreign flag vessel); United States v. Toscanino, 500 F.2d 267, 271, 275 (2d Cir. 1974) (holding U.S. officials' illegal conduct of torturing and forcibly bringing to United States accused, invalidated victim's trial in United States); Greenham Women Against Cruise Missiles v. Reagan, 591 F. Supp. 1332 (S.D.N.Y. 1984) (refusing case for being political and nonjusticiable; involving citizens of Great Britain asserting constitutional rights on British soil), *aff'd*, 755 F.2d 34 (2d Cir. 1985); United States v. Tiede, 86 F.R.D. 227, 242-44 (U.S. Ct. Berlin 1979) (holding Constitution applies to criminal proceedings and alien has right to jury trial in U.S. court abroad).

215. *See* Neuman, *Whose Constitution*, *supra* note 30, at 912 (criticizing Justice Rhenquist's decision in *Verdugo-Urquidez*).

216. *Id.* at 984-85 (relying on THOMAS HOBBES, LEVIATHAN 272-73 (C.B. Macpherson ed., 1985)).

217. *Id.* at 984. A Hobbesian justifies this approach on the basis of a concern for national security. *Id.* As the nation-state operates in a state of nature, i.e., war, survival is the predominate concern. *Id.*

218. *Id.* at 985. A Hobbesian might argue that the impossibility of getting actual or tacit consent from an alien when a nation exercises its authority abroad removes a nation's use of power abroad from the social contract theory. *Id.* Yet, many would argue that this idea has no distinction from the social contract the-

Justice Marshall, dissenting in both *Mandel* and *Fiallo*, recognized the absurdity of allowing the government to restrict fundamental rights by the mere showing of a "facially legitimate and bona fide reason," when such rights are normally limited only by a "compelling governmental interest."[267] Discussing the distinctions among citizens through the parent-child definition, Justice Marshall found that "[w]hen Congress grants a fundamental right to all but an invidiously selected class of citizens, and it is abundantly clear that such discrimination would be intolerable in any context but immigration, it is our duty to strike the legislation down."[268]

Congress should not be given unquestioning deference when the rights of U.S. citizens are at stake.[269] As recognized by Martin

267. *Fiallo*, 430 U.S. at 807-09, 816 (Marshall, J., dissenting); *Mandel*, 408 U.S. at 775 (Marshall, J., dissenting). The majority in *Mandel* held that a U.S. citizen's First Amendment rights can be restricted by the Attorney General's assertion of a "facially legitimate and bona fide reason." *Mandel*, 408 U.S. at 761-70. As Justice Marshall acknowledged, however, "[m]erely 'legitimate' governmental interests cannot override constitutional rights." *Id.* at 777 (Marshall, J., dissenting). Properly considering the First Amendment rights of the appellees, Justice Marshall did not see a "compelling governmental interest" that would override their First Amendment rights and argued:

> At least when the rights of Americans are involved, there is no basis for concluding that the power to exclude aliens is absolute. When Congress' exercise of one of its enumerated powers clashes with those individual liberties protected by the Bill of Rights, it is our 'delicate and difficult task' to determine whether the resulting restriction on freedom can be tolerated. . . . [A]ll governmental power—even the war power, the power to maintain national security, or the power to conduct foreign affairs—is limited by the Bill of Rights. When individual freedoms of Americans are at stake, we do not blindly defer to broad claims of the Legislative Branch or Executive Branch, but rather we consider those claims in light of individual freedoms.

Id. at 782-83 (Marshall, J., dissenting) (citation omitted); *see also* Scaperlanda, *Marshall's Jurisprudence*, *supra* note 25, at 58-61 (discussing Justice Marshall's approach to fundamental rights for aliens).

It has been suggested, however, that the majority's decision in *Mandel* may not controvert attempts to have the rights of U.S. citizens or lawful permanent family members considered in challenges to U.S. family unification laws. *Id.* at 59. *Mandel* can be viewed as a controversial and distinguishable decision, as it does not involve the rights of an alien with direct ties to the United States or its citizens. *See Mandel*, 408 U.S. at 756-60 (reviewing claim of alien who had no substantial ties to United States and had previously violated conditions of his temporary visa). The group of citizens involved in *Mandel* can be characterized as "ill-defined." Matsumoto-Power, *supra* note 59, at 85.

268. *Fiallo*, 430 U.S. at 816 (Marshall, J., dissenting).

269. *See* United States *ex rel.* Knauff v. Shaughnessy, 338 U.S. 537, 549 (1950) (Frankfurter, J., dissenting) (arguing against unquestioning deference); Matsumoto-Power, *supra* note 59, at 77 (same). Justice Frankfurter in *Knauff* chastised such an approach by the Court stating:

> It should not be assumed that Congress gave with a bountiful hand but allowed its bounty arbitrarily to be taken away . . . . An alien's opportunity of entry into the United States is of course a privilege which Congress

and Aleinikoff, as U.S. citizens are the most protected members of our society, their constitutional rights are deserving of the utmost protection, regardless of the government's assertion of the plenary power doctrine.[270] When the rights of U.S. citizens are "implicated," absolute deference to the political branches and its sovereign interest becomes "inapplicable."[271] As the fundamental rights of lawful permanent residents have traditionally been recognized as deserving nearly, if not the exact, protection provided to U.S. citizens, then, just like in the case of a citizen, when these rights are at stake absolute deference to the political branches is inappropriate.[272]

When the fundamental rights of U.S. citizens or residents are at stake, and the absolute defense of controlling sovereign interest is removed, the recent case of *Adarand Constructors, Inc. v. Pena*[273] lends support to subjecting the federal government to the same level of scrutiny as the states in creating alienage classifications.[274] The Court in *Adarand* indicated its willingness to hold the federal

---

> may grant or withhold. But the crux of the problem before us is whether Congress having extended the privilege for the benefit not of the alien but of her American husband, left wide open the opportunity to ruthlessly take away what it gave.

Knauff, 338 U.S. at 549.

270. Aleinikoff, *Citizens, Aliens, Membership*, *supra* note 40, at 20-21; Martin, *supra* note 28, at 208.

271. *Mandel*, 408 U.S. at 783 (Marshall, J., dissenting). Marshall distinguishes this case from all of the cases invoking the plenary power doctrine as "all of them involved only the rights of the excluded aliens themselves." *Id.* at 782 (Marshall, J., dissenting); *see also* Fong Yue Ting v. United States, 149 U.S. 698 (1893) (evaluating claim of excluded alien); Chinese Exclusion Case, 130 U.S. 581 (1889) (reviewing claim of excluded alien). Later, Justice Marshall in his dissent in *Fiallo* argued that any attempt to limit citizens' fundamental rights must comport with the Fifth Amendment principles of due process and equal protection. *Fiallo*, 430 U.S. at 800 (Marshall, J., dissenting). Despite the fact that *Fiallo* challenged an immigration law, Justice Marshall's dissent was consistent with the Court's previous holdings requiring strict scrutiny of legislation affecting "suspect" classifications. *Id.*

272. *See* Aleinikoff, *Citizens, Aliens, Membership*, *supra* note 40, at 26 (suggesting that lawful permanent residents may have membership rights similar, if not equal to citizens). Aleinikoff questions the distinctive rights of citizens versus residents in the current family immigration system. *Id.*; *see also* Guendelsberger, *Family Unification*, *supra* note 14, at 82-83 (recognizing many inequities which have existed in treatment of alien spouse and children from early immigration laws to present day).

273. 115 S. Ct. 2097 (1995).

274. *See id.* (holding that question of whether government's use of subcontractor compensation clause should be subject to strict scrutiny of Court); Kurfis, *supra* note 86, at 134 (providing history of strict scrutiny of alienage classifications and its development from lower standards). For a further discussion of the fact that state and federal governments are being held to different standards of scrutiny regarding alienage classifications, see *supra* notes 82-87 and accompanying text.

lygamy, the constitutionally humane approach is limited.[281] Consequently, a criticism of this approach may be that it does not demonstrate respect for relationships the judiciary is not ready to protect or for the beliefs and customs of other cultures.[282] While this approach is constitutionally bound, it can develop with the legal interpretation of fundamental rights. If, for example, *Romer v. Evans*[283] or *Baehr v. Miike*[284] were to become a springboard for homosexual marital rights, an argument could be made for the family unification rights in immigration law of a homosexual married couple.[285] Following a constitutionally humane approach, any attempt to limit these rights through immigration policies would become subjected to a "compelling interest" standard.

X. CONCLUSION

As noted, applying a constitutionally humane approach does not guarantee a final victory for the individual.[286] The constitutionally humane approach, like the plenary power approach, considers the government's interest in sovereignty.[287] Under the constitutionally humane approach, however, the government's interest will not predictably become the overriding concern. The interest of the persons affected by the law will also be fully and fairly evaluated. Following a constitutionally humane approach, the fundamental right of the alien and his or her lawful family will begin to be properly assessed along with the rights of the government. Hopefully then, this discussion will have served its limited purpose of initiating an open dialogue regarding the proper assessment of rights.[288]

281. *See generally* Anderson, *supra* note 257, at 310-11 (recognizing fact that Refugee Act of 1980 only extends protection to individuals falling within statute's narrow definition of refugee).

282. *But see* Guendelsberger, *Family Unification*, *supra* note 14, at 54-57 (discussing respect France's immigration system has for other cultures).

283. 116 S. Ct. 1620 (1996).

284. 65 U.S.L.W. 2399 (1st Cir. Dec. 3, 1996) (No. 91-1394)

285. *Gays' Right to Marry Upheld*, NEWSDAY, Dec. 4, 1996, at A5; *The Message from Hawaii*, N.Y. TIMES, Dec. 6, 1996, at A38.

286. *See* Aleinikoff, *Community Ties*, *supra* note 29, at 245 (discussing community ties). Even in acknowledging the ties of different groups of individuals to the United States and in balancing the rights of individuals against the remaining *Mathews v. Eldridge*, 424 U.S. 319 (1972) factors, reasonable people might ultimately differ as to the degree the government versus the individual is affected. *Id.* For a further discussion of the *Eldridge* factors, see *supra* note 132 and accompanying text.

287. For a further discussion of the notion of sovereignty, see *supra* notes 38-42 and accompanying text.

288. *See* Jean v. Nelson, 472 U.S. 846, 880 (1985) (Marshall, J., dissenting) (noting this may not be appropriate place to set "the precise contours" of U.S.

In so doing, the inhumane results which have been reached in allowing an unbridled deference to the plenary power can be prevented.[289] Such a constitutionally humane approach may lead towards the treatment of aliens by federal authorities from the Constitution's fundamental perspective of protecting the rights of the individual.

---

immigration law's family unification policy); *see also* Aleinikoff, *Citizens, Aliens, Membership*, *supra* note 40, at 26-27 (discussing Court's careful hedging in its statements regarding theory of membership); Scaperlanda, *Marshall's Jurisprudence*, *supra* note 25, at 67 (discussing Justice Marshall's failure to provide formula for determining relationship between government's plenary immigration power and rights of aliens).

289. *See* Shaughnessy v. United States *ex rel.* Mezei, 345 U.S. 206 (1953) (stating individual excluded from United States by Court's strict adherence to will of Congress and refusal to exercise discretion in permitting him to stay); United States *ex rel.* Knauff v. Shaughnessy, 338 U.S. 537 (1950) (noting Court's reliance on immigration laws passed in wartime and observing that Congress did not intend to permit members of armed services to marry and bring into United States aliens that Congress had specifically excluded); *see also Jean*, 472 U.S. at 875 (Marshall, J., dissenting) (discussing bridled nature of immigration power); Martin, *supra* note 28, at 192 (commenting on mistakes of *Knauff* and *Mezei*).

The Limits of Borders: A Moderate Proposal for Immigration Reform

by

Frank H. Wu

From Franz Kafka, "Before the Law":

> *Before the Law stands a door-keeper. To this doorkeeper there comes a man from the country and prays for admittance to the Law. But the doorkeeper says that he cannot grant admittance at the moment . . . The doorkeeper gives him a stool and lets him sit down at one side of the door. There he sits for days and years. He makes many attempts to be admitted, and wearies the doorkeeper by his importunity. The doorkeeper frequently has little interviews with him, asking him questions about his home and many other things, but the questions are put indifferently, as great lords put them, and always finish with the statement that he cannot be let in yet . . . "Everyone strives to reach the Law," says the man, "so how does it happen that for all these many years no one but myself has ever begged for admittance?" The doorkeeper recognizes that the man has reached his end, and, to let his failing sense catch the words, roars in his ear: "No one else could ever be admitted here, since this gate was made only for you, I am now going to shut it."*[1]

This article presents a moderate proposal for immigration reform: the Supreme Court should apply the same standards to immigration laws that it applies to all other laws.

Frank H. Wu is an Assistant Professor at Howard University School of Law. Prior to becoming a professor, Mr. Wu was a Teaching Fellow at Stanford Law School. He received his degrees from Johns Hopkins University and University of Michigan Law School. Professor Wu also writes for The New York Times Syndicate *and* Asian Week.

INTRODUCTION

This article presents a moderate proposal for immigration reform: the Supreme Court should apply the same standards to immigration laws that it applies to all other laws. The constitutional limits that govern at the borders should be similar to the constitutional limits which are accepted everywhere else.

The proposal rests on textual and structural rationales. A literalist interpretation of the Constitution supports the proposal, because many of the rights articulated in the document are attributed to individuals and not necessarily limited to citizens. A structural approach to the Constitution also supports the proposal, because under even a restrictive reading of equal rights, the equality of citizens is compromised by immigration legislation.

As an initial matter, the Court should abolish the archaic doctrine of "plenary power," which it developed a century ago in a series of cases upholding immigration policies that today a consensus would regard as being based on race in the most objectionable sense. The plenary power doctrine is a judicial creation from an era the constitutional theory of which has been superseded in almost all other respects. It rests on an erroneous understanding of challenges to immigration policies, which takes them to be efforts by and for foreigners rather than citizens. Efforts to restrict immigration across the national border and efforts to limit migration over state and local boundaries share the same objectionable features, and the Court has recognized the problems at the latter levels.

This article describes some effects of applying domestic constitutional norms in the area of immigration. A Supreme Court that chose to follow this course would overrule some earlier precedent, but it likely would validate much contemporary immigration law and all but the most extreme pending legislation. It may even strengthen, rather than weaken, the distinction between citizens and aliens.

As a corollary to the change in substantive standards, citizens would more clearly have standing to challenge immigration statutes for their impact on native communities. In turn, citizen standing forms part of a reconception of how the immigration debates impinge upon the status on citizens, especially racial minorities perceived as foreign. The relationship of immigration and civil rights, captured by the so-called "blacks versus browns" dilemma, shows how immigration law should alter our understanding of color-blindness as a constitutional theory. In the greatest departure from prior thinking, but closest alignment with political realities, the constitutional change would reinforce a corresponding conceptual change: immigration issues should be understood as intimately related to civil rights issues.

The article responds to current conservative efforts to restrict immigration. But in a sense it is addressed to the liberal who has been sympathetic to immigrants though also ambivalent about the relatively high numbers of immigrants that the United States is now receiving and the accompanying social changes, real and perceived. In a response to restrictionists who have attempted to portray their opposition as motivated by self-interest or emotions, the article offers a set of principles that are extended from conventional constitutional theory and applied in a new manner. This proposal falls between the philosophical extremes, on the one hand that the sovereign nation can make any decisions whatsoever with respect to outsiders, and on the other hand that a liberal democracy lacks moral authority to refuse entry to anyone. The article is an attempt to advance an agenda for positive social change, rather than merely defending against extreme reactionary proposals.

The article is organized into three sections. Section I summarizes the current debate over immigration and provides an overview of the dynamics of that debate. Section II describes social and political trends which connect the debates on the national border to debates over state and local boundaries. Section III analyzes the application of domestic constitutional standards to immigration law.

I. WITH LIBERALS LIKE THESE, WHO NEEDS CONSERVATIVES?

Proponent of a military presence on the U.S.-Mexico border:

I've been a liberal Democrat all my life.[2]

A. The Ascendant Reactionary View of Immigration

As "the American Century" approaches its end, immigration issues have become so divisive that reform can mean anything from abolishing immigration to abolishing immigration laws.[3] Immigration policies are means of defining the national community and giving meaning to the concept of citizenship. In their contradictory efforts to develop immigration policies, liberals have become scared of the straw man of "political correctness." In contrast to the confused reactions of liberals, conservatives have consistently appealed to color-consciousness, not color-blindness, in developing their vision of an immigration policy.[4]

Under the guise of attacking "political correctness," immigration restrictionists have appealed to a racialized vision of citizenship. Their arguments have attracted wide popular support. Whether it is called "politically correct" or "politically incorrect," however, the troubling trend is toward closing the borders and prohibiting further immigration, legal or otherwise.[5]

Today, the most prominent proponent of immigration restriction is Peter Brimelow. Brimelow — himself an immigrant from England[6] — has authored the polemical tract, *Alien Nation: Common Sense About America's Immigration Disaster.*[7] A few years earlier, Brimelow had written a magazine article that would serve as a preliminary draft of *Alien Nation.*[8] His concern then was whether immigrants would assimilate.[9] His distress has now sharpened, as he has concluded that immigrants are racially inassimilable.[10]

By making his arguments both more expansive and more extreme in book form, Brimelow has shaped the substance and the style of the immigration debate.[11] He says nothing new in his work.[12] His book has its roots in a long line of arguments that have been made since the founding of the nation.[13]

During the decade preceding publication of Brimelow's book, a few other advocates for lowering levels of immigration had operated at the margins of mainstream politics.[14] But overall, anti-immigrant activities had been in a lull since 1965,[15] when Congress finally replaced with a new system an immigration system borne of the turn-of-the-century eugenics and Social Darwinist movements. The pre-reform statutory scheme discriminated against not only people of color but also white ethnic groups. It did so intentionally and explicitly through national origin quotas designed to maintain a racial balance equivalent to the early twentieth century composition of the country.[16]

Following passage of the 1965 Immigration and Nationality Act,[17] immigration increased, especially Asian and Latino immigration. Immigration again became a divisive issue in the early 1990s. It was then that the Census revealed that whites might become a racial minority group in the foreseeable future.

Accompanying the change in the color of immigrants, the recent round of the battle over immigration began during the 1992 Presidential elections. Adopting an "America First" attitude in an aggressive challenge to then incumbent President George Bush, conservative candidate Pat Buchanan casually remarked on the David Brinkley television show that "I think God made all people good, but if we had to take a million immigrants in, say Zulus, next year, or Englishmen, and put them in Virginia, what group would be easier to assimilate and would cause less problems for the people of Virginia?"[18] As Buchanan explained at greater length in his syndicated column, America had become "so uncivil and angry" because "a flood tide of immigration has rolled in from the Third World."[19]

Anti-immigrant arguments prevailed in the 1994 California elections. By ballot referendum, a majority of voters in the state passed Proposition 187 (Prop. 187), a measure which was ostensibly focused on "illegal" immigrants but expressly covered any individual "suspected" of being an "illegal" immigrant.[20] Prop. 187 echoed Brimelow's magazine article arguments with its call-to-arms preamble. Through Prop. 187, "the People of California [found and declared] that they have suffered and are suffering economic hardship caused by the presence of illegal aliens."[21] As proponents of Prop. 187 declared to voters, "you are the posse and [the proposal] is the rope."[22]

After their victory, the hard-core backers of Prop. 187 went on to attack legal immigrants as well, much to the chagrin of some of their supporters who had believed campaign promises that the targets were "illegal" immigrants only. The hard-core view reflects the belief that an astute observer ascribed to the Immigration and Naturalization Service (INS): "a legal immigrant is merely an illegal alien with papers."[23]

Inspired by Prop. 187, pending federal legislation, which has a high likelihood of passing (or having already passed prior to publication of this symposium issue), may be the most significant revision of immigration laws in a generation. The leading bills share as their primary feature lower limits on legal immigration.[24] Some restrictionists are advocating amending the Constitution to end birthright citizenship.[25] The restrictionist policies envisioned by Brimelow would become law through these proposals.[26] It would be an understatement to say that if immigration restrictionists succeed in the legislative process and the statutes subsequently survive court challenges, the new era of immigration policy will significantly alter the future of the United States — for better or for worse.

In its latest form, immigration law has expanded in its reach. Just as it does not end with "illegal" immigrants, it also does not stop at the border. Whatever its merits, Prop. 187 does not touch on the event of crossing the border and entering the United States, but instead reaches the conduct of citizens and those presumed to be aliens in their daily lives within the community.[27]

And so it is that Brimelow, by reintroducing a vision of America as racially white and culturally homogeneous, has captured public attention with his anti-immigrant attacks. If the title of his book were not signal enough, his thesis is stated succinctly: "America needs another time-out from immigration."[28] He is forthright in declaring his allegiance to an America that is in conception racial rather than political; his nation is one of white men, not one of laws.

Brimelow's primary argument purposefully blends the racial and the cultural: "Race is destiny in American politics" because "[c]ulture is a substitute for ethnicity."[29] As he makes similar statements throughout his book,[30] never bothering to define race, ethnicity or culture, or critically question the meaning of those concepts, he can be taken quite fairly as assuming that race and culture are essentially equivalent.

Even to another immigration restrictionist, Brimelow's argument should appear to be curiously missing the crucial link between race and culture. He has only to say, in response to another writer who asserted that he was promoting "the racial hegemony of white Americans": "I was immediately stricken by guilt . . ."[31]

Brimelow's guilt did not last long:

> But then it occurred to me: Suppose I had proposed more immigrants who looked like me? [Until 1950] nine out of ten Americans looked like me . . . And in those days, they had another name for this thing dismissed so contemptuously as "the racial hegemony of white Americans." They called it "America."[32]

As for any inquiry about whether an American who failed to look like Brimelow could assimilate to become more like him, his response is threatening: "the only possible answer is: *they'd better*."[33]

Brimelow repeats himself often enough to dispel doubt that he means to "set forth," as Michael Lind noted, "what looks very much like a defense of old-fashioned white racial nationalism."[34] Brimelow writes, "The American nation has always had a specific ethnic core. And that core has been white."[35] To be more precise, "the American stew of 1790 . . . for better or worse . . . tasted distinctly British."[36] His complaint is that Americans are unwilling to think in terms of racial group generalizations, even when he (and implicitly they) believe them to be true.[37]

Brimelow opens and closes by arguing that Asian Americans[38] and Latinos[39] who are immigrants and support immigration are alienated from America;[40] they threaten to "break down white America's sense of identity."[41] Furthermore, blacks, in whose economic condition Brimelow professes to take an interest,[42] fare poorly in Brimelow's racial analysis. In particular, Zulus have not reached the level of "Alfred the Great, let alone . . . Elizabeth II or any civilized society," as Brimelow is compelled to add.[43] Haitian refugees should not be "embraced" (a figurative phrase used by New York Times columnist Abe Rosenthal) because "some 3 percent of the Haitian refugees at Guantanamo tested HIV-positive."[44]

Likewise, Brimelow disparages white ethnic groups. He remarks, "[i]n recent years the Mafia or Cosa Nostra has been in decline, not least because of the acculturation of Italian Americans."[45] The Irish immigrants of the nineteenth century "displayed social pathologies striking similar to those of the contemporary American black ghetto," but they improved over the next several generations because "America changed the Irish — and they changed themselves."[46]

Of course, Brimelow sees some positive points in immigration. He is "sentimental" about Asian immigration, in part because, as he recounts it, "the young female students I see every morning entering the Parsons School of Design [in New York City, next to his office] are very charming, and fashionable."[47]

Brimelow's secondary argument is economic: immigration "is a luxury. And like all luxuries, it can help — or it can hurt."[48] He devotes many pages to a cost-benefit analysis of immigration,[49] but admits that rational calculations can conceal racial beliefs.[50]

In later presentations of his proposals, Brimelow has varied. On some occasions, he has been more outrageous, and on other occasions more circumspect. He has called the move toward race-neutral immigration policies the "absurd end of the anti-Nazi crusade" and described the resulting shifts in the racial composition of the country as "Hitler's posthumous revenge."[51] He also has argued for lowering immigration levels with only an uncharacteristic passing reference to the racial characteristics of current immigrants.[52]

In finishing off his attack on immigrants, Brimelow has the gall to suggest that he and other critics of immigration be called — one might imagine the requisite drumroll — "Patriots."[53] As self-important as he is, it would be difficult to write a better parody of Brimelow than Brimelow himself has done.[54] If only he were making mischief with his italicized warning, "*Remember — practically until the Civil War, white Protestants were America.*"[55]

Unintentionally, Peter Brimelow has done liberals a service by revealing what is wrong with the conservative view of immigration. Unfortunately, his will be the prevailing view unless liberals take up the issue aggressively.

B. An Alternative View of Immigration

Instead of reacting to Brimelow and his peers, liberals should advance their own agenda for positive social change. Liberals may be currently divided on immigration issues, but liberal principles should reunite them.[56]

While it may seem less than an ideal moment in American history to suggest that the borders should be more open than closed, the country has always had an ambivalent attitude toward immigration, seeing it through an opposed pair of traditions.[57] The positive myth, symbolized by the Statue of Liberty, celebrates the contributions of innumerable ethnic groups. The negative myth, contained in metaphors of a floodtide, an invasion, and the Tower of Babel, condemns the literal and symbolic costs associated with absorbing newcomers.

It may be heartening, then, to remember that anti-immigrant forces were regarded as extremist until recently. Whether these trends run in cycles, the arguments here are offered with the hope that over time reason will prove persuasive.

The dormant fissure among liberals on immigration, especially "illegal" immigration, erupted again during the campaign for Prop. 187.[58] The ballot measure introduced a theme that resonated in the ensuing public discourse: "I am a liberal — BUT . . ."[59]

Like everyone else, liberals filled in the blank with reactions ranging from "this is a country of laws and there's a right way and a wrong way to become a citizen," to "immigration hurts the most disadvantaged among us." Liberals rationalized their litany of complaints as a principled form of selfishness. By their negative image, immigrants compete for jobs, consume affirmative action benefits, or become dependent on welfare entitlements. They might refuse to learn English and assimilate, and instead become militant multi-culturalists. They are among the sources of crime, terrorism, disease, pollution, and overpopulation.[60] Many politicians, pundits and voters expressed their feeling defensively, as the mayor of a California city did. Well before the Prop. 187 campaign was underway, when immigration was an issue of local concern, this politician argued for posting the military on the U.S.-Mexico border, insisting as he did so, "I've been a liberal Democrat all my life."[61]

Against this movement of the majority, the moderate proposal that should persuade liberals is as follows: in considering "reform" options, apply the same standards at the border that apply within the borders.[62] Stated in terms of constitutional law: eliminate the plenary power doctrine and permit challenges to immigration laws that discriminate based on suspect classifications such as race.[63] There is nothing wrong with limiting immigration, but it should be troubling if the limits are racial, either explicitly or implicitly.[64]

By such standards, the racial justifications used to define outsiders and keep them out, which might seem seductive at the national border, appear as repulsive as they would at any other border. Many ideas that are considered within the mainstream where the national border is concerned would be rejected as racist by any definition of that term and beyond the pale if applied at any other border: taking military measures,[65] building a wall,[66] violent vigilante actions,[67] and routine detention.[68] These ideas are all the more disturbing where internal migrants are racially different — as they often are — outsiders literally and metaphorically. Every argument advanced by Brimelow applies with the same force to new residents of a state or would-be neighbors in a suburb. That Brimelow dislikes the conception of the nation as a civil society with a unifying political identity should make it easier to transfer his arguments from the national level to state and local levels. If anything, the realities of the situation should compel a reversal in thinking: the national border is less, not more, critical than state and local boundaries to the extent that a genuine community wishes to maintain its identity and well-being.[69] Many Americans,[70] however, would balk at adopting Brimelow's suggestions at borders within the United States, either state or local. That inconsistency is the potential source of progressive social change.

Set alongside one another, as Joseph Carens has argued,[71] arguments for limiting immigration are virtually the same as the arguments used to prevent "Okie" farmers displaced from the dustbowl from moving to California during the Depression, and prohibiting African Americans from moving into suburban neighborhoods during the civil rights era. It is inconsistent, and should be subject to legal scrutiny, to believe that the national border can be controlled in a manner that would be indisputably unconstitutional and deemed unwise at a local or state boundary line. It would be consistent, although subject to legal scrutiny for other reasons, to believe that all borders can be controlled by equally extreme measures.

Immigration restrictionists have used various rhetorical tricks to distinguish between borders. These procedural and structural moves have neither logical nor moral significance. They deserve little legal consideration. The argument of national sovereignty, their favorite device, has historical counterparts that carry little intellectual weight, among progressives at any rate. "National sovereignty" finds an equivalent in "states' rights," invoked by the South during the Confederacy and a century later in the reaction against the civil rights movement.[72] "National sovereignty" has another equivalent in the "local control" repeatedly asserted by counties, townships and municipalities as an ineffective bulwark against external influences.

As Bruce Ackerman has observed, the assumption that the national border has special significance eventually must fall back on the assertion that it is different by nature.[73] It rests, at bottom, on little more than its own definition — power rather than principle. At best, it depends on priority in time as a compelling claim; i.e., the people who arrived earlier are entitled to exclude the people who appeared later.[74] Even then, Brimelow's approach reads into priority in time an implicit guarantee of racial group entitlement. Without this racial link, the immigration restrictionist position makes no sense. It is the racial group, not the individual, whose arrival counts for the creation of rights.[75]

Yet it would be naive verging on utopian to argue for open borders and against the existence of nations. In a world with severe socioeconomic differences among nations, and for a country that has an extensive welfare system, it would be impossible to adopt a policy of allowing entry to every potential immigrant.

Nothing so extreme need be proposed. National sovereignty must be accepted.[76] National sovereignty, however, establishes only that the nation can regulate its borders. National sovereignty, by itself, does not establish that the nation can regulate its borders by standards that a consensus would hold absurd applied everywhere else. Thus, even if national sovereignty establishes that the United States can and should distinguish among potential new citizens, it does not directly follow that race-based restrictions on immigration are natural or any more acceptable at the border than elsewhere.[77]

Understood in this manner, national sovereignty speaks to challenges by aliens or by foreign governments to United States immigration policy. At the same time, national sovereignty in a liberal democracy ought to encourage challenges by citizens to immigration policy.[78] A nation that is a constitutional democracy may especially be expected to uphold its intrinsic values at the limits.

Liberals who take the political position that national sovereignty forecloses questioning restrictive immigration policies should acknowledge that they are diverging greatly from their ideals. Better yet, they could return to those ideals.

The best path back toward liberal ideals is viewing immigration as part of domestic politics, looking at it from the inside out, while also viewing immigration as part of foreign policy, looking at it from the outside in.[79] Exclusive use of the foreign policy perspective only ensures that immigration will be likened to invasion.[80]

Immigration issues have always fragmented political parties and failed to divide neatly along the political spectrum,[81] thereby demonstrating the inadequacy of traditional labels and metaphors. Some conservatives have argued in favor of immigration as an extension of laissez-faire economic principles. They also have been less sanguine about attacking "illegal" immigration, if not actually tolerant of it. Their philosophy is based on an opposition to welfare entitlements as a more important problem (although with an apparent acceptance of the notion that "illegal" immigrants take advantage of those benefits and services as well).[82]

In this vein, William Bennett and Jack Kemp, stalwarts of the Reagan and Bush administrations, placed themselves among the opponents of Prop. 187.[83] Joining them was California gubernatorial candidate Ron Unz, who positioned himself to the "right" of incumbent Pete Wilson in the 1994 Republican primaries; Unz opposed Prop. 187 while Wilson served as one of its backers.[84] Aside from Bennett, Kemp and Unz, about the only people whose arguments for unrestricted immigration are taken seriously are pure libertarians who believe in free markets and free movement of labor, unregulated by government in any form.[85] They may have the wrong principle, but they do have a principle, which is better than can be said of many others.

Brimelow may base his argument on race confused with culture, but there are individuals who have legitimate reasons for wishing to limit immigration.[86] People ought to be able to find a middle ground upon which to resolve their disagreements. The challenge lies in finding that place.

II. MEMBERSHIP HAS ITS PRIVILEGES

From an internal memorandum written by the founder of the Federation for American Immigration Reform (FAIR):

— on whites becoming a racial minority:

Will they simply go quietly into the night? Or will there be an explosion?

— on the birthrates of whites compared to nonwhites:

Perhaps this is the first instance in which those with their pants up are going to be caught by those with their pants down.[87]

The rush to close the gates — local, state and national — is driven by several trends. These trends shape the context within which any discussion of immigration policy must take place. They form the subtext of Brimelow's *Alien Nation* and lie beneath the surface in many discussions of immigration policies. The five phenomena are: (1) the changing role of whites in the United States; (2) the changing role of the United States in the world; (3) mass migration worldwide; (4) the unimportance of being anywhere; (5) apocalyptic predictions for the turn of the millennium. These social and political forces, as much as any intellectual arguments, generate nativism. Any legal response must account for them.

A. The New Face of America

The first two phenomena are linked. The dramatic demographic changes sweeping across the country have become a cliched concept.[88] The shifts in the balance of power among nations have become perhaps equally cliched.[89] Together, these phenomena have created twin trends of perceived decline. Some whites worry that they will cease to be the dominant racial group in the United States.[90] Many Americans fear that the United States will lose its position as the dominant superpower of the world.[91]

These acute anxieties are connected through immigration. Brimelow and Buchanan make the connection. As the latter has written, "Does this First World nation wish to become a Third World country? Because that is our destiny if we don't build a wall against the waves of immigration rolling over our shores."[92] Or as one supporter of Prop. 187 put it, "People are saying, 'I don't like this Third World takeover.' It is literally an invasion and very upsetting."[93]

The common complaint that "we" are becoming "Third World" is ambiguous.[94] The risk of becoming a "Third World" nation refer both to an internal condition and an external position. It is as rooted in the belief that whites are diminishing in power as it is in the feeling that the country is declining in influence.

These perceptions of change have the proverbial grain of truth to them.[95] The nation has entered an unprecedented phase in race relations, as a result of immigration and intermarriage.[96] At the turn of the century, the population consisted of approximately ninety-percent nonHispanic whites.[97] Before the turn of the millennium, the population already consists of less than seventy-five percent nonHispanic whites.[98] The numbers of immigrants in the population is higher than ever before, but the proportion is lower than during the entire period between the Civil War and the Depression.[99] The number of mixed marriages has doubled in the past decade.[100] Still, the grain of truth has grown into a weed of distortions and exaggerations: social science research shows that white Americans, like all other Americans (to different degrees), overestimate the extent to which demographic changes have already occurred.[101]

Until the relatively recent past, the country could plausibly be mythologized as a unified community. In fact, it was predominantly white racially and Anglo-Saxon Protestant culturally. Today, the society could be perceived as a mosaic of communities occasionally in conflict. Regardless, it is undeniably multi-racial and multicultural. Non-white racial groups and individuals are increasing not only their numbers, but also their presence and participation in economic, political and cultural spheres. Coinciding with these changes, many citizens have come to see the United States as a slowly sinking lifeboat.[102]

It is more than a coincidence though. Although it would be simplistic to attribute resistance to immigration solely to racism or nativism (or false consciousness on the part of those immigrants who are less enthusiastic about admitting others after them), it would be wrong to deny that there is a complex relationship between efforts to restrict immigration and the race of the immigrants. The immigration debate is about the numbers of new arrivals, but it also is about their races and their cultures.

B. On the Road to Nowhere

The third and fourth phenomena also are connected, but in opposition to one another. Everyone is moving; or more accurately, groups and individuals are more mobile than ever before are mobile. Simultaneously, thanks to technology it is increasingly irrelevant where a person is located physically (if the person is well-situated socioeconomically). These contradictory trends are global as well as local.

Human migration may well be a natural and timeless phenomenon. Individual mobility today is restricted by abstract laws, rather than primitive territoriality, physical barriers or practical constraints. According to recent United Nations estimates, in 1985 there were over 100 million migrants throughout the world.[103] People depart from their homelands destined for the United States, but people leave for other nations as well — much of the worldwide pattern of migration consists of movement from developing nations to other developing nations.[104] Within overall migration patterns, another countertrend is emerging which suggests the rise of a transnational class: upwardly-mobile young Americans are working overseas temporarily and settling elsewhere permanently.[105]

In contrast with the compulsion to migrate, individuals who have the means are able to rely on technological advances and the integration of communications to conduct their business affairs and personal lives from almost anywhere. While a generation ago media prophet Marshall McLuhan forecast a "global village,"[106] today Internet enthusiasts speak of the forthcoming virtual community.[107] *The Economist*, the cosmopolitan London-based newsmagazine that promotes a libertarian philosophy, asked in a provocative cover article, "Does it matter where you are?"[108] *The Economist* concluded that geography remains economically important, but increasingly less so.[109]

The sense that people are free of their physical location, even if based more on optimism than fact, presents a means of overcoming immigration restrictionism. The divergent trends in the importance of location are metaphorical as well: as Benjamin Barber has observed, based on basic ideological conflict increasing even as mass culture becomes more influential, "the planet is falling precipitantly apart and coming reluctantly together at the very same moment."[110]

C. Apocalypse Now

Finally, the fifth phenomenon presents itself as overshadowing all else. The popular culture has been inundated by a variety of neo-Malthusian doomsday scenarios.[111]

The themes of overpopulation, overdevelopment and overconsumption form the basis for an environmental objection to immigration. The argument seems to be that if everyone stays in place, people will lose their opportunities to deplete natural resources and generate waste — at least in the manner to which Americans have become accustomed.[112] In his controversial book *Living Within Limits*, Garret Hardin argues against allowing migration from poorer to wealthier societies on biological and ecological grounds.[113] As a leading environmental organization, the Sierra Club has published a book raising similar claims.[114] In doing so, it lent its reputation to the cause of immigration restriction. By these means, immigration restrictionists acquire scientific credibility and liberal credentials.

Meanwhile, *The Atlantic Monthly*, an intellectual mass media magazine that is moderate in its politics, has published several cover stories in the past few years describing impending chaos the world over and in this country as well. The myriad predictions, all of them negative, have been based on historical, social scientific and scientific data. These articles, which have been well received, have asked whether it "must be the rest against the west;"[115] and whether the end of the world is near because of breakdown of the social order,[116] overpopulation,[117] or fundamentalism of many forms.[118] Such a bleak intellectual climate has fostered the growth of anti-immigrant feelings.

D. THE COMMUNITY AS A COMMODITY

The five trends apply at all levels, local, state and national. The similarity of the levels is as empirical as it is analytic. Immigration and internal migration form different levels of the same subject.

Migration crosses borders and borders within borders. Here in the United States, internal migration has always been the norm rather than the exception. The levels of internal migration are so high that people who move around within the country outnumber immigrants coming into the country.[119]

Coupling the positive myth of immigration with the frontier myth, arrival in this country typically is only one step in a long series of moves.[120] The local, state and national levels also are connected through "white flight": as nonwhite immigrants move to the specific regions of the country, white natives move elsewhere within the country.[121] One supporter of Prop. 187 displayed his regional rather than national concerns by stating, "Someone is going to be leaving the state. It will either be them or us."[122]

As people move across all forms of boundaries, people react adversely at each of those boundaries. Communities are becoming closed, in the local, state and national spheres. At the local level, literal gates are being built and closed around exclusive developments, some of which are so large-scale as to be entire towns that have been basically privatized.[123] At the state level, factions within the Deep South have attempted to reassert a states' rights movement, as a revival of antebellum traditions to the extent of secession, though ostensibly free of their racial components.[124] The aspirations of these local and state movements show that the real risk of national disintegration lies with whites, not Latinos. The local and state developments mirror Brimelow's proposals for the national border.

The resurgence of communitarianism as such has not been tested legally, but some of its elements have faced and failed constitutional scrutiny already. At a local level, the Constitution has been interpreted to forbid official decisions to physically divide communities by race.[125] At a state level, the Constitution creates a right to interstate travel that trumps official decisions to exclude migrants because of economic status or assumed economic status.[126]

There is no question that constitutional standards exist for the control of local and state boundaries.[127] As with all constitutional standards, these limits restrain political actions that are supported by a majority, in this case if they are based on racial or economic motivations.

Immigration law raises many of the same issues of membership in the national community as arise at the local and state levels.[128] However, immigration law at the constitutional level differs from other border-related law because it lacks guiding principles.

There was a time when immigration law was animated by nativist principles. Before passage of the 1965 Immigration and Nationality Act, immigration statutes had passed through phases when Eastern and Southern Europeans were limited by strict quotas, especially if their countries of origin were more heavily Catholic or Jewish; Latinos were recruited as workers when needed and repatriated when convenient; and Asians were barred.[129] There was a time, too, when immigration practices were integral to racist policies. Forced migration of Africans as slaves, for all its scale and severity, "the largest known migration over such a distance in world history up to that time,"[130] is usually conspicuously absent from the stories of immigration.[131]

All of that changed with the 1965 Act, which established more or less neutral principles, by replacing national origin quotas with hemispheric quotas.[132] The 1965 Act was imperfect. By imposing hemispheric caps, it reduced permissible levels of Mexican immigration.[133] But it was revolutionary as a repudiation of a race-based immigration policy.

In the post-1965 era, continuing minor alterations of immigration policies have caused it to steadily drift away from somewhat neutral principles. A series of political bargains resulted in the programs allowing wealthy investors to buy their citizenship,[134] and the lottery that provides players from designated countries with the chance to win their citizenship.[135] In the best light, the former suggests that people may earn citizenship, the latter that they may be rewarded for their luck. Reflecting the worst aspects of American culture, they might send the cynical message that benefits are distributed as much by luck as by work. Together, they are at odds with one another, and not part of a cohesive public policy.

Perhaps appropriately, the highly technical substance of the existing statutory scheme is weakened by its convoluted procedure.[136] The immigration process is so arcane as to benefit nobody except lawyers and con artists.[137] The bureaucracy of the INS has been plagued by scandals such as bribery.[138]

Now, Prop. 187 and related proposals threaten to return immigration policy to a pre-1965 racial basis. Unlike in other areas of the law, the lack of principles governing immigration policy assumes constitutional dimensions because of the plenary power doctrine.

III. SOVEREIGNTY AS THE LAST REFUGE OF THE SCOUNDREL

> *[I]n the exercise of its broad power over immigration and naturalization, 'Congress regularly makes rules that would be unacceptable if applied to citizens.'*[139]

[O]ur country would be overrun by them.[140]

A. The History of the Plenary Power Doctrine

Before considering the possible constitutional analysis that could be applied to immigration, the sources and weaknesses of the extraordinarily durable plenary power doctrine must be revisited and explained. The plenary power doctrine has enjoyed a long life for a constitutional theory.[141] The Constitution itself states no more than that Congress, among its enumerated powers, "shall have the power to . . . establish an uniform Rule of Naturalization."[142] The Supreme Court has construed the clause to mean that Congress has "plenary power" over immigration if not immigrants, beyond constitutional norms and judicial review.

1. *The Anti-Asian Cases*

The plenary power doctrine has its origins in cases challenging race-based immigration restrictions which formed the beginnings of federal immigration legislation. The Court offered its interpretation of the doctrine in the late nineteenth century in the course of upholding the outright exclusion of Chinese immigrants. Since then, the Court has continued to adhere to its view that it will defer to whatever the federal legislature chooses to do with respect to immigration. Normal constitutional review vanishes.

The Supreme Court introduced the plenary power doctrine in what is known aptly as the Chinese Exclusion Case. In the case, *Chae Chan Ping v. United States,*[143] the Court upheld an 1888 Congressional act prohibiting Chinese residents of the United States who had visited China to return to the United States.[144] The 1888 act was itself an amendment to the 1882 legislation that forbade further Chinese immigration to the United States.[145] That earlier legislation, in turn, had been the political outcome of a nationwide movement blaming Chinese immigrants for an economic downturn.

Before the Exclusion Act, Chinese men had been recruited to the Reconstruction South and in Northeastern factories as laborers, and for work crews building the transcontinental railroad. They were pitted against freed black slaves and white ethnic minorities in an attempt to replace those groups as a source of controlled labor, especially as freedmen began to assert their rights and unions began to organize.[146] During the time period shortly before the Chinese Exclusion Act was passed, Chinese communities were attacked by white mobs, with dozens of fatalities in numerous incidents.[147] Significantly, the popular slogan used by anti-Chinese forces was directed not only at immigrants but also at residents: "The Chinese Must Go!"[148]

The Chinese Exclusion Act and its later amendments prevented further immigration, while also making it much more difficult for those already within the United States to travel overseas to see their wives and families.[149] With the artificial absence of Chinese women in the United States, along with miscegenation laws enforced by societal norms, the Chinese American community would have died out had the Exclusion Act been as effective as intended.

The racial motivations of the Chinese Exclusion Act were unremarkable in the eyes of the Supreme Court. In the Chinese Exclusion Case, Justice Stephen J. Field, writing for the majority, identified the fundamental issue as national sovereignty and not racial discrimination. With that approach, he found the issue beyond debate. That the United States government "can exclude aliens from its territories is a proposition which we do not think open to controversy."[150] He reasoned that this power was derived directly from the principle of national sovereignty. "Jurisdiction over its own territory . . . is an incident of every independent nation."[151] Otherwise, Justice Field continued, the United States, "if it could not exclude aliens . . . would be to that extent subject to the control of another power."[152] The passage suggests that Justice Field perceived the tension in the case as being between the United States controlling its own borders, and foreigners having power over the borders — the foreign individuals involved in litigation coming to embody their homelands.[153] Framed this way, the tension is not between legislative choice and constitutional limits, as represented by Congress and the Court, respectively.

Notwithstanding the importance of control over the borders, Justice Field was somewhat ambiguous about the extent of constitutional constraints on this power. He provided a lengthy list of the "sovereign powers" — "to declare war, make treaties, suppress insurrection, repel invasion, regulate foreign commerce, secure republication governments to the States, and admit subjects of other nations to citizenship . . ." To this, however, he added what might seem to be a constitutional caveat, that those powers were "restricted in their exercise only by the Constitution itself."[154]

The racialization of immigration law was explicit in the Chinese Exclusion Act, but only implicit in the Supreme Court case. While the Chinese Exclusion Act singled out a racial group by name, the Supreme Court assumed, without addressing the issue, that the power of the legislature to regulate immigration included the power to regulate it based on race. Insofar as the Court considered race, it gave its approval to the Congressional conclusion. The majority opinion asserted that "the differences of race added greatly to the difficulties of the situation,"[155] in the decidedly unsympathetic sense that "our country would be overrun by them"[156] without the Exclusion Act. "The existence of war would render the necessity of the proceeding only more obvious and pressing."[157]

The reasoning went straight from the reality of war to the possibility of war to immigration: "The same necessity, in a less pressing degree, may arise when war does not exist, and the same authority which adjudges the necessity in one case must also determine it in the other."[158] Whether the majority understood the war to be literal or metaphorical, it understood the racial issue to pose the risk of war and the risk of war to justify exclusion. It is doubtful that Justice Field distinguished much between a literal war — military invasion by Chinese soldiers — and a metaphorical war — racial invasion by Chinese immigrants.

A few terms later, the Supreme Court clarified its theory in *Fong Yue Ting v. United States*.[159] Much as *Chae Chan Ping* is the Chinese Exclusion case, *Fong Yue Ting* might be called the Chinese Deportation Case. In *Fong Yue Ting*, the Court upheld another revision of the anti-Chinese legislation, which specifically provided for the deportation of individuals who by definition were aliens unable to naturalize.[160] "The power to exclude aliens and the power to expel them . . . are in truth but parts of one and the same power."[161]

Writing for the majority, Justice Horace Gray expressed himself with even more conviction than had Justice Field: "The Constitution of the United States speaks with no uncertain sound upon this subject."[162] Justice Gray limited judicial review to instances where "it has been authorized by treaty or by statutes or is required by the paramount law of the Constitution."[163] Again, the exception seems stronger than the rule, despite the reference to the "paramount law of the Constitution."

Justice Gray concluded that "it behooves the Court to be careful that it does not undertake to pass upon political questions."[164] More than that, Justice Gray recited another lengthy list of responsibilities entrusted to the President. Harkening back to war, the list opened with the President's role as "the commander-in-chief of the army and navy." A similar list attributed to the Congress began with its "power to regulate commerce with foreign nations."[165] Within the powers attributed to Congress was the power of "bringing of persons into the ports of the United States."[166] With that line of reasoning, the Court's authority was limited by the Constitution, but immigration laws were not.

As with the Chinese Exclusion Case, the Court understood the Chinese Deportation case as raising no racial issues worth considering. The statutory provision that was challenged in the case was a requirement during deportation proceedings that "at least one credible white witness" attest to a Chinese individual's residency in the United States prior to the enactment of the Chinese Exclusion Act.[167] Far from evoking any concern about unfairness, the racial discrimination was regarded as reasonable. Congress had had experience with "the loose notions entertained by the witnesses of the obligation of an oath" when Chinese individuals were permitted to testify.[168] Thus, the provision was an example of what might be termed reasonable racism.

Writing in dissent, Justice David J. Brewer corrected the majority's version of the facts: The Chinese individuals were "resident aliens" and not sojourners through the country and that they had been in the country "almost as long a time as some of those who were members of the Congress that passed this act of punishment and expulsion."[169] Justice Brewer argued in vain that "the governments of other nations have elastic powers — ours is fixed and bounded by a written Constitution."[170] Under that Constitution, it was improper to "drive from our territory" people "for no crime, but that of their race and birthplace."[171]

Presaging later developments in immigration law, Justice Brewer distinguished the result reached in Chinese Exclusion Case on what were to him "obvious" grounds. The Chinese Exclusion Case had concerned immigrants who were outside of the community — not people already part of the community — and "[t]he Constitution has no extraterritorial effect."[172] Justice Brewer was not quite progressive by today's standards, for he admitted in a well-known piece of dicta that "it is true that this statute is directed only against the obnoxious Chinese."[173] Justice Brewer transformed his prejudice against the Chinese into an appeal to universal standards of sorts, for he argued, "if the power exists, who shall say it will not be exercised tomorrow against other classes and other people?"[174]

Justice Field, who recalled that he "had the honor to be the organ of the court in announcing" the earlier Chinese Exclusion Case, numbered himself among the dissenters in this later case. Introducing an argument that has gone undeveloped in immigration law, Justice Field argued that "the government of the United States is one of limited and delegated powers" and the actions of expelling the Chinese without due process of law exceeded those powers.[175]

The language of the majority opinions in the two cases appear almost to impose an affirmative duty on the executive and legislative branches to protect the country from foreign invasion, if only symbolic, by military action if necessary and immigration laws in any event. The plenary power doctrine, at this high point, goes well beyond a limitation on the judicial branch. The plenary power doctrine is asserted as a defense against a potential racial war. When the court turned away from foreign policy to domestic politics, the debate over the plenary power doctrine focused on the division of authority among branches of the federal government, or federalism concerns over the allocation of authority between the federal government and the respective state governments.[176] Any discussion about the justice of discriminatory restrictions against a racial minority never began.

There would be nothing unusual about this judicial attitude toward race in general and the Chinese in particular, were it not for a decision the Court had issued prior to either of the immigration cases but after the Chinese Exclusion Act of 1882 had already become the law of the land. In the celebrated case of *Yick Wo v. Hopkins*, the Supreme Court struck down a San Francisco regulation of laundries that while neutral on its face had been discriminatorily applied against the Chinese for racial reasons alone.[177] The case remains "good law" for the proposition that a facially neutral law cannot be the product of impermissible legislative intent, nor can it be applied in a discriminatory manner.[178]

In contrast to *Yick Wo*, the Chinese Exclusion Case suppressed the racial references in the law. The difference in the approach to immigration is all the more striking because *Yick Wo* involved a statute that contained no overt racial references while the Chinese Exclusion Case involved a statutory scheme that consisted of nothing but racial references.

This contradiction continued over time. As immigration law evolved toward greater reliance on race, the Court emphasized the irrelevance of race. If there were doubts about the racial basis of an immigration law, the Court resolved them as a matter barely worth comment in dicta. In its 1903 decision of what is known as the Japanese Immigrant Case, *Yamataya v. Fisher*,[179] the Court issued the pronouncement making explicit what had been implicit: "That Congress may exclude aliens of a particular race from the United States . . . and commit the enforcement of . . . provisions, conditions and regulations [for deportation] exclusively to executive officers, without judicial intervention, are principles firmly established by the decisions of this court."[180] Appropriately, the Court made its statement while applying constitutional due process standards to deportation and holding that there was no violation of those standards despite, among other things, the plaintiff's inability to understand English, the consequences of the proceedings, lack of assistance of counsel, and denial of an opportunity to contest the findings.[181]

2. *The Twentieth Century Cases*

As a recurring theme throughout the nineteenth century of immigration case law, the plenary power doctrine has more recently been strangely submerged.[182] It has receded from view without diminishing in influence. Over time, though, it has lost complexity. Immigration law has developed other peculiarities to be sure, but the plenary power doctrine has become all the simpler.

At the turn of the century, the Court stated, "[O]ver no conceivable subject is the legislative power of Congress more complete than it is over [immigration]."[183] Since then, plenary power doctrine has continued to be a set of stock citations bereft of further reasoning.

Over the latter half of the twentieth century, the Court has continued to make similar statements about the plenary power doctrine regardless of whether its decision was favorable to the immigrant challenging a statute. During the Cold War, for example, the nonidentical twin decisions of *Knauff* and *Mezei*, each of which upheld the exclusion of an alien with strong legal arguments grounded in compelling circumstances, contained a concise if facile statement of the view: "Whatever the procedure authorized by Congress is, it is due process as far as an alien denied entry is concerned."[184]

In that same era, immigration discrimination moved beyond race to include ideology. In a concurring opinion in the 1952 case of *Harisiades v. Shaughnessy*,[185] concerning deportation of an individual for his membership in the Communist Party, Justice Felix Frankfurter recited the plenary power doctrine as follows: "[T]he underlying policies of what classes of aliens shall be allowed to enter and what classes of aliens shall be allowed to stay, are for Congress exclusively to determine even though such determination may be deemed to offend American traditions and may, as has been the case, jeopardize peace."[186]

Nearly one hundred years after introducing the plenary power doctrine, the Supreme Court restated it. In 1972, the Court stated in *Kleindienst v. Mandel*[187] that "the Court's general reaffirmations of [the plenary power doctrine] have been legion" and "[t]he Court without exception has sustained [it] . . . ."[188] In 1977, the Court declared in *Fiallo v. Bell*:[189] "at the outset, it is important to underscore the limited scope of judicial inquiry into immigration legislation."[190] The Court wrote, "our recent decisions have not departed from this long-established rule."[191] The consequence, as the Court conceded freely, was that "in the exercise of its broad power over immigration and naturalization, "Congress regularly makes rules that would be unacceptable if applied to citizens."[192]

The majority approach adopted in *Fiallo* is the best example of the plenary power doctrine retreating while retaining its vitality.[193] There, the statute at issue distinguished by legitimacy and gender: children born within wedlock were treated better than children born out of wedlock. Furthermore, the relationship of an illegitimate child to the mother was recognized but not the relationship of the same child to her putative father.[194] The majority reasoned that "it could be argued that the line should have been drawn at a different point . . . [b]ut it is clear from our cases that these are policy questions entrusted exclusively to the political branches of our government. . . ."[195] Justice Thurgood Marshall dissented, writing "this case, unlike most immigration cases . . . directly involves the rights of citizens, not aliens."[196] He continued, "once it is established that this discrimination among citizens cannot escape traditional constitutional scrutiny simply because it occurs in the context of immigration legislation, the result is virtually foreordained."[197]

The majority's treatment of the dissent is unresponsive. It purported to address the discriminatory nature of the challenged provision, but overlooked the type of discrimination that would be unconstitutional if applied to citizens. The majority mischaracterized the dissent of Justice Marshall as directed against any "line drawing" among family members. The majority responded in a footnote that "there are widely varying relationships and degrees of kinship" and "in the inevitable process of 'line drawing,' Congress has determined that certain classes of aliens are more likely than others to satisfy national objectives without undue cost, and it has granted preferential status only to those classes."[198]

The majority, by defending distinctions on the basis of abstract family relationships which it did not further specify, avoided the problem of discrimination on the concrete bases of legitimacy and gender. Whether other distinctions, such as those between immediate family and distant cousins would be acceptable in domestic law, the discrimination between legitimate and illegitimate children, and mothers and fathers, are invidious and would merit heightened scrutiny if enforced against citizens.[199] The question remains, and the constitutional moment is suspended, when the distinction is sanctioned in immigration law. The problem is rendered especially compelling because, even though the statute regulates immigration, it is applied to and affects directly the interests of citizens.

Recent decisions in the immigration area have not presented a serious threat to the plenary power doctrine because they have assumed its existence without addressing its effects. The Court has decided a batch of cases in the 1990s on immigration, none of which do more with the plenary power doctrine than mention it: While immigration issues have appeared on the docket repeatedly, majority opinions have failed to criticize, defend or even explain the plenary power doctrine.[200]

The Court has been quiet about its chief analytic principle in high-profile immigration matters. In the politicized and publicized immigration litigation which led to the *Haitian Centers Council* case,[201] the Court upheld an Executive Order that the Coast Guard "interdict" boats on the high seas and turn away refugees with colorable claims to legal immigration status. The Executive Order, facially neutral, was directed at a specific group of refugees — Haitians.[202] An unprecedented form of immigration restriction, the Executive Order also violated of the plain language of international treaty obligations.[203] The Court held that the federal government, through the executive branch, could take official actions outside of the borders for the purpose of preventing aliens from arriving on U.S. shores and applying for legal status (along the way gaining access to procedural due process protections).[204] There is no language in the majority opinion that would limit its application to immigrants presumed to be "illegal" nor which imposes any apparent limit on the extraterritorial powers of the government over immigration.

As many observers noted, the Congressional Black Caucus among them, the treatment of black refugees from Haiti differed from the treatment of white refugees from Cuba.[205] Aside from race, the primary difference in these situations were the ideologies of the regimes from which they were fleeing — hardly a better basis for the different treatment.[206]

In reviewing the interdiction program, the Court relied on the precedent established in *Mezei*.[207] It did not quite adhere to the plenary power doctrine. It did worse than that. As Justice Harry A. Blackmun argued in dissent, if the plenary power doctrine were applied, it ought to have compelled the Court to choose the Congressional policy expressed in the statute over the Executive Order which disregarded it.[208] Consequently, plenary power proved to be of little use to immigrants on the rare occasion when it would have favored them.

The only exceptions to the plenary power doctrine that are likely to have any significance have been identified by Hiroshi Motomura, building on work by Stephen Legomsky. In a pair of law review articles, Professor Motomura has reoriented the constitutional dimensions of immigration law.

First, Professor Motomura has argued that "phantom" constitutional norms have been developed by the Supreme Court through statutory interpretation.[209] This tactic is illustrated by *Jean v. Nelson*.[210] There, the plaintiffs alleged that the defendants, federal immigration authorities, had discriminated on the basis of race and national origin.[211] The Court held that the challenged parole statutes and regulations barred race and national origin discrimination, and accordingly remanded for a determination of whether the statutes and regulations were being violated.[212] It avoided altogether the much more difficult issue of whether the statutes and regulations could have been written the other way around.

Second, Professor Motomura has argued that lower courts have sometimes avoided the plenary power doctrine by characterizing a particular constitutional challenge as procedural rather than substantive.[213] This occurred in the vacated District of Columbia Circuit decision on the marriage fraud sections of the immigration statutes, *Escobar v. INS*.[214] There, the court struck down a two-year exile waiting period for naturalization that applied when a marriage was entered into by an immigrant while he was in exclusion or deportation proceedings.[215] The court reasoned that the time period was a procedural requirement, which in effect established an irrebutable presumption of fraudulent marriage.[216]

Together, as Professor Motomura argues, the two approaches to immigration law give the Court a means of evading constitutional concerns that are taken as central to domestic law. The approaches create doctrinal distortions. Where it denies right to immigrants, the Court moves the border into the interior of the country.

In effect, instead of the border determining whether an individual is an immigrant, whether an individual is an immigrant locates the border. Other than a handful of exclusion cases, immigration decisions rarely concern individuals who are outside of the country at the time of the events in question. Where it grants immigrants rights, the Court divides laws pertaining to immigration itself and laws concerning immigrants as individuals in a way divorced from legislative intent and reality. That is, Supreme Court case law can be reconciled as stating that people have no right to immigrate, but immigrants have rights as people.[217] By ruling favorably for immigrants in cases that do not concern deportation or exclusion,[218] the Court has recognized that Congress is capable of regulating immigration by regulating immigrants; however, the Court has not noticed that Congress can govern immigration directly with effects that are much more devastating.[219]

Professor Motomura is not optimistic about the potential for progressive reform through either statutory interpretation or procedural approaches.[220] Nor is there reason to be. The resurgence of restrictionist attitudes toward immigration, and impending legislation lowering levels of immigration with a possible racial motivation, suggest that judicial willingness to extend civil rights protection to legal immigrants (never mind illegal immigrants) will not last long without constitutional authority — if not constitutional mandate.

3. *The Power of Stare Decisis*

The plenary power doctrine is a relic. When the Supreme Court decided the Chinese Exclusion Case, it had yet to articulate any concept of strict scrutiny or suspect classification. Accordingly, the judicial deference to the legislative branch, and its accompanying lack of interest in protecting the civil rights of racial minorities, were normal and not anomalous for their time. They are abnormal and anomalous today, though.

In the late nineteenth century, the Supreme Court had not even propounded the color-blindness principle that the conservatives of today would advance to give meaning to the Equal Protection Clause. The Supreme Court had still to entertain the attack on racial segregation presented in *Plessy v. Ferguson*,[221] much less render its ruling striking down separate-but-equal in *Brown v. Board of Education*.[222] Even a cursory review of Supreme Court precedent turns up numerous concepts that commanded a place in constitutional theory then but have been jettisoned since: the notion that equal protection is "the usual last resort of constitutional arguments" and that forced sterilization of the disabled was progressive;[223] the natural law basis of gender discrimination;[224] the idea that political dissent could pose a "clear and present" danger beyond First Amendment protection;[225] the whole of substantive due process;[226] and the limits on federal government authority pursuant to the commerce clause (which also has since seen its resurrection).[227]

The plenary power doctrine belongs to this same company. Indeed, it has occupied a dubious place in constitutional law since its invention. The Court itself has recognized that "much could be said for the view" that it is ill-considered, "but the slate is not clean."[228]

The *stare decisis* argument for the plenary power doctrine is weak for three reasons.[229] First, *stare decisis* can be best justified as a check on raw political power shaping judicial decisionmaking. Its application is appropriate where a reversal of precedent is urged quickly. This is not such an instance. Second, the erosion of the entire surrounding terrain of constitutional theory leaves little support for this last remaining piece of nineteenth-century racial case law. If the other doctrines were rightly repudiated, so too the plenary power doctrine should be "as application of constitutional principles to facts as they had not been seen by the Court before."[230] The Chinese Exclusion case stands as a "decision [that] has been proved manifestly erroneous" in its characterization of Asian immigrants and "its underpinnings [have been] eroded by subsequent decisions of the Court."[231] Third, the plenary power doctrine is an especially peculiar constitutional theory to defend by the device of *stare decisis*. *Stare decisis* protects the legitimacy of judicial review by insisting that courts be bound by their decisions, but the plenary power doctrine itself is an abdication of the function of judicial review. To use *stare decisis* to defend the plenary power doctrine is to persist in a refusal to take action. While implicating constitutional concerns, as distinguished from statutory interpretation, the plenary power doctrine has also resulted in no private reliance that would counsel against its reversal.[232]

Not surprisingly, the plenary power doctrine finds few defenders. Since its introduction, Supreme Court

Justices have written strong dissents casting doubt on its validity and wisdom.[233] Generally, academics have condemned it as a misguided gloss on the Constitution in a "sustained shelling" of critical commentary.[234] Nobody is heard to contend that a contemporary counterpart to the Chinese Exclusion Case, or other early decisions following its plenary power doctrine, could or would be decided with the same outcome or by similar reasoning.[235] Ironically, there is nothing to the plenary power doctrine. The powerful force it exerts is hidden. It preempts as a constitutional matter almost any challenges on substantive grounds to laws applicable to immigrants, certainly at the time or place of their actual admission to the country, and possibly in their later encounters with straightforward discrimination.

Even for immigration restrictionists, including those activists who espouse restriction for racial reasons, the Supreme Court has done a frustrating disservice with respect to the plenary power doctrine. The Court has taken the worst possible course as an institution of final authority in constitutional interpretation, by neither overruling the plenary power doctrine, nor reaffirming it with any analysis. If it intends to follow the plenary power doctrine, the Supreme Court should say so. It should declare that a renewal of the Chinese Exclusion Act would be constitutional. It should be forced to articulate its own institutional weakness and acknowledge its willingness to countenance racial discrimination. If it cannot do so, it has a responsibility as the arbiter of constitutional boundaries to present an alternative.

B. The Future of the Plenary Power Doctrine

The Supreme Court could follow a better course. The Supreme Court should abolish the plenary power doctrine. The Constitution should apply to immigration.[236] Aside from consistency, which, standing alone, is less than compelling as a constitutional principle, there are two primary reasons for applying the Constitution to immigration. Both of these reasons have been raised in the case law, but neither has been clearly adopted by a majority of Justices.

1. *The Potential of Citizenship*

The first rationale for abolishing the plenary power doctrine is a plain language reading of the text: many of the rights guaranteed by the Constitution belong to persons, not citizens.[237] Most importantly, the Constitution prohibits the state from "deny[ing] to any person within its jurisdiction the equal protection of the laws."[238] Alexander Bickel provided the leading analysis of the constitutional importance of personhood and the relative insignificance of citizenship.[239] In a work which would be characterized as more conservative than liberal in conventional terms, Bickel traced the problems of citizenship to "the contradiction of slavery."[240] According to Bickel, because the Supreme Court's reasoning in *Dred Scott*[241] equated "people" with "citizens" in the course of denying that blacks were either, the precedent "had to be effectively, which is to say constitutionally, overruled by a definition of citizenship in which race played no part."[242] After the *Slaughter-House Cases*[243] rendered the Equal Protection Clause more authoritative than the Privileges and Immunities Clause, the reference to "persons" in the former was elevated over the reference to "citizens" in the latter.[244]

As the Court stated in *Yick Wo* before it had announced the plenary power doctrine: "The Fourteenth Amendment to the Constitution is not confined to the protection of citizens."[245] Or as the Court has stated almost a century after *Yick Wo*, "There are literally millions of aliens within the jurisdiction of the United States. The Fifth Amendment, as well as the Fourteenth Amendment, protects every one of these persons from deprivation of life, liberty or property without due process of law."[246]

Although its later pronouncement seems to offer strong civil rights protection to persons without regard to citizenship, the Court in that very case and on other occasions has drawn a distinction with immigration that it has withdrawn from elsewhere as a constitutional matter, between rights and privileges.[247] The Court distinguished between participation in the political process and receipt of governmental entitlements, protecting the right of immigrants with regard to the former but not the latter (presumably because immigrants could use the political process to obtain governmental entitlements; maybe so, but that reasoning would apply to any plaintiff in an entitlements case).[248] The constitutional distinction is reflected roughly in the political assertion by many immigration restrictionists that the problem with which they are concerned is not immigration itself but use of public benefits.[249] The constitutional problem that must be resolved is for the most part the right-privilege dichotomy, and only to a lesser extent the citizen-immigrant dichotomy.

Thus, the argument turns more on the level of constitutional scrutiny that should be applied to immigration laws than on whether there should be any review whatsoever.[250] A few aspects of applying the Constitution to immigration should be clarified. The change would necessarily be toward permitting challenges to immigration laws that discriminated on the basis of a suspect classification — aside from alienage — such as race. Logically, the change could not be to allow challenges to immigration laws that discriminated on the basis of the ambiguous classification of alienage, as all immigration laws inherently draw lines between citizens and aliens.[251]

It may well be that immigration proponents would relent on the citizen-alien distinction, and the Court would approve alienage discrimination (including perhaps discrimination against permanent resident aliens), if discrimination on the basis of race in immigration were established as unconstitutional.[252] In this sense, alienage discrimination serves as a proxy for race discrimination.[253] After the change, alienage discrimination might become permissible precisely because race discrimination vis a vis immigrants would be prohibited. It would no longer be possible for immigration restrictionists to work through alienage to reach race, nor necessary for responses to follow the same route.

Admittedly, immigration enthusiasts may not be of one mind about the consequences of constitutional review of immigration. There are approaches other than those suggested here, but whatever path is followed is likely to lead away from the makeshift devices that have developed under the plenary power doctrine.[254]

The change fits well with mainstream constitutional thinking: if an individual can easily alter the characteristic (alienage), and it is not immutable, then it becomes much more acceptable to use it as a classificatory trait.[255] Any change that provided greater protection for immigrants at the border than they receive now need not necessarily reduce the level of protection available to them after they have passed within the borders.[256] The change, in sum, would not require extreme results such as either open borders or extending domestic standards beyond the borders,[257] although those more robust possibilities would remain available as public policy options.[258]

2. *The Standing of Citizens*

The Constitution itself — and civic culture as a result — is strengthened if it is applied to immigration. The commitment to the Constitution is affirmed by its application to immigration; it will have positive ripple effects on rights elsewhere.[259] The converse also is true, that the commitment to the Constitution is weakened by creating an exception for immigration; that, too, has ripple effects on rights elsewhere. Specifically, one of the impacts of immigration legislation is on citizens who are or are perceived as members of the same racial groups that, as immigrants, are being excluded.[260]

In other words, the second rationale for abolishing the plenary power doctrine is based on the rights of members of the community, not outsiders to it: citizens stand to benefit directly and indirectly from the proposed change.[261] As a practical matter, citizens and not aliens, would become the likely primary plaintiffs in much of the ensuing litigation. Citizens could challenge immigration policies that, either facially or as applied, discriminated by race rather than alienage.

Those laws that were intended to focus on race or in operation did focus on race rather than alienage should be flushed out. Laws of this type are of immediate concern to citizens who may be mistaken as immigrants — particularly, as "illegal" immigrants — and disadvantaged as a result. Consider the following scenario. High proportions of the Asian and Latino population are foreign-born.[262] The cultural stereotypes elevate the real proportions. If Prop. 187 were to operate anything at all like the Immigration Reform and Control Act (IRCA) — and Prop. 187 is likely to be more harmful than IRCA, because IRCA contained specific anti-discrimination safeguards which Prop. 187 lacks — it would be reasonable to predict that reasonable suspicion would focus on Asians and Latinos who are citizens.[263] Those citizens should be allowed to sue under traditional constitutional theories of race discrimination.[264]

Although a survey of the citizen standing issue lies beyond the scope of this article, there are immigration cases in which citizens have been the co-plaintiffs, notably in *Fiallo* and *Kleindienst*.[265] These cases were failures for the citizen standing approach, but lesser-known cases have brought success to citizens and their immigrant family members.

Earlier in the century, the Court invalidated the California Alien Land Law — again facially neutral but indisputably aimed at Japanese immigrants and their Japanese American children — by analyzing part of it as a case of citizen standing to challenge alienage discrimination.[266] In the tradition of analyzing state restrictions based on alienage in a federalism mode, the Court wrote, "This case presents the conflict between a state's right to formulate a policy of landholding within its bounds and the right of American citizens to own land anywhere in the United States."[267] But then the Court wrote, "When these two rights clash, the rights of a citizen may not be subordinated merely because of his father's [ineligibility for citizenship]."[268]

More recently, the Ninth Circuit has found that two individuals met standing requirements when they brought suit seeking injunctive relief in the form of a declaration that they were citizens.[269] The two plaintiffs had been born outside of the United States to mothers who were United States citizens and fathers who were foreign nationals, at a time when the statutes conferring citizenship on foreign-born offspring of citizens discriminated between mothers and fathers; the children of citizen mothers did not automatically become citizens, but the children of citizen fathers did.[270] The statute was amended prospectively, leaving the plaintiffs no remedy, short of their claim of an equal protection violation for the failure to treat them like others similarly situated but whose citizen parent had been male. The court found standing and held for them on the merits. In its standing analysis, the court reasoned that the plaintiffs "have suffered a concrete injury" and "their interests coincide with their mothers and are equally as intense."[271] The court mentioned that the plaintiffs' mothers were deceased, but it did not rely solely or primarily on that fact.[272]

On the surface, the Ninth Circuit case may appear to be the reverse of citizen standing. Below the surface, the case is stronger than an affirmation of citizen standing. It assumes that citizen standing would be permissible, if the deceased mothers were to have been joined as plaintiffs. It then goes further because it accepts not only standing but also an argument on the merits from an immigrant who is bringing the claim based on the rights of a citizen.

Citizens would also benefit indirectly, though concretely, because of their family ties to immigrants. The relationship of immigrant parents and their citizen children were weighed in the balance in *Plyler v. Doe*,[273] where the Court applied rationality review and struck down a Texas state law that prohibited children who could not provide documentation of their status or their parents' status from attending public schools. As already discussed, the relationship of immigrant children to their citizen parents failed to persuade a majority in *Fiallo*.[274] This particular argument should have broad appeal. Family "reunification" should be a prime example of family values that cultural conservatives presumably wish to encourage and the type of tradition and institution communitarians believe need to be affirmed and supported.[275] The connection between citizens and their family members may serve to offset the tendency within communities of color to impose internal distinctions that disfavor immigrants among them. At the most theoretical level, the citizen standing problem turns on the basic question of who belongs to the community and can assert her rights within it; denying citizen standing in immigration matters means that members of the community lose their ability to contest its norms.

3. *The Limits of Limits*

In the end, applying constitutional limits to immigration would have relatively modest effects.[276] The change would offer an opportunity to aggrieved parties to challenge immigration statutes and regulations; it would be far from an assurance that they would succeed in litigation. The potential plaintiffs would face the same extreme difficulties of any civil rights litigant under the applicable doctrine.[277] Following *Adarand v. Pena*,[278] the affirmative action case decided by the Supreme Court in its 1994-95 term, suspect classifications may trigger strict scrutiny, but strict scrutiny is not always fatal.[279]

As the Prop. 187 litigation continues through the courts, it remains to be seen whether *Plyler* will remain good law. Whatever the outcome of the new case, *Plyler* remains a rarity: an immigration case where plaintiffs prevail by demonstrating the irrationality of a statute under the most deferential standard of review available.[280] The anomalous status of *Plyler* underscores the evolutionary, rather than revolutionary, nature of the likely results from applying the Constitution to immigration. What would happen is as important as what would not happen.

The most important positive result would be that courts would strike down any restrictions based on a racial rationale, in the same manner that a locality or state could not rely on race to exclude individuals. They also conceivably could strike down some, though by no means all, restrictions based on a cultural rationale, to the relatively limited extent that the First and Fourteenth Amendments offer protection of cultural rights or may be interpreted to do so in the future.[281] The Chinese Exclusion case, the source of the plenary power doctrine, would be reversed, both as to the general principle and the specific holding.[282] In short, Brimelow's approach to immigration could not be constitutionally legislated.

Neither race and culture, nor race and socioeconomic status, should be equated with respect to immigration any more than they can be collapsed as a general matter. Brimelow's tendency to equate race and culture would be problematic under constitutional doctrine outside of the immigration area. Absent a nexus that would satisfy strict scrutiny, race cannot be justified as a classificatory device because of the asserted difficulties associated with an individual determination regarding culture.[283] Individuals making the counterargument that race and culture are not necessarily the same sometimes serve as an example of their claim. For example, Francis Fukuyama, who happens to be Japanese American, is a leading neo-conservative working within an historically Anglo-American tradition — though without stated self-consciousness of the fact.[284]

An equally important negative result is that courts would apply the very deferential standard of rationality review to limitations on immigration based on nonracial factors. Essentially, these forms of discrimination would remain constitutional.[285] As iconoclast Michael Lind has proposed, we could have lower limits on immigration that are race-neutral, along with strong civil rights protection for permanent resident aliens.[286] Or as one sympathetic reviewer of *Alien Nation* suggested, substituting class for race, "We could easily have a much more discriminatory immigration policy aimed at raising the average level of human and financial capital of new entrants, while maintaining the current, high proportion of non-Europeans."[287] That these options would be permissible as a constitutional matter does not mean that they would be wise as a legislative choice.

Most immigration restrictions based on economic rationales would be left intact. Needless to say, the economic impact of immigrants is important.[288] However, it bears emphasizing that similar considerations about migrants cannot constitutionally be given full consideration at local and state levels. Therefore, at the national level, the proposed change to the plenary power doctrine may be incomplete. Accepting some difference between national and other borders might result in a standard of review which permits economic factors to be weighed against allowing immigration, provided that they are not purely pretextual. If Congress were to provide an economic basis for restrictive immigration laws, and a plaintiff challenging the laws could not demonstrate that the economic reasons concealed racial reasons, then the plaintiff would need to carry the burden of regular rationality review. Only a limited number of plaintiffs would be able to meet that standard.

Again, what distinguishes the current doctrine is that plaintiffs are precluded from even trying to show irrationality much less invoking strict scrutiny. But as Brimelow candidly concedes, "People habitually justify their immigration preferences in economic terms, but really they are motivated by a wide range of ethnic, moral and even psychological agendas."[289] A covert version of Brimelow's racial agenda would be equally unconstitutional.

To take specific existing case law that would have a positive impact if brought to bear on immigration, the principle derived from *Palmore v. Sidotti* would prevent prejudice from being used as its own justification.[290] In *Palmore*, the Court held that a white woman who was living with a black man could not be denied custody of her child from a former marriage on the basis of possible prejudice against interracial relationships from the community.[291] The Court found unpersuasive the circular argument that potential discrimination by the public at large justified discrimination by the government — even if the former prejudice could be proven.[292] Likewise, under the proposed reform, it would not be enough to save an otherwise racially discriminatory immigration law by arguing that a consensus supported it. The means would not justify the ends.

Coming full circle, the Prop. 187 campaign demonstrates the importance of constitutional standards and judicial review.[293] In the campaign for Prop. 187, proponents frequently argued that a vote in favor of the measure would "send a message" without harming anyone, because the courts would apply constitutional safeguards.[294] Whether this was a blithe or cynical assumption that constitutional limits applied to immigration, sponsors of the measure complained after it passed that judicial review would be undemocratic.[295]

C. Immigration and Other Civil Rights

Finally, there is important cultural meaning to accepting immigrants as people within the protection of the Constitution and immigration as an issue within the purview of judicial review.[296] Within constitutional limits, immigration issues should be viewed as integral to the civil rights movement — for Asian American and Latino communities certainly, but for all racial groups in some sense.[297] Understanding immigration issues as related to civil rights, if not understanding immigration itself as a civil right, strengthens immigration rights as much as it strengthens traditional civil rights. It enhances the claim that civil rights are universal rights rather than special interests. The current discussion of immigration and civil rights has the relationship backwards.

Politicians of all persuasions have sometimes argued against immigration on the grounds that it harms the most disadvantaged native-born citizens.[298] Conservatives have recently developed an especially potent strain of this argument. Their inflammatory claim is that immigrants, most of whom today are Asian and Latino, are taking advantage of affirmative action, which was originally meant for African Americans.[299] This claim forms the basis of the "blacks versus browns" dilemma.[300]

Needless to say, the relationship between immigration and affirmative action presents complex issues.[301] To take examples from litigation, the named defendant in the *Adarand* decision was a Latino member of the Clinton administration Cabinet,[302] but the plaintiff in a recent appellate case challenging affirmative action also was Hispanic.[303] Chinese Americans have challenged the consent decree that desegregated the San Francisco schools,[304] while an African American has challenged the inclusion of Asian Indians in an Ohio affirmative action program.[305] Significant numbers of Latinos and African Americans voted for Prop. 187 (though a lower proportion than among whites).[306] As these situations show, people of color face great internal tensions — even over whether they form any cohesive community within racial groups before they build coalitions across racial groups. The "blacks versus browns" dilemma creates as much as it describes the situation.

Progressive individuals and communities, whether people of color or whites, can and should address their disagreements cooperatively and constructively. The opposition of immigration and affirmative action, however, divides communities with common interests in civil rights and exacerbates their differences.

The opposition of immigration and affirmative action serves political purposes.[307] Its central claim is curious if not paradoxical because it is used to attack not only immigration, but also affirmative action. The two issues — and respective racial groups who are represented

— can be played off of one another only until one of them gives way.[308]

1. What the Immigration Debate Tells Us About Affirmative Action

The argument that immigrants should be excluded from affirmative action, assuming it accepts that immigrants are entitled to civil rights otherwise, implies that affirmative action is an aberration, unrelated to civil rights as a whole. The dynamics of immigration and affirmative action may be difficult, and one or the other may need public policy revisions, but the interplay between the two deserves more careful consideration than it has received.

The arguments for exclusion of immigrants from affirmative action programs are self-defeating. The argument that focuses on excluding immigrants because of affirmative action presents the circular and paternalistic logic that discrimination against racial minorities within a society justifies their exclusion from it. The perverse result is that efforts to remedy discrimination need never include immigrants. Immigrants are deemed to have consented to assuming a subordinate status.[309] Some politicians have gone so far as to suggest that immigrants be barred for their lifetimes from receiving any government entitlements, not only those with a race-based component.[310]

Brimelow himself would create a lower caste of citizen. He objects that the citizens who sponsor immigrants sometimes are not "native born" but "immigrants who have simply graduated to citizenship."[311] If he had his way, they would never effectively graduate to citizenship, or having done so, would remain in significant respects inferior to the native born. Immigrants would be forced to sacrifice not simply allegiance to another nation, but also the possibility of family reunification — that is, the possibility of family reunification that would be taken for granted by native-born citizens with respect to their native nuclear families as well as their foreign-born extended families. Accepting for the sake of argument that this regime may be a defensible conception of immigration, it is not so by any theory of liberal democracy that allows immigrants to become citizens with the implicit promise that the status once conferred will be regarded in an equal and meaningful manner.

The racial arguments against immigration show the emptiness of color-blindness. Color-blindness has content only within its context.[312] As the United States did for several generations, a community could appear to be color-blind among its members by the expedient means of being highly color-conscious at the threshold. It would exclude nonwhites from entry and membership.

Correspondingly, the Court can become color-blind jurisprudentially by adopting a principle such as the plenary power doctrine, which renders legislative color-consciousness invisible. As a result, color-conscious immigration policies would transform Justice Antonin Scalia's recent pronouncement: "In the eyes of the government, we are just one race here. It is American."[313]

The result is to equate being American with being white, under the guise of color-blindness. Toward the end of his book, Brimelow cautiously expresses goodwill toward Asian immigrants because "[t]heir ethnic message . . . may be different" than that of other non-whites, thanks to the similarity of their beliefs to whites' beliefs.[314] Demonstrating knowledge of an obscure part of American history, he recounts the arrival of Asian immigrants "in the South directly after the Civil War."[315] What Brimelow admires about these Asian immigrants was that they "seem to have graduated . . . in the era of segregation, to a sort of honorary white status."[316] Brimelow likes them all the more because they further graduated "to an actual white status" as "unreinforced by immigration, the Chinese communities . . . intermarried . . . and essentially vanished from the Census returns."[317] One may be in favor of assimilation — and indeed quite assimilated — and regard this vision of what it means to be a citizen as markedly inferior to the promise held out by America.

The idea that some Americans have been here longer and should have more power to determine who enters the country rests on their racial ancestry rather than their individual right.[318] It is people as racial groups and not as individuals who are presumed to have a greater stake in American identity due to their lengthier presence in the country. Under this theory, lineage, not longevity, is what counts.

The immigrants and natives are groups which have identities that survive over generations; if they are not groups, it is difficult to see how an individual native could demonstrate his "arrival" several generations prior to his birth. One might optimistically believe that they could be groups, without assuming that they are racial groups, but given American history and Brimelow's "common sense," it is difficult to conceive of them as anything else. Hence Brimelow's concern with his son and his appeal to children collectively — or, rather, the children of the white Founders of the Republic, and the children of Brimelow's readership.[319]

With a color-blind world view, it would be nonsensical to state, as another leading restrictionist has written: "racial justice means that the majority in a country treats minorities fairly and equally; it does not mean that the majority is required to turn *itself* into a minority."[320] Even with a color-conscious world view, it is not clear that racial justice is meaningful when people of color must remain always and everywhere racial minorities.

The argument that immigrants from some nations, but not other nations, have more in common with citizens is rooted in racial group generalizations. Even the argument that newer immigrants are assimilating more slowly than older immigrants rests on racial group generalizations, as the conclusion is not reached on an individual basis. Again, the reasonable response might be something along the lines of, "well, yes, but we must make some generalizations." This reaction fails to answer either of the two questions it raises: why the generalizations must be racial generalizations, and if they must be, why they cannot be in other areas of the law.[321]

In immigration, it also becomes clear that conservatives can recognize neutral standards that lack invidious intent as having disproportionate impact in practice, and that they can complain of the same. For critics of immigration who hold racial concerns, the facial neutrality of immigration laws is less persuasive than their as-applied impact. The 1965 reforms, which were more or less neutral standards, were passed with a mix of intentions that was at worst benign toward whites and at best (from the white perspective) favorable toward whites.[322]

As Brimelow has argued, the neutral standards have had an effect that is anything but racially neutral.[323] Due to migration patterns over which the United States has little control (white Europeans from developed countries have fewer incentives to emigrate) immigrants are predominantly Asian and Latino. The critics of immigration legislation are not assuaged by good intentions and neutral language if the outcomes favor Asians and Latinos. In response, Congress has adopted an immigration counterpart to affirmative action, borrowing the buzzword of "diversity."[324] The "diversity" lottery is a visa quota based on national origin. It functions through a set-aside of extra visas for countries that are "underrepresented" within the immigrant pool, thereby benefiting Europeans and Africans (the former purposefully; the latter as a side effect) and for the most part disadvantaging Asians and Latinos.[325] In 1995, for example, 24,549 extra visas were allocated to Europe; 20,200 to Africa; 8 to North America; 2,589 to South America; and 6,837 to Asia.[326]

Concern about immigration can be concern about race. Peter Brimelow is right about that.[327] If the public is persuaded by Brimelow, and Asian and Latino immigrants are deemed undesirable, it would follow that Asian and Latino citizens also would be rendered less than desirable.[328] Though the latter may remain in the eyes of many aliens within the community, there are constitutional protections that should prevent their mistreatment. But as what could not be done within the community is being done at the borders, there is an undesirable impact within. Asian Americans and Latinos are rendered perpetual guests in their own country.

In this way, immigration issues illustrate the tendency of conservatives, rather than liberals, to think along the lines of racial group entitlement. Immigration law presents the strong form of racialization of the law: arguments based on race are not only permitted, they are accepted as the norm; they are not only private beliefs, but also embedded in public actions. Immigration shows the weakness of color-blindness and intent-based approaches to equal protection. While color-blindness conceals racial motivations, an intent-based approach overlooks them. Brimelow can agitate for racial restrictions, and politicians may be persuaded but offer other reasons for lower limits on immigration. Courts and commentators, in their zealous watch for openly racial restrictions on immigration, ignore programs with undisputed but hidden racial motivations — such as the diversity lottery for visas.

The success of efforts to limit immigration may undermine the attacks on affirmative action.[329] If anything, the attempts to end immigration when it has become predominantly colored show that color-blindness is far from a universally shared ideal. The people who would prefer immigrants who are racially Caucasian and culturally Anglo-Saxon Protestant can hardly complain about remedial programs such as affirmative action because they rely on racial characteristics. They may oppose the measures on other grounds, but the principled claim of color-blindness is irretrievably undermined. The concerns raised by the white majority with respect to colored immigration carry over to affirmative action: it is not procedural justice that is paramount, but resulting substantive changes, not the number of people who are to be allowed to enter, but their racial and cultural identity and their political power that matters.

For those reasons, constitutional limits are critical. Immigration is unique because the Court has recognized that the Constitution is silent on basic facets of government structure and federal power. The Court has sought to interpret the text. Its mistake is in the specific interpretation, not in the act of interpretation itself. The arguments over affirmative action also show how constitutional limits shape political outcomes. Alongside the contentious debate on what affirmative action, if any, is desirable, effective, or counterproductive, there is a parallel constitutional discourse about what affirmative action, if any, is required, permitted, or forbidden. Whatever their position, virtually all participants in the political process recognize that the public policy which results is still bounded by constitutional norms. In this way, constitutional theory informs and contributes to political action; a civic culture is created which also is a constitutional culture.[330] We are creating a constitutional culture; our immigration laws can contribute toward that constitutional culture, rather than contradicting it. The constitutional constraints can and should be flexible, but they must exist if there is to be a more deliberative democracy and principled political choices.

2. *What the Affirmative Action Debate Tells Us About Immigration*

The rhetorical similarities between anti-immigrant and anti-affirmative action campaigns emerge in the juxtaposition of Prop. 187 with the cleverly misnamed California Civil Rights Initiative (CCRI)[331] — the anti-affirmative action referendum that will follow it in the 1996 elections. Prop. 187 and CCRI share something pernicious. Each contains an appeal to racial minority groups at the expense of other people of color.[332]

Perhaps the most galling aspect of the Prop. 187 campaign was the false promise made to African Americans.[333] Without evidence, advocates for Prop. 187 asserted loudly and repeatedly that Asian and Latino immigrants were taking jobs from blacks or using government services intended for underprivileged citizens. Backers of Prop. 187 implied that excluding Asians and Latinos from the country would benefit blacks directly. What was never mentioned is that there were no plans to spend the purported savings from passage of Prop. 187 on either creating employment opportunities for blacks or increasing benefits for the poor.

In an almost perfect reversal,[334] CCRI is targeted at the rapidly growing and increasingly powerful Asian American community.[335] Proponents of CCRI argue to Asian American audiences that they are limited in their upward mobility because African Americans receive racial preferences. In particular, the argument goes, Asian Americans stand to gain greatly in their representation on college campuses if African Americans and Latinos are excluded. What is never revealed is the practice of affirmative action for whites in the form of preferences for alumni children or outright quotas for whites such as at the prestigious Lowell High School in San Francisco.[336]

Taken together, Prop. 187 and CCRI send the message to racial minority groups that they must compete for the crumbs left on the table after the pie has been eaten by the majority. They also send the message that political problems should be solved by blaming them on parts of the population traditionally seen as outsiders. Moreover, Prop. 187 and CCRI implicitly urge racial minority groups to turn upon themselves. Asian and Latino immigrants and African Americans who have assimilated, prospered and moved to the suburbs are welcomed as good minorities. The others become the "illegal" immigrants and the "unqualified" who are to be left behind.

It is important to note that one can be ambivalent about immigration and affirmative action, but also be appalled at the disingenuous and manipulative manner in which they have been bound together. It is possible to oppose immigration without being "racist," however that term may be defined. The more important inquiries, politically and constitutionally, look beyond blame and intent, good intentions and bad faith; victims and wrongdoers; they are directed, instead, toward identifying the real economic and structural problems — and possible solutions to them. Along the way, though, individuals who are concerned about justice in immigration would do well to ask themselves whether they believe what they are being asked to believe about immigrants. All of this is to point out contradictions in the immigration restrictionist position when it is asserted with an anti-affirmative action position; none of this should be taken to suggest that increased color-consciousness, in a conventional sense, is required or preferable.

In the volume of cases and the contentiousness of the decisions, immigration law has developed as a leading field for development of constitutional theory.[337] This has occurred despite the persistence of the plenary power doctrine. It may well be that the plenary power doctrine has been weakened over time, but the current legislative proposals are likely to bring its return with a vengeance. Even if it were considered moribund, it is far from certain what if any norms have taken its place. The plenary power doctrine has distorted constitutional discourse, by excepting an entire area of law from normal review. Major immigration cases that presented an opportunity to overturn the plenary power doctrine have been settled, which, while beneficial to the litigants, has prevented the development of standards favorable to all immigrants.[338] If the Supreme Court is unwilling to impose constitutional limits on Congress, the legislature will have the opportunity to assert its independent role in evaluating the Constitution by adopting a more moderate course in immigration reform.

One last caveat is in order. Contrary to their references to reason, immigration restrictionists have employed a galling strategy which should be resisted. That *ad hominem* strategy is the characterization of advocates of liberal immigration policies as motivated merely by bias due to their own personal circumstances, and able to argue only in emotional terms as a consequence.[339] The same could be said of proponents of conservative immigration policies — who would be as adamant, if not outraged, if their right to take part in the political process were denied and their right even to remain in the country of their birth denigrated. Immigration enthusiasts have as much of a claim to the national interest.

CONCLUSION

The change proposed here would bring to the immigration debate the limits which are recognized in every other sphere of American law. In the face of contested normative judgments, whether immigration is racially desirable or not, and disputed facts, whether immigration is economically beneficial or detrimental, the Constitution should mark the limits of the law. It is commonplace to suggest that the treatment of strangers reveals most deeply the morality of a society. It would be remarkable if the treatment of its potential members reflected as well the confidence of a society.

ACKNOWLEDGMENTS

I thank the following individuals for comments and encouragement: Gabriel Chin, Janet Halley, Kevin Johnson, Jerry Kang, Shaun Martin, Karen Musalo, Hiroshi Motomura, Gerald Neuman, Jamin Raskin, Rogers Smith, Andrew Taslitz, George Wright, Elizabeth Henderson and Mark Johnston. Vanessa Abrahams and Eleanore Irwin, Howard University law school students who worked as my research assistants, and Erin O'Neal, Dean Jablonski and Nalini Philipose, my editors, deserve thanks as well for their invaluable assistance. I also thank participants in the second annual Mid-Atlantic People of Color Legal Scholarship Conference, Feb. 15-17, in Washington, D.C., where this article was presented as a work in progress.

NOTES

[1] FRANZ KAFKA, *Before the Law*, *in* THE COMPLETE STORIES 3 (Willa & Edwin Muir trans., 1971).

[2] Barbara Koh, *Close the U.S. Border, Mayor Says; Culver City: Steven Gourley Urges the Country to 'Draw a Line' Against Illegal Immigrants. His Comments Spark Cries of Racism*, L.A. TIMES, Mar. 28, 1991, at J1.

[3] For an overview of the immigration debate, I have relied on ARGUING IMMIGRATION: THE DEBATE OVER THE CHANGING FACE OF AMERICA (Nicolaus Mills ed., 1994) [hereinafter ARGUING IMMIGRATION], *especially* Nathan Glazer, *The Closing Door*, *id.* at 37, Toni Morrison, *On the Backs of Blacks*, *id.* at 97; Jack Miles, *Blacks vs. Browns*, *id.* at 101, *especially* 133-38; Francis Fukuyama, *Immigrants and Family Values*, *id.* at 15; Lawrence Auster, *The Forbidden Topic*, *id.* at 169.

[4] The diverse range of views is represented by and described in the following articles: Steven A. Holmes, *Surprising Rise In Immigration Stirs Up Debate*, N.Y. TIMES, Aug. 30, 1995, at A1 (describing Census Bureau's latest report on the size of the foreign-born population); Sam Fulwood III & Craig Turner, *Customs Rejects Plan to Relax Border Checks*, L.A. TIMES, Aug. 31, 1995, at A1 (discussing proposal for "open border" with Canada); Jerry Adler & Steven Waldman, *What is an American?*, NEWSWEEK, July 10, 1995, at 18 (arguing that multiculturalism and class divisions have split national the character); Editorial, *Immigration: Not Fixed Yet*, NAT'L REV., June 26, 1995, at 21 (proposing moratorium on immigration, including legal immigration); Editorial, *Closing the Doors: U.S. Resumes Deportation of Cuban Refugees*, NEW REPUBLIC, May 29, 1995, at 7 (supporting repatriation of Cuban immigrants); Jeffrey Rosen, *The War On Immigrants: Why the Courts Can't Save Us*, NEW REPUBLIC, Jan. 30, 1995, at 22 (analysis of the current debate suggesting legislative action is necessary; criticizing *Plyler* decision and Alexander Bickel's analysis of citizen-alien distinction); Nancy Gibbs, *Keep Out, You Tired, You Poor . . . Around the Country, and Especially in California, Outrage Over Immigration Is Becoming Electoral Dynamite*, TIME, Oct. 3, 1994, at 46 (arguing that Prop. 187 would make a "bad situation worse" and supporting stronger border enforcement measures); Paul Offner, *Solid Noncitizens: Don't Toss Legal Immigrants off the Dole*, NEW REPUBLIC, June 20, 1994, at 10 (proposing few changes to welfare eligibility except for elderly immigrants); Fred Barnes, *No Entry: The Republicans' Immigration War*, NEW REPUBLIC, Nov. 8, 1993, at 10, 12 (concluding "[c]autious Democrats are dead meat in this climate."); Daniel Choi, *Border-lines: An Immigration Debate Guide*, NEW REPUBLIC, Sept. 13, 1993, at 14 (describing different views on immigration across political spectrum); Michael Lind, *Aliens Among Us; Politics of Immigration*, NEW REPUBLIC, Aug. 23, 1993, at 22 (presenting mixed view of immigration); S.C. Gwynne, *The Unwelcome Mat*, TIME, Nov. 28, 1994, at 35 (describing border enforcement on U.S.-Mexico border). Additional articles are cited throughout.

[5] The following provide useful summaries of politicians' positions on immigration: Ronald Brownstein, *Immigration Debate Roils G.O.P. Presidential Contest; Politics: Ideas Range From Halting All New Arrivals to Increasing Them; Prop. 187 Brought Issues to Forefront*, L.A. TIMES, May 14, 1995, at A1; Roy Beck, *Right of Silence: Of Ten Leading Republicans, Two Favor Keeping Our Current Immigration Policy, Two Favor Changing It More or Less Radically, and Six Are Agnostic; Position of Possible Presidential Candidates on Immigration Policy*, NAT'L REV., July 11, 1994, at 27; Michael Lind, *Liberals Duck Immigration Debate*, N.Y. TIMES, Sept. 7, 1995, at A19; Roberto Suro, *White House Pressured By Immigration Politics*, WASH. POST, Mar. 28, 1994, at A1 (describing Clinton administration policies as being developed in response to Republican agenda; quoting officials as stating that they would rely on the Jordan Commission for proposals); John M. Broder, *Immigration Delicate Issue for Clinton*, L.A. TIMES, Sept. 7, 1993, at A1.

[6] This is to make nothing more of Brimelow's personal status than he himself would. Neither the fact that he is an immigrant nor the fact that he is an Englishman should be held against him. To the contrary, he offers those characteristics to enhance his arguments. In an attempt to establish authority for his arguments by reference to himself, Brimelow has a habit of invoking his immigrant status and refers at least a half-dozen times to his concern about "politically correct" persecution of "my little son Alexander," who is white. *See* PETER BRIMELOW, ALIEN NATION: COMMON SENSE ABOUT AMERICA'S IMMIGRATION DISASTER 9, 11, 20, 103, 221, 249-50 (1995).

[7] *Id.*

[8] Peter Brimelow, *Time to Rethink Immigration? The Decline of the Americanization of Immigrants*, NAT'L REV., June 22, 1992, at 30.

[9] *Id.*

[10] *See infra* notes 34-41 and accompanying text.

[11] For major reviews of the book in mass media publications, see, e.g., Nicholas Lemann, *Too Many Foreigners*, N.Y. TIMES, Apr. 16, 1995, § 7 (Book Review), at 3; Christopher Hitchens, *From Melting Pot to Potpourri*, L.A. TIMES, May 21, 1995, Book Review at 4; Michael Lind, *American By Invitation: A Conservative Call to Arms on a Coming Issue*, NEW YORKER, Apr. 24, 1995, at 107; Jack Miles, *Book Review, "Alien Nation,"* ATLANTIC, Apr. 1995, at 130. A set of reviews also appeared in one of the journals of which Brimelow is an editor: Nathan Glazer, *Book Review, Alien Nation: Common Sense About America's Immigration Disaster*, NAT'L REV., May 1, 1995, at 78; Francis Fukuyama, *Book Review, Alien Nation: Common Sense About America's Immigration Disaster*, NAT'L REV., May 1, 1995, at 77; Glenn C. Loury, *Book Review, Alien Nation: Common Sense About America's Immigration Disaster*, NAT'L REV., May 1, 1995, at 80.

[12] In recent history, Brimelow was preceded by, among others, the former Governor of Colorado in RICHARD D. LAMM & GARY IMHOFF, THE IMMIGRATION TIME BOMB: THE FRAGMENTING AND DESTRUCTION OF AMERICA BY IMMIGRATION (1985) and LAWRENCE AUSTER, THE PATH TO NATIONAL SUICIDE: AN ESSAY ON IMMIGRATION AND MULTICULTURALISM (1990).

Brimelow is apparently unaware that his book shares a title with a popular science fiction movie, starring James Caan and Mandy Patinkin, in the story of aliens from outer space arriving in contemporary Los Angeles and struggling to assimilate. ALIEN NATION (20th Century Fox Film Corp. 1988). The very term "alien," and the association of science fiction aliens with real aliens is a method of demonizing the latter. H.G. Wells, among other authors, recognized the power of alien invasion as a metaphor. *Cf.* Gerald L. Neuman, *Aliens as Outlaws: Government Services, Proposition 187, and the Structure of Equal Protection Doctrine*, 42 UCLA L. REV. 1425, 1428 (1995) (discussing imagery of "nonhuman invaders from outer space" used in immigration context).

[13] For historical information concerning immigrants, see generally JOHN HIGHAM, STRANGERS IN THE LAND: PATTERNS OF AMERICAN NATIVISM, 1860-1925 (Rev. ed. 1963) [hereinafter HIGHAM, STRANGERS IN THE LAND]; JOHN HIGHAM, SEND THESE TO ME: IMMIGRANTS IN URBAN AMERICA (Rev. ed. 1984), *especially* 3-70; LAWRENCE H. FUCHS, THE AMERICAN KALEIDOSCOPE: RACE, ETHNICITY AND THE CIVIC CULTURE (1990). *Cf.* BILL ONG HING, MAKING AND REMAKING ASIAN AMERICA THROUGH IMMIGRATION POLICY, 1850-1990 (1993) (analyzing the impact of immigration policies on the Asian American communities). *See also* SELECT COMMISSION ON IMMIGRATION AND REFUGEE POLICY (SCIRP), U.S. IMMIGRATION POLICY AND THE NATIONAL INTEREST, STAFF REPORT, 92, 93, 161-216 (1981) [hereinafter SCRIP], *excerpted in* THOMAS ALEXANDER ALEINIKOFF ET AL., IMMIGRATION: PROCESS AND POLICY 41-61 (3rd ed. 1995). The Aleinikoff casebook, the first in the immigration area, is an excellent source for general information and excerpts of secondary materials cited herein.

[14] *See* Miles, *supra* note 3, at 134 (describing Neo-Nazis and others who hold restrictionist views on immigration). *See generally* RITA J. SIMON & SUSAN H. ALEXANDER, THE AMBIVALENT WELCOME: PRINT MEDIA, PUBLIC OPINION AND IMMIGRATION 197 (1993) (useful summary of leading anti-immigrant groups active in the late 1980s and early 1990s).

[15] For early articles anticipating the current debate, *see* Michael Kinsley, *TRB: Gatecrashers — U.S. Immigration Policy*, NEW REPUBLIC, Dec. 28, 1992, at 6; Deborah Sontag, *Calls to Restrict Immigration Come From Many Quarters*, N.Y. TIMES, Dec. 13, 1992, § 4, at 5; *Return of the Nativist*, ECONOMIST, June 27, 1992, at 25. Immigration scholars have dated the revival of restrictionism to the Marielito Cuban crisis which occurred during the 1980 Presidential campaign. *See, e.g.*, Aristide R. Zolberg, *From Invitation to Interdiction: U.S. Foreign Policy and Immigration Since 1945*, *in* THREATENED PEOPLES, THREATENED BORDERS: WORLD MIGRATION AND U.S. POLICY, 117, 157 (Michael S. Teitelbaum & Myron Weiner eds., 1995) [hereinafter THREATENED PEOPLE, THREATENED BORDERS].

In the past few years, there have been more optimistic views on immigration, *see, e.g.*, BEN J. WATTENBERG, THE FIRST UNIVERSAL NATION: LEADING INDICATORS AND IDEAS ABOUT THE SURGE OF AMERICA IN THE 1990S (1991), as well as more mixed views on immigration, *see, e.g.*, MICHAEL LIND, THE NEXT AMERICAN NATION: THE NEW NATIONALISM AND THE FOURTH AMERICAN REVOLUTION (1995). *See also* FUCHS, *supra* note 13 (arguing for a pluralist democracy with a shared civic culture); Richard Rayner, *What Immigration Crisis?*, N.Y. TIMES, Jan. 7, 1996, § 6 (Magazine), at 26 (recent article with balanced view of immigrants, discusses problems faced by and related to undocumented immigration using personal profiles). These articles and books, along with oral histories of immigrants, autobiographies and biographies, appear to have had much less of an impact on public opinion than Brimelow.

For general information about debates immediately before Brimelow appeared on the scene, I have consulted THOMAS MULLER, IMMIGRANTS AND THE AMERICAN CITY (1993) and ELLIS COSE, A NATION OF STRANGERS: PREJUDICE, POLITICS AND THE POPULATING OF AMERICA (1992). The Muller book, as the title suggests, focuses on immigration to urban areas; it includes summaries of many of the leading economic studies through 1992. The Cose book presents the historical information is a lively manner, and provides a general account of legislative efforts through the passage of the Immigration Reform and Control Act (IRCA).

I have, however, only selectively examined the fast-growing social science scholarship on immigration. *See, e.g.*, IMMIGRATION RECONSIDERED: HISTORY, SOCIOLOGY, AND

POLITICS 21, 27 (Virginia Yans-McLaughlin ed., 1990) [hereinafter IMMIGRATION RECONSIDERED], *especially* Ewa Morawska, *The Sociology and Historiography of Immigration*, *id.* at 187 (describing interdisciplinary work and discussing a paradigm shift toward analysis of collectivist and ethnic perspectives).

[16] Immigration Act of 1924, ch. 190, § 11(b), 43 Stat. 153, 159.

[17] Immigration and Nationality Act Amendments of 1965, Pub. L. No. 89-236, § 2, 79 Stat. 911, *codified* at 8 U.S.C. § 1152 (1988).

[18] *In Buchanan's Words*, WASH. POST, Feb. 29, 1992, at A2 (quoting from appearance by Buchanan on *This Week With David Brinkley*, ABC television broadcast, Dec. 8, 1991).

[19] Patrick Buchanan, *Looking Back With Longing*, WASH. TIMES, Oct. 30, 1991, at D1.

[20] Although the suspicion must be "reasonable," no standards are provided for determining reasonableness. CAL. WELF. & INST. CODE § 10001.5(c) (West 1995) (as revised by Prop. 187); HEALTH & SAFETY CODE § 130(c) (West 1995) (same); GOV'T. CODE § 53069.65 (West 1995) (same). The key effect of Prop. 187 is to challenge the *Plyler v. Doe* decision. By denying not only undocumented immigrant children but also children of undocumented immigrant parents (and those suspected of such status), the measure contravenes the decision holding unconstitutional a Texas statute which was limited to the former group. The remainder of Prop. 187 is symbolic. Prop. 187 affects not only undocumented immigrant children but also children of undocumented immigrant parents (and those "suspected" of such status), it denies to individuals "suspected" of being "illegal" immigrants a range of government services, including services that they already are ineligible for under state law, as well as services to which they are entitled under federal law. It also requires that public employees who come into contact with these "suspected" individuals report them to the Immigration and Naturalization Service (INS).

The United States District Court has enjoined Prop. 187. League of United Latin American Citizens v. Wilson, 908 F. Supp. 755 (C.D. Cal. 1995).

[21] Cal. Prop. 187, § 1: Findings and Declaration (1994).

[22] *See* Patrick J. McDonnell, *Prop. 187 Turns Up the Heat in U.S. Immigration Debate; Education: Backers Seek Revolution in National Policy; Foes Predict Ill-Educated, Disease-Prone Underclass*, L.A. TIMES, Aug. 10, 1994, at A1.

[23] *See* Faye Fiore, *Split-Up of Immigration Bill Urged; Politics: Ten G.O.P. Congressmen from California Want Separate Measures on Legal and Illegal Migrants; Request Divides Republicans*, L.A. TIMES, Nov. 13, 1995, at A3. The quote concerning the INS can be found in Weston Kosova, *The INS Mess: How Immigration Became a Nightmare*, NEW REPUBLIC, Apr. 13, 1992, at 15.

[24] H.R. 2202, 104th Cong., 1st Sess. (1995) (Immigration in the National Interest Act of 1995); S. 1394, 104th Cong., 1st Sess. (1995).

[25] Marc Lacey, *Move to Limit Citizenship Gains Support*, L.A. TIMES, June 11, 1995. *See, e.g.*, H.R. 2162, 705, 375, H.J.R. 93, 88, 64, 56, *all* 104th Cong., 1st Sess. (1995).

Peter Schuck and Rogers Smith's influential work on birthright citizenship is discussed briefly, *infra* note 56. *Cf.* David A. Martin, *The Civic Republican Ideal for Citizenship, and for Our Common Life*, 35 VA. J. INT'L L. 301 (1994) (moderating the liberal democratic ideal and arguing in favor of birthright citizenship because individuals otherwise "will suffer a kind of functional statelessness.").

[26] BRIMELOW, *supra* note 6, at 262 (proposing drastic or total reduction in immigration immediately) and 265 (proposing abolition of birthright citizenship).

[27] Four symposium issues of law reviews have been published on Prop. 187 or on immigration since the passage of Prop. 187. 42 UCLA L. REV. 1425 (1995); *Forming Immigration Policy in the Media Spotlight: Rhetoric and Reality*, 70 WASH. L. REV. 589 (1995); *Immigration Law and the New Century: The Developing Regime*, 35 VA. J. INT'L L. 1 (1995); *Demography and Distrust: The Latino Challenge to Civil Rights and Immigration Policy*, 8 LA RAZA L.J. 1 (1995). *See also* Ignatius Bau, *Immigrant Rights: A Challenge to Asian Pacific American Political Influence*, 5 ASIAN AM. POL'Y REV. 7 (1995).

[28] BRIMELOW, *supra* note 6, at 262.

[29] *Id.* at 264.

[30] *See id.* at 11 ("*Race and* ethnicity *are destiny in American politics.*") (emphasis in original); *id.* at 121 ("Once again, ethnicity, and demography, is destiny in American politics.").

[31] *Id.* at 58-59.

[32] *Id* at 59.

[33] *Id.* at 48 (emphasis in original).

[34] Lind, *supra* note 11, at 108. Brimelow himself defines racism as winning an argument with a liberal. BRIMELOW, *supra* note 6, at 10-11. It is tempting to respond by defining political correctness as winning an argument against a conservative. But the more important point is that such facile and glib sound bites fail to advance understanding and cooperation. As for Brimelow, I do not call him a "racist" and should not be taken as implying that he is one. That term is much too simple to describe Brimelow's views.

[35] BRIMELOW, *supra* note 6, at 10.

[36] *Id.* at 18.

[37] *Id.* at 11, 116-17, 178-81, 215-16.

[38] *Id.* at 271-72 (criticizing historian Ronald Takaki for his anecdote about being perceived as foreign, because "to the extent that there is any content to Takaki's complaint, it is because he is Asian in a predominantly white society. *And there is no cure for that except radically increasing the numbers of minorities and breaking down white America's sense of identity.*") (emphasis added).

[39] *Id.* at 105-07 (criticizing Raoul Lowery Contreras for "his emotional attitudes" toward immigration).

[40] Brimelow does not pause for fine distinctions such as Asian Americans and Latinos who in fact are native-born citizens, or who oppose immigration; it *is* unclear, however, that his argument would be any different if he did.

[41] *Id.* at 271-72.

[42] *Id.* at 64-65 (loss of political power for blacks), 173-75 (negative economic impact on blacks), 249 (arguing that "it is immediately obvious that . . . the plight of poor American blacks must be considered before that of landless laborers in Latin America.").

[43] *Id.* at 108-09.

[44] *Id.* at 113.

[45] *Id.* at 185.

[46] *Id.* at 215.

[47] *Id.* at 189-90.

[48] *Id.* at 139.

[49] *Id.* at 137-77.

[50] *Id.* at xvii.

[51] Peter Brimelow, *National Transformation in the Making?*, WASH. TIMES, May 30, 1995, at A13 (discussing immigration as a cause of disease and terrorism). The Hitler reference is the first line of ALIEN NATION. BRIMELOW, *supra* note 6, at xv.

[52] Peter Brimelow, *Perspective on Immigration: Keep Reform Focused on Fact*, L.A. TIMES, June 20, 1995, at B9 (mentioning that contemporary immigration flows have been from nations "whose populations are racially quite different from most Americans.").

[53] *Id.* at 254. It follows, in Brimelow's view, that liberal elites who favor immigration have committed "a species of treason." *Id.* at 114.

[54] A few miscellaneous points about Brimelow's book are noteworthy. Brimelow indulges in amateur psychological explanations for pro-immigrant views, *see, e.g.*, BRIMELOW, *supra* note 6, at 14 (characterizing "Americans favoring immigration" as "stress[ing] the emotional experience of an issue over its rational aspect"), but becomes angered by that same approach toward anti-immigrant views. *Id.* at 96 (criticizing *New York Times* article, for implying that "any public concern about immigration . . . had to be explained . . . in vulgar psychoanalytic terms."). *See also id.* at 98-100. Brimelow has an aside that is bizarre in a work that has some scholarly pretense. Explaining the difference between American and British debate techniques, he argues for the superiority of the latter tradition, in which he works. He observes that British debaters, who speak extemporaneously and not from prepared texts, are "expected to succeed by quickness of wit and whatever facts they can dredge (or *make) up*." *Id.* at 89-90 (emphasis added). Finally, Brimelow argues, interestingly, that homogeneity and not heterogeneity correlates to liberalism on race. *Id.* at 120-23. He may be right in the sense that homogeneous societies are tolerant of racial minorities if they are clearly outsiders who present no threat.

[55] *Id.* at 197.

[56] The two leading scholarly works that accept the possibility a more restrictive immigration policy within an internally liberal democracy are MICHAEL WALZER, SPHERES OF JUSTICE: A DEFENSE OF PLURALISM AND EQUALITY 31-63 (1983) (arguing that liberal societies can restrict membership using standards that deviate from internal norms to preserve its values) and PETER H. SCHUCK & ROGERS M. SMITH, CITIZENSHIP WITHOUT CONSENT: ILLEGAL ALIENS IN THE AMERICAN POLITY (1987) (arguing against birthright citizenship especially for children of undocumented aliens). *Cf.* Frederick G. Whelan, *Citizenship and Freedom of Movement: An Open Admission Policy?*, *in* OPEN BORDERS? CLOSED SOCIETIES? THE ETHICAL AND POLITICAL ISSUES 3, 6-7 (Mark Gibney ed., 1988).

While each of the works deserves, and has received, significant scholarly response, whether they are persuasive depends almost entirely on whether their premise is accepted, namely that nations should have different standards externally than internally. The debate concerns not only the normative standards that govern the community after it has been constituted, but also the normative standards that define how the community comes into being to begin with. The levels cannot be separated without assumptions about sovereignty, because the process of defining membership is continually ongoing and self-fulfilling.

There are flaws in WALZER and SCHUCK & SMITH. Neither of the two major works, with their emphasis on abstract consent of the polity to newcomers, addresses at length the realities of prejudice and discrimination based on race and ethnicity faced by those who are already members of the community.

Moreover, Walzer, while insisting that entry is a "political decision" made by members of the community, recognizes that "decisions of this sort are subject to constraint." WALZER, *supra* note 56, at 40. I have no quarrel with either argument, that immigration is subject to a "political decision" or that it can legitimately be made by those already part of the society. My point is to examine who is considered a part of the society, and where the constraints might reasonably be set.

[57] This is hardly an original point. Virtually every history of immigration notes the conflicting national myths and native responses surrounding immigration and immigrants.

[58] This Article does not consider the circular reasoning used to define "illegal" immigrants, or the contradictory political factors that have caused the immigration debate to focus on them. Two excellent articles on the subject are Gerald P. Lopez, *Undocumented Mexican Migration: In Search of a Just Immigration Law and Policy*, 28 UCLA L. REV. 615 (1981) and Linda S. Bosniak, *Exclusion and Membership: The Dual Identity of the Undocumented Worker Under United States Law*, 1988 WIS. L. REV. 955 (1988).

Suffice it to say that the image of the "illegal" immigrant is constructed poorly; it is a proxy for race, class, welfare use, etc. Consider that a California politician, from Europe, who was an "illegal" immigrant in a strict sense of entering the country in violation of immigration laws by "jumping ship" while docked, campaigned for Prop. 187. He considered himself something other than the "illegal" immigrant meant by the measure. Carl Ingram, *California Elections: 4th Senate District; Prop. 187 Serving as Backdrop in Yet Another Race*, L.A. TIMES, Nov. 7, 1994, at A3. The image of the "illegal" immigrant is almost exclusively nonwhite, (basically, Mexican), and the manner of entry portrayed is crossing the Southern border on foot or in a smugglers' van. The majority of "illegal" immigrants, however, are neither Mexican nor did they arrive from Mexico via an illegal entry. MICHAEL FIX & JEFFREY S. PASSEL, IMMIGRATION AND IMMIGRANTS: SETTING THE RECORD STRAIGHT 24-25 (1994).

[59] A few examples. One of the leading liberal politicians of the 1960s, Eugene McCarthy, has come to restrictionist conclusions. EUGENE MCCARTHY, A COLONY OF THE WORLD: THE UNITED STATES TODAY: AMERICA'S SENIOR STATESMAN WARNS HIS COUNTRYMEN (1992). Two of today's leading liberal politicians have also come to restrictionist conclusions. United States Senator Barbara Boxer of California has proposed a military presence on the U.S.-Mexico border. Glenn F. Bunting, *Boxer's Bid to Put National Guard at Border is Stymied; Immigration: Pentagon Refuses to Implement Senator's Plan, Which It Says Lacks Legal Authority*, L.A. TIMES, Aug. 6, 1994, at A1. United States Senator Dianne Feinstein also has supported increased Border Patrol presence on the border and a national identification card, but would not decrease legal levels of immigration. James Bornemeier, *Feinstein Introduces Immigration Bill*, L.A. TIMES, Mar. 22, 1995, at A10. The late Barbara Jordan, formerly a United States Representative and later chair of the bipartisan Commission on Immigration Reform, proposed that everyone be issued a national identification card. U.S. COMMISSION ON IMMIGRATION REFORM, U.S. IMMIGRATION POLICY: RESTORING CREDIBILITY 90-101 (1994).

[60] I encountered these arguments while working on the campaign against Prop. 187. Some of the difficulties faced by liberal candidates during the Prop. 187 campaign are discussed in Greg Krikorian & Amy Wallace, *Prop. 187 Rises as Key Theme In Top 2 Races*, L.A. TIMES, Oct. 25, 1994, at A1; B Drummond Ayres, Jr., *The 1994 Campaign: California: Candidates Hedge Their Bets on an Immigration Measure*, N.Y. TIMES, Oct. 25, 1994, at B8.

[61] Koh, *supra* note 2.

[62] My article may be read as a dialogue with and extension from Joseph H. Carens, *Aliens and Citizens: The Case for Open Borders*, 49 REV. OF POL. 251, 264-70 (1987) [hereinafter Carens, *Open Borders*] (the essay is a contemporary classic in its articulation of the open borders argument, considering Nozick, Rawls and Walzer). Carens is concerned with the universal nature of liberal values. *Id.* at 265, 269. Carens also argues that the national, state and local borders are comparable. *Id.* at 258, 266-67. *See also* Joseph H. Carens, *Immigration and the Welfare State*, in DEMOCRACY AND THE WELFARE STATE 207 (Amy Gutmann ed., 1988).

For a recent version of the open borders argument, *see* R. George Wright, *Federal Immigration Law and the Case for Open Entry*, 27 LOY. L.A. L. REV. 1265 (1994); *see also* ALAN DOWTY, CLOSED BORDERS: THE CONTEMPORARY ASSAULT ON FREEDOM OF MOVEMENT (1987) (discussing right to emigrate as well to immigrate, using international perspective); *contra* Whelan, *supra* note 56, at 27.

[63] In developing my legal analysis, I have been guided most by Hiroshi Motomura, *Immigration Law After a Century of Plenary Power: Phantom Constitutional Norms and Statutory Interpretation*, 100 YALE L.J. 545 (1990) [hereinafter Motomura, *Plenary Power*] and Hiroshi Motomura, *The Curious Evolution of Immigration Law: Procedural Surrogates for Substantive Constitutional Rights*, 92 COLUM. L. REV. 1625 (1992) [hereinafter Motomura, *Curious Evolution*]. I also have been aided by the following law review articles on immigration policies: T. Alexander Aleinikoff, *Rights — Here and There: Federal Regulation of Aliens and the Constitution*, 83 A.J.I.L. 862 (1989); T. Alexander Aleinikoff, *Citizens, Aliens, Membership and the Constitution*, 7 CONST. COMMENT. 9 (1990) [hereinafter Aleinikoff, *Citizens*]; Louis Henkin, *The Constitution and United States Sovereignty: A Century of Chinese Exclusion and its Progeny*, 100 HARV. L. REV. 853 (1987); Bill Ong Hing, *Beyond the Rhetoric of Assimilation and Cultural Pluralism: Addressing the Tension of Separatism and Conflict in an Immigration-Driven Multiracial Society*, 81 CAL. L. REV. 863 (1993); Kenneth L. Karst, *Paths to Belonging: The Constitution and Cultural Identity*, 64 N.C. L. REV. 303 (1986); Stephen H. Legomsky, *Immigration Law and the Principle of Plenary Congressional Power*, 1984 SUP. CT. REV. 255 [hereinafter Legomsky, *Plenary Power*]; STEPHEN H. LEGOMSKY, IMMIGRATION AND THE JUDICIARY — LAW AND POLITICS IN BRITAIN AND AMERICA (1987); Gerald L. Neuman, *The Lost Century of American Immigration Law (1776-1875)*, 93 COLUM. L. REV. 1833 (1993) [hereinafter Neuman, *The Lost Century*]; Gerald L. Neuman, *Whose Constitution?*, 100 YALE L.J. 909 (1991); Jamin Raskin, *Legal Aliens, Local Citizens: The Historical, Constitutional and Theoretical Meanings of Alien Suffrage*, 141 U. PENN. L. REV. 1391 (1993); and Peter H. Schuck, *The Transformation of Immigration Law*, 84 COLUM. L.

REV. 1 (1984). One of the few articles analyzing immigration within a comprehensive constitutional framework is Michael J. Perry, *Modern Equal Protection: A Conceptualization and Appraisal*, 79 COLUM. L. REV. 1023, 1060-65 (1979) (analysis of immigration legislation as preemption problem rather than equal protection issue). *Cf.* Gerald M. Rosberg, *The Protection of Aliens from Discriminatory Treatment by the National Government*, 1977 SUP. CT. REV. 275; LAWRENCE H. TRIBE, AMERICAN CONSTITUTIONAL LAW 361 (2d ed. 1988) (discussing positivist theory of national sovereignty as unrealistic), 1544-53 (analyzing alienage discrimination cases within equal protection theory and characterizing *Plyler* as the right result but "problematic" in reasoning). Additional articles are cited throughout.

[64] I hasten to emphasize this point: my concern is with racial motivations for lowering the numbers of immigrants or selecting them. I am concerned about cultural arguments as well, but only insofar as culture masks race, or culture is protected within domestic constitutional standards. I am not concerned with economic arguments, except to note that they, too, may be economic arguments only on the surface and something else altogether below the surface; as discussed throughout the notes, the empirical evidence for an objective argument against immigration is weak.

[65] *See, e.g.*, Koh, *supra* note 2 (mayor of Culver City supports military on border); Bunting, *supra* note 59 (Democratic Senator from California supports military on border).

[66] *See, e.g.*, Dwight Silverman, *Buchanan Backs Barrier on Border with Mexico*, HOUSTON CHRON., Dec. 12, 1991, at A1 (quoting Presidential candidate Pat Buchanan as advocating building a "ditch and fence" on U.S.-Mexico border).

[67] Michael J. Nunez, Note, *Violence at Our Border: Rights and Status of Immigrant Victims of Hate Crimes and Violence Along the Border Between the United States and Mexico*, 43 HASTINGS L.J. 1573 (1992) (describing Border Patrol and vigilante violence); Jerry Kang, Note, *Racial Violence Against Asian Americans*, 106 HARV. L. REV. 1926 (1993) (discussing racialized violence against Asian Americans).

[68] *See, e.g.*, Jean v. Nelson, 472 U.S. 846 (1985) (no need to reach constitutional issues possibly presented by detainees who may have been excludable, because of statutory ground for decision).

[69] *Cf.* Aleinikoff, *Citizens*, *supra* note 63, at 33-34 ("But our immigration laws are not primarily concerned with the construction or maintenance of a particular kind of community"); *contra* WALZER, *supra* note 56, at 35-42 (considering analogies for the nation).

[70] The use of the term "Americans," rather than U.S. citizens is intentional. Brimelow uses the term to mean U.S. citizens; and U.S. citizens tend to view themselves as "Americans" to the exclusion of Canadians, Mexicans and others in the Western Hemisphere. I am sensitive to the claim that just as American does not mean white, it also does not mean U.S. citizen.

[71] Carens, *Open Borders*, *supra* note 62.

[72] In an historical reflection of the equivalence between federal and state immigration restriction, Professor Gerald Neuman discusses the 1803 federal statute that forbade importation of foreign blacks into states whose laws contained the same prohibition; he suggests that the congruence at federal and state levels "may hereafter occupy a prominent place in the history of our legislation." Neuman, *The Lost Century*, *supra* note 63, at 1869-70. Neuman is a notable exception in that he clearly links slavery-related anti-immigrant legislation directed at blacks with other anti-immigrant legislation such as the Chinese Exclusion Act. *Id.* at 1872.

The normative arguments made in this article do not depend on the romanticized notion that the nation had "open borders" in the past. *See* Neuman, *The Lost Century*, *supra* note 63 (describing numerous state statutes and regulations governing immigration and immigrants prior to the Chinese Exclusion Act).

[73] BRUCE ACKERMAN, SOCIAL JUSTICE IN THE LIBERAL STATE 4, 89-95 (1980) (describing rationality principle whereby "whenever anybody questions the legitimacy of another's power, the power holder must respond not by suppressing the questioner but by giving a reason that explains why he is more entitled to the resource than the questioner is" and imagining dialogue in which native defends right to exclude immigrant based on earlier arrival). Ackerman would tolerate limits on immigration if they were necessary to ensure the "liberal dialogue." Though this may prove to be a dangerous exception, susceptible to claims of crisis, it at least indicates that Ackerman cannot be dismissed as an absolute proponent of open borders.

[74] *See* WALZER, *supra* note 56, at 34 ("there are certain similarities between strangers in political space (immigrants) and descendants in time (children).").

[75] *See*, *infra* note 318 and accompanying text.

[76] Or as Louis Henkin stated, "[t]here is no reason to resist . . . [the] suggestion that control over immigration is a right of every sovereign state and that it is inherent . . ." Henkin, *supra* note 63, at 857.

[77] National sovereignty is invoked often and uncritically as "directly" justifying immigration policies. *See, e.g.*, Peter H. Schuck, *The Message of 187: Facing Up to Illegal Immigration*, 21 AM. PROSPECT, Spring 1995, at 85, 88 (1995) (arguing that "harsh options" for illegal aliens "follow directly from the premise of national territorial sovereignty.").

[78] Carens, *Nationalism*, *supra* note 56, at 49, 54 (distinguishing between arguments made by outsiders and insiders).

[79] For the latter view, see, e.g., Joan Fitzpatrick & William M. Bennett, *A Lion in the Path? The Influence of International Law on the Immigration Policy of the United States*, 70 WASH.

L. REV. 589 (1995). *See also* THREATENED PEOPLES, THREATENED BORDERS, *supra* note 15 (proceedings of the American Assembly at Columbia University), *especially* at 13 (immigration "has created a major foreign policy challenge to the United States and other population-receiving countries") and 299 ("international migration is rising to the top of the foreign policy agenda."). The concluding recommendations of the American Assembly, which include the use of "domestic policy instruments" to control immigration, omit any mention of constitutional norms. The legal version of this view is found in justifications of the plenary power doctrine based on the foreign affairs power, the war powers, or the commerce power (with respect to commerce with foreign nations). A useful summary of the different justifications offered for the plenary power doctrine can be found in ALEINIKOFF, *supra* note 13, at 7-15 and Legomsky, *supra* note 63, at 261-78.

[80] *See* Carens, *Open Borders*, *supra* note 62, at 271.

[81] On the side that supports immigrants, former New York Governor Mario Cuomo, a leading Democrat, and current New York City mayor Rudolph Guliaiani, a law and order Republican, have been willing to extend their welcomes to legal immigrants together with undocumented immigrants. *See* Michael S. Teitelbaum & Myron Weiner, *Introduction*, *in* THREATENED PEOPLES, THREATENED BORDERS *supra* note 15, at 20.

For examples of contemporary divisions on immigration issues, see Steven A. Holmes, *The Strange Politics of Immigration*, N.Y. TIMES, Dec. 31, 1995, § 4, at 3; Matthew Purdy, *Unlikely Allies Battle Congress Over Anti-Immigration Plans*, N.Y. TIMES, Oct. 11, 1995, at B1; Choi, *supra* note 4.

[82] By and large, contrary to the premise of Prop. 187, immigrants do not immediately enjoy the same entitlements as citizens; this is all the more true of "illegal" immigrants. Legal immigrants underutilize benefits and services to which they are entitled, with the possible exception of elderly refugees whose immigration to the United States arises from unique circumstances — in many cases a result of U.S. foreign policy. On legal immigration and welfare, *see* Richard A. Boswell, *Restrictions on Non-Citizens' Access to Public Benefits: Flawed Premise, Unnecessary Response*, 42 UCLA L. REV. 1475, 1482-87 (explaining virtually absolute discretion of United States embassies in denying visas to applicants deemed likely to become "a public charge," citing 8 U.S.C. § 1182 (a)(4) (1994)). On "illegal" immigration and welfare, *see* Stephen H. Legomsky, *Immigration, Federalism, and the Welfare State*, 42 UCLA L. Rev. 1453, *especially* 1468-70 (1995) (discussing principles that might be used to "draw the line"). For empirical data concerning the use of government entitlements, see FIX & PASSEL, *supra* note 58 (concluding that immigrants, legal and illegal, create a net economic gain); JULIAN SIMON, IMMIGRATION: THE DEMOGRAPHIC AND ECONOMIC FACTS (1995).

[83] *See* Ronald Brownstein & Patrick J. McDonnell, *Kemp, Bennett and INS Chief Decry Prop. 187*, L.A. TIMES, Oct. 19, 1994, at A1.

[84] *See* Ron K. Unz, *Immigration or The Welfare State; Which Is Our Real Enemy?*, HERITAGE FOUND. POL'Y REV., Fall 1994, at 33 (arguing for higher immigration levels but reduced entitlements).

[85] *See* Choi, *supra* note 4.

[86] I take racial considerations to be "illegitimate," because they generally are considered to be illegitimate by the common culture and constitutional doctrine with respect to local and state borders. I am willing to concede the argument, at least in this Article, to anyone who takes both the position that Brimelow is right and the position that racial considerations are morally legitimate with respect to the internal borders of a liberal democracy.

[87] ELLIS COSE, A NATION OF STRANGERS: PREJUDICE, POLITICS AND THE POPULATING OF AMERICA 194 (1992). Brimelow refers to the founder of FAIR rather frighteningly as "truly a citizen who has taken up arms for his country." BRIMELOW, *supra* note 6, at 278.

[88] *See, e.g.*, William A. Henry III, *Beyond the Melting Pot*, TIME, Apr. 9, 1990, at 28; Tim Mathews et al., *America's Changing Face*, NEWSWEEK, Sept. 10, 1990, at 46; Special Issue (Multiculturalism), TIME, Fall 1993; Felicity Barringer, *Census Shows Profound Change in Racial Makeup of the Nation*, N.Y. TIMES, Mar. 11, 1991, at A1; Edward B. Fiske, *Minorities a Majority in New York*, N.Y. TIMES, Mar. 20, 1991, at B1; Martha F. Riche, *We're All Minorities Now*, AM. DEMOGRAPHICS, Oct. 1991, at 26; Barbara Vobejda, *Births, Immigration Revise Census View of 21st Century U.S.*, WASH. POST, Dec. 4, 1992, at A10 (reporting that whites would become a racial minority group faster than expected because of comparatively lower birth rates). *See generally* SAM ROBERTS, WHO WE ARE: A PORTRAIT OF AMERICA BASED ON THE LATEST U.S. CENSUS 65-117 (Rev. ed. 1995); FIX & PASSEL, *supra* note 58, at 25-28, 39-44, 70-71; Jeffrey S. Passel & Barry Edmonston, *Immigration and Race: Recent Trends in Immigration the United States in* IMMIGRATION AND ETHNICITY: THE INTEGRATION OF AMERICA'S NEWEST ARRIVALS 34 (Barry Edmonston & Jeffrey S. Passel eds., 1994) [hereinafter IMMIGRATION AND ETHNICITY].

[89] The 21st century has been described as "The Pacific Century." *See, e.g.*, FRANK GIBNEY, THE PACIFIC CENTURY: AMERICA AND ASIA IN A CHANGING WORLD (1992); Special Report, *The Pacific Century*, NEWSWEEK, Feb. 22, 1988, at 42; James A. Baker, III, *Just What Should the Role of the United States Be in the Pacific Century?*, L.A. TIMES, Nov. 20, 1994, at M2 (former Secretary of State arguing that the United States can and should play an active role in the Pacific Century).

[90] *See* BRIMELOW, *supra* note 6, at 62-65, 72-78, 137, 191-201.

[91] For an influential statement of the view that ideological conflict among nations would increase in the next century, with many countries set against the United States, *see* Samuel P. Huntington, *The Clash of Civilizations?*, FOREIGN AFF., Summer

1993, at 22.

[92] *See* Stephen Glass, *Pat Speaks*, NEW REPUBLIC, Mar. 18, 1996, at 17.

[93] Sam Enriquez, *Valley Chambers Vote to Support Prop. 187*, L.A. TIMES, Sept. 17, 1994, at A1.

[94] Supporters of Prop. 187 repeatedly referred to the "Third World" in derogatory terms. *See* Kevin R. Johnson, *Public Benefits and Immigration: The Intersection of Immigration Status, Ethnicity, Gender, and Class*, 42 UCLA L. REV. 1509, 1548 n.178 (1995) (describing views of Prop. 187 supporters, including negative references to "Third World" origins of immigrants) [hereinafter Johnson, *Public Benefits*]; Kevin R. Johnson, *An Essay on Immigration Politics, Popular Democracy, and California's Proposition 187: The Political Relevance and Legal Irrelevance of Race*, 70 WASH. L. REV. 629, 654-58 (same) [hereinafter Johnson, *Race*]; *see, e.g.*, Gebe Martinez & Patrick J. McDonnell, *Prop. 187 Backers Counting on Message, Not Strategy*, L.A. TIMES, Oct. 30, 1994, at A1 (quoting supporter as stating that "We are becoming a Third World state.").

[95] Some of the issues related to these perceptions are discussed in Hing, *supra* note 63; Karst, *supra* note 63; and Frank H. Wu, *Changing America: Three Arguments About Asian Americans and the Law*, AM. UNIV. L. REV. (forthcoming 1996).

[96] Of course, the nation has never been wholly white, or even simply black and white. ROBERTS, *supra* note 88, at 73. Differences among white ethnic groups were considered significant until relatively recently. *See* MICHAEL NOVAK, THE RISE OF THE UNMELTABLE ETHNICS: POLITICS AND CULTURE IN THE SEVENTIES (1972); *see also* HIGHAM, STRANGERS IN THE LAND, *supra* note 13; NOEL IGNATIEV, HOW THE IRISH BECAME WHITE (1995).

[97] ROBERTS, *supra* note 88, at 67.

[98] *Id.* at 70.

[99] *See* SIMON, *supra* note 82, at 7-10; U.S. CENSUS BUREAU, THE FOREIGN BORN POPULATION: 1994 (1995).

[100] Mixed marriages constitute two percent of all marriages. Some of the apparent increase over time may be due to better survey methodology. *See* ROBERTS, *supra* note 91, at 48. *See also* FIX & PASSEL, *supra* note 58, at 43; Antonio McDaniel, *The Dynamic Racial Composition of the United States: An American Dilemma Revisited*, DAEDULUS, Jan. 1995, at 179 (comparing intermarriage rates of African Americans with intermarriage rates of Asian Americans).

[101] *See* Richard Morin, *A Distorted Image of Minorities; Poll Suggests That What Whites Think They See May Affect Beliefs*, WASH. POST, Oct. 8, 1995, at A1.

[102] *See* Adler & Waldmann, *supra* note 4. Although I am skeptical of the distinction, arguably racism and nativism are diverging, and presumably most clearly among immigrants who oppose immigration. Their views, which warrant further consideration, appear to be among the least persuasive arguments to immigrants who disagree but also the most persuasive for natives who agree. Derrick Bell's analysis of the "super-standing" acquired by racial minorities who espouse conservative political views may explain this dichotomy. *See* DERRICK BELL, FACES AT THE BOTTOM OF THE WELL 109-26 (1992).

[103] *See* Sharon S. Russell, *Migration Patterns of U.S. Foreign Policy Interest*, *in* THREATENED PEOPLES, THREATENED BORDERS, *supra* note 15, at 41 (*citing* UNITED NATIONS, TRENDS IN THE TOTAL MIGRANT STOCK (database)). *See also* Hal Kane, *Leaving Home*, *in* STATE OF THE WORLD 1995: A WORLDWATCH INSTITUTE REPORT ON PROGRESS TOWARD A SUSTAINABLE SOCIETY (Lester R. Brown ed., 1995) (general overview of worldwide migration patterns).

[104] Only 16% of migrants can be found in the United States. Russell, *supra* note 103, at 41. To be fair, 33% of migrants to the developed world resided in the United States. *Id.* The United States is also unique within the developed world in experiencing increasing immigration in the past generation. *Id.* at 45.

[105] FIX & PASSEL, *supra* note 58, at 23; Passel & Edmonston, *Immigration and Race*, *supra* note 88, at 34-36; William Echikson, *Young Americans Go Abroad To Strike It Rich*, FORTUNE, Oct. 17, 1994, at 185; Gary Belsky, *Escape from America*, MONEY, July 1994, at 60. Fix and Passel, who are based at the Urban Institute, estimate 200,000 American emigrants annually. FIX & PASSEL, *supra* note 58, at 23.

[106] *See* MARSHALL MCLUHAN, THE GLOBAL VILLAGE (1968).

[107] *See* HOWARD RHEINGOLD, THE VIRTUAL COMMUNITY: HOMESTEADING ON THE ELECTRONIC FRONTIER (1994).

[108] Editorial, *Does It Matter Where You Are?*, ECONOMIST, July 30, 1994, at 13. The editorial was accompanied by a special section on technological changes.

[109] *Id.*

[110] Benjamin R. Barber, *Jihad vs. McWorld*, ATLANTIC, Mar. 1992, at 53. The article has recently been expanded into a book of the same name.

[111] *See, e.g.*, Nick Ervin, *Immigration and the Environment*, *in* ARGUING IMMIGRATION, *supra* note 3, at 90. *See generally* Peter L. Reich, *Environmental Metaphor in the Alien Benefits Debate*, 42 UCLA L. REV. 1577 (1995). *Cf.* JULIAN SIMON, THE ECONOMIC CONSEQUENCES OF IMMIGRATION 187-93 (1989) (arguing that immigration has not harmed the environment). The following section is developed from the Reich article.

[112] Reich, *supra* note 111.

[113] GARRETT HARDIN, LIVING WITHIN LIMITS: ECOLOGY, ECONOMICS AND POPULATION TABOOS (1994). Hardin is also author of the famous essay, *The Tragedy of the Commons*, 162 SCIENCE 142 (1968).

[114] LEON F. BOUVIER & LINDSAY GRANT, HOW MANY AMERICANS? POPULATION, IMMIGRATION AND THE ENVIRONMENT (1994).

[115] Matthew Connelly & Paul Kennedy, *Must It Be the Rest Against the West? Immigration and Relations Between Western and Developing Nations*, ATLANTIC, Dec. 1994, at 61, 69 (arguing that "we are heading into the twenty-first century in a world consisting for the most part of a relatively small number of rich, satiated, demographically stagnant societies and a large number of poverty-stricken, resource-depleted nations whose populations are doubling every twenty-five years or less" and proposing a global New Deal).

[116] Robert D. Kaplan, *The Coming Anarchy: How Scarcity, Crime, Overpopulation, Tribalism, and Disease Are Rapidly Destroying the Social Fabric of Our Planet*, ATLANTIC, Feb. 1994, at 44 ("Disease, overpopulation, unprovoked crime, scarcity of resources, refugee migrations, the increasing erosion of nation-states and international borders, and the empowerment of private armies, security firms, and international drug cartels are now most tellingly demonstrated through a West African prism. West Africa provides an appropriate introduction to the issues, often extremely unpleasant to discuss, that will soon confront our civilization.").

The Kaplan article has been incorporated into a recent book. ROBERT D. KAPLAN, THE ENDS OF THE EARTH: A JOURNEY AT THE DAWN OF THE TWENTY-FIRST CENTURY (1996).

[117] Charles C. Mann, *How Many is Too Many? Population Growth*, ATLANTIC, Feb. 1993, at 47 (describing history of overpopulation studies and contrasting biological-ecological with demographic-economic approaches; concluding that there probably is a problem with overpopulation).

[118] Barber, *supra* note 110.

[119] ROBERTS, *supra* note 88, at 114 (more than half of the population changed residences between 1985 and 1990); FIX & PASSEL, *supra* note 58, at 29-30 (reporting that between 1985 and 1990 New York City gained 600,000 immigrants but lost 800,000 natives for a net population reduction); Steven A. Holmes, *Now, Home Is Where the Job Is*, N.Y. TIMES, Jan. 2, 1994, § 4, at 3. *Cf.* SIMON, *supra* note 111, at 15-17.

[120] BRIMELOW, *supra* note 6, at 68-70. Brimelow recognizes white flight and racial polarization geographically, apparently meaning to support the reactions of white natives who have fled the arrival of nonwhite immigrants. *See* Kristin E. Neuman & Martin Tienda, *The Settlement and Secondary Migration Patterns of Legalized Immigrants: Insights from Administrative Records*, *in* IMMIGRATION AND ETHNICITY, *supra* note 88, at 184-226.

[121] *See* BRIMELOW, *supra* note 6, at 68-70.

[122] Martinez & McDonnell, *supra* note 94.

[123] *See* EVAN MCKENZIE, PRIVATOPIA (1994).

[124] Michael Hill & Thomas Fleming, *The New Dixie Manifesto: State's Rights Shall Rise Again*, WASH. POST, Oct. 29, 1995, at C3 (statement from leaders of secessionist Southern League); SOUTHERN PARTISAN, Fourth Quarter 1994, at 34 (interview with Michael Hill, leader of the Southern League).

[125] *See* Memphis v. Greene, 451 U.S. 100 (1981) (holding that segregation at a local level is unconstitutional but rejecting challenge to the building of a public wall separating predominantly black and predominantly white areas for lack of showing of intent). For scholarly commentary on the case, see Richard T. Ford, *The Boundaries of Race: Political Geography in Legal Analysis*, 107 HARV. L. REV. 1841 (1994); Charles R. Lawrence, III, *The Id, the Ego, and Equal Protection: Reckoning with Unconscious Racism*, 39 STAN. L. REV. 317 (1987). There also are Fair Housing Act protections and other statutes that forbid and attempt to ameliorate residential segregation.

[126] *See* Shapiro v. Thompson, 394 U.S. 618, 630 (1969) (recognizing right to interstate travel without attributing it to a specific Constitutional clause, in considering a challenge to state welfare restrictions); Anderson v. Greene, 115 S. Ct. 1059 (1995) (declining on ripeness grounds to consider merits of challenge to California welfare entitlements differential between long-term residents and new incoming residents).

[127] The Supreme Court has occasionally compared impairment of the right to interstate travel with discrimination against immigrants. In one of its decisions most favorable toward immigrants, *Graham v. Richardson*, 403 U.S. 365 (1971), the Court unanimously struck down state public assistance provisions that discriminated against noncitizens, citing *Shapiro v. Thompson* throughout the opinion. Whatever these decisions meant, they were limited by the later decision in *Mathews v. Diaz*, 426 U.S. 67, 85, 87 (1976). Although emigration is different than immigration, and temporary travel overseas different further still, *see* Regan v. Wald, 468 U.S. 222, 241 n.25 (1984) (upholding limitations on international travel by citizens, stating that earlier cases had treated "the constitutional right to travel within the United States and the right to travel abroad . . .indiscriminately. That position has been rejected in subsequent cases."). *See also* Zobel v. Williams, 457 U.S. 55, 68 (1982) (Brennan, J., concurring) (in striking down Alaska oil pipeline divided distribution plan which discriminated based on residential duration, a comparison of equality between naturalized and native-born citizens and equality between recent and long-term state residents); Kent v. Dulles, 357 U.S. 116, 126 (1958) (restricting Secretary of State's ability to deny passports, stating that "[t]ravel abroad, like travel within the country, may be necessary for a livelihood.").

[128] In a principled and moderate manner, for example, Professor Peter Schuck has expressed concern over high levels of immigration based on a communitarian outlook. *See* SCHUCK & SMITH, *supra* note 56; Schuck, *supra* note 63; Peter H. Schuck, *Membership in the Liberal Polity: The Devaluation of American Citizenship*, *in* IMMIGRATION AND THE POLITICS OF CITIZENSHIP IN EUROPE AND NORTH AMERICA 51 (W.R. Brubaker ed., 1989). The nascent communitarian movement with respect to immigration is analyzed in Rogers M. Smith, *American Conceptions of Citizenship and National Service*, *in* NEW COMMUNITARIAN THINKING: PERSONS, VIRTUES, INSTITUTIONS, AND COMMUNITIES 233 (Amitai Etzioni ed., 1995) [hereinafter Smith, *American Conceptions*] and Daniel J. Tichnor, *in Immigration and Political Community in the United States*, *id.* at 259.

The Smith article is especially perceptive. Smith argues that Americans have used not only liberal democratic and civic republican models of citizenship and membership, but also an "Americanist" view. This "Americanist" view "holds that ascriptive characteristics, such as ethnicity, race, religion, gender, language, and cultural customs and heritage, are quite relevant for deciding who should be full American citizens." Thus, "American citizens should possess the characteristics of native-born WASP males or some none too distant approximation thereof." Smith, *American Conceptions*, at 237. Other peoples "they might wise to avoid, could chose to assimilate, but also could rightly dominate." *Id.* at 244. The problem is that "today many Americans still want to feel they have a meaningful national identity, with common values" in this "Americanist" sense, but "older notions of that common nationality that were hierarchical and exclusionary are much less viable . . . though far from absent." *Id.* at 251. To make the United States a pure liberal democracy "would have seriously disrupted existing social and political hierarchies and customary ways of life. It still would do so." *Id.* at 252. Smith suggests that national service can serve as a means of introducing Americans to diversity.

[129] *See, e.g.*, SCIRP, *supra* note 13.

[130] Philip D. Curtin, *Migration in the Tropical World*, *in* IMMIGRATION RECONSIDERED, *supra* note 15, at 21, 27.

[131] The Constitution mandated an "open borders" period with respect to Congressional control over the importation of slaves. U.S. CONST., art. I, § 9, cl. 1. *See also* Smith v. Turner, 48 U.S. 283 (1849) (The Passenger Cases).

The slavery issue may have prevented Congress from being able to take up federal legislation over immigration. *See* Neuman, *The Lost Century*, *supra* note 63, at 1865-66 (discussing the historical role of slavery in shaping state immigration law prior to the Civil War).

[132] Immigration and Nationality Act Amendments of 1965 (INA), Pub. L. No. 89-236, § 2, 79 Stat. 911, *codified* at 8 U.S.C. § 1152 (1988). Technically, it was a national origins based policy. Actually, even national origins have been reduced to race in immigration law. Prior to the 1965 reforms, the Second Circuit held that a Brazilian citizen born of Brazilian parents of Japanese ancestry was not Brazilian, but Japanese for quota purposes. Hitai v. INS, 343 F.2d 466 (2d Cir. 1965).

The increasing divergence of national origin and race, even in what might be regarded broadly as the Old World, exposes the constructed and indeterminate nature of the concepts — when there are enough individuals who are, say, Arab or African racially, French as a matter of national origin and citizenship, and some combination culturally, it is no longer an academic assertion that race, national origin, citizenship and culture are not biological matters of blood. A worthwhile area of inquiry for future scholarship would be immigration cases presenting this type of divergence. Some would-be immigrants strategically emigrate initially to another country from which further emigration to the United States is easier than from their original homeland.

[133] Mexico would be further affected by per-country ceilings. 8 U.S.C. § 1152.

[134] INA § 203(b)(5).

[135] INA § 203(c).

[136] *See* Kosova, *supra* note 23; Robert D. Kaplan, *Frontier Justice: U.S. Immigration and Naturalization Service Bureaucracy*, NEW REPUBLIC, Apr. 13, 1992, at 24.

[137] As a result of the complexity of immigration law, the field is crowded with purveyors of fraudulent documents. *See* Bill Miller, *INS Cracks Down on Immigration Fraud for Profit; Consultants Who Falsify Documents, Arrange Phony Marriages Are Target of Federal Probes*, WASH. POST, Jan. 15, 1995, at A8; Patrick McDonnell, *Victimized Brothers Help End Immigration Scam; Fraud; Illegal Immigrants from Oaxaca Were Central to Suit That Unmasked Firm Selling Worthless Papers to Foreigners*, L.A. TIMES, Aug. 4, 1991, at B1.

[138] Stephen Engelberg, *In Immigration Labyrinth, Corruption Comes Easily*, N.Y. TIMES, Sept. 12, 1994, at A1 (part of a series; describes bribery scandals in Arlington, Va., office of INS, and other similar situations throughout the agency). Some authors propose that the INS would better serve its contradictory dual purposes of immigrant service and law enforcement if it were divided into two separate agencies. *See* DANIEL W. SUTHERLAND, CENTER FOR EQUAL OPPORTUNITY (CEO) POLICY BRIEF, ABOLISH THE INS: HOW FEDERAL BUREAUCRACY DOOMS IMMIGRATION REFORM (1996).

[139] Fiallo v. Bell, 430 U.S. 787, 792 (1977).

[140] Chae Chan Ping v. United States, 130 U.S. 58, 595 (1889) (The Chinese Exclusion Case).

[141] I have benefited greatly from the analyses of the plenary power doctrine by other scholars. *See especially* Motomura, *Plenary Power*, *supra* note 63, at 545-59 (tracing course of "classical" immigration law); Motomura, *Curious Evolution*, *supra* note 63, at 1632-38 (discussing *Chae Chan Ping* and *Fong Yue Ting*); *see also* Henkin, *supra* note 63 (considering

international law perspective); Legomsky, *Plenary Power*, *supra* note 63 (discussing possible justifications for plenary power doctrine); Schuck, *supra* note 63 (distinguishing between "classical" immigration law and contemporary communitarian immigration law).

This article does not analyze each of the possible justifications for the plenary power doctrine, a task which Stephen Legomsky performed admirably in his article. I have tried to take up where Legomsky left off, considering how the Court could progress beyond the plenary power doctrine, and what the constitutional consequences might be. *See* Legomsky, *Plenary Power*, *supra* note 63, at 305 ("[The] next stage [of constitutional review of immigration law] will be marked by a return to general principles of constitutional law.") *Cf.* Schuck, *supra* note 63, at 83-85 (discussing some possible approaches in the absence of plenary power).

[142] U.S. CONST., art. I, § 8, cl. 4. If anything, "uniform Rule" should be read to prevent racial discrimination. The other enumerated power of that clause is to set "uniform Laws on the subject of Bankruptcies." Nobody contends that Congress possess "plenary power" over bankruptcy, beyond constitutional limits.

[143] 130 U.S. 581 (1889).

[144] *Id.* at 599-600.

[145] *Id.* at 596-98.

[146] The racial animosity that formed the background for the Chinese Exclusion Act is described at length in the following historical works. STUART C. MILLER, THE UNWELCOME IMMIGRANT: THE AMERICAN IMAGE OF THE CHINESE, 1785-1882 (1969); ALEXANDER SAXTON, THE INDISPENSABLE ENEMY: LABOR AND THE ANTI-CHINESE MOVEMENT IN CALIFORNIA (1971); *see also* Charles J. McClain, Jr., *The Chinese Struggle for Civil Rights in Nineteenth Century America: The First Phase*, 1850-1870, 72 CAL. L. REV. 529 (1984); Shirley Hune, *The Politics of Chinese Exclusion: Legislative-Executive Conflict*, 1876-1882, 9 AMERASIA J. 5 (1982). *See generally* RONALD TAKAKI, STRANGERS FROM A DIFFERENT SHORE: A HISTORY OF ASIAN AMERICANS 79-131 (1989).

[147] *See* Frank H. Wu, *Neither Black Nor White: Asian Americans and Affirmative Action*, 15 B.C. THIRD WORLD L. REV. 225, 232 (1995) and sources cited therein.

[148] *Id.*

[149] *See* Hing, *supra* note 63, at 44-46.

[150] Chae Chan Ping v. United States, 130 U.S. 581, 603 (1889).

[151] *Id.*

[152] The interpretation that follows is developed from Motomura, *Plenary Power*, *supra* note 63, at 551. *Cf.* Aleinikoff, *Rights*, *supra* note 63, at 863 (describing international law perspective on immigration as "understandable.").

[153] The foreign relations aspect of the Chinese Exclusion Act are described in Henkin, *supra* note 63, at 863-86 and Fitzpatrick & Bennett, *supra* note 79, at 594-608. If immigration is evaluated by international norms, the irony is that the Chinese Exclusion Act breached international law obligations and agreements.

[154] *Chae Chan Ping*, 130 U.S. at 604.

[155] *Id.* at 595. Brimelow believes the case to have been decided rightly. *See* BRIMELOW, *supra* note 6, at 214-15 (characterizing argument as "maybe" having a "dark, nativistic motive" but being "highly rational and a very specific complaint about the difficulty of assimilating immigrants from what was then a pre-modern society.").

[156] *Id.* at 595.

[157] *Id.* at 606.

[158] *Id.*

[159] 149 U.S. 698 (1893).

[160] *Id.* at 706.

[161] *Id.* at 713.

[162] *Id.* at 711.

[163] *Id.* at 713.

[164] *Id.* at 712.

[165] *Id.* at 711-12.

[166] *Id.* at 712.

[167] *Id.* at 729.

[168] *Id.* at 730 (quoting Chae Chan Ping v. United States, 130 U.S. 581, 598 (1889).

[169] Fong Yue Ting v. United States, 149 U.S. 698, 734 (1893). Scholars have shown that Asian immigrants and European immigrants displayed similar return rates to their homelands. *See, e.g.*, TAKAKI, *supra* note 146, at 11; Chan, *European and Asian Immigration into the United States in Comparative Perspective, 1820s to 1920s*, *in* IMMIGRATION RECONSIDERED, *supra* note 15, at 37, 38.

[170] *Fong Yue Ting*, 149 U.S. at 734.

[171] *Id.* at 738.

[172] *Id.* at 737.

[173] *Id.* at 743.

[174] *Id.*

[175] *Id.* at 757.

[176] *Cf.* LEGOMSKY, *supra* note 63, ch. 3; Michael Scaperlanda, *Justice Thurgood Marshall and the Legacy of Dissent in Federal Alienage Cases*, 8 GEO. IMMIG. L.J. 1, 17-18 (1994).

[177] 118 U.S. 356 (1886). *See also* Aleinikoff, *Rights*, *supra* note 63, at 864. A recent commentator, based on an exhaustive survey of anti-Chinese case law, has concluded that *Yick Wo* was a decision much more focused on economic rights of corporations than equal protection of racial minorities. *See* Thomas W. Joo, *New "Conspiracy Theory" of the Fourteenth Amendment: Nineteenth Century Chinese Civil Rights Cases and the Development of Substantive Due Process Jurisprudence*, 29 U.S.F.L. REV. 353 (1995). *Cf.* Wong Wing v. United States, 163 U.S. 228 (1896) (striking down imprisonment without jury trial provisions of Chinese Exclusion Act by distinguishing between those immigrants who "came into the country with consent" and those who came "in disregard of the law.").

[178] *See, e.g.*, Shaw v. Reno, 113 S. Ct. 2816, 2825 (1993).

[179] 189 U.S. 86 (1903) (The Japanese Immigrant Case).

[180] *Id.* at 97.

[181] *Id.* at 101-02.

[182] The Court has ignored the plenary power doctrine on plenty of occasions.

Unable to simply defer to Congress, the Court intervened actively in a remarkable series of early twentieth century cases defining what it meant to be a "white" person able to naturalize. *See* Ozawa v. United States, 260 U.S. 178 (1922) (Japanese individual not permitted to naturalize because he was not white); United States v. Thind, 261 U.S. 204 (1922) (Asian Indian individual not permitted to naturalize because he was not white). *See* IAN F. HANEY-LOPEZ, WHITE BY LAW: THE LEGAL CONSTRUCTION OF RACE (1996).

More recently, the Supreme Court invalidated the legislative veto in the immigration context. INS v. Chadha, 462 U.S. 919 (1983). As Stephen Legomsky noted shortly after the decision, its discussion ignored the plenary power doctrine. Legomsky, *Plenary Power*, *supra* note 63, at 301-03. Legomsky predicted that *Chadha* would "speed the demise of the plenary power doctrine." *Id.* at 302. He has been incorrect, alas. *See* Stephen H. Legomsky, *Ten More Years of Plenary Power: Immigration, Congress, and the Courts*, 22 HASTINGS CONST. L.Q. 925 (1995) (more cautious prediction that the Supreme Court may "soften" the plenary power doctrine in the future).

[183] Oceanic Steam Navigation Co. v. Stranahan, 214 U.S. 320, 339 (1909) (upholding levy on carriers who had transported inadmissible aliens).

[184] United States ex rel. Knauff v. Shaughnessy, 338 U.S. 537, 544 (1950); Shaughnessy v. United States ex rel. Mezei, 345 U.S. 206, 212 (1953).

[185] 342 U.S. 580 (1952).

[186] *Id.* at 597 (Frankfurter, J., concurring).

[187] 408 U.S. 753 (1972).

[188] *Id.* at 765-766.

[189] 430 U.S. 787 (1977).

[190] *Id.* at 792.

[191] *Id.*

[192] *Id.* (quoting Mathews v. Diaz, 426 U.S. 67, 80 (1976)).

[193] *Fiallo*, 430 U.S. at 787.

[194] *Id.*

[195] *Id.* at 798.

[196] *Id.* at 806 (Marshall, J., dissenting).

[197] *Id.* at 809.

[198] *Id.* at 795 n.6.

[199] *See* Legomsky, *Plenary Power*, *supra* note 63, at 298. *See also* Scaperlanda, *supra* note 176.

[200] *See* Stone v. INS, 115 S. Ct. 1537 (1995) (interpreting statutory time period for filing appeal from deportation order as not being tolled by motion for administrative reconsideration); Reno v. Flores, 507 U.S. 292 (1993) (rejecting claim that juvenile aliens unaccompanied by parents and awaiting resolution of deportation proceedings had a right to be released to the custody of responsible adults, with traditional recitation of plenary power doctrine); INS v. National Ctr. for Immigrants' Rights, 502 U.S. 183 (1991) (explicitly narrow decision on strictly statutory grounds concerning regulations that prohibited aliens unable to work from working during pendency of deportation proceedings).

Some earlier and similarly cursory statements of the plenary power doctrine include: United States v. Valenzuela-Bernal, 458 U.S. 858, 864 (1982) (rejecting claim of Fifth or Sixth Amendment violation by criminal defendant whose potential witnesses were deported); Toll v. Moreno, 458 U.S. 1, 26 (1982) (striking down state regulation of aliens that prevented them from acquiring state resident status for college tuition purposes, observing in passing that plenary power does not preempt all state regulation of aliens).

Kevin Johnson has offered another explanation. He refers to *Chevron* deference to administrative agencies as possibly more powerful than the plenary power doctrine in insulating immigration decisions from judicial review. *See* Kevin R. Johnson, *Responding to the "Litigation Explosion": The Plain Meaning of Executive Branch Primacy Over Immigration*, 71 N.C. L. REV. 413 (1993).

[201] Sale v. Haitian Ctrs. Council, Inc., 113 S. Ct. 2549 (1993). While the opinion labeled the Haitian immigrants "illegal," they might have been "legal" at the end of the process on which they were embarking, as they had a strong argument for asylum. As Justice Blackmun pointed out, if the majority accepted that the Haitian immigrants were "illegal," then the statute would have limited the discretion of the executive branch. *Id.* at 2568 (Blackmun, J., dissenting).

[202] *Id.* at 2555 n.13 (Executive Order reproduced; facially neutral); *id.* at 2549 (characterizing order as directed at Haitians). I have relied on two articles written by Harold H. Koh, who was counsel of record in the case. Harold H. Koh, *The "Haiti Paradigm" in United States Human Rights Policy*, 103 YALE L.J. 2391 (1994) [hereinafter Koh, *Haiti Paradigm*]; Harold H. Koh, *Reflections on Refoulement and Haitian Centers Council*, 35 HARV. INT'L L.J. 1 (1994).

[203] *Sale*, 113 S. Ct. at 2569 (Blackmun, J., dissenting); *see also* Koh, *Haiti Paradigm*, *supra* note 202, at 2416-19.

[204] 113 S. Ct. at 2558-62, 2567.

[205] *See, e.g.*, Brief of the NAACP, Transafrica and Congressional Black Caucus, Amici Curiae in Support of Respondents in Sale v. Hatian Ctrs., Council, Inc., 113 S. Ct. 2549 (1993). *Cf.* Peter J. Boyer, *The Rise of Kweisi Mfume*, NEW YORKER, Aug. 1, 1994, at 27, 27 (quoting head of Congressional Black Caucus as stating "if Haitians were not black, we would not sit back and watch this murder occur."); Koh, *Haiti Paradigm*, *supra* note 202, at 2413.

[206] *See* Kevin R. Johnson, *Judicial Acquiescence to the Executive Branch's Pursuit of Foreign Policy and Domestic Agendas in Immigration Matters: The Case of the Haitian Asylum-Seekers*, 7 GEO. IMMIG. L.J. 1, 12-13, 26 (1993).

[207] *Sale*, 113 S. Ct. at 2561 (*citing* Shaughnessy v. United States ex rel. Mezei, 345 U.S. 206, 212 (1953).

[208] *Id.* at 2577 (Blackmun, J., dissenting). *See* Koh, *Haiti Paradigm*, *supra* note 202, at 2411-16.

[209] Motomura, *Plenary Power*, *supra* note 63.

[210] Jean v. Nelson, 472 U.S. 846 (1985).

[211] *Id.* at 849.

[212] *Id.* at 857.

[213] Motomura, *Curious Evolution*, *supra* note 63.

[214] 896 F.2d 564 (D.C. Cir. 1990), *vacated without opinion*, 925 F.2d 488 (D.C. Cir. 1991) (original opinion available on-line only, 1990 WL 6857 (D.C. Cir., Feb. 2, 1990).

[215] 1990 WL 6857, at *1.

[216] *Id.* at *2-4.

[217] This would reconcile the discrimination against immigrants at the border with the protection offered to them as immigrants within the border, as expressed by *Graham v. Richardson*, 403 U.S. 365 (1971) (striking down state public assistance provisions that discriminated against noncitizens).

[218] *Id.*; *see also* Bosniak, *supra* note 58 (analyzing decisions in labor law that protect undocumented workers).

[219] This again may be nothing more than an argument for consistency: the Court could be less protective of immigrants across the board.

[220] *See* Motomura, *Plenary Power*, *supra* note 63, at 574, 600-13; Motomura, *Curious Evolution*, *supra* note 63, at 1690-92, 1702-04.

[221] 163 U.S. 537 (1896). This point is made by Motomura, *Plenary Power*, *supra* note 63, at 551.

[222] 347 U.S. 483 (1954).

[223] Buck v. Bell, 274 U.S. 200 (1927); *compare* Skinner v. Oklahoma, 316 U.S. 535 (1942).

[224] Bradwell v. Illinois, 83 U.S. 130, 141 (1873) (affirming denial of law license to married woman with dicta concerning the "wide difference in the respective spheres and destinies of man and woman" which is "recognized" in "the civil law, as well as nature herself."). *Compare* Frontiero v. Richardson, 411 U.S. 677 (1973) (heightened scrutiny for gender discrimination).

[225] *See* Schenck v. United States, 249 U.S. 47 (1919); Gitlow v. New York, 268 U.S. 652 (1925); Whitney v. California, 274 U.S. 357 (1927); *compare* Brandenburg v. Ohio, 395 U.S. 444 (1969); Texas v. Johnson, 491 U.S. 397 (1989).

[226] Lochner v. New York, 198 U.S. 25 (1905). The age of the plenary power doctrine can be measured against substantive due process: the latter came into existence after the plenary power doctrine and ceased to exist while the plenary power doctrine continued to flourish. *Cf.* Henkin, *supra* note 63, at 859 n.26 (noting early traces of substantive due process at time of the Chinese Exclusion Case).

[227] United States v. Lopez, 115 S. Ct. 1624 (1995).

[228] Galvan v. Press, 347 U.S. 522, 530-31 (1954) (upholding deportation on basis of Communist Party membership).

[229] For an extended discussion of the three arguments addressed

here, see Planned Parenthood of Southeastern Pennsylvania v. Casey, 505 U.S. 833, 854-64 (1992) (joint opinion of Justices O'Connor, Kennedy and Souter, declining to overrule *Roe v. Wade*, 410 U.S. 113 (1973), on *stare decisis* grounds).

See Henry P. Monaghan, *Stare Decisis and Constitutional Adjudication*, 88 COLUM. L. REV. 723, *especially* 740-53 (1988) (describing a coherent theory of *stare decisis*).

[230] *Casey*, 505 U.S. at 863 (explaining appropriate departure from *stare decisis* in abandonment of substantive due process and in *Brown v. Board of Education*, 347 U.S. 483 (1954)).

[231] United States v. Gaudin, 115 S. Ct. 2310, 2319 (1995).

[232] *Compare* Adarand v. Pena, 115 S. Ct. 2097, 2114-17 (1995).

[233] Fong Yue Ting v. United States, 149 U.S. 698, 732 (1893) (Brewer, J., dissenting); *id.* at 744 (Field, J., dissenting); *id.* at 762 (Fuller, C.J., dissenting); Kleindienst v. Mandel, 408 U.S. 753, 769 (1972) (Douglas, J., dissenting); Fiallo v. Bell, 430 U.S. 787, 800 (1977) (Marshall, J., dissenting).

[234] The phrase is Stephen Legomsky's. Legomsky, *supra* note 63, at 929. *See, e.g.*, Motomura, *Plenary Power*, *supra* note 63; Motomura, *Curious Evolution*, *supra* note 63; Henkin, *supra* note 63; Legomsky, *Plenary Power*, *supra* note 63.

[235] Nobody, that is, except Peter Brimelow and others who believe as he does. *But see* Peter J. Spiro, *The States and Immigration in an Era of Demi-Sovereignities*, 35 VA. J. INT'L L. 121 (1994) (arguing that states should have greater leeway in passing immigration legislation and focusing on federalism concerns with apparent willingness to tolerate what would be equal protection violations in other contexts).

Some scholars are confident that the Chinese Exclusion Act, or its counterpart, could not be passed today as a political matter, and also would not be sustained by the Court. *See, e.g.*, ALEINIKOFF, *supra* note 13, at 160.

[236] *Cf.* Viet Dinh, *Law and Asylum*, *in* ARGUING IMMIGRATION, *supra* note 3, at 215, 220 (arguing without elaboration that "the standards that we employ to exclude aliens have to reflect the values of our society.").

[237] U.S. CONST., amend. V, XIV. Another elaboration of the argument that should appeal to judicial conservatives who are consistent in their views is the reluctance to recognize implied powers, rendered all the stronger here because the implied power over immigration would seem to overpower express guarantees of rights. *See* Harisiades v. Shaughnessy, 342 U.S. 580, 599 (1952) (Douglas, J., dissenting); *cf.* Fong Yue Ting v. United States, 149 U.S. 698, 757-58 (1893) (Field, J., dissenting).

[238] U.S. CONST., amend. XIV, § 1.

[239] ALEXANDER M. BICKEL, THE MORALITY OF CONSENT 33-54 (1975). *Cf.* JUDITH N. SHKLAR, AMERICAN CITIZENSHIP: THE QUEST FOR INCLUSION 16 (1991); Gerald L. Neuman, *Justifying U.S. Naturalization Policies*, 35 VA. J. INT'L LAW 237 (1995) (presenting different theories for understanding citizenship as a concept); Stephen H. Legomsky, *Why Citizenship?*, 35 VA. J. INT'L LAW 279, *especially* 285-88, 290 (discussing why citizenship is important as a means of inquiring who is eligible to become a citizen). The short answer to Legomsky's query is that citizenship can be better than race as a means of classifying individuals.

[240] BICKELL, *supra* note 239, at 36. As Bickel stated, "that is not quite an end of the matter." *Id.* at 48. In a more difficult passage to interpret, he then argued that "conditions may be attached to entry permits" and "in time of war even resident enemy aliens may be subject to fairly harsh restrictions" (presumably a reference to the Japanese-American internment cases). He suggested "that is a consequence . . . or our perception of the meaning of foreign citizenship and of the obligations it may impose more than it is a consequence of our own domestic law." *Id.* Bickel is much more helpful for articulating the rights of immigrants than he is for the right to immigrate. He implicitly distinguishes, as the Court has done, between cases involving immigrants and cases involving immigration.

[241] Dred Scott v. Sandford, 60 U.S. 393 (1857).

[242] BICKELL, *supra* note 239, at 41.

[243] 83 U.S. 36 (1873).

[244] *Id.* at 42-43.

[245] Yick Wo v. Hopkins, 118 U.S. 356 (1886) (holding that facially neutral ordinance that had been applied in a racially discriminatory manner could be struck down as unconstitutional).

[246] Mathews v. Diaz, 426 U.S. 67, 77 (1976) (unanimous decision holding that strict scrutiny did not apply to alienage in the context of restrictions on Medicare entitlements).

[247] *See, e.g.*, Goldberg v. Kelly, 397 U.S. 254 (1970); *cf.* Cleveland Bd. of Educ. v. Loudermill, 470 U.S. 532 (1985).

[248] *See especially* Cabell v. Chavez-Salido, 454 U.S. 432, 438-40 (1982) (explaining distinction between "membership in the political community" and "distribution of economic benefits."). *Cf.* Landon v. Plascencia, 459 U.S. 21 (1982) (applying procedural due process standards for exclusion proceedings involving permanent resident alien); Sugarman v. Dougall, 413 U.S. 634, 647-48 (1973) (distinguishing between state alienage discrimination in civil service positions and higher political offices, or as voters, because the latter constitute "participation in [the state's] democratic political institutions.") *See generally* Motomura, *Curious Evolution*, *supra* note 63, at 1626 ("The stunted growth of constitutional immigration law contrasts sharply with the flowering of constitutional protections for aliens in areas other than immigration law."), and at 1650-51 (arguing that the right-privilege distinction explains the

characterization of deportation as civil rather than criminal).

Were the court (or legislatures) serious about the distinction, they would consider granting permanent resident aliens the right to vote at least in local elections. *See* Raskin, *supra* note 63. In another example of constitutional doctrine being blind to political practice, the advocates of restricting immigration characterize violations of immigration law as criminal or quasi-criminal. The political significance of describing some immigrants as being "illegal" (rather than "undocumented") should give the Court pause before it asserts again that deportation is civil. But if the Court recognized that deportation was criminal or quasi-criminal, it also might be forced to apply constitutional principles to the process. *Cf.* INS v. Lopez-Mendoza, 468 U.S. 1032 (1984), *especially* at 1056-57 (White, J., dissenting).

[249] *See* Unz, *supra* note 84.

[250] *Cf.* LEGOMSKY, *supra* note 63, at 273.

[251] This renders inconsequential the point made by Chief Justice Rehnquist that the citizen-alien distinction is mandated by the Constitution. *See Sugarman*, 413 U.S. at 651 (Rehnquist, J., dissenting) ("That distinction is constitutionally important in no less than 11 instances in a political document noted for its brevity.").

[252] The Court is ready to revisit the issue of alienage as a suspect classification. In its 1994-1995 term, it accepted certiorari in a case where an insurance carrier had discriminated against an Australian citizen who was a permanent resident alien, but dismissed the case after it had settled. Geico v. Duane, 37 F.3d 1036 (4th Cir. 1994), *cert. granted* 115 S. Ct. 1251 (1995) *and cert. dismissed* 115 S. Ct. 2272 (1995) (42 U.S.C. § 1981 bars alienage discrimination). *Cf.* Neuman, *supra* note 12, at 1426-30.

[253] *Cf.* Mari J. Matsuda, *Voices of America: Accent, Antidiscrimination Law, and a Jurisprudence for the Last Reconstruction*, 100 YALE L.J. 1329 (1991) (analyzing permissible accent discrimination as a proxy for prohibited race discrimination).

[254] In my opinion, it is worth taking the risk that the few victories for immigrant rights achieved under plenary power will be rendered less persuasive, because they are not likely to endure without modification anyway. The greatest risk is the so-called race-to-the-bottom, where governments faced with the choice between offering an entitlement to everybody or nobody choose the latter. *See* Spiro, *supra* note 235, at 151 n.128 (arguing that equal protection analysis would be incoherent applied to aliens and would result in detriment to them due to a race-to-the-bottom scenario). A more subtle risk is that domestic constitutional standards will be weakened. It is difficult to believe that equal protection doctrine could be so undone as to reach the level of the plenary power doctrine; the more likely problem is that other forms of deference will paralyze the court. *See* Johnson, *supra* note 200.

[255] The result in one pro-immigrant case might be reversed as a result if First Amendment grounds could not be found as an alternative basis to protect the individual. The Court rejected the argument by the state of New York that it was acceptable to discriminate against aliens unwilling to naturalize as soon as they were qualified to do so. *See* Nyquist v. Mauclet, 432 U.S. 1 (1977).

[256] This border-interior distinction has been recognized in immigration law for quite some time. *See, e.g.*, Landon v. Plascencia, 459 U.S. 21, 32 (1982) ("once an alien gains admission to our country and begins to develop the ties that go with permanent residence his constitutional status changes accordingly.") Thus, if equal protection doctrine developed along the lines suggested by critical race theorists, looking toward subjugation or cultural meaning or other factors, alienage may still be a candidate for suspect classification status.

For a discussion of problems with a more complex approach to alienage, see Neuman, *supra* note 12, at 1426-40.

[257] It would not run afoul of Sale v. Haitian Ctrs. Council, Inc., 113 S. Ct. 2549 (1993); United States ex rel. Knauff v. Shaughnessy, 338 U.S. 537, 544 (1950); Shaughnessy v. United States ex rel. Mezei, 345 U.S. 206, 212 (1953); or cases in other contexts in which the Supreme Court has for all practical purposes indicated that constitutional standards have limited extraterritorial effect. *See, e.g.*, United States v. Verdugo-Urquidez, 494 U.S. 259, 274-75 (1990) (no Fourth Amendment rights applicable when U.S. officials conduct a search in Mexico). In this respect, the arguments advanced here differ from those offered by Professor Henkin. They do not depend on any understanding that the Constitution governs foreign affairs. *See* Henkin, *supra* note 63; Legomsky, *Plenary Power*, *supra* note 63, at 275-77.

[258] *See* Carens, *Open Borders*, *supra* note 62, *especially* at 270.

[259] The relationship between traditional civil rights and immigrant rights would bear a family resemblance to the relationships among anti-discrimination laws covering race, gender, disability, and sexual orientation.

[260] These impacts have always existed, but are acknowledged only occasionally. Schuck, for example, stated that Prop. 187 would likely result in "many U.S. citizens and legal aliens" being "caught up in the dragnet" along with "families in which some members have legal status . . . while others . . . do not." Schuck, *supra* note 77, at 89. Although Schuck recognized the link between immigration and citizens who are racial minorities, and also identified himself as a "friend of immigration," he nonetheless analyzed the measure in familiar terms when he presented the question "Do Outsiders Have Claims on Us?" *Id.* at 85, 91. Judith Shklar has argued persuasively for considering the "standing of citizens," defining standing in a broad and colloquial sense rather than a technical legal sense. *See* SHKLAR, *supra* note 239, at 2.

[261] *See* Fiallo v. Bell, 430 U.S. 787, 800 (1977) (Marshall, J., dissenting).

[262] *See* U.S. CENSUS BUREAU, *supra* note 99, at 1.

[263] *See* U.S. GENERAL ACCOUNTING OFFICE, IMMIGRATION REFORM-EMPLOYER SANCTIONS AND THE QUESTION OF DISCRIMINATION 5-7 (1990) (concluding that after IRCA, national origin discrimination presented "a serious pattern of discrimination"). The "suspicion" of Asian Americans calls forth the nineteenth-century presumption that Chinese laborers were not entitled to be in the United States unless they produced a certificate required by the Chinese Exclusion Act.

[264] *Cf.* Motomura, *Curious Evolution*, *supra* note 63, at 1657-58 (presenting hypothetical cases contrasting claim of race discrimination in mainstream constitutional law and immigration constitutional law).

[265] *See Fiallo*, 430 U.S. at 787; Kleindienst v. Mandel, 408 U.S. 753 (1972); Escobar v. INS, 896 F.2d 564 (D.C. Cir. 1990), *vacated without opinion* 925 F.2d 488 (D.C. Cir. 1991); *cf.* Peter H. Schuck & Theodore H. Wang, *Continuity and Change: Patterns of Immigration Litigation in the Courts, 1979-1990*, 45 STAN. L. REV. 115, 147-49 (1992) (describing affirmative challenges to immigration statutes brought by citizens, including citizens seeking to restrict immigration by curtailing employment of alien workers); Patricia D. Rudloff, *In Re Oluloro: Risk of Female Genital Mutilation as "Extreme Hardship" in Immigration Proceedings*, 26 ST. MARY'S L.J. 877 (1995) (reporting unpublished opinion of immigration judge suspending deportation of foreign national who was the mother of citizen children, who if they accompanied their mother to her homeland, would have faced female genital mutilation as ritual practice).

There also are cases in which citizen co-plaintiffs have escaped attention. *See, e.g.*, INS v. Delgado, 466 U.S. 210, 213 n.1 (1984) (holding that INS workplace search was not a detention or seizure subject to constitutional constraints).

Immigration restrictionists who sued seeking to accomplish their goals might attempt to invoke citizen standing, but they have been unsuccessful in the past for reasons that should still preclude their efforts, e.g., lack of injury in fact. *See* FAIR v. Reno, 897 F. Supp. 595 (D.D.C. 1995). *See also* Northwestern Forest Workers Ass'n. v. Lyng, 688 F. Supp. 1 (D.D.C. 1988) (holding without analysis that citizen plaintiffs had standing to challenge pro-immigrant administrative agency interpretation of Special Agricultural Workers program), *later proceedings sub. nom;* Wint v. Yuetter, 902 F.2d 76 (D.C. Cir. 1990). The *FAIR* case offers support for abolishing the plenary power doctrine from an unusual source. Although ultimately ruling in favor of the government, which was in the unusual position of ostensibly defending its relatively pro-immigrant stance, the court rejected the government's argument that immigration legislation presented a nonjusticiable political question. *Id.* at 9.

On standing in race-related cases, see Reggie Oh & Frank Wu, *The Evolution of Race in the Law: The Supreme Court Moves from Approving Internment of Japanese Americans to Disapproving Affirmative Action for African Americans*, 1 MICH. J. LAW & RACE (forthcoming 1996); Girardeau A. Spann, *Color-Coded Standing*, 80 CORNELL L. REV. 1422 (1995) (arguing that Supreme Court standing analysis in race cases has discriminated due to results-oriented bias disfavoring minorities).

[266] Oyama v. California, 332 U.S. 633 (1948).

[267] *Id.* at 647.

[268] *Id.*

[269] Wauchope v. United States, 985 F.2d 1407 (9th Cir. 1993).

[270] *Id.* at 1409.

[271] *Id.* at 1411.

[272] *Id.* The *Wauchope* decision has been followed with respect to standing and distinguished on the merits. In *Ablang v. Reno*, another Ninth Circuit panel reasoned that a *Fiallo* type claim could be brought by a child seeking to establish citizenship through her relationship to her father, but that *Fiallo* also controlled and required minimal rationality review. Accordingly, the case was dismissed. Ablang v. Reno, 52 F.3d 801, 805 n.4 (9th Cir. 1995), *cert. denied*, 64 U.S.L.W. 3465 (1996). The *Ablang* court characterized the *Wauchope* decision in a manner that supports citizen standing but contradicts *Fiallo*: "*Wauchope* concerned the right of United States citizen mothers to transmit citizenship to their children born abroad according to the same standards set for United States citizen fathers." *Id.* at 804, 805-06. *See also* Aguayo v. Christopher, 865 F. Supp. 479 (N.D. Ill. 1994) (following *Wauchope*); Le Brun v. Thornburgh, 777 F. Supp. 1204, 1209-10 (D.N.J. 1991) (holding in favor of citizen standing); *contra* Tranter v. Secretary of State, 1994 U.S. Dist. LEXIS 8824 (D.D.C. May 17, 1994) (holding against citizen standing due to inability to redress any alleged harm, because courts could not confer citizenship); *compare* Acosta v. Gaffney, 413 F. Supp. 827 (D.N.J. 1976) (withholding deportation of alien parents because deportation of citizen child would result), *rev'd* 558 F.2d 1153 (3d Cir. 1977).

[273] Plyler v. Doe, 457 U.S. 202 (1982).

[274] Fiallo v. Bell, 430 U.S. 787 (1977); *Cf* Kleindienst v. Mandel, 408 U.S. 753 (1972); (rejecting claim that citizens interested in being an audience for a Marxist author had a First Amendment right to hearing him speak).

[275] Francis Fukuyama, for example, has made the futile and likely infuriating claim that the new immigrants espouse traditional American and especially conservative values, almost more than many native-born citizens. *See* Fukuyama, *supra* note 3; Fukuyama, *supra* note 11. A negative reaction anticipating these arguments can be found in James J. Treires, *The Dark Side of the Dream*, NEWSWEEK, Mar. 20, 1989, at 10; *cf.* BRIMELOW, *supra* note 6, at 180-81, 269-72.

[276] Professor Motomura has argued persuasively that constitutional standards have worked their way into immigration

law, in the form of statutory construction abrogating the plenary power doctrine. *See* Motomura, *Curious Evolution*, *supra* note 63.

[277] *See* Johnson, *Race*, *supra* note 94, at 661-72 (describing difficulties of challenging immigration laws on constitutional grounds).

[278] 115 S. Ct. 2097 (1995). *Adarand*, incidentally, emphasizes consistency between federal and state equal protection analysis. This suggests that the Court may be willing to depart from its federal-state distinction in immigration regulation, though whether it would tend toward the former or the latter is unclear.

[279] *Id.* at 2117.

[280] Plyler v. Doe, 457 U.S. 202 (1982).

[281] *See* Karst, *supra* note 63.

[282] Likewise, *Fiallo*, if it presented itself again, would be resolved by reference to then prevailing standards for discrimination on the basis of birth, legitimacy and gender.

[283] *See Adarand*, 115 S. Ct. at 2117.

[284] *See* Fukuyama, *supra* note 11, at 77 (arguing that race, culture and socioeconomic status are different, and that "the common American culture . . . is actually a sectarian Protestant Anglo-Saxon culture that was somehow detached from its ethnic roots, mixed with universalistic Lockean-liberal principles, and adopted by the non-Anglo-Saxon, non-Protestant immigrants from Europe who arrived subsequently, and who then intermarried to such an extent that it is no longer meaningful to try to determine what proportion of the country is descended from Italians, Swedes, and the like.").

[285] Even Carens agrees that some limitations might be appropriate. Carens, *Open Borders*, *supra* note 62, at 260, 270; Joseph H. Carens, *Nationalism and the Exclusion of Immigrants: Lessons From Australian Immigration Policy*, *in* OPEN BORDERS? CLOSED SOCIETIES? THE ETHICAL AND POLITICAL ISSUES 41, 59 (Mark Gibney ed., 1988).

[286] Lind, *supra* note 5, at A19 (also arguing that "pro-labor liberals and non-racist populists on the right should unite to demand an immigration policy that puts the interests of American workers above the interests of the native rich."). *Cf.* SIMON, *supra* note 111, at 318-19, 320 (policy recommendations including anti-discrimination laws and also cuts in welfare entitlements).

[287] Loury, *supra* note 11.

[288] The economic impact of immigration is not considered here, save to note that it is the economic impact of migrants that leads to legislation which violates the right to interstate travel. I have relied on the following major studies on the many sides of the issues: FIX & PASSEL, *supra* note 58; SIMON, FACTS, *supra* note 87; SIMON, *supra* note 111. *See also* GEORGE J. BORJAS, FRIENDS OR STRANGERS: THE IMPACT OF IMMIGRANTS ON THE U.S. ECONOMY (1990); George J. Borjas, *The Economics of Immigration*, 32 J. ECON. LIT. 1667 (1994) (updating Borjas' earlier study); George J. Borjas, *Know the Flow; Economics of Immigration*, NAT'L REV., Apr. 17, 1995, at 7 (presenting mass media version of his research results); DONALD HUDDLE, THE COST OF IMMIGRATION (1993) (the Huddle study, which was widely reported in the media, is critiqued in FIX & PASSEL, *supra* note 58, and SIMON, *supra* note 82. *See also* BRIMELOW, *supra* note 6, at 137-77; *see generally* THOMAS MULLER, IMMIGRANTS AND THE AMERICAN CITY (1993). For information concerning estimates of the undocumented immigrant population, one of the most controversial areas of the debate, see U.S. GENERAL ACCOUNTING OFFICE, ILLEGAL ALIENS: DESPITE DATA LIMITATIONS, CURRENT METHODS PROVIDE BETTER POPULATION ESTIMATES (1993).

[289] BRIMELOW, *supra* note 6, at xvii.

[290] 466 U.S. 429 (1984).

[291] *Id.* at 431.

[292] *Id.* at 433.

[293] Some sophisticated writers also assume that constitutional standards apply to immigration. *See, e.g.*, James C. Clad, *Slowing the Wave*, FOREIGN POL'Y, Summer 1994, at 139, 150 ("The United States has the sovereign right, if it *constitutionally* reflects the majority view, to exclude others from coming here. It is that simple; it is that awkward.") (emphasis added).

[294] *See* Paul Feldman, *Uncertainty, Lawsuits Would Greet Prop. 187; Election: Many Hospitals, Clinics Have Yet to Prepare Contingency Plans; Disobedience and Confusion Predicted*, L.A. TIMES, Oct. 31, 1994, at A1, A1 (quoting sponsor of measure, "The purpose of the initiative is to have the court revisit and reconsider the *Plyler* case. Passage of the initiative will provide that vehicle."); Doreen Carrajal, *Prop. 187 Has Even Backers a Bit Uneasy; Although It Still Has Substantial Appeal, 62% Say They Would Not Turn in an Undocumented Student — Which Initiative Would Require*, L.A. TIMES, Oct. 31, 1994, at A1, A1 (quoting voter who supported the measure, "it's just to send a message . . . it will be ruled unconstitutional.").

[295] *See* H. Eric Schockman, *Why Prop. 187 Needs Judicial Review: The "Voices of the People" May Mandate the Law, But Constitutional Principles Form the Rule of Law*, L.A. TIMES, Jan. 22, 1995, at B19. *Cf.* Schuck, *supra* note 77, at 92 (observing that Governor Pete Wilson "surely knows that Prop. 187 could have dire practical consequences for his state" and speculating "he may secretly hope that an activist court will rescue him by striking it down.").

[296] *Cf.* Motomura, *Curious Evolution*, *supra* note 63, at 1631. Two other articles from Latino perspectives have focused on the relationship of progressive immigration reform to traditional civil rights. Rachel F. Moran, *Foreward — Demography and*

Distrust: The Latino Challenge to Civil Rights and Immigration Policy in the 1990s and Beyond, 8 LA RAZA L.J. 1 (1995) (suggesting that *Brown v. Board of Education* model of civil rights litigation is inappropriate for Latinos and may be anachronistic for African Americans as well); Kevin R. Johnson, *Civil Rights and Immigration: Challenges for the Latino Community in the Twenty-First Century*, 8 LA RAZA L.J. 42, *especially* 55-65 (1995) (analyzing "immigration as a dividing line" in the civil rights coalition). Ignatius Bau has written an article from an Asian American perspective based on his experience in the Prop. 187 campaign. Bau, *supra* note 27. *See also* William R. Tamayo, *When the Colored are Neither Black Nor Citizens: The United States Civil Rights Movement and Global Migration*, 2 ASIAN L.J. 1 (1995).

[297] Bill Ong Hing has argued at length that the Asian American community must be understood as having been constituted by immigration policies. *See* HING, *supra* note 13. *Cf.* Steven A. Holmes, *Anti-Immigrant Mood Moves Asians to Organize*, N.Y. TIMES, Jan. 3, 1996, at A1, A1 (quoting Karen Narasaki, Asian American civil rights leader, "For Asian Americans, because of their history, [immigration] is a cornerstone of what civil rights means to the community.").

[298] *See, e.g.*, COSE, *supra* note 15, at 205 (quoting U.S. Representative Smith, "no other nation in the world has the delusion that it can ignore its own poor while importing a whole generation of poor people every year" and arguing that the nation has a choice between importing workers or training "our own underclass.").

[299] *See, e.g.*, BRIMELOW, *supra* note 6, at 173-75; Lawrence Fuchs, *What Do Immigrants Deserve? A Warm Welcome and the Usual Benefits — But Not Affirmative Action*, WASH. POST, Jan. 29, 1995, at C2; Mark Krikorian, *Affirmative Action and Immigration*, *in* DEBATING AFFIRMATIVE ACTION: RACE, GENDER, ETHNICITY, AND THE POLITICS OF INCLUSION 300 (Nicolaus Mills ed., 1994) (FAIR representative arguing that affirmative action for some racial groups effectively subsidizes immigrants at the expense of native-born citizens). The Fuchs article is significant because the author, the former executive director of SCIRP, is considered more moderate on immigration issues. In an odd bit of dicta, Justice Stevens in an affirmative action case alluded to undocumented immigration. He stated that unlike blacks who had been enslaved, "the 'Spanish-speaking' subclass [of the program] came voluntarily, *frequently without invitation* . . ." Fullilove v. Klutznick, 448 U.S. 448, 538 (1980) (Stevens, J., dissenting) (emphasis added).

[300] The article that introduced the "blacks versus browns" dilemma is Miles, *supra* note 3, *especially at* 138-41. *See also* Peter H. Schuck, *The Evolving Civil Rights Movement: Old Civil Rights and New Immigration*, CURRENT, Jan. 1994, at 13. *Cf.* BRIMELOW, *supra* note 6, at 103-04, 242-43.

[301] *See* Wu, *supra* note 147, at 263 and accompanying notes.

[302] *See* Adarand v. Pena, 115 S. Ct. 2097 (1995).

[303] Podberesky v. Kirwan, 38 F.3d 147, 152 (4th Cir. 1994), *cert. denied*, 115 S. Ct. 2001 (1995).

[304] Memorandum Decision and Order, Ho v. San Francisco Unified Sch. Dist., Case No. C-94-2418 (N.D. Cal., Sept. 28, 1995) (denying motion to dismiss filed by defendant) (order marked as not for publication; on file with author); Selena Dong, Note, *"Too Many Asians": The Challenge of Fighting Discrimination Against Asian Americans and Preserving Affirmative Action*, 47 STAN. L. REV. 1027 (1995).

[305] Sandy Theis, *Suit Targets Minority Set-Asides: Black Claims Asian Indians Not Eligible*, CINCINNATI ENQ., May 23, 1995, at B1; *see also* Frank H. Wu, *Race Dynamics: The Case of Two Asian American Schoolgirls in Maryland Proves a Landmark for Affirmative Action*, ASIAN WEEK, Sept. 22, 1995, at 9 (describing controversy over the enrollment of two children of mixed Caucasian-Asian background in suburban Washington, D.C. magnet school in a district seeking to maintain racial balance); Dan Boyers, *Montgomery Reverses Itself, Lets Asian Girls Switch Schools*, WASH. POST, Sept. 14, 1995, at A1 (same).

[306] Daniel M. Weintraub, *Crime, Immigration Issues Helped Wilson, Poll Finds; Election: Proposition 187 Wins Among Whites, But Loses Among All Other Ethnic Groups, Exit Survey Shows*, L.A. TIMES, Nov. 19, 1994, at A1.

[307] Brimelow owns up to his political agenda. BRIMELOW, *supra* note 6, at 195-201. The real problem with "the immigration pincers" is the possibility that "the Clinton administration's electoral coalition may be a harbinger of politics to come." That coalition — "Southerners used to call them 'scalawags'" consists of blacks, Hispanics, Jews and minority whites. *Id.* at 197.

[308] The tensions among people of color, especially African Americans and recent immigrants (some of whom are of African origin or are considered black within American society), can be acute. *See* Morrison, *supra* note 3; Wanda Coleman, *Blacks, Immigrants and America: Remembering Latasha*, NATION, Feb. 13, 1993, at 187 (arguing "as a price of entry, the majority of immigrants buy into the lie of American apartheid: Black people are inferior."). *Cf.* COSE, *supra* note 15, at 151 (NAACP endorsed early version of IRCA) and 214 (Los Angeles African American clergyman argued that Latinos brought in to weaken black voting power); MULLER, *supra* note 288, at 56 (NAACP opposition to undocumented immigration), 91-98 (historical views of African Americans), 167-94 (economic impact of immigration on African Americans); Lawrence H. Fuchs, *The Reactions of Black Americans to Immigration*, *in* IMMIGRATION RECONSIDERED, *supra* note 15, at 293; Bill Ong Hing, *Immigration Policies: Messages of Exclusion to African Americans*, 37 HOW. L.J. 237 (1994); ARNOLD M. SHANKMAN, AMBIVALENT FRIENDS: AFRO-AMERICANS VIEW THE IMMIGRANT (1982).

[309] *See* Legomsky, *Plenary Power*, *supra* note 63, at 269-70 (discussing guest theory of immigration restriction). Walzer

rejects this view that members, once accepted, can continue to be distinguished. WALZER, *supra* note 57, at 62.

[310] In the 1996 Republican Presidential primary season, U.S. Senator Phil Gramm made this suggestion, prompting rival U.S. Senator Bob Dole to criticize him for proposing a form of second-class citizenship. *See* Brownstein, *supra* note 5.

[311] Peter Brimelow, *Whose Country Is It Anyway?*, WASH. POST, Oct. 15, 1995, at C4.

[312] *Cf.* Neil Gotanda, *A Critique of "Our Constitution is Color-Blind,"* 44 STAN. L. REV. 1 (1991); Cheryl I. Harris, *Whiteness as Property*, 106 HARV. L. REV. 1707 (1993); Ian H. Lopez, *The Social Construction of Race: Some Observations on Illusion, Fabrication, and Choice*, 29 HARV. C.R.-C.L. L. REV. 1 (1994).

[313] Adarand v. Pena, 115 S. Ct. 2097, 2101 (1995) (Scalia, J., concurring). Justice Scalia's statement should be read against earlier formulations of color-blindness. *See* Wu, *supra* note 95. Gabriel Chin has exposed an overlooked aspect of the first Justice Harlan's celebrated dissent exalting color-blindness in *Plessy v. Ferguson*. While Justice Harlan proclaimed that color-blindness should be the constitutional norm, he also contrasted Chinese immigrants unfavorable with African Americans. *See* Gabriel Chin, *A Streetcar Named Harlan: Asian Americans and John Marshall Harlan's Dissent in Plessy v. Ferguson* (forthcoming 1996; manuscript on file with author).

Ian Haney Lopez also has pointed out that "the alien land law, which transformed the phrase 'alien ineligible for citizenship' into a tool for discrimination against Japanese noncitizens, shows the ease with which discriminatory statutes can be drafted without explicit reference to race." *See* Lopez, *supra* note 312, at 141. By excluding Japanese immigrants from citizenship for racial reasons, the law could continue to discriminate against them without the need for any racial reference.

[314] BRIMELOW, *supra* note 6, at 270.

[315] *Id.*

[316] *Id.*

[317] *Id.*; *see also id.* at 274 (arguing that intermarriage cannot work "two ways" if it is to be effective, but must be of nonwhites into the white majority). Where all of this leaves African Americans is anybody's guess, but Brimelow provides no answer on that score. *See* Glazer, *supra* note 11, at 78 ("one reason [Brimelow] spends so little time on the issue [of the impact of immigration on blacks] is that he makes so much of the white and European ethnic and racial character of the American nation. He is therefore at a loss as to how to make his argument if he gives full weight to the fact that at its founding the nation was 20% black, and it is now 12% and modestly rising.").

[318] *See, e.g.*, BRIMELOW, *supra* note 6, at 215-16 (distinguishing today's immigrants from "the Orient" from nineteenth century Irish immigrants, because "Irish Americans have earned the hard way their right to opinions about who and how many their country can absorb."). Brimelow's argument fails factually, for large numbers of Irish and large numbers of Chinese arrived in America simultaneously.

[319] BRIMELOW, *supra* note 6, at xviii-xix, 209 (Constitution being designed to form a more perfect Union for "'ourselves and our posterity' — the Founder's posterity, not posterity in general.").

[320] Auster, *supra* note 3, at 175.

[321] Sympathetic readers of the manuscript version of this article have noted that this argument, though compelling, may be thought to cast doubt on historical rationales for affirmative action. Without addressing at length the different rationales for affirmative action, and the meaning of that debate, I accept the consequences of consistency here because I am convinced that contemporary rather than historical justifications for affirmative action are both more compelling and more likely to be held constitutional. Like the arguments about immigration, the arguments about affirmative action must take account of history in order to understand, not to blame.

[322] Brimelow concedes as much. BRIMELOW, *supra* note 6, at 76-84.

[323] Brimelow asserts that the 1965 Act discriminates against European immigrants. This claim is credible only if one accepts that the prior system — which intentionally and clearly discriminated in favor of European immigrants — was somehow neutral. *Id.* at 79.

[324] *See* Stephen Legomsky, *Immigration, Equality and Diversity*, 31 COLUM. J. TRANSNAT'L L. 319 (1993); COSE, *supra* note 15, at 195-208 (discussing legislative history of "diversity" lottery).

[325] Immigration and Nationality Act Amendments of 1965 (INA), Pub. L. No. 89-236, § 203(c), 79 Stat. 911, *codified* at 8 U.S.C. § 1152 (1988).

"Diversity" benefiting whites in immigration and "diversity" benefiting any particular group in affirmative action share an equally weak justification. If proportionate representation were the only goal, diversity should benefit whites in immigration. But given that proportionate representation as a sole measurement of racial justice has long since been rejected by the courts and abandoned as an argument for affirmative action, it cannot serve to justify "diversity" in immigration for groups already advantaged within the polity. Washington v. Davis, 426 U.S. 229 (1976); Wards Cove Packing Co. v. Atonio, 490 U.S. 642 (1989); William Bradford Reynolds, *Individualism vs. Group Rights: The Legacy of Brown*, 93 YALE L.J. 995 (1984); U.S. DEP'T OF JUSTICE, OFF. OF LEGAL POL'Y, REDEFINING DISCRIMINATION: "DISPARATE IMPACT" AND THE INSTITUTIONALIZATION OF AFFIRMATIVE ACTION (1988).

To be fair, Brimelow seems no happier about the benefits to Irish foreign nationals, because the lottery "pass[ed] up any chance to ensure that these immigrants met American needs," and he attacks Sen. Edward Kennedy for sponsoring the measure "above all for relatives of [his] Massachusetts constituents." BRIMELOW, *supra* note 6, at 83. Brimelow also acknowledges that the benefit to African foreign nationals was incidental rather than intentional. *Id.*

[326] 71 INTERP. REL. 451 (1994).

[327] *Cf.* Peter Schuck, *supra* note 64, at 44 ("In a democracy, demography is political destiny."). This is not to equate Peter Schuck with Peter Brimelow.

[328] *See* Neil Gotanda, *"Other Non-Whites" in American Legal History: A Review of Justice at War*, 85 COLUM. L. REV. 1186 (1985) and Neil Gotanda, *Asian American Rights and the "Miss Saigon Syndrome,"* in ASIAN AMERICANS AND THE SUPREME COURT: A DOCUMENTARY HISTORY 1087 (Hyung-chan Kim ed., 1992). In both articles, Professor Gotanda argues that Asian Americans have been cast in a citizen-foreigner paradigm rather than a black-white paradigm which makes it easier to approve of discrimination against them. *See, e.g.*, Korematsu v. United States, 323 U.S. 214 (1944).

[329] Alternatively, the success of attacks on affirmative action should make it much more difficult to sustain limits on immigration. As philosopher Frederick Whelan observes with a rhetorical question, classical liberalism would seem to prefer allocation of job opportunities based on merit "regardless of international borders or the nationality of the applicant." Whelan, *supra* note 56, at 8-9.

[330] *See* Louis Henkin, *Immigration and the Constitution: A Clean Slate*, 35 VA. J. INT'L L. 333, 333 (1994) ("[t]he ideology of our time is 'the rule of law' or, better, 'constitutionalism.'"). *Cf.* Koh, *Haiti Paradigm*, *supra* note 207, at 2398 (describing transnational public law litigation, which immigration cases may sometimes be, as exhibiting a distinctive feature: "the litigants' strategic awareness of the transportability of [transnational] norms" to domestic "political bargaining."); LEGOMSKY, *supra* note 63, at 273-80, 298-30 (discussing general theories of judicial review within constitutional democracy).

[331] CCRI will be replaced with a proposition number if it appears on the ballot. Prop. 187 started as "S.O.S." — "Save Our State" — the initials being interpreted in parodies very quickly.

[332] For analysis of the role of race in the Prop. 187 campaign, I have relied primarily on Johnson, *Race*, *supra* note 94; Kevin R. Johnson, *Civil Rights and Immigration: Challenges for the Latino Community in the Twenty-First Century*, 8 LA RAZA L.J. 42 (1995); Ignatius Bau, *Immigrant Rights: A Challenge to Asian Pacific American Political Influence*, 5 ASIAN AM. POL'Y REV. 7 (1995); William R. Tamayo, *When the Colored are Neither Black Nor Citizens: The United States Civil Rights Movement and Global Migration*, 2 ASIAN L.J. 1 (1995); Charles R. Lawrence, *Foreword: Race, Multi-Culturalism and the Jurisprudence of Transformation*, 47 STAN. L. REV. 819 (1995) (introduction to symposium issue on race and remedy in a multicultural society).

[333] For perspectives during the campaign on Prop. 187 and African Americans, see Kevin Ross, *Prop. 187, Is Brown-Latino Friction a Voting Booth Issue? Yes; The Initiative Is Horrible Legislation, But It's Still a Focal Point for Legitimate African American Resentments*, L.A. TIMES, Oct. 24, 1994, at B5; John W. Mack, *Prop. 187, Is Brown-Latino Friction a Voting Booth Issue? No; The Initiative's Backers Would Put All Minorities in the Same Boat; African Americans Won't Escape Harm*, L.A. TIMES, Oct. 24, 1994, at B7; Evelyn C. White, *Immigration a Tough Call for Blacks: Proposition 187 Debate Has Stirred Deep Feelings*, S.F. CHRON., Oct. 10, 1994, at A1.

[334] The role of Hispanics, to use the Census classification, renders the reversal somewhat incomplete, because they may be victims of Prop. 187 and CCRI. It may be that internal ethnic divisions and generational divisions among Hispanics, however, resemble the African American-Asian American tensions. *See* Johnson, *supra* note 332, at 65-72.

[335] Benjamin Pimentel, *Asian Americans' Awkward Status: Some Feel Whites Use Them as 'Racial Wedge' With Others*, S.F. CHRON., Aug. 22, 1995, at A1.

[336] *See* Wu, *supra* note 147; Dong, *supra* note 304.

[337] *See* Schuck & Wang, *supra* note 272 (empirical analysis of immigration litigation, both INS enforcement actions and affirmative challenges brought by immigrants showing rise over the time period studied).

[338] *See, e.g.*, American Baptist Churches v. Thornburgh, 760 F. Supp. 796 (N.D. Cal. 1991) (The ABC Case), *discussed in* Motomura, *Curious Evolution*, *supra* note 63, at 1675-78; Russell, *supra* note 103, at 51.

[339] While it should be unnecessary, along the lines of Brimelow's attempt to cloak himself in his immigrant status to preempt any argument that he is a racist, I point out that I am a native-born American citizen to dispel any suspicion that I may be biased by my status. In the interest of disclosure, I also mention that from June to September 1994 I worked as a full-time volunteer for Californians United Against Prop. 187, a grassroots campaign centered in the San Francisco Bay Area.

Partial Membership: Aliens and the Constitutional Community

*Michael Scaperlanda**

Abstract

In the midst of one of the largest waves of legal immigration in our nation's history, a strong anti-immigrant undertow threatens to pull us from our constitutional commitment to equality and from our national mythology of open arms and golden doors. The debates concerning noncitizens in the "public square" of the 1990s provide a good occasion and excellent backdrop for re-examining the noncitizen's status in our constitutional order.

Although noncitizens are "a discrete and insular minority" in need of heightened judicial protection, the U.S. Supreme Court has applied a panoply of standards when reviewing government actions that classify based on "alienage." The Court's review ranges from the strict scrutiny normally associated with suspect classifications to a near abdication of any judicial review responsibilities. Two paradigms emerge: membership and personhood.

The membership paradigm provides the baseline, unifying a seemingly incoherent alienage jurisprudence. When the Court perceives that a governmental entity is engaged in the process of communal formation, the Court applies a deferential "membership" standard allowing the political branches to go about their substantive work unencumbered by noncitizens' claims of constitutional protection. Where membership issues are absent, the Court shifts its focus to the rights of the individual noncitizen, more aggressively reviewing political choices under the "personhood" paradigm.

After examining these two paradigms and the complex set of doctrines developed within them, this Article explores membership's border. In the coming years, as litigation arises from renewed anti-immigrant legislation, this border will be critical. The Court confines state membership issues to questions of formation of the political community. In contrast, it reads federal membership issues expansively to include formation of the economic, social, and cultural community in addition to the political.

The federal membership cases are unpersuasively based on supposed unlimited and inherent sovereign powers. Here, I suggest that the Court, where it has not already done so, should make explicit that its federal alienage jurisprudence rests on the process of communal formation, not on unbridled and inherent governmental

---

* Professor of Law, University of Oklahoma College of Law. B.A., J.D., University of Texas. I am thankful to Kevin Johnson, Hiroshi Motomura, Gerald Neuman, Margaret Taylor, and the participants at the AALS Immigration Law Conference, Albuquerque, N.M., June 1994, for their insightful comments at earlier stages of this Article. Taraneh Astani, Myong Chun, and Michele Glenn-Seiger provided excellent research assistance.

power. Given judicial absence from the ongoing conversation concerning communal formation, I conclude that the public, which has the primary responsibility for ensuring that our membership rules are commensurate with our a priori commitments, should engage in constitutional dialogue concerning the place of noncitizens in the American community.

Table of Contents

Over a hundred poems are on the walls.
Looking at them, they are all pining at the delayed progress.
What can one sad person say to another?
Unfortunate travellers everywhere wish to commiserate.
Gain or lose, how is one to know what is predestined?
Rich or poor, who is to say it is not the will of heaven?
Why should one complain if he is detained and imprisoned here?
From ancient times, heroes often were the first ones to face adversity.[1]

I. INTRODUCTION

An anti-immigrant tide currently rages against this country's shores. Proposition 187, which denies illegal aliens access to publicly funded social services, nonemergency health care, and education, received overwhelming support from the voters of California in the 1994 elections.[2] Several states

---

1. Poem by One Named Xu, From Xiangshan, Consoling Himself, *in* Him Mark Lai et al., Island: Poetry and History of Chinese Immigrants on Angel Island 1910-1940 62 (HOC DOI 1980).

2. Proposition 187 passed by a margin of 59% to 41%. California Secretary of State, Statement of Vote, Nov. 8, 1994 115 (1994). Proposition 187's provisions can be found scattered throughout California's statutes. *See, e.g.*, Cal. Educ. Code § 48215 (West Supp. 1995) (excluding illegal alien children from public elementary and secondary schools); Cal. Educ. Code § 66010.8 (West Supp. 1995) (excluding illegal aliens from public post secondary schools); Cal. Health & Safety Code § 130 (West Supp. 1995) (excluding illegal aliens from publicly funded health care); Cal. Welf. & Inst. Code § 10001.5 (West Supp. 1995) (excluding illegal aliens from public social services). Several lawsuits have been filed in an attempt to overturn many of these provisions. *See, e.g.*, U.S. Judge Bars Enforcement of Anti-Immigration Measure, Wash. Post, Dec. 15, 1994, at A4 (declaring that California's Proposition 187 raises serious constitutional questions). For a thorough discussion of Proposition 187 and its provisions, see generally Kevin R. Johnson, Public Benefits and Immigration: The Intersection of Immigration Status, Ethnicity, Gender, and Class, 42 UCLA L. Rev. 1509 (1995). *See also* Carl E. Goldfarb, Note, Allocating the Local Apportionment Pie: What Portion for Resident Aliens?, 104 Yale L.J. 1441, 1463-1470 (1995) (arguing that states may not constitutionally single out legal aliens in apportionment plans); Note, Unenforced Boundaries: Illegal Immigration and the Limits of Judicial Federalism, 108 Harv. L. Rev. 1643 (1995) (arguing that illegal immigration unfairly burdens certain states). Several other states are contemplating Proposition 187 type legislation. *See, e.g.*, 1995 Fla. House Bill No. 476, Fla 1995 Reg. Sess. (prohibiting adult illegal aliens from receiving public social services); 1995 Fla. House Bill No. 245, Fla 1995 Reg. Sess. (prohibiting illegal aliens from receiving "any public social services or benefits"); N.Y. Senate Bill No. 3092, N.Y. 218th Gen. Assmebly, 1st Reg. Sess. (excluding illegal aliens from receiving public health benefits); N.Y. Senate Bill No. 3090, N.Y. 218th Gen. Assmebly, 1st Reg. Sess. (excluding illegal aliens from public elementary and secondary schools); 1995 N.Y. Senate Bill No. 3089, N.Y. 218th Gen. Assembly, 1st Reg. Sess. (excluding illegal aliens from public post-secondary education). Texas, the state with the longest southern border, has not followed California's anti-immigrant lead. Governor George Bush of Texas

have sued the federal government, alleging that lack of border enforcement has cost the states millions of dollars in services provided to illegal aliens.[3] Extending beyond disdain for the undocumented, the current anti-immigrant backlash blurs the distinction between legal and illegal migration, stigmatizing legal permanent resident aliens who have settled here with permission and have begun the process of becoming full members in our national community.[4] This backlash also threatens our national commitment to generous and orderly legal immigration. Welfare reform proposals in Congress would exclude aliens from eligibility for welfare benefits and would allow states to adopt similar discriminatory restrictions.[5] Other proposals would restrict the administrative and judicial process for some aliens facing deportation.[6] Still other potential legislation would restructure the number and characteristics of noncitizens allowed to immigrate to the United States.[7] Proposals have even been introduced to amend the Constitution to restrict the birthright citizenship granted by the Fourteenth Amendment.[8]

---

stated: "We will tolerate no bashing of Mexico or immigrants." Anti-Immigrant Talk Angers Texas Governor, Wash. Post, Aug. 11, 1995, at A7; *see* Roberto Suro, Two Political Realities: Immigration Effect—Texas, California, Wash. Post, Oct. 27, 1994, at A25 (stating that because Texas has a different political, cultural, and historical relationship with immigrants, "in Texas illegal immigration does not produce the kind of outrage that has so thoroughly inflamed politics in California").

3. Arizona, California, Florida, New Jersey, New York, and Texas have sued the federal government seeking reimbursement for the cost of services provided to illegal aliens, claiming that the federal government failed to properly secure the border. *See, e.g.*, Reimbursement Denied, Wash. Post, Feb. 14, 1995, at A11 (dismissing California suit); *see also* Padavan v. United States, 82 F.3d 23 (2nd Cir. 1996) (holding New York's suit failed to state a claim upon which relief could be granted); Chiles v. United States, 874 F. Supp. 1334 (S.D. Fla. 1994) (dismissing Florida's lawsuit). Additionally, nonjudicial avenues may be available to states seeking reimbursement. Several bills have been introduced in Congress that would reimburse states for various expenditures associated with an immigrant population. *See, e.g.*, H.R. 205, 104th Cong., 1st Sess. (1995) (reimbursing state and local governments for the cost of imprisoning deportable criminals).

4. *See* U.S. Commission on Immigration Reform, U.S. Immigration Policy: Restoring Credibility, 1994 Executive Summary 2 1995 ("[F]ailure to develop effective strategies to control unlawful immigration has blurred the public perception of the distinction between legal and illegal immigrants.").

5. *See, e.g.*, H.R. 605, 104th Cong., 1st Sess. (1995) (requiring certain legal aliens to reside in the United States for five consecutive years to be eligible for preferential public housing and rental assistance); H.R. 4, 104th Cong., 1st Sess. § 402 (1995) (restricting permanent resident alien eligibility under several welfare programs and authorizing states to follow suit as part of comprehensive welfare reform).

6. *See, e.g.*, S. 735, 104th Cong., 1st Sess. (1995) (authorizing partially secret deportation proceedings); S. 269, 104th Cong., 1st Sess. (1995) (restricting judicial review of deportation orders).

7. *See, e.g.*, H.R. 373, 104th Cong., 1st Sess. (1995) (proposing an immigration moratorium, narrowing the scope of both family-sponsored and employment-based immigrants, decreasing family-sponsored immigration from a maximum of 226,000 to 10,000 persons a year and employment-based immigration from 140,000 to 5,000 persons a year, and eliminating the diversity immigrant category).

8. *See, e.g.*, H.R.J. Res. 64, 104th Cong., 1st Sess. (1995) (restricting birthright citizenship

This phenomenon is not new. Although we are, in many respects, a nation of immigrants, xenophobia and nativism have afflicted us in times past, manifest in different ways at different times.[9] Additionally, genuine dialogue concerned with developing an immigration policy consistent with our national interest has ebbed and flowed over the last century.[10] During these periods of robust—and sometimes nasty—debate, the judiciary was often called upon to mediate between the interests of the government and the rights of the noncitizen. In response, the Supreme Court developed a rich, complex, and seemingly incoherent jurisprudence of the noncitizen. The current national and regional debate on immigration policy serves as a timely backdrop for re-examining the constitutional status of the noncitizen.

Alienage jurisprudence operates within at least five separate distinct levels of judicial review ranging from strict scrutiny to something approaching the nonjusticiability of the political question doctrine.[11] At

---

to children of mothers who are legal residents); H.R.J. Res. 56, 104th Cong., 1st Sess. (1995) (restricting birthright citizenship to children of legal residents). Other proposals would eliminate birthright citizenship by statute. *See* H.R. 1363, 104th Cong., 1st Sess. (1995) (children born in the United States to parents who are not citizens or permanent resident aliens are not "subject to the jurisdiction of the United States" and not automatic citizens); H.R. 375, 104th Cong., 1st Sess. 301 (1995) (declaring that children born to illegal alien mothers are not born "subject to the jurisdiction of the United States"). For an argument that a constitutional amendment is not necessary to deny birthright citizenship to children of illegal aliens, see Peter H. Schuck & Rogers M. Smith, Citizenship Without Consent 116 (1985) (arguing for a "reinterpretation of the Citizenship Clause of the Fourteenth Amendment. Its guarantee of citizenship to those born 'subject to the jurisdiction' of the United States should be read to . . . refer only to children of those legally admitted to permanent residence in the American community"). *See generally* Robert J. Shulman, Children of a Lesser God: Should the Fourteenth Amendment be Altered or Repealed to Deny Automatic Citizenship Rights and Privileges to American Born Children of Illegal Aliens?, 22 Pepp. L. Rev. 669 (1995); Note, The Birthright Citizenship Amendment: A Threat to Equality, 107 Harv. L. Rev. 1026 (1994).

9. *See, e.g.*, Richard O. Curry & Thomas M. Brown, Conspiracy: The Fear of Subversion in American History (1972) (presenting a collection of essays on American xenophobia); Roger Daniels, Anti-Chinese Violence in North America (1978) (presenting a collection of previously printed essays); Alexander Saxton, The Indispensable Enemy: Labor and the Anti-Chinese Movement in California (1971) (exploring the expansive effect of California's treatment of the "indispensable enemy," which permeated the political and economic scene throughout the country).

10. *Cf.* U.S. Commission on Immigration Reform, supra note 4, at 1:

> The Commission decries hostility and discrimination against immigrants as antithetical to the traditions and interests of the country. At the same time, we disagree with those who would label efforts to control immigration as being inherently anti-immigrant. Rather, it is both a right and a responsibility of a democratic society to manage immigration so that it serves the national interests.

11. When a state entity classifies persons on the basis of alienage, the classification will normally be reviewed under the "strict scrutiny" standard, and the state classification will be struck down. *See* infra notes 215-32 and accompanying text. (discussing the review of classification under the "strict scrutiny" standard). When, however, the state engages in the sovereign function of defining its political community, the Court abandons strict scrutiny

one extreme, the Court treats aliens as a "discrete and insular" minority entitled to heightened judicial protection.[12] At the other end of the spectrum, the Court allows the political branches broad policy making discretion, while consciously discarding long standing constitutional principles.[13] These two opposing approaches—strict scrutiny and unbridled discretion— reflect the tenuous position occupied by noncitizens within the American constitutional community.

In exploring this tension, I offer a model that attempts to pull the multifarious strands of the alienage jurisprudence into a unified whole.[14] For all of its doctrinal complexity, the Court frames alienage cases around two broad categories: one marked by extreme deference to the political branches of government, and the other, in stark contrast, marked by heightened suspicion of invidious governmental action. I refer to these

---

review, preferring to defer to the state's lawmakers with a modified "rational basis review." *See* infra notes 159-68 and accompanying text. When faced with a state classification denying illegal alien children a free public education, the Court employed intermediate scrutiny to strike down the law. *See* infra notes 233-54 and accompanying text (analyzing the application of the intermediate scrutiny standard in the realm of denying alien children access to tuition-free public education). Most federal alienage classifications are upheld pursuant to standards of review that grant unusual deference to the judgment of the political branches of the national government. When the federal government acts with respect to core immigration issues, the Court's deference is at its greatest, bordering on nonjusticiability under the guise of the "political question" doctrine. *See* infra notes 80-123 and accompanying text. Aside from issues of admission, exclusion, and expulsion of aliens, the Court remains extremely deferential, applying rational basis review to federal alienage classifications. *See* infra notes 124-45 and accompanying text (discussing the application of the "rational basis" standard in classifying aliens). When, however, the federal government attempts to treat aliens differently with respect to certain civil and criminal procedural rights, the Court is much less deferential. *See* infra notes 183-205 and accompanying text (discussing situations where procedural rights trump membership concerns).

12. *See, e.g.*, Graham v. Richardson, 403 U.S. 365, 372 (1971) ("[A]liens as a class are a prime example of a 'discrete and insular' minority for whom such heightened judicial solicitude is appropriate." (citation omitted)).

13. *See, e.g.*, Reno v. Flores, 507 U.S. 292, 305-06 (1993); Kleindienst v. Mandel, 408 U.S. 753 (1972) (holding that the Attorney General may exclude aliens who advocate "the economic, international, and governmental doctrines of world communism").

14. It is here that I first part company with fellow travelers who, like me, are attempting to make sense of our alienage jurisprudence. Alex Aleinikoff states that "the two lines of cases are not part of a coherent whole, but rather reflect conflicting strands in our constitutionalism: one concerned with affirming the importance of membership in the national community; the other pursuing a notion of fundamental human rights that protects individuals regardless of their status." T. Alexander Aleinikoff, Citizens, Aliens, Membership and the Constitution, 7 Const. Commentary 9, 19 (1990) [hereinafter Alienikoff, Citizens]; *see, e.g.*, Linda S. Bosniak, Membership, Equality, and the Difference Alienage Makes, 69 N.Y.U. L. Rev. 1047, 1056 (1994) [hereinafter Bosniak, Membership, Equality, and Difference (contending "that the law has contructed alienage as a hybrid legal status category that lies at the nexus of two legal - and moral - worlds. It lies, first of all, in the world of borders, sovereignty, and national community membership; . . . [it] also lies in the world of social relationships among territorially present persons"). Although I agree that these two traditions grow out of conflicting constitutional origins, the argument that I develop in this Article is that an overarching principle exists that draws them together into a coherent whole.

categories as the membership[15] and personhood[16] paradigms, respectively.

Although many others have contrasted these seemingly inconsistent traditions, they usually distinguish immigration law—the law of admission, exclusion, and expulsion[17]–from the larger alienage jurisprudence.[18] To

---

15. Membership as used here encompasses those issues faced by a sovereign people as they struggle with issues of communal formation, in determining the characteristics of those who would be desirable newcomers to the community. It also includes issues of preservation of the community from external threats. Professor Aleinikoff has argued that "constitutional norms defining the federal immigration power are shaped by a membership model of citizenship and alienage." *See* Aleinikoff, Citizens, supra note 14, at 9-10 (suggesting that permanent resident aliens be considered members of the national community and arguing that the federal immigration power ought to be decoupled from membership notions and reconceptualized as "one of many powers Congress exercises in pursuit of the national welfare"); *see also* Peter H. Schuck, The Transformation of Immigration Law, 84 Colum. L. Rev. 1, 54-58 (1984) (viewing Plyler v. Doe, 457 U.S. 202 (1982), as plausibly a judicially mandated expansion of "the national community" to persons who are unlawfully present in the Untied States).

In the interest of clarity, I should note my use of the term "membership" differs from the use of others who write in this area. For them, the membership concept provides a tool or a rationale for inclusion, supplying an argument that noncitizens who have gained entrance and developed ties to the United States should receive a portion of the benefits of membership. *See, e.g.*, Linda S. Bosniak, Exclusion and Membership: The Dual Identity of the Undocumented Worker Under United States Law, 1988 Wis. L. Rev. 955, 1042 (1988) ("[W]e must acknowledge [the undocumented's] vital place in the community."); David A. Martin, Due Process and Membership in the National Community: Political Asylum and Beyond, 44 U. Pitt. L. Rev. 165, 201 (1983) (arguing that the Court's due process analysis should reflect that "notions of membership in the national community" are more complex and multi-layered than can be captured in the concept of citizenship alone). In contrast, I use "membership" as a shorthand way of expressing the judiciary's reluctance to interfere with the membership choices made by the political community. *Cf.* Bosniak, Membership, Equality and Difference, supra note 14, at 1057 n.28 (now characterizing "the sphere of membership" as encompassing "border regulation, or admission").

16. Personhood denotes constitutional status. Persons have constitutional rights, nonpersons do not. *See* Roe v. Wade, 410 U.S. 113, 156-57 (1973) (conceding that its holding that the constitutional right to privacy encompassed the right to terminate pregnancy collapses if the fetus is a "person"); *cf.* Scott v. Sandford, 60 U.S. 393, 407 (1856) (holding that when the Constitution was adopted, African-Americans were not considered "people" and thus the protection of the Constitution did not apply to them, even if they were free). Where the Court's emphasis is on the noncitizen as a constitutionally constituted person, it takes seriously the alien's claim to constitutional protection. *See, e.g.*, Michael Scaperlanda, Justice Thurgood Marshall and the Legacy of Dissent in Federal Alienage Cases, 8 Geo. Immigr. L.J. 1, 3-4 (1994) (identifying the *Yick Wo* and *Graham* cases as models of the personhood approach).

17. *See, e.g.*, Stephen H. Legomsky, Immigration Law and the Principle of Plenary Congressional Power, 1984 Sup. Ct. Rev. 255, 256 [hereinafter Legomsky, Plenary Congressional Power] ("For purposes of my argument, the term 'immigration law' will be used to describe the body of law governing the admission and exclusion of aliens. That is the sphere in which plenary power has operated. It should be distinguished from the more general law of aliens' rights and obligations.").

18. *See, e.g.*, Legomsky, supra note 18, at 256 (distinguishing alienage jurisprudence, which includes alien eligibility for social programs, certain forms of employment, or special legal duties, from immigration law, which is concerned only with the admission, expulsion,

them, "the stunted growth of constitutional immigration law contrasts sharply with the flowering of constitutional protections for aliens in areas other than immigration law."[19] I agree with them that the judiciary's refusal to "review federal immigration statutes for compliance with substantive constitutional restraints"[20] makes immigration law a "constitutional oddity."[21]

Immigration law, with its "plenary power doctrine,"[22] however, provides only one part of this complex puzzle. The sharp contrast does not exist between immigration law, "in its strict sense,"[23] and the larger alienage jurisprudence. In my analysis, the contrast lies between the law of membership, which transcends the immigration field,[24] and those alienage cases where membership issues are absent.

While I agree that plenary power marks the outer edges of the deferential membership paradigm, the constitutional anomaly it creates, far from being cabined within immigration law, pervades the entire alienage jurisprudence.[25]

Professor Bosniak succinctly illuminates this point.[26] She argues that the traditional analysis, with its focus on whether a case is "inside" or "outside" immigration law, "tends to obscure the complex and contested nature of the status of aliens." [27]Like me,[28] she recognizes that "wholly

---

and exclusion of aliens).

19. *See, e.g.*, Hiroshi Motomura, The Curious Evolution of Immigration Law: Procedural Surrogates for Substantive Constitutional Rights, 92 Colum. L. Rev. 1625, 1626 (1992); *see also* Legomsky, Plenary Congressional Power, supra note 17, at 256 (terming the difference a "mild contrast").

20. Id. at 255.

21. Id.

22. Plenary power allows the political branches of the federal government to formulate immigration policy without "constitutional limitations." *See, e.g.*, Lenni B. Benson, By Hook or By Crook: Exploring the Legality of an INS Sting Operation, 31 San Diego L. Rev. 813, 839 n.124 (1994); Louis Henkin, The Constitution and the United States Sovereignty: A Century of Chinese Exclusion and its Progeny, 100 Harv. L. Rev. 853, 859 (1987); Legomsky, Plenary Congressional Power, supra note 17, at 255; Michael Scaperlanda, Polishing the Tarnished Golden Door, 1993 Wis. L. Rev. 965, 967 (1993) [hereinafter Scaperlanda, Polishing]; Margaret Taylor, Detained Aliens Challenging Conditions of Confinement and the Porous Border of the Plenary Power, 22 Hastings Const. L.Q. 1087, 1128 (1995).

23. Legomsky, Plenary Congressional Power, supra note 17, at 256.

24. Membership and membership's deference even apply to the review of state laws affecting the formation of the state's political community. *See* infra text accompanying notes 159-68.

25. *See* Scaperlanda, Polishing, supra note 22, at 994-1002 (exploring the expansion of plenary power to issues of noncitizen entitlement to welfare and Fourth Amendment rights of noncitizens); Taylor, supra note 22, at 1153-56 (exploring plenary power's subconscious influence on cases involving conditions at noncitizen detention facilities).

26. Bosniak, Membership, Equality, and Difference, supra note 14, at 1056-58.

27. Id. at 1058.

28. In an earlier article, I stated that "[o]utside the immigration context, in the context of economic opportunity, the Court has spurned the *Yick Wo* [personhood] tradition in favor of allowing the executive branch and Congress broad powers to discriminate against lawfully resident aliens." Scaperlanda, Polishing, supra note 22, at 996, 971 n.20 ("The political

apart from questions of admission, expulsion and naturalization, the law continues to treat alienage as the rightful basis for less favorable treatment of persons in a variety of contexts, notwithstanding the *Yick Wo* tradition."[29] To account for this complexity, she envisions the alienage jurisprudence more broadly as involving a "'jurisdictional' dispute" between "the domains of membership and equal personhood."[30]

Bosniak views the "defining question"[31] as "whether government treatment of aliens beyond the border broadly construed–beyond questions of admission, exclusion, deportation, and naturalization–is itself to be viewed as an incident or extension of the immigration power. To the extent that the immigration power is understood to represent the power to define membership in the national community, how far does that power extend? Does it extend to regulation of the status of aliens in the economic, social and political spheres of life within our society?"[32] *Membership, Equality, and the Difference that Alienage Makes* provides a useful framework for structuring the debate. Bosniak, however, does not venture an answer to her question beyond the observation that "the cases will likely turn on the question of where immigration—or membership—regulation legitimately begins and ends. Percisely how the courts will respond is, of course uncertain."[33] In thiArticle, I attempt to answer the question by suggesting an expansive reading of membership.

The membership and personhood traditions collapse into a unified whole[34] because of the Court's approach to prioritizing these categories.

---

branches of the federal government have the broadest power over aliens in the immigration context, but even outside this context, the Court has afforded the political branches great latitude.").

29. Bosniak, Membership, Equality, and Difference, supra note 14, at 1064.

30. Id. at 1056-57 ("To what degree, in short, is the status of aliens to be understood as a matter of national borders, to what degree a matter of personhood, and how are we to tell the difference?").

31. 'Id. at 1143 ("The defining question in the current politics of alien status is just how far the government's power to regulate immigration legitimately extends.").

32. Id. at 1094. Bosniak reformulates this question several times throughout the article. *E.g.*, id. at 1055 ("What legitimate bearing should the country's interests in regulating immigration have on the general treatment of aliens in our society?"); id. at 1067 ("What are the contours of that body of law we call immigration law; where does it legitimately begin and end? Likewise, what are the parameters of the law regulating alien status beyond immigration law; where does it end and begin?"); id. at 1087 ("What is the legitimate scope, or jurisdiction, of the membership sphere? When do membership principles appropriately shape the status of aliens residing within the national community, and when is their status subject instead to broad principles associated with the 'sphere of equal personhood.'").

33. Id. at 1148 ("Given the judiciary's change in personnel in recent years, many observers predict things will go badly for the immigrants."). Descriptively, Bosniak views the law as having one of two responses to the question of membership's reach: (1) the "convergence" model treats membership broadly, extending beyond immigration issues to "the regulation of social relationships among all territorially present persons;" and (2) the "seperation" model maintains a restrictive view of membership and "urges a relatively strict separation between the membership domain and the domain of territorial personhood." Id. at 1138.

34. Process values, however, do not fall within this unified model. *See* infra text

Where membership issues are present, the Court categorically ignores or severely discounts the noncitizen's interests, deferring instead to the policy developed by the political arms of government.[35] When, however, membership issues are absent, the Court generally heightens its scrutiny allowing the noncitizen's personhood to trump any asserted state interest.[36] Simply put, membership interests trump and render negatory any substantive rights claimed by aliens. Sections II-IV sketch the development of these paradigms and explore the doctrinal framework that brings them out of formless abstraction and into concrete law.

My thesis is that membership provides the baseline norm governing all aspects of our alienage jurisprudence, with the personhood tradition subordinated to a secondary status. Assuming no change from the judiciary, it is imperative in this time of fervent immigration debate for the political branches to explore membership's borders to determine what interests legitimately belong in the membership category and what interests are more properly addressed within the personhood framework. For the most part, the Court has taken an expansive view of membership. At the federal level, all issues pertaining to entry into the social, economic, and political community fall within membership's parameters.[37] The state cases reflect shifting notions of membership. At one time the membership paradigm applied to the distribution of the state's resources,[38] but today it operates solely within the context of a state's attempt to form its political community.[39] Even here, the Court defers to any state policy choice that is arguably within the state's interest in communal formation. Section V explores the parameters of the membership paradigm.

Finally, in Section VI, I look to the rhetoric used to construct the membership paradigm. State membership cases are built on the affirmative responsibility of the people to form a political community. In contrast, the federal membership cases rest on a negative, unwritten, absolute, and even arbitrary power of the governing bodies to set policy. If the membership paradigm remains as the cornerstone of our alienage jurisprudence, and there is no indication otherwise, the community building rationale of the

---

accompanying notes 182-205.

35. *See* infra text accompanying notes 76-168.

36. *See* infra notes 206-53 and accompanying text (describing cases where aliens receive heightened judicial scrutiny).

37. For instance, outside the immigration context, the federal government can deny noncitizens welfare benefits. Mathews v. Diaz, 426 U.S. 67, 85 (1976). *See* infra notes 124-32 and accompanying text.

38. For instance, a state could prohibit noncitizens from hunting the wildlife found within the state. Patsone v. Pennsylvania, 232 U.S. 138, 145-46 (1914). *See* infra notes 146-53 and accompanying text (pointing out the constitutionality of a state's ability to reserve its resources only for its citizens).

39. For example, states can bar aliens from serving as public school teachers because teachers perform functions that are central to a state's political identity. Ambach v. Norwick, 441 U.S. 68, 76-82 (1979). *See* infra notes 160-69 and accompanying text (describing the jobs that are excluded from being performed by aliens due to the position's political function).

state cases provides the better model for two reasons. First, it fits more squarely with our democratic traditions than a rationale rooted in the "powers inherent in sovereignty." Second, it explicitly signals to the community's members that they assume the responsibility for fulfilling or undermining constitutional values in the realm of communal formation.[40] The Court's deferential membership policy has clearly left to the People, as members of the national community, not only the opportunity, but more importantly the responsibility, to participate in the building of a membership scheme that reflects the nation's constitutional values and aspirations. In substance, the Court has refused this role.[41] We the People must accept the challenge or lose, for this generation, coherence between our membership goals and our constitutional commitments.[42]

---

40. "Judges are not the only constitutional decisionmakers in the United States. It is necessary, therefore, to move beyond widespread preoccupation with the Constitution's *judicial* interpretation and enforcement." Wayne D. Moore, Reconceiving Interpretative Autonomy: Insights From the Virginia and Kentucky Resolutions, 11 Const. Comm. 315, 315 (1994); *see, e.g.*, Cass R. Sunstein, The Partial Constitution 350 (1994):

> [T]he identification of constitutional law with the decisions of the Supreme Court is a damaging and ahistorical mistake. This identification, fueled by the Warren Court, is inconsistent with the democratic goals of the American constitutional tradition. Those goals call for nonjudicial actors—Congress, the President, state officials, ordinary citizens—to engage in deliberation about the meaning of the Constitution's broad guarantees.

41. Some would say that the Court has abdicated its responsibility. *See* Henkin, supra note 22, at 854 (concluding that "courts are prepared to abdicate their responsibility to ensure that the executive act in conformity with international law"). Although the Court refuses to reconcile plenary power with the constitutional rights tradition, it continues to arrogate to itself the constitutional decision making power. Instead of committing immigration issues to the judicial nadir of the political question doctrine and admitting that it has neither the tools nor the will to respond to constitutional issues arising in this context, it concludes that the Congressional exercise of the immigration power, no matter how far removed from our constitutional norms, is constitutional. *See, e.g., Mathews*, 426 U.S. at 81-82 ("The reasons that preclude judicial review of political questions also dictate a narrow standard of review of decisions made by the Congress or the President in the area of immigration and naturalization.") (footnote omitted).

42. This task is not new. The founding generation struggled profoundly with the application of our constitutional values toward noncitizens. Prior to Marbury v. Madison, 5 U.S. (1 Cranch) 137 (1803), and the establishment of judicial review of constitutional issues, Congress passed the Alien Act of 1798, ch. 58 § 1, 1 Stat. 570, (1798) (authorizing the President to deport aliens he considers dangerous to the United States). Madison argued against the constitutionality of the Act. *See* 4 Jonathan Elliot, The Debates in the Several State Conventions on the Adoption of the Federal Constitution 554-56 (1881) (2d ed. 1866) ("If aliens had no rights under the Constitution, they might not only be banished, but even capitally punished, without a jury or the other incidents to a fair trial."). Virginia and Kentucky passed resolutions condemning the Alien Act and its sibling, the Sedition Act. Kentucky Resolutions of 1798 and 1799, *reprinted in* 4 Elliot, supra, at 540-45; Virginia Resolutions of 1798, *reprinted in* 4 Elliot, supra, at 528-32 (pronouncing the Alien and Sedition Acts unconstitutional and "defining the rights of the states"). With the benefit of robust constitutional dialogue, the Act expired after two years. *See* Charles Gordon & Stanley Mailman, Immigration Law and Procedure § 2.02 (1) (1994) ("[T]he Alien Act of 1798 . . . was allowed to expire at the end of its two-year term.").

II. A CONFLICT OF TRADITIONS

Like the noncitizen, the Court finds itself straddling two worlds, the one rooted in individual rights (whether the rights tradition of the Founders or the one created by the Court in the Warren era) and the other deeply concerned with communal formation. From the time the Supreme Court first involved itself with immigration issues,[43] it's alienage jurisprudence has produced two distinct traditions. Two cases from the foundational period in federal jurisprudence—*Yick Wo v. Hopkins* and *Fong Yue Ting v. United States*—illuminate both the personhood tradition and the membership tradition.[44]

Yick Wo v. Hopkins[45] illustrates the founding of the personhood tradition. Long before the Equal Protection Clause provided meaningful protection for Blacks,[46] the Court utilized it to protect aliens of Chinese origin. *Yick Wo* involved a San Francisco ordinance requiring a special permit to operate a laundry in any structure not made of brick or stone. The city granted permits to eighty non-Chinese nationals, but denied them to the more than two hundred Chinese nationals who applied.[47] In concluding that the discriminatory application of the ordinance violated the Equal Protection Clause, the Court stated:

> The rights of the petitioners . . . are not less because they are aliens and subjects of the Emperor of China. . . . The Fourteenth Amendment to the Constitution is not confined to the protection of citizens. . . . [Its] provisions are universal in their application, to all persons within the territorial jurisdiction, without regard to

43. My analysis begins with cases decided in the 1880s, which mark the genesis of the two lines of cases that I refer to as the membership and personhood traditions. Prior to that time, immigration restrictions were largely matters of state law. Professor Gerald Neuman has brought this "lost century" to life in a thorough historical analysis. *See generally* Gerald L. Neuman, The Lost Century of American Immigration Law (1776-1875), 93 Colum. L. Rev. 1833 (1993) (examining the major categories of state immigration law during the first century of American history).

44. For an article exploring three periods of profound judicial activity reviewing federal action adversely affecting noncitizens, see generally Scaperlanda, Polishing, supra note 22, at 975. The foundational period was marked by judicial acquiescence to racially discriminatory congressional immigration policies. Id. at 976-84. The entrenchment period witnessed a similar acquiescence to ideological discrimination. Id. at 984-91. In the modern period, the court has held steadfast to its doctrines of the past, transcending the border to encompass issues outside of the core immigration concerns of admission, exclusion, and expulsion. Id. at 991-1002.

45. 118 U.S. 356 (1886).

46. *See, e.g.*, Plessy v. Ferguson, 163 U.S. 537 (1896) (upholding Louisiana statute requiring "equal but separate" accommodations on passenger railroads); The Civil Rights Cases, 109 U.S. 3 (1883) (striking down civil rights law that required "equal enjoyment" of privately owned public accommodations on the ground that the Fourteenth Amendment only protected against state, not private, discrimination). *But see* Strauder v. West Virginia, 100 U.S. 303 (1879) (striking down state statute that barred blacks from serving on juries).

47. *Yick Wo*, 118 U.S. at 374.

> any differences of race, of color, or of nationality . . . .[48]

Yick Wo, together with *Wong Wing v. United States,*[49] established the personhood tradition: noncitizens, "having our common humanity, . . . are protected by all the guaranties of the Constitution."[50] Under this tradition, the constitutional rights[51] of the individual, including the noncitizen, restrict the power of the government to act.[52]

Fong Yue Ting, in contrast, ignores the possible constitutional rights of the noncitizen, subordinating any such interests to Congress's plenary power to expel those not possessing membership in the national community. This case illustrates the founding of the membership tradition. In *Fong Yue Ting,* three Chinese laborers, who had resided in the United States for nineteen, sixteen, and fourteen years, respectively,[53] faced deportation for failure to obtain the requisite certificate of residence.[54] In affirming the deportation orders, the Court explored the nature of the noncitizens' rights and the federal government's power to expel. The Court concluded that the power to expel, like the power to exclude, derives from international law and is an "absolute and unqualified" power "inherent in [a nation's] sovereignty."[55] Therefore, if:

> the government of the United States, through its legislative department, considers the presence of foreigners of a different

---

48. Id. at 368-69.

49. 163 U.S. 228, 238 (1896) (stating that aliens are "persons" and are protected by the Fifth Amendment).

50. Fong Yue Ting v. United States, 149 U.S. 698, 754 (1893) (Field, J., dissenting).

51. At times I refer to constitutional rights as constitutional first principles or *a priori* commitments because "[t]he strident rights rhetoric that currently dominates American political discourse poorly serves the strong tradition of protection for individual freedom for which the United States is justly renowned." Mary A. Glendon, Rights Talk: The Impoverishment of Political Discourse 171 (1991) ("Our stark, simple rights dialect puts a damper on the processes of public justification, communication, and deliberation upon which the continuing vitality of a democratic regime depends."). Id.

52. This point might seem obvious outside of the alienage context. The right to be free from governmental racial discrimination restricts the power of the government, prohibiting race based policy choices. *See, e.g.,* Adarand Constructors, Inc. v. Pena, 115 S. Ct. 2097, 2100 (1995) ("[A]ny person, of whatever race, has the right to demand that any governmental actor subject to the Constitution justify any racial classification subjecting that person to unequal treatment under the strictest judicial scrutiny."). The right to freely express oneself restricts the governmental power to prohibit an offensive demonstration. *See, e.g.,* R.A.V. v. City of St. Paul, 505 U.S. 377, 382 (1992) ("The First Amendment generally prevents government from proscribing speech.").

53. Interestingly, this period was "almost as long a time as some of those who were members of the Congress that passed this act of punishment and expulsion." *Fong Yue Ting,* 149 U.S. at 734 (Brewer, J., dissenting).

54. Id. at 702-04. In one of the cases, the petitioner had proved, to the satisfaction of the judge, that he had resided in the United States for a time sufficient to be eligible for a certificate; he was held deportable, however, because the proof was not established by the testimony of a "credible white witness," which was required by statute. Id. at 704.

55. Id. at 705, 707.

> race in this country, who will not assimilate with us, to be dangerous to its peace and security, their exclusion is not to be stayed because at the time there are not actual hostilities with the nation of which the foreigners are subjects.[56]

Values of communal formation and protection, with deference to the political branches' judgment on the ability of foreign peoples to assimilate and on their potential threat as outsiders to the security and stability of the nation, proved determinative.

The majority dismissed the noncitizens' constitutional claims holding that "aliens residing in the United States . . . are entitled, so long as they are permitted by the . . . United States to remain . . . , to the safeguards of the constitution . . . ."[57] In other words, Congress may expel aliens—because of their lack of membership in the community—whenever it decides that their removal is in the public interest.[58] The Court distinguished *Yick Wo* and the personhood tradition: *Yick Wo* addressed the constitutional limits to a state's power over continually residing noncitizens; *Fong Yue Ting*, in contrast, addressed the federal government's plenary power "to put an end to their residence."[59]

The three dissenting opinions strongly rejected the creation of the membership tradition and its divergence from *Yick Wo's* personhood tradition. These justices found inherent sovereign powers antithetical to the structure of our form of government.[60] Even assuming that the power to expel is "among the powers implied," the dissent suggests, "it can be exercised only in subordination to the limitations and restrictions imposed by the constitution."[61] Further, the Bill of Rights generally, and the Fifth Amendment specifically, limit the scope of federal power; therefore, the federal immigration power must succumb to the limitations imposed by those first amendments. If not, the dissent asserts, the guarantees of the Constitution belong to noncitizens "by sufferance and not of right."[62]

---

56. Id. at 706 (quoting Chae Chan Ping v. United States, 130 U.S. 581, 606 (1889).

57. Id. at 724.

58. *Fong Yue Ting*, 149 U.S. at 724.

59. Id. at 725.

60. Id. at 737-38 (Brewer, J., dissenting); 757-58 (Field, J., dissenting); 762 (Fuller, C.J., dissenting).

61. Id. at 738 (Brewer, J., dissenting). Chief Justice Fuller, in his dissent, recited the majority's argument "that friendly aliens, who have lawfully acquired a domicil [sic] in this country, are entitled to avail themselves of the safeguards of the constitution only while permitted to remain, and that the power to expel them and the manner of its exercise are unaffected by that instrument." Id. at 762. For him—and me—"[i]t is difficult to see how this can be so . . . [because it] import[s] a condition not recognized by the fundamental law." Id.

62. Id. at 743 (Brewer, J., dissenting).

> [Noncitizens] differ only from citizens in that they cannot vote or hold any public office. As men having our common humanity, they are protected by all the guaranties of the constitution. To hold that they are subject to any different law or are less protected in any particular than other persons, is in my judgment to ignore the teachings of our history, the practice of our government, and the language of our Constitution.

For these dissenters, *Yick Wo* established the authoritative precedent.

> If the use of the word "person" in the fourteenth amendment protects all individuals lawfully within the state, the use of the same word, "person," in the fifth must be equally comprehensive, and secures to all persons lawfully within the territory of the United States the protection named therein; and a like conclusion must follow as to the sixth.[63]

In many respects, *Fong Yue Ting* presented the more compelling case for judicial intervention. *Yick Wo* invalidated a facially neutral statute that had been discriminatorily administered to prevent relatively few people from pursuing their chosen occupation.[64] *Fong Yue Ting*, on the other hand, involved a federal law that subjected "a hundred thousand people . . . to arrest and forcible deportation."[65] If the lesser wrong receives judicial rebuke, the *Fong Yue Ting* dissent suggests that the "greater wrong" should receive no less.[66]

As these cases demonstrate, the Court proceeds from a membership baseline in its alienage jurisprudence. Where membership issues are present, the Court has consistently refused to seriously consider the constitutional claims made by noncitizens or their citizen families,[67] much less balance those claims against purported governmental interests. With respect to core federal membership issues (those involving admission, exclusion, and expulsion), the Court has consistently held that the government's sovereign power to develop immigration restrictions is plenary, rendering any rights claims irrelevant.[68] And, with respect to state membership issues, the Court has held that while rights claims are not irrelevant, its "scrutiny will not be so demanding."[69]

When a case implicates membership issues, this categorical approach ignores the constitutional values of liberty and equality, along with the "rights" of noncitizens and their families. Only in the absence of membership issues does the Court provide constitutional protection to noncitizen persons. The choice of the membership baseline is rooted in the last century's understanding of sovereignty.[70] Although this historical

---

Id. at 754 (Field, J., dissenting). Since the provisions of the Fifth and Fourteenth Amendments, guaranteeing certain rights "are . . . universal in their application to all persons within the territorial jurisdiction, . . . the rule laid down [in *Yick Wo*, 118 U.S. 356 (1886)] as much applies to Congress, under the Fifth Amendment, as to the States under the Fourteenth." Id. at 761-62 (Fuller, C.J., dissenting).

63. *Fong Yue Ying*, 149 U.S. at 739 (Brewer, J., dissenting).

64. *See* id. at 744 (restating the Court's holding in *Yick Wo*).

65. Id.

66. *See* id. (arguing that the Court in *Fong Yue Ting* should provide at least as much constitutional protection as it did in *Yick Wo*).

67. *See* infra notes 77-169.

68. *See* infra notes 88-124.

69. Foley v. Connelie, 435 U.S. 291, 296 (1978) (quoting Sugarman v. Dougall, 413 U.S. 634, 648 (1973)). *See* infra notes 146-69 (discussing membership in a state community).

70. Scaperlanda, Polishing, supra note 22, at 974; *see also* Fiallo v. Bell, 430 U.S. 787, 795 n.6 (1977) ("[T]he fallacy of the assumption [that domestic constitutional norms apply in the

link provides a weak justification for ignoring our constitutional text and tradition, it does explain the initial divergence of the membership and personhood traditions. At the founding of these two traditions and for much of the ensuing century, doctrinal and theoretical coherence could be forged from these seemingly inconsistent paradigms; the Court could be viewed as engaging in categorical balancing of interests, with personhood interests subordinated to membership issues, but prevailing over other governmental interests.

This alluring coherence disintegrated with the Court's decision in *Graham v. Richardson.*[71] The *Graham* Court's use of strict scrutiny within the personhood paradigm precludes doctrinal consistency.[72] The characteristics of the noncitizen that led the Court to apply the "discrete and insular" label do not abate merely because membership issues are present.[73] Justice Marshall, in elaborating on the "spectrum of standards" for reviewing equal protection claims, stated that the level of scrutiny depends on "the constitutional and societal importance of the interest adversely affected and the recognized invidiousness of the basis upon which the particular classification is drawn."[74] When a law adversely

---

immigration context] is rooted deeply in fundamental principles of sovereignty."); United States *ex rel.* Knauff v. Shaughnessy, 338 U.S. 537, 542 (1950) ("The exclusion of aliens is a fundamental act of sovereignty."); *Fong Yue Ting,* 149 U.S. at 705, 707 (1893):

> It is an accepted maxim of international law, that every sovereign nation has the power, as inherent in sovereignty, and essential to self-preservation, to forbid the entrance of foreigners within its dominions. . . . The right of a nation to expel or deport foreigners . . . rests upon the same grounds, and is as absolute and unqualified, as the right to prohibit and prevent their entrance into the country.

71. 403 U.S. 365 (1971).

72. *See* Michael J. Perry, Modern Equal Protection: A Conceptualization and Appraisal, 79 Colum. L. Rev. 1023, 1064 (1979) (characterizing the alienage equal protection jurisprudence as doctrinally incoherent); *cf.* Peter J. Spiro, The States and Immigration in an Era of Demi-Sovereignties, 35 Va. J. Int'l L. 121, 151 (1994) ("*Graham* failed to work through implications of its equal protection construct for discrimination on the part of the federal government . . . ."). Doctrinal coherence should be distinguished from theoretical coherence. Doctrinal coherence requires that the various doctrines employed to bring the Court's theoretical underpinnings to life be reconciled into a unified whole. In contrast, theoretical coherence demands that the theory, which transcends the doctrine but is manifest in doctrine, be reconciled in a unified whole.

73. *See* Gerald M. Rosberg, The Protection of Aliens from Discriminatory Treatment by the National Government, 1977 Sup. Ct. Rev. 275, 294 (stating that although the federal government's unique concern with immigration matters might constitute a "compelling need for a particular classification," the presence of the immigration power "does not in any obvious way explain why the burdern of justification on the federal government should be any different from the burden on the state").

74. San Antonio Indep. Sch. Dist. v. Rodriguez, 411 U.S. 1, 98-99 (1973) (Marshall, J., dissenting). Although Marshall was arguing against categorical balancing in favor of sliding scale balancing, he agrees that the Court reserves its strictest scrutiny for classifications that impinge fundamental rights or discriminate against suspect classes. Id. at 99. *See also* United States v. Carolene Prod., Co., 304 U.S. 144, 152-53 n. 4 (1938). In the alienage context, at least, Marshall got it backwards; the degree of scrutiny depends on the nature of the government's interests, not the interests or characteristics of the individual. Only in the

affects a "suspect class," it is presumed invidious and strict scrutiny applies.[75] Therefore, doctrinal consistency would require the Court to strictly scrutinize all alienage cases—a result both unlikely and unwise—or refrain from calling noncitizens a "discrete and insular" minority. In the next two sections of the Article, I develop the membership paradigm and the personhood paradigm in greater detail. Taken together, these paradigms transcend the doctrinal morass, providing a model explaining alienage jurisprudence as a whole, not just its constituent parts.

III. THE MEMBERSHIP MODEL

Even before *Graham*, troubling questions arose from the Court's refusal to apply constitutional first principles to many alienage cases. For example, in the *Chinese Exclusion Case*,[76] the Court upheld the exclusion of Chae Chan Ping[77] by recognizing the government's power to formulate membership policy along racial lines.[78] The Court ignored the constitutional constraints present in the personhood tradition, which emphasizes the rights of individual noncitizens under our Constitution, preferring, instead, the membership tradition with its emphasis on the rights of the sovereign in the areas of communal formation and security. This section will sketch the doctrinal framework shaping the membership tradition, first at the federal level and then at the state level.

A. *Membership in the American Community*

In contrast to the heightened review attending most state alienage cases,[79] the Court grants extreme deference when reviewing federal alienage cases. The intersection of alienage issues and criminal trial rights, where domestic constitutional norms apply, provides the only real

absence of communal formation interests will the Court apply strict scrutiny to laws that intentionally discriminate against noncitizens. *See, e.g.*, Cabell v. Chavez-Salido, 454 U.S. 432, 439 (1982) (holding strict scrutiny inapplicable in determining whether employment as probation officer could be limited to citizens).

75. *See, e.g.*, Batson v. Kentucky, 476 U.S. 79, 89 (1986) (applying strict scrutiny equal protection analysis to a state prosecutor's use of a peremptory challenge to strike a juror based on that juror's race); Washington v. Seattle Sch. Dist. No. 1, 458 U.S. 457, 483 (1982) (applying strict scrutiny equal protection analysis to a state initiative terminating mandatory bussing for desegregation that burdened "all future attempts to integrate" schools throughout Washington).

76. Chae Chan Ping v. United States, 130 U.S. 581 (1889).

77. Chae Chan Ping was no stranger to the United States. He had resided in the United States for twelve years prior to returning to China for a visit. Before leaving the United States he obtained a certificate from the United States ensuring his re-entry. Id. at 582.

78. Id. at 606. The Fourteenth Amendment, which overruled *Dred Scott*, prohibited the use of racial classifications in drawing internal membership policy. *See* U.S. Const. amend. XIV.

79. *See* infra notes 214-32 and accompanying text (surveying state case law applying strict scrutiny to alienage cases).

deviation from the principle of deference.[80] When, however, the Court addresses immigration issues—issues of admission, exclusion, or expulsion—its analysis treads perilously close to the political question doctrine.[81] And, in cases that fall between the immigration context and the criminal context, the Court, at its most stringent, applies a rational basis test.[82]

Deference is due, the Court has said, because "any policy toward aliens is vitally and intricately interwoven with contemporaneous policies in regard to the conduct of foreign relations, the war power, and the maintenance of a republican form of government."[83] Despite criticism from the bench[84] and from many commentators,[85] the Court has consistently[86] refused to assimilate federal alienage cases into mainstream constitutional law.

---

80. *See* infra text at notes 182-91.

81. *See* infra notes 87-123.

82. *See* infra notes 124-44 and accompanying text.

83. *E.g.*, Harisiades v. Shaughnessy, 342 U.S. 580, 588-89 (1952) ("Such matters are so exclusively entrusted to the political branches of government as to be largely immune from judicial inquiry or interference."); *see also* Fiallo v. Bell, 430 U.S. 787, 792 (1977) ("[I]t is important to underscore the limited scope of judicial inquiry into immigration legislation. This Court has repeatedly emphasized that 'over no conceivable subject is the legislative power of Congress more complete that it is over' the admission of aliens." (quoting Oceanic Navigation Co. v. Stranahan, 214 U.S. 320, 339 (1909))); Mathews v. Diaz, 426 U.S. 67, 81 (1976):

> For reasons long recognized as valid, the responsibility for regulating the relationship between the United States and our alien visitors has been committed to the political branches of the Federal Government. Since decisions in these matters may implicate our relations with foreign powers, and since a wide variety of classifications must be defined in the light of changing political and economic circumstances, such decisions are frequently of a character more appropriate to either the Legislature or the Executive than to the Judiciary.

84. *See, e.g.*, Fong Yue Ting v. United States, 149 U.S. 698, 732 (Brewer, J., dissenting). For a look at the history of dissent in federal alienage cases, see generally Scaperlanda, supra note 6.

85. *See, e.g.*, T. Alexander Aleinikoff, Federal Regulation of Aliens and the Constitution, 83 Am. J. Int'l L. 862, 866 (1989) [hereinafter Aleinikoff, Federal Regulation] ("The analysis and implications of *Chinese Exclusion* and *Fon Yue Ting* are so patently inconsistent with modern constitutional principles that a thoroughgoing reconceptualization of the immigration power is in order."); James A. R. Nafziger, Review of Visa Denials By Consular Officers, 66 Wash. L. Rev. 1, 51 (1991) ("[T]he plenary power doctrine is illogical . . . .").

86. *See, e.g.*, Galvan v. Press, 347 U.S. 522, 531-32 (1954):

> "In light of the expansion of the concept of substantive due process as a limitation upon all powers of Congress, even the war power, much could be said for the view, were we writing on a clean slate, that the Due Process Clause qualifies the scope of political discretion . . . in regulating the entry and deportation of aliens. . . . But the slate is not clean. As to the extent of the power of Congress under review, there is not merely a page of history but a whole volume." (citations omitted).

1. Plenary Immigration Power

The Court's deference to the judgment, whim, or fancy of the political branches reaches its apex when the Court confronts immigration issues. "Over no conceivable subject is the legislative power of Congress more complete than it is over" the admission, exclusion, and expulsion of aliens.[87] Although aliens are "persons" entitled to the protection of the Constitution,[88] in the immigration context, neither the Constitution itself nor the Supreme Court's ruminations about the document entitle the noncitizen to substantive constitutional guarantees.

Plenary immigration power was founded on the back of blatant racial discrimination. The *Chinese Exclusion Case*,[89] which affirmed the exclusion of Chinese nationals from the United States, established within the political branches the absolute power to develop a profile of the "desirable" immigrant unfettered by any provision of our higher law.[90] As Professor Henkin has noted, "[w]hatever the Court intended [in the *Chinese Exclusion Case*], both its holding and its sweeping dictum have been taken to mean that there are no constitutional limitations on the power of Congress to

---

87. *Oceanic Navigation Co.*, 214 U.S. at 339.

88. Wong Wing v. United States, 163 U.S. 228, 238 (1896).

89. The Chinese Exclusion Case, 130 U.S. 581 (1889).

90. The "exclusive and absolute" power to exclude foreigners, which emanates from sovereignty, rests with the political branches of the federal government and is "conclusive upon the judiciary." The *Chinese Exclusion Case*, 130 U.S. at 606. "The right of a nation to expel or deport foreigners . . . rests upon the same grounds, and is as absolute and unqualified as the right to prohibit and prevent their entrance into the country." *Fong Yue Ting*, 149 U.S. at 707. Several commentators have noted that the Court, while not rejecting the *Chinese Exclusion Case* and its rationale, has softened its stand that the political branches' immigration decisions are "conclusive upon the judiciary." *See, e.g.*, Schuck, supra note 15, at 65 (noting that the Court's language in *Diaz* and *Fiallo* suggests that "the seeds of judicial intervention have been planted"). The Court's language suggests that the commentators are correct; the Court has retired the language of total abdication. *See, e.g.*, Reno v. Flores, 507 U.S. 292, 306 (1993) (reaffirming an expansive plenary power on immigration matters, and stating that, "[o]f course, the INS regulation must still meet the (unexacting)" rational basis test); *Fiallo*, 430 U.S. at 793 n.5 ("Our cases reflect acceptance of a limited judicial responsibility under the Constitution even with respect to [core immigration matters]."). Many lower courts apply the rational basis standard in reviewing Congress's immigration laws. *E.g.*, Perez-Oropeza v. INS, 56 F.3d 43, 45 (9th Cir. 1995); Ablang v. Reno, 52 F.3d 801, 804 (9th Cir. 1995). Despite the appearance of less deferential review, the results in the Supreme Court have remained the same; the government prevails in constitutional immigration cases. Additionally, the opinions that suggest less deference often contain conflicting language. For instance, in *Fiallo* the Court said "these are policy questions entrusted exclusively to the political branches of our Government, and we have no judicial authority to substitute our political judgment for that of the Congress." *Fiallo*, 430 U.S. at 798. The second Justice Marshall ably summed up the current state of affairs. He concluded that the Court's review remained "completely 'toothless'" because "the majority concludes: [B]ut the decision nonetheless remains one 'solely for the responsibility of the Congress and wholly outside the power of this Court to control.' Such 'review' reflects more than due deference; it is abdication." Id. at 805 (Marshall, J., dissenting) (citations omitted).

regulate immigration."[91] From racial discrimination, plenary immigration power grew without bounds, allowing Congress to reflect the mood of an often anxious and fearful nation, unencumbered by the dictates of the Constitution.[92] During the "red scare" of McCarthyism, Congress wielded this power to deport long time resident aliens for their thoughts and associations.[93] Today it continues to stand as a sentry at our gates, allowing the political branches to formulate immigration policy without the restrictions that would otherwise be required by our constitutional traditions.[94]

The immigration power, an unenumerated[95] "incident of sovereign-

91. Henkin, supra note 22, at 859

92. "The Chinese Exclusion doctrine and its extensions have permitted, and perhaps encouraged, paranoia, xenophobia, and racism, particularly during periods of international tension." Henkin, supra note 22, at 859.

93. *See* Galvan v. Press, 347 U.S. 522, 531 (1954); *Harisiades*, 342 U.S. at 591. "The four defendants in *Harisiades* and *Galvan* had a collective 142-year presence in the United States, with each defendant residing here for over 30 years. One defendant had been associated with the Communist Party for only six years, his membership having ceased 23 years prior to his deportation." Scaperlanda, Polishing, supra note 22, at 988 n.102. Ideological exclusions and deportations have continued sporadically in recent years. The Supreme Court has not spoken on the issue in two decades; in its last case, involving the exclusion of a Marxist journalist, it upheld the order of exclusion despite a recognized First Amendment claim. *See* Kleindienst v. Mandel, 408 U.S. 753, 756 (1972). *But see* American-Arab Anti-Discrimination v. Reno, 70 F.3d 1045, 1064-66 (9th Cir. 1995) (concluding that aliens in deportation are entitled to the protections of the First Amendment); Rafeedie v. INS, 795 F. Supp. 13, 21 (D.D.C. 1992) (striking down ideological exclusions, holding that aliens present in this country possessed First Amendment rights on par with citizens); American-Arab Anti-Discrimination Committee v. Meese, 714 F. Supp. 1060, 1082 (C.D. Cal. 1989), *rev'd on other grounds*, 940 F.2d 445 (9th Cir. 1991) (striking down ideological exclusions, holding that aliens present in this country possessed First Amendment rights on par with citizens). Several commentators have criticized ideological exclusions or deportations. *See, e.g.*, John Scanlan, Alien in the Marketplace of Ideas: The Government, The Academy, and the McCarran-Walter Act, 66 Tex. L. Rev. 1481 (1988); Robert R. Shapiro, Ideological Exclusions: Closing the Border to Political Dissidents, 100 Harv. L. Rev. 930 (1987); Courtney E. Pelligrino, Comment, A Generously Fluctuating Scale of Rights: Resident Aliens and First Amendment Free Speech Protections, 46 SMU L. Rev. 225, 233-44 (1992).

94. *See, e.g.*, Sale v. Haitian Ctrs. Council, Inc., 509 U.S. 155, 201 (1993) (Blackmun, J., dissenting) (discussing plenary power over immigration matters); Reno v. Flores, 507 U.S. 292, 305 (1993) (citing *Fiallo* to support congressional authority); *Fiallo*, 430 U.S. at 788 (challenging constitutionality of Immigration & Nationality Act); Parades-Urrestarazu v. INS, 36 F.3d 801, 807 (9th Cir. 1994) (discussing plenary power); United States v. Cupa-Guillen, 34 F.3d 860, 862 (9th Cir. 1994) (describing judicial review as "exceedingly narrow" because of Congress's plenary power); U.S.A. *ex rel.* Tiep Cuong Chau v. McElroy, No. 95 Civ. 1042, 1995 WL 92319, at *4 (S.D.N.Y. Mar. 6, 1995) ("The Fifth Amendment does not affect, in any degree, Congress' plenary power over exclusion proceedings.") (citations omitted); Aliens for Better Immigration Laws v. United States, 871 F. Supp. 182, 185 (S.D.N.Y 1994) (citing *Fiallo* "to underscore the limited scope of judicial inquiry into immigration legislation"); United States v. Phetchanphone, 863 F. Supp. 1543, 1546 (D. Utah 1994) (describing congressional power over aliens as plenary); Cruz-Elias v. Attorney General, 870 F. Supp. 692, 698 (E.D. Va. 1994) (finding no constitutional violation for indefinite detention of alien excludable for serious crime).

95. *See, e.g.*, Ira J. Kurzban, Immigration Law Sourcebook 12-13 (5th ed. 1995) (stating

ty,"[96] belongs to both Congress[97] and the Executive.[98] The Constitution does not provide internal limitations to this power ;[99] moreover, the Court has consistently refused to supply external constitutional constraints, such as the Bill of Rights, to limit the power's scope.[100] A modern example of plenary power will illustrate its immense breadth.

Fiallo v. Bell[101] serves as a useful guide. It discusses and rejects modern domestic equal protection doctrine within the immigration context despite the presence of gender, illegitimacy, and alienage

---

that the Commerce Clause, the Naturalization Clause, the Migration and Importation Clause, The War Power, as well as the implied power to conduct foreign policy, and the implied powers accruing to a sovereign have all been used as justifications for the federal government's immigration power); Thomas A. Aleinikoff et al., Immigration Process and Policy 7-17 (3d ed. 1995) (same and adding a discussion on "constructional and structural" arguments for sources of federal immigration power); Stephen H. Legomsky, Immigration Law and Policy 8-12 (1992) [hereinafter Legomsky, Immigration Law] (same).

96. *See, e.g.*, *Chae Chan Ping*, 130 U.S. at 609; *see also* Nafziger, supra note 85, at 46 (criticizing inherent sovereign powers justification for plenary power); Scaperlanda, Polishing, supra note 22, at 968 (criticizing the inherent sovereign powers justification of plenary power in light of evolving international law norms).

97. The Court has "repeatedly emphasized that 'over no conceivable subject is the legislative power of Congress more complete than it is over' the admission of aliens." *E.g.*, *Fiallo*, 430 U.S. at 792.

98. "When Congress prescribes a procedure concerning the admissibility of aliens, it is not dealing alone with a legislative power. It is implementing an inherent executive power." *E.g.*, United States *ex rel.* Knauff v. Shaughnessy, 338 U.S. 537, 542 (1950); *cf.* Youngstown Sheet & Tube Co. v. Sawyer, 343 U.S. 579, 635-37 (1952) (Jackson, J., concurring) (discussing the relationship between executive power and congressional power).

99. United States v. Curtiss-Wright, 299 U.S. 304, 316 (1936) (stating that with respect to external sovereignty, the United States government is not a government of limited and defined enumerated powers, "[S]ince the states severally never possessed international powers, such powers could not have been carved from the mass of state powers but obviously were transmitted to the United States from . . . the Crown"). Therefore, "[t]he power to expel undesirable aliens . . . which is [not] expressly affirmed by the Constitution, nevertheless exist[s] as inherently inseparable from the conception of nationality." Id. at 318.

100. *See, e.g.*, *Kleindienst*, 408 U.S. at 753-54 (holding that the First Amendment provides no protection for American scholars wanting to hear an alien speaker whom the Attorney General has excluded from entry). For noncitizens, a constitutional framework anchored by a commitment to protect the individual lives in suspended animation, just past the second star to the right. *See* Kikuyo Matsumoto-Power, Comment, Aliens, Resident Aliens, and U.S. Citizens in the Never-Never Land of the Immigration and Nationality Act, 15 U. Haw. L. Rev. 61 (1993); *see also* Henkin, supra note 22, at 861 ("[T]he offspring of *Chinese Exclusion* still reign to deny constitutional protection to many thousands of aliens against new indecencies . . . ."); Legomsky, Plenary Congressional Power, supra note 17, at 255 ("In immigration cases, the American courts have been their most restrained on constitutional issues."); Schuck, supra note 15, at 1 ("Immigration has long been a maverick, a wild card, in our public law. Probably no other area of American law has been so radically insulated and divergent from those fundamental norms of constitutional right . . . that animate the rest of our legal system."). For a thorough examination of the minority of justices who would have used the Bill of Rights to restrict Congress' plenary power in immigration matters, see Scaperlanda, supra note 16.

101. 430 U.S. 787, 787 (1977) (holding that excluding an illigitimate child and his natural father, though not the natural mother, from special preference status is constitutional).

questions. *Fiallo* involved claims by three illegitimate children and their natural fathers that then existing immigration laws violated the "equal protection" component of the Fifth Amendment's Due Process Clause. The problem: Although the parent-child relationship provided the best avenue to obtain immigration benefits,[102] the immigration laws recognized only the parent-child relationship between a mother and her illegitimate child and ignored the relationship between a father and his illegitimate child.[103] The fathers and their illegitimate offspring could not obtain immigration benefits based on their familial relationship, scuttling their desire for family reunification in the United States.

Following a strategy first employed in *Kleindienst v. Mandel*,[104] the plaintiffs in *Fiallo* claimed that the discriminatory immigration law violated the rights of the family member currently in the United States, not the one seeking entrance.[105] They argued that the challenged provision "involved 'double-barreled' discrimination based on sex and illegitimacy," which "infringed upon . . . the rights of citizens and legal permanent residents. . . ."[106] Because the *Kleindienst* Court upheld Congress's plenary

102. Where either the parent or adult child is a citizen, the noncitizen parent or minor child can immigrate without regard to the annual numerical limitations placed on the immigrants, which can lead to long delays. *See* 8 U.S.C. § 1151(b) (West Supp. 1995) (defining immediate relatives). For example, a married son or daughter of a United States citizen seeking to immigrate from the Philippines to the United States was eligible to immigrate in July of 1995 if she applied to immigrate before January 1, 1984. *See* 72 Inter. Releases 829, 862 App. IV (June 26, 1995) (quoting State Department Visa Preference Numbers for July 1995). Brothers and sisters of United States citizens immigrating from the Philippines in July 1995 applied before September 2, 1977. *See* id. Although adult unmarried sons and daughters of citizens are subject to numerical limitations, 8 U.S.C. §1153(a)(1) (West Supp. 1995), this category is current. *See* 72 Inter. Releases at 862 App. IV (June 26, 1995) (listing visa preference statistics for July 1995). For spouse and unmarried sons and daughters of permanent residents, who are subject to numerical limitations, 8 U.S.C. at §1153(a)(2), there is a backlog of between two and five years. *See* 72 Inter. Releases at 862 App. IV (June 26, 1995) (listing visa preference statistics for July 1995).

103. The illegitimate child father relationship can now provide the basis for family based immigration benefits provided a bona fide parent-child relationship exists. *See* The Immigration Reform and Control Act of 1986, Pub. L. No. 99-603, § 315(a), 100 Stat. 2613, 3359 (1986), (codified at 8 U.S.C. §1101(b)(1)(D) (West Supp. 1993)) (defining eligible illegitimate children).

104. 408 U.S. 753, 769 (1972) (acknowledging that American academics had a First Amendment right to hear the Marxist journalist they had invited to speak, yet subordinating this right to the government's plenary power to exclude).

105. Previous cases had addressed the issue of whether the noncitizens' constitutional rights were violated by the denial of admission or the order of expulsion. For example, see Shaughnessy v. Mezei, 345 U.S. 206, 209 (1953) (although alien had immediate family in the United States, he claimed that his substantive and procedural constitutional rights were violated by indefinite detention pending removal from the United States). In an attempt to distinguish their cases from earlier failed attempts to break plenary power's stronghold on immigration law, the plaintiffs in *Kleindienst* and *Fiallo* attempted, albeit unsuccessfully, to shift the focus away from the adverse affect on the aliens to the harm visited upon those already lawfully in the United States.

106. *Fiallo*, 430 U.S. at 794.

power to override the First Amendment rights of citizens and legal permanent residents in the immigration context, the plaintiffs distinguished *Kleindienst*. Unlike the statutory provisions in *Kleindienst*, in *Fiallo* "the statutory provisions were designed to reunite families wherever possible."[107] Therefore, the plaintiffs argued, Congress intended to grant rights to United States citizens and legal permanent residents.[108] The Court, however, was unpersuaded by this "unique coalescing of factors."[109] Following the long line of plenary power cases, stretching back to the *Chinese Exclusion Case*, the Court concluded that "[i]n any event, it is not the judicial role in cases of this sort to probe and test the justifications for the legislative decision."[110]

Why did the Court refuse to "probe and test" the legislative rationale underlying the discriminatory classification? This law discriminated against aliens[111] and their citizen family. Even if *Chinese Exclusion*'s plenary power doctrine subordinates *Graham v. Richardson*'s characterization of aliens as members of a "discrete and insular" minority, how does the Court justify denying the citizen family members equal protection of the law? After all, the classification did involve "double-barreled" discrimination; both gender and illegitimacy classifications normally receive intermediate scrutiny review.[112] The Court, which takes upon itself the role of shedding "increasingly outdated misconceptions concerning the role of females in the home rather than in the 'marketplace of ideas,'"[113] told the families in *Fiallo* that their argument[114] "should be addressed to the Congress

107. Id. at 793, 794 (discussing *Kleindienst* and declining to reconsider the case). The plaintiffs charged that this discrimination undermined a major policy of our immigration legislation, which "was concerned with the problem of keeping families of United States citizens and immigrants united." House Judiciary Comm., Facilitating the Entry into the United States of Certain Adopted Children, and Other Relatives of United States Citizens, H.R. Rep. No. 1199, 85th Cong., 1st Sess., pt. 1, at 7 (1957), *reprinted in* 1957 U.S.C.C.A.N. 2016, 2020. In contrast, the statute at issue in *Kleindienst* was not designed to enhance the ability of United States citizens to exercise their First Amendment right to hear diverse viewpoints. Instead, that law was designed to protect the country and its citizens from perceived threats to the national security. *See Fiallo*, 430 U.S. at 806-08 (Marshall, J. dissenting) (noting that the instant case was distinguishable because here the government was not concerned with the influx of "undesirables" and the large potential audience for the "probity of [their] ideas").

108. *Fiallo*, 430 U.S. at 793.

109. Id. (quoting brief of appellants).

110. Id. at 799.

111. Graham v. Richardson, 403 U.S. 365 (1971); Yick Wo v. Hopkins, 118 U.S. 356 (1886).

112. *See, e.g.*, Clark v. Jeter, 486 U.S. 456 (1988) (describing the intermediate scrutiny analysis as applied to claims of illegitimacy); Craig v. Boren, 429 U.S. 190 (1976) (holding that equal protection claims based on gender are subject to intermediate scrutiny).

113. *Craig*, 429 U.S. at 198-99.

114. Their argument was precisely the argument that had received favorable treatment in *Craig*: "that the statutory distinction [denying them immigration benefits] is based on an overbroad and outdated stereotype concerning the relationship of unwed fathers and their illegitimate children." *Fiallo*, 430 U.S. at 799 n.9.

rather than the courts."[115] Why did the Court refuse to "probe and test" in this particular case?

Citing the *Chinese Exclusion Case* and its progeny, the Court began its analysis by synthesizing a century of plenary power: "At the outset, it is important to underscore the limited scope of judicial inquiry into immigration legislation."[116] Immigration involves "an exercise of the Nation's sovereign power to admit or exclude foreigners in accordance with perceived national interests. . . . [L]imits and classifications as to who shall be admitted are traditional and necessary elements of legislation in this area."[117]

The Court hovers near, but never on, the judicial nadir known as the "political question" doctrine. Quoting *Galvan v. Press*,[118] the Court stated that "the formulation of these '[p]olicies pertaining to the entry of aliens' . . . is entrusted exclusively to Congress.'"[119] In the same paragraph, the Court continued: "This is not to say . . . that the Government's power in this area is never subject to judicial review, . . . only to limited judicial review."[120] Equivocating further, the Court stated that "the reasons that preclude judicial review of political questions also dictate a narrow standard of review of decisions made by the Congress or the President in the area of immigration and naturalization."[121] Doctrinally, immigration law's plenary power grants more deference, if possible, than rational basis review and less deference than a full embrace of the political question doctrine would entail.

Plenary power, with its near total deference to the political branches, continues to serve as the cornerstone of our alienage jurisprudence. Many commentators have echoed the sentiment of Professor Henkin when he wrote: "*Chinese Exclusion*—its very name is an embarrassment—must go."[122] Yet the Court has shown no signs of relenting.[123] Taking this reluctance as a given, this Article attempts to explore the parameters of the doctrine. With that in mind, I turn to another line of cases within the membership model; cases where the Court has slightly moderated the force of plenary power.

---

115. Id.

116. Id. at 792.

117. Id. at 795 n.6.

118. 347 U.S. 522, 531 (1954).

119. *Fiallo*, 430 U.S. at 795 n.6.

120. Id. at 795-96 n.6

121. Id. at 796 (quoting Mathews v. Diaz, 426 U.S. 67, 81-82 (1976)).

122. Henkin, supra note 22, at 863.

123. *See Reno*, 507 U.S. at 305-06 (recognizing a long line of plenary power cases as authoritative).

2. *Rational Basis*

Outside the immigration context, a semblance of domestic constitutional decisionmaking appears. Plenary power loses much of its rhetorical thrust as the Court appears to take semi-seriously the review of these alienage cases by utilizing the rational basis test. Companion cases, *Mathews v. Diaz*[124] and *Hampton v. Mow Sun Wong*,[125] involved federal alienage classifications outside of the immigration context. Both cases had state counterparts: *Mathews*, which involved eligibility for welfare benefits, found its corollary in *Graham v. Richardson*,[126] and *Hampton*, which involved citizenship requirements for the federal civil service, followed *Sugarman v. Dougall*.[127] Forging new constitutional doctrine, the Court rejected both the judicial abstinence of plenary power and the strict scrutiny of the state alienage cases. Instead, these federal classifications, which adversely affected a "discrete and insular" minority, received deferential but not abdicational review. Some commentators hoped that these cases signaled the beginning of the end for the plenary power doctrine.[128] In my opinion, they strengthen and broaden its force.

In *Mathews v. Diaz*, the Court confronted the issue of "whether Congress may condition an alien's eligibility for participation in a federal medical insurance program on continuous residence in the United States for a five-year period and admission for permanent residence."[129] In reaching an affirmative conclusion, the Court rejected *Graham*'s strict scrutiny test and employed a rational basis test, placing the burden on the

---

124. 426 U.S. 67 (1976).

125. 426 U.S. 88 (1976).

126. 403 U.S. 365 (1971); *see* id. at 382 n.14 ("We have no occasion to decide whether Congress . . . could itself enact a statute imposing on aliens a uniform nationwide residency requirement as a condition of federally funded welfare benefits."). *Graham*, which used strict scrutiny to strike down a state statute excluding aliens from receiving welfare, specifically left unanswered whether the same level of review would apply to a similar alienage classification adopted by the federal government. For a discussion of *Graham*, see supra notes 71-73 and accompanying text.

127. 413 U.S. 634 (1973); *see* infra notes 159 and 164 and accompanying text.

128. *See, e.g.*, Schuck, supra note 5, at 65-66:

> *Diaz* seemed to concede that even federal alienage classifications were reviewable, albeit under a 'narrow standard of review.' . . . Great and imposing structures of judicial power have been built upon far less prepossessing foundations than these. It seems likely that, just as the Court earlier imposed constitutional limits on Congress's broad power to regulate the acquisition and loss of American citizenship, the Court will not continue indefinitely to tolerate, as it did in *Diaz*, unprincipled discrimination against aliens who . . . have become vital members of the community.;

cf. Stephen H. Legomsky, Immigration and the Judiciary: Law and Politics in Britain and America 219 (1987) ("[T]here is evidence that the plenary power doctrine is beginning to warp."). Professor Legomsky has recently revised his predictions on the demise of plenary power, believing now that the Court will only slowly undermine the century-old doctrine. Stephen H. Legomsky, Ten More Years of Plenary Power: Immigration, Congress, and the Courts 22 Hastings Const. L.Q. 925, 937 (1995).

129. *Mathews*, 426 U.S. at 69.

law's challenger. It concluded that "it is unquestionably reasonable for Congress to make an alien's eligibility depend on both the character and the duration of his residence."[130] The Court distinguished *Graham* because of "significantly different considerations" present in the relationship between federal government and alien but absent in the relationship between state government and alien.[131] Unlike the states, "it is the business of the political branches of the Federal Government . . . to regulate the conditions of entry and residence of aliens."[132]

In a rare move, the Court, in *Hampton v. Mow Sun Wong*,[133] struck down a federal rule prohibiting aliens from competing for federal civil service positions. In reaching its conclusion, the Court did not follow *Sugarman v. Dougall*, which used strict judicial scrutiny to strike down state civil service eligibility requirements; instead, it adopted a rationale that defies easy characterization. Perhaps the dissent put it best: "[T]he Court does not rely on an equal protection analysis . . . . [It] instead inexplicably melds together the concepts of equal protection and procedural and substantive due process to produce" its holding.[134] Because of the federal government's "overriding national interests" in immigration,[135] the Court jettisoned "traditional equal protection analysis."[136] In its stead, the Court inserted a two prong melding. First, if a state's adoption of the discriminatory rule would violate the Fourteenth Amendment, then "due process requires that there be a legitimate basis for presuming that the rule was actually intended to serve" an overriding national interest.[137]

---

130. Id. at 82-83. The Court reasoned:

> Since neither requirement is wholly irrational, this case essentially involves nothing more than that it would be more reasonable for Congress to select somewhat different requirements of the same kind . . . . Since appellees have not identified a principled basis for prescribing a different standard than the one selected by Congress, they have, in effect, merely invited us to substitute our judgment for that of Congress. . . . We decline the invitation.

Id. at 83-84.

131. Id. at 84-85. This rationale, which drew distinctions based on the type of government making the decision, originated in Fong Yue Ting v. United States, 149 U.S. 698, 725 (1893). In contrast, the Court of the middle period focused on the type of power wielded, promoting deference to the federal government's immigration decisions, but counseling greater review outside the immigration context. *See* Harisiades v. Shaughnessy, 342 U.S. 580, 586-87 (1952).

132. *Mathews*, 426 U.S. at 84.

133. 426 U.S. 88 (1976).

134. Id. at 119 (Rehnquist, J., dissenting). The Court held:

> The added disadvantage resulting from the enforcement of the rule—ineligibility for employment in a major sector of the economy—is of sufficient significance to be characterized as a deprivation of an interest in liberty. Indeed, we deal with a rule which deprives a discrete class of persons of an interest in liberty on a wholesale basis. By reason of the Fifth Amendment, such a deprivation must be accompanied by due process.

Id. at 102-03.

135. Id. at 100-01.

136. Id. at 103.

137. Id. at 103. "[I]f the rule were expressly mandated by the Congress or the President,

Second, if an agency with no foreign affairs responsibility promulgates the discriminatory rule, the Court balances the governmental interest against the interests of those harmed by the rule.[138]

In this case the balance was struck for noncitizens. "Any fair balancing of the public interest in avoiding the wholesale deprivation of employment opportunities caused by the Commission's indiscriminate policy, as opposed to what may be nothing more than a hypothetical justification, requires rejection of the argument of administrative convenience in this case."[139] Therefore, the Civil Service Commission's regulations were invalid.[140] The Court assumed a different outcome if the classification had been made by Congress or the President.[141] Three federal court decisions upholding President Ford's subsequent executive order excluding aliens from civil service positions ratified the Court's assumption.[142]

Reading between the lines, the Court seems to hold that if the political branches of the federal government adopt a discriminatory posture adversely affecting aliens or a group of aliens outside the immigration context, the Court will apply at most a rational basis review. Where, however, a federal agency possessing no residual immigration power adopts the discriminatory rule, the Court will apply some form of heightened scrutiny, but its review will still fall short of the strict scrutiny analysis applied in the state cases.

The membership paradigm remains operative justifying broad judicial deference to the political branches of the federal government when classifying in ways that disadvantage this "discrete and insular" minority. This paradigm, and not the personhood paradigm, applies because:

> [T]he responsibility for regulating the relationship between the United States and our alien visitors has been committed to the political branches of the Federal Government. Since decisions in these matters may implicate our relations with foreign powers,

---

we might presume that any interest which might rationally be served by the rule did in fact give rise to its adoption." Id. This dicta follows the rationale of *Hampton*'s companion case, Mathews v. Diaz, 426 U.S. 67 (1976), where the Court applied a rational basis test to a congressionally adopted rule that excluded certain aliens from welfare benefits. *Mathews*, 426 U.S. at 82-83.

138. *Hampton*, 426 U.S. at 114-16.

139. Id. at 115-16.

140. Id. at 116-17.

141. *See* id. at 105 (discussing the fact that the civil service commission's adoption of citizenship as a requirement for employment in the federal civil service is without congressional or presidential authorization.).

142. *See* Vergara v. Hampton, 581 F.2d 1281 (7th Cir. 1978), *cert. denied*, 441 U.S. 905 (1979) (upholding executive order barring lawfully admitted resident aliens from the federal competitive civil service); Mow Sun Wong v. Hampton, 435 F. Supp. 37 (N.D. Cal. 1977) (upholding executive order explicitly excluding aliens from the civil service), *aff'd sub nom.* Mow Sun Wong v. Campbell, 626 F.2d 739 (9th Cir. 1980), *cert. denied*, 450 U.S. 959 (1981); Santin Ramos v. United States Civil Serv. Comm'n 430 F. Supp. 422 (D. P.R. 1977) (upholding executive order barring aliens from taking competitive civil service exams).

> and since a wide variety of classifications must be defined in the light of changing political and economic circumstances, such decisions are frequently of a character more appropriate to either the Legislature or the Executive than to the Judiciary.[143]

In regulating this relationship between the national community and the noncitizen, the dual membership concerns of communal formation and protection reign paramount, permitting discriminatory classifications as an "incentive" to noncitizens to become full participatory members of the community through naturalization.[144] Membership is not, however, within the exclusive province of the federal government.

B. *Membership in a State Community*

From *Yick Wo* through *Graham*, the personhood paradigm finds its strongest roots in the state alienage cases. Unlike the federal counterpart, where membership provides the point of embarkation, in state cases membership "appears" as an exception to the personhood tradition.[145] The membership exception has surfaced under two distinct doctrines: the special public interest doctrine and the public function doctrine.

1. *Special Public Interest Doctrine*

Prior to 1948, when a state reserved its resources for its own citizens, denying noncitizens access to those resources, no constitutional violation existed. This line of cases had its roots in the now largely discarded right versus privilege distinction.[146] Where the discrimination pertained "to the

143. *Mathews*, 426 U.S. at 81.

144. *See Hampton*, 426 U.S. at 105 ("[I]f the Congress or the President had expressly imposed the citizenship requirement it would be justified . . . [as] an incentive for aliens to become naturalized . . . . ").

145. Analyzing the state alienage cases without the benefit of the federal cases is like examining the source of the moon's "light" without knowledge of the sun—the perspective is skewed by incomplete data. If we examine the state cases in isolation, personhood appears as the norm and membership the exception. Stepping back and viewing the alienage jurisprudence as a whole allows us to see that membership, like the sun, sits at the center providing the energy for the whole mechanism, while personhood is relegated like the moon to a secondary role, giving the illusion that it is casting its own light.

146. *See* William W. Van Alstyne, The Demise of the Right-Privilege Distinction in Constitutional Law, 81 Harv. L. Rev. 1439, 1444 (1968) (explaining that to a large extent, the right versus privilege distinction has been relegated to the jurisprudential graveyard in many cases, including those involving state alienage classifications); Goldfarb, supra note 2, at 1460 ("[In state alienage cases], the Court rejected the special public interest doctrine as part of a dated and discredited right versus privilege distinction . . . ."). *But see* Rodney A. Smolla, The Reemergence of the Right-Privilege Distinction in Constitutional Law: The Price of Protesting Too Much, 35 Stan. L. Rev. 69, 70 (1982) (noting the "astounding ability of the right versus privilege distinction to rebound from discredit"). The right versus privilege distinction maintains vitality in the federal alienage cases. *See* Landon v. Plasencia, 459 U.S. 21, 32 (1982) ("[A]n alien seeking initial admission to the United States requests a privilege and has no constitutional rights regarding his application. . . . "); Alfred C. Aman, Jr. & William T. Mayton, Admin. Law 158 (1993); Aleinikoff, Federal Regulation, supra note 85, at 865 ("News of the decline of the "rights/privilege distinction has not yet reached immigration law. . . . ").

regulation or distribution of the public domain, or of the common property or resources of the people of that State, the enjoyment of [such] may be limited to its citizens as against both aliens and citizens of other States."[147] Therefore, states could prohibit noncitizens from hunting wildlife,[148] owning land,[149] and leasing land for agricultural pursuits.[150] This special public interest doctrine extended to private employment on public projects.[151] The line between the public domain and private enterprise blurred when the Court extended this doctrine to purely private activity in upholding a law that prohibited aliens from owning and operating a billiard parlor.[152] Applying a rational basis standard of review, the Court in *Clarke v. Deckebach* concluded that it was not irrational to prohibit aliens from engaging in this occupation because billiard parlors were potential locations for depravity.[153]

The special public interest doctrine's influence in state alienage cases was short lived. In *Torao Takahashi v. Fish & Game Comm'n*,[154] the Court struck down a California statute that denied Japanese citizens living in California the opportunity to obtain a commercial fishing license.[155] After

---

147. *Cabell*, 454 U.S. at 437

148. *See Patsone*, 232 U.S. at 143 (describing the contemporary statute prohibiting noncitizens from hunting wildlife).

149. *See* Frick v. Webb, 263 U.S. 326, 326 (1923) (citing the law prohibiting noncitizens from owning land); Webb v. O'Brien, 263 U.S. 313, 315 (1923) (same); Porterfield v. Webb, 263 U.S. 225, 225 (1923) (same).

150. *See* Terrace v. Thompson, 263 U.S. 197, 220-21 (1923) (upholding a law that denied the right to lease land to aliens not seeking citizenship in good faith).

151. *See* Crane v. New York, 239 U.S. 195, 198 (1915) (following result in *Heim*); Heim v. McCall, 239 U.S. 175, 194 (1915) (holding that New York City may exclude aliens from public construction projects). This result was partially foreordained by the right versus privilege distinction. Justice Cardozo, on behalf of the New York Court of Appeals, said:

> The state in determining what use shall be made of its own moneys, may legitimately consult the welfare of its own citizens rather than that of aliens. Whatever is a privilege rather than a right, may be made dependent upon citizenship. In its war against poverty, the state is not required to dedicate its own resources to citizens and aliens alike.

People v. Crane, 108 N.E. 427, 430 (N.Y. 1915), *aff'd sub nom.* Crane v. New York, 239 U.S. 195 (1915).

152. Ohio *ex rel.* Clarke v. Deckebach, 274 U.S. 392, 396 (1927).

153. Id. at 397.

154. 334 U.S. 410 (1948). Tarao Takahashi became a permanent resident of California in 1907. Between 1915 and 1942 he earned his living as a fisherman off California's coast pursuant to a fishing license granted to him by the state. While he and other Japanese residents of California were interred during World War II, California passed several anti-Japanese measures including one "prohibiting issuance of a [commercial fishing] license to any 'alien Japanese.'" Id. at 413. Fearing that the law might be unconstitutional, California amended it to prohibit the "issuances of licenses to any 'person ineligible to citizenship.'" Id. Although the Court did not treat this classification as race based, it is clear that the law had deep racial overtones. Id. at 418, 422 (Murphy, J., concurring).

155. Under the statute, any resident of California who was ineligible for United States citizenship was prohibited from obtaining a commercial fishing license. Id. at 413. Japanese immigrants were prevented, until 1952, from becoming citizens pursuant to our formerly

noting that a state's power to classify along alienage lines "is confined within narrow limits,"[156] the Court rejected California's public domain argument concluding that: "To whatever extent the fish . . . off California may be 'capable of ownership' by California, we think that 'ownership' is inadequate to justify . . . excluding any or all aliens who are lawful residents of the State from making a living by fishing in the ocean . . . while permitting all others to do so."[157] In refusing to distinguish the right to fish from the right to hunt or *Takahashi* from the previous special public interest cases, the Court signaled the decline of that doctrine.[158]

The transferral of all state alienage jurisprudence to the personhood paradigm did not follow this decline. Instead, the "public function" exception replaced the special public interest doctrine as the membership prong of the state cases. The two doctrines differ significantly on the underlying meaning of citizenship. Although both are membership centered, special public interest emphasizes the rewards of full membership–reaping the fruits of a state's bounty; public function, in contrast, emphasizes the participatory process value of communal formation.

2. *Public Function*

The special public interest doctrine had its foundations in economic protectionism by the state legitimized through the vehicle of the right versus privilege distinction. In contrast, the public function doctrine finds its moorings in an exclusionary theory of the political community. The Court will not employ strict scrutiny to protect this discrete and insular minority in cases where the state, by the challenged classification, is merely engaging in the ongoing process of "defin[ing] its political

---

racially discriminatory naturalization process. The first Congress declared that only "free white persons" were eligible for citizenship. *See* Act of Mar. 26, 1790, ch. III, § 1, 1 Stat. 103 (1845) (describing the procedures for a free white person to become a U.S. citizen). This "only 'free whites' need apply" rule was whittled away over the years. *See* 16 Stat. 254, 256 (1870) (making aliens of African nativity or descent eligible for naturalization); 54 Stat. 1137, 1140 (1940) (declaring "races indigenous to the Western Hemisphere" eligible for naturalization); Act of Dec. 17, 1943, ch. 344, § 1, 57 Stat. 601 (making aliens of Chinese origins eligible for naturalization); 60 Stat. 416 (1946) (making "races indigenous to India" and Filipinos eligible for naturalization). In 1952, Congress ended its racially discriminatory naturalization policies. *See* Act of June 27, 1952, ch. 477, § 311, 66 Stat. 163, 239 (1952) (codified as amended at 8 U.S.C.A. § 1422 (West Supp. 1995). The 1952 repeal accrued primarily to the benefit of Japanese immigrants, who at that time were the largest group of aliens living in the United States but ineligible for citizenship. *Cf.* Oyama v. California, 332 U.S. 633 (1948) (holding that an American citizen's right to equal protection was violated when his land escheated to the state because his father was a Japanese alien). *See generally* 4 Gordon & Mailman, supra note 42, § 15.12; Charles Gordon, The Racial Barrier to American Citizenship, 93 U. Pa. L. Rev. 237 (1945) (arguing that the U.S. should repeal all racial exclusion laws because they are anachronistic and unjust).

156. *Takahashi*, 334 U.S. at 420.

157. Id. at 421.

158. Id. at 420-21.

community."[159] This exception to the use of strict scrutiny "applies to laws that exclude aliens from positions intimately related to the process of democratic self-government."[160]

The Court's scrutiny in these cases becomes less demanding because:

> The act of becoming a citizen is more than a ritual with no content beyond the fanfare of ceremony. A new citizen has become a member of a Nation, part of a people distinct from others. The individual, at that point, belongs to the polity and is entitled to participate in the processes of democratic decisionmaking. Accordingly, we have recognized "a State's historical power to exclude aliens from participation in its democratic political institutions," as part of the sovereign's obligation "to preserve the basic conception of a political community."[161]

Because the Court refuses to strictly scrutinize all state laws affecting this discrete and insular minority, it has developed a test for determining when to employ the less demanding rational basis standard and when to retain the strict scrutiny standard:

> First, the specificity of the classification will be examined: a classification that is substantially overinclusive or underinclusive tends to undercut the governmental claim that the classification services legitimate political ends. . . . Second, even if the classification is sufficiently tailored, it may be applied in the particular case only to "persons holding state elective or important nonelective executive, legislative, and judicial positions," those officers who "participate directly in the formulation, execution, or review of broad public policy" and hence "perform functions that go to the heart of representative government."[162]

If a classification is over or underinclusive, the law receives strict scrutiny review. If the classification, even though not over or underinclusive, is not tailored to encompass only those positions that "go to the heart of

---

159. *Sugarman*, 413 U.S. at 642-43.

160. Bernal v. Fainter, 467 U.S. 216, 220 (1984). In *Sugarman*, the Court had stated:

> Neither do we hold that a State may not, in an appropriately defined class of positions, require citizenship as a qualification for office. . . . Such power inheres in the State by virtue of its obligation . . . 'to preserve the basic conception of a political community'. . . . [O]ur scrutiny will not be so demanding where we deal with matters resting firmly within a State's constitutional prerogatives.

Sugarman, 413 U.S. at 647-48 (citation omitted).

161. Foley v. Connelie, 435 U.S. 291, 295-96 (1978) (citations omitted). Excluding aliens from the political community is a matter of state discretion, not constitutional mandate. *See* Gerald L. Neuman, "We are the People": Alien Suffrage in German and American Perspective, 13 Mich. J. Int'l L. 259, 311-12 (1992) (reciting history of alienage suffrage in the United States until the 1970s and arguing that it is a permissible and defensible position today); Gerald Rosberg, Aliens and Equal Protection: Why Not the Right to Vote?, 75 Mich. L. Rev. 1092, 1093, 1135-36 (1977) (advocating including aliens in the political community by extending the vote).

162. Cabell v. Chavez-Salido, 454 U.S. 432, 440 (1982).

representative government," the law receives strict scrutiny. If, however, the classification is sufficiently narrow to restrict access to only those jobs involving development, implementation, and execution of "broad public policy," then the Court will employ rational basis review. Teachers, peace officers, and parole officers all perform important political functions,[163] and states may prohibit noncitizens from working in those fields. Civil servants,[164] engineers,[165] notary publics,[166] and attorneys[167] do not perform such functions, and states may not bar noncitizens from pursuing these careers.

If the Court seriously considers aliens as members of a discrete and insular minority who are entitled to greater judicial protection, the level of judicial scrutiny should not be dependent on the nature and strength of the government's interest. The Court's opinions should counsel strict scrutiny review and the state should have the burden of showing that it had a compelling state interest and that the classification was necessary to meet the compelling interest. The state may have a compelling interest in reserving jobs essential to defining the political community to its citizenry. And, it is theoretically possible to draw a classification narrowly enough to be necessary to achieve that compelling interest. The Court, however, refuses to engage in this inquiry, preferring instead to change the rules of analysis for this particular type of alienage issue.[168] This result is partly a product of the outcome determinative nature of categorical balancing, which possesses a rigidness that cannot account for nuance.

More importantly, whether the Court employs a categorical approach or an ad hoc balancing approach, the public function doctrine represents the scales tilting away from the "rights" of the individual in favor of the interests of the community precisely because membership issues are present. In the next section, I survey the personhood model marked by its categorical presumption in favor of protecting the noncitizen.

---

163. *See* Ambach v. Norwick, 441 U.S. 68, 75 (1979) (teachers); *Foley*, 435 U.S. at 300 (police officers); *Cabell*, 454 U.S. at 447 (parole officers).

164. *See Sugarman*, 413 U.S. at 640 (discussing various federal and New York state laws excluding noncitizens from public employment).

165. *See* Examining Board v. Flores de Otero, 426 U.S. 572, 603 (1976) (finding that Puerto Rico's prohibition of noncitizen employment in the private practice of engineering is unconstitutional).

166. *See Bernal*, 467 U.S. at 225 (holding that Texas law precluding noncitizens from employment as a notary public to be unconstitutional).

167. *See In re* Griffiths, 413 U.S. 717, 727 (1973) (holding that Connecticut's exclusion of aliens from the practice of law violates the Equal Protection Clause).

168. "Unless the Court was prepared to strike down every manner and form of distinction between citizens and aliens, it would have to acknowledge that alienage is no garden-variety suspect classification and then construct a rationale to support some of those distinctions." Gerald Rosberg, Discrimination Against the "Nonresident" Alien, 44 U. Pitt. L. Rev. 399, 400 (1983).

IV. THE PERSONHOOD PARADIGM

The personhood tradition, dating back to *Yick Wo v. Hopkins*,[169] has existed in tandem with the *Chinese Exclusion Case*'s[170] membership paradigm, generating a century long dissonance in our alienage jurisprudence.[171] Although most pronounced at the state level, the personhood paradigm has found a limited, but significant, home in the federal cases. During the 1950s and its period of ideological exclusions, the Court often assumed that noncitizens shared the same rights as citizens outside of the immigration context. Without marking a distinction between federal and state treatment of aliens, the Court in *Harisiades v. Shaughnessy*[172] stated:

> [T]he Constitution assures [the alien] a large measure of equal economic opportunity; he may invoke the writ of habeas corpus to protect his personal liberty; in criminal proceedings against him he must be accorded the protections of the Fifth and Sixth Amendments; and, unless an enemy alien, his property cannot be taken without just compensation.[173]

In reality, personhood remains the subsidiary paradigm, garnering a majority support in the Supreme Court only in the absence of broadly construed membership issues (with one notable exception[174]). Its presence, however, is critically important. Whether finding voice in majority opinions or in dissents, the personhood tradition serves to force the courts and those of us who think about these issues "to reconsider the

169. 118 U.S. 356 (1886).

170. Chae Chan Ping v. United States, 130 U.S. 581 (1889).

171. Aleinikoff, Citizens, supra note 14, at 19 (describing the two paradigms as "conflicting strands").

172. 342 U.S. 580 (1952).

173. Id. at 586 n.9 ("Under our law, the alien in several respects stands on an equal footing with citizens, but in others has never been conceded legal parity with citizens. Most importantly, to protract this ambiguous status within the country is not his right but is a matter of permission and tolerance."); *see also* Kwong Hai Chew v. Colding, 344 U.S. 590, 596 n.5 (1953) ("[O]nce an alien lawfully enters and resides in this country he becomes invested with the rights guaranteed by the Constitution to all people within our borders."); Carlson v. Landon, 342 U.S. 524, 534 (1952) ("When legally admitted, they have come at the Nation's invitation, as visitors or permanent residents, to share with us the opportunities and satisfactions of our land. As such visitors and foreign nationals they are entitled in their persons and effects to the protection of our laws."). Following Michael Walzer, this is what Professor Bosniak refers to as the "separation" model, where there is "a strict sepraration between the sphere of membership and the spheres internal to the national society in which aliens conduct their lives." Bosniak, Membership, Equality, and Difference, supra note 14, at 1095. In contrast, both earlier and later cases use the state versus federal distinction to demarcate the line between the personhood and membership paradigms. *See, e.g.*, Plyler v. Doe, 457 U.S. 202, 225 (1982) ("[T]he States enjoy no power with respect to the classification of aliens. This power is 'committed to the political branches of the Federal Government.'") (citations omitted); *Fong Yue Ting*, 149 U.S. at 725 (distinguishing *Yick Wo* because the "question there was of the power of a state over aliens continuing to reside within its jurisdiction, not of the power of the United States to put an end to their residence").

174. *See* infra note 182 (discussing procedural rights exception).

fundamental questions and to rethink the result[s]"[175] of the Court's alienage jurisprudence.

A. *Noncitizen as "Person" Under the Fifth Amendment*

As an exercise of sovereignty, the executive and the legislative branches have almost absolute authority and power to adopt any immigration policy, even those that offend our most basic constitutional principles. The further removed the issues are from the immediate substantive decisions to admit, exclude, or expel, the more likely the Court will backpedal from this near total abdication. As we saw with *Hampton* and *Mathews*, the Court will apply domestic norms, albeit still an extremely deferential rational basis review, to federal discrimination against aliens in the distribution of government benefits. Justice Thurgood Marshall identified two areas where even unadmitted aliens enjoy constitutional protection: First, nonenemy aliens can employ the Fifth Amendment's Takings Clause to protect their property against unlawful takings by the federal government. Second, aliens subject to criminal prosecution "enjoy at trial all of the protections that the Constitution provides to criminal defendants."[176]

1. *Alien Property and the Takings Clause*

Membership issues are largely absent from Takings Clause questions; therefore, domestic constitutional norms apply. In *Russian Volunteer Fleet v. United States*,[177] a Russian corporation sought compensation for two shipbuilding contracts requisitioned by the United States. Relying on the archetypical personhood cases, *Yick Wo* and *Wong Wing*, the Court concluded that the Russian Corporation, as "an alien friend, . . . was entitled to the protection of the Fifth Amendment."[178] Domestic norms flourished here under a personhood regime because questions of admission, exclusion, expulsion, and protection of society's members from outsiders were not present.

If the case had involved enemy aliens or acquisition or retention of

---

175. William J. Brennan, Jr., In Defense of Dissents, 37 Hastings L.J. 427, 436 (1986).

176. Jean v. Nelson, 472 U.S. 846, 873 (1985) (Marshall, J., dissenting).

177. 282 U.S. 481 (1931).

178. Id. at 489. Constitutional protection did not depend on reciprocity from the foreign government:

> The Fifth Amendment gives to each owner of property his individual right. The constitutional right of owner A to compensation when his property is taken is irrespective of what may be done somewhere else with the property of owner B. As alien friends are embraced within the terms of the Fifth Amendment, it cannot be said that their property is subject to confiscation here because the property of our citizens may be confiscated in the alien's country. The provision that private property shall not be taken for public use without just compensation establishes a standard for our government which the Constitution does not make dependent upon the standards of other governments.

Id. at 491-92.

property by noncitizens in violation of U.S. law, the case may have had a different outcome.[179] Enemy aliens threaten the security of the community, compelling the use of membership standards.[180] Violating property laws designed to restrict foreign ownership may be seen as an external threat to the integrity of the process of communal formation.[181] *Russian Volunteer Fleet* demonstrates that where no such membership issues arise, the Court will treat aliens as constitutional persons. In the next section, I explore a true exception to plenary power, application of personhood principles in the presence of membership policy.

2. *Process Values: Personhood's Stronghold*

If immigration law is a constitutional oddity, then the procedural aspects of immigration law present a plenary power doctrine oddity. In the procedural realm, the Court, at times, shifts paradigms and takes the rights of noncitizens seriously within the context of immigration law, limiting the sovereign's otherwise inherent and exclusive power to develop immigration policy. The lesson seems to be that process values, where practicable,[182] trump membership concerns. Procedural issues arise within the context of the decision to admit, exclude, or expel and also within the context of criminal prosecutions of aliens.

From plenary power's beginnings, the Court has consistently held that noncitizens are entitled to domestic criminal trial rights before being criminally sanctioned. After concluding that noncitizens are persons entitled to the protections of the Fifth and Sixth Amendments, the Court,

---

179. *Cf.* id. at 489 ("There was no legislation which prevented it from acquiring and holding the property in question. The petitioner was an alien friend . . . .").

180. *See* Johnson v. Eisentrager, 339 U.S. 763, 771-72 (1950) ("It is war that exposes the relative vulnerability of the alien's status. . . . [D]isabilities this country lays upon the alien who becomes also an enemy are imposed temporarily as an incident of war and not as an incident of alienage."); *see also* Gerald L. Neumann, Whose Constitution?, 100 Yale L.J. 909, 936 n.149 (1991) (noting difference between "alien friends" and "alien enemies"); Douglass I. Koff, Note, Post-Verdugo-Urquidez: The Sufficient Connection Test—Substantially Ambiguous, Substantially Unworkable, 25 Colum. Hum. Rts. L. Rev. 435, 451-52(1994) (discussing parameters of *Eisentrager*).

181. *See Mathews*, 426 U.S. at 80 ("The decision to share [our country's] bounty with our guests may take into account the character of the relationship between the alien and this country: Congress may decide that as the alien's tie grows stronger, so does the strength of his claim to an equal share of that munificence."); *cf. Takahashi*, 334 U.S. at 421 ("To whatever extent the fish in the three-mile belt off California may be 'capable of ownership' by California, we think that 'ownership' is inadequate to justify California in excluding any or all aliens who are lawful residents of the State from making a living by fishing in the ocean off its shores while permitting all others to do so.").

182. The provision of procedural rights is ever bounded by practical concerns. In the immigration context, the essential problem is developing a framework that limits the number of people entitled to benefit from constitutionally mandated procedural minimum. "The main difficulty is probably an obvious one. We are talking about literally everyone in the world—four billion people." Martin, supra note 15, at 180.

in *Wong Wing v. United States*,[183] held that although an alien could suffer deportation upon a summary executive proceeding, it was unconstitutional for the state to first sentence the alien to hard labor without benefit of a judicial trial. Many criminal cases raise no membership issues. Likewise, the criminal alien normally poses no threat to the security of society's members distinct from that provided by our own home grown rabble. One might be tempted to conclude, on the basis of lack of membership concerns, that the personhood paradigm applies.

Wong Wing defies such a simple answer because *Wong Wing* was an immigration case.[184] In formulating membership policy, Congress made a deliberate choice to impose, as part of a package aimed at stemming Chinese migration, criminal sanctions on Chinese nationals residing unlawfully within the United States.[185] The statute allowed the government to impose the criminal penalty administratively without indictment, trial by jury, or judicial involvement.[186] Assuming that the mere threat of deportation would not provide an adequate incentive for the targeted group to voluntarily leave the country, Congress decided that it needed the threat of a relatively quick and cheap punishment that could be imposed upon a summary hearing. Membership's plenary power doctrine would dictate deference to the policy judgments of Congress because "any policy toward aliens is vitally and intricately interwoven with contemporaneous policies in regard to the conduct of foreign relations, the war power, and

---

183. 163 U.S. 228, 238 (1896).

184. Bosniak reads the *Wong Wing* case as a classic example of the Court separating immigration issues from other issues involving the life of the noncitizen within the United States. She says:

> In effect, *Wong Wing* stands for the following proposition: The mere fact that the object of government power is an alien does not mean that the government is exercising its immigration power. The proper domain of immigration regulation has its limits. There is immigration power, and there is governmental power in spheres not directly connected with admission and exclusion; the two are not coextensive and must be kept separate. . . . In other words, power in one sphere does not necessarily entail power in the other. This is a profound and not immediately intuitive holding. . . . [The immigration] domain governs matters of admission, exclusion, and deportation; beyond it, the alien inhabits the domain of territorially present persons where different and more protective rules against government power apply.

Bosniak, Membership, Equality, and Difference, supra note 5, at 1097-98. Here, I think Bosniak has it wrong. *Wong Wing* is not what she terms a separation case; it is, as I state above in the text, a core immigration case. Since *Wong Wing* cannot be justified or explained on the theory that it is a nonimmigration case, some other rationale is needed to explain the presence of meaningful judicial review. I argue that *Wong Wing* reflects the Court's willingness to impose a minimum procedural regime within which the political branches can carry out their substantive immigration policy.

185. Act of May 5, 1892, ch. 60, § 4, 27 Stat. 25 (1893) ("[A]ny such Chinese person or person of Chinese descent convicted and adjudged to be not lawfully entitled to be or remain in the United States shall be imprisoned at hard labor for a period of not exceeding one year and thereafter removed from the United States.").

186. *Wong Wing*, 163 U.S. at 235.

the maintenance of a republican form of government."[187]

Wong Wing squarely addressed Congress's attempt to streamline the removal of those who were not welcome as members or even visitors to our national community.[188] The Court, relying on plenary power precedent, clearly recognized that it could place "*[n]o limits* . . . upon the power of congress to protect, by summary methods, the country from the advent of aliens whose race or habits render them undesirable as citizens, or to expel such if they have already found their way into our land."[189] Nonetheless, the Court rejected the membership rationale and proceeded to impose limits using the personhood paradigm.[190] Congress's underlying substantive decision to punish these aliens did not trouble the Court, but it found the process used to adjudicate the question of punishment unacceptable. "[W]hen Congress sees fit to further promote [its expulsion] policy by subjecting the persons of such aliens to infamous punishment at hard labor, or by confiscating their property, we think such legislation, to be valid, must provide for a judicial trial to establish the guilt of the accused."[191] At least with respect to process in criminal proceedings incident to immigration policy, the Court will enforce domestic norms.

Process values have also displaced plenary power in the context of deportation, and to a lesser extent, in the context of exclusion.[192] Unlike the criminal procedure arena, with its constitutionally enumerated trial rights, the process owed to noncitizens in deportation and exclusion derives from the amorphous Due Process Clause. In the *Japanese Immigrant Case*,[193] the Court established that before the government could deport a noncitizen, she must be given "all opportunity to be heard upon the questions involving his [sic] right to be and remain in the United States. No such arbitrary power can exist where the principles involved in due process of law are recognized."[194]

---

187. *Mathews*, 426 U.S. at 81 (quoting *Harisiades*, 342 U.S. at 588-89; *Reno*, 507 U.S. at 305 ("'[O]ver no conceivable subject is the legislative power of Congress more complete.'"(quoting *Fiallo*, 430 U.S. at 792)).

188. "The question now presented is whether Congress can promote its policy in respect to Chinese persons by adding to its provisions for their exclusion and expulsion punishment by imprisonment at hard labor, to be inflicted . . . without a trial by jury." *Wong Wing*, 163 U.S. at 235.

189. *Wong Wing*, 163 U.S. at 237 (emphasis added).

190. The same reasoning that led to the protection of noncitizens in *Yick Wo*, 118 U.S. at 369, applies to the Fifth and Sixth Amendments as well, requiring an equality of treatment of aliens with respect to the process of trying and punishing them in the United States. *Wong Wing*, 163 U.S. at 238.

191. *Wong Wing*, 163 U.S. at 237.

192. "The one partial exception to the absolute character of Congress's power over immigration concerns procedural due process. . . . [I]t is now accepted that aliens undergoing deportation proceedings are entitled to procedural due process. The same principle seems to extend to those exclusion proceedings in which aliens are returning residents, although again the cases are in conflict." Legomsky, Plenary Congressional Power, supra note 17, at 259.

193. Yamataya v. Fisher, 189 U.S. 86 (1903).

194. Id. at 101. Finding the minimal due process requirements satisfied, the court affirmed

For the most part, the Court takes a territorial approach with little or no regard for the strength of an alien's ties to the United States. Noncitizens who are within our borders legally or illegally,[195] for short or extended periods of time,[196] possess a liberty interest in remaining in this country; therefore, they are entitled to due process prior to deportation. Noncitizens who are outside this country, no matter how strong their ties to the United States,[197] have no similar liberty interest in gaining admittance and, therefore, are entitled to none of the Constitution's procedural guarantees[198] unless the alien falls within the purview of *Landon v. Plasencia*.[199]

Landon involved the Immigration and Naturalization Service's attempt to exclude Plasencia from the United States on grounds of her involvement in smuggling illegal aliens into the United States.[200] Plasencia, a permanent resident alien, made two procedural claims. First, she claimed an entitlement to have her immigration status determined in a deportation hearing rather than an exclusion hearing.[201] Second, she claimed that her status as a returning permanent resident entitled her to the constitutional protections found in the Due Process Clause of the Fifth Amendment, regardless of whether she received a deportation hearing or an exclusion hearing. After denying her claim to a deportation hearing on statutory construction grounds,[202] the Court concluded "that under the

---

the deportation order. Id. at 102. "If the appellants want of knowledge of the English language put her at some disadvantage in the investigation . . . that was her misfortune . . . ." Id.

195. "Aliens, even aliens whose presence in this country is unlawful, have long been recognized as 'persons guaranteed due process of law by the Fifth and Fourteenth Amendments." *Plyler*, 457 U.S. at 210.

196. *See Yamataya*, 189 U.S. at 86 (four days).

197. *See, e.g.*, Shaughnessy v. United States *ex rel.* Mezei, 345 U.S. 206, 208 (1953) (involving a 25-year resident of the United States).

198. *See, e.g.*, id. at 215; United States *ex rel.* Knauff v. Shaughnessy, 338 U.S. 537, 544 (1950) ("Whatever the procedure authorized by Congress is, it is due process as far as an alien denied entry is concerned."); *see also* Nafziger, supra note 85, at 51 (discussing the plenary power doctrine, which "is illogical" and should not bar judicial review of visa denials).

199. 459 U.S. 21 (1982).

200. At the time an alien "who at any time shall have, knowingly and for gain, encouraged, induced, assisted, abetted, or aided any other alien to enter or to try to enter the United States in violation of law" was excludable. Id. at 23 (quoting 8 U.S.C. § 1182 (a)(31)). The "for gain" language has been deleted from the statutes, allowing for the exlusion of volunteer alien smugglers. *See* 8 U.S.C. § 1182 (a)(6)(E)(i) (1994) ("Any alien who at any time knowingly has encouraged, induced, assisted, abetted, or aided any other alien to enter or to try to enter the United States in violation of law is excludable.").

201. Following Rosenberg v. Fleuti, 374 U.S. 449 (1963), which held that an "innocent, casual, or brief" absence from the country does not trigger "the consequences of an "entry" on return, Plasencia argued that her trip to Mexico fit within the *Fleuti* exception, and, therefore, she was entitled to a deportation hearing. *Landon*, 459 U.S. at 30. The Court disagreed, stating that *Fleuti* "only defined 'entry' and did not designate the forum for deciding questions of entry." Id. at 31-32.

202. *Landon*, 459 U.S. at 32 ("The Statutory scheme is clear: Congress intended that the

circumstances of this case, she can invoke the Due Process Clause on returning to this country, although we do not decide the contours of the process that is due or whether the process accorded Plasencia was insufficient."[203] The Court found that the sovereign was obligated to provide a constitutionally prescribed procedural minimum because Plasencia's prior residence in the United States strengthened her constitutional status.[204]

In *Landon*, as with the other cases granting noncitizens procedural relief, the Court saw its role as limited. "The role of the judiciary is limited to determining whether the procedures meet the essential standard of fairness under the Due Process Clause and does not extend to imposing procedures that merely displace congressional choices of policy."[205] This limited role, however, is significantly broader than the one played by the judiciary under plenary power. Some aliens (those present in the United States and those who fall within Plasencia) receive treatment as persons under the procedural due process component of the Fifth Amendment even at the expense of Congress' membership scheme. We will return briefly to the procedural exceptions to plenary power in Section IV of the Article. As the only true exceptions to plenary power's hold on membership policy, these cases may contain the formula for those desiring to loosen the grip of plenary power on the Court's alienage jurisprudence.

B. Noncitizen as "Person" Under the Fourteenth Amendment

Yick Wo v. Hopkins[206] created the personhood paradigm. During the next half century, the state alienage cases developed along two distinct lines. One line of cases addressed classifications imposing burdens on aliens in the private sphere. The other line addressed classifications involving the special public interest.[207] *Truax v. Raich*,[208] is a typical example of the former line. In *Truax*, the challenged Arizona law prohibited most employers from employing more than twenty percent noncitizens. The Court struck down the law on equal protection grounds:

It requires no argument to show that the right to work for a living

---

determinations of both 'entry' and the existence of grounds for exclusion could be made at an exclusion hearing.").

203. Id. at 32. The Court recognized that the balancing test developed in Matthews v. Eldridge, 424 U.S. 319, 334-35 (1976), was the appropriate test to determine the process due. *Landon*, 459 U.S. at 34. Here, the "weighty" competing interests, Plasencia's interest in staying in the United States with her family and the government's "sovereign prerogative" to control immigration, hung in the balance. Id.

204. Id. at 32. ("[O]nce an alien gains admission to our country and begins to develop the ties that go with permanent residence, his constitutional status changes accordingly," at least with respect to procedural due process.).

205. Id. at 34-35.

206. *See* supra notes 169-175 and accompanying text (discussing the personhood paradigm).

207. *See* supra notes 146-158 and accompanying text.

208. 239 U.S. 33 (1915).

> in the common occupations of the community is of the very essence of the personal freedom and opportunity that it was the purpose of the Amendment to secure. . . . If this could be refused solely upon the ground of race or nationality, the prohibition of the denial to any person of the equal protection of the laws would be a barren form of words.[209]

Yick Wo, its early progeny, and its exceptions provide the necessary backdrop for examining the modern state alienage cases. Before moving on to those cases, it is important to mention the two distinct theories that underlie and support the results in *Yick Wo* and its progeny. First, aliens, like citizens, are "persons" entitled to equal protection. Second, the federal government possesses exclusive power over alienage issues.[210]

For my purposes, it does not matter whether the Court's state alienage cases rest on equal protection or federalism grounds. Rather, what matters is that the Court applies strict scrutiny in many state alienage cases precisely because of the absence of membership issues; the rationale—equality or preemption—is irrelevant to the outcome. As an explanatory tool, however, preemption has greater force by staying clear of the hopelessly tangled web the Court created by characterizing aliens as a suspect class. Doctrinally, this latter approach, based on federalism, is clearer; it recognizes that the citizen and the alien are not similarly situated for purposes of parceling out the benefits of membership, while also recognizing that the primary responsibility for drawing distinctions rests with the federal government. Despite the attractiveness of the federalism approach, the Court continues to emphasize the equal protection rationale in its alienage cases.[211]

Choosing between these two theoretical approaches to the alienage cases does not resolve one other important issue—the intensity with which the Court will review the government's alienage classifications.[212] As the

---

209. Id. at 41 (citations omitted).

210. Id. at 42.

> The underpinnings of the Court's constitutional decisions defining the circumstances under which state and local governments may favor citizens of this country by denying lawfully admitted aliens equal protection rights and opportunities have been two. The first, *based squarely on the concepts embodied in the Equal Protection Clause of the Fourteenth Amendment and in the Due Process Clause of the Fifth Amendment*, recognizes that "[a]liens as a class are a prime example of a 'discrete and insular' minority . . . for whom . . . heightened judicial solicitude is appropriate. The second, grounded in the Supremacy Clause and in the naturalization power, recognizes the Federal Government's primary responsibility in the field of immigration and naturalization.

Examining Bd. of Eng'rs v. Flores, 426 U.S. 572, 602 (1976) (emphasis added)(citations omitted); *see, e.g.*, Michael J. Perry, Equal Protection, Judicial Activism, and the Intellectual Agenda of Constitutional Theory: Reflections on, and Beyond, Plyler v. Doe, 44 U. Pitt. L. Rev. 329, 334 (1983) (suggesting "that constitutional doctrine regarding alienage-based classifications is better understood in terms, not of equal protection, but of federalism").

211. *See, e.g.*, *Bernal*, 467 U.S. at 219 (holding that a Texas statute violates the Equal Protection Clause by denying aliens the opportunity to become notaries public).

212. Even if the personhood approach provides a sound legal alternative to the federal

Court has stated, aliens are persons and, at least in some limited context, are entitled to equal protection. However, states may have various interests in treating aliens and members of their own political community similarly or dissimilarly. The formula for reconciling these competing interests remained elusive until *Graham v. Richardson*.[213]

1. Strict Scrutiny

Modern equal protection law affecting aliens has retained strands of both the *Yick Wo* tradition and its exception, the special public interest doctrine. The progeny of *Yick Wo* solidified protection for aliens, subjecting most state classifications that discriminate on alienage grounds to strict scrutiny review. The exception, narrowed and refocused, reappeared as the public function doctrine.[214] This subsection discusses the strict scrutiny cases.

Building on *Takahashi* and the creation of two-tiered equal protection analysis,[215] the Court in *Graham v. Richardson* concluded that "classifications based on alienage, like those based on nationality or race, are inherently suspect and subject to close judicial scrutiny. Aliens as a class are a prime example of a 'discrete and insular' minority for whom such heightened judicial solicitude is appropriate."[216] Applying strict scrutiny, the Court will strike down any state law that discriminates against aliens unless the classification is necessary to achieve a compelling state interest.[217] The Court has used this test to strike down laws that deny permanent resident aliens welfare benefits,[218] financial aid for higher education,[219] the opportunity to compete for state civil service jobs,[220] and the opportunity to work as an attorney,[221] civil engineer,[222] and

---

supremacy rationale, the Court is not bound to intensely review state discrimination against aliens. "Decisions of this Court holding that an alien is a "person" within the meaning of the Equal Protection Clause of the Fourteenth Amendment are simply irrelevant to the question of whether that Amendment prohibits legislative classifications based upon this particular status." Sugarman v. Dougall, 413 U.S. 634, 653 (1973) (Rehnquist, J., dissenting); *cf.* Williamson v. Lee Optical, 348 U.S. 483, 491 (1955) (explaining that although opticians are "persons" under the Fourteenth Amendment, classification that places them at a competitive disadvantage to ophthalmologists and optometrists is deferentially scrutinized under the rational basis test).

213. 403 U.S. 365 (1971).

214. *See* supra notes 159-68 (discussing when strict scrutiny will be applied to state laws affecting a "discrete and insular minority" and when such scrutiny by the Court is less demanding).

215. *See* United States v. Carolene Prods. Co., 304 U.S. 144, 152-53 n.4 (1938).

216. Id. at 372 (citation omitted). The Court did cite *Carolene Product's* footnote 4. *See Carolene Prods.*, 304 U.S. at 152 n.4; *see also Hampton*, 426 U.S. at 102 (describing aliens as "an identifiable class of persons . . . subject to disadvantages not shared by the remainder of the community").

217. *See* Washington v. Davis, 426 U.S. 229, 248 (1976).

218. Graham v. Richardson, 403 U.S. 365 (1971).

219. Nyquist v. Mauclet, 432 U.S. 1 (1977).

220. *Sugarman*, 413 U.S. at 643.

221. *In re* Griffiths, 413 U.S. 717 (1973).

notary public.[223]

Sugarman v. Dougall,[224] like its federal counterpart, *Hampton v. Mow Sun Wong*,[225] involved a government attempt to restrict civil service employment to citizens. The state's discriminatory classification failed strict scrutiny because the "citizenship restriction [swept] indiscriminately," prohibiting noncitizen employment as garbage collectors and typists.[226] Although the Court's analysis fell solidly within the personhood paradigm, the dicta presaged membership in the form of the public function doctrine. In disavowing any suggestion that it would reject a state's attempt to develop citizenship requirements for "an appropriately defined class of positions," the Court said that "our scrutiny will not be so demanding where we deal with matters resting firmly within a State's constitutional prerogatives."[227]

Justice Rehnquist dissented. He did not quarrel with the Court's characterization of the noncitizen as a "person" entitled to equal protection; rather, he took issue with the Court's choice of strict scrutiny as the prism with which to review the classification. Rehnquist saw no constitutional ground to treat aliens as a "suspect" class; he would have upheld the classifications using a rational basis analysis. According to Rehnquist, the Court, by applying the greatest degree of judicial protection to noncitizens, seriously undervalued the importance of citizenship. "In constitutionally defining who is a citizen of the United States, Congress obviously thought it was doing something important. Citizenship meant something, a status in and relationship with society which is continuing and more basic than mere presence or residence."[228] Because membership issues were present, even at the state level, Rehnquist would strike the categorical balance toward the community and place the case in the membership category.[229]

---

222. Examining Bd. v. Flores de Otero, 426 U.S. 572 (1976).

223. Bernal v. Fainter, 467 U.S. 216 (1984).

224. 413 U.S. 634 (1973).

225. For a discussion of *Hampton*, see supra text at notes 133-42.

226. *Sugarman*, 413 U.S. at 643.

227. Id. at 647-48.

228. Id. at 652 (Rehnquist, J., dissenting). The most disturbing part of the opinion "is the intimation, if not statement, that [citizens] are really not any different from aliens." Id. at 658. "The Court simply ignores the purpose of the process of assimilation into and dedication to our society . . . ." Id. at 661.

229. Rehnquist's concern extended beyond the alienage sphere to what he saw as the Court's indiscriminate use of "strict scrutiny." He saw no support for treating any minorities other than racial minorities as "discrete and insular." Id. at 650.

> Our society, consisting of over 200 million individuals of multitudinous origins, customs, tongues, beliefs, and cultures is, to say the least, diverse. It would hardly take extraordinary ingenuity for a lawyer to find "insular and discrete" minorities at every turn in the road. Yet, unless the Court can precisely define and constitutionally justify both the terms and analysis it uses, these decisions today stand for the proposition that the Court can choose a "minority" it "feels" deserves "solicitude." . . . I cannot find, and the Court does not cite, any constitutional authority for

By employing the rigid and dichotomous equal protection doctrine, and by casting noncitizens as a discrete and insular minority, the Court commits itself to a highly intensive level for reviewing state alienage claims. Echoing the spirit of *Carolene Products*'s Footnote 4,[230] *Graham* and its progeny assign paramount weight to the noncitizen's personhood,[231] placing great emphasis on the values of human dignity and equality. Against equality, the state's interests are insignificant. The state's interests merit no weight unless compelling. Even then, the state has the insurmountable task of proving that its classification is necessary to achieve that compelling state interest. This method of assigning relative weight to the competing interests works fairly well where the Court is willing to summarily dismiss the state's interests. Complications arise in the alienage field because the Court is unwilling, in all cases, to discard the governmental interest, as evidenced by the "public function doctrine" at the state level and plenary power at the federal level.

Classifying aliens as a discrete and insular minority and tying the Court to a personhood approach in alienage classifications cemented the dissonance in an already polarized field. Although the class of aliens presumably retain the characteristics that earned this legally privileged label, close judicial scrutiny has never applied to substantive questions falling within the membership paradigm. In Section V, I will turn to exploring what Margaret Taylor has described as the "pourous border" between membership and personhood.[232]

2. *Intermediate Scrutiny: Education and Undocumented Children*

Perhaps *Plyler v. Doe*,[233] is best understood as a constitutional anomaly.[234] In *Plyler*, the state's ability to allocate its limited education dollars collided with the purported rights of undocumented alien children to receive tuition-free access to education on an equal basis with citizens and legal aliens. In resolving this issue in favor of the alien children, the Court blended strands from both the personhood and membership paradigms. Doctrinally, the Court created yet another standard of review in alienage cases. Aliens, even those illegally in the United States, are

---

such a "ward of the Court" approach to equal protection.

Id. at 657.

230. *Carolene Products*, 304 U.S. at 152-53 n.4.

231. The *Graham* Court did not forget federalism issues. "An additional reason why the state statutes at issue in these cases do not withstand constitutional scrutiny emerges from the area of federal-state relations." *Graham*, 403 U.S. at 376-77.

232. *Taylor*, supra note 22, at 1145.

233. 457 U.S. 202 (1982).

234. "[B]y patching together bits and pieces of what might be termed quasi-suspect-class [illegal alien children] and quasi-fundamental-rights [education] analysis, the Court spins out a theory custom-tailored to the facts. . . . " Id. at 244 (Burger, C.J., dissenting); *see also* Spiro, supra note 71, at 153 n.136 ("*Plyler* is but a small twig on the jurisprudential tree, one which would be readily broken off with disturbing other rulings, for other decisions have not followed from it.").

"persons" entitled to the protections of the Constitution.[235] The question then became the intensity of judicial oversight. The Court found that strict scrutiny was inappropriate for two reasons: First, the illegal alien children could not be considered a "suspect class because their presence in this country in violation of federal law is not a 'constitutional irrelevancy.'"[236] Second, public education, although "a most vital civic institution,"[237] is not a fundamental constitutional right. Minimum rational basis review, however, inadequately protected the important educational interests of these "special members of this underclass"[238] who are in the United States involuntarily. Denying these children free public education would "impose[] a lifetime hardship on a discrete class of children not accountable for their disabling status. The stigma of illiteracy will mark them for the rest of their lives."[239] Additionally, since these undocumented children will likely spend their lives in this country, the state has a long term interest in having them educated.

The Court, therefore, settled for the middle ground, applying intermediate scrutiny review. The law, which burdened illegal alien children in a significant way, would not be found rational and upheld "unless it furthered some substantial goal of the State."[240] The Court found that none of the state's "three colorable" interests met the constitutional burden.[241] First, the Court thought "it clear that charging tuition to undocumented children constitutes a ludicrously ineffectual attempt to stem the tide of illegal immigration."[242] Second, the Court

---

235. *Plyler*, 457 U.S. at 210. A person illegally in the United States "is subject to the full range of obligations imposed by the State's civil and criminal laws. And until he leaves . . . he is entitled to the equal protection of the laws that a State may choose to establish." Id. at 215.

236. Id at 223.

> We reject the claim that "illegal aliens" are a "suspect class," . . . Unlike most of the classifications that we have recognized as suspect, entry into this class, by virtue of entry into this country, is a product of voluntary action. Indeed, entry into the class is itself a crime. . . . [U]ndocumented status is [not] a "constitutional irrelevancy." With respect to the actions of the Federal Government, alienage classifications may be intimately related to the conduct of foreign policy. . . . No State may independently exercise a like power.

Id. at 219 n.19.

237. Id. at 221 (citing Abington Sch. Dist. v. Schempp, 374 U.S. 203, 230 (1963) (Brennan, J., concurring).

238. *Plyler*, 457 U.S. at 219.

239. Id. at 223; *see also* Elizabeth Hull, Undocumented Children and Free Public Education: An Analysis of Plyler v. Doe, 44 U. Pitt. L. Rev. 409, 432 (1983) ("To deny them the equal protection of the laws would . . . compound an injustice, and create for the first time since the demise of Jim Crow legislation an institutionalized underclass.").

240. *Plyler*, 457 U.S. at 224. "'Intermediate' scrutiny permits [the Court] to evaluate the rationality of the legislative judgment with reference to well-settled constitutional principles: by inquiring whether [the classification] may fairly be viewed as furthering a substantial interest of the State." Id. at 217-18, n.16.

241. *See* id. at 227, 230 (labeling the state's three interests as "colorable" and deciding these interests are "wholly insubstantial in light of the costs involved to these children").

242. Id. at 228-29.

found undocumented children to be similarly situated with children lawfully in the country with respect to educational funding issues.[243] Third, since "[t]he State has no assurance that any child, citizen or not, will employ the education provided by the State within the confines of the State's borders," likely future contributions to the state is an inadequate justification for the disparate treatment.[244]

With its heightened scrutiny, *Plyler* clearly and squarely falls within the personhood paradigm. Membership concerns, obscure, but present nevertheless, played a supporting role in advancing the case for the undocumented children. The Court recognized that many of these children "will remain here permanently and that some indeterminate number will eventually become citizens."[245] The Court could not fathom "precisely what the State hope[d] to achieve by promoting the creation and perpetuation of a subclass of illiterates within its boundaries, surely adding to the problems and costs of unemployment, welfare, and crime."[246] In addition to providing "the basic tools by which individuals might lead economically productive lives to the benefit of us all[,]"[247] education plays a central role in communal formation. "[P]ublic schools [serve] as a most vital civic institution for the preservation of a democratic system of government."[248] They serve as a vital forum where students are inculcated with the "fundamental values necessary to the maintenance of a democratic political system."[249] Education "is the very foundation of good citizenship. Today it is a principal instrument in awakening the child to cultural values."[250]

To justify its protection of the individual, the Court relied heavily on the membership concerns of communal formation beginning with the education of the young. Although membership issues were present, the Court unequivocally rejected the membership paradigm. The Court, not the state legislature, made the policy determination that the membership concerns it valued, coupled with the concerns for the innocent child, merited close scrutiny of Texas's legislative scheme.[251] In contrast, the Court dismissed the state's asserted membership interests as ludicrous[252]

243. Id. at 229.
244. Id. at 230.
245. *Plyler*, 457 U.S. at 222 n.20.
246. Id. at 230.
247. Id. at 221.
248. Id. (citing Abington Sch. Dist. v. Schempp, 374 U.S. 203, 230 (Brennan, J., concurring)).
249. Id. (quoting Ambach v. Norwick, 441 U.S. 68, 77 (1979)).
250. *Plyler*, 457 U.S. at 223 (quoting Brown v. Board of Educ., 347 U.S. 483, 493 (1954)).
251. Scott D. Livingston, Plyler v. Doe: Ilegal Aliens and the Misguided Search for Equal Protection, 11 Hastings. Const. L.Q. 599, 635 (1984) (criticizing the Court's aproach, the author concludes: "[I]t is not the result, but the process, not the resolution but the investigation, not the outcome but the struggle to reach an effective political consensus that are fundamental to our democracy.").
252. *See Plyer*, 457 U.S. at 228.

and "difficult to understand."[253]

This section and the previous one explored the various doctrinal manifestations of the membership and personhood paradigms. In the next section, I explore the broad parameters of membership.

V. MEMBERSHIP'S BORDERS

The alienage cases are unique because they exhibit the full range of doctrinal options currently used by the judiciary. Broadly summarized, the Court uses strict scrutiny to review most alienage classifications made by the states; however, the political function exception to strict scrutiny allows the Court to apply a rationality test to state alienage classifications that are intimately associated with the state's definition of its political community. The Court employed intermediate scrutiny where the state denied illegal alien children equal access to free public education. The Court uses some form of heightened scrutiny in reviewing federal action that denies noncitizens, who are present in the United States, criminal trial rights and other procedural protections, but it uses rational basis review for federal alienage classifications that do not involve immigration's core. Finally, the Court gives deferential review, bordering on use of the political question doctrine, in cases of federal classifications involving questions of noncitizen admission, exclusion, and expulsion from the United States.

Generally, when a case involves sovereign interests of immigration and communal formation, the Court examines the issues through membership's lens, allowing lawmakers broad flexibility in policy development. In the absence of these membership concerns, the Court generally focuses on the noncitizen as an individual protected by the Constitution. The Court refuses to engage in ad hoc balancing of the interests of the government and of the noncitizen, preferring instead the categorical balancing so prevalent in modern constitutional analysis. When a case is catalogued within the membership sphere, the Court has made an a priori determination that membership issues outweigh personhood issues, obviating the need for a delicate balancing of the competing interests. Conversely, when the Court applies the personhood approach, it has made a prior determination that personhood concerns outweigh any purported governmental interests. This methodology is too rigid to accommodate meaningful exploration into the relative strengths of the competing individual and governmental interests. It forces the Court to undervalue the interests of either the government or the individual. Given the fact that the categorization almost always proves outcome determinative, it is imperative to explore the borderland between membership and personhood.

It seems obvious "that as the alien's tie [to the United States] grows stronger, so does the strength of his claim to an equal share of [this

253. Id. at 230.

country's] munificence."[254] Equally obvious is that the government's interests gain strength, reaching an apex "with decisions that lie at the heart of immigration policies."[255] When does one interest dominate the other?

> In general, national-origin classifications have a stronger claim to constitutionality when they are employed in connection with decisions that lie at the heart of immigration policy. When central immigration concerns are not at stake, however, the Executive must recognize the individuality of the alien, just as it must recognize the individuality of all other persons within our borders.[256]

How wide and deep is the "heart of immigration?" Stated more broadly, what is the scope of the membership sphere? And, who—the Courts or the policy makers—gets to decide these parameters?

Justice Marshall explored these issues in his dissent in *Jean v. Nelson*.[257] That case presented an equal protection claim by Haitians who claimed that they were denied parole into the United States, pending the determination of their admissibility as refugees, on the basis of race and national origin.[258] The Court based its decision on nonconstitutional grounds, a position Marshall saw as "untenable."[259] He concluded that the Fifth Amendment's equal protection component prohibited the government from discriminating on the basis of race or national origin in its decision whether to parole unadmitted aliens pending the determination of their admissibility.[260] In reaching this conclusion, Marshall took a narrow view of immigration's core and would have required the

254. *Mathews*, 426 U.S. at 80.

255. Jean v. Nelson, 472 U.S. 846, 881 (1985) (Marshall, J., dissenting).

256. Id.

257. Id. at 858-82.

258. For many years, the INS paroled undocumented aliens into the country pending a determination of their admissibility. Id. at 849. Pursuant to our entry fiction, these parolees although physically present have not made an entry into the United States and therefore remain subject to the procedural and substantive law of exclusion. *See* Kathrin S. Mautino, Entry: What Mama Never Told You About Being There, 31 San Diego L. Rev. 911, 933-36 (1994) (discussing the parole of excludable aliens); Charles D. Weisselberg, The Exclusion and Detention of Aliens: Lessons From the Lives of Ellen Knauff and Ignatz Mezei, 143 U. Penn. L. Rev. 933, 951-52 (1995) (exploring the entry fiction and the detention of excludable aliens). As a result of the increased flux of refugees flowing into South Florida from the Caribbean, the INS began a policy of detaining the undocumented aliens pending a determination of admissibility. *Jean*, 472 U.S. at 849 (Marshall, J., dissenting). In *Jean v. Nelson*, the Haitians claimed that the detention policy was being applied adversely to them based on their race and national origin. Id.

259. *Jean*, 472 U.S. at 868 (Marshall, J., dissenting). Avoiding the constitutional issues, the majority concluded that the applicable statutes and regulations did not permit parole decisions to be based on race or national origin grounds. Id. at 857. Marshall viewed the Court's nonconstitutional argument as a "house of cards," because he saw no "nonconstitutional constraints on the Executive's authority to make national-origin distinctions in the statutes and regulations." Id. at 859 (Marshall, J., dissenting).

260. Id. at 868-69.

government to show that its discriminatory acts fall within that core. For him, the issue of parole into the United States pending a determination of admissibility, which necessarily includes temporary admission, was not a core immigration question.[261] If Congress or the Executive demonstrates that its discriminatory parole policy is "sufficiently related to [a] valid immigration goal . . . then arguably it should be upheld, provided of course that it is not too underinclusive."[262] As the cases explored in the previous sections reveal, Marshall's position is the minority position: membership's core is broad and the political branches receive wide latitude in formulating its policy.

A. Substantive Values

The Court gives both the federal and the state governments much discretion regarding the parameters of membership. More discretion flows to the federal government because of its status as a sovereign nation and its obligations to set immigration policy, but ample discretion is still given to the states. The public function exception to strict scrutiny, as seen in the contrast between *Sugarman v. Dougall*[263] and *Cabell v. Chavez-Salido*[264] illustrates this proposition. In *Sugarman*, the Court recognized New York's "substantial" interest in prohibiting nonmembers from taking part in the shaping of the political community.[265] A statute limiting employment in the competitive civil service to citizens failed under strict scrutiny, however, because the means chosen were not "precisely drawn in light of the acknowledged purpose; . . . [t]he citizenship restriction sweeps indiscriminately."[266] The citizenship requirement was both over and underinclusive: the statute barred noncitizens from many state jobs, such as sanitation worker and typist, that do not touch upon important sovereign functions of the state, but it did not bar noncitizens from "holding elective and high appointive offices."[267] The Court left open the possibility of

261. Id. at 877-78.

262. Id. at 880-81. Marshall also took a narrow view of membership in the state cases. First, he would have preferred to strictly scrutinize any state policy choice that placed citizenship restrictions on employment, even when the state sought to justify the classification on communal formation grounds. *See* Foley v. Connalie, 435 U.S. 291, 303 n.1 (1978) (Marshall, J., dissenting) ("The Court did not explain why the level of scrutiny should vary with the nature of the job from which aliens are being excluded."). Second, Marshall read the political function exception much more narrowly than the majority. *See* id. at 304-05 (explaining that a state trooper is not a policy maker); *see also* Cabell v. Chavez-Salido, 454 U.S. 432, 455 (1982) (Blackmun, J., joined by Marshall, Brennan and Stevens, dissenting) ("California's statutory exclusion of aliens is fatally overinclusive and underinclusive."); Ambach v. Norwick, 441 U.S. 68, 90 (1979) (Blackmun, J. joined by Marshall, Brennan and Stevens, dissenting) (remarking that New York's exclusion of aliens from teaching school children is "repugnant" to the values the state is trying to teach).

263. 413 U.S. 634 (1973).

264. 454 U.S. 432 (1982).

265. 413 U.S. at 643.

266. Id.

267. Id.

citizen restrictive laws by stating: "Neither do we hold that a State may not, in an appropriately defined class of positions, require citizenship as a qualification for office."[268] In constrast, the Court applied the political function exception in upholding California's requirement that "peace officers be citizens of the United States."[269]

Under a strict scrutiny analysis, an appropriately defined class must be narrowly drawn to achieve the state's sovereignty interests. As we have seen,[270] the Court rejected such a rigid analysis when reviewing a state's attempt to prohibit noncitizens from occupying jobs that go to the heart of governing.[271] As a threshold for determining whether to apply the membership approach, the Court inquires into "the specificity of the classification . . . a classification that is substantially overinclusive or underinclusive tends to undercut the governmental claim that the classification serves legitimate political ends."[272] In other words, the Court will look at substantial overbreadth as a sign that the state's true motive was something other than fostering the political community.

If the Court had used strict scrutiny in *Chavez-Salido* or if the Court had even taken seriously the political function exception's test for deference, it would not have upheld California's law prohibiting noncitizens from becoming peace officers. California had classified "[c]emetery sextans, furniture and bedding inspectors, livestock identification inspectors, and toll service employees" as well as several other types of "law enforcement" officials under the rubric "peace officer."[273] These positions certainly are not important to California's identity as a political community. The severe overinclusiveness of the citizenship restriction undermined California's argument that the law served the purportedly important political function interest; instead, a fairly clear inference could be drawn that the state was merely engaged in impermissible economic protectionism.[274]

Without probing the invidious and prejudicial nature of the

268. Id. at 647 (citing Cal. Penal Code §830.5 (West Supp. 1981)).

269. *Cabell*, 454 U.S. at 445.

270. *See* supra notes 206-23 and accompanying text (discussing the Supreme Court's decision that strict "scrutiny will not be so demanding . . . with matters resting firmly within the state's constitutional prerogatives").

271. *See Foley*, 435 U.S. at 296-97 (recognizing that citizenship can be a relevant qualification for government jobs).

272. *Cabell*, 454 U.S. at 440. Additionally, "even if the classification is sufficiently tailored, it may be applied in the particular case only to 'persons holding state elective or important nonelective executive, legislative, and judicial positions,' those officers who 'participate directly in the formulation, execution, or review of broad public policy' and hence 'perform functions that go to the heart of representative government.'" Id. at 440 (quoting *Sugarman*, 413 U.S. at 647. *See* supra text at notes 159-68 for a more detailed analysis of the public function doctrine.

273. *Cabell*, 454 U.S. at 442.

274. At the least, "the [s]tatutes at issue here represent . . . an unthinking and haphazard exercise of state power." Id. at 454.

classification, as evidenced by the law's overinclusiveness and underinclusiveness, the Court jettisoned strict scrutiny analysis, concluding that such a high standard "is out of place when the restriction primarily serves a political function."[275] Instead, the Court employed the "public function" exception to strict scrutiny review. Since law enforcement officers generally serve important public functions, the Court did not press the state to justify each constituent peace officer position.[276] Although some peace officer jobs "may have only a tenuous connection to traditional police functions of law enforcement," the Court found that the statute's classification is "sufficiently tailored . . . to pass the lower level of scrutiny . . . articulated as the appropriate equal protection standard for such an exercise of sovereign power . . . ."[277] Noncitizens remain a suspect class and alienage classifications remain "inherently suspect" because noncitizens fall within the judicially constructed category of discrete and insular minority.[278] Because, however, the "[d]efinition of the important sovereign functions of the political community is necessarily the primary responsibility of the representative branches of government," the Court will engage in only "limited judicial review."[279]

The rigid tiered analysis cannot adequately accommodate both the alien and the government where both have important interests on the line. The strict scrutiny test falters under the weight of the state's asserted interest in defining and shaping its political community. Under traditional strict scrutiny, the Court explores whether the state is engaged in invidious discrimination by first inquiring into the compellingness of the state's interest. If the state has no compelling interest in its classification, the Court might suspect a wrongful and prejudicial purpose behind the law. In

---

275. Id. at 439.

276. *See* id.

277. Id. at 444. The Court admits that some of the jobs placed in the categorical umbrella of peace officer "have only a tenuous connection to traditional police functions of law enforcement." Id. at 443.

278. *See* Bernal v. Fainter, 467 U.S. 216, 219 n.5 (1984) (quoting Graham v. Richardson, 403 U.S. 365, 372 (1971)); *see also Cabell*, 454 U.S. at 438 (1982) (defining areas in which state government may distinguish between its citizens and aliens). In *Flores*, the Court suggests that strict scrutiny applies to all alienage cases (at least non-immigration cases):

> We do not suggest, however, that a State, Territory, or local government, or certainly the Federal Government, may not be permitted some discretion in determining the circumstances under which it will employ aliens or whether aliens may receive public benefits or partake of public resources on the same basis as citizens. In each case, the governmental interest claimed to justify the discrimination is to be carefully examined in order to determine whether that interest is legitimate and substantial, and inquiry must be made whether the means adopted to achieve the goal are necessary and precisely drawn.

Examining Bd. v. Flores, 426 U.S. 572, 604-05 (1976).

279. *Cabell*, 454 U.S. at 445. "[A]lthough citizenship is not a relevant ground for the distribution of economic benefits, it is a relevant ground for determining membership in the political community;" therefore, "strict scrutiny is out of place when the restriction primarily services a political function." Id. at 438-39.

Chavez-Salido, we can assume, arguendo, that the state's interest is compelling. Next, the Court would inquire into the classification's necessity in achieving the compelling state interest of defining the political community. The classification would be examined under the judicial microscope for possible under and overinclusive tendencies, which would undermine the state's claim that its law was not invidious. Here, in the means testing, the process breaks down. Almost all classifications can be drawn with more precision. But, the instruments necessary to calibrate the law with such precision raise the cost of legislation above that which the Court is willing to demand. Therefore, the Court's "scrutiny will not be so demanding where [they] deal with matters resting firmly within a State's constitutional prerogatives."[280]

With respect to the state alienage jurisprudence, I do not want to overstate the case for deference. *Graham v. Richardson,* with its strict scrutiny doctrine, operates in a wide sphere, placing strict equal protection limitations on state actors. My point, informed by the Court's reasoning in *Chavez-Salido,* is that when membership issues are arguably present, the Court retreats, allowing the states broad authority to discriminate in the name of communal formation.[281] Two components are present: the Court's decision to create an exception to the strict scrutiny analysis, and the Court's deferential posture toward the state legislatures when the issues reside in the borderland between membership and personhood.

The federal government has even broader authority. With the demise of the special public interest doctrine, the Court has limited the states' membership concerns to the political formation of the community and not the distribution of the community's goods.[282] At the federal level, nearly every action affecting noncitizens is considered part of the membership scheme. It is here that I seem to part company with other scholars who cabin the plenary power doctrine solely within immigration law.[283] In my analysis, the Court discards burdensome domestic constitutional norms whenever and wherever membership issues are found.[284]

280. *Sugarman,* 413 U.S. at 648.

281. *Cabell,* 454 U.S. at 445. "Definition of the important sovereign functions of the political community is necessarily the primary responsibility of the representative branches of government, subject to limited judicial review." Id.

282. It is probably no coincidence that the demise of the special public interest doctrine paralleled the Court's acceptance of a national economy. *See generally* Wickard v. Filburn, 317 U.S. 111 (1942) (maintaining that all of the wheat produced and consumed on a farm is "far from trivial" and thus should fall within the scope of federal regulation); United States v. Darby, 312 U.S. 100 (1941) (holding that while manufacture itself may not be interstate commerce, the interstate shipment of such goods is commerce and, thus, is controlled by congressional regulations); NLRB v. Jones & Laughlin Steel Corp., 301 U.S. 1 (1937) (holding that "acts which directly burden or obstruct interstate or foreign commerce, or its free flow, are within the reach of the congressional power . . . .").

283. *See* supra note 18 (recognizing that plenary power, strictly speaking, applies only in cases of admission, exclusion, and deportation, but its effects are felt throughout the alienage jurisprudence, and it serves as the centerpiece for the membership paradigm).

284. Procedural due process is the exception. *See* supra notes 182-205 and accompanying

Aside from the issues of admission and exclusion, which lie at membership's core, Congress acts in two other ways that can significantly and adversely impact an alien's status as a partial member in the American community: First, Congress may place conditions on continued residence in the form of affirmative conditions and negative consequences. Second, it may deny permanent resident aliens complete access to our economic union.[285]

Most new immigrants to the United States receive unqualified permanent residence. Coupled with a fairly short and light path to citizenship,[286] this allows for the process of integration to begin in earnest immediately. When immigration is based on a new marriage or a substantial investment in this country, Congress chooses to confer "conditional" permanent residence, which the government can revoke within two years after entry.[287] In addition to these affirmative conditions applying to a small group of immigrants, the government can remove all noncitizens for misbehavior or other undesirable characteristics. Current law grants the power to deport on a variety of grounds including criminal activity,[288] document fraud,[289] terrorist activity,[290] and on the ground

text.

285. Additionally, for those unfortunate aliens who find themselves incarcerated as a result of our immigration laws, there is the question of their "conditions of confinement." Taylor, supra note 22, at 1089.

286. In general, permanent resident aliens who have resided continuously in the United States for five years are eligible for naturalization, provided that they are "of good moral character, attached to the principles of the Constitution of the United States, and well disposed to the good order and happiness of the United States." 8 U.S.C.A. §1427(a) (West Supp. 1995). Additionally, applicants for citizenship must have minimal competency in English and minimal knowledge of United States history and government. *See* id. at § 1423 (waiving English requirement for elderly and disabled, and waiving government and history requirement for disabled).

287. *See* 8 U.S.C.A. § 1186(a) (West Supp. 1995) (providing that a noncitizen who immigrates based on a marriage that is less than two years old is a permanent resident on a "conditional basis," which can be terminated for various reasons in the first two years); id. at §1186(b) (providing that alien entrepreneurs, who gain immigrant status based on capital investment and employment creation obtain permanent resident status "on a conditional basis," which can be terminated for various reasons during the first two years of residence). For a discussion of these provisions, see generally Janet M. Calvo, Spouse-Based Immigration Laws: The Legacies of Coverture, 28 San Diego L. Rev. 593 (1991); Gary Endelman & Jeffrey Hardy, Uncle Sam Wants You: Foreign Investment and the Immigration Act of 1990, 28 San Diego L. Rev. 671 (1991); Ronald R. Rose, Fixing the Wheel: A Critical Analysis of the Immigrant Investor Visa, 29 San Diego L. Rev. 615 (1992); Joe A. Tucker, Assimilation to the United States: A Study of the Adjustment of Status and Immigration Marriage Fraud Statutes, 7 Yale L. & Pol'y Rev. 20 (1989).

288. *See* 18 U.S.C.A. § 1251 (a)(2) (West Supp. 1995) (including deportability for crimes involving moral turpitude, multiple criminal convictions, aggravated felonies, controlled substances, and certain firearms offenses.).

289. *See* id. at § 1251(a)(3) (consisting of failing to register and falsifying documents).

290. *See* id. at § 1251(a)(4) (listing criminal activities which endanger public safety or national welfare). Our immigration laws have often reflected a close nexus between exclusion-deportation for terrorism and exclusion-deportation on ideological grounds causing some to

that the alien has become a "public charge."[291] These are conditions subsequent to the admission decision. Additionally, a partial member suffers several constitutional encumbrances[292] and other statutorily imposed encumbrances.[293] These measures may derive from a desire to reserve certain benefits for full members or to encourage aliens to acquire full membership.[294]

Imagine membership as a process.[295] The government screens

---

question the "chill" placed on noncitizens' speech and political activities. *See, e.g.*, Scanlan, supra note 93, at 1485 (arguing the government has considerable discretionary authority to take ideological considerations into account in determining an alien's immigration status); Philip Monrad, Comment, Ideological Exclusion, Plenary Power, and the PLO, 77 Cal. L. Rev. 831 (1989)). For a discussion of recent relaxation of ideological deportations, see generally George C. Beck, Note, Deportation on Security Grounds and the First Amendment: Closing the Gap Between Resident Aliens and Citizens, 6 Geo. Immigr. L.J. 803 (1992). For the relationship between deportation and extradition, see generally Michael J. Bowe, Note, Deportation as De Facto Extradition: The Matter of Joseph Doherty, 11 N.Y.L. Sch. J. Int'l & Comp. L. 263 (1990).

291. 8 U.S.C.A. § 1251(a)(5) (West Supp. 1995). *See generally* Aba Heiman, Aliens Under Social Security, Medicare, and Supplemental Security Income, 19 Soc. Sec. Rep. Serv. 777 (1988).

292. *See Sugarman*, 413 U.S. at 651 (Rehnquist, J., dissenting) (listing the encumbrances, Rehnquist states, "the distinction [between alien and citizen] is constitutionally important in no less than 11 instances in a political document known for its brevity").

293. *See, e.g.*, Mathews v. Diaz, 426 U.S. 67 (1976) (upholding denial of welfare benefits to certain aliens). *See also* supra note 5 (discussing a proposal in Congress to curtail benefits to noncitizens).

294. *See, e.g.*, Hampton v. Mow Sun Wong, 426 U.S. 88, 116 (1976) (holding that residents legally admitted by decisions from Congress or the President cannot, as a class, be denied opportunities for employment by Civil Service Commission).

295. David Martin characterizes "[m]embership, in short, as a matter of degree." Martin, supra note 15, at 201. Citizens, permanent resident aliens, and even illegal aliens are all part of the everwidening "circle of concentric communities that make up the nation." Id. at 201-02. His metaphor provides a useful description of the varying ties different noncitizens have with the United States. From this he concludes that permanent resident aliens" are *entitled* by virtue of that [degree of] membership alone to enter *fully* into virtually all other aspects of community life." Id. at 202 (emphasis added). Even with respect to undocumented persons who may be "denied many benefits" of membership, "as to other advantages of life in this political community, denial is not allowed." Id. This conclusion of entitlement simply does not follow from a recognition that the heterogeneous body of noncitizens have differing degrees of attachment to the United States. In fact, because membership is the controlling paradigm, all "entitlements" for this class of persons are to a large extent "illusory." *See Harisiades*, 342 U.S. at 600 (Douglas, J., dissenting).

At a constitutional law level, membership as "process" more closely captures the Court's work than "degrees" of membership. Marriage provides an illustrative metaphor. Dating, courtship, and betrothal are all part of a process leading up to and culminating in the marriage commitment. As the relationship progresses from a casual date, through "going steady," to engagement, the young man's membership in his future wife's family changes by degrees. This change will most likely carry with it certain rights and responsibilities. At first he may wait to be invited for Sunday dinner, later he may assume he is welcome at Sunday dinner, and finally he may even find himself posing for the family portrait. As in the state alienage cases, a certain family member, possibly a sibling, has no jurisdictional authority over the question of whether he can sit for the portrait. But, no matter how attached he becomes

prospective members for their desirable characteristics, which will allow them to immigrate,[296] and for any undesirable characteristics, which will preclude immigration, even for those who are otherwise qualified.[297] Upon admission, the process of becoming a member is far from complete; on the contrary, admission signals the beginning of the membership process. Prior to the decision to admit, the noncitizen is, in no way, a member or even a member in process. Instead, she is a prospective member–a member wannabe. If she happens to have the statutorily required characteristics, the government will stamp her membership application with approval. At this point, she begins the journey toward full membership—citizenship. As a partial member, a novice, her continued membership is not assured. If she fails to meet a condition or misbehaves in a serious way, her membership may be terminated. Additionally, until she qualifies for and chooses full membership, she is not entitled to all the privileges of membership. Once she acquires citizenship, she has the full right[298] to participate in the community's decisions, including the decision of who to admit and under what circumstances.

Every action uniquely affecting aliens involves membership. As noncitizens proceed along the journey toward full membership, do personhood concerns at some point outweigh membership concerns?[299] Stated differently, at some point does the Court shift paradigms, seriously enforcing constitutional restrictions on governmental action? Starting with

---

to this new family, no matter how much he is treated as a member, and no matter how much he relies on this relationship for economic, intellectual, emotional, or spiritual support, he can be cast aside and discarded by this community, for any reason or no reason at all. Additionally, some family policymaker or group of policymakers have unfettered authority to decide what membership benefits will accrue to his benefit and at what point in the process they will accrue. It is only after he has completed the process and taken the culminating oath that he has legal rights that cannot be ignored. Although an imperfect analogy, this more closely approaches what the Court is and has been telling us in its alienage jurisprudence.

296. *See* 8 U.S.C.A. §§ 1151, 1153 (West Supp. 1995). United States immigration laws have developed three profiles of desirable immigrants: (1) those with close family in the United States; (2) those with education and training that would benefit the United States; and (3) those who would add diversity to the immigration pool. *See* id. The most preferred group are immediate relatives of United States citizens. *See* id. at § 1151(b) (stating that immediate relatives of citizens can immigrate outside the numerical system that places limits on the number of immigrants admitted each year).

297. *See* 8 U.S.C.A. § 1182 (West Supp. 1995) (including excludability on health related grounds, on criminal and related grounds, on security and related grounds, among others).

298. The only exception is the constitutional bar to her becoming president. *See* U.S. Const. art. II, §1, cl. 5 ("No Person except a natural born Citizen . . . shall be eligible to the Office of President . . . .").

299. Precedent establishes "that aliens receive constitutional protections when they have come within the territory of the United States and developed substantial connections with this country." United States v. Verdugo-Urquidez, 494 U.S. 259, 271 (1990). *See* Aleinikoff, Citizens, supra note 14, at 10 ("[*I*]*f* membership is to be the guiding principle for constitutional analysis of the immigration power, then the circle of membership should include permanently residing aliens.").

United States v. Fong Yue Ting,[300] dissenting opinions have argued that the act of removal is fundamentally different in kind from the question of admission, requiring a readjustment of the constitutional balance between membership and personhood.[301]

> The view that the power of Congress to deport aliens is absolute and may be exercised for any reason which Congress deems appropriate rests on *Fong Yue Ting v. United States*. . . . That decision seems to me to be inconsistent with the philosophy of constitutional law which we have developed for the protection of resident aliens . . . .
>
> An alien, who is assimilated in our society, is treated as a citizen so for as his property and his liberty are concerned. He can live and work here and raise a family. . . . Those guaranties of liberty and livelihood are the essence of the freedom which this country from the beginning has offered the people of all lands. If those rights, great as they are, have constitutional protection, I think the more important one–the right to remain here–has a like dignity.[302]

A majority of the Court has consistently disagreed, maintaining that the removal power and the admission power are closely intertwined and that no substantive constitutional guaranties limit either power.[303] Even away from the border, in areas of economic opportunity supposedly protected by the Constitution,[304] the Court employs the membership paradigm because Congress can "make an alien's eligibility [for many privileges of membership] depend on both the character and the duration of his residence."[305]

The *Chinese Exclusion Case* and *Graham v. Richardson* provide the archetypes for membership and personhood, respectively. If noncitizens are discrete and insular and in need of special judicial intervention, what compels the Court to abandon its aid in the membership cases? The character of the class–aliens–undergoes no transformation in the shift from

---

300. 149 U.S. 698 (1893).

301. *See* supra notes 60-63.

302. *Harisiades*, 342 U.S. at 598-99 (Douglass, J., dissenting). "Unless they are free from arbitrary banishment, the 'liberty' they enjoy while they live here is indeed illusory." Id. at 600. "I am unwilling to say [that a resident alien] may be driven from our land because he joined a political party that California and the Nation then recognized as perfectly legal." Galvan v. Press, 347 U.S. 522, 533 (1954) (Black, J., dissenting). "If [resident aliens] are to be deported, it must be for what they are and do, not for what they once believed." Id. at 534 (Douglas, J., dissenting).

303. *See, e.g., Fiallo*, 430 U.S. at 796 (stating that there is no distinction made between exclusion and deportation); *Harisiades*, 342 U.S. at 587 (1952) ("Government's power to terminate its hospitality has been asserted and sustained by the Court since the question first arose." (quoting Fong Yue Ting v. United States, 149 U.S. 698, 707 (1893)); *Fong Yue Ting*, 149 U.S. at 711-14 (observing that both powers rest on one foundation).

304. *See, e.g., Harisiades*, 342 U.S. at 586 n.9 ("This court has held that the Constitution assures [the alien] a large measure of equal economic opportunity.").

305. *E.g., Mathews*, 426 U.S. at 83.

issues contemplating the distribution of state benefits to the issues of communal formation. Similarly, no transformation occurs in the shift from the state to the federal context; aliens remain discrete and insular. The last hundred years are replete with occasions where the federal government acted with invidious prejudice against some portion of this politically powerless discrete and insular minority.[306] The change, and it is significant, lies in the character of the government's interest.

When the government, whether state or federal, articulates a plausible argument that its classification involves fundamental question of membership in the national or state community, the Court abandons its lofty ideals of protecting the dispossessed. It subordinates the noncitizen's constitutional interests as a protected person to society's interest in making important membership decisions. Membership issues–plenary power's long arm—pass through the border, extending to almost all federal issues uniquely affecting aliens and to all state issues that arguably affect the formation of the political community.

B. *Procedural Cracks?*

Procedural due process rights provide the only true relief to membership's dominance. In the criminal area, noncitizens benefit from the criminal trial rights provided by the Fifth and Sixth Amendments. Since immigration has always been characterized as "civil" in nature, those protections are not available in the deportation context.[307] The Court has, however, applied the amorphous concepts of procedural due process found in the Fifth Amendment to protect noncitizens in immigration proceedings.[308] This practice is not surprising given the qualitative differences between procedural rules and substantive policy choices.[309]

Since the due process arena marks the only place in our alienage

---

306. *See, e.g.*, *Fiallo*, 430 U.S. at 799-800 (allowing discrimination on the basis of gender and illegitimacy); Kleindienst v. Mandel, 408 U.S. 753 (1972) (condoning discrimination on the basis of political beliefs); Shaughnessy v. United States *ex rel.* Mezei, 345 U.S. 206, 215 (1953) (allowing the indefinite detention and exclusion of an alien on secret national security grounds); *Chinese Exclusion Case*, 130 U.S. at 609 (discriminating against an alien on the basis of race).

307. *See, e.g.*, *Harisiades*, 342 U.S. at 594 ("Deportation, however severe its consequences, has been consistently classified as a civil rather than criminal procedure."); Bugajewitz v. Adams, 228 U.S. 585, 591 (1913) (holding that deportation is not punishment); Fong Yue Ting v. United States, 149 U.S. 698, 730 (1893). This view has, from the beginning, met with ardent dissent. *See, e.g.*, *Harisiades*, 342 U.S. at 600 (Douglas, J., dissenting) ("Banishment is punishment in the practical sense. It may deprive a . . . family of all that makes life worthwhile."); *Fong Yue Ting*, 149 U.S. at 759 (Field, J., dissenting) (arguing that not only is deportation punishment, it is "beyond all reason in its severity. . . . It is cruel and unusual.").

308. *See* supra notes 192-204 and accompanying text.

309. Due process "must be a specialized responsibility within the competence of the judiciary on which they do not bend before the political branches of the Government, as they should on matters of policy which compromise substantive law." *Mezei*, 345 U.S. at 224 (Jackson, J., dissenting) ("Only the untaught layman or the charlatan lawyer can answer that procedures matter not.").

jurisprudence where the personhood paradigm applies when membership issues are present, those seeking to weaken membership's grip on the rights of aliens should focus their efforts here.[310] Only a cursory overview of the procedural possibilities is necessary in this Article because Professor Hiroshi Motomura has thoroughly explored this issue.[311] In addition to providing procedural due process protection to affected aliens, Motomura convincingly demonstrates how courts use procedural claims at times as surrogates for substantive constitutional claims. These procedural surrogates operate at two levels. First, marginal claims, ones that are not clearly "substantive" or "procedural," can be cast as procedural making it possible to enforce rights that would not be recognized in a substantive context.[312] Second, substantive constitutional norms inform even clearly procedural analysis.[313] For Motomura, "procedural surrogates are a natural outgrowth of the tension between the plenary power doctrine in immigration law and the *Yick Wo* tradition's more humane treatment of aliens in other contexts."[314]

---

310. "While it is a widely accepted idea that procedural rules often reflect substantive values, the anomalous structure that the plenary power doctrine imposes on constitutional immigration law means that procedural decisions are often the only vehicle for taking substantive rights seriously." Motomura, supra note 19, at 1656.

311. *See* id. at 1656.

312. Section 5 of the Immigration Marriage Fraud Amendments ("IMFA") of 1986, Pub. L. No. 99-639, § 5, 100 Stat. 3537, 3543 (1986) (codified at 8 U.S.C.A. §§ 1154(g), 1255(e) (West Supp. 1995)), which prohibits aliens who were married during deportation or exclusion proceedings from using the marital status to immigrate to the United States until they have resided outside the United States for two years, illustrates Motomura's point. *See* Motomura, supra note 19, at 1659-65. Although most courts reviewing § 5's constitutionality upheld the provision, *e.g.*, Anetekhai v. INS, 876 F.2d 1218 (5th Cir. 1989), two courts adjudged it unconstitutional, concluding that "Section 5 was 'procedural' because it interposed a two-year delay before the government would decide the [bona-fides of the] marriage." Motomura, supra note 19, at 1661 (citing Escobar v. INS, 896 F.2d 564 (D.C. Cir. Feb. 2, 1990) (opinion withdrawn) and Manwan v. United States, 736 F. Supp. 1367 (W.D.N.C. 1990)). *See also* Edward L. Rubin, Generalizing the Trial Model of Procedural Due Process: A New Basis for the Right to Treatment, 17 Harv. C.R. - C.L. L. Rev. 61, 69 (1982) ("[T]he boundary between [substance and procedure] is far from sharp.").

313. Motomura examines the *Orantes-Hernandez* litigation to make this point. In this case, the district court concluded that INS summary removal procedures denied Salvadorans their right to due process by effectually denying their ability to apply for asylum. Motomura, supra note 19, at 1673-75 (citing Orantes-Hernandez v. Smith, 541 F. Supp. 351 (C.D. Cal. 1982) (prelim. inj.); Orantes-Hernandez v. Meese, 685 F. Supp. 1488 (C.D. Cal. 1988) (perm. inj.), *aff'd sub nom.*, Orantes-Hernandez v. Thornburg, 919 F.2d 549 (9th Cir. 1990) (affirming on nonconstitutional grounds)). "In *Orantes-Hernandez*, the procedural policies and practices of the INS were troubling largely because asylum seekers from countries other than El Salvador apparently received better treatment without congressional authority for the difference. . . . This disparity in treatment would have raised serious equal protection problems but for the plenary power doctrine. With direct equal protection claims barred, the next best alternative for the plaintiffs and the court was to take the procedural due process claims in *Orantes* seriously—as a procedural surrogate for equal protection." Motomura, supra note 19, at 1674-75.

314. Id. at 1700.

Procedural surrogate use may only be a "transitional stage" between plenary power's nonrecognition of the rights of aliens and an "open and direct approach to aliens' substantive constitutional claims."[315] This stage probably holds the key to any attempt to open plenary power's lock on judicially enforceable substantive constitutional rights of noncitizens. I doubt, however, the sustained success of such ventures. Although immigrant advocates may win a few victories here and there, I do not see the Court abandoning what I term, more broadly, the membership paradigm, which keeps much of alienage jurisprudence at the margins of domestic constitutional law.[316] I offer two reasons for my prediction.

First, I disagree with Motomura and others over the nature of the tension in alienage law: the tension does not exist between immigration law and the larger body of alienage law;[317] instead, in my analysis, the apparent tension arises from the doctrinal incoherence occasioned by labeling noncitizens a discrete and insular minority. This tension dissolves into a hundred years of consistency if we step back from the doctrine and take a broad look at the whole of alienage jurisprudence.[318] Judicial deference to the subsantive choices of the political branches transcends the bounds of immigration law, extending to a larger body of membership cases. From *Yick Yo* and *Chinese Exclusion* to the present, the Court has consistently and emphatically reconciled the membership and personhood traditions in favor of membership, with a steadfast refusal to displace the political branches' substantive value judgments in the field of communal formation. There is simply little or no evidence to suggest that the

315. Id.

316. A major judicial victory came in American-Arab Anti-Discrimination Committee v. Reno, 70 F.3d 1045 (9th Cir. 1995), where the court clearly rejected the membership paradigm, favoring the personhood approach even in the deportation context. In holding that First Amendment protections apply in deportation, the court said that:

> Because we are a nation founded by immigrants, this underlying principle is especially relevant to our attitude toward current immigrants who are part of *our community*. . . . It is thus especially appropriate that our First Amendment principle of tolerance for different voices restrain our decisions to expel *a participant in that community* from our midst.

Id. at 1064 (emphasis added).

317. *But see* Motomura, supra note 19, at 1688-89 ("[T]he more generous constitutional treatment of aliens outside immigration law has exerted considerable pressure on the courts toward greater recognition of constitutional guarantees in immigration matters as well. The plenary power doctrine is fundamentally opposed to this trend. Procedural surrogates reflect the failure of immigration law to reckon openly with the consequences of the resulting tension.").

318. I mean only that the apparent doctrinal tension disappears into a century old jurisprudence that consistently places membership concerns above personhood concerns. The fundamental tension between the rights of the American community to draft more or less exclusionary membership rules and the rights of individual noncitizens to the enjoyment of the benefits of American residence remain central to immigration politics and this tension remains alive in the courts by a minority of justices who would cabin the membership paradigm within the core immigration issues of admission, exclusion and deportation.

personhood tradition is chiseling away at this structure.

Second, and of equal importance, procedural due process claims will not serve as a wedge prying immigration claims free from plenary power's chokehold on the development of substantive constitutional protections. Motomura's argument that procedural due process might serve this role is based on a misconception of the place of procedural claims in the constitutional order. He imagines "a pattern of concentric circles, the radius of which represents a spectrum of constitutional claims. The most substantive constitutional claims are in the inner most rings, and the most procedural claims are in the outer most ones."[319]

In this view, a new vision–that aliens have protectable rights–seeps into the circle of constitutional claims at the margins, slowly and guardedly working its way toward the center.[320] I do not dispute Motomura's conclusion that at times "the substance-procedure distinction is vague and unpredictable."[321] Likewise, I have no quarrel with the argument that procedural decisions often "reflect substantive value judgments."[322] However, I do question Motomura's intermingling of procedure and

---

319. Motomura, supra note 19, at 1657:

> At the center we find the most "substantive" rights, such as freedom of speech, the right to travel, and possibly the right to marry. These rights compel the legislature to grant certain benefits to everyone, and they bar the legislature from imposing certain burdens on anyone. Just further out, as we move into the second ring, we see "substantive" constitutional claims of a different type. These are not claims that the legislature must grant a benefit or may not impose a burden. Instead, they are claims that in granting benefits and imposing burdens the legislature may not transgress a different kind of substantive norm—embodied in the Equal Protection Clause—that constrains legislative choice. . . .
>
> Proceeding outward to the third ring, we find "procedural" constitutional claims . . . . On the inside part of this third ring, close to the second ring of substantive equal protection claims, we find claims of extensive procedural protection. In the middle of the third ring, fewer procedures are claimed, and at the outer edge of the third ring, the only procedural claim is that the government must give reasons for its decision. As we move beyond the outer edge of the third ring, we come to claims like that in *Roth*, in which there was no valid procedural claim at all because the Court declined to find a constitutionally protected entitlement.

Id. at 1657-58 (footnote omitted).

320. Professor Motomura states:

> From a broader historical perspective then, the use of procedural surrogates may be a transitional stage, the sort of awkward accommodation that results when courts are unwilling to acknowledge that one area of law is badly out of touch with the rest. The next step in this natural evolution may be to adopt an open and direct approach to aliens' substantive constitutional claims.

Id. at 1700.

321. *See e.g.*, Motomura, supra note 19, at 1703-04 (citing Laurence H. Tribe, American Constitutional Law §§ 10-12, at 711 (2d. ed. 1988) (criticizing attempts to distinguish procedure and substance)). "Although much ink has been spilled by courts and commentators in the the attempt to separate questions of substance and process, the attempt can never be wholly successful because the questions are functionally inseperable." Jerry L. Mashaw, Due Process In the Administrative State 5 (1985).

322. Motomura, supra note 19, at 1704.

substance in "a spectrum of constitutional claims," and his placement of procedural claims in the third ring, at the margins of recognizable constitutional law.[323]

Although the Constitution embodies both types of claims, procedure and substance serve the constitutional order in fundamentally different ways. To conceptualize these claims as part of a spectrum (concentric circles) with substance at the "core" and procedure at the margins misconstrues and undermines the important and *distinct* mission of procedural protections. If the concentric circle metaphor is used, I would argue that procedure, not substance, belongs at the core. As Justice Jackson said in his *Mezei* dissent, "[p]rocedural fairness and regularity are of the indispensable essence of liberty. Severe substantive laws can be endured if they are fairly and impartially applied. Indeed if put to the choice, one might well prefer to live under Soviet substantive law applied in good faith by our common-law procedures than under our substantive law enforced by Soviet procedural practices."[324]

Procedural due process works to ensure that our substantive laws, whatever they may be, are administered fairly, not by some arbitrary and tyranical hand.[325] For these reasons, in all areas of constitutional law (not just alienage jurisprudence), the courts are more likely to enforce their own procedural regime, while remaining more reticent about displacing the substantive value judgments of others.[326]

---

323. Id. at 1657. Motomura's concentric circles analysis is useful in explaining those cases where a court has chosen to affirm a substantive right indirectly by recognizing and giving force to a procedural penumbra surrounding the substantive right. *See* id. at 1659-79. My point is that in treating questions of procedure as questions of substance and in using the metaphor of concentric circles to describe the relationship between procedural and substantive constitutional questions, important attributes of procedural due process are lost. *See* George Lakoff & Mark Johnson, Metaphors We Live By 10 (1980) ("The very systemicity that allows us to comprehend one aspect of a concept in terms of another will necessarily hide other aspects of the concept. In allowing us to focus on one aspect of a concept, a metaphorical concept can keep us from focusing on other aspects of the concept that are inconsistent with the metaphor.").

324. *Mezei*, 345 U.S. at 224 (Jackson, J., dissenting) ("Procedural due process is more elemental and less flexible than substantive due process."). Jackson's dissent forcefully and clearly sets out the distinctive roles of process and substance under our constitution, placing process not substance at the core of constitutional protections. Id. at 218-28.

325. *See e.g.*, William Burnham, Separating Constitutional and Common-Law Torts: A Critique and a Proposed Constitutional Theory of Duty, 73 Minn. L. Rev. 515, 529 (1989) ("The fairness concern of procedural due process is that the government will cause a loss that is erroneous under substantive law without providing sufficient attendant procedural safeguards for preventing or correcting that error."); Rubin, supra note 313, at 71 ("The fact that the State acts in a general manner ensures that it will not single out a particular individual for unfair or arbitrary treatment. But when the state focuses its power upon an individual, that person is potentially subject to all the abuses which arbitrary, resentful, or corrupt state agents may inflict, and only judicial review can provide sufficient protection.").

326. *See, e.g.*, T.M. Scanlon, Due Process, *in* Due Process Nomos XVIII 104-05 (J. Roland Pennock and John W. Chapman eds., 1977) ("[D]ecisions of substantive due process deserve to be considered a more controversial form of judicial activity, for in making them courts

This basic distinction, which reveals not one but two separate spheres of constitutional protection, has been recognized in the alienage context from plenary power's infamous origins.[327] As Justice Jackson concluded in his *Mezei* dissent, "Congress has ample power to determine" substantive immigration policy.[328] "The only limitation is that it may not do so by authorizing United States officers to take without due process of law the life, the liberty, or the property of an alien who has come within our jurisdiction."[329] Because of this fundamental distinction between the work of substantive and procedural protections, I doubt that procedural surrogates are a temporary phase on the journey to judicial recognition of substantive constitutional rights for aliens.

Given my prognosis of membership's health (of course I could be proven wrong tomorrow) and given my dissatisfaction with the Court's story of plenary power,[330] I have sought an alternative way to tell the story. A way that, while not achieving the substantive outcome hoped for by some, would not be antithetical to our constitutional traditions. In the next section, I offer a sketch of that alternative.

VI. THE STATE CASES: A MODEL FOR MEMBERSHIP

"[O]nly . . . the Constitution itself" restricts Congress's sovereign immigration power.[331] Nonetheless, constitutional law has never imposed substantive limits on this power. The unsatisfying story perpetuated by the Court is that Congress and the Executive have inherent plenary power to construct a membership regime. "The right to exclude or expel" is "an inherent and inalienable right of every sovereign and independent nation."[332] However, unlike some other nations, we are a nation that lives by the rule of law, and because our paramount law—the Constitution—places restrictions on the operation of government, this inherent

---

exercise a further and more intrusive form of authority over the institutions concerned."); Rubin, supra note 312, at 72 ("[J]udicial reliance on the broad mandate of the due process clause to protect individuals is more justified than reliance on the clause to protect larger groups.").

327. In the *Japanese Immigrant Case*, the Court reaffirmed a still young plenary power doctrine: "It has been settled that the power to exclude or expel aliens belonged to the political department." Yamataya v. Fisher, 189 U.S. 86, 100 (1903). In contrast, "this court has never held, nor must we now be understood as holding, that administrative officers, when executing the provisions of a statute involving the liberty of persons, may disregard the fundamental principles that inhere in 'due process of law.'" Id.

328. *Mezei*, 345 U.S. at 228.

329. Id. ("It is inconceivable to me that this measure of simple justice and fair dealing would menace the security of this country. No one can make me believe that we are that far gone.").

330. Scaperlanda, Polishing, supra note 22, at 970-72.

331. The Chinese Exclusion Case, 130 U.S. 581, 604 (1889).

332. Fong Yue Ting v. United States, 149 U.S. 698, 711 (1892). Although the Court went on to question whether the immigration power was being exercised in a manner consistent with the Constitution, the Court has never seriously entertained restrictions. Id.

power rationale should not stand as a benchmark for judicial reasoning. Yet, it continues to find its way into cases, justifying results that are at odds with our domestic constitutional norms.

From plenary power's beginnings, dissenting judges have accurately and succinctly exposed the misplaced nature of the Court's logic:

> It is said that the power here asserted is inherent in sovereignty. This doctrine of powers inherent in sovereignty is one both indefinite and dangerous. Where are the limits to such powers to be found, and by whom are they to be pronounced? Is it within legislative capacity to declare the limits? If so, then the mere assertion of an inherent power creates it, and despotism exists. May the courts establish the boundaries? Whence do the obtain the authority for this? Shall they look to the practices of other nations to ascertain the limits? The governments of other nations have elastic powers—ours are fixed and bounded by a written constitution. . . . Now, the power to remove resident aliens is, confessedly, not expressed. Even if it be among the powers implied, yet still it can be exercised only in subordination to the limitations and restrictions imposed by the Constitution.[333]

Plenary power, with its inherent sovereign power, exists in complete defiance of a constitutional order built on limited and delegated powers, which the Bill of Rights further restrict. Although plenary power's results often seem harsh by contemporary constitutional standards, it is this theory of inherent sovereign powers, not the outcome of a particular case, that causes plenary power's illegitimacy.[334] Is there an alternative?

Constitutional law involves the practice of prioritizing and balancing competing interests within a given framework.[335] The competing claims of the individual noncitizen to the constitutional protections afforded persons and of the collective citizenry to fashion membership rules free from binding constitutional restraint create the tension addressed here. On the one hand, the Court recognizes noncitizens as "persons" entitled to protection, and the noncitizens desire more than illusory protection. On the other hand, the Constitution gives Congress the naturalization power,[336] which in a broader sense gives Congress policy making authority over membership issues, since naturalization completes the legal assimilation process. How should these interests be balanced?

One could argue that the Court should subordinate the express naturalization power to constitutionally imposed restrictions. And, since

---

333. Id. at 737-38 (Brewer, J., dissenting).

334. *Cf.* Nafziger, supra note 85, at 46 ("[A]ny plenary power of Congress must be derived from the Constitution and not from some transcendental concept of inherent sovereignty.").

335. *Cf.* Kathleen M. Sullivan, Governmental Interests and Unconstitutional Conditions Law: A Case Study in Categorization and Balancing, 55 Alb. L. Rev. 605 (1992) (describing the roles of categorization and balancing in modern constitutional law and the characteristic moves between those two modes of reasoning).

336. U.S. Const. art. I, § 8, cl. 4 (granting Congress the power "to establish a Uniform Rule of Naturalization").

aliens as a class are a discrete and insular minority, the constitutional restrictions should apply with their strongest level of review.[337] This, however, will not occur because it would strip Congress of any flexibility in formulating immigration policy. Some other accommodation of these competing interests must be made. Another possibility would be for the Court to engage in an *ad hoc* balancing of interests in the vein of *City of Cleburne v. Cleburne Living Center*,[338] which developed an active rational basis review. Where the Court perceives that Congress or the Executive has acted out of "mere negative attitudes, or fear, unsubstantiated by factors which are properly cognizable," the Court's rational basis review might require a more intrusive inquiry into whether the classification is truly rationally related to legitimate governmental interests.[339]

Over the past one hundred years, the Court has clearly expressed its preference for categorical balancing over *ad hoc* balancing in its alienage jurisprudence. Where membership issues are involved, broad deference to the appropriate political body, and, in the absence of such issues, strong protection for alien persons. Given this preference for categorical balancing, the federal membership story needs retelling to make it consistent with our constitutional commitments.

The state membership cases provide a model, albeit rather crude, for re-envisioning the tension between communal formation and the rights' claims of the noncitizen. Instead of casting the conflict in terms of a clash between inherent sovereign power (an alien concept in our jurisprudence) and the rights of recognized persons, it could be recast as a conflict between the rights of "We the People" to create a constitutional community and the rights of nonmembers and partial members to the benefits of constitutional protection.

In *Cabell v. Chavez-Salido*,[340] the Court said:

> [t]he exclusion of aliens from basic governmental processes is not a deficiency in the democratic system but a necessary consequence of the community's process of political self-definition. Self-government . . . begins by defining the scope of the community and thus the governors as well: Aliens are by definition those outside of this community.[341]

At the state level, this task is limited to the formation of the political

---

337. Not even the most ardent dissenters from plenary power have advocated this position. "None of plenary powers dissenters has ever suggested that a noncitizen's rights are equal to those of a citizen. They all recognize that an alien's constitutional claim strengthens when she is in the United States and developing ties here. They also recognize that the federal government's power is extensive in the immigration context, rising to an apex in the admissions decisions." Scaperlanda, supra note 16, at 21.

338. 473 U.S. 432 (1985).

339. Id. at 448. *See generally* Harry F. Tepker, Jr., Separating Prejudice from Rationality in Equal Protection Cases: A Legacy of Thurgood Marshall, 47 Okla. L. Rev. 93, 103-07 (discussing Marshall's disagreement with the Majority's opinion in *Cleburne*).

340. 454 U.S. 432 (1982).

341. Id. at 439.

community since the states lack the power to police the border.[342] At the federal level membership touches a broader array of issues,[343] and its reach extends further than limitations on governmental employment to issues of admission and exclusion, to questions of deportation, and beyond the border and immigration law to the benefits and burdens attendant to partial membership, and the qualifications for full membership.

Alexander Bickel once wrote that "[r]emarkably enough–and as I suggest, happily–the concept of citizenship plays only the most minimal role in the American constitutional scheme."[344] The Court, it seems, would dispute this characterization of citizenship's role. "The act of becoming a citizen is more than a ritual with no content beyond the fanfare of cermony. A new citizen has become a member of a Nation, part of a people distinct from others."[345] Prior to this, the resident alien enjoys "such advantages as accrue from residence here without renouncing his foreign allegiance or formally acknowledging adherence to the Constitution."[346] Justice Rehnquist identified at least eleven constitutional provisions, "in a political document noted for its brevity," where the concept of citizenship is important.[347] The Fourteenth Amendment's definition of a citizen suggests that "[c]itizenship meant something, a status in and relationship with a society which is continuing and more basic than mere presence or residence."[348]

The Court has been telling us for a hundred years that in most instances it will not resolve the tension between membership and personhood by subordinating membership issues to the constitutional claims of nonmembers or partial members. With respect to federal alienage cases, the Court has unconvincingly relied on a theory of inherent sovereign powers. The whole of alienage jurisprudence reveals another explanation–that, in the Court's eyes, the unfettered process of communal formation reigns paramount over the concerns of individual noncitizens and their claims to substantive constitutional protection. Either the Naturalization Clause[349] or the political question doctrine[350] (or both),

---

342. The political function exception to strict scrutiny "represents the choice, and right, of the people to be governed by their citizen peers. . . . [A]lthough we extend to aliens the right to education and public welfare, along with the ability to earn a livelihood . . . , the right to govern is reserved for citizens." *Foley*, 435 U.S. at 296-97.

343. *See* supra notes 77-144 and accompanying text.

344. Alexander M. Bickel, The Morality of Consent 33 (1975).

345. *Foley*, 435 U.S. at 295; *cf.* United States v. Manzi, 276 U.S. 463, 467 (1928) ("Citizenship is a high privilege . . . .").

346. Harisiades v. Shaughnessy, 342 U.S. 580, 585 (1952). *See generally* Sanford Levinson, Constitutional Faith 180-94 (1988) (discussing the question of putting one's own signature on the Constitution).

347. Sugarman v. Dougall, 413 U.S. 634, 651 (1973) (Rehnquist, J., dissenting).

348. Id. at 652.

349. U.S. Const. art. I, § 8, cl. 4. *But see* Aleinikoff, Citizens, supra note 14, at 9 ("One might well distinguish between regulation of the *physical entry* of the aliens into the *territory* of the United States and regulation of the entry into the *political community* of the United

might justify tilting the balance strongly toward membership. In any event, it provides a more legitimate explanation of the Court's behavior in its alienage cases. Implicit within this understanding of plenary power as part of a larger membership paradigm is the realization that it is our responsibility, as community members, to ensure that our membership rules correspond to our constitutional commitments.

VII. CONCLUSION: CONSTITUTIONAL DIALOGUE

From the *Chinese Exclusion Case* to the present, the Court has clearly and unequivocally stated that when membership and personhood clash, it will not judicially enforce the substantive constitutional rights tradition. The Court likely will retain this posture if called upon to address the pressing immigration issues of today. With respect to the proposed amendments to limit birth right citizenship, the Court has no role.[351] The Court, relying on precedent, will likely conclude that federal proposals to exclude noncitizens from welfare eligibility fall within the membership paradigm. Even with respect to measures like Proposition 187 that prohibit the undocumented from receiving state benefits available to all other people, the Court might overrule *Plyler* or distinguish it on the grounds that it involved the unique combination of factors–involuntary presence and the denial of a vitally important educational opportunity. Do any of these current measures conflict with this country's constitutional values? The Court refuses to answer this question in its alienage jurisprudence. In the end, We the People must square immigration policy with cherished constitutional values.[352]

States.").

350. *See* Fiallo v. Bell, 430 U.S. 787, 796 (1977) (quoting *Mathews*); Mathews v. Diaz, 426 U.S. 67, 81-82 (1976) ("The reasons that preclude judicial review of political questions also dictate a narrow standard of review . . . in the area of immigration and naturalization."). For thoughtful criticism of the Court's use of the political question doctrine rhetoric and justification in immigration cases, see Nafziger, supra note 85, at 46-49; Legomsky, Immigration Law, supra note 95, at 261-69.

351. Unlike Germany, our constitutional law regime does not visualize unconstitutional constitutional amendments. *See* Donald P. Kommers, German Constitutionalism: A Prolegomenon, 40 Emory L.J. 837, 852 (1991) ("In the German constitutionalist view, accepted and propogated by the Constitutional Court itself, any constitutional amendment conflicting with the core values or spirit of the Basic Law as a whole would itself be unconstitutional.").

352. We won't be the first generation to undertake such a task. Before the Constitution came to be owned by the judiciary, the People took responsibility for debating whether a proposed law was constitutional—not necessarily in a legally binding way, but with respect to our budding constitutional traditions. *See* supra note 40. I recognize that I may be taken as naive by some, especially those who have come to rely almost exclusively on the Court for development and enforcement of our constitutional values. My reply is simply that, whether one likes it or not, there is no practical alternative. Constitutional dialogue concerning the place of noncitizens in our society must proceed primarily outside the courthouse because the Court continues to refuse to engage in the dialogue from the bench. The Court here recognizes what it has forgotten elsewhere, that "the democratic faith is this: that the most

This path will not be easy. Like Johnson,[353] Motomura,[354] and others, I question whether the political branches will react positively to the claims of noncitizens. The consitutional values dialogue will take place in a larger debate over immigration policy, competing with a host of other voices–pragmatists, utilitarians, internationalists, racists, organized labor, and anyone else concerned with immigration and communal formation. Many times, maybe even most of the time, more immediate and less lofty concerns will carry the day. But, the outcome of any particular debate is far less important than the process. What is imperative, especially given judicial absence, is that we begin to develop a culture of constitutonal dialogue with respect to our membership decisions.

This dialogue represents a shift from judicially enforced constitutional law[355] to a broader concept of constitutional values, embracing "that web of understandings, myths, symbols, and documents out of which [is] woven interpretative narratives"[356] defining the American constitutional experiment. Free from the limitations imposed by treating the constitution as binding law,[357] the constitutional canon might even include documents

---

terribly important things must be left to ordinary [people] themselves." G. K. Chesterton, Orthodoxy 47 (1908) ("[T]his is democracy; and in this I have always believed.").

353. Kevin R. Johnson, *Los Olvidados*: Images of the Immigrant, Political Power of Noncitizens, and Immigration Law and Enforcement, 1993 B.Y.U. L. Rev. 1139, 1147 (1993) ("*[E]ven when the interests of noncitizens are supported by a majority of the electorate*, they may well lose in the political process. In other words, a dysfunctional political system molds immigration law and enforcement.").

354. *Motomura*, supra note 19, at 1703 ("In any given case, however, the promise of congressional correction is too remote and unreliable.").

355. Chief Justice Marshall established the Constitution as law in Marbury v. Madison, 5 U.S. (1 Cranch) 137, 177-78 (1803). *See* Louis Henkin, The Age of Rights 90 (1990) [hereinafter Henkin, Age] ("In establishing judicial review [John Marshall] helped make the courts what they are today, the final arbiters of what the Constitution means, and the rock and the redeemer of our rights. But Marshall achieved his success by establishing the Constitution as law, the thing of courts and lawyers.").

356. Levinson, supra note 346, at 10. Although speaking of "constitutional adjudication", I would place Ronald Garet's The Resolution of Independence with this tradition. *See* Ronald R. Garet, The Resolution of Independence, 29 Hous. L. Rev. 867, 868 (1992) (discussing the "contribution that the Declaration [of Independence] might make to a certain kind of thought: reflective, intuitive, almost meditative. There is a place for such contemplative thoughts in our efforts to understand the Constitution's provisions and to apply them to some of the issues of our day.").

357. Certain freedom of interpretation was lost in the process of characterizing the Constitution as law and of casting the courts as "the final arbiters of what [it]means." *See* Henkin, Age, supra note 355, at 90-91 ("We were condemned to be textualists, 'interpretivists'; other parts of our hariography—notably the Declaration of Independence—were excluded from the jurisprudential canon; ancestral theory might sneak in, but only occasionally, and in the guise of construction of the constitutional text."). Rule 8 of The Bluebook, 15th ed. mandates that the "C" in constitution be capitalized when referring to the United States Constitution. I have deliberately not capitalized it here to emphasize the shift from constitutional "law," which limits the canon to the text and to judicial opinions interpreting the text, to a broader concept of what I have referred to as constitutional values, which legitimately includes many other writings, both official and unofficial, that contribute to

such as Emma Lazarus's *The New Colossus*, which has come to symbolize America as a nation of immigrants, still welcoming others who by choice or by force have left their homelands to build a new life in this country.[358] At this level, I believe, like Levinson, that the constitution is "less a series of propositional utterances than a commitment to taking political conversation seriously."[359] The Court, by its abdication, has given us–those who care about such matters–the field of developing, articulating, debating, and attempting to implement a constitutional vision of the noncitizen in our polity. The task will be difficult, the answers usually tentative, but the process of dialogue will be rewarding; "the answers can emerge, if at all, only out of conversation."[360] In the end, constitutional dialogue within the realm of politics provides the most viable vehicle for establishing immigration and alienage policies that balance the legitimate interest of the national community (and its local constituent parts) with the human dignity and value of the noncitizen person.[361] Let us continue the conversation in earnest.

---

the American myth. Here I draw an analogy to the Nicene Creed, which refers to "one holy catholic and apostolic church." Catechism of the Catholic Church 197 (1994). The small "c" in catholic encompasses the universe of Christian believers, not solely adherents to Roman Catholicism. *See* id. at 220-222 (stating that the Church is "on a mission to the whole of the human race").

358. In contrast to a textual "protestant" nature of the constitution, Professor Levinson finds "more meaningful a 'catholic' view of the Constitution that adds to the parchment ratified in 1788 (and formally amended thereafter) not only key decisions of the Supreme Court, Congress, and the president, but also fundamental documents such as the Declaration of Independence and the Gettysburg Address and, beyond that, aspects of the American experience that cannot be reduced to a text at all." Levinson, supra note 346, at 185.

359. Id. at 193. Cardinal Roger Mahony of Los Angeles exemplifies this serious discourse. In a homily given during an annual Multi-Ethnic Mass and Celebration, he said: "The Catholic tradition proposes certain moral and ethical principles which should guide a reasonable analysis of the issues and the development of fair and just solutions. The rights of immigrants are a theme of extraordinary importance in Catholic social teaching and follow from basic principles of this teaching which affirm human life and human dignity. The right to move across borders to escape political persecution or in search of economic survival is explicitly part of that tradition. . . Much is at stake in the way we respond . . . ." Cardinal Roger Mahony, You Have Entertained Angels—Without Knowing It, The Tidings, Oct. 10, 1993, at 10-12.

360. Levinson, supra note 346, at 194.

361. *Cf.* Johnson, supra note 353, at 1240-41 (discussing the need for innovative strategies to bring about social change for the benefit of noncitizens). Stating that "[p]olitical mobilization and organization that *empowers* noncitizens offers the only meaningful opportunity for change," Johnson advocates a strategy to put a human face on the noncitizen by sharing the "facts, the stories, and the truth" about their lives. Id. at 1240. Until the full members of the national community come to know the stories of the partial members, the "noncitizens, a significant part of the national community, will continue to be *Los Olvidados*, The Forgotten. Although this strategy for change may fail, and may be doomed from the outset by its underlying optimism, if not naivete, we will never know unless we try." Id. at 1240-41. *See generally* Robert Coles, The Call of Stories: Teaching and the Moral Imagination (1989)(a wonderful book about the importance of stories–personal narratives–in the development of moral understanding).

EXPANDING THE CIRCLE OF MEMBERSHIP BY RECONSTRUCTING THE "ALIEN"†: LESSONS FROM SOCIAL PSYCHOLOGY AND THE "PROMISE ENFORCEMENT" CASES

Victor C. Romero*

Recent legal scholarship suggests that the Supreme Court's decisions on immigrants' rights favor conceptions of membership over personhood. Federal courts are often reluctant to recognize the personal rights claims of noncitizens because they are not members of the United States. Professor Michael Scaperlanda argues that because the courts have left the protection of noncitizens' rights in the hands of Congress and, therefore, its constituents, U.S. citizens must engage in a serious dialogue regarding membership in this polity while considering the importance of constitutional principles of personhood. This Article takes up Scaperlanda's challenge. Borrowing from recent research in social psychology, this Article contends that "We the People" can better inform our ideas of polity membership by resisting existing invidious stereotypes of the noncitizen as the "alien" and by embracing instead the notion of equal personhood. This Article also urges citizens to demand the repeal of the "court-stripping" provisions of the Illegal Immigration Reform and Immigrant Responsibility Act of 1996. These provisions encourage the federal government to renege on promises not to deport noncitizen defendants in exchange for assistance in criminal prosecutions. Without fear of judicial review, the government is free to enter into cooperation agreements with noncitizen defendants and then breach those agreements with impunity so as to achieve its dual goals of criminal prosecution and deportation. The federal government should not be allowed to break its promises, especially when the goal of the agreement with the noncitizen is to facilitate a criminal prosecution, not to impact immigration law.

---

† Except to make a statement in this title, I prefer the terms "noncitizen" to "alien" and "undocumented immigrant" to "illegal alien" because there are pejorative connotations attached to the word "alien." However, I favor the term "alienage jurisprudence" rather than "citizenship jurisprudence" because the former captures the dehumanizing nature of such categorizations. *See* Victor C. Romero, *The Congruence Principle Applied: Rethinking Equal Protection Review of Federal Alienage Classifications After* Adarand Constructors, Inc. v. Peña, 76 OR. L. REV. 425, 426 n.4 (1997) [hereinafter Romero, *Congruence*]; Victor C. Romero, *Equal Protection Held Hostage: Ransoming the Constitutionality of the Hostage Taking Act*, 91 NW. U. L. REV. 573, 573 n.4 (1997) [hereinafter Romero, *Equal Protection*]; *see also* Kevin R. Johnson, *"Aliens" and the U.S. Immigration Law: The Social and Legal Construction of Nonpersons*, 28 U. MIAMI INTER-AM. L. REV. 263, 268 (1996–97) (discussing "how the term alien masks the privilege of citizenship and helps to justify the legal status quo").

* Associate Professor of Law, Pennsylvania State University, Dickinson School of Law. B.A., 1987, Swarthmore College; J.D., 1992, University of Southern California Law Center; e-mail: vcr1@psu.edu.

As always, I appreciate the support of the following friends and colleagues whose insightful comments on previous drafts helped sharpen my thinking on this difficult subject: Jack Chin, Harvey Feldman, Kevin Johnson, Hiroshi Motomura, Eric Muller, Michael Scaperlanda, Laurel Terry, and Frank Wu. I would also like to thank Penny Rebert, Bill Dorgan, and Amy Phillips for their invaluable research assistance; Dean Peter Glenn for the generous funding for this Article; and most importantly, my wife, Corie, and my family in the Philippines for their untiring love and support.

INTRODUCTION

Estrella Santiago, a Mexican citizen, is arrested for her involvement as a drug courier in an international cocaine-smuggling conspiracy. She is tried in federal court for her drug offense, and if convicted, she will likely be haled into immigration court as a deportable[1] person for her involvement in drug trafficking.[2] The Assistant United States Attorney (AUSA) prosecuting her criminal case agrees to recommend a reduced sentence and promises that Ms. Santiago will not be deported if she testifies against her co-conspirators and waives any objections to deportation. Ms. Santiago, after consulting with her attorney, agrees to the deal. After pleading guilty and waiving objections to her deportability, Ms. Santiago receives a deportation order from a U.S. immigration judge requiring her to surrender to the Immigration and Naturalization Service (INS) authorities. When Ms. Santiago complains to the INS that the federal prosecutor offered her immunity from deportation, the INS replies that the AUSA had no authority to promise immunity and that the INS is therefore not bound by the federal prosecutor's promise. Terrified at the idea of being sent back to Mexico only to be killed by henchmen of angry co-conspirators convicted by her testimony, Ms. Santiago decides to seek to enforce the AUSA's promise in federal court. However, upon the government's motion, the district court judge dismisses Ms. Santiago's "promise enforcement" suit for lack of jurisdiction, citing Congress's recent enactment of the Illegal Immigration Reform and Immigrant Responsibility Act of 1996 (IIRIRA),[3] which limits the jurisdiction of federal courts over challenges to immigration deportation orders.[4]

This fictional scenario, based in reality,[5] captures the crucial difference between the citizen and noncitizen in the United States:[6] A

1. While the Illegal Immigration Reform and Immigrant Responsibility Act of 1996 (IIRIRA) uses the term "removal" rather than "deportation," *see* IIRIRA, Pub. L. No. 104-208, § 304, 110 Stat. 3009-546, 3009-587 (1996) (codified as amended in scattered sections of 8 U.S.C.), "deportation" is a term more commonly used in immigration literature, *see, e.g.*, 8 U.S.C. § 1101(a)(47)(A) (Supp. II 1996) (defining "order of deportation"), and therefore, I use it here.

2. *See* Immigration and Nationality Act (INA) § 241(a)(2)(B)(I), 8 U.S.C. § 1227(a)(2)(B)(I) (Supp. II 1996) (originally codified at 8 U.S.C. § 1251 (1994)) (requiring a noncitizen convicted of a crime to be deported under some circumstances).

3. 110 Stat. 3009-546.

4. *See* 8 U.S.C. § 1252 (Supp. II 1996).

5. *See infra* Part II.B.

6. For more information on the trials of noncitizens, see generally Kevin R. Johnson, Los Olvidados: *Images of the Immigrant, Political Power of Noncitizens, and Immigration Law and*

citizen would never be subject to deportation and would never be faced with Ms. Santiago's dilemma. Moreover, generally, a citizen would be able to avail herself of an effective remedy in the face of intentional or negligent government deception because she would be entitled to have her conviction vacated, and she would be allowed to enter a new plea.[7] In contrast, a noncitizen lacks such a remedy because Congress's recent enactment of the IIRIRA effectively deprives any court of jurisdiction over deportation orders.[8] Our hypothetical Ms. Santiago potentially represents many others who will never get their day in court as Congress "clear[s] the decks"[9] of pending cases covered by the new statute. Like Ms. Santiago, many of these former government witnesses may be exposed to grave bodily harm after being deported to their home countries when the U.S. government fails to live up to its promises. If there is one principle for which the Bill of Rights stands, it is limiting government action against persons, especially when the government fails to follow rules of fair play in the enforcement of its laws.[10] Yet this foundational principle of fair play does not protect Ms. Santiago.

Enforcement, 1993 BYU L. REV. 1139, 1146 [hereinafter Johnson, Los Olvidados] (discussing the difficulties faced by immigrants in both the political and judicial spheres); Michael A. Olivas, *The Chronicles, My Grandfather's Stories, and Immigration Law: The Slave Traders Chronicle as Racial History*, 34 ST. LOUIS U. L.J. 425 (1990) (comparing the immigration histories of Native Americans, Chinese, and Mexicans in America); Margaret H. Taylor, *Detained Aliens Challenging Conditions of Confinement and the Porous Border of the Plenary Power Doctrine*, 22 HASTINGS CONST. L.Q. 1087 (1995) (describing the treatment of immigrants held in U.S. detention centers); Patricia Zavella, *The Tables Are Turned: Immigration, Poverty, and Social Conflict in California Communities*, *in* IMMIGRANTS OUT!: THE NEW NATIVISM AND THE ANTI-IMMIGRANT IMPULSE IN THE UNITED STATES 136 (Juan F. Perea ed., 1997) [hereinafter IMMIGRANTS OUT!] (describing the rise of social conflict in California in the face of increased immigration and a changing economy).

7. *See, e.g.*, Santobello v. New York, 404 U.S. 257, 262–63 (1971) (holding that the government's failure to abide by a promise that induces a guilty plea requires that the conviction be vacated and the case remanded to the lower court).

8. *See* IIRIRA § 306(a), Pub. L. No. 104-208, 110 Stat. 3009-546, 3009-612 (codified as amended at 8 U.S.C. § 1252(g) (Supp. II 1996)). Section 1252 now reads, in pertinent part, as follows:

> EXCLUSIVE JURISDICTION.—Except as provided in this section and notwithstanding any other provision of law, no court shall have jurisdiction to hear any cause or claim by or on behalf of any alien arising from the decision or action by the Attorney General to commence proceedings, adjudicate cases, or execute removal orders against alien under [the INA].

Id. § 1252(g) (Supp. II 1996).

9. Ramallo v. Reno, 114 F.3d 1210, 1213 (D.C. Cir. 1997) (*Ramallo III*).

10. *See, e.g.*, U.S. CONST. amends. IV (right to be free from unreasonable searches and seizures), V (right to due process), VI (right to counsel), VII (right to a jury trial), VIII (right to be free from cruel and unusual punishments), XIV, § 1 (right to equal protection of the laws).

This horrible result arises from the distinctions our country draws between the citizen and noncitizen. At first blush, differentiating between citizen and foreigner appears reasonable. Indeed, any sovereign nation should have the power to determine who qualifies to join its polity. In fact, the power to distinguish between citizen and noncitizen rests in the U.S. Constitution's charge that Congress create a "uniform Rule of Naturalization."[11] The framers, however, surely did not intend or foresee the disastrous consequences of the citizen/noncitizen distinction for foreigners such as Ms. Santiago, especially in the context of promise enforcement cases. Although immigration consequences flow from the government's breach of its promise, the essential purpose of the cooperation agreement is to facilitate law enforcement, not to regulate immigration.[12] It would be easy to attribute Ms. Santiago's fateful plight to the doctrine of unintended consequences,[13] but the consequences may be particularly grave in this instance. A conscientious America must ensure that such consequences do not materialize.

How did we get here? Why does current immigration and due process law allow for such an unjust outcome? More importantly, how can we work to avoid such undesirable results? This Article seeks to answer these important questions by examining current immigrants' rights theory, reviewing recent due process case law on promise enforcement suits, and borrowing from Professor Jody Armour's theories on enhancing legal decision-making and recent psychological research on people's attitudes toward new immigrant groups. By recognizing that, like racial stereotypes, immigrant group stereotypes have been used to create a permanent out-group of noncitizens, American society can begin to retreat from its current xenophobic stance and adopt policies that value the inherent humanity of all. Citizens might start this process by demanding Congress repeal the "court-stripping" provisions of the IIRIRA, thus providing a check on the government's reneging on cooperation agreements made with noncitizens like Ms. Santiago.

---

11. U.S. CONST. art. I, § 8, cl. 4.

12. *See, e.g.*, Thomas v. INS, 35 F.3d 1332, 1337 (9th Cir. 1994) (analogizing the cooperation agreement to a traditional plea agreement).

13. *See generally* Thomas O. Depperschmidt, *Unintended Consequences and Perverse Effects in Forensic Economic Award Calculations*, J. LEGAL ECON., Summer 1994, at 65, 65 ("[U]nintended consequences contain actions yielding a variety of unplanned results, often somewhat serendipitously."); *cf. generally* Cass R. Sunstein, *Political Equality and Unintended Consequences*, 94 COLUM. L. REV. 1390 (1994) (describing the unintended consequences that result from well-meaning campaign finance regulations). Of course, my use of the term here is not so benign.

Part I examines the history of several immigrant groups in the United States and the current legal theories that explain how and why American law draws distinctions between the citizen and noncitizen. American history reveals, and contemporary scholars assert, that there are two competing views of noncitizens' rights in U.S. law: one views the noncitizen as someone not entitled to constitutional protection (the "membership" paradigm), and the other values the personhood of the noncitizen and the citizen equally and thus entitles the noncitizen to constitutional protection (the "personhood" paradigm). Professor Michael Scaperlanda argues that courts view membership claims as superior to personhood claims. He advocates that citizens seek strategies to ensure that constitutional notions of personhood are not forgotten in our discussions of polity membership. Part II looks at three recent promise enforcement suits like Ms. Santiago's and illustrates how current theories of membership and personhood may be used to explain the results in those cases. Drawing from contemporary critical race theory and social psychology research about invidious immigrant group stereotypes, Part III begins the membership dialogue Scaperlanda suggests in an effort to move away from ideas of segregation, alienation, and subordination to those of integration, acceptance, and equality. Specifically, this Part contends that by acknowledging the existence of anti-immigrant stereotypes in contemporary society, citizens might reconstruct their image of the noncitizen deportee by calling for the repeal of the IIRIRA's court-stripping provisions and by insisting that the federal government abide by its promises and respect the noncitizen's equal personhood.

I. HISTORICAL AND LEGAL PERSPECTIVES ON IMMIGRANTS' RIGHTS

Despite the rapid globalization of the world economy, the countries of *terra firma* are unlikely to abandon the concept of individual, sovereign nations in favor of a world of free borders and unrestricted migration.[14] Thus, every sovereign nation will

14. Note, however, that some scholars have argued for open border immigration policies for the United States and elsewhere. *See, e.g.*, Joseph H. Carens, *Aliens and Citizens: The Case for Open Borders*, 49 REV. OF POL. 251, 252 (1987) (finding support for open borders from the assumption that individuals are of equal moral worth); R. George Wright, *Federal Immigration Law and the Case for Open Entry*, 27 LOY. L.A. L. REV. 1265, 1265 (1994) ("[A]

continue to struggle with immigration and naturalization policy in an effort to decide who should join the polity and enjoy all the rights and privileges of citizenship and who should be excluded.[15]

For the United States, the immigration issue is particularly difficult because two competing values lie at the core of American legal history and culture: the conception of the United States as an immigrant nation and the notion of limiting resources and rights to U.S. citizens only. Images of the former include the Statue of Liberty, Ellis Island,[16] the poetry of Emma Lazarus,[17] multiculturalism,[18] and the melting pot concept.[19] In contrast, the latter notion conjures up visions of the Chinese Exclusion Act,[20] World War II internment camps,[21] current anti-

---

carefully crafted version of an open entry policy need not involve costs to current citizens so substantial as to practically disqualify such a policy.").

15. The European Community might be the exception to this statement. Under the Treaty on European Union, the community has begun to experiment with a single immigration policy governing movement of union nationals within the member states. *See* Treaty on European Union, Feb. 7, 1992, art. 8a, § 1, 31 I.L.M. 247, 259; Giovanna I. Wolf, Note, *Efforts Toward "An Ever Closer" European Union Confront Immigration Barriers*, 4 IND. J. GLOBAL LEGAL STUD. 223, 223 (1996).

16. *See* New Jersey v. New York, 118 S. Ct. 1726, 1733 (1998) (discussing Ellis Island's role in U.S. immigration from 1892 until 1954).

17. Emma Lazarus's words adorn the pedestal of Lady Liberty: "Give me your tired, your poor, / Your huddled masses yearning to breathe free, / The wretched refuse of your teeming shore. / Send these, the homeless, tempest-tost to me, / I lift my lamp beside the golden door!" Emma Lazarus, *The New Colossus*, *in* THE POEMS OF EMMA LAZARUS 203 (1888).

18. *See generally* THOMAS J. LA BELLE & CHRISTOPHER R. WARD, MULTICULTURALISM AND EDUCATION: DIVERSITY AND ITS IMPACT ON SCHOOLS AND SOCIETY (1994) (evaluating the desirability of multicultural education through an analysis of history, immigration, and culture). La Belle and Ward believe that "multiethnic and multiracial societies should make efforts to ensure equity and justice for individuals whose minority background, physical features, economic status, and goals differ from dominant groups." *Id.* at 1. They also believe that societies need to use "differences in lifestyles, values, and beliefs as a means to enrich all individuals and groups by studying other cultures, learning other languages, establishing fair and equitable methods of treatment, and generally making an effort to understand the behavior and thought of others through their eyes and value systems." *Id.* This Article attempts to provide one method by which citizens can learn to value noncitizens' personhood by examining recent social psychology research on perceptions of outgroups. *See* discussion *infra* Part III.

19. *See* Kenneth L. Karst, *Paths to Belonging: The Constitution and Cultural Identity*, 64 N.C. L. REV. 303, 311–13 (1986) (discussing the origins of the melting pot concept in U.S. history).

20. Act of May 6, 1882, ch. 126, 22 Stat. 58 (1882) (repealed 1943).

21. *See, e.g.*, Korematsu v. United States, 323 U.S. 214, 219 (1944) (upholding order excluding persons of Japanese ancestry from areas on the West Coast during World War II); Hirabayashi v. United States, 320 U.S. 81, 100–02 (1943) (determining that World War II curfew order directed at persons of Japanese ancestry did not unconstitutionally discriminate against U.S. citizens of Japanese ancestry); Yasui v. United States, 320 U.S. 115, 117 (1943) (upholding conviction of American-born person of Japanese descent for violating

Asian violence,[22] Proposition 187,[23] and welfare reform.[24] Not surprisingly, the U.S. Supreme Court's jurisprudence in the area of

curfew order in light of *Hirabayashi*); *see also* PETER IRONS, JUSTICE DELAYED: THE RECORD OF THE JAPANESE AMERICAN INTERNMENT CASES (1989) (collecting materials discussing *Korematsu*, *Hirabayashi*, and *Yasui*). The irony of the internment camps is that most of those interned were American citizens who were perceived to be foreigners. *See* MICHI WEGLYN, YEARS OF INFAMY: THE UNTOLD STORY OF AMERICA'S CONCENTRATION CAMPS 29 (1976) ("[O]f those interned some 73 percent were American citizens, born in this country and entitled to the full protection of our laws. These citizens were imprisoned for no reason other than their race."); *see also infra* note 44.

22. While anti-Asian violence has long been a sad part of America's history, one recent incident galvanized the Asian-American community: the 1982 killing of Vincent Chin. Chin was a young Chinese-American engineer who "was brutally beaten to death with a baseball bat by two white auto workers who thought he was Japanese and blamed him for the recession of the American auto industry." NATIONAL ASIAN PACIFIC AMERICAN LEGAL CONSORTIUM, 1995 AUDIT OF VIOLENCE AGAINST ASIAN PACIFIC AMERICANS: THE CONSEQUENCES OF INTOLERANCE IN AMERICA 6 (1996). Chin's killers served no jail time. *See id.*

23. Proposition 187 is a California initiative that restricts undocumented immigrants' access to various state benefits. *See* Lolita K. Buckner Inniss, *California's Proposition 187—Does It Mean What It Says? Does It Say What It Means? A Textual and Constitutional Analysis*, 10 GEO. IMMIGR. L.J. 577, 617–22 (1996) (describing provisions of Proposition 187). California voters passed the proposition in 1994 with a fifty-nine percent to forty-one percent vote. *See id.* at 578. Racially-tinged appeals to American patriotism were typical of the campaign to pass the initiative. *See, e.g.*, Letter to the Editor, *Illegal Students Given Preferential Coverage*, L.A. TIMES, Oct. 30, 1994, at B16, *available in* 1994 WL 2360440 ("[T]he state of California is not a province of Mexico. The victory of Proposition 187 will be proof that the state of California belongs to the United States of America."). Through correspondence with the Author, Professor Kevin Johnson has suggested that "Proposition 187, which limited benefits to *undocumented* immigrants, was simply a precursor to the limitation of benefits to legal immigrants as well," as evidenced by the 1996 welfare reform bill. Letter from Kevin R. Johnson, Professor, University of California, Davis, to Victor C. Romero, Associate Professor, Dickinson School Law 2 (Sept. 8, 1997) (emphasis added) (on file with the *University of Michigan Journal of Law Reform*). Thus, the anti-immigrant sentiment behind Proposition 187 was not limited to "illegal aliens." *See* Kevin R. Johnson, *An Essay on Immigration Politics, Popular Democracy, and California's Proposition 187: The Political Relevance and Legal Irrelevance of Race*, 70 WASH. L. REV. 629, 651 (1995) ("It also is possible that the passage of Proposition 187 resulted from sheer frustration with immigration.").

24. Last year's welfare reform bill included a provision that would deny "aliens" certain welfare benefits. *See* Restricting Welfare and Public Benefits for Aliens, Pub. L. No. 105-33, tit. V, subtit. D, 111 Stat. 251, 597-603 (1998). The INS has seen a surge in the number of citizen applications as a result of this and other anti-immigrant measures. *See* William Booth, *In a Rush, New Citizens Register Their Political Interest*, WASH. POST, Sept. 26, 1996, at A1 ("[T]he anti-immigrant mood of the country is pushing many to become citizens."); Matt McKinney, *Welfare Reform Spurs Citizenship "Panic,"* PROVIDENCE J. BULL., Sept. 24, 1996, at C1, *available in* 1996 WL 12465785 ("Applications nationwide have climbed sharply. Immigration officials received more than 1 million applications for citizenship between Oct. 1, 1994, and Sept. 30, 1995, the fiscal year for the INS. That was a 300 percent increase over 1994.").

This year, recent efforts by the Clinton administration to repeal some of the anti-immigrant welfare measures have relieved some of the panic among immigrants rushing to become citizens. *See* Annie Nakao, *Rush to Become Citizens Slowing, Aid Groups Say Many Immigrants Believe Threatened Benefits Won't Be Taken Away After All*, S.F. EXAMINER, July 30, 1997, at A5. Immigrants' rights groups, however, are continuing to urge noncitizens to naturalize, in case Congress decides to pass other anti-immigrant legislation. *See id.* In the meantime, a federal district judge in New York recently upheld, against an equal protection challenge,

noncitizens' rights illustrates this dichotomy between the celebration of immigrants' personhood and the denial of equal status for noncitizens.

In an effort to better understand the challenges U.S. citizens face in balancing the need to restrict membership in this country against the interest in protecting the rights of all people who enter, Part A briefly examines the history of three immigrant groups in America and the competing theories underlying the Supreme Court's jurisprudence.

A. A Historical Perspective: Non-English Whites, Chinese, and Mexican Immigrants

Throughout American history, immigration and alienage law has reflected a tension between welcoming the immigrant as a person entitled to the same legal protections and benefits as citizens and denigrating the immigrant as one outside the circle of national membership. To illustrate this tension, this section will briefly discuss how three groups in the United States' history—the non-English whites, the Chinese, and the Mexicans—have been treated alternately as insiders and outsiders by the United States' citizenry. In reviewing this history, two patterns emerge. Where the out-group can be characterized by the majority as possessing attributes similar to the majority's or as helping to further the majority's interests, then discrimination abates. Where the out-group is viewed as different and threatening, however, discrimination escalates.

1. Non-English European Immigration—In early America, there was no federal immigration law as it currently exists today. Rather, America was "the New World," free to be populated by those fleeing religious persecution in Europe.[25] In the 1700s, many of the

---

the Welfare Reform Act's provisions disqualifying many lawful permanent residents from receiving supplemental security income benefits and food stamps. *See* Abreu v. Callahan, 971 F. Supp. 799, 821 (S.D.N.Y. 1997). For a more detailed analysis of the welfare reform legislation, see generally Michael Scaperlanda, *Who Is My Neighbor?: An Essay on Immigrants, Welfare Reform, and the Constitution*, 29 CONN. L. REV. 1587 (1997) (explaining the effect of the Personal Responsibility and Work Opportunity Reconciliation Act of 1996 on resident aliens); Charles Wheeler, *The New Alien Restrictions on Public Benefits: The Full Impact Remains Uncertain*, 73 INTERPRETER RELEASES 1245 (1996) (arguing that the language of the Personal Responsibility and Work Opportunity Reconciliation Act of 1996 remains open to interpretation but will likely have the greatest negative impact on resident alien children and the elderly and states with large resident alien populations).

25. Although he acknowledges that there was neither a quantitative restriction on immigration nor a federal mandate against it, Professor Gerald Neuman contends that

immigrants were of English or Scottish descent, often members of dissenting Protestant sects.[26] Tied by a bond of common culture and purpose, many of these new settlers came to prefer things English[27] and likely felt no need to discourage immigration of others like themselves. With the influx of other Europeans, however—the non-English, the poor, the Catholics, the Jews—the first wave of immigrants began to resent the newcomers' intrusion and made them feel unwelcome.[28] Interestingly, early "immigration law" restricted entry into the various states rather than into America itself. These state-imposed rules differed from modern federal immigration law in that the former applied to other states' citizens as well as to foreigners and were often ostensibly concerned with regulating the spread of disease or with crime rather than with excluding undesirable non-English Europeans.[29] Similarly, the first federal immigration laws enacted in the late 1800s appeared to be racially and ethnically neutral,[30] although anti-Catholic sentiment was rampant.[31]

Over time, however, the English settlers began to accept the non-English.[32] Despite the initial classification of the non-English as "the other," ultimately the Europeans' shared "whiteness" constituted a sufficient basis for constructing a unified community with a new "other," the non-Whites. Congress might have foreshadowed this eventual merger of the English and non-English whites in 1790 when it restricted naturalization to "white persons,"

qualitative restrictions on transborder movement existed, primarily at the state level and supplemented by federal legislation. *See* GERALD L. NEUMAN, STRANGERS TO THE CONSTITUTION 19 (1996).

26. *See* Joe R. Feagin, *Old Poison in New Bottles: The Deep Roots of Modern Nativism*, *in* IMMIGRANTS OUT!, *supra* note 6, at 15.

27. *See id.* at 15–16.

28. *See id.* at 17.

29. *See* THOMAS ALEXANDER ALEINIKOFF ET AL., IMMIGRATION: PROCESS AND POLICY 1 (3d ed. 1995) (noting that early immigration law restricted entry by other states' citizens and foreigners and also regulated specific concerns such as public health); *see also* NEUMAN, *supra* note 25, at 21–34 (describing restrictionist policies by various colonies, including the control of disease and the entry of convicts).

30. *See* Act of Mar. 3, 1875, ch. 141, 18 Stat. 477 (repealed 1974); Act of Aug. 3, 1882, ch. 376, 22 Stat. 214 (1883); *see also* ALEINIKOFF ET AL., *supra* note 29, at 2 ("The first federal statutes limiting immigration, enacted in 1875 and 1882, prohibited the entry of criminals, prostitutes, idiots, lunatics, and persons likely to become a public charge.").

31. *See* Feagin, *supra* note 26, at 19, 21–22, 25.

32. *See id.* at 25 ("The Irish, however, did share certain cultural mores with the English and most did assimilate relatively easily to many aspects of the dominant culture."). On the concept of "whiteness" as a social construct, see generally IAN F. HANEY LÓPEZ, WHITE BY LAW: THE LEGAL CONSTRUCTION OF RACE (1996).

thus formally recognizing the common bond between the two groups.[33]

2. *Chinese Immigration*—Like the non-English whites, the Chinese in America have also experienced membership in the in-group and out-group. Initially brought to California to work on the railways, Chinese laborers outlived their usefulness in the eyes of the European-Americans once the transcontinental railroad was completed.[34] In the ensuing Panic of 1873, a drought and the depression of 1877, the Chinese became easy targets of anti-immigrant sentiment.[35] In the 1880s, Congress passed the so-called "Chinese Exclusion Laws,"[36] which were designed to prohibit Chinese immigration.[37] Further, in *Chae Chan Ping v. United States*,[38] the U.S. Supreme Court held that Congress possessed plenary constitutional power over immigration and therefore could exclude noncitizens on the basis of race.[39] The plenary power doctrine was born with this decision, and it has remained a resilient,

---

33. *See* Act of Mar. 26, 1790, ch. 3, 1 Stat. 103 (1845) (repealed 1795). Feagin correctly notes, however, that white-on-white ethnic conflict has not completely disappeared from American society, citing 1984 vice-presidential candidate Geraldine Ferraro's and former New York Governor Mario Cuomo's need to defend themselves against allegations that their Italian heritage suggested Mafia links. *See* Feagin, *supra* note 26, at 27. Unfortunately, the often white-on-white prejudice of anti-Semitism still also occurs. *See id.* at 27–28.

34. *See* ALEINIKOFF ET AL., *supra* note 29, at 2.

35. *See id.* Authors disagree as to whether the Chinese were consigned to the margins of society from the outset or whether they were gradually resented as their numbers grew. *Compare id.* at 2–3 ("The Chinese had been victims of discriminatory legislation in California since the 1850's. They were subjected to entry, license and occupation taxes, originally to raise money for the California treasury and later as a means to deter immigration."), *and* HYUNG-CHAN KIM, A LEGAL HISTORY OF ASIAN AMERICANS, 1790–1990 47 (1994) ("[T]he Chinese became immediate targets of both legal and extralegal actions taken by white miners against them to discourage their presence in California."), *with* MARY ROBERTS COOLIDGE, CHINESE IMMIGRATION 21 (1909) (describing Chinese as having been "welcomed, praised and considered almost indispensable"). For more on the early history of the Chinese in America, see generally LUCY E. SALYER, LAW HARSH AS TIGERS: CHINESE IMMIGRANTS AND THE SHAPING OF MODERN IMMIGRATION LAW (1995); Charles McClain, Jr., *The Chinese Struggle for Civil Rights in Nineteenth Century America: The First Phase, 1850–1870*, 72 CAL. L. REV. 529 (1984).

36. *See* Act of Nov. 3., 1893, ch. 14, 28 Stat. 7 (repealed 1943); Act of May 5, 1892, ch. 60, 27 Stat. 25 (repealed 1943); Act of Oct. 1, 1888, ch. 1064, 25 Stat. 504 (repealed 1943); Act of Sept. 13, 1888, ch. 1015, 25 Stat. 476 (repealed 1943); Act of July 5, 1884, ch. 220, 23 Stat. 115 (repealed 1943); Act of May 6, 1882, ch. 126, 22 Stat. 58 (repealed 1943).

37. *See* ALEINIKOFF ET AL., *supra* note 29, at 2 (discussing the history of Chinese immigration); *see also* KIM, *supra* note 35, at 70–91 (discussing the statutes and court cases regarding Chinese exclusion); Gabriel J. Chin, *Segregation's Last Stronghold: Race Discrimination and the Constitutional Law of Immigration*, 46 UCLA L. REV. 1, 12–16 (1998) (discussing the plenary power doctrine arising out of the Chinese exclusion cases).

38. 130 U.S. 581 (1889).

39. *See id.* at 601–11.

important organizing principle of immigration law.[40] Justice Field chillingly captured the nativists' view of the Chinese as the "outsider" during that time:

> The differences of race added greatly to the difficulties of the situation. . . . [T]hey remained strangers in the land, residing apart by themselves, and adhering to the customs and usages of their own country. It seemed impossible for them to assimilate with our people or to make any change in their habits or modes of living. As they grew in numbers each year the people of the coast saw, or believed they saw, in the facility of immigration, and in the crowded millions of China, where population presses upon the means of subsistence, great danger that at no distant day that portion of our country would be overrun by them . . . .[41]

After classifying the Chinese as the "outsider," Justice Field found it easy to justify their harsh treatment at the hands of the government:

> If, therefore, the government of the United States, through its legislative department, considers the presence of foreigners of a different race in this country, who will not assimilate with us, to be dangerous to its peace and security, their exclusion is not to be stayed because at the time there are no actual hostilities with the nation of which the foreigners are subjects.[42]

Like the non-English whites before them, the Chinese were viewed as outsiders who chose not to assimilate into the American culture and who therefore posed a threat to the security of the majority. According to the Court's analysis, there were only two ways by which the perceived threat of "invasion" could be abated:

---

40. *See* Stephen H. Legomsky, *Ten More Years of Plenary Power: Immigration, Congress, and the Courts*, 22 HASTINGS CONST. L.Q. 925, 925–26 (1995) [hereinafter Legomsky, *Ten More Years*]; *see also* Peter H. Schuck, *The Transformation of Immigration Law*, 84 COLUM. L. REV. 1, 3 (1984) ("Classical immigration law proved to be remarkably durable.").

Many scholars have called for the dismantling of the plenary power doctrine and have been disappointed by its continued acceptance. *See* Legomsky, *Ten More Years*, *supra*, at 936–37 (predicting future erosion and emasculation of the plenary power doctrine); *see also* Stephen H. Legomsky, *Immigration Law and the Principle of Plenary Congressional Power*, 1984 SUP. CT. REV. 255, 303, 305 [hereinafter Legomsky, *Immigration Law*] (predicting that the plenary power doctrine will eventually be frankly disavowed); Frank H. Wu, *The Limits of Borders: A Moderate Proposal for Immigration Reform*, 7 STAN. L. & POL'Y REV., Summer 1996, at 35, 35 (calling for elimination of the plenary power doctrine).

41. *Ping*, 130 U.S. at 595.

42. *Id.* at 606.

through assimilation (the route traversed by the non-English whites) or through exclusion. Viewing the Chinese as incapable of assimilating to the white culture, the dominant majority chose exclusion.[43] Just as the English settlers used facially objective laws to keep social "undesirables" out of the colonies, the white majority utilized the fiction of sovereign power to justify its overtly racist policies.[44]

Despite the continued prejudice and violence against Chinese-Americans today,[45] the dominant society has come to view the Chinese as having assimilated in some areas of American life. For example, Chinese and other East Asians often do very well on college entrance examinations and are viewed as "model minority" groups that succeed by virtue of traditional "American" values like industry and loyalty.[46] Thus, just as the non-English whites have

---

43. Anti-Asian sentiment in America historically has affected groups other than the Chinese. Americans of Japanese heritage also suffered the indignity of exclusion and isolation by being interned in camps during World War II, while Americans of German and Italian descent remained free. *See* Neil Gotanda, *Asian American Rights and the "Miss Saigon Syndrome," in* ASIAN AMERICANS AND THE SUPREME COURT: A DOCUMENTARY HISTORY 1087, 1098 (Hyung-chan Kim ed., 1992) ("The evacuated Japanese Americans, including U.S. citizens, were presumed to be sufficiently foreign for an inference by the military that such racial-foreigners might be disloyal.... With the presence of racial foreignness, a presumption of disloyalty was reasonable and natural."); *see also* Neil Gotanda, *"Other Non-Whites" in American Legal History: A Review of* JUSTICE AT WAR, 85 COLUM. L. REV. 1186, 1190–92 (1985) (book review) (discussing *Korematsu* and other wartime "concentration camp cases").

44. *See* Ibrahim J. Wani, *Truth, Strangers, and Fiction: The Illegitimate Uses of Legal Fiction in Immigration Law,* 11 CARDOZO L. REV. 51, 83 (1989) ("There is also a sinister ideological purpose served by the fiction of sovereignty. The Court was undoubtedly caught up in the nativist xenophobia of the era.... The fiction of sovereignty masked the Court's underlying bigotry by providing the decision with a seemingly objective disinfectant.") (footnote omitted). By drawing analogies between the experiences of the non-English whites and the Chinese, I do not mean to ignore the role racism played in the subordination of the Chinese. I compare these two groups, however, not to determine which has suffered more, but to emphasize the injustices that both sets of newcomers endured at the hands of the earlier arrivals, themselves European immigrants.

45. *See supra* note 22 (discussing the murder of Vincent Chin).

46. In an interesting twist in group dynamics, some universities have placed ceilings on Asian-American admissions to increase admissions of members of other racial groups. *See generally* Pat K. Chew, *Asian Americans: The "Reticent" Majority and Their Paradoxes,* 36 WM. & MARY L. REV. 1 (1994) (discussing treatment of Asian Americans in university admission policies and the distortions in societal perceptions that lead to this treatment); Grace W. Tsuang, Note, *Assuring Equal Access of Asian Americans to Highly Selective Universities,* 98 YALE L.J. 659 (1989) (discussing admission ceilings on Asian-Americans at some universities). Such admission ceilings have led some Asian-Americans to question affirmative action policies as anti-Asian, generating much scholarly commentary. *See, e.g.,* Frank H. Wu, *Neither Black nor White: Asian Americans and Affirmative Action,* 15 B.C. THIRD WORLD L.J. 225 (1995) (arguing that Asian-Americans have become pawns in the affirmative action debate because of their success in the American education system); Selena Dong, Note, *"Too Many Asians": The Challenge of Fighting Discrimination Against Asian-Americans and Preserving Affirmative Action,* 47 STAN. L. REV. 1027 (1995) (proposing constitutional arguments for Chinese-

assimilated into the dominant culture, the Chinese have been accepted where they have reflected values held by American society.

3. Mexican Immigration—Mexican laborers, like the Chinese coolies before them, have been welcomed and shunned at different times based upon their perceived usefulness by the larger American majority. While the Chinese were imported to build railroads, the Mexicans concentrated on agricultural work, mostly in the southwestern United States.[47] Based on economic demand for their services, the Mexicans alternately were recruited through formal and informal immigration arrangements[48] and rejected by American agricultural businesses.

U.S. immigration policy frequently has reflected business demand for Mexican labor. For example, World War II created an increased need for agricultural workers. Accordingly, the United States negotiated a treaty with Mexico, popularly known as the "*Bracero* Program," under which Mexican citizens were temporarily allowed entry into the United States to work on agricultural lands.[49] Once the United States government realized that it could not control its businesses' continued recruitment of cheaper, undocumented non-*Bracero* labor, however, the INS initiated "Operation Wetback" in 1954 to expel over 1,000,000 undocumented Mexican workers.[50] Rather than designing a coherent immigration policy that also punished American businesses for hiring undocumented immigrants, the federal government forced the workers to bear the ignominy of deportation.[51] In 1986, some

---

American students who must meet higher admission standards at a San Francisco high school because enrollment exceeded desegregation quotas).

47. *See* Olivas, *supra* note 6, at 432–41 (comparing the immigration histories of the Chinese and Mexicans in America).

48. Professor Gerald López asserts that while the evidence is incomplete, early commentaries support his conclusion that "the majority of Mexicans recruited after the 1880s were undocumented." Gerald P. López, *Undocumented Mexican Migration: In Search of a Just Immigration Law and Policy*, 28 UCLA L. REV. 615, 668 & n.302 (1981).

49. *See* Agreement Respecting the Temporary Migration of Mexican Agricultural Workers, Aug. 4, 1942, U.S.-Mex., 56 Stat. 1759, 1766 [hereinafter *Bracero* Program]; *see also* López, *supra* note 48, at 664–67 (discussing the *Bracero* Program).

50. *See* López, *supra* note 48, at 670; *see also* ELIZABETH HULL, WITHOUT JUSTICE FOR ALL 84–85 (1985) (describing Operation Wetback); Olivas, *supra* note 6, at 438–39 (same).

51. *See* López, *supra* note 48, at 707–08. López states:

> If we were really serious about making . . . a [sic] effective deterrent to undocumented entry, we might be able to do something about it. . . . [T]here is no reason to suppose that sanctioning those employing undocumented Mexicans would be ineffective. . . . [but] sanctions would harm the economic interests of employers and the documented population.

Id.

thirty years after Operation Wetback, Congress decided to amend the INA to include employer sanctions for hiring undocumented persons.[52] Rather than value and respect the industry of Mexican workers, many of whom have toiled in agricultural jobs not taken by citizens,[53] the United States has often affirmed the primacy of one's legal immigration status over one's desire to put in an honest day's work.[54]

Even the most cursory review of the immigration histories of the non-English whites, the Chinese, and the Mexicans in the United States reveals that their acceptance by the dominant culture, both inside and outside the law, depended greatly on their perceived similarity or usefulness to the larger society. The non-English whites shared their skin color and some cultural mores with the original English settlers; the Chinese were able to excel scholastically; the Mexicans provided vital, inexpensive agricultural labor. Just as each immigrant group has achieved varying degrees of acceptance,[55] the United States' immigration policies toward group members have vacillated depending on the citizenry's ability to

---

52. *See* Immigration Control and Reform Act of 1986, Pub. L. No. 99-603, tit. I, § 10, INA § 274A, 100 Stat. 3360–74 (codified as amended at 8 U.S.C. § 1324a (1994)). Section 1324a makes it "unlawful for a person or other entity [] to hire, or to recruit or refer for a fee, for employment in the United States [a noncitizen] knowing the [noncitizen] is an unauthorized [noncitizen] . . . with respect to such employment . . . ." *Id.* § 1324a(a)(1)(A).

53. Professor Kevin Johnson describes this attitude toward Mexican workers as "schizophrenic": "On the one hand, Mexicans often are characterized as hardworking and performing labor that many 'Americans' will not. On the other hand, they serve as convenient scapegoats when the U.S. economy turns for the worse." Kevin Johnson, *The New Nativism: Something Old, Something New, Something Borrowed, Something Blue*, *in* IMMIGRANTS OUT!, *supra* note 6, at 165, 171 (endnotes omitted).

54. As one subway commuter acknowledged in a recent *New York Times* article about undocumented immigrant workers: "These guys work very hard, even if they are here illegally." Clyde Haberman, *Immigrants: In Plain Sight, but Not Seen*, N.Y. TIMES, July 22, 1997, at B1; *see also* Linda S. Bosniak, *Exclusion and Membership: The Dual Identity of the Undocumented Worker Under United States Law*, 1988 WIS. L. REV. 955 (discussing the identity of undocumented workers in the United States).

55. Indeed, some commentators contend that the recent nativism directed at noncitizens of color may be more resilient than that directed at their white counterparts:

> Many of today's "legal" and "illegal" immigrants are people of color, especially from Mexico. As has been the case with past immigrant generations, they have been subject to discrimination. Unlike their European predecessors, however, the animus directed at the new immigrants may enjoy greater resilience. The color of their skin indefinitely ensures their weakness in the political process, even for those "illegals" who navigate the arduous process to become "legal."

Johnson, Los Olvidados, *supra* note 6, at 1145 (citations omitted); *see also* Robert S. Chang, *A Meditation on Borders*, *in* IMMIGRANTS OUT!, *supra* note 6, at 244, 245 (discussing the concept of nativistic racism as it applies to discrimination against Asian-Americans).

recognize in the noncitizens values held by the dominant American culture.

This section has examined the historical tension between the acceptance and rejection of the foreigner by the citizen. The next section will examine how the Supreme Court's alienage jurisprudence reflects this tension. Specifically, the next section describes two competing paradigms in Supreme Court precedent to explain the Court's opinions about noncitizens: the membership and personhood paradigms.

B. A Legal Perspective: Membership Versus Personhood

Two important law review articles succinctly summarize the Supreme Court's jurisprudence regarding the membership and personhood status of immigrants in American society.

In *Membership, Equality, and the Difference that Alienage Makes,*[56] Professor Linda Bosniak contends that the Court's alienage decisions may best be understood through the prisms of "separation" and "convergence."[57] Drawing from the work of political scientist Michael Walzer,[58] Bosniak describes the separation model[59] as one that assumes that the government's plenary power[60] over immigration—the admission and exclusion of noncitizens—exists separate from its limited power over immigrants' personal rights.[61] Therefore, a government that has the power to deny a noncitizen admission to this country does not have the power to beat a confession out of an immigrant accused of committing a crime.[62] The convergence model asserts the converse: the government's power over immigration converges with its power over immigrants'

56. Linda S. Bosniak, *Membership, Equality, and the Difference that Alienage Makes*, 69 N.Y.U. L. REV. 1047 (1994).

57. *Id.* at 1059.

58. *See id.* at 1057 (discussing MICHAEL WALZER, SPHERES OF JUSTICE: A DEFENSE OF PLURALISM AND EQUALITY (1983)).

59. *See id.* at 1138.

60. *See id.* at 1059–65.

61. *See id.* at 1094–95.

62. *See* Franco de Jerez v. Burgos, 876 F.2d 1038, 1042 (1st Cir. 1989) (noting that the Constitution guarantees noncitizens the same constitutional rights possessed by citizens charged with crimes); Lynch v. Cannatella, 810 F.2d 1363, 1374 (5th Cir. 1987) (holding that noncitizens have the right to be free from gross physical abuse at the hands of state or federal agents).

rights.[63] For example, the government may fairly restrict the right to vote to citizens only, but deny the franchise to foreigners.[64]

Despite these distinctions, Bosniak acknowledges that the boundary between these two models is not, at the margin, clearly delineated: "The defining question in the current politics of [noncitizen] status is just how far the government's power to regulate immigration legitimately extends."[65] In other words, does the government's power to deny a foreigner entry into the United States also include the power to deny the noncitizen access to public benefits once in the United States? In the case of our fictional Ms. Santiago, does the government's immigration power extend so completely over noncitizens that the government can deny Ms. Santiago the right to enforce a plea agreement? Ultimately, Bosniak chooses not to predict how courts will respond to the ever-increasing number of rights claims by noncitizens in the current anti-immigrant climate, but she is satisfied that, for now, her two models provide a useful framework from which to evaluate these claims.[66]

In *Partial Membership: Aliens and the Constitutional Community*,[67] Professor Michael Scaperlanda picks up where Bosniak leaves off. Using the term "personhood" in place of "separation" and "membership" in lieu of "convergence," Scaperlanda contends that the Supreme Court favors membership over personhood.[68] In reviewing a noncitizen's rights claim, the Court will first determine whether membership issues are present.[69] If so, then the noncitizen's claim will be summarily denied, and the Court will defer to the political arm which has chosen to differentiate between citizen and foreigner.[70] For instance, in *Mathews v. Diaz*,[71] the Court held that Congress's plenary power over immigration extended into the realm of the distribution of Medicare benefits.[72] Accordingly, the Court upheld the statutory scheme that made a noncitizen's length of continued residence in the United States a condition for par-

63. *See* Bosniak, *supra* note 56, at 1138.

64. *See infra* note 138 and accompanying text (discussing limits on the voting rights of noncitizens); *cf.* Bosniak, *supra* note 56, at 1064 (noting that alienage is often a legitimate basis for denying certain rights to noncitizens).

65. Bosniak, *supra* note 56, at 1143.

66. *See id.* at 1148–49.

67. Michael Scaperlanda, *Partial Membership: Aliens and the Constitutional Community*, 81 IOWA L. REV. 707 (1996).

68. *See id.* at 716, 752.

69. *See id.*

70. *See id.* at 716.

71. 426 U.S. 67 (1976).

72. *See id.* at 80 (applying rational basis review to the federal alienage classification).

ticipation in a federal medical insurance program.[73] Diaz was not a citizen, so Congress could legitimately exercise its plenary immigration power over him to deny him certain federal benefits.[74] His claim of personhood did not trump his status as a foreigner.

If membership is not an issue, however, then the Court closely scrutinizes the discriminatory governmental conduct, often validating the noncitizen's claim to equal personhood.[75] In another benefits case, *Graham v. Richardson*,[76] the Court invalidated an Arizona statute that deprived noncitizens of certain welfare benefits, stating that "classifications based on alienage, like those based on nationality or race, are inherently suspect and subject to close judicial scrutiny."[77] In *Graham*, national membership was not an issue; therefore, Arizona, which, unlike Congress, possesses no plenary power over immigration, could not deny noncitizens their rights to equal personhood absent a compelling reason.[78] Equal personhood trumps governmental claims where national membership is a non-issue.[79]

Given the Court's preference for the membership model, Scaperlanda argues for a redefinition of the debate over membership from one that pits the plenary power of the legislature against the noncitizen's claim to equal rights, to a debate that weighs the rights of the citizenry "to create a constitutional community"[80] against the rights of the noncitizen to equal personhood. Scaperlanda cites the Court's "political function" cases to illustrate his theory.[81] In these cases, the Court found that a state's right to define who is part of its community overrides any personhood claims the noncitizen might have.[82] For example, in *Cabell v. Chavez-Salido*,[83] the Court sustained a California requirement that all peace officers be citizens.[84] The Court stated the following:

> [The] exclusion of [noncitizens] from basic governmental processes is not a deficiency in the democratic system but a necessary consequence of the community's process of political

73. *See id.* at 83–84.
74. *See id.* at 84.
75. *See* Scaperlanda, *supra* note 67, at 716, 752.
76. 403 U.S. 365 (1971).
77. *Id.* at 372 (citations omitted).
78. *See* Scaperlanda, *supra* note 67, at 731 & n.126.
79. *See id.* at 716.
80. *Id.* at 769.
81. *See id.* at 767–71.
82. *See id.* at 769–70.
83. 454 U.S. 432 (1984).
84. *See id.* at 447.

> self-definition. Self-government ... begins by defining the scope of the community of the governed and thus of the governors as well: [noncitizens] are by definition those outside of this community.[85]

Scaperlanda specifically cites this passage in *Cabell* to emphasize that the Court should justify its preference for membership over personhood only when membership involves the citizenry's attempt at self-definition in accordance with constitutional mandates.[86] Thus, Scaperlanda maintains, the current plenary power or the "inherent sovereign power" paradigm is essentially unbounded.[87] His alternative—a model that requires that communal formation be tempered by the Constitution and then weighed against the noncitizen's personhood claim—forces the government to recognize that it has limited power. The primacy of the Constitution prevents the government from playing the membership card to trump personhood.[88]

Scaperlanda concludes by calling for a constitutional dialogue among "We the People."[89] While he questions whether the political branch will act to protect the rights of noncitizens,[90] he hopes that the process of engaging in a frank discussion about citizenship and personal rights will help shape "the place of noncitizens in our society ... ."[91]

---

85. *Id.* at 439–40.

86. *See* Scaperlanda, *supra* note 67, at 769–71.

87. *See id.* at 754 ("[T]he membership's core is broad and the political branches receive wide latitude in formulating its policy.").

88. Arguably, Scaperlanda's reliance on the political function cases begs the issue. If Scaperlanda seeks to bound both the federal and state governments by the Constitution, current equal protection law arguably does just that. Even in cases where membership is an issue, the Court has employed, for the most part, a rational basis test to scrutinize the government action. *See* Scaperlanda, *supra* note 67, at 731–34. While this may not seem like much scrutiny, it remains constitutional scrutiny nonetheless. *See* Mathews v. Diaz, 426 U.S. 67, 81–82 (1976) ("The reasons that preclude judicial review of political questions also dictate a narrow standard of review of decisions made by the Congress or the President in the area of immigration and naturalization.") (citations omitted). In correspondence I have received from him, Scaperlanda responds that he is concerned that the current rational basis review undervalues the personhood interests of the noncitizen. *See* Electronic Mail from Michael Scaperlanda, Professor, University of Oklahoma Law Center, to Victor C. Romero, Associate Professor, Dickinson School of Law (Dec. 12, 1997) (on file with *University of Michigan Journal of Law Reform*). I agree with that assessment and, in fact, argue for greater judicial scrutiny of alienage classifications within the immigration law context. *See* Romero, *Congruence*, *supra* note †, at 441–54.

89. *See* Scaperlanda, *supra* note 67, at 771.

90. Kevin Johnson has expressed a similar fear that the U.S. citizenry will be unsympathetic to noncitizen concerns. *See* Johnson, Los Olvidados, *supra* note 6, at 1147.

91. Scaperlanda, *supra* note 67, at 771 n.352. Certainly, the public could decide to amend the Constitution to eliminate the distinction between citizen and noncitizen. So long as the United States and other nations favor territorial boundaries over borderless

Part II, through its discussion of the recent promise enforcement cases, provides one recent example of how membership preempts personhood and how Scaperlanda's fears of an unsympathetic Congress have been realized. After acknowledging the problem that the primacy of membership poses, Part III proposes a way to engage in the constitutional dialogue Scaperlanda suggests by examining recent research in critical race theory and social psychology.

II. PERSONHOOD VERSUS MEMBERSHIP: THE "PROMISE ENFORCEMENT" CASES

A. *The Due Process Rights of Noncitizens*

The Due Process Clauses of the Fifth and Fourteenth Amendments preclude the federal government and the states, respectively, from denying life, liberty, or property to any person without due process.[92] Although the Supreme Court decided long ago that the term "person" in both amendments applies to certain groups of noncitizens[93] and that noncitizens enjoy a right to trial in criminal proceedings,[94] within the context of immigration law, the Court has been reluctant to ascribe constitutional significance to any procedural protections granted immigrants in civil deportation proceedings.

Professor Hiroshi Motomura contends that the Court has not held that the Constitution requires procedural due process protection for noncitizens in deportation hearings. Instead, the Court has relied on subconstitutional statutory interpretations of the INA[95] that favor the noncitizen.[96] For example, Motomura asserts

---

jurisdictions, however, the distinction between citizen and noncitizen will remain. *See supra* text accompanying notes 14–15. My goal is less ambitious: using the promise enforcement cases as examples, I seek to convince citizens to value fundamental rights concomitant with the idea of personhood rather than to assert the primacy of their polity membership.

92. "No person shall . . . be deprived of life, liberty, or property, without due process of law . . . ." U.S. CONST. amend. V. "No State shall . . . deprive any person of life, liberty, or property, without due process of law . . . ." *Id.* amend. XIV, § 1.

93. *See* Kwong Hai Chew v. Colding, 344 U.S. 590, 596 (1953) (holding that permanent residents are "persons" within the context of the Fifth Amendment's Due Process Clause); Yick Wo v. Hopkins, 118 U.S. 356, 369 (1886) (holding that permanent residents are "persons" protected by the Fourteenth Amendment).

94. *See* Wong Wing v. United States, 163 U.S. 228, 237 (1896).

95. 8 U.S.C. §§ 1101–1557 (1994).

96. *See* Hiroshi Motomura, *The Curious Evolution of Immigration Law: Procedural Surrogates for Substantive Constitutional Rights*, 92 COLUM. L. REV. 1625, 1645 (1992) [hereinafter Motomura, *Evolution*] ("The few judicial decisions [of the 1950s and 1960s] that fostered

that in *Woodby v. INS*,[97] the Court's decision that the applicable INA statute required the showing of clear and convincing evidence of deportability, rather than a simple preponderance, incorporated constitutional due process reasoning, despite the Court's insistence that it was merely engaging in statutory interpretation.[98]

The Court has been reluctant to apply constitutional law due to the primacy of the membership paradigm, as embodied in Congress's plenary power over immigration. The use of this paradigm restricts the Court and renders it reluctant to encroach upon Congressional conceptions of citizenship by erecting constitutional requirements and barriers. The only way the Court is willing to subvert Congressional power is through the occasional use of clandestine subconstitutional due process norms masquerading as neutral statutory interpretation.

Arguably, the use of what Motomura describes as "phantom" or "surrogate" procedural rules[99] to achieve what constitutional norms of personhood readily accomplish, reinforces the concept of the noncitizen as the "other" by underenforcing our traditional constitutional norms. Every court decision that favors the membership paradigm over the personhood theory further alienates the noncitizen.

The next section describes how the primacy of membership over personhood can lead a federal court to completely abdicate its role as protector of the marginalized in deference to legislative conceptions of citizenship.

B. Membership Trumps Personhood: The "Promise Enforcement" Cases

Each of the three cases described below highlights the tensions between the membership and personhood paradigms in a judicial milieu that generally favors membership concerns.

1. The Personhood Paradigm Applied: Thomas v. INS—Clive Charles Thomas arrived in the United States in 1954 and was admitted

---

the expansion of procedural due process review did so primarily through statutory interpretation, not constitutional law."); *see also* Hiroshi Motomura, *Immigration Law After a Century of Plenary Power: Phantom Constitutional Norms and Statutory Interpretation*, 100 YALE L.J. 545, 564–75 (1990) [hereinafter Motomura, *Century*] (arguing that the plenary power doctrine has constrained courts from applying constitutional law in immigration cases).

97. 385 U.S. 276 (1966).

98. *See* Motomura, *Evolution*, *supra* note 96, at 1645 & n.106 (citing *Woodby*, 385 U.S. at 284–85).

99. *See id.* at 1645 n.100.

as a lawful permanent resident.[100] In 1983, Thomas, still a noncitizen, pled guilty to conspiracy to possess cocaine for sale and was sentenced to seven years' imprisonment.[101] Because Thomas cooperated with the U.S. Attorney's Office in a major narcotics investigation, he was released after serving only two years of his sentence.[102]

As part of his deal with the government, Thomas entered into a written cooperation agreement in which he agreed to turn over a sworn statement about his drug trafficking and to serve as a prosecution witness for two years.[103] In exchange, the government promised to advise Thomas's parole board of his cooperation and agreed not to oppose motions made by Thomas's attorney for reduction of sentence and relief from deportation.[104]

After his conviction, the INS issued an order for Thomas to show cause why he should not be deported.[105] Thomas's attorney moved for discretionary relief under section 212(c) of the Immigration and Nationality Act (INA).[106] Notwithstanding the government's express promise not to do so, the INS opposed the request for relief, calling two witnesses at the immigration court hearing who testified to Thomas's criminal activities.[107] Despite Thomas's testimony about his reformed behavior and his cooperation with the government, the immigration judge denied Thomas's request. Thomas also lost his appeal before the Board of Immigration Appeals (BIA).[108]

Thomas then brought his case before the Ninth Circuit, claiming that the government had violated his due process rights by reneging on its promise not to contest his motion for relief from deportation.[109] In a 2-1 decision, the Ninth Circuit panel agreed with Thomas and remanded the case to the immigration judge for

100. *See* Thomas v. INS, 35 F.3d 1332, 1335 (9th Cir. 1994).

101. *See id.*

102. *See id.*

103. *See id.*

104. *See id.* Under the agreement, if the U.S. Attorney determined that Thomas had lied, the government could terminate the agreement. The government, however, was required to give Thomas an opportunity to confront his accusers prior to the agreement's termination. *See id.*

105. *See id.* at 1336.

106. *See id.* INA section 212(c) provides that "[noncitizens] lawfully admitted for permanent residence who temporarily proceeded abroad voluntarily and not under an order of deportation, and who are returning to a lawful unrelinquished domicile of seven consecutive years, may be admitted in the discretion of the Attorney General . . . ." 8 U.S.C. § 1182(c) (1994).

107. *See Thomas*, 35 F.3d at 1336.

108. *See id.*

109. *See id.* at 1336–37.

a new section 212(c) proceeding for discretionary relief from deportation.[110]

Citing well-known and long-standing Supreme Court precedent, the Ninth Circuit began the heart of its opinion strongly in Thomas's favor: "It has long been the law that the government's failure to keep a commitment which induces a guilty plea requires that judgment be vacated and the case remanded."[111] Noting that a cooperation agreement is analogous to a plea agreement,[112] the court stated that the government would be held to the literal terms of the agreement and would ordinarily bear responsibility for any lack of clarity.[113] For the agreement to be enforceable, however, the promisee must rely detrimentally on the promise, and the promisor must be authorized to make the agreement.[114]

The INS offered two arguments in opposition to Thomas's appeal. First, it contended that the INS was neither a party to the agreement, nor bound by it, nor did the agreement specify that the government would not oppose Thomas's request.[115] Second, it "argue[d] that the United States Attorney lacked authority to enter into an agreement on [behalf of the INS]."[116]

The court rejected outright the first argument regarding the INS's alleged non-participation in the agreement negotiations.[117] Although acknowledging the reasonableness of the INS's wish not to be bound by an agreement crafted without its consultation, the court nonetheless focused on the harm to Thomas caused by the U.S. Attorney's gaffe: "Thomas was entitled to performance by the government of its promise."[118] Moreover, the court stated the following:

> The agreement plainly and unambiguously spoke to the issue of deportation and expressly bound the INS. In the first paragraph, the agreement says that "Government," designated as the promisor, "includes its departments, officers, agents, and agencies." . . . The eighth paragraph bound "[t]he Government," so defined, not to oppose motions for "relief from deportation to the . . . U.S. Immigration Service." . . . Motions for relief from deportation are made and heard before the

110. *See id.* at 1337.
111. *Id.* (citing Santobello v. New York, 404 U.S. 257, 262 (1971)).
112. *See id.* (citing United States v. Carrillo, 709 F.2d 35, 36 (9th Cir. 1983)).
113. *See id.* (citing United States v. Anderson, 970 F.2d 602, 607 (9th Cir. 1992)).
114. *See id.* (citing Johnson v. Lumpkin, 769 F.2d 630, 633 (9th Cir. 1985)).
115. *See id.*
116. *Id.*
117. *See id.*
118. *Id.*

INS, and opposed by INS lawyers, so this particular promise, to mean anything, had to mean that the INS would not oppose such a motion.[119]

The court spent considerably more time analyzing the INS's second argument, that the U.S. Attorney lacked authority to bind the INS.[120] Applying common law agency principles, the court stated that an agent may bind the principal only if it has actual authority—express or implied—to do so:

> Therefore, the United States Attorney's promise that the government would not oppose Thomas's § 212(c) application is binding on the INS if the United States Attorney had either an express grant of authority to make such a promise, or his authority for making the promise is incidental to some other express grant of authority.[121]

Examining the duties of the U.S. Attorneys, the court noted that Congress expressly conferred upon them the power to "prosecute for all offenses against the United States."[122] Congress, however, specifically delegated to the Attorney General the power to administer and enforce the INA.[123] In turn, the Attorney General has delegated much of this power to officials of the INS, leading the court to conclude that "[s]o far as we have found in the Code of Federal Regulations, no delegation of that authority has been made to United States Attorneys."[124]

After finding no *express* delegation, the court next considered whether the U.S. Attorney's Congressionally-sanctioned power to prosecute gives her *implied* authority to prevent the government, including the INS, from opposing motions for relief from deportation.[125] The court ruled that the U.S. Attorney has such implied authority.[126] Again citing common law agency principles, the court held that the power to enter a cooperation agreement and consequently bind the government is an incident of the same prosecutorial power that gives U.S. Attorneys the implied authority

119. *Id.* at 1337–38 (citations omitted).
120. *See id.* at 1338–42.
121. *Id.* at 1338.
122. *Id.* at 1339 (citing 28 U.S.C. § 547(1) (1988)).
123. *See id.* at 1338 (citing 8 U.S.C. § 1103(a) (1994)).
124. *Id.*
125. *See id.* at 1339.
126. *See id.* at 1339–40.

to negotiate plea bargains.[127] The court specified three reasons for its holding:

> First, deportation commonly arises from the context of criminal prosecution. It is likely to be a central issue in many criminal cases involving [noncitizens]. Second, the terms of a plea or cooperation agreement will commonly affect deportation. The attorneys will negotiate the offenses of conviction and sentences partly by considering the effects of these determinations on deportation. Third, there is no reason why, in the absence of regulations or orders to the contrary, we should doubt that Congress implied this grant of authority.[128]

This holding does not mean that the INS is without a remedy. The court noted that the Attorney General, if she wished, could limit the authority of the U.S. Attorneys through an appropriate section in the Code of Federal Regulations, but she has chosen not to do so.[129]

This case is a marvelous example of the personhood theory of noncitizens' rights. Specifically, this case demonstrates three characteristics of the personhood paradigm: (1) the focus is on constraining government power rather than determining the extent to which the noncitizen may enjoy the rights of a citizen; (2) the government is seen as a unified entity rather than separate branches in instances where it seeks to limit a noncitizen's rights; and (3) the paradigm recognizes the reality that noncitizens should be accorded more protection in some instances, especially since the threat of deportation is a constant in noncitizens' lives. Let us examine these lessons in turn.

First, the court did not begin by looking at Thomas's noncitizenship in order to determine what process was due. Instead, it focused on Thomas's claim that the government failed to satisfy its end of the bargain, which caused a direct harm to Thomas.[130] While it sympathized with the INS's plight owing to the agency's non-participation in the cooperation agreement talks, the court stressed that, ultimately, it was Thomas who was "entitled to performance by the government"[131]—whether that obligation was fulfilled by the U.S. Attorney or the INS. Thomas's personhood, and therefore, his claim against the government, was not dimin-

127. *See id.*
128. *Id.* at 1340.
129. *See id.* at 1341.
130. *See id.* at 1337.
131. *Id.*

ished by his noncitizenship. In the court's eyes, he was entitled to the same due process as citizens subject to prosecution by the government and its entities.[132]

The personhood paradigm is especially applicable here because membership issues are of secondary concern in the promise enforcement scenario. The primary object of the cooperation agreement between the government and the noncitizen is to facilitate the prosecution of a criminal case, not to affect immigration law.[133] Put another way, in cooperation agreements, the government's main concern is the defendant's cooperation, not the defendant's citizenship. The *Thomas* court properly kept its focus on the government's obligation to keep its promises rather than be distracted by the defendant's irrelevant citizenship status.

Second, this case is instructive because the court correctly understood that, in the noncitizen's eyes, the government is monolithic. When the government purports to negotiate with any person, noncitizens included, it should not be allowed to feign ignorance when one of its branches fails to communicate with another branch. Thus, drawing an artificial boundary between the government's immigration arm and its criminal prosecutorial arm means little to the noncitizen who negotiates in good faith. Viewing the government as monolithic makes sense, especially when the government's negotiating arm seeks to acquire from the noncitizen cooperation that benefits the general public. If the government wants to reap the benefits of its negotiated deal, it must also be willing to accept the accompanying burdens.

At one level, "distaste" for the monolithic government also mirrors the general sentiment held by some scholars that there should be little difference between state and federal discrimination against noncitizens. Commentators have long recognized that plenary power over immigration effectively immunizes the federal government from equal protection scrutiny when it treats noncitizens worse than citizens, while state governments engaging in the same discriminatory conduct are generally subject to heightened scrutiny.[134] This federal/state dichotomy in alienage jurisprudence has led some to urge that the plenary power doctrine be

132. *See id.* (accepting Thomas's due process claim); *see also* Santobello v. New York, 404 U.S. 257, 262 (1971) (discussing the importance for due process considerations that the government abide by its promises in the plea agreement context).

133. *See Thomas*, 35 F.3d at 1337 (analogizing cooperation agreements to plea bargains).

134. *See* Legomsky, *Immigration Law, supra* note 40, at 256, 305 n.254; Gerald M. Rosberg, *The Protection of Aliens from Discriminatory Treatment by the National Government*, 1977 SUP. CT. REV. 275, 275–77.

rejected,[135] while others have suggested that, at the very least, some congruence be sought between the levels of scrutiny currently used to examine federal versus state action.[136] From the noncitizen's perspective, the view of the government is the same in the *Thomas* case as in the plenary power debate: all the noncitizen knows is that she is being confronted by an American government seeking somehow to restrict her liberty.

Finally, the court correctly observed that, as a practical matter, cooperation agreements in criminal law proceedings affect noncitizens more than citizens because of the "everpresent threat of deportation."[137] Perhaps second only to the inability to vote,[138] the constant threat of deportation divides the noncitizen from the citizen. Because noncitizens cannot exercise the franchise, they are unable to vote for procedural safeguards to temper prosecutorial zeal in deportation hearings.[139] Therefore, courts must pay atten-

---

135. *See supra* note 40.

136. *See* T. Alexander Aleinikoff, *Federal Regulation of Aliens and the Constitution*, 83 AM. J. INT'L L. 862, 870 (1989) (suggesting that rather than invoking Congress's plenary power, "courts ought to examine the justifications offered on behalf of federal regulations based on alienage to see if they meet traditional constitutional standards of permissibility" and recommending courts review strictly regulations burdening fundamental constitutional rights); Gilbert Paul Carrasco, *Congressional Arrogation of Power: Alien Constellation in the Galaxy of Equal Protection*, 74 B.U. L. REV. 591, 603 n.52 (1994) (arguing that the Court has failed to articulate a viable reason for why state and federal laws would be subject to different levels of scrutiny); Romero, *Congruence*, *supra* note †, at 428–29 (arguing that Justice O'Connor's "congruence principle" in the *Adarand* case may serve as the starting point for requiring generally stricter scrutiny of some federal alienage classifications); Rosberg, *supra* note 134, 316–36 (arguing that constitutional limits on classification by alienage should apply to federal as well as state government). *But see* Michael J. Perry, *Modern Equal Protection: A Conceptualization and Appraisal*, 79 COLUM. L. REV. 1023, 1060–65 (1979) (arguing that conceptualizing the distinction between levels of scrutiny using the Supremacy Clause, not equal protection, explains the Court's general deference to federal actions).

137. MICHAEL WALZER, SPHERES OF JUSTICE: A DEFENSE OF PLURALISM AND EQUALITY 58 (1983). Ironically, even though deportation is viewed as the enforcement activity most closely associated with the INS, many noncitizens that the INS expels are undocumented immigrants caught and repelled at the border. *See* Patrick J. McDonnell, *Formal Departure Is Much Less Common than Expulsion*, L.A. TIMES, June 23, 1997, at A14.

138. *See* Hampton v. Mow Sun Wong, 426 U.S. 88, 102 (1976) (noting that noncitizens are denied the right to vote); JOHN HART ELY, DEMOCRACY AND DISTRUST 161 (1980) (same); *see also* U.S. CONST. amend. XV, § 1 (protecting the right to vote of citizens only). Professor Gerald Rosberg has argued that noncitizens with permanent resident status should be allowed to vote. *See* Gerald M. Rosberg, *Aliens and Equal Protection: Why Not the Right to Vote?*, 75 MICH. L. REV. 1092, 1110–15 (1977); *see also* Jamin B. Raskin, *Legal Aliens, Local Citizens: The Historical, Constitutional and Theoretical Meanings of Alien Suffrage*, 141 U. PA. L. REV. 1391, 1441–60 (1993) (arguing that no logical distinction exists between citizens and resident aliens for purposes of the voting franchise).

139. While Thomas arguably could have naturalized so he could enjoy the full panoply of citizens' rights, naturalization is not an option for the vast majority of permanent residents who are either waiting to apply or are in the process of applying for U.S. citizenship. *See* INA § 316(a), 8 U.S.C.A. § 1427 (West 1998) (noting that legal permanent residents

tion to the double threat facing a noncitizen charged with a crime: criminal prosecution and deportation. The *Thomas* court did just that. It acknowledged that, when a noncitizen is a criminal defendant, deportation must be considered because any plea or cooperation agreement could very well involve deportation considerations.[140]

In sum, the *Thomas* decision captures the essence of the personhood paradigm: the belief that due process rights require the government to act fairly in its dealings with both citizens and noncitizens.[141]

2. *The Membership Paradigm Applied:* San Pedro v. United States—This next subsection examines a case whose facts, though similar to the facts in *Thomas*, led the court to deny the noncitizen protection and implicitly, though likely unintentionally, to assert the primacy of the membership theory of noncitizens' rights.

Alberto San Pedro is a Cuban citizen, but he has been a lawful permanent resident of the United States for over forty years.[142] He was indicted for bribing, and for conspiracy to bribe, a federal public official.[143] After entering into a plea agreement with the U.S. Attorney's Office, San Pedro pled guilty to the conspiracy charge in exchange for transactional immunity.[144] The government promised not to prosecute San Pedro for any other offenses based upon evidence revealed during the investigation leading to the bribery charges.[145]

It is at this point that San Pedro's and Thomas's stories converge. As in *Thomas*, the INS issued an order for San Pedro to show

---

must have lived in the United States for five years before they are eligible to apply for naturalization).

140. *See Thomas*, 35 F.3d at 1340.

141. In a case involving similar facts, the Eighth Circuit followed the same reasoning as the *Thomas* court in holding that an AUSA could bind the INS to a plea agreement. *See* Margalli-Olvera v. INS, 43 F.3d 345, 353 (8th Cir. 1994). The Eighth Circuit panel stated the following:

> [A]n Assistant United States Attorney enters into a plea agreement on behalf of the United States government as a whole. Accordingly, promises made by an Assistant United States Attorney bind all agents of the United States government. Therefore, we hold that unless a plea agreement uses specific language that limits the agents bound by the promise, ambiguities regarding the agencies bound by the agreement are to be interpreted to bind the agency at issue.

Id.

142. *See* San Pedro v. United States, 79 F.3d 1065, 1067 (11th Cir. 1996), *cert denied*, 519 U.S. 980 (1996).

143. *See id.*

144. *See id.*

145. *See id.* at 1067 & n.1.

cause why he should not be deported because of his conviction.[146] San Pedro responded by filing a petition for writ of mandamus in federal district court, contending, as did Thomas, that the government's promise in the plea agreement prevented the INS from deporting him.[147] The government filed a motion to dismiss, arguing, as did the government in *Thomas*, that it never promised San Pedro non-deportation, and even if it did, that the promise did not bind the INS because the U.S. Attorney did not have the authority to make such a promise.[148]

Converting the motion to dismiss into one for summary judgment,[149] the court ruled that although there was a factual issue as to whether the government made the non-deportation promise, the crucial legal issue was whether the U.S. Attorney "had the authority to promise not to deport a criminal defendant as a condition of a plea bargain."[150] The court held that neither the U.S. Attorney's manual nor the INA vested the U.S. Attorney with the power to bind the INS through a non-deportation clause; accordingly, the court granted summary judgment in the government's favor.[151]

On appeal, the Eleventh Circuit grappled with the same issues as the *Thomas* court, and indeed, cited *Thomas* as prior authority.[152] While it agreed with the *Thomas* court that Congress did not expressly grant the U.S. Attorney power to bind the INS or any other governmental agency,[153] the Eleventh Circuit disagreed with the *Thomas* court's interpretation of the controlling law:

> We believe *Thomas* incorrectly harmonized the statutes that empower the United States attorneys and the attorney general, and failed to consider that *the express authority to enforce immigration law is concentrated solely in the attorney general.* It is unclear to this court, as it was to the district court, why Congress would have granted United States attorneys the authority to enter into agreements with criminal defendants that bind the INS while simultaneously granting the authority

146. *See id.* at 1067.

147. *See id.*

148. *See id.*

149. *See id.*

150. *Id.* at 1068.

151. *See id.*; *see also* United States v. Igbonwa, 120 F.3d 437, 444 (3d Cir. 1997) ("We hold that the United States Attorney's Office lacks the authority to make a promise pertaining to deportation in the prosecution of a criminal matter that will bind INS without its express authorization.").

152. *See* San Pedro v. United States, 79 F.3d 1065, 1069 (11th Cir. 1996). The panel also noted that the Eighth Circuit had followed the *Thomas* court's reasoning in a 1994 decision. *See id.* (citing Margalli-Olvera v. INS, 43 F.3d 345, 353 (8th Cir. 1994)).

153. *See id.*

> to enforce the specific provisions of the immigration laws to the attorney general in the INA. We therefore follow the principle, upheld by the Supreme Court on numerous occasions, that a specific statute takes precedence over a more general one.[154]

Unlike the Ninth Circuit's affirmation of Thomas's personhood, the Eleventh Circuit implicitly upheld the theory of membership by emphasizing the separate, unique status of immigration law enforcement. By extension, the *San Pedro* court also highlighted the practical disadvantage separate immigration enforcement creates for noncitizens like San Pedro who cannot rely on a monolithic government to abide by its promises but instead must specifically adhere to the INS's rules and requirements, regardless of what other government agencies might guarantee.

The *San Pedro* decision emphasizes two other important points that appear in the Supreme Court's alienage jurisprudence about membership. First, the court was quick to rely on a seemingly neutral rule of interpretation—that specific statutes take precedence over more general ones—without examining the adverse consequences to San Pedro. Similarly, the Supreme Court in *Mathews v. Diaz* invoked another neutral rule—the plenary power doctrine—to deny Medicare benefits to certain noncitizens.[155] Arguably, the distribution of public benefits has little to do with the admission or expulsion of people,[156] which is the basic province of immigration

154. *Id.* (citing Simpson v. United States, 435 U.S. 6, 15 (1978); Brown v. General Servs. Admin., 425 U.S. 820, 834 (1976)) (emphasis added).

155. *See* Mathews v. Diaz, 426 U.S. 67, 81–84 (1976).

156. Some may argue, as I am sure the proponents of Proposition 187 did, that a legitimate way to deter immigration is to create disincentives to immigrate. Thus, the proponents of California's Proposition 187 would contend that one purpose of denying Mexican undocumented immigrants medical care is to deter them from crossing the border illegally. Recent research, however, has affirmed prior studies that most Mexican immigrants come to the United States to work and not to avail themselves of government benefits. *See* WAYNE A. CORNELIUS ET AL., CENTER FOR U.S.-MEXICAN STUDIES, MEXICAN IMMIGRANTS IN THE SAN FRANCISCO BAY AREA: A SUMMARY OF CURRENT KNOWLEDGE 43–56 (1982) (noting that although undocumented Mexican immigrants in the Bay Area are commonly thought to be heavy social services users, the available evidence does not support this characterization); WAYNE A. CORNELIUS ET AL., CENTER FOR U.S.-MEXICAN STUDIES, MEXICAN IMMIGRANTS AND SOUTHERN CALIFORNIA: A SUMMARY OF CURRENT KNOWLEDGE 52–56, 57 (1982) (noting that first generation undocumented Mexican immigrants tend to come to the United States to accumulate capital to return to Mexico and discussing the health care costs associated with undocumented immigrants); Patrick J. McDonnell, *Immigrants Not Lured by Aid, Study Says*, L.A. TIMES, Jan. 29, 1997, at A3 (citing a report by the Public Policy Institute of California which found that half of all documented Mexican immigrants return home within two years, and less than one-third stay as long as ten years, while undocumented immigrants return home even sooner); *see also* T. Alexander Aleinikoff, *The Tightening Circle of Membership*, *in* IMMIGRANTS OUT!, *supra* note 6, at 324–26

law. Invoking the plenary power doctrine became even more frustrating when the Supreme Court held that alienage is a suspect classification like race and that states may not discriminate against noncitizens in the distribution of state-sponsored public benefits.[157] The plenary power doctrine, like the specific statute rule used in *San Pedro*,[158] provides the court with an apparently legitimate and neutral way to discriminate against noncitizens but simultaneously ignores the real hardship such a rule inflicts.[159]

Second, the *San Pedro* court characterized the government as being multidimensional rather than monolithic by emphasizing the differences between the immigration and prosecutorial powers of the federal government: The immigration power focuses on the admission and expulsion issue, while the prosecutorial power examines the criminal liability of those subject to U.S. law.[160] Yet, in contrast, the *Mathews* court chose not to separate the immigration question (should a noncitizen be admitted or expelled) from the immigrants' rights question (should a noncitizen be entitled to public benefits) and instead invoked the plenary power doctrine to assert a united government's power over immigrants as long as they are in the United States.[161] *Mathews* illustrates how courts can manipulate their characterization of the government from a singular entity to a fragmented structure to avoid government responsibility for noncitizens' welfare. The end result is the same, whether intended or not: the failure to focus on the personhood of the noncitizen tightens the circle of membership, excluding those who are not full citizens.

3. Membership Trumps Personhood: Ramallo v. Reno—As a final illustration of the workings of the personhood/membership dichotomy in recent lower court decisions, this section examines the curious case of *Ramallo v. Reno*[162] in which Congress intervened

---

(arguing that denials of public benefits to permanent residents send the message that the circle of citizenship is growing ever smaller).

157. *See* Graham v. Richardson, 403 U.S. 365, 372 (1971).

158. *See San Pedro*, 79 F.3d at 1069.

159. Moreover, the *San Pedro* court could have invoked some of Motomura's phantom norms of statutory interpretation to achieve justice, but it chose not to do so. *See supra* text accompanying notes 96–99.

160. *See San Pedro*, 79 F.3d at 1069–70 & n.3; *see also* Thomas v. INS, 35 F.3d 1332, 1346 n.5 (9th Cir. 1994) (Kozinski, J., dissenting) (noting that Congress chose to give both the Attorney General and U.S. Attorneys prosecutorial power, but authority over immigration matters rests with the Attorney General alone).

161. *See* Mathews v. Diaz, 426 U.S. 67, 79–80 (1976).

162. 931 F. Supp. 884 (D.D.C. 1996) (*Ramallo I*), *order entered by* 934 F. Supp. 1 (D.D.C. 1996) (*Ramallo II*), *vacated by* 114 F.3d 1210 (D.C. Cir. 1997) (*Ramallo III*).

to reestablish the primacy of the membership theory after the lower court had implicitly endorsed the idea of personhood.

Marlena Ramallo is a Bolivian citizen who entered the United States in 1972.[163] She became a permanent resident in 1978.[164] In August 1986, she pled guilty to the charge of conspiracy to import cocaine.[165] Three months after Ramallo's conviction, the INS initiated deportation proceedings against her.[166] During the course of the deportation proceedings, the government entered into an agreement with Ramallo in which she promised to assist in prosecuting other drug traffickers.[167] In return, the government, with approval of the AUSA, the Drug Enforcement Agency, and the INS District Director, agreed not to deport Ramallo.[168] Pursuant to her understanding of the agreement, Ramallo withdrew her objection to deportability in the INS proceedings.[169] In apparent violation of the agreement, an INS judge subsequently issued a deportation order.[170] When the government later attempted to enforce the order, Ramallo filed suit in federal district court, claiming violation of her due process rights[171] and seeking to enforce the cooperation agreement to restore her to permanent resident status.[172]

After several rounds of briefing, the parties filed cross-motions for summary judgment.[173] Ramallo claimed that the government had violated her constitutional rights by breaching its agreement and, therefore, it was promissorily and equitably estopped from deporting her.[174] In response, the government argued that, among other things, the government representatives who dealt with Ramallo did not have the authority to bind the government[175]—the

163. *See Ramallo III*, 114 F.3d at 1211.

164. *See id.*

165. *See id.*

166. *See id.*

167. *See Ramallo I*, 931 F. Supp. at 898–99.

168. *See Ramallo II*, 934 F. Supp. at 2. In *Ramallo I*, the court noted that Ramallo also contended that the government agreed to restore her status as a lawful permanent resident. *See Ramallo I*, 931 F. Supp. at 889.

169. *See Ramallo III*, 114 F.3d at 1211.

170. *See id.*

171. *See id.*

172. *See id.*

173. *See Ramallo I*, 931 F. Supp. at 888.

174. *See id.*

175. *See id.* Although it did not dispute that a cooperation agreement was reached, the government also claimed that it promised Ramallo only a temporary stay of deportation. *See id.* Alternatively, the government asserted that Ramallo had modified the original agreement and therefore was barred from receiving equitable relief under the doctrine of "unclean hands." *See id.*

same argument the government raised before the *Thomas* and *San Pedro* courts.

On the issue of agency, the court cited its approval of *Thomas*[176] and its rejection of *San Pedro.*[177] Ultimately, however, the court decided that it did not need to choose definitively between these conflicting precedents because an INS agent was directly involved in the negotiations along with the U.S. Attorney.[178] If anyone has authority to bind the INS, "an INS attorney, whose job is to represent the INS ... in matters of deportation proceedings,"[179] must have that power. Soon thereafter,[180] the court granted judgment in Ramallo's favor, ruling that fundamental due process concerns required the government to restore Ramallo's status as a lawful permanent resident.[181]

At first blush, *Ramallo* appears to be a much easier case than either *Thomas* or *San Pedro.* The *Ramallo* district court did not have to choose between the conflicting theories of *Thomas*'s personhood paradigm and monolithic government on the one hand and *San Pedro*'s membership paradigm and multidimensional government on the other. The D.C. District Court simply applied general principles of agency law to hold that an INS agent who promises a noncitizen that she will not be deported binds the INS by that promise[182]—a rather uncontroversial statement.

This obvious truth, however, would not hold sway for long. The government appealed this case to the District of Columbia Circuit, claiming that the lower court lacked jurisdiction when it found for the plaintiff.[183] Although the appellate court did not reach the jurisdictional issue, it vacated the decision of the lower court.[184] After the district court heard the case, Congress enacted the IIRIRA,[185] which amended the INA to deprive federal courts of jurisdiction to

176. *See id.* at 893–94 (citing Thomas v. INS, 35 F.3d 1332, 1339, 1345 (9th Cir. 1994)). The court also cited *Margalli-Olvera* with approval. *See id.* (citing Margalli-Olvera v. INS, 43 F.3d 345 (8th Cir. 1994)). In *Margalli-Olvera,* the Eighth Circuit held that the U.S. Attorney's Office had authority to bind the INS to a plea agreement. *See Margalli-Olvera,* 43 F.3d at 355.

177. *See Ramallo I,* 931 F. Supp. at 894 (citing San Pedro v. United States, 79 F.3d 1065 (11th Cir. 1996)).

178. *See id.*

179. *Id.*

180. The court denied both sides' motions for summary judgment on the narrow factual issue of whether the government promised Ramallo that she would not be deported. *See id.* at 892. At the ensuing hearing, the court resolved this factual issue in Ramallo's favor and granted judgment for the plaintiff. *See Ramallo II,* 934 F. Supp. at 2.

181. *See id.*

182. *See Ramallo I,* 931 F. Supp. at 894.

183. *See Ramallo III,* 114 F.3d at 1211.

184. *See id.* at 1213–14.

185. Pub. L. No. 104-208, div. C, 110 Stat. 3009-546 (1996) (codified as amended in scattered sections of 8 U.S.C.).

decide cases like *Ramallo*. Section 306(a) of the IIRIRA amends section 242 of the INA[186] by depriving federal courts of jurisdiction over noncitizens' claims that arise out of proceedings brought against the noncitizens by the Attorney General.[187] Because Ramallo's case was a claim arising out of the INS's efforts to deport her, the IIRIRA barred the federal courts from entertaining her claim.[188]

What started out as a decision closely tracking the personhood paradigm was transformed into a membership case by Congressional fiat! Indeed, *Ramallo* did not begin as a controversial case. Just as a citizen should be able to insist that a prosecutor's promise bind the prosecuting office, so should a noncitizen be able to surmise that an INS agent's word will obligate the INS. Unfortunately, Congress, with its plenary power over immigration, invoked the membership paradigm to quash any claims of equal personhood Ramallo could have made.[189]

Ramallo is the most recent example of the American government using its power over immigration and naturalization to deny even the most basic due process rights to noncitizens. So long as the government continues to value the membership paradigm (and its enforcer—the plenary power doctrine) over equal personhood for noncitizens, the circle of membership will continue to

---

186. Section 242 of the INA deals with the apprehension and deportation of noncitizens. *See* INA § 242, 8 U.S.C. § 1252 (1994 & Supp. II 1996).

187. *See* 8 U.S.C. § 1252(g) (Supp. II 1996). Section 1252 now reads in pertinent part:

> EXCLUSIVE JURISDICTION.—Except as provided in this section and notwithstanding any other provision of law, no court shall have jurisdiction to hear any cause or claim by or on behalf of any alien arising from the decision or action by the Attorney General to commence proceedings, adjudicate cases, or execute removal orders against alien under [the INA].

Id. § 1252(g) (Supp. II 1996). Because this Article focuses on fostering constitutional dialogue through the use of social psychology techniques, the constitutionality of the IIRIRA's court-stripping provision is beyond the scope of this discussion. For an analysis of this latter point, see generally Lenni B. Benson, *Back to the Future: Congress Attacks the Right to Judicial Review of Immigration Proceedings*, 29 CONN. L. REV. 1411 (1997) (discussing possible judicial reaction to the jurisdiction stripping provision of the IIRIRA).

188. *See Ramallo III*, 114 F.3d at 1213.

189. In *Ramallo III*, the circuit court noted that Ramallo was not entirely without a remedy; she could file a habeas claim. *See id.* at 1214. But this statement rings hollow. Aside from the difficulty of winning habeas claims, the very fact that this case could turn from an easy, obvious, and just win for the noncitizen into a denial of jurisdiction for what are important constitutional claims sends a very strong message that the government has unbridled discretion as to noncitizens. On the difficulty of pursuing habeas relief, see generally Stephen B. Bright, *Is Fairness Irrelevant?: The Evisceration of Federal Habeas Corpus Review and Limits on the Ability of State Courts to Protect Fundamental Rights*, 54 WASH. & LEE L. REV. 1, 4 (1997).

tighten. What does that mean for people like Marlena Ramallo and Alberto San Pedro? If they fulfill their promises to the U.S. government and bring their co-conspirators to justice, not only will they be denied the right to remain in the United States, they also face almost certain retaliation upon return to their home countries.[190]

III. Reasserting the Importance of Personhood

The previous two parts of this Article demonstrate the prominence of the membership paradigm in both Supreme Court jurisprudence and in recent promise enforcement cases brought before the lower federal courts. Professor Scaperlanda's challenge still must be met as the paramount question remains: What can be done to redefine and expand the circle of membership? The work of Professor Jody Armour and recent social psychology research on attitudes about immigrants may help effect a paradigm shift: If we can all acknowledge the stereotypes we have about others—immigrants included—we may begin to dismantle those stereotypes, debunk those myths, and, ultimately, welcome and value the equal personhood of those who are different.

A. Armour on Stereotype Reduction in Judicial Decision-making

Critical race theorist Professor Armour's work on effective legal decision-making provides us with a framework for understanding society's views about the "other." Armour has challenged the approach adopted by most courts, and advocated by many commentators, that leaves descriptions of race, gender, and sexual orientation out of the courtroom because doing so appeals to the prejudices of the jury.[191] Indeed, defense lawyer Johnnie Cochran often was criticized in the press for "playing the race card" during

---

190. Despite the potentially greater harm to noncitizens from deportation than from incarceration, the Supreme Court has held that deportation is a "purely civil action," and therefore, noncitizens at deportation hearings are not given the same constitutional and procedural safeguards as in criminal trials. *See* INS v. Lopez-Mendoza, 468 U.S. 1032, 1038–39 (1984); *see also* U.S. COMM'N ON CIVIL RIGHTS, THE TARNISHED GOLDEN DOOR: CIVIL RIGHTS ISSUES IN IMMIGRATION 97–101 (1980) (discussing the characterization of deportation hearings as civil in nature).

191. *See* Jody Armour, *Stereotypes and Prejudice: Helping Legal Decisionmakers Break the Prejudice Habit*, 83 CAL. L. REV. 733, 736–38 (1995).

the O.J. Simpson trial.[192] When Cochran sought to paint Mark Fuhrman as racist, critics viewed the accusation as irrelevant to whether Simpson was guilty of double murder and asserted that it would make the black jurors empathize with Simpson. Rather than seeing the acquittal as a reflection of reasonable doubt in the jurors' minds, some commentators thought the Simpson verdict was the product of black people acting prejudicially in favor of a fellow black, ignoring what in critics' minds was overwhelming evidence of Simpson's guilt.[193]

To enhance the legal decision-making process, Armour challenges conventional wisdom by drawing distinctions between constructive and destructive uses of stereotypes about social outgroups.[194] Borrowing from recent social psychology theory, Armour distinguishes between prejudice and stereotype: "Stereotypes consist of well-learned sets of associations among groups and traits established in children's memories at an early age, before they have the cognitive skills to decide rationally upon the personal acceptability of the stereotypes."[195] For example, a three-year-old child, upon seeing a black infant, might describe the infant as a "baby maid," demonstrating a recognition of the social stereotype

---

192. *See* Rob Morse, *The Gospel According to Cochran*, S.F. EXAMINER, Sept. 28, 1995, at A1 ("Cochran didn't just play the race card before the jury of nine African Americans, two whites and one Latino. He played the whole race deck."). Indeed, one of Cochran's own "critics was co-counsel Robert Shapiro who has berated Cochran for playing the race card 'from the bottom of the deck.'" Lynda Gorov, *Cochran Becomes Celebrity, Draws Criticism*, BOSTON GLOBE, Oct. 5, 1995, at 31 (quoting Robert Shapiro). Even Senator Arlen Specter considered probing Cochran's "playing the race card" during closing arguments. *See White House '96—Specter: Considers Probe of Cochran's Conduct in O.J. Trial* (visited Oct. 28, 1998) <http.www.cloakroom.com/pubs/hotline/db2/1995/10/h951011.18 .html>.

193. *See, e.g.*, Martin Gottlieb, *Racial Split at End as at Start*, N.Y. TIMES, Oct. 4, 1995, at A1 ("'The case turned when the black jurors pivoted from looking at the murder to looking at the police . . . . O.J. should have burned and the cops should have lost their jobs . . . .'"); Elsa McDowell, *O.J. Trials Say More About Us than Judiciary*, POST & COURIER (Charleston, SC), Feb. 6, 1997, at B1, *available in* LEXIS, News Library, PSTCUR File ("People who decry the criminal acquittal as racially motivated may not be altogether wrong."); Roger Rosenblatt, *The Simpson Verdict*, TIME, Oct. 16, 1995, at 40, 43 ("'Think of it,' a young man said bitterly. 'O.J.'s lawyer tried to separate the races, and it worked.' He shook his head. 'It's a payback for Rodney King; that's all it is. Everybody was so stunned to see that police beating on tape.'"); Jim Steinberg, *Fresno Reaction Takes on Racial Overtone*, FRESNO BEE, Oct. 4, 1995, at A1 ("White workers by a curb along California Avenue dismissed the trial and verdict with a word denoting bulls' excrement. . . . 'It was a done deal,' [said one man], who [was] white.").

194. *See* Armour, *supra* note 191, at 768–69.

195. *Id.* at 741 (citing Patricia G. Devine, *Stereotypes and Prejudice: Their Automatic and Controlled Components*, 56 J. PERSONALITY & SOC. PSYCHOL. 5, 6 (1989)). Armour has incorporated many of these arguments in his recent book. *See* JODY DAVID ARMOUR, NEGROPHOBIA AND REASONABLE RACISM: THE HIDDEN COSTS OF BEING BLACK IN AMERICA 115–53 (1997). On the nature of prejudice generally, Professor Gordon Allport's treatise on the subject is a classic. *See* GORDON W. ALLPORT, THE NATURE OF PREJUDICE (1954).

without having the cognitive wherewithal to approve or disapprove of the ascription.[196] "In contrast, prejudice consists of derogatory *personal beliefs*," those "that people endorse and accept as being true."[197] Thus, the three-year-old in our hypothetical who grows up to reject the stereotype of the black maid is not "prejudiced" under this definition.[198]

Aside from highlighting the distinction between "stereotype" and "prejudice," Armour notes that social psychologists also differentiate between "low prejudiced" individuals (those who have personally rejected cultural stereotypes as inappropriate) and "high prejudiced" individuals (those who know and endorse cultural stereotypes).[199] He argues that people commonly err by labeling "low prejudiced" individuals who exhibit stereotype-congruent responses as "racist" when, as social psychologists point out, "nonprejudiced beliefs and stereotype-congruent thoughts and feelings may coexist within the same individual."[200] For example, some Southerners, despite rejecting prejudice against blacks, have expressed feeling squeamish when shaking African Americans' hands—a product of residual feelings from their childhood, social scientists say.[201]

Armour next points to empirical evidence that suggests that unless they monitor their behavior, low prejudiced people may fall easily into stereotype-congruent responses and habits because negative cultural stereotypes are environmentally well-established and reinforced by the mass media.[202] Thus, prejudice-like responses

---

196. *See* Armour, *supra* note 191, at 741 (citing Phyllis A. Katz, *The Acquisition of Racial Attitudes in Children*, *in* TOWARDS THE ELIMINATION OF RACISM 125, 147 (Phyllis A. Katz ed., 1976)).

197. *Id.* at 742 (citing Anthony R. Pratkanis, *The Cognitive Representation of Attitudes*, *in* ATTITUDE STRUCTURE AND FUNCTION 71, 91 (Anthony R. Pratkanis et al. eds., 1989)). Similarly, Professor Allport opines that an adequate definition of prejudice must contain an "*attitude* of favor or disfavor" that "must be related to an overgeneralized (and therefore erroneous) *belief*." ALLPORT, *supra* note 195, at 13.

198. *See* Armour, *supra* note 191, at 742.

199. *See id.* (citing Patricia G. Devine et al., *Prejudice with and Without Compunction*, 60 J. PERSONALITY & SOC. PSYCHOL. 817, 817–19 (1991)).

200. *Id.* at 743 (citing Devine, *supra* note 199, at 817)). This distinction between low- and high-prejudiced individuals might help reduce feelings of defensiveness among those in the white majority who, sometimes justifiably, feel like scapegoats every time the question of white racism is raised. On the issue of affirmative action, for example, some white males see the issue as one of class rather than race. *See, e.g.*, David Thomas, *Initiative Will Level Playing Field*, L.A. TIMES, Mar. 10, 1996, at B4, *available in* 1996 WL 5249221 ("I'm sick and tired of the bashing from all the groups who are still crying about lack of opportunities in education and business, and who characterize all white males as racist, sexist animals whose only job on Earth is to deny others their due.").

201. *See* Armour, *supra* note 191, at 743 (citing Daniel [G]oleman, *"Useful" Modes of Thinking Contribute to the Power of Prejudice*, N.Y. TIMES, May 12, 1987, at C1).

202. *See id.* at 755–57.

that are sometimes labeled "racist" may simply be the product of a bad habit rather than a personal belief in the inferiority of a given race.[203]

Armour uses this research to argue against the tendency of many courts to disallow arguments to the jury relating to race, gender, sexual orientation, or other group characteristics on the ground that such evidence engenders prejudice.[204] He contends that legal decisionmakers should be reminded of their non-prejudiced personal beliefs so that they may guard against unconscious discrimination.[205] Armour cites the example of a 1920s case in which Clarence Darrow effectively utilized this strategy in his defense of a black doctor, the doctor's relatives, and friends accused of murdering a white man.[206] Two days after Dr. Ossian Sweet and his family moved into a white Detroit neighborhood in 1925, an angry white mob gathered outside their home, shouting racial epithets and throwing rocks.[207] As the mayhem intensified, the police officers who were dispatched to keep the peace did nothing.[208] After seeing a big rock crash through an upstairs window and the crowd make a sudden movement, Dr. Sweet and his brother fired a warning shot above the mob; one of the crowd's members was killed, and all eleven household members were charged with murder.[209]

In his summation before an all-white jury, Darrow challenged them to resist giving in to their racial prejudices:

> I haven't any doubt but that every one of you is prejudiced against colored people. I want you to guard against it. I want you to do all you can to be fair in this case, and I believe you will. . . .
>
> . . . Here were eleven colored men, penned up in the house. Put yourselves in their place. Make yourselves colored for a

203. *See id.* at 756–59. Armour explains: "[T]he research demonstrating disassociation of stereotypes and personal beliefs in low-prejudiced people argues against the conclusion that 'we are all racists.' Instead, I suggest that it is more accurate and useful to say that 'we are all creatures of habit.'" *Id.* at 759.

204. *See id.* at 759–60.

205. *See id.*

206. *See id.* at 762 (citing Arthur Weinberg, *You Can't Live There!*, *in* ATTORNEY FOR THE DAMNED 229, 229 (Arthur Weinberg ed., 1957) (compiling excerpts of Clarance Darrow's closing arguments and supplying editorial commentary)).

207. *See id.* (internal citation omitted).

208. *See id.* (internal citation omitted).

209. *See id.* (internal citation omitted).

> little while. It won't hurt, you can wash it off. They can't, but you can; just make yourself black for a little while; long enough, gentlemen, to judge them, and before any of you would want to be judged, you would want your juror to put himself in your place. That is all I ask in this case, gentlemen. . . .[210]

The jury acquitted Dr. Sweet, and the prosecution dropped the charges against the remaining defendants.[211]

Darrow's triumph provides an inspiring narrative of the power of social psychology. As Armour's theory suggests, Darrow's reminder to the jury members—all white males—of their unconscious proclivity for prejudice forced them to suppress this irrational emotion in favor of a just verdict.

More importantly, Armour's research serves as a useful starting point for engaging in a more informed dialogue about citizenship and membership in the U.S. polity along the lines envisioned by Scaperlanda: If social psychologists are correct, American citizens can train themselves to guard against any lingering stereotypes they may have against immigrant groups—such as those maintained against non-English whites, Chinese, and Mexicans[212]—and reject the primacy of membership in cases where personhood should prevail, as in the promise enforcement cases discussed above. Thus, when the government makes a promise in a criminal proceeding and the promisee upholds her side of the bargain, it should not matter whether the promisee is a citizen or a foreigner. Because the IIRIRA currently permits differential treatment on the basis of citizenship, citizens should act to ensure that noncitizens receive the same bargain from the government by calling for the repeal of the Act's court-stripping provisions.

The next section examines recent social psychology scholarship that explores a citizenry's reactions to new immigrant groups with an eye toward learning how to reassert the importance of personhood in our own constitutional dialogue.

B. Maio et al.'s Research on Attitudes Toward New Immigrant Groups

Strong parallels may be drawn between Armour's references to race prejudice and the anti-immigrant sentiment in the United

---

210. *Id.* at 762–63 (internal citation omitted).
211. *See id.* at 763 (internal citation omitted).
212. *See supra* Part I.A.

States today. First, just as deep-seated historical biases and the media have contributed to the stereotype of the black male as hostile or prone to violence,[213] the media have also perpetuated the stereotype of the "illegal alien" as a young, unskilled Mexican male, although Mexicans comprised only thirty-nine percent of all undocumented immigrants in 1992.[214] Further, despite the persistence of these racial and immigrant stereotypes, most people are low-prejudiced individuals. A recent poll of 1,314 whites, blacks, and Hispanics, all citizens or residents of the United States since 1980, revealed that while the respondents were divided on the issue of whether immigrants benefit or burden the nation overall, only one in three respondents offered negative views toward individual immigrant groups.[215] In an interesting commentary on how alienage serves as a proxy for race, the respondents viewed European immigrants in the most favorable light, while Cubans, Mexicans, Middle Easterners, and people from the Carribean were perceived most unfavorably.[216] Finally, given this intersection of race and alienage,[217] Armour's research may prove useful in identifying and confronting racial prejudice masquerading as politically more palatable anti-immigrant sentiment.[218] Armour's work may

---

213. *See* Armour, *supra* note 191, at 752–53 (discussing various studies regarding group trait stereotypes).

214. *See, e.g.*, Kevin R. Johnson, *Public Benefits and Immigration: The Intersection of Immigration Status, Ethnicity, Gender, and Class*, 42 UCLA L. REV. 1509, 1545–46 (1995) [hereinafter Johnson, *Public Benefits*]. Professor Johnson states the following:

> The stereotypical 'illegal alien,' the term that replaced 'wetback,' is a Mexican who has snuck [sic] into the United States in the dark of night. The image in the minds of many is that of a poor, brown, unskilled, young male. . . . Despite the stereotype, only about thirty-nine percent (1.3 million) of the total [number of undocumented immigrants in 1992] were from Mexico.

See id. (footnotes omitted).

215. *See Poll Shows Americans Softening on Immigration*, Assoc. Press, June 15, 1997, *available in* Westlaw, ASSOCPR Database [hereinafter *Poll*]; *see also New Immigrants Winning Much Wider Acceptance—More Americans Meeting, Learning About Newcomers*, ORLANDO SENTINEL, June 15, 1997, at A12, *available in* 1997 WL 2785222 (explaining how people's encounters with immigrants, as well as their personal circumstances, shape their attitudes toward newcomers).

216. *See Poll, supra* note 215. Japanese were viewed as the next most favorable group, followed by Chinese and Africans. *See id.*

217. I explore the race-alienage dynamic in other articles on equal protection and immigrants' rights. *See* Romero, *Congruence, supra* note †, at 445–49; Romero, *Equal Protection, supra* note †, at 601–02.

218. Karen K. Narasaki, Executive Director of the National Asian Pacific American Legal Consortium, noted the following in an immigration law symposium at Georgetown University: "My feeling has been that talking about immigrants is really sort of the last acceptable way to talk about race without actually talking about race." Symposium, *Reforming*

enrich Scaperlanda's constitutional dialogue about membership by forcing U.S. citizens to confront their stereotypes regarding immigrant groups, knowing that the root of some stereotypes may be in racial bias.

Armour's work is just the beginning. Two recent social psychology articles specifically address the issue of people's attitudes toward new immigrant groups and may help advance Scaperlanda's proposed constitutional dialogue. The first is a study conducted by Gregory R. Maio et al. to examine how indirect information regarding a new immigrant group affects people's attitudes toward that group.[219] This experiment started with the premise that many people first receive information about a new group indirectly—e.g., through the media—rather than through direct interpersonal contact.[220] In the study, over two hundred residents of Ontario, Canada were asked their views regarding the impending arrival of a fictitious group of new immigrants, the "Camarians," who were fleeing to various countries because of natural disasters in their nation.[221] The subjects were told that the Canadian Statistics on Immigration Agency expected 7,000 Camarians to arrive in Canada within seven months.[222] To examine the extent to which the subjects' views might be influenced by the perceived impact the impending immigration might have on their lives, some subjects were told the Camarians would immigrate to Ontario (high personal relevance), while others were told the immigrants would settle in British Columbia (low personal relevance).[223] The subjects were also told that their views were of interest because the Camarians might cause a shift in provincial employment and economic conditions.[224] Finally, the subjects received tables that contained fictitious information regarding the emotions Camarians elicit from others, their personality traits, and their values.[225] The respondents were told that these tables were

---

the Administrative Naturalization Process: Reducing Delays While Increasing Fairness—March 6, 1996 Transcript, 10 GEO. IMMIGR. L.J. 5, 27 (1996).

219. *See* Gregory R. Maio et al., *The Formation of Attitudes Toward New Immigrant Groups*, 24 J. APPLIED SOC. PSYCHOL. 1762 (1994).

220. *See id.* at 1762–63.

221. *See id.* at 1767.

222. *See id.*

223. *See id.*

224. *See id.*

225. *See id.* The six emotions listed were "comfortable," "curious," "happy," "proud," "relaxed," and "respect." *Id.* at 1768. "Friendly," "hardworking," "honest," "intelligent," "loyal," and "polite" were the six personality traits used. *Id.* The six values included "economic development," "education," "equality," "family," "freedom," and "law and order." *Id.* The fictitious survey reflected the extent to which the Camarians elicited the emotion, possessed the personality trait, or promoted the value listed. *See id.*

taken from a survey of perceptions about Camarians in England and the Southwestern United States.[226] Each subject was randomly given either uniformly positive information, uniformly negative information, or a mixture of both positive and negative information regarding these three characteristics.[227] After reviewing the fictitious survey information, the subjects were asked to indicate their attitudes toward Camarians using an attitude thermometer with a scale from zero degrees (extremely unfavorable) to 100 degrees (extremely favorable).[228]

The study revealed that people formed more favorable attitudes toward the new immigrant group when they were provided uniformly positive information about the emotions elicited by the group's members, their personality traits, and their values.[229] Thus, those who received uniformly positive information about the Camarians were most receptive to their immigration.[230] People who believed that they would be most affected by the Camarians' immigration acted less favorably—but still positively—to the uniformly positive information than those for whom the immigration was less relevant.[231] For example, the Ontarian subjects who were told that the Camarians would settle in Ontario favored the immigration, but did so at a lower attitude reading than those who believed the Camarians would settle in British Columbia, even though both groups received uniformly positive information regarding the Camarians.[232] Despite its moderating effect on the perception of uniformly positive information, personal relevance had no noticeable effect on subjects' views toward the Camarians based on the immigrants' fictitious values.[233] Maio et al. hypothesize that the subjects may have perceived the emotions elicited by Camarians and their personality traits as having a more immediate,

226. *See id.* at 1767–68.

227. *See id.* at 1768.

228. *See id.*

229. *See id.* at 1772.

230. *See id.* at 1770 fig. 1. Although those participants who received uniformly positive information were more receptive in absolute numbers, while the effect was statistically significant for those subjects in the "low relevance" category, *see id.* at 1769, for those in the "high relevance" category, the difference between those who received uniformly positive information and those who received mixed information was not statistically significant. *See id.* at 1771.

231. *See id.* at 1772. Interestingly enough, where mixed positive and negative information was received, the respondents actually responded more favorably to immigration when they perceived it to be more relevant to their lives, although not as favorable as their response to uniformly positive information. *See id.* at 1772–73.

232. *See id.* at 1772.

233. *See id.* at 1773.

personal effect on the respondents' lives than the more abstract notion of values.[234]

In constructing our dialogue about membership, we should consider Maio et al.'s findings. Their study teaches us that while imparting positive consensus information is important in fostering favorable attitudes toward new immigrants, it is even more important to recognize that personal relevance bias plays a significant role. To convince citizens of the value of the personhood of immigrants, one must find a way to convey positive images of "the immigrant as person" that will resonate with the citizens so that the natives becomes personally vested in the immigrant's plight. This "connection" between in-group and out-group members is what Darrow successfully accomplished in obtaining Dr. Sweet's acquittal, and this is the challenge faced by those seeking to restore personhood's importance in the debate over immigrants' rights.

How do we achieve this "connection" in our constitutional dialogue? The second study by Maio et al. provides support for Armour's position that informing decision-makers of their inherent biases may enhance their evaluative processes.[235] Psychological research has shown that while most people do not subscribe to racial discrimination, they unconsciously retain certain negative stereotypes about many out-groups.[236] Other research has shown that people may hold both positive and negative views of an out-group. For example, while some white Americans hold negative views toward blacks, they may simultaneously sympathize with their plight.[237] As a follow-up to the above-mentioned study, Maio et al. decided to test the effect this kind of ambivalence might have on the way people process persuasive messages about certain minority groups.[238] Like many of the studies Armour cites, Maio et al.'s experiment addressed the issue of how people with conflicting attitudes process information.[239]

This study was conducted in two parts: First, over 113 psychology undergraduates were evaluated on the ambivalence of their attitudes toward "Oriental" people, defined by the researchers as

234. *See id.*

235. *See* Gregory R. Maio et al., *Ambivalence and Persuasion: The Processing of Messages About Immigrant Groups*, 32 J. EXPERIMENTAL & SOC. PSYCHOL. 513, 532–33 (1996).

236. *See supra* Part III.A.

237. *See* Maio et al., *supra* note 235, at 514 (citing Irwin Katz & R. Glen Hass, *Racial Ambivalence and American Value Conflict: Correlational and Priming Studies of Dual Cognitive Structures*, 55 J. PERSONALITY & SOC. PSYCHOL. 893 (1988)).

238. *See id.* at 514. Although describing the research in terms of "minority" groups, the study provided subjects with information about immigrant minority groups. *See id.* at 516.

239. *See id.* at 514.

persons from China, Japan, and Hong Kong.[240] Next, each subject was given either a "strong" or "weak" persuasive message in favor of immigration from Hong Kong: The strong message described a strong tendency for Hong Kong residents to elicit positive emotions from people, possess positive personality traits, and favor positive values; the weak message described a weak, but still positive, tendency.[241] The researchers then examined the effect of these messages on the subjects' agreement with immigration from Hong Kong, favorability toward Hong Kong residents, and the immigration-related thoughts the subjects listed in response to the messages.[242]

The study demonstrated that those people who possessed "ambivalent attitudes toward [the immigrants were] more likely to systematically process persuasive messages about the group than [those] people who [held] unambivalent attitudes toward the group."[243] Thus, the ambivalent participants given the strong positive message about immigration from Hong Kong favored this immigration more than those who received the weak positive message, while unambivalent respondents were not affected differentially by the strong and weak messages.[244] Maio et al. posited that because they had conflicting views of the out-group, ambivalent persons would not only be more motivated to pay attention to new information about that group but also be better able to process such new information.[245]

It is at this point that Armour's and Maio et al.'s theories complement each other. If both theories are correct in assuming that most people are, in varying degrees, ambivalent about out-group members, and that ambivalent people are more effective than unambivalent people in processing information about the out-group, then it behooves us all to develop strategies to communicate positive messages about personhood to citizens acting to define membership in this polity.

For example, throughout history, many U.S. businesses have been ambivalent about employing undocumented Mexican immigrants.[246] On the one hand, the industries enjoy the fruits of cheap

240. *See id.* at 516.
241. *See id.* at 517.
242. *See id.*
243. *Id.* at 528.
244. *See id.*
245. *See id.* at 530.
246. *See* Linda S. Bosniak, *Exclusion and Membership: The Dual Identity of the Undocumented Worker Under United States Law*, 1988 WIS. L. REV. 955, 956; López, *supra* note 48, at 657. The ambivalence exists to this day in California, which has recently been in need of farm workers. Indeed, John Ledbetter, an officer of Vino Farms, Inc., in Lodi, California, stated that

labor; on the other, the businesses do not want to encourage undocumented immigration.[247] So when an undocumented worker is sexually harassed by her employer and reports the abuse to the authorities, should she be subject to deportation because of her status? Should the immigrant's lack of membership in the polity preempt her personal claim to protection from abuse? What is more important: discouraging "illegal" immigration or preventing employer abuse? The average citizen holds little sympathy for the stereotype of the "illegal alien" as the unskilled, dark-skinned Mexican laborer sneaking into the United States,[248] but the citizen decision-maker must fight against that stereotype by considering three additional points. First, regardless of how one feels about undocumented immigration, the immigrant in this case is a person who suffered sexual harassment. Second, by deporting the immigrant, the United States sends the message that it discourages the reporting of similar incidents of sexual abuse. Third, and perhaps most importantly, the definition of whether one is a "legal" or "illegal alien" may depend upon the country from which one hails. For instance, a Mexican citizen who enters the United States without a valid visa is automatically an "illegal alien," while many Western European citizens may remain in the United States for up to ninety days without one.[249]

With this new information, the ambivalent citizen, aware that she is influenced by the media-driven image of the "illegal alien" stereotype, might be able to process this positive data effectively to reach a decision valuing personhood over membership. One good example of a citizen who decided to reassert the importance of personhood is Rudolph Giuliani, the Republican mayor of New York City. Giuliani, who is sometimes criticized for being unsympa-

---

the federal government might want to consider "[s]ome type of a program that allows people to legally come to this country to work on a temporary basis . . . ." Lynn Graebner, *Farmers Face Shortage of Laborers*, BUS. J.-SACRAMENTO, Oct. 31, 1997, at 3, *available in* 1997 WL 15017468.

247. Michael Posner, Executive Director of the Lawyers Committee for Human Rights, recently stated the following: "We're schizophrenic about immigration . . . . On the one hand, we want control of our borders, and I think that's right. On the other hand, we want cheap immigrant labor. That's what keeps whole industries alive. That is the bargain, and we should be honest about it." Haberman, *supra* note 54, at B1.

248. *See supra* note 214 and accompanying text.

249. *See* Berta Esperanza Hernández-Truyol, *Reconciling Rights in Collision: An International Rights Strategy*, *in* IMMIGRANTS OUT!, *supra* note 6, at 254, 255. Professor Kevin Johnson notes that one-half of all undocumented immigrants were visa overstays; thus, the failure to address this issue, while simultaneously beefing up the U.S.-Mexico border, signifies a desire to reduce only undocumented Mexican immigration, not all undocumented immigration. *See* Johnson, *Public Benefits*, *supra* note 214, at 1547.

thetic to minority concerns,[250] believes that it is more important to encourage the reporting of abuse suffered by immigrants than to worry about the "illegal" presence of undocumented persons.[251] Indeed, he recently vowed to appeal a lower federal court decision invalidating an executive order that prohibited city employees from turning in undocumented immigrants who sought basic services such as police protection.[252] By adopting the strategies outlined by Armour and Maio et al., "We the People" might be in a better position to reach decisions on immigrants' rights matters unfettered by the stereotypes that might cause us to discount the value of equal personhood. In turn, this should lead to legislative action consistent with these ideals.

The final section applies the social psychology research outlined here to articulate a model for re-injecting personhood into the discussion of the promise enforcement cases discussed above.

C. Application of Social Psychology Research to the "Promise Enforcement" Cases

Like the issue of undocumented immigrant employment, the promise enforcement cases raise the issue of balancing membership and personhood concerns. In the promise enforcement cases, the question is whether a noncitizen should be precluded from receiving the benefit of her bargain with the government simply because of her foreign status. Put another way, does her foreign, nonmembership status preempt her personal right to enforce her claim that the government promised not to deport her in exchange for her cooperation?

Assuming that the federal courts have abdicated the membership decision to the citizenry, as Scaperlanda suggests, how does the social psychology research cited here help "We the People" value personhood in the midst of a discussion about membership? First, citizens must, as Armour's research indicates, acknowledge their deep-rooted, media-influenced biases, which include anti-immigrant sentiment, as well as the United States' long and sordid

---

250. In one infamous incident, Giuliani went head-to-head with the flamboyant Reverend Al Sharpton and his followers over the use of the Brooklyn Bridge for a march to celebrate Reverend Dr. Martin Luther King, Jr.'s birthday. *See* Kirk Johnson, *Words of Peace and Protest on King Holiday*, N.Y. TIMES, Jan. 16, 1996, at B1. Giuliani prohibited the marchers from using the entire bridge because they would impede the flow of traffic. *See id.* Sharpton compared Giuliani to a southern segregationist. *See id.*

251. *See id.*

252. *See* Haberman, *supra* note 54, at B1.

history of alienating newcomers.[253] Related to this first point, citizens must reflect upon whether any anti-immigrant stereotypes they harbor have roots in racial bias. Second, citizens must, as Darrow suggested in his defense of Dr. Sweet, put themselves in the shoes of the noncitizen. After all, many of their ancestors were once noncitizens. Do not citizens expect that a government will abide by its promises to them? Third, citizens must ask themselves whether the primary purpose of due process as it relates to promise enforcement cases is to restrain government action against citizen and noncitizen alike or to ensure the primacy of a citizen's rights over those of a noncitizen. Because Maio et al.'s work reveals that ambivalent people are better at processing new information than unambivalent people, and current data suggest that most Americans are ambivalent about immigration and immigrants, adopting the social psychology techniques outlined here may lead to a more self-aware citizenry better able to engage in a dialogue about membership without forgetting the importance of personhood.[254] Unlike Armour's application of such research to judicial decision-makers, this Article advocates that U.S. citizens use these techniques to help construct fair alienage policies that value equal personhood. Hopefully, a reflective and thoughtful citizenry will call for the repeal of the court-stripping provisions of the IIRIRA and will ensure that, at a minimum, the U.S. government abides by its promises to all, citizen and noncitizen alike.

---

253. *See supra* Part I.A.

254. I am aware that some may not share my view that citizens should show empathy toward criminal noncitizens. *See* Anthony Lewis, *Accent the Positive*, N.Y. TIMES, Oct. 10, 1997, at A29. The article discusses Senator Spencer Abraham's view that to make the case for legal immigration, one must also "make clear that you're going to address the negatives, especially criminal [noncitizens]. There is a public feeling against those who come here and commit crimes." *Id.* As mentioned earlier, however, the wrongdoing in the promise enforcement context is committed by the government, not the noncitizen. It is the government that reneges on its promises in these cases, benefits from the noncitizen's performance, and then acts to deport the noncitizen simply because it can do so under the law. I contend that the government should be constrained in promise enforcement cases in a manner similar to the limitations on government activity in other criminal contexts. For example, government agents may not beat confessions out of defendants under the Fourteenth Amendment, *see* Brown v. Mississippi, 297 U.S. 278, 285–86 (1936), and they may not illegally search a person's property under the Fourth Amendment. *See* Weeks v. United States, 232 U.S. 383, 391–93, 398 (1914). Society as a whole benefits from such restraints on government activity. *See, e.g.*, Mapp v. Ohio, 367 U.S. 643, 659 (1961) ("Nothing can destroy a government more quickly than its failure to observe its own laws, or worse, its disregard of the charter of its own existence.").

CONCLUSION

The tension between membership and personhood in the realm of immigrants' rights law has been, and will continue to be, of paramount concern to U.S. citizens. Because this issue is so important, we, the citizens of this country, must tread cautiously as we try to define what it means to be an American. Although membership will probably always be the starting point for determining questions of citizenship, it need not be the endpoint. We live in a society steeped in a culture of xenophobia and invidious anti-immigrant stereotypes, some of which are rooted in racial bias. It behooves us all to acknowledge and then transcend these prejudices if we are to ensure that the value of equal personhood retains true constitutional significance in our society. Otherwise, someone we know and hold dear might be the next Ms. Santiago—an "alien" whose personhood is sacrificed at the altar of non-membership.

Race, the Immigration Laws, and Domestic Race Relations: A "Magic Mirror"† into the Heart of Darkness

KEVIN R. JOHNSON*

TABLE OF CONTENTS

† The "magic mirror" metaphor is from *Lennon v. INS*, 527 F.2d 187 (2d Cir. 1975), in which the court stated that the list of grounds for exclusion of noncitizens from admission into the United States "*is like a magic mirror, reflecting the fears and concerns of past Congresses*." *Id.* at 189 (emphasis added).

* Professor of Law, University of California at Davis. A.B., University of California at Berkeley; J.D., Harvard University. This paper, which is part of a larger project analyzing the implications of the immigration laws for U.S. citizens, was prepared for the Critical Race Theory Conference at Yale Law School in November 1997. I thank the participants at that conference, especially Mary Romero, Margaret Montoya, Leslie Espinoza, Chris Cameron, Deborah Waire Post, Jo Carrillo, John Park, Maria Ontiveros, and Neil Gotanda, for their comments and support. Correspondence with Richard Delgado on preliminary ideas focused my thinking; his encouraging comments on a draft proved valuable. I am indebted to Michael Olivas for his continued encouragement and support as I test new academic waters. Conversations with George A. Martinez, as well as his comments on a draft, assisted greatly in the evolution and development of the arguments in this paper. I also thank John Scanlan, Sylvia Lazos, Stephen Shie-Wei Fan, Guadalupe Luna, Jack Chin, Victor Romero, Jan Ching-An Ting, Gil Gott, and Alex Aleinikoff for helpful, though often critical, comments on a draft. Frank Valdes offered insightful suggestions on an adapted version of this paper. I, of course, am responsible for all errors. Christine Shen, Melissa Corral, and Sushil Narayanan provided first-rate research assistance.

Well Papa go to bed now it's getting late
Nothing we can say can change anything now
Because there's just different people coming down here now
and they see things in different ways
And soon everything we've known will just be swept away.[1]

INTRODUCTION

In the face of persistent, often virulent attacks in the popular press,[2] as well as academia,[3] the critical study of the impact of race on the social fabric of the United States continues. Despite the rich analysis of race in critical scholarship, a body of law chock full of insights remains largely unexplored.[4] Immigration law traditionally has been considered a specialty area of practitioners spurned by academics. However, the treatment of "aliens," particularly noncitizens of color, under the U.S. immigration laws reveals volumes about domestic race relations in the nation. A deeply complicated, often volatile, relationship exists between racism directed toward citizens and that aimed at noncitizens. Peter Brimelow's anti-immigrant book, *Alien Nation*,[5] exemplifies this relationship; while ostensibly criticizing the state of U.S. immigration law, the book attacks affirmative action, "Hispanics," multiculturalism, bilingual education, and virtually any program designed to remedy discrimination in the United States.

As the legacy of chattel slavery and forced migration from Africa would have it, the United States has a long history of treating racial minorities in the United States harshly, at times savagely. Noncitizen racial minorities, as foreigners not part of the national community, generally have been subject to similar cruelties

1. BRUCE SPRINGSTEEN, *Independence Day*, *on* THE RIVER (Columbia Records 1980).

2. *See, e.g.*, Alex Kozinski, *Bending the Law*, N.Y. TIMES, Nov. 2, 1997, § 7, at 46 (reviewing *Beyond All Reason* by Daniel A. Farber and Suzanna Sherry); Neil A. Lewis, *For Black Scholars Wedded to Prism of Race, New and Separate Goals*, N.Y. TIMES, May 5, 1997, at B9; Richard A. Posner, *The Skin Trade*, NEW REPUBLIC, Oct. 13, 1997, at 40 (reviewing *Beyond All Reason*); Jeffrey Rosen, *The Bloods and the Crits*, NEW REPUBLIC, Dec. 9, 1996, at 27.

3. *See, e.g.*, DANIEL A. FARBER & SUZANNA SHERRY, BEYOND ALL REASON (1997); Randall L. Kennedy, *Racial Critiques of Legal Academia*, 102 HARV. L. REV. 1745, 1749 (1989); Mark Tushnet, *The Degradation of Constitutional Discourse*, 81 GEO. L.J. 251 (1992); *see also* Keith Aoki, *The Scholarship of Reconstruction and the Politics of Backlash*, 81 IOWA L. REV. 1467, 1471-72 (1996) (observing that Critical Race Theory has been the subject of "'attack' scholarship" designed "to preempt and shut down debate").

4. There are, of course, some works that consider the relationship between immigration and race relations. *See, e.g.*, Bill Ong Hing, *Beyond the Rhetoric of Assimilation and Cultural Pluralism: Addressing the Tension of Separatism and Conflict in an Immigration-Driven Multiracial Society*, 81 CAL. L. REV. 863 (1993).

5. PETER BRIMELOW, ALIEN NATION (1995).

but also have suffered deportation,[6] indefinite detention,[7] and more. The differential treatment is permitted, if not encouraged, by the disparate bundles of legal rights afforded domestic minorities and noncitizen minorities.

In analyzing the treatment of noncitizens in the United States, immigration law offers an invaluable vantage point because of its unique characteristics vis-à-vis traditional constitutional law. The so-called "plenary power" doctrine, which historically has shielded substantive immigration judgments by the political branches of government from meaningful judicial review, bestows great discretion on the U.S. Government to establish rules regulating the admission of noncitizens into the country.[8] Born in an era when Congress acted with a vengeance to exclude Chinese immigrants from this nation's shores,[9] the plenary power doctrine remains the law, though perhaps narrowed somewhat in scope.[10] Moreover, the Supreme Court has invoked the doctrine to permit the federal government, and at times the states, to discriminate against immigrants with the lawful right to remain permanently in this country.[11]

In sharp contrast to the limited constitutional rights of noncitizens, citizens enjoy a full array of protections under the Constitution and a multitude of other laws.[12] Racial minorities, for example, may rely on the Equal Protection Clause of the Fourteenth Amendment to challenge discriminatory governmental action[13] and the Civil Rights Act of 1964 to fight racism in the workplace.[14] Although the

---

6. *Cf.* Bridges v. Wixon, 326 U.S. 135, 147 (1945) (emphasizing that deportation of a noncitizen "may result in the loss 'of all that makes life worth living'") (quoting Ng Fung Ho v. White, 259 U.S. 276, 284 (1922)).

7. *See, e.g.*, Barrera-Echavarria v. Rison, 44 F.3d 1441 (9th Cir. 1995) (en banc) (holding that the Attorney General had legal authority to indefinitely detain a Cuban noncitizen whom Cuba refused to allow to return).

8. *See infra* text accompanying notes 231-41 (describing doctrine).

9. *See infra* text accompanying notes 52-54 (analyzing genesis of plenary power doctrine in Chinese exclusion cases).

10. *See infra* text accompanying notes 231-41 (discussing modern significance of doctrine); *see, e.g.*, Fiallo v. Bell, 430 U.S. 787, 792 (1977) (upholding gender and legitimacy classifications in immigration laws); Kleindienst v. Mandel, 408 U.S. 753, 765-67 (1972) (rejecting constitutional challenge to denial of nonimmigrant visa to Marxist academic on ideological grounds); Boutilier v. INS, 387 U.S. 118, 122-23 (1967) (allowing exclusion of homosexuals).

11. *See* Mathews v. Diaz, 426 U.S. 67, 78-84 (1976) (upholding discrimination against lawful permanent residents in federal medical benefits program); *infra* note 235 (citing decisions permitting states to discriminate between citizens and lawful permanent residents).

12. For a communitarian critique of the proliferation of rights, see MARY ANN GLENDON, RIGHTS TALK (1991).

13. *See, e.g.*, Brown v. Board of Educ., 347 U.S. 483, 493 (1954); *cf.* United States v. Virginia, 518 U.S. 515, 531-58 (1996) (holding that Virginia's exclusion of women from Virginia Military Institute violated Equal Protection Clause). The Fourteenth Amendment, however, offers uncertain protections to noncitizens. *See infra* text accompanying notes 41-46 (analyzing law in this regard).

14. *See, e.g.*, Robinson v. Shell Oil Co., 117 S. Ct. 843 (1997) (reversing dismissal of Title VII claim alleging racial discrimination by employer). In contrast, the Supreme Court held that Title VII does not bar discrimination on the basis of alienage status. *See* Espinoza v. Farah Mfg. Co., 414 U.S. 86, 95 (1973).

close of the twentieth century has been marked by rollbacks in legal protections for minorities,[15] the law, at least in theory, serves to protect discrete and insular minorities from the excesses of the political process.[16]

Rather than just a peculiar feature of U.S. public law, the differential treatment of citizens and noncitizens serves as a "magic mirror" revealing how dominant society might treat domestic minorities if legal constraints were abrogated. Indeed, the harsh treatment of noncitizens of color reveals terrifying lessons about how society views citizens of color. For example, the era of exclusion of Chinese immigrants in the 1800s occurred almost simultaneously with punitive, often violent, action against the Chinese on the West Coast.[17] Efforts to exclude and deport Mexican citizens from the United States, which accelerated over the course of the twentieth century, tell much about how society generally views Mexican American citizens.[18] Similarly, the extraordinarily harsh policies directed toward poor, Black, Haitian persons, seeking refuge from violent political and economic turmoil in Haiti, leave little room for doubt—if there were any—about how this society as a whole views its own poor Black citizens.[19] The out-group homogeneity thesis from psychology, in which in-groups generally view out-groups, such as racial minorities, as homogeneous, lends support to this insight.[20]

Oddly enough, even while the attacks on immigrants of color pervade the national consciousness, some informed observers claim that racism is a historical

---

15. *See, e.g.*, Adarand Constructors, Inc. v. Peña, 515 U.S. 200, 225 (1995) (holding that all racial classifications, including those in federal program designed to foster minority enterprise, are subject to strict scrutiny); City of Richmond v. J.A. Croson Co., 488 U.S. 469, 498 (1989) (invalidating city's minority business program as violation of equal protection); Taxman v. Board of Educ., 91 F.3d 1547 (3d Cir. 1996) (holding that affirmative action plan was unlawful), *cert. granted*, 117 S. Ct. 2506, *cert. dismissed*, 118 S. Ct. 595 (1997); *see also infra* note 23 (citing cases upholding end of and invalidating affirmative action programs).

16. *See* United States v. Carolene Prods. Co., 304 U.S. 144, 152-53 n.4 (1938) (recognizing that "prejudice against discrete and insular minorities may be a special condition, which tends seriously to curtail the operation of those political processes ordinarily to be relied upon to protect minorities, and which may call for a correspondingly more searching judicial inquiry"); *see also* JOHN HART ELY, DEMOCRACY AND DISTRUST 75-77 (1980) (exploring importance of *Carolene Products*'s footnote 4 to constitutional theory of judicial review). This is not to suggest that legal remedies for minorities have proven to be problem-free. Some argue that liberalism's belief that law will promote meaningful social change is misplaced. *See, e.g.*, DERRICK BELL, FACES AT THE BOTTOM OF THE WELL (1992) (contending that racism is endemic to United States); RICHARD DELGADO & JEAN STEFANCIC, FAILED REVOLUTIONS (1994) (analyzing limits of achieving social reform through law); George A. Martínez, *Legal Indeterminacy, Judicial Discretion and the Mexican-American Litigation Experience: 1930-1980*, 27 U.C. DAVIS L. REV. 555 (1994) (analyzing limits of litigation in achieving meaningful social change for Mexican Americans in the United States).

17. *See infra* text accompanying notes 47-54 (analyzing circumstances surrounding Chinese exclusion).

18. *See infra* text accompanying notes 150-78 (scrutinizing U.S. Government's efforts to exclude and deport Mexican immigrants as well as Mexican American citizens).

19. *See infra* text accompanying notes 179-206 (evaluating significance of Haitian interdiction and repatriation for African Americans in the United States).

20. *See infra* text accompanying notes 258-60 (discussing theory).

artifact in the United States,[21] or at least has greatly diminished as a driving force behind policymaking as the twentieth century comes to a close.[22] Based in part on this premise, political forces attack affirmative action,[23] multiculturalism,[24] language minorities,[25] and ameliorative programs created in response to the civil rights struggles of the 1960s. At the same historical moment, Congress, with minimal resistance, has passed increasingly restrictive immigration laws, in the name of fighting a range of social ills from welfare fraud to crime to terrorism to "illegal" immigration.[26] This Article contends that the fact that anti-immigrant sentiment caught fire in tandem with the anti-minority backlash in the United States is no coincidence.

Besides analyzing the history surrounding legal exclusions in the immigration laws, I argue that the exclusionary laws reveal majority sentiment about racial minorities in the United States. Subordination of Asian immigrants and the use of quotas to exclude racialized peoples,[27] among other devices, evolved into more

---

21. *See, e.g.*, DINESH D'SOUZA, THE END OF RACISM 3, 22-24 (1995).

22. *See, e.g.*, Peter H. Schuck, *Alien Rumination*, 105 YALE L.J. 1963, 1966 (1996) (book review) ("Racism in the United States has declined dramatically in recent decades, despite frequent denials of this fact. *I believe . . . that [though arguable] racism as such no longer plays a crucial role in immigration law; certainly it plays a less significant role than it did before 1965*.") (emphasis added) (footnotes omitted).

23. *See, e.g.*, Coalition for Econ. Equity v. Wilson, 122 F.3d 692, 701 (9th Cir.) (rejecting constitutional challenges to California's Proposition 209, which prohibits consideration of race and gender in any state program), *cert. denied*, 118 S. Ct. 397 (1997); Hopwood v. Texas, 78 F.3d 932, 934 (5th Cir.) (holding that affirmative action by the University of Texas in law school admissions violated Fourteenth Amendment), *cert. denied*, 116 S. Ct. 2580 (1996).

24. *See, e.g.*, ARTHUR M. SCHLESINGER, JR., THE DISUNITING OF AMERICA (1992) (contending that multiculturalism is destructive force in the United States); *see also* J. HARVIE WILKINSON III, ONE NATION INDIVISIBLE (1997) (contending that ethnic separatism threatens the nation).

25. *See infra* text accompanying notes 226-28 (discussing speak-English-only rules).

26. *See, e.g.*, Illegal Immigration Reform and Immigrant Responsibility Act of 1996, Pub. L. No. 104-208, §§ 501-553, 110 Stat. 3009, 3670-81 (limiting immigration and facilitating deportation in number of ways); Personal Responsibility and Work Opportunity Reconciliation Act of 1996, Pub. L. No. 104-193, §§ 400-451, 110 Stat. 2105, 2260-77 (limiting the receipt of public benefits by legal immigrants); Antiterrorism and Effective Death Penalty Act of 1996, Pub. L. No. 104-132, §§ 423, 502, 110 Stat. 1214, 1259, 1272 (providing, inter alia, that noncitizens convicted of criminal offenses would receive limited or no judicial review of deportation orders and creating a special tribunal responsible for deporting so-called terrorists).

27. *See* MICHAEL OMI & HOWARD WINANT, RACIAL FORMATION IN THE UNITED STATES (2d ed. 1994) (analyzing how ideology and history contribute to the construction of races). This contextual definition of "race" is particularly appropriate in analyzing the immigration laws. Restrictionist immigration laws historically sought to limit immigration of groups of persons today thought of as "white ethnics," such as Jewish or Irish immigrants, because they were of a different "race." *See infra* notes 97-120 and accompanying text. Moreover, the international law on which the asylum and refugee provisions of the U.S. immigration laws permitting persons fleeing persecution on account of race are based, *see* Immigration & Nationality Act, ch. 477, 66 Stat. 163 (1952) (as amended), §§ 101(a)(42), 241(b)(3) (codifed at 8 U.S.C.A. §§ 1101(a)(42), 1231(b)(3) (West 1970 & Supp. 1998)), requires a liberal definition of "race." *See* OFFICE OF THE UNITED NATIONS HIGH COMM'R FOR REFUGEES, HANDBOOK ON PROCEDURES AND CRITERIA FOR DETERMINING REFUGEE STATUS ¶ 68, at 18 (re-edited ed. 1992) (offering

subtle forms of exclusion with the transformation of racial sensibilities in modern times. Besides analyzing the treatment of minorities under the immigration laws, this Article posits that the harsh treatment of immigrants of color suggests how this nation might treat citizens of color if afforded the opportunity. Absent the Constitution and other legal protections, domestic minorities could expect no better treatment than their foreign brothers and sisters. This is no idle concern. Not all that long ago, the United States Supreme Court declared that African Americans "had no rights which the white man was bound to respect."[28] Though racial sensibilities have changed, this nation at times has denied rights to racial minorities. To avoid the repetition of such events, everyone, not just immigrant rights activists and immigration law scholars, concerned with race relations in the United States should take interest in the exclusionary aspects of our immigration laws.

This Article, however, is more than simply a summary of how racism has infected immigration law and policy in the United States and how citizens as well as noncitizens should be gravely concerned. It instead demonstrates how the harsh treatment of *noncitizens* reveals just how this society views *citizens* of color. As psychological theory suggests, the virulent attacks on noncitizens in effect represent transference and displacement of animosity for racial minorities generally.[29] Because direct attacks on minorities on account of their race is nowadays taboo, frustration with domestic minorities is displaced to foreign minorities. A war on noncitizens of color focusing on their immigration status, not race, as conscious or unconscious cover, serves to vent social frustration and hatred.[30] Hatred for domestic minorities is displaced to an available, more publicly palatable, target for antipathy. These psychological devices help society reconcile the view that "U.S. society is not racist" with the harsh treatment of noncitizens of color. Noncitizens, so the story goes, deserve different treatment because of their immigration status, not race.

Psychological theory also helps explain some historical oddities about U.S. society's seemingly contradictory treatment of different minority groups, particularly African Americans, and groups historically classified as "foreign," such as Asian Americans and Latinos. Congress passed the anti-Chinese exclusionary laws in the 1800s on the heels of the abolition of slavery and the ratification of the Reconstruction Amendments, ostensibly intended to eliminate

---

interpretive guidance on relevant international law and stating that "[r]ace . . . has to be understood in its widest sense to include all kinds of ethnic groups that are referred to as 'races' in common usage").

28. Dred Scott v. Sandford, 60 U.S. (19 How.) 393, 407 (1856).

29. *See infra* text accompanying notes 261-88 (analyzing psychological theory as tool for understanding relationship between anti-immigrant and anti-minority sentiment).

30. *See, e.g.*, BRIMELOW, *supra* note 5. Though ostensibly complaining about immigrants and immigration, Brimelow expresses deeper frustrations with multiculturalism, affirmative action, and race relations in the United States. *See* Kevin R. Johnson, *Fear of an "Alien Nation": Race, Immigration, and Immigrants*, STAN. L. & POL'Y REV., Summer 1996, at 111, 113-17 (criticizing Brimelow's analysis of these issues).

all vestiges of this nation's "peculiar institution."[31] What legal rights the country formally extended to Blacks, it ruthlessly denied Chinese immigrants. Similarly, a landmark achievement for African Americans, *Brown v. Board of Education*,[32] and its rejection of the "separate but equal" doctrine, was decided the same year that the U.S. Government commenced "Operation Wetback," a massive campaign resulting in the deportation of tens of thousands of Mexican immigrants, as well as U.S. citizens of Mexican ancestry.[33] Both examples reflect the appearance of generosity toward African Americans, on the one hand, and a crackdown against "foreigners" on the other. When law constrained attacks on the domestic minority, animosity was displaced to foreign minorities in our midst and at our borders. Maintenance of the racial status quo serves as the unifying theme explaining these historical phenomena.[34]

One might wonder why interrelationships such as these have gone unexplored to this point. The subordination of non-Black racial minorities often has remained invisible.[35] Issues of race, being parsed into hues of Black and white,

---

31. KENNETH M. STAMPP, THE PECULIAR INSTITUTION at vii (1956); *see infra* text accompanying notes 69-82 (analyzing relationship between these historical developments).

32. 347 U.S. 483, 495 (1954).

33. *See infra* text accompanying notes 150-78 (considering various anti-Mexican campaigns, including infamous "Operation Wetback").

34. *See generally* TOMÁS ALMAGUER, RACIAL FAULT LINES: THE HISTORICAL ORIGINS OF WHITE SUPREMACY IN CALIFORNIA (1994) (analyzing central organizing principle of white supremacy in race relations in California); REGINALD HORSMAN, RACE AND MANIFEST DESTINY (1981) (analyzing importance of belief of Anglo-Saxon racial superiority to doctrine of Manifest Destiny).

Nothing in this Article should be read to suggest that racial discrimination is the exclusive factor shaping the U.S. immigration laws. Rather, as I analyze in other work, *see, e.g.*, Kevin R. Johnson, *An Essay on Immigration Politics, Popular Democracy, and California's Proposition 187: The Political Relevance and Legal Irrelevance of Race*, 70 WASH. L. REV. 629, 650-51 (1995), other factors not directly linked to race, such as concerns with the perceived costs of immigration and its impact on the labor market, obviously have influenced the development of the immigration laws. Nor does the Article take the extreme position that every immigration law, intentionally or not, discriminates against racial minorities. Rather, I modestly contend that race has influenced—and continues to influence —U.S. immigration law and policy. Consequently, this Article analyzes how race, as one variable in a complex multivariate equation, has affected the policymaking process and studies the relationship between exclusionary immigration laws and the civil rights of domestic racial minorities.

35. *See* Richard Delgado, *Rodrigo's Fifteenth Chronicle: Racial Mixture, Latino-Critical Scholarship, and the Black-White Binary*, 75 TEX. L. REV. 1181, 1185 (1997) (book review). "The Black/white framing of race issues must give way to a fuller, more differentiated understanding of a multiracial, multiethnic society divided along the lines of race, class, gender, and other axes in order to . . . contribute to the long-term empowerment of [racial minorities]." Sumi K. Cho, *Korean Americans vs. African Americans: Conflict and Construction*, *in* READING RODNEY KING, READING URBAN UPRISING 196, 196-97 (Robert Gooding-Williams ed., 1993); *see* Kevin R. Johnson, *Civil Rights and Immigration: Challenges for the Latino Community in the Twenty-First Century*, 8 LA RAZA L.J. 42, 64 (1995) (noting "tendency . . . to frame civil rights as an almost exclusively black/white issue") (footnote omitted); Margaret E. Montoya, *Of "Subtle Prejudices," White Supremacy, and Affirmative Action: A Reply to Paul Butler*, 68 U. COLO. L. REV. 891, 925 (1997) ("Race relations in this country are extremely complex. White supremacy is experienced by non-white

have obscured the relationship between various forms of subordination of different racial minorities.[36] In moving beyond this vision of race relations, we must take care not to "dilute or obscure . . . [the] claims and interests [of African Americans]."[37] This Article contends that it is impossible to fully appreciate the subordination of any particular racial minority group without understanding the oppression of all minority groups.[38] To this end, Part I of the Article analyzes the long history of racial and national origin exclusion in the immigration laws. Part II focuses on the teachings of this exclusionary history for minority citizens as well as noncitizens.

In the end, we peer into a heart of darkness where the deepest fears of racial minorities—that a majority of society desires and has consistently strived for Anglo-Saxon homogeneity and hegemony—are demonstrated to be more than justified. One is left to ponder the frailties of the human condition, what we are as a society, and the possibilities, if any, for racial harmony in the twenty-first

---

groups in *different* ways in *different* geographic regions under *different* historical conditions.") (emphasis in original).

36. George A. Martínez has made this point from a philosophical perspective. *See* George A. Martínez, *African-Americans, Latinos, and the Construction of Race: Toward an Epistemic Coalition*, 19 CHICANO-LATINO L. REV. (forthcoming 1998); *see also* Angela P. Harris, *The Jurisprudence of Reconstruction*, 82 CAL. L. REV. 741, 774-78 (1994) (contending that Critical Race Theory, which has tended to focus on African American subordination, may benefit from the study of subordination of women, lesbians and gay men, Asian Americans, Latinos, indigenous peoples, and the poor); *cf.* Lynn M. LoPucki, *The Systems Approach to Law*, 82 CORNELL L. REV. 479 (1997) (describing how "systems" analysis in non-legal disciplines applies to study of law).

37. John O. Calmore, *Exploring Michael Omi's "Messy" Real World of Race: An Essay for "Naked People Longing to Swim Free"*, 15 LAW & INEQ. J. 25, 61 (1997); *see* Leslie Espinoza & Angela P. Harris, *Afterword: Embracing the Tar-Baby—LatCrit Theory and the Sticky Mess of Race*, 85 CAL. L. REV. 1585, 1596-605 (1997) (articulating case for "black exceptionalism," that is, the uniqueness of the African American experience in the United States).

38. I elaborate on this argument in Kevin R. Johnson, *Racial Hierarchy, Asian Americans and Latinos as "Foreigners," and Social Change: Is Law the Way to Go?*, 76 OR. L. REV. 347 (1997). Two examples help illustrate the central point. The U.S.-Mexican War, which culminated in the Treaty of Guadalupe Hidalgo in 1848, resulted from expansionist desires, including the hope by some to protect the institution of slavery in the United States. *See* 1 RICHARD HOFSTADTER ET AL., THE UNITED STATES 230-31 (4th ed. 1976) (noting that Whigs contended that war was designed to expand slavery to new territories). Thus, an effort to maintain slavery and the subjugation of African Americans, was part of a chain of events culminating in a treaty that many claim resulted in the subordination of Mexican Americans in the Southwest. *See, e.g.*, RODOLFO ACUÑA, OCCUPIED AMERICA 28-39, 105-08 (1972); RICHARD GRISWOLD DEL CASTILLO, THE TREATY OF GUADALUPE HIDALGO (1990); Guadalupe T. Luna, *"Agricultural Underdogs" and International Agreements: The Legal Context of Agricultural Workers Within the Rural Economy*, 26 N.M. L. REV. 9, 13-21 (1996). Similarly, race relations in Texas cannot be fully understood without analyzing the history of the interactions between Anglo, Mexican American, and African American communities; analysis of Mexican American/Anglo or African American/Anglo relations, for example, would offer an incomplete picture. *See generally* NEIL FOLEY, THE WHITE SCOURGE: MEXICANS, BLACKS, AND POOR WHITES IN TEXAS COTTON CULTURE (1997) (analyzing history of race relations in central Texas).

century. As Roberto Unger said about the legal academy, "[w]hen we came, they were like a priesthood that had lost their faith and kept their jobs. They stood in tedious embarrassment before cold altars. But we turned away from those altars and found the mind's opportunity in the heart's revenge."[39]

I. THE HISTORY OF RACIAL EXCLUSION IN THE U.S. IMMIGRATION LAWS

Racism, along with nativism,[40] economic, and other social forces, has unquestionably influenced the evolution of immigration law and policy in the United States. It does not exist in a social and historical vacuum. Foreign and domestic racial subordination instead find themselves inextricably linked.

In untangling this history, keep in mind critical differences between traditional immigration law and ordinary public law. Although the Equal Protection Clause generally requires strict scrutiny of racial classifications in the laws,[41] the Supreme Court long ago—in a decision undisturbed to this day—upheld discrimination on the basis of race and national origin in the admission of noncitizens into the country.[42] Similarly, even though discrimination on the basis of alienage status in modern times may mask an intent to discriminate against racial minorities,[43] the Supreme Court ordinarily defers to alienage classifications made by Congress.[44] Because the substantive provisions of the immigration laws

---

39. ROBERTO MANGABEIRA UNGER, THE CRITICAL LEGAL STUDIES MOVEMENT 119 (1986).

40. "Nativism" is the "intense opposition to an internal minority on the ground of its foreign (i.e., 'un-American') connections." JOHN HIGHAM, STRANGERS IN THE LAND 4 (2d ed. 1992). The classic historical study of nativism in the United States is *id.* For a summary of nativism's influence on the development of U.S. immigration laws, see Berta Esperanza Hernández-Truyol, *Natives, Newcomers and Nativism: A Human Rights Model for the Twenty-First Century*, 23 FORDHAM URB. L.J. 1075, 1083-97 (1996).

41. *See generally* LAURENCE H. TRIBE, AMERICAN CONSTITUTIONAL LAW § 16-14, at 1466-74 (2d ed. 1988).

42. *See, e.g.*, Chae Chan Ping v. United States (Chinese Exclusion Case), 130 U.S. 581 (1889).

43. Though the Supreme Court has held it impermissible to discriminate against minority immigrants in the country, *see* Yick Wo v. Hopkins, 118 U.S. 356 (1886), it must be proven that the state actor *intentionally* used alienage as a proxy for race. *See* Washington v. Davis, 426 U.S. 229 (1976). This formidable burden can rarely be satisfied. *See* Theodore Eisenberg & Sheri Lynn Johnson, *The Effects of Intent: Do We Know How Legal Standards Work?*, 76 CORNELL L. REV. 1151 (1991) (demonstrating empirically that the discriminatory intent requirement deters the filing of claims and results in a high loss rate for plaintiffs).

44. *See* Mathews v. Diaz, 426 U.S. 67, 84-87 (1976). *But see* Hampton v. Mow Sun Wong, 426 U.S. 88 (1976) (invalidating federal civil service rule barring employment of lawful, permanent residents). State alienage classifications sometimes have been subject to strict scrutiny. *Compare* Graham v. Richardson, 403 U.S. 365, 371-72 (1971) (applying strict scrutiny to alienage classification in state welfare scheme), *with* Foley v. Connelie, 435 U.S. 291, 294-95 (1978) (declining to apply strict scrutiny in upholding a New York requirement that police officers be U.S. citizens).

historically have been immune from legal constraint,[45] the political process allows the majority to have its way with noncitizens.[46]

A. From Chinese Exclusion to General Asian Subordination

The horrendous treatment of Chinese immigrants in the 1800s by federal, state, and local governments, as well as by the public at large, represents a bitter underside to U.S. history.[47] Culminating the federalization of immigration regulation,[48] Congress passed the infamous Chinese exclusion laws barring virtually all immigration of persons of Chinese ancestry[49] and severely punishing Chinese immigrants who violated the harsh laws.[50] Discrimination and violence, often rooted in class conflict as well as racist sympathies, directed at Chinese immigrants already in the United States, particularly in California, fueled passage of the laws.[51] The efforts to exclude future Chinese immigrants from our shores can be seen as linked to the deeply negative attitude toward Chinese persons already in the country.

The Supreme Court emphasized national sovereignty as the rationale for not disturbing the laws excluding the "obnoxious Chinese"[52] from the United States. In the famous *Chinese Exclusion Case*, the Supreme Court stated that "[t]he

---

45. For an analysis of how the plenary power doctrine has caused courts to invoke procedural due process norms and liberally interpret the immigration laws, see Hiroshi Motomura, *Immigration Law After a Century of Plenary Power: Phantom Constitutional Norms and Statutory Interpretation*, 100 YALE L.J. 545 (1990), and Hiroshi Motomura, *The Curious Evolution of Immigration Law: Procedural Surrogates for Substantive Constitutional Rights*, 92 COLUM. L. REV. 1625 (1992).

46. *See generally* Kevin R. Johnson, *Los Olvidados: Images of the Immigrant, Political Power of Noncitizens, and Immigration Law and Enforcement*, 1993 BYU L. REV. 1139 (analyzing the vulnerability of noncitizens in the political process).

47. *See generally* RONALD TAKAKI, STRANGERS FROM A DIFFERENT SHORE 79-130 (1989) (documenting the treatment of Chinese immigrants in nineteenth century America). Not willing to be passive victims, the Chinese community aggressively posed sophisticated legal challenges to the various state and federal barriers placed in their paths. *See generally* CHARLES J. MCCLAIN, IN SEARCH OF EQUALITY (1994) (chronicling resistance).

48. *See generally* GERALD L. NEUMAN, STRANGERS TO THE CONSTITUTION 19-43 (1996) (tracing the shift from state to federal immigration regulation over the course of the 1800s).

49. *See infra* text accompanying notes 52-54 (discussing Chinese exclusion cases).

50. *See* Wong Wing v. United States, 163 U.S. 228, 233 (1896) (invalidating law providing that a Chinese immigrant unlawfully in the country "shall be imprisoned [without a jury trial] at hard labor").

51. *See generally* ROGER DANIELS, ASIAN AMERICA 9-99 (1988); ELMER CLARENCE SANDMEYER, THE ANTI-CHINESE MOVEMENT IN CALIFORNIA (2d ed. 1991). In 1871, for example, mob violence against Chinese persons in Los Angeles resulted in the killing of at least 18 people. *See id.* at 48; *see also* DANIELS, *supra*, at 58-66 (describing anti-Chinese violence on the West Coast during this period).

52. Fong Yue Ting v. United States, 149 U.S. 698, 743 (1893) (Brewer, J., dissenting); *see* Frank H. Wu, *The Limits of Borders: A Moderate Proposal for Immigration Reform*, STAN. L. & POL'Y REV., Summer 1996, at 35, 43-45 (summarizing Supreme Court decisions, denominated as the "anti-Asian cases," which upheld the Chinese exclusion laws).

power of exclusion of foreigners [is] an incident of sovereignty belonging to the government of the United States, as a part of [its] sovereign powers delegated by the Constitution."[53] Similarly, in *Fong Yue Ting v. United States*, the Court reasoned that "[t]he right of a nation to expel or deport foreigners . . . is as absolute and unqualified as the right to prohibit and prevent their entrance into the country."[54]

Congress later extended the Chinese exclusion laws to bar immigration from other Asian nations and to prohibit the immigration of persons of Asian ancestry from *any* nation.[55] The so-called Gentleman's Agreement between the U.S. and Japanese Governments in 1907-08 greatly restricted immigration from Japan.[56] The Immigration Act of 1917 expanded Chinese exclusion to prohibit immigration from the "Asiatic barred zone."[57] A 1924 law, best known for creating the discriminatory national origins quota system,[58] allowed for the exclusion of noncitizens "ineligible to citizenship," which affected Asian immigrants who as non-whites were prohibited from naturalizing.[59]

Other aspects of the immigration and nationality laws reinforced the anti-Asian sentiment reflected in the exclusion laws. For example, the Supreme Court interpreted the naturalization law, which allowed "white" immigrants as well as (after the Civil War) persons of African ancestry to naturalize, as barring Asians from naturalizing.[60] In *United States v. Thind*,[61] the Court held that an immigrant from India was not "white" and therefore was ineligible for naturalization. Similarly, in *Ozawa v. United States*,[62] the Court held that a Japanese immigrant, as a non-white, could not naturalize. This manipulation of the citizenship rights of racial minorities harkens back to *Dred Scott v. Sandford*,[63] in which the

---

53. Chae Chan Ping v. United States (Chinese Exclusion Case), 130 U.S. 581, 609 (1889).

54. 149 U.S. at 707.

55. For an analysis of the impact of the immigration laws on the evolution of the Asian American community in the United States, see BILL ONG HING, MAKING AND REMAKING ASIAN AMERICA THROUGH IMMIGRATION POLICY, 1850-1990 (1993).

56. *See* DANIELS, *supra* note 51, at 123-28.

57. Ch. 29, § 3, 39 Stat. 874, 875-76 (repealed 1952); *see* HING, *supra* note 55, at 32.

58. *See infra* text accompanying notes 97-120 (analyzing the social forces resulting in the passage of a national origins quota system in 1924).

59. Immigration Act of 1924, ch. 190, § 11(d), 43 Stat. 153, 159 (repealed 1952); *see also* TAKAKI, *supra* note 47, at 209-10 (observing the impact of this restrictive exclusion ground on immigration from Japan).

60. *See generally* IAN F. HANEY LÓPEZ, WHITE BY LAW (1996) (analyzing cases applying the naturalization prerequisite that a noncitizen be "white"). The impact of the racial prerequisite to the naturalization laws was ameliorated to some extent by the birthright-citizenship rule, which bestows citizenship on virtually all persons born in the United States. *See* United States v. Wong Kim Ark, 169 U.S. 649 (1898); *see also* Kevin R. Johnson, *Racial Restrictions on Naturalization: The Recurring Intersection of Race and Gender in Immigration and Citizenship Law*, 11 BERKELEY WOMEN'S L.J. 142, 152-53 (1996) (reviewing *White by Law* and commenting on impact of birthright citizenship on children of noncitizens born in United States).

61. 261 U.S. 204 (1923).

62. 260 U.S. 178 (1922).

63. 60 U.S. (19 How.) 393 (1856).

Supreme Court held that a freed Black man was not a citizen for the purpose of invoking the jurisdiction of the federal courts.

Incorporating the racial discrimination encoded in federal naturalization law, state laws buttressed the racial hierarchy. A number of states, most notably California, passed so-called "alien land laws" early in the twentieth century that barred the ownership of certain real property by noncitizens "ineligible to citizenship."[64] The measures were directed at Japanese immigrants, who as non-whites barred from naturalization, were "ineligible to citizenship." The political and social milieu in which these laws were passed demonstrates their racial animus. For example, anti-Japanese venom dominated the campaign culminating in the alien land law by initiative in California.[65] Despite the obvious racial overtones, the Supreme Court rejected the contemporary challenges to the land laws.[66]

Racism unquestionably influenced the anti-Asian exclusion in the immigration laws.[67]

> The national climate of opinion, pervaded by racism and a burgeoning feeling of ethnic superiority or what [has been] called the "Anglo-Saxon complex," certainly contributed not just to the violence but also to the virtual unanimity with which the white majority put its seal of approval on anti-Chinese ends if not means.[68]

1. Chinese Exclusion and Reconstruction

Congress passed the first wave of discriminatory immigration laws not long after the Fourteenth Amendment, which bars states from denying any person equal protection of law, and other Reconstruction Amendments went into effect.[69] With the harshest treatment generally reserved for African Americans

---

64. *See* Cockrill v. California, 268 U.S. 258 (1925); Terrace v. Thompson, 263 U.S. 197 (1923). For a further discussion of the alien land laws of California and other states, see Edwin E. Ferguson, *The California Alien Land Law and the Fourteenth Amendment*, 35 CAL. L. REV. 61 (1947), and Dudley O. McGovney, *The Anti-Japanese Land Laws of California and Ten Other States*, 35 CAL. L. REV. 7 (1947).

65. *See* Oyama v. California, 332 U.S. 633, 658-59 (1948) (Murphy, J., concurring) (describing a "spirited campaign . . . waged to secure popular approval, a campaign with a bitter anti-Japanese flavor" resulting in the passage of a land law by initiative in California); Ferguson, *supra* note 64, at 62-73 (reviewing the anti-Japanese animus that motivated the initiative's passage). *See generally* DANIELS, *supra* note 51, at 100-282 (analyzing the growth of anti-Japanese sentiment in the United States).

66. *See supra* note 64 (citing cases).

67. *See* THOMAS ALEXANDER ALEINIKOFF ET AL., IMMIGRATION PROCESS AND POLICY 2 (3d ed. 1995) (observing that the Chinese exclusion laws "like many later immigration laws . . . were the product of economic and political concerns laced with racism and nativism").

68. DANIELS, *supra* note 51, at 65 (citing BARBARA MILLER SOLOMAN, ANCESTORS AND IMMIGRANTS (2d ed. 1972)); *see* MALDWYN ALLEN JONES, AMERICAN IMMIGRATION 227 (2d ed. 1992) (noting that later anti-Japanese hysteria in California resulted in part from a "belief in Anglo-Saxon superiority").

69. *See* TRIBE, *supra* note 41, § 5-12, at 330; *see also* John Hayakawa Torok, *Reconstruction and Racial Nativism: Chinese Immigrants and the Debates on the Thirteenth, Fourteenth, and Fifteenth Amendments and Civil Rights Laws*, 3 ASIAN L.J. 55 (1996)

formally declared unlawful, the nation transferred animosity to another discrete and insular racial minority whose immigration status, combined with race, made such treatment more socially acceptable and legally defensible.[70] This issue arose in the congressional debates over ratification of the Fourteenth Amendment when a member of Congress declared that Chinese persons could be treated less favorably than African Americans because "[the Chinese] are foreigners and the negro is a native."[71]

The relationship between Chinese exclusion and the revolutionary improvements for African Americans during Reconstruction often goes ignored, even though pre-Civil War state laws regulating the migration of slaves served as precursors to the Chinese exclusion laws.[72] Congress enacted the national exclusion laws with the support of southerners interested in rejuvenating a racial caste system as well as self-interested Anglos from California.[73]

It was no coincidence that greater legal freedoms for African Americans were tied to Chinese misfortunes. As one historian observed, "[w]ith Negro slavery a dead issue after 1865, greater attention was focused [on immigration from China]."[74] Political forces quickly reacted to fill the racial void in the political arena. In California, partisan political concerns, along with labor unionism, in the post-Civil War period figured prominently in the anti-Chinese movement.[75]

> In 1867 [the year after the Fourteenth Amendment went into effect] California Democrats launched their offensive against the Chinese. *The result . . . was a bonanza.* The party laid hands on an issue of enormous potential in its own right—a new issue, uncontaminated by the sad history of the civil

---

(analyzing how issues surrounding Chinese immigration and immigrants affected the debate over Reconstruction Amendments).

70. *See infra* text accompanying notes 266-83 (analyzing psychological theories of transference and displacement).

71. CONG. GLOBE, 39th Cong., 1st Sess. 1056 (1866) (comments of Rep. Higby). In discussing why Blacks should be able to naturalize under the Fourteenth Amendment and Chinese could not, Representative Niblack asked the following:

> If a Chinaman is one of the human race, why should he be degraded below the negro? Why should he not receive the same right as the negro? I should like to understand it. The negro is of pagan race, and is a pagan before he comes here. . . . I want to understand why we should exclude one race and include another, why we should deny to these people the right of naturalization, for instance, and allow it to others.

Id. (comments of Rep. Niblack). Congress ultimately extended birthright citizenship under the Fourteenth Amendment to persons of Chinese, as well as African, ancestry born in the United States. *See* Gerald L. Neuman, *Back to* Dred Scott?, 24 SAN DIEGO L. REV. 485, 491-92 (1987) (reviewing PETER H. SCHUCK & ROGERS M. SMITH, CITIZENSHIP WITHOUT CONSENT (1985), and considering congressional debate on this point).

72. *See* NEUMAN, *supra* note 48, at 39-40.

73. *See* MILTON R. KONVITZ, THE ALIEN AND THE ASIATIC IN AMERICAN LAW 10-12 (1946).

74. STUART CREIGHTON MILLER, THE UNWELCOME IMMIGRANT 151 (1969).

75. *See generally* ALEXANDER SAXTON, THE INDISPENSABLE ENEMY (2d ed. 1995). However, while the exclusion of Asian immigrants resulted in a marked decline in violence directed at Asians in this country, African Americans, who as citizens could not be removed from the country, were subject to horrible violence well into the twentieth century. *See* SUSAN OLZAK, THE DYNAMICS OF ETHNIC COMPETITION AND CONFLICT 219-20 (1992).

> war, yet evocative of that entire syndrome of hatreds and loyalties which still could not quite openly be declared.[76]

The relationship between the treatment of African Americans and other racial minorities can be seen in a constitutional landmark of the nineteenth century. In his dissent in *Plessy v. Ferguson*, often lauded for its grand pronouncement that "[o]ur Constitution is color-blind,"[77] Justice Harlan noted the irony that the "separate but equal" doctrine applied to Blacks, who unquestionably were part of the political community, but not Chinese immigrants, "a race so different from our own that we do not permit those belonging to it to become citizens of the United States" and who generally are excluded from entering the country.[78] Seeking to protect Blacks by denigrating the Chinese, Justice Harlan left no doubt about his sympathies on the question of racial superiority:

> The white race deems itself to be the dominant race in this country. And so it is, in prestige, in achievements, in education, in wealth and in power. So, I doubt not, it will continue to be for all time, if it remains true to its great heritage and holds fast to the principles of constitutional liberty.[79]

Some might contend that this analysis fails to recognize that the courts at various times invoked the law to protect Chinese immigrants. A most prominent example is *Yick Wo v. Hopkins*, in which the Supreme Court held that discriminatory enforcement of a local laundry ordinance against "aliens and subjects of the Emperor of China" violated the Equal Protection Clause of the Fourteenth Amendment.[80] Though often cited for the proposition that a facially neutral law enforced in a racially discriminatory manner violates the Constitution,[81] the decision, rather than a commitment to racial equality, represented an early foray by the Supreme Court in invalidating economic regulation, which reached its high-water mark during the *Lochner* era.[82] In any event, as the Court's treatment of the exclusion laws reveals, *Yick Wo* is far from representative of the prevailing judicial attitude toward the rights of persons of Chinese ancestry during the late 1800s.

2. Japanese Internment and *Brown v. Board of Education*

The historical context of the infamous decision to intern Japanese Americans, as well as Japanese immigrants, during World War II sheds light on the interrelationship between society's treatment of different minority groups. The

---

76. SAXTON, *supra* note 75, at 260 (emphasis added).

77. 163 U.S. 537, 559 (1896) (Harlan, J., dissenting). For a critique of Justice Harlan's so-called color-blindness jurisprudence, see Gabriel J. Chin, *The* Plessy *Myth: Justice Harlan and the Chinese Cases*, 82 IOWA L. REV. 151 (1996).

78. *Plessy*, 163 U.S. at 561 (Harlan, J., dissenting).

79. *Id.* at 559 (Harlan, J., dissenting).

80. 118 U.S. 356, 368 (1886).

81. *See, e.g.*, TRIBE, *supra* note 41, § 16-17, at 1483.

82. *See* Thomas Wuil Joo, *New "Conspiracy Theory" of the Fourteenth Amendment: Nineteenth Century Chinese Civil Rights Cases and the Development of Substantive Due Process Jurisprudence*, 29 U.S.F. L. REV. 353, 356 (1995).

Supreme Court ruling in *Korematsu v. United States*[83] shows how, absent the protection of law, disfavored racial minority *citizens* might be treated. In that case, the Supreme Court allowed U.S. citizens of Japanese ancestry, including some born and bred in this country, to be detained in internment camps. This decision reveals the inherent difficulties in drawing fine legal distinctions between noncitizens and citizens who share a common ancestry. In attempting to defuse the Japanese threat to national security, the U.S. Government refused to distinguish between noncitizens who immigrated from Japan and citizens of Japanese ancestry. Lumped together as the monolithic "Japanese" enemy, all were interned. The U.S. Government classified all persons of Japanese ancestry, regardless of their immigration status, as "foreign."

As the Japanese suffered from internment during World War II, African Americans, due in no small part to increased labor demand during the war, experienced improved employment opportunities and less discrimination.[84] As in the nineteenth century, Asian American exclusion from the national community was combined with some improvements for African Americans.

The timing of the Supreme Court's decision in *Korematsu*, one of the most well-known equal protection cases of the twentieth century, should not be ignored. *Korematsu* (1944) is an infamous case, while *Brown v. Board of Education*[85] (1954), which vindicated the rights of African Americans, is much revered. Though close in time, these cases reveal the very best and worst of American constitutional law. While persons of Japanese ancestry were rebuilding the remnants of their lives after the turmoil of legally sanctioned internment,[86] African Americans saw hope in being told that "separate but equal" was no longer the law of the land.

Ultimately, some of the harshest aspects of the anti-Asian laws were relaxed. Pressures to end exclusion of Chinese immigrants to the United States grew during World War II as it became increasingly embarrassing for the nation to prohibit immigration from a valued ally, China, in the war effort. Japanese propaganda efforts during World War II made much of the Chinese exclusion laws.[87] In the end, foreign policy concerns, not humanitarian ones, caused Congress in 1943 to allow China a minimum quota of immigrant visas and to

---

83. 323 U.S. 214 (1944).

84. *See* MANNING MARABLE, RACE, REFORM AND REBELLION: THE SECOND RECONSTRUCTION IN BLACK AMERICA, 1945-1982, at 12-15 (1984).

85. 347 U.S. 483 (1954). Even closer in time to *Korematsu*, President Truman in 1948 ordered the desegregation of the armed forces in response to pressures from African American activists. *See generally* RICHARD M. DALFIUME, DESEGREGATION OF THE U.S. ARMED FORCES 148-74 (1969) (analyzing political forces surrounding desegregation order); MORRIS J. MACGREGOR, JR., INTEGRATION OF THE ARMED FORCES, 1940-1965, at 291-314 (1981) (same).

86. *See* Eugene V. Rostow, *The Japanese American Cases—A Disaster*, 54 YALE L.J. 489 (1945).

87. *See* DANIELS, *supra* note 51, at 186-98; *see also* J. Donald Kingsley, *Immigration and Our Foreign Policy Objectives*, 21 LAW & CONTEMP. PROBS. 299, 303-06 (1956) (analyzing U.S. foreign policy problems resulting from the exclusion of Asian immigrants).

allow Chinese immigrants to naturalize.[88] In this way, the United States relaxed the Chinese exclusion laws for foreign policy reasons similar to those that helped bring about *Brown v. Board of Education*.[89]

The Vietnam War also reveals a relationship between Asian subordination and improvements for African Americans. While the civil rights movement of the 1960s achieved improvements for African Americans, the escalation of the war in Vietnam during this time was accompanied by the growth of racism directed at the Vietnamese people, which lingers to this day.[90] Seeing the racial roots of the war, as well as the impact on domestic people of color, two of the most prominent African American leaders of their generation, Martin Luther King, Jr. and Malcolm X, though of different political persuasions, opposed U.S. involvement in Vietnam.[91]

As this sad history demonstrates, Asian Americans—whatever their immigration status and however long they or their ancestors have lived in the United States—historically have been treated as foreigners in this land.[92] Some claim that the immigration laws discriminate against Asians to this day.[93] Besides

---

88. *See* Act of Dec. 17, 1943, ch. 344, 57 Stat. 600 (amended 1946); *see also* Gabriel J. Chin, *The Civil Rights Revolution Comes to Immigration Law: A New Look at the Immigration and Nationality Act of 1965*, 75 N.C. L. REV. 273, 282-86 (1996) (analyzing foreign policy reasons for the elimination of the ban on Chinese immigration). In 1945, 109 Chinese immigrants came to the United States and 233 in 1946. *See* DANIELS, *supra* note 51, at 199 tbl.6.3. In 1946, Congress extended similar privileges to Filipinos and Indians. *See* Act of July 2, 1946, ch. 534, 60 Stat. 416 (amended 1952). The Immigration & Nationality Act of 1952 (INA) granted these minimum rights to all Asian nationalities. *See* Immigration & Nationality Act, ch. 477, §§ 201(a), 311, 66 Stat. 163, 175, 239 (1952) (codified as amended at 8 U.S.C.A. §§ 1151(a), 1422 (West Supp. 1998)).

89. *See* Mary L. Dudziak, *Desegregation as a Cold War Imperative*, 41 STAN. L. REV. 61 (1988) (contending that U.S. foreign policy interests spurred desegregation efforts in 1950s); *see also* Derrick A. Bell, Jr., Brown v. Board of Education *and the Interest-Convergence Dilemma*, 93 HARV. L. REV. 518, 524 (1980) ("[T]he [*Brown*] decision helped to provide immediate credibility to America's struggle with Communist countries to win the hearts and minds of emerging third world peoples. At least this argument was advanced by lawyers for both the NAACP and the federal government. And the point was not lost on the news media.") (footnote omitted); Mary L. Dudziak, *The Little Rock Crisis and Foreign Affairs: Race, Resistance, and the Image of American Democracy*, 70 S. CAL. L. REV. 1641 (1997) (analyzing relationship between U.S. foreign affairs and civil rights during Eisenhower administration).

90. *See, e.g.*, United States v. Piche, 981 F.2d 706, 710 (4th Cir. 1992) (affirming conviction of the murderer of an Asian American who told victim that he hated the Vietnamese because his brother had been killed in Vietnam and that the Vietnamese should not have come to United States); *see also* Vietnamese Fishermen's Ass'n v. Knights of Ku Klux Klan, 518 F. Supp. 993 (S.D. Tex. 1981) (enjoining Ku Klux Klan and affiliates from harassing and intimidating Vietnamese fishermen).

91. *See* MARABLE, *supra* note 84, at 111-16.

92. *See* Cynthia Kwei Yung Lee, *Race and Self-Defense: Toward a Normative Conception of Reasonableness*, 81 MINN. L. REV. 367, 429-38 (1996); Natsu Taylor Saito, *Alien and Non-Alien Alike: Citizenship, "Foreignness" and Racial Hierarchy in American Law*, 76 OR. L. REV. 261 (1997).

93. *See* Jan C. Ting, *"Other than a Chinaman": How U.S. Immigration Law Resulted from and Still Reflects a Policy of Excluding and Restricting Asian Immigration*, 4 TEMP. POL. & CIV. RTS. L. REV. 301 (1995); *see also infra* text accompanying notes 121-49 (offering

suffering from efforts to exclude persons who shared their ancestry from the national community,[94] Asian Americans stood accused of the high crime against the American "melting pot" mythology of refusing to assimilate.[95] Ironically, the law prevented full assimilation and equal citizenship. For example, due to the bar to naturalization, immigrants from Asia (as non-whites) were disenfranchised and prohibited from exercising political power as citizens, which in the long run detrimentally affected Asian American political involvement.[96] Barred from the political community, Asian Americans were denied the possibility of more fully assimilating into the mainstream and then suffered criticism for failing to assimilate.

B. The National Origins Quota System

In 1924, Congress established the much-reviled national origins quota system, a formulaic device designed to ensure stability in the ethnic composition of the United States.[97] Specifically, the system served to prefer white immigrants. It initially permitted annual immigration of up to two percent of the number of foreign-born persons of a particular nationality in the United States as set forth in the 1890 census.[98] In operation, the quota system "materially favored

---

examples of disparate impact that modern immigration laws have on Asian immigration).

94. *See infra* text accompanying notes 242-60 (explaining stigma attached to citizens as the result of exclusion of certain races and nationalities who share similar characteristics).

95. *See, e.g.*, Hirabayashi v. United States, 320 U.S. 81, 96-97 (1943) (observing in Japanese internment case that many factors "prevented [Japanese] assimilation as an integral part of the white population"); Chae Chan Ping v. United States (Chinese Exclusion Case), 130 U.S. 581, 595 (1889) (justifying law excluding Chinese immigration by stating that "[i]t seemed impossible for [the Chinese] to assimilate with our people"). In this vein, the Supreme Court refused to allow an immigrant from India to naturalize and become a citizen, and thus assimilate into the U.S. political community, because he could not assimilate:

> It is a matter of familiar observation and knowledge that the physical group characteristics of the Hindus render them readily distinguishable from the various groups of persons in this country commonly recognized as white. . . . [I]t cannot be doubted that the children born in this country of Hindu parents would retain indefinitely the clear evidence of their ancestry. . . . What we suggest is merely racial difference, and it is of such character and extent that the great body of our people instinctively recognize it and reject the thought of assimilation.

United States v. Thind, 261 U.S. 204, 215 (1923).

For a historical analysis of how persons advocating immigration restriction have relied on the argument that immigrants fail to assimilate, see Kevin R. Johnson, *The New Nativism: Something Old, Something New, Something Borrowed, Something Blue*, *in* IMMIGRANTS OUT! THE NEW NATIVISM AND THE ANTI-IMMIGRANT IMPULSE IN THE UNITED STATES 165 (1997). *See also* Kevin R. Johnson, *"Melting Pot" or "Ring of Fire"?: Assimilation and the Mexican-American Experience*, 85 CAL. L. REV. 1259 (1997) (analyzing barriers to Mexican American assimilation in the United States).

96. *See* Robert S. Chang, *Toward an Asian American Legal Scholarship: Critical Race Theory, Post-Structuralism, and Narrative Space*, 81 CAL. L. REV. 1241, 1300-03 (1993).

97. *See* Immigration Act of 1924, ch. 190, § 11(a), 43 Stat. 153, 159 (repealed 1952).

98. *See id.* The 1924 Act was a successor to the Immigration Act of 1921, which had a more liberal quota of three percent of the persons from a particular country as determined by the 1910 census. *See* Act of May 19, 1921, ch. 8, § 2(a), 42 Stat. 5, 5 (repealed 1952). Under

immigrants from Northern and Western Europe because the great waves from Southern and Eastern Europe did not arrive until after 1890."[99] Congress enacted the quota system in the wake of passing the literacy test in 1917; this test excluded "[a]ll aliens over sixteen years of age, physically capable of reading, who can not read the English language, or some other language or dialect, including Hebrew or Yiddish."[100] In operation, the test, as intended, restricted the immigration of non-English speakers, including Italians, Russians, Poles, Hungarians, Greeks, and Asians.[101]

A House report offers a clear articulation of the purposes of the national origins quota system:

> "With full recognition of the material progress which we owe to the races from southern and eastern Europe, *we are conscious that the continued arrival of great numbers tends to upset our balance of population, to depress our standard of living, and to unduly charge our institutions for the care of the socially inadequate.*
>
> If immigration from southern and eastern Europe may enter the United States on a basis of substantial equality with that admitted from the older sources of supply, *it is clear that if any appreciable number of immigrants are to be allowed to land upon our shores the balance of racial preponderance must in time pass to those elements of the population who reproduce more rapidly on a lower standard of living than those possessing other ideals.*"
>
> . . . .
>
> ". . . *[The quota system] is used in an effort to preserve, as nearly as possible, the racial status quo in the United States. It is hoped to guarantee, as best we can at this late date, racial homogeneity* . . . ."[102]

---

the law, the quota system was based on U.S. population demographics as of 1920 beginning in 1927. *See* Immigration Act of 1924 § 11(b), 43 Stat. at 159.

99. Hiroshi Motomura, *Whose Alien Nation?: Two Models of Constitutional Immigration Law*, 94 MICH. L. REV. 1927, 1933 (1996) (footnote omitted); *see also* Chin, *supra* note 88, at 279-97 (discussing how quota system limited immigration from Asia). *See generally* HIGHAM, *supra* note 40, at 264-330 (analyzing social forces resulting in passage of restrictionist quota system). Interestingly, the national origins quota system did not impose restrictions on immigration from the Western Hemisphere, *see* Motomura, *supra*, at 1934, which was not expressly restricted until much later, *see infra* text accompanying notes 125-26 (discussing restrictions on Western Hemisphere immigration).

100. Immigration Act of Feb. 5, 1917, ch. 29, § 3, 39 Stat. 874, 877 (repealed 1952).

101. *See* HIGHAM, *supra* note 40, at 300-30; *see also* E.P. HUTCHINSON, LEGISLATIVE HISTORY OF AMERICAN IMMIGRATION POLICY, 1798-1965, at 465-68, 481-83 (1981) (discussing genesis of literacy test).

102. HUTCHINSON, *supra* note 101, at 484-85 (emphasis, omissions, and alterations added) (quoting STAFF OF HOUSE COMM. ON IMMIGRATION AND NATURALIZATION, REPORT ON RESTRICTION OF IMMIGRATION, H.R. REP. NO. 68-350, pt. 1, at 13-14, 16 (1924)); *see also* ROY L. GARIS, IMMIGRATION RESTRICTION at vii (1927) (expressing similar views and emphasizing that "our capacity to maintain our cherished institutions stands diluted by a stream of alien blood, with all its inherited misconceptions respecting the relationships of the governing power to the governed"). Some in the modern immigration debate have made similar calls for greater homogeneity among immigrants. *See, e.g.*, BRIMELOW, *supra* note 5, at 232 ("[B]y introducing diverse populations, [immigration] strikes at the nation-state's Achilles' heel: the need for

As one commentator remarked approvingly in 1924, the national origins quota system was "a scientific plan for keeping America American."[103] Implicit in these rationales, of course, was the view that persons of northern European stock were superior to persons of other groups. In a similar vein, the conventional wisdom was that "[t]he real assimilation of aliens depends to a very large extent upon their associates after entering—'we can easily assimilate' them 'if their origins resemble the origins of the people they find when they get here.'"[104]

The racial hierarchy endorsed by proponents of the national origins quota system was entirely consistent with the academic literature of the day, which viewed the "races" of southern and eastern Europe as inferior to northern European ones.[105] In effect, southern and eastern European immigrants, commonly thought of today as white ethnics, were "racialized" as non-white, and therefore unworthy of joining the national community.[106]

A heavy dose of anti-Semitism fueled the demand for the national origins quota system. Proponents hoped to limit the immigration of Jewish persons to the United States.[107] This anti-Semitism mirrored the discrimination suffered by Jewish Americans in this country.[108] During World War II, anti-Semitism, enforced and reinforced by the quota system, unfortunately influenced the U.S. Government's refusal to accept many Jewish refugees fleeing the Holocaust, one of the tragedies of the twentieth century.[109]

---

homogeneity."). *But see* Howard F. Chang, *Liberalized Immigration as Free Trade: Economic Welfare and the Optimal Immigration Policy*, 145 U. PA. L. REV. 1147, 1210-19 (1997) (contending that personal preferences for the ethnic status quo are not legitimately considered in immigration law and policymaking).

103. A. Warner Parker, *The Quota Provisions of the Immigration Act of 1924*, 18 AM. J. INT'L L. 737, 740 (1924).

104. *Id.*

105. *See* HIGHAM, *supra* note 40, at 149-56. An influential book in this regard is MADISON GRANT, THE PASSING OF THE GREAT RACE (4th rev. ed. 1923). *See* HIGHAM, *supra* note 40, at 271 (analyzing nativism's influence on immigration legislation during this period and observing that "[i]ntellectually the resurgent racism of the early twenties drew its central inspiration from [this book]").

106. *See* HIGHAM, *supra* note 40, at 156-57 (analyzing racial hierarchies popular in science during that time with Jews and other "non-Nordics" classified as of inferior racial stock). The racialization of white ethnic immigrants was in no way unprecedented. For example, mainstream U.S. society classified early Irish immigrants as non-white. *See* Ronald Takaki, The Tempest *in the Wilderness: The Racialization of Savagery*, *in* DISCOVERING AMERICA 58 (David Thelen & Frederick E. Hoxie eds., 1994).

107. *See generally* JOHN HIGHAM, SEND THESE TO ME: IMMIGRANTS IN URBAN AMERICA 81-174 (Johns Hopkins Univ. Press, rev. ed. 1984) (1975) (analyzing impact of anti-Semitism on immigration restrictions and discrimination against Jews in the United States).

108. *See* NATHAN GLAZER & DANIEL PATRICK MOYNIHAN, BEYOND THE MELTING POT 137-85 (1963). *See generally* ROBERT S. WISTRICH, ANTISEMITISM (1991) (analyzing roots of anti-Semitism around the world).

109. *See* RITA J. SIMON & SUSAN H. ALEXANDER, THE AMBIVALENT WELCOME 31 (1993) (summarizing poll data indicating that, in 1939, vast majority of public opposed allowing large number of Jewish refugees from Germany into United States). *See generally* HENRY L. FEINGOLD, THE POLITICS OF RESCUE (1970) (analyzing the Roosevelt administration's response to Jewish refugees); SAUL S. FRIEDMAN, NO HAVEN FOR THE OPPRESSED (1973) (studying U.S.

Other "races" also were affected by the quota system. Although Asian Americans were excluded from immigrating to the United States well before 1924,[110] an oft-overlooked impact of the quota system was that it discouraged immigration from Africa, historically the source of precious little immigration to the United States.[111] This is entirely consistent with anti-Black subordination in the country and this nation's later refusal to accept refugees fleeing political turmoil in Haiti, a country populated primarily by persons of African ancestry.[112]

Despite persistent criticisms, including claims that it adversely affected U.S. foreign policy interests,[113] the Anglo-Saxon, northern European preference in the immigration laws remained intact until 1965. Congress, though it tinkered somewhat with the quota system, maintained the quotas in the Immigration & Nationality Act (INA), the comprehensive immigration law that (as frequently amended) remains in place today.[114] President Truman vetoed the INA (a veto that Congress overrode) because it carried forward the discriminatory quota system.[115] In defending the INA's version of the quota system, one commentator of the day claimed that the nation's ethnic composition should not be changed and that, because some known Communists opposed the law, opponents should be circumspect before joining the fray.[116] A Senate report concluded that the national origins quota system "preserve[d] the sociological and cultural balance in the United States," which was justifiable because northern and western Europeans "had made the greatest contribution to the development of [the]

---

refugee policy toward Jewish refugees during World War II); GORDON THOMAS & MAX MORGAN WITTS, VOYAGE OF THE DAMNED (1974) (documenting U.S. Government's refusal to accept Jewish refugees on the SS *St. Louis* during World War II and forcing the ship to return to Nazi Germany).

110. *See supra* text accompanying notes 47-82 (analyzing the significance of various laws designed to exclude immigration from China).

111. *See* Bill Ong Hing, *Immigration Policies: Messages of Exclusion to African Americans*, 37 HOW. L.J. 237, 240 (1994).

112. *See infra* text accompanying notes 179-206 (analyzing U.S. response to Haitian refugees).

113. *See* PRESIDENT'S COMM'N ON IMMIGRATION AND NATURALIZATION, WHOM SHALL WE WELCOME 52-56 (1953).

114. *See* INA, ch. 477, § 201(a), 66 Stat. 163, 175 (1952) (codified as amended at 8 U.S.C.A. § 1151(a) (West Supp. 1998)) (providing nations with quotas equal to one-sixth of one percent of the number of current U.S. inhabitants who traced their ancestry to that country in 1920).

115. *See* PUBLIC PAPERS OF THE PRESIDENTS OF THE UNITED STATES: HARRY S. TRUMAN 441 (1952-53) [hereinafter TRUMAN PAPERS] (explaining veto of INA because it perpetuated discriminatory national origins quota system and emphasizing that "immigration policy is . . . important to the conduct of our foreign relations and to our responsibilities of moral leadership in the struggle for world peace").

116. *See* Robert C. Alexander, *A Defense of the McCarren-Walter Act*, 21 LAW & CONTEMP. PROBS. 382, 385-86 (1956). Some, however, claimed that the public at large opposed the INA, particularly the national origins quota system. *See* Harry N. Rosenfield, *The Prospects for Immigration Amendments*, 21 LAW & CONTEMP. PROBS. 401, 411 (1956). The passage of the INA in the face of public opposition might be explained by the political strength of an anti-immigrant minority. *See* Johnson, *supra* note 46, at 1158-61 (contending that, due to politics of immigration, vocal anti-immigrant minority may prevail in political process).

country" and the nation should "admit immigrants considered to be more readily assimilable because of the similarity of their cultural background to those of the principal components of our population."[117]

In sum, the national origins quota system reflects this nation's preoccupation with its ethnic balance. The system was based on the desire to limit the immigration of inferior "races" from southern and eastern Europe.[118] Domestic discrimination accompanied the exclusion in the laws. Long-standing anti-Semitism, as well as prejudice against other immigrant groups,[119] existed in the United States.

The life of the national origins quota system spanned a period when domestic racial minorities enjoyed some improvements under the law. While domestic minorities gained formal legal rights, noncitizens at best remained in the same rightless place in American society. Many noncitizens lost rights with the INA, which besides maintaining the quota system, also included some draconian provisions punishing noncitizen political minorities in the name of fighting Communism.[120]

C. Modern Racial Exclusion

In the wake of the Civil Rights Act of 1964,[121] Congress passed the Immigration Act of 1965.[122] This new law abolished the national origins quota system[123] and barred racial considerations from expressly entering into decisions about immigrant visas;[124] it also imposed for the first time a ceiling (120,000) on migration from the Western Hemisphere.[125] Immigration from the Western

---

117. STAFF OF SENATE COMM. ON THE JUDICIARY, REPORT ON THE IMMIGRATION AND NATURALIZATION SYSTEMS OF THE UNITED STATES, S. REP. NO. 81-1515, at 455 (1951).

118. This lends support to the concept that race is a social, not a biological, construction. *See generally* OMI & WINANT, *supra* note 27 (analyzing racial formation in the United States).

119. *See* GLAZER & MOYNIHAN, *supra* note 108, at 181-218 (documenting the Italian-immigrant experience in New York City).

120. *See* John A. Scanlan, *Aliens in the Marketplace of Ideas: The Government, the Academy, and the McCarren-Walter Act*, 66 TEX. L. REV. 1481, 1489-505 (1988) (analyzing the history of ideological exclusions in U.S. immigration laws with a focus on INA). *See generally* Kevin R. Johnson, *The Antiterrorism Act, the Immigration Reform Act, and Ideological Regulation in the Immigration Laws: Important Lessons for Citizens and Noncitizens*, 28 ST. MARY'S L.J. 833 (1997) (analyzing how noncitizen political minorities historically have been treated in a way that would be patently unconstitutional if they were citizens).

121. Pub. L. No. 88-352, 78 Stat. 241 (codified as amended in scattered sections of 28 and 42 U.S.C.).

122. Pub. L. No. 89-236, 79 Stat. 911 (codified as amended in scattered sections of 8 U.S.C.).

123. *See id.*, sec. 1, 79 Stat. at 911 (codified as amended at INA § 201, 8 U.S.C.A. § 1151 (West Supp. 1998)).

124. *See id.*, sec. 2, 79 Stat. at 911-12 (codified as amended at INA § 202, 8 U.S.C.A. § 1152).

125. *See id.*, sec. 21(e), 79 Stat. at 921 (repealed 1976); *see also* Rep. Lamar Smith & Edward R. Grant, *Immigration Reform: Seeking the Right Reasons*, 28 ST. MARY'S L.J. 883, 888 (1997) ("Unfortunately, just as the immigration debate in the 1920s had been unduly

Hemisphere previously had been restricted not through quotas but through vigorous enforcement of the exclusion and deportation grounds. The limitation on Western Hemisphere immigration was part of a compromise to those who feared a drastic upswing in Latin American immigration.[126] Consequently, Congress coupled more generous treatment of those outside the Western Hemisphere with less generous treatment of Latin Americans.

With the demise of the quota system, the racial demographics of the immigration stream changed significantly.[127] Increasing numbers of immigrants of color came to the United States.[128] Not coincidentally, concern with

---

affected by the rise of nativism, the debate in 1965 was unduly influenced by a very different movement, that to secure civil rights of all Americans."). Interestingly, criticism of the discriminatory nature of the quota system in the House and Senate reports is muted with emphasis placed on the benefits of the new system rather than the deficiencies of the old. *See* STAFF OF HOUSE COMM. ON THE JUDICIARY, REPORT ON AMENDING THE IMMIGRATION AND NATIONALITY ACT, AND FOR OTHER PURPOSES, H.R. REP. NO. 89-745, at 12 (1965) ("In place of the national origins system the bill establishes a new system of selection designed to be fair, rational, humane, and in the national interest."); STAFF OF SENATE COMM. ON THE JUDICIARY, REPORT ON AMENDING THE IMMIGRATION AND NATIONALITY ACT, AND FOR OTHER PURPOSES, S. REP. NO. 89-748, at 13 (1965), *reprinted in* 1965 U.S.C.C.A.N. 3328, 3332 (same). Indeed, the House report states that "[t]he national origins system has failed to maintain the ethnic balance of the American population," thereby suggesting that the goal was not necessarily inappropriate. H.R. REP. NO. 89-745, at 11.

126. *See* Motomura, *supra* note 99, at 1934; *see, e.g.*, H.R. REP. NO. 89-745, at 48 (noting that the "most compelling reason" for imposing the Western Hemisphere quota was fear of increased immigration from Latin America resulting from projected population growth); S. REP. NO. 89-748, at 17-18, *reprinted in* 1965 U.S.C.C.A.N. 3328, 3336 (expressing concern with the level of immigration from Western Hemisphere). The blue ribbon Select Commission on Immigration and Refugee Policy summarized the history:

> The United States was . . . far from free of prejudice . . . and one part of the 1965 law reflected change in policy that was in part due to antiforeign sentiments. Prejudice against dark-skinned people . . . remained strong. *In the years after World War II, as the proportion of Spanish-speaking residents increased, much of the lingering nativism in the United States was directed against those from Mexico and Central and South America. . . . Giving in to . . . pressures as a price to be paid for abolishing the national origins system, Congress put into the 1965 amendments a ceiling [on Western Hemisphere immigration] to close the last remaining open door of U.S. policy.*

U.S. SELECT COMM'N ON IMMIGRATION AND REFUGEE POLICY, STAFF REPORT: U.S. IMMIGRATION POLICY AND THE NATIONAL INTEREST 208 (1981) (emphasis added) (footnote omitted).

127. For essays on this subject, see IMMIGRATION AND ETHNICITY (Barry Edmonston & Jeffrey S. Passel eds., 1994). Whether Congress envisioned the change in the racial demographics of immigration has been a subject of debate. *See* Chin, *supra* note 88 (contending that, contrary to conventional wisdom, Congress understood the implications of the 1965 law).

128. *See* IMMIGRATION AND NATURALIZATION SERV., U.S. DEP'T OF JUSTICE, 1995 STATISTICAL YEARBOOK OF THE IMMIGRATION AND NATURALIZATION SERVICE 23 tbl.D (1997) [hereinafter 1995 INS STATISTICAL YEARBOOK] (presenting statistical data showing that the top five countries of birth of immigrants in fiscal year 1995 were Mexico, the Philippines, Vietnam, the Dominican Republic, and the People's Republic of China).

immigration, particularly the race of the immigrants, grew over the coming decades.[129]

Importantly, the abolition of the national origins quota system, though removing blatant discrimination from the immigration laws, failed to cleanse all remnants of racism. Various characteristics of the modern immigration laws, though facially neutral, disparately impact noncitizens of color from developing nations. The 1965 Act replaced the national origins quotas with an across-the-board annual numerical limit of 20,000 immigrants from each nation.[130] This ceiling in operation creates lengthy lines for immigrants from developing nations, such as Mexico, the Philippines, and India, and relatively short, or no, lines for people from most other nations. For example, as of March 1998, fourth-preference immigrant visas (brothers and sisters of adult citizens)[131] were being granted to Philippine nationals who applied in April 1978, compared to October 1987 for virtually all other nations.[132] For third-preference immigrant visas (married sons and daughters of citizens),[133] the applications of Mexican citizens filed in May 1989 were being processed in March 1998, compared to September 1994 for applicants from almost every other nation.[134] Thus, similarly situated persons (e.g., siblings and children of U.S. citizens) may face radically different waits for immigration depending on their country of origin, with accompanying racial impacts.[135]

---

129. *See, e.g.*, BRIMELOW, *supra* note 5, at 11 (expressing concern with increased immigration of racial minorities because "[r]ace and ethnicity are destiny in American politics") (emphasis omitted); RICHARD D. LAMM & GARY IMHOFF, THE IMMIGRATION TIME BOMB 76-98 (1985) (expressing fear of immigration of non-Anglo-Saxon immigrants who fail to assimilate).

130. *See* Immigration Act of 1965, Pub. L. No. 89-236, sec. 2, 79 Stat. 911, 911-12 (codified as amended at INA § 202(a), 8 U.S.C.A. § 1152(a) (West Supp. 1998)). Congress changed the quota somewhat in 1990. *See* STEPHEN H. LEGOMSKY, IMMIGRATION AND REFUGEE LAW AND POLICY 123-24 (2d ed. 1997) (explaining changes). The per country quotas were not extended to nations in the Western Hemisphere until 1976. *See* INA Amendments of 1976, Pub. L. No. 94-571, sec. 2, 90 Stat. 2703, 2703 (codified as amended at INA § 201(a), 8 U.S.C.A. § 1151(a)).

131. *See* INA § 203(a)(4), 8 U.S.C.A. § 1153(a)(4).

132. *See Immigrant Numbers for May 1997*, VISA BULL. (Bureau of Consular Affairs, U.S. Dep't of State, Washington, D.C.), May 1997, at 1, 2.

133. *See* INA § 203(a)(3), 8 U.S.C.A. § 1153(a)(3).

134. *See Immigrant Numbers for May 1997*, *supra* note 132, at 2.

135. *See* Stephen H. Legomsky, *Immigration, Equality and Diversity*, 31 COLUM. J. TRANSNAT'L L. 319, 333 (1993) ("[T]he Mexican individual is treated *less* favorably than his or her Austrian counterpart, because the per-country limit already subjects immigrants from high-demand countries to longer waits.") (emphasis in original); Ting, *supra* note 93, at 308 (contending that per-country caps disparately affect immigrants from Asia, many whom face long waits to immigrate). Some restrictionists recognize, and in fact embrace, the racial impacts. *See* LAMM & IMHOFF, *supra* note 129, at 21-22 (noting that "[c]ountry ceilings on legal immigration exist only to ensure that there is a mixture in our migrant stream, that no one country or group of countries will again dominate the stream to the exclusion of others").

Some might argue that the family reunification policy underlying the INA, *see* LEGOMSKY, *supra* note 130, at 168-70, erroneously favors immigrants from nations with larger families, which is the case in many developing nations populated by people of color. *See* ROY BECK, THE

Other changes to the immigration laws reflect racial concerns. Many have lauded the Refugee Act of 1980,[136] which for the very first time created a general right to apply for asylum in the United States for noncitizens fleeing political and related persecution in their homelands.[137] The Act, however, was motivated in part by a desire to limit the number of Vietnamese refugees accepted by the United States, whom the President had admitted liberally after the fall of Saigon in 1975.[138] The law established numerical limits on refugee admissions and generally restricted the power of the President to admit refugees, with the hope of preventing future mass migrations. Years after Congress passed the law, Vietnamese citizens brought suit charging that the U.S. Government discriminates against them based on nationality in processing visa applications.[139]

Similarly, the immigration laws allow for the exclusion of persons likely to become public charges,[140] an inadmissibility ground given more teeth in 1996 amendments to the immigration laws.[141] The public charge exclusion has a disproportionate effect on noncitizens of color from developing nations.[142]

CASE AGAINST IMMIGRATION 40-41 (1996); LAMM & IMHOFF, *supra* note 129, at 192-93; *see also* BRIMELOW, *supra* note 5, at 79-81 (advocating change to family reunification policy). They claim that this results in "chain migration." However, "[t]he extent to which . . . 'chain migration' really takes place is hotly disputed." ALEINIKOFF ET AL., *supra* note 67, at 191 (citing authorities).

136. Pub. L. No. 96-212, 94 Stat. 102 (codified in scattered sections of 8, 22, and 42 U.S.C.).

137. *See, e.g.*, 126 CONG. REC. 4501 (1980) (comments of Rep. Rodino) (characterizing this law as "one of the most important pieces of humanitarian legislation ever enacted").

138. *See* Deborah E. Anker & Michael H. Posner, *The Forty Year Crisis: A Legislative History of the Refugee Act of 1980*, 19 SAN DIEGO L. REV. 9, 34 (1981) (reviewing legislative history of Refugee Act and concluding that "commitment [to numerical limits on refugee admissions] reflected a growing antagonism within the United States to increased immigration in general, a feeling crystallized by the very large number of Indochinese admitted into the country since 1975"); *see also* GIL LOESCHER & JOHN A. SCANLAN, CALCULATED KINDNESS 102-69 (1986) (documenting growing public concern from 1975 to 1980 with the large number of Indochinese refugees resettling in the United States and general fear of mass migration).

139. *See* Legal Assistance for Vietnamese Asylum Seekers v. Department of State, 104 F.3d 1349 (D.C. Cir. 1997) (dismissing claims on jurisdictional grounds).

140. *See* INA § 212(a)(4)(A), 8 U.S.C.A. § 1182(a)(4)(A) (West Supp. 1998) ("Any alien . . . likely at any time to become a public charge is inadmissible.").

141. *See* Juan P. Osuna, *The 1996 Immigration Act: Affidavits of Support and Public Benefits*, 74 INTERPRETER RELEASES 317 (1997) (summarizing changes to the public charge inadmissibility ground in the 1996 amendments to immigration laws).

142. *See* Charles Wheeler, *The New Affidavit of Support and Sponsorship Requirements*, 74 INTERPRETER RELEASES 1581, 1590-91 (1997) (noting that certain nationality groups, particularly Mexicans and Central Americans, will be disparately affected by new income requirements (125% of poverty level) imposed on sponsors of immigrants by Congress in 1996, in INA § 213A(f)(1), 8 U.S.C.A. § 1183a(f)(1)) (citing Michael Fix & Wendy Zimmermann, *Welfare Reform: A New Immigrant Policy for the U.S.* (Apr. 1997) (report commercially available from the Urban Institute, Washington, D.C.)). *See generally* Kevin R. Johnson, *Public Benefits and Immigration: The Intersection of Immigration Status, Ethnicity, Gender, and Class*, 42 UCLA L. REV. 1509, 1519-28 (1995) (summarizing the history of the public charge exclusion and deportation grounds and other racial impacts).

For a recent example of alleged discrimination in the granting of visas to noncitizens, see

Passed before the heated immigration debates of the 1990s, the Immigration Act of 1990 reflects congressional concerns with the racial composition of the immigrant stream.[143] The law created a new immigrant visa program that effectively represents affirmative action for white immigrants, a group that benefitted from preferential treatment under the national origins quota system until 1965.[144] Congress, in an ironic twist of political jargon, established the "diversity" visa program, which though facially neutral prefers immigrants from nations populated primarily by white people.[145] As congressional proponents envisioned, many Irish immigrated under the program.[146] Indeed, a transitional diversity program required that forty percent of the visas would be issued to Irish immigrants.[147] In fiscal year 1995, the leading source of immigrants under the permanent diversity visa program was Poland.[148]

In short, the modern immigration laws have disparate racial impacts. As Professor Howard Chang has observed in a related vein, "[n]ativism . . . is not merely a shameful feature of our past . . . . Nativism afflicts our politics *today*,

---

Olsen v. Albright, 990 F. Supp. 31 (D.D.C. 1997) (granting summary judgment in favor of State Department consular officer, formerly based in Brazil, who claimed he was unlawfully terminated for failing to discriminate on basis of visa applicant's race, ethnicity, national origin, economic class, and physical appearance).

143. Pub. L. No. 101-649, 104 Stat. 4978 (codified as amended primarily in scattered sections of 8 U.S.C.).

144. *See id.*, sec. 131, 104 Stat. at 4997-99 (codified as amended at INA § 203(c), 8 U.S.C.A. § 1153(c)); *see also* Legomsky, *supra* note 135, at 321 ("[T]he diversity program is merely the latest in a series of congressional attempts, spanning more than a century, to influence the ethnic composition of the United States immigrant stream.") (footnote omitted).

145. *See* LEGOMSKY, *supra* note 130, at 204-10 (explaining the genesis and operation of diversity visa program). "Since many more Americans already trace their ancestry to Europe than to Asia or Latin America, the statutory 'diversity' program is in truth an '*anti-diversity*' program; it causes the resulting population mix to be *less* diverse than it would otherwise be." *Id.* at 210 (emphasis in original); *see also* Ting, *supra* note 93, at 309 ("The expansion of diversity visas as part of the Immigration Act of 1990 reflects continuing Congressional unhappiness with the predominantly Asian and Latin American character of immigration and corresponding satisfaction with the success of diversity visa programs in leavening the immigration mix with more Europeans and other Caucasians."). Before passage of the 1990 Act, Congress tinkered with a pilot "diversity" program. *See* ALEINIKOFF ET AL., *supra* note 67, at 130 (noting that the Immigration Reform & Control Act of 1986, Pub. L. No. 96-603, 100 Stat. 3359 (codified as amended primarily in 8 and 42 U.S.C.), created pilot diversity visa program "to ameliorate the steep reduction in European migration that [was a] byproduct of the 1965 amendments"); Legomsky, *supra* note 135, at 329-30 (explaining temporary predecessors to diversity visa program of Immigration Act of 1990 and explaining how diversity visas are allocated).

146. *Compare* Patricia I. Folan Sebben, Note, *U.S. Immigration Law, Irish Immigrants and Diversity: Céad Míle Fáilte (A Thousand Times Welcome?)*, 6 GEO. IMMIGR. L.J. 745 (1992) (recognizing and defending the diversity immigrant program's benefits to Irish), *with* Walter P. Jacob, Note, *Diversity Visas: Muddled Thinking and Pork Barrel Politics*, 6 GEO. IMMIGR. L.J. 297 (1992) (reviewing the legislative history of 1990 Act, demonstrating how diversity visas were designed to benefit Irish, and criticizing the program).

147. *See* 1995 INS STATISTICAL YEARBOOK, *supra* note 128, at 21.

148. *See id.*

posing a clear and present danger of new anti-immigrant legislation."[149] The same is true for racial discrimination in the immigration laws. Other examples bring this point home.

1. The War on "Illegal Aliens" a/k/a Mexican Immigrants

One cannot fully appreciate the current debate over undocumented immigration in the United States without understanding how it fits into a long history. Especially in the Southwest,[150] the immigration laws have helped ensure a disposable labor force.[151] For example, during the Great Depression when the supply of unskilled labor dwarfed demand, Mexican immigrants as well as citizens of Mexican ancestry were "repatriated" to Mexico at the behest of governmental authorities.[152] Later, under the Bracero Program in the 1940s and 1950s, an estimated one million Mexican workers were temporarily admitted into the country to work in agriculture.[153]

At times, the call for immigration restrictions has been expressly anti-Mexican. For example, in 1956, the Duke Law School's *Law & Contemporary Problems* published an article ironically entitled "A Critical Analysis of the Wetback Problem,"[154] which referred to the 1950s as the "wetback decade" and blamed undocumented immigration from Mexico with "displacement of American workers, depressed wages, increased racial discrimination toward Americans of Mexican ancestry, illiteracy, disease, and lawlessness."[155] Though the term "wetbacks" has been replaced in today's parlance with "illegal aliens," the

---

149. Howard F. Chang, *Immigration Policy, Liberal Principles, and the Republican Tradition*, 85 GEO. L.J. 2105, 2115 (1997) (emphasis in original).

150. *See generally* ACUÑA, *supra* note 38; CAREY MCWILLIAMS, NORTH FROM MEXICO (rev. ed. 1990).

151. *See generally* MARIO BARRERA, RACE AND CLASS IN THE SOUTHWEST (1979) (analyzing history of labor control devices used in Southwest). For a summary of the history of Mexican immigration to the United States and an argument that the United States owes moral obligations to undocumented Mexican immigrants living in the country, see Gerald P. López, *Undocumented Mexican Migration: In Search of a Just Immigration Law and Policy*, 28 UCLA L. REV. 615 (1981).

152. *See* FRANCISCO E. BALDERRAMA & RAYMOND RODRÍGUEZ, DECADE OF BETRAYAL: MEXICAN REPATRIATION IN THE 1930S, at 98-99 (1995) (analyzing deportation of persons of Mexican ancestry during Great Depression).

153. *See* KITTY CALAVITA, INSIDE THE STATE 218 (1992) (analyzing and criticizing U.S. Government's role in the program of ensuring control over Mexican labor). For a summary of the anti-Mexican policies during this period, see Michael A. Olivas, *The Chronicle, My Grandfather's Stories, and Immigration Law: The Slave Traders Chronicles as Racial History*, 34 ST. LOUIS U. L.J. 425, 435-39 (1990).

154. Eleanor M. Hadley, *A Critical Analysis of the Wetback Problem*, 21 LAW & CONTEMP. PROBS. 334 (1956). The pejorative term "wetback" was commonplace vernacular at the time and present in legal as well as popular discourse. *See, e.g.*, Henry M. Hart, Jr., *The Power of Congress to Limit the Jurisdiction of the Federal Courts: An Exercise in Dialectic*, 66 HARV. L. REV. 1362, 1395 (1953) (lamenting dicta in Supreme Court decision "say[ing], in effect, that a *Mexican wetback* who sneaks successfully across the Rio Grande is entitled to the full panoply of due process in his deportation") (emphasis added).

155. Hadley, *supra* note 154, at 344.

modern restrictionist movement plays on remarkably similar—though often sanitized—themes.[156]

Despite the fact that undocumented persons come from nations all over the world, the near exclusive focus of governmental and public attention at the tail end of the twentieth century has been on undocumented immigration from Mexico.[157] The racial impact of the recent push to crack down on "illegal aliens" is unmistakable.[158] Well-publicized border enforcement operations, little different from military operations, in El Paso, Texas (Operation Blockade, later renamed Operation Hold the Line due to protests from the Mexican Government)[159] and San Diego, California (Operation Gatekeeper)[160] have been aimed at sealing the U.S.-Mexico border and keeping undocumented Mexican citizens from entering the United States.[161] Indeed, U.S. military forces assisted the Immigration & Naturalization Service (INS) in policing the border.[162] At the same time, reported abuses against Mexican nationals along the border continue unabated.[163] For example, in 1997, a U.S. Marine on patrol shot and killed a teenager, Esequiel Hernandez, Jr. (a U.S. citizen who had no criminal record) while he was herding his family's goats near the border.[164] The U.S. General

156. *See, e.g.*, BRIMELOW, *supra* note 5, at 262-63 (expressing similar concerns in arguing for dramatic reductions in levels of immigration).

157. *See* 1995 INS STATISTICAL YEARBOOK, *supra* note 128, at 185-86 (estimating that, as of October 1996, about 54% of the undocumented population was of Mexican origin and that 15 countries contributed 50,000 or more persons to undocumented population in the United States).

158. For analysis of the importance of language as a tool for rationalizing limitations on the rights of noncitizens under the immigration laws, see Kevin R. Johnson, *"Aliens" and the U.S. Immigration Laws: The Social and Legal Construction of Nonpersons*, 28 U. MIAMI INTER-AM. L. REV. 263 (1996-97).

159. *See* U.S. COMM'N ON IMMIGRATION REFORM, U.S. IMMIGRATION POLICY: RESTORING CREDIBILITY 10-19 (1994) (lauding Operation Hold the Line in El Paso and advocating expansion of this enforcement strategy).

160. *See President's Report Reviews Initiatives, "Accepts Immigration Challenge"*, 71 INTERPRETER RELEASES 1469 (1994) (describing operation).

161. *See generally* TIMOTHY J. DUNN, THE MILITARIZATION OF THE U.S.-MEXICO BORDER, 1978-1992 (1996) (documenting increased militarization of border enforcement).

162. *See* H.G. Reza, *Military Silently Patrols U.S. Border*, L.A. TIMES, June 29, 1997, at A3 (reporting on National Guard unit patrolling U.S.-Mexico border).

163. *See* U.S. COMM'N ON CIVIL RIGHTS, FEDERAL IMMIGRATION LAW ENFORCEMENT IN THE SOUTHWEST 80 (1997) (reporting on evidence of pattern of violence by Border Patrol); Amnesty Int'l, *United States of America: Human Rights Concerns in the Border Region with Mexico* (visited May 26, 1998) <http://www.amnesty.org/ailib/aipub/1998/AMR/25100398 .htm> (documenting human rights abuses by INS); *see also* ALFREDO MIRANDÉ, GRINGO JUSTICE 100-45 (1987) (analyzing abuses of Chicanos in name of border enforcement); Bill Ong Hing, *Border Patrol Abuse: Evaluating Complaint Procedures Available to Victims*, 9 GEO. IMMIGR. L.J. 757 (1995) (analyzing need for improved complaint procedure for Border Patrol abuses).

164. *See* Sam Howe Verhovek, *After Marine on Patrol Kills a Teen-Ager, a Texas Border Village Wonders Why*, N.Y. TIMES, June 29, 1997, § 1, at 16. An archeologist who knew Hernandez his entire life commented that "'I'm telling you, the only way they could have botched this up more was if they shot Mother Teresa. If there was one truly innocent man on the border, it was this young man. And he's the one who got killed.'" *Id.*; *see also* Elvia R.

Accounting Office found that, despite the border enforcement build-up, the evidence was inconclusive about whether the strategy had proven effective.[165]

Public concern with undocumented Mexican immigration heightened at the same time that the population of persons of Mexican ancestry grew in the United States.[166] In return, the resistance of Mexican Americans to anti-immigrant sentiment represents a fight for status. Similar to the often-heated debate over bilingual education[167] and crime,[168] restrictionist proposals are but another battlefield for Anglos and Mexican Americans to fight for status in the U.S. social hierarchy.[169]

Besides conflict over social status, Mexican Americans, and Latinos more generally, have a self-interest in fighting overzealous border enforcement. In the fervor to locate and deport undocumented Mexican citizens, Mexican Americans, often stereotyped as "foreigners" by the national community, may fall within the enforcement net.[170] In the infamous deportation campaign known as "Operation Wetback" in 1954, for example, "[t]he Mexican American community was affected because the campaign was aimed at only one racial group, which meant that the burden of proving one's citizenship fell totally upon people of Mexican descent. Those unable to present such proof were arrested and returned to Mexico."[171] Similarly, evidence suggests that provisions of the immigration laws

---

Arriola, *LatCrit Theory, International Human Rights, Popular Culture, and the Faces of Despair in INS Raids*, 28 U. MIAMI INTER-AM. L. REV. 245, 256-62 (1996-97) (relaying human stories of undocumented Mexican immigrants in INS workplace raids).

165. *See* U.S. GEN. ACCOUNTING OFFICE, GAO/GGD-98-21, ILLEGAL IMMIGRATION: SOUTHWEST BORDER STRATEGY RESULTS INCONCLUSIVE; MORE EVALUATION NEEDED (1997).

166. *See* FREDRIC C. GEY ET AL., CALIFORNIA LATINA/LATINO DEMOGRAPHIC DATA BOOK 8-9 tbls.1-2 to 1-3 (1993) (examining data showing that the population of California was 19% Latino in 1980 and 25% in 1990, with 80% of the Latinos in 1990 identifying themselves as of Mexican ancestry). The Bureau of the Census has projected that "Hispanics" will be the largest minority group in the United States by 2005. *See* Katharine Q. Seelye, *U.S. of Future: Grayer and More Hispanic*, N.Y. TIMES, Mar. 27, 1997, at B16.

167. *See generally* Rachel F. Moran, *Bilingual Education as a Status Conflict*, 75 CAL. L. REV. 321 (1987) (analyzing controversy over bilingual education as conflict over status between Anglos and Latinos).

168. *See, e.g.*, People *ex rel.* Gallo v. Acuna, 14 Cal. 4th 1090 (1997) (upholding broad injunction limiting conduct of Latino "gang" members not convicted of any crime).

169. *Cf.* John Cassidy, *The Melting-Pot Myth*, NEW YORKER, July 14, 1997, at 40, 40 ("The immigration debate has become a surrogate for arguments about everything from eugenics to welfare reform to economic growth."). For analysis of the conflict over status and its relevance to constitutional interpretation, see J.M. Balkin, *The Constitution of Status*, 106 YALE L.J. 2313 (1997).

170. *See* Kevin R. Johnson, *Some Thoughts on the Future of Latino Legal Scholarship*, 2 HARV. LATINO L. REV. 101, 117-29 (1997) (analyzing significance of classification of Latinos as "foreigners"); *see also* Luis Angel Toro, *"A People Distinct from Others": Race and Identity in Federal Indian Law and the Hispanic Classification in OMB Directive No. 15*, 26 TEX. TECH L. REV. 1219, 1245-51 (1995) (summarizing history of racialization of Chicanos in United States).

171. JUAN RAMON GARCÍA, OPERATION WETBACK 230-31 (1980); *see* JULIAN SAMORA, LOS MOJADOS: THE WETBACK STORY 52 (1971) (noting that in "Operation Wetback," "the Border Patrol launched the greatest maximum peacetime offensive against a highly exploited, unorganized and unstructured 'invading force' of Mexican migrants").

that allow for the imposition of sanctions on those who employ undocumented persons,[172] have resulted in "'a serious pattern of discrimination'" by employers against persons of Latin American, as well as Asian, ancestry.[173]

The historical relationship between subordination of Mexican Americans, a "foreign" minority, and African Americans, viewed as a domestic minority, is telling. During the New Deal, while the government scrambled to help citizens and provided public benefits to citizens who satisfied eligibility requirements,[174] Mexican American citizens as well as Mexican immigrants were effectively deported to Mexico.[175] In 1954, the same year that the Supreme Court handed down the much-lauded *Brown v. Board of Education*[176] decision, the U.S. Government commenced "Operation Wetback," the mass-deportation campaign directed at undocumented Mexicans.[177] Ironically, the war on Mexican immigrants, as well as Mexican American citizens, began at the same time that the formal legal rights of African Americans were finally being recognized. At that time, it was far from clear that the Equal Protection Clause of the Fourteenth Amendment on which *Brown* rested even protected Mexican Americans.[178]

---

172. *See* U.S. COMM'N ON IMMIGRATION REFORM, *supra* note 159, at 50-88 (finding current enforcement of employer sanctions to be ineffective); *see also* Cecelia M. Espenoza, *The Illusory Provisions of Sanctions: The Immigration Reform and Control Act of 1986*, 8 GEO. IMMIGR. L.J. 343 (1994) (arguing for elimination of sanctions because of their ineffectiveness and because they have increased discrimination against persons of Mexican ancestry).

173. U.S. GEN. ACCOUNTING OFFICE, GAO/GGD-90-62, IMMIGRATION REFORM: EMPLOYER SANCTIONS AND THE QUESTION OF DISCRIMINATION 5-6 (1990) (quoting a nationwide GAO survey); *see* U.S. COMM'N ON CIVIL RIGHTS, THE IMMIGRATION REFORM AND CONTROL ACT at iv (1989) (finding "no doubt that the employer sanctions have caused many employers to implement discriminatory hiring practices"). Such discrimination occurs despite the existence of provisions prohibiting it. *See* INA § 274B, 8 U.S.C.A. § 1324b (West Supp. 1998).

174. *See* WILLIAM C. BERMAN, THE POLITICS OF CIVIL RIGHTS IN THE TRUMAN ADMINISTRATION 4 (1970) ("Negroes voted for Roosevelt in 1936 and 1940 largely because their economic deprivation, stemming from unemployment and discrimination, had been lessened through the work of [the] . . . New Deal agencies . . . ."); *see also* WALTER I. TRATTNER, FROM POOR LAW TO WELFARE STATE 249-75 (4th ed. 1989) (summarizing various social welfare programs developed for citizens during New Deal). Indeed, "in spite of the large number of white women on [welfare], 'welfare' . . . has become a '. . . code word' for race. And the 'typical' [welfare] mother is widely—though erroneously—believed to be an unmarried, unemployed urban woman of color with many children." Lucie E. White, *No Exit: Rethinking "Welfare Dependency" from a Different Ground*, 81 GEO. L.J. 1961, 1966 (1993) (omission added) (quoting Marian Wright Edelman, head of the Washington-based Children's Defense Fund). This is not to suggest that the administration of welfare during the New Deal was racially neutral. *See* FRANCES FOX PIVEN & RICHARD A. CLOWARD, REGULATING THE POOR 133-35 (2d ed. 1993) (discussing racial discrimination by southern states administering the federal welfare program).

175. *See supra* text accompanying note 152.

176. 347 U.S. 483 (1954).

177. *See supra* text accompanying note 171.

178. *See* Hernandez v. Texas, 347 U.S. 475 (1954) (reversing finding that Mexican Americans failed to constitute a cognizable class for equal protection purposes); *see also* Ian F. Haney López, *Race, Ethnicity, Erasure: The Salience of Race to LatCrit Theory*, 85 CAL. L. REV. 1143 (1997) (analyzing *Hernandez* in terms of racialization of Mexican Americans in Texas); George A. Martínez, *The Legal Construction of Race: Mexican-Americans and*

During a period when the law promised (though perhaps failed to deliver) new legal protections to African Americans, a legally sanctioned deportation campaign struck with a vengeance at persons of Mexican ancestry.

2. Asylum, Haitian Interdiction, and the Politics of Race

U.S. law and policy toward noncitizens who have fled civil war, political and other persecution, and genocide in their native lands historically have been influenced by nativism and racism. Domestic anti-Semitism, for example, unfortunately contributed to the Roosevelt administration's decision to turn its back on Jewish refugees fleeing the horrors of Nazi Germany.[179] Congress passed the Refugee Act of 1980, among more humanitarian purposes, with the hope of reducing the number of refugees that the President admitted from Vietnam.[180]

It has not only been race, however, that has influenced U.S. refugee and asylum policy. Persons from China and Cuba, for example, in the latter half of the twentieth century received generous treatment from the U.S. Government in no small part due to foreign policy concerns, namely that the U.S. Government was at odds with the government of their homelands; admitting refugees from China and Cuba implicitly condemned their governments.[181] The United States generally denied asylum to Central Americans fleeing regimes with abominable human rights records that were U.S. allies, while granting relief to Poles fleeing a harsh communist government at odds with our own.[182]

Policy conflicts occasionally resulted in confused and inconsistent U.S. policies. For example, the treatment of Chinese refugees, including many who claimed persecution because of resistance to China's one-child rule, was erratic at best.[183] This results from the fact that, while foreign policy interests favored

---

Whiteness, 2 HARV. LATINO L. REV. 321, 328 (1997) (analyzing lower court decision in *Hernandez* and treatment of Mexican Americans under law as "white" to their disadvantage).

179. *See supra* text accompanying notes 108-09.

180. *See supra* text accompanying notes 136-38.

181. *See generally* LOESCHER & SCANLAN, *supra* note 138, at 6-84 (documenting how various presidents employed asylum and refugee decisions to further U.S. foreign policy goals).

182. *See* Kevin R. Johnson, *A "Hard Look" at the Executive Branch's Asylum Decisions*, 1991 UTAH L. REV. 279, 343-48 (presenting statistical data reflecting phenomenon); *see also* Joan Fitzpatrick & Robert Pauw, *Foreign Policy, Asylum and Discretion*, 28 WILLAMETTE L. REV. 751 (1992) (analyzing impact of foreign policy on asylum and refugee decisions); Katherine L. Vaughns, *Taming the Asylum Adjudication Process: An Agenda for the Twenty-First Century*, 30 SAN DIEGO L. REV. 1, 28 (1993) (noting that, although Refugee Act "was hailed as a significant milestone in human rights, . . . the widely held view [is] that the present system is politically biased, compromising the intended goal of neutrality").

183. *See* Di v. Carroll, 842 F. Supp. 858, 866-67 (E.D. Va. 1994) (tracing inconsistency in treatment by U.S. Government of Chinese persons fleeing one-child rule), *rev'd without opinion*, 66 F.3d 315 (4th Cir. 1995). Congress in 1996 changed the law to expressly make persons fleeing such policies eligible for relief. *See* INA § 101(a)(42), 8 U.S.C.A. § 1101(a)(42) (West Supp. 1998) (as amended by the Illegal Immigration Reform and Immigrant Responsibility Act of 1996, Pub. L. No. 104-208, sec. 601(a)(1), 110 Stat. 3009, 3689, which provides that a person who has been subject to, or fears being subject to, forced abortion or involuntary sterilization, is deemed to have been persecuted on account of political opinion and therefore is eligible for asylum).

liberal admissions (and thus implicitly condemned China's communist government), domestic fears militated in favor of numerical limits. The U.S. Government initially showed sympathy for Chinese refugees.[184] However, fearing a mass migration from China in the 1990s, the executive branch began to detain all Chinese migrants who came to the United States on ships, including the much-publicized Golden Venture in 1993, and to interdict Chinese ships outside U.S. territorial waters before they reached the mainland.[185]

Despite the fluctuations on policy, the U.S. Government not infrequently went to extraordinary lengths to halt feared mass migrations of people of color. It implemented special detention policies directed at Central Americans and made concerted efforts to encourage potential asylum applicants to forego their claims and "voluntarily" depart.[186] No U.S. policy approached, however, the government's extraordinary treatment of Black persons fleeing the political violence in Haiti. An oft-ignored fact is that, by stigmatizing African American citizens, "U.S. immigration policy toward Haiti may *harm* a historically disadvantaged group—namely, black Americans."[187]

For much of recent history, the U.S. Government generally has supported the Haitian Government, in large part because the various regimes were stridently anticommunist.[188] In stark contrast, both Democratic and Republican administrations have had notoriously poor relations with Haiti's neighbor, Cuba, since Fidel Castro came to power in 1959. The different relationships visibly influenced asylum and refugee policy toward persons fleeing the two nations: Cubans received much more favorable treatment than Haitians.[189]

---

184. *See, e.g., In re* Chen, 20 I. & N. Dec. (BIA) 16 (1989) (granting asylum to Chinese refugee based on past persecution during Cultural Revolution despite minimal threat of future persecution).

185. *See* Ting, *supra* note 93, at 310-11 (contending that treatment of Chinese immigrants on Golden Venture and interdiction of Chinese ships represent selective enforcement of immigration laws to limit Asian immigration); *see, e.g.*, Zhang v. Slattery, 55 F.3d 732 (2d Cir. 1995) (affirming denial of asylum claim of Chinese national apprehended on Golden Venture); Chai v. Carroll, 48 F.3d 1331 (4th Cir. 1995) (same).

186. *See* Orantes-Hernandez v. Thornburgh, 919 F.2d 549 (9th Cir. 1990) (affirming permanent injunction barring INS from engaging in a pattern and practice of coercing Salvadoran noncitizens into signing voluntary departure forms and interfering with right to counsel); *see also* ROBERT S. KAHN, OTHER PEOPLE'S BLOOD 209-19 (1996) (documenting increased use of detention by INS in the 1980s, particularly detention of Central Americans).

187. Motomura, *supra* note 99, at 1950 (emphasis in original); *see infra* text accompanying notes 242-60 (analyzing stigma attached to domestic minorities when immigration law excludes immigrants sharing similar ancestry).

188. *See* THOMAS CAROTHERS, IN THE NAME OF DEMOCRACY 183 (1991); *see also* Jorge I. Domínguez, *Immigration as Foreign Policy in U.S.-Latin American Relations*, *in* IMMIGRATION AND U.S. FOREIGN POLICY 150, 157-58 (Robert W. Tucker et al. eds., 1990) (discussing the U.S. Government's relationship with Haiti).

189. *See* Kevin R. Johnson, *Judicial Acquiescence to the Executive Branch's Pursuit of Foreign Policy and Domestic Agendas in Immigration Matters: The Case of the Haitian Asylum-Seekers*, 7 GEO. IMMIGR. L.J. 1, 12-14 (1993) (analyzing significance of double standard). This has not always been the case. For example, refugees who came over in large numbers on the Mariel boatlift were detained with some even facing indefinite detention because the United States would not admit them, and the Cuban Government would not allow

In the late 1970s, an increasing number of Haitians in makeshift boats sailed to south Florida. In 1981, the Reagan administration, to diminish the flow of refugees and to deter others from following, initiated a program in which the U.S. Coast Guard interdicted Haitian boats and allowed INS officers to screen applicants to determine whether they had plausible claims for asylum and withholding of deportation.[190] Between 1981 and 1991, the Coast Guard interdicted about 25,000 Haitians.[191]

After the military coup toppled the democratically elected government in September 1991, the Bush administration imposed economic sanctions on Haiti and suspended interdiction; in November 1991, interdiction recommenced.[192] As a result of the coup, "'hundreds of Haitians [were] killed, tortured, detained without a warrant, or subjected to violence and the destruction of their property because of their political beliefs. Thousands [were] forced into hiding.'"[193] In the six months after October 1991, the Coast Guard halted over 34,000 Haitians on

---

them to return. *See, e.g.*, Barrera-Echavarria v. Rison, 44 F.3d 1441 (9th Cir. 1995) (en banc) (upholding indefinite detention of Cuban national who came to the United States in Mariel boatlift). *See generally* Richard A. Boswell, *Rethinking Exclusion—The Rights of Cuban Refugees Facing Indefinite Detention in the United States*, 17 VAND. J. TRANSNAT'L L. 925 (1984) (discussing the detention of Cubans arriving since 1980); Mark D. Kemple, Note, *Legal Fictions Mask Human Suffering: The Detention of the Mariel Cubans*, 62 S. CAL. L. REV. 1733 (1989) (summarizing the intolerable conditions Cuban detainees must endure during confinement). One salient difference between the Mariel Cubans and previous Cuban immigrants was that many more of the Mariel Cubans were Black. *See* MARÍA CRISTINA GARCÍA, HAVANA USA 68 (1996) (observing that 15-40% of Mariel Cubans were Black compared to 3% of the 1959-1973 stream of Cuban immigrants). Race thus helps explain the differential treatment of distinct waves of Cuban immigrants.

In 1994, the U.S. and Cuban Governments agreed to take steps to limit migration from Cuba to the United States. *See* LEGOMSKY, *supra* note 130, at 58-62 (summarizing evolution of U.S. policy toward persons fleeing Cuba). The United States' willingness to enter the agreement was influenced by concerns of a mass migration. *See id.* at 61-62 (observing that nations agreed to treaty after "new exodus" of "[t]housands of rafters" embarked for the United States).

190. *See* Sale v. Haitian Ctrs. Council, Inc., 509 U.S. 155, 160-62 (1993) (describing evolution in U.S. Government's treatment of Haitians during the 1980s and early 1990s). Under U.S. law, Haitians, once in the country, could have applied for asylum and withholding of deportation (now known as nonreturn). *See* INA § 208(a)(1), 8 U.S.C.A. § 1158(a)(1) (West Supp. 1998) (asylum); *id.* § 241(b)(3)(A), 8 U.S.C.A. § 1231(b)(3)(A) (nonreturn). Claims were made that screening on Coast Guard cutters was insufficient to satisfy obligations under international law to protect Haitians fleeing persecution. *See* Arthur C. Helton, *The Mandate of U.S. Courts to Protect Aliens and Refugees Under International Human Rights Law*, 100 YALE L.J. 2335, 2341 (1991).

For challenges to other policies directed specifically at Haitian asylum-seekers, see *Jean v. Nelson*, 472 U.S. 846 (1985) (reviewing claims of racial and national origin discrimination and finding that applicable regulation did not permit such discrimination), *Haitian Refugee Center v. Civiletti*, 503 F. Supp. 442 (S.D. Fla. 1980), *aff'd as modified sub nom. Haitian Refugee Center v. Smith*, 676 F.2d 1023 (5th Cir. 1982) (finding discrimination by INS in processing asylum claims of Haitians), and *Louis v. Meissner*, 530 F. Supp. 924 (S.D. Fla. 1981) (finding to the same effect as *Haitian Refugee Center*).

191. *See Sale*, 509 U.S. at 161.

192. *See id.* at 162.

193. *Id.* (alterations added) (quoting district court's "uncontested finding of fact").

the high seas,[194] which exceeded the number interdicted during the previous ten years.[195]

To stop the flow of refugees, President Bush in May 1992 began immediately repatriating all Haitians without screening to determine whether they might be eligible to remain in the United States.[196] Despite campaign promises to the contrary, President Clinton continued Haitian interdiction and repatriation and forcefully defended the policy against legal challenge.[197]

The Supreme Court ultimately upheld the executive branch's unprecedented Haitian repatriation policy.[198] The Court did so without squarely addressing the claim made in an amicus curiae brief of the NAACP, TransAfrica, and the Congressional Black Caucus that the policy was discriminatory and that the Haitians were subject to "separate and unequal" treatment.[199]

Besides African American activist groups, others condemned the executive branch's harsh policies toward the Haitians as race-based.[200] True enough, people of color from Haiti apparently were the first group of refugees ever singled out for interdiction on the high seas by U.S. armed forces, as well as for a series of extraordinary policies.[201] The issue is complex, however. Cubans, who have received much more favorable treatment, also are people of color. The executive branch's foreign policy goals, in addition to race and concerns of a mass migration, may explain the disparate treatment between Haitians and Cubans.[202]

---

194. *See id.* at 163.

195. *See id.* at 161 (stating that, in decade after commencement of interdiction in 1981, "the Coast Guard interdicted approximately 25,000 Haitian migrants") (footnote omitted).

196. *See* Exec. Order No. 12,807, 3 C.F.R. 303 (1993), *reprinted in* 8 U.S.C. § 1182 (1994).

197. *See* Elaine Sciolino, *Clinton Says U.S. Will Continue Ban on Haitian Exodus*, N.Y. TIMES, Jan. 15, 1993, at A1.

198. *See Sale*, 509 U.S. at 188. In so doing, the Court relied on a version of the plenary power doctrine. *See id.* (emphasizing need for deference to President when "construing treaty and statutory provisions that may involve foreign and military affairs") (citing United States v. Curtiss-Wright Export Corp., 299 U.S. 304 (1936)).

199. *See* Brief of the National Association for the Advancement of Colored People, TransAfrica, and the Congressional Black Caucus as Amici Curiae in Support of Respondents, *Sale*, 509 U.S. 155 (No. 92-344).

200. *See* Joyce A. Hughes & Linda R. Crane, *Haitians: Seeking Refuge in the United States*, 7 GEO. IMMIGR. L.J. 747, 749 & n.12 (1993); Malissia Lennox, Note, *Refugees, Racism, and Reparations: A Critique of the United States' Haitian Immigration Policy*, 45 STAN. L. REV. 687, 688 (1993); *see also* Haitian Refugee Ctr. v. Civiletti, 503 F. Supp. 442, 451 (S.D. Fla. 1980) (stating that a "possible underlying reason" why Haitians were treated differently than any other refugees fleeing repressive regimes was that they are Black), *aff'd as modified sub nom.* Haitian Refugee Ctr. v. Smith, 676 F.2d 1023 (5th Cir. 1982).

201. *See* SARAH IGNATIUS, NATIONAL ASYLUM STUDY PROJECT, AN ASSESSMENT OF THE ASYLUM PROCESS OF THE IMMIGRATION AND NATURALIZATION SERVICE 141-66 (1993) (documenting special policies geared only toward Haitian asylum applicants by INS asylum officers).

202. *See supra* text accompanying notes 181-82. This suggests a hierarchy of racial discrimination in the United States, with the strongest racist sentiment directed at persons of African ancestry. *See* Saito, *supra* note 92 (analyzing racial hierarchy in the United States); *see also* Linda Kelly, Defying Membership: The Evolving Role of Immigration Jurisprudence 53-58 (unpublished manuscript on file with author) (analyzing Nicaraguan Adjustment and Central

Nonetheless, subtle racism inevitably reduced the potential for significant resistance to an interdiction program directed exclusively at Haitian refugees. As law professor Steve Legomsky declared, "'[t]he public would never [have stood] for this if the boat people were Europeans.'"[203] The race, class, language, and culture of the Haitians, as well as the popular belief that many had the HIV virus, unquestionably contributed to the domestic resistance to their admission.[204]

In the end, asylum-seekers from Haiti, one of the few nations near the United States with a large Black population, suffered some of the harshest treatment imaginable from the U.S. Government. The Supreme Court's sanctioning of that treatment occurred in the aftermath of the violence in Los Angeles after the Rodney King verdict,[205] a time when the nation's focus was on building racial harmony to avoid a repeat of violence in the future.[206] At the same historic moment, the nation was striving to improve the place of African Americans at home while it was excluding Blacks from abroad.

3. Proposition 187 and Race

Race played a prominent role in the passage of California's Proposition 187, one of the racial milestones of the 1990s.[207] To bolster his sagging re-election campaign, California Governor Pete Wilson capitalized on public dissatisfaction with immigration by staunchly supporting the initiative. Television advertisements emphasizing Wilson's unqualified support for Proposition 187 showed shadowy Mexicans crossing the border in large numbers.[208] Supporters blamed undocumented Mexicans for California's economic woes that were more

---

American Relief Act, Pub. L. No. 105-100, §§ 201-204, 111 Stat. 2160, 2193-201 (1997) (codified in 8 U.S.C.A. §§ 1101, 1153, 1229b, and 1255 (West Supp. 1998)), which afforded lawful permanent residency to certain Nicaraguans, Cubans, and others but not to similarly situated Haitians).

203. James Harney, *Critics of U.S. Policy See Racist Overtones*, USA TODAY, Feb. 3, 1992, at 2A (alterations added) (quoting Professor Legomsky).

204. *See* Janice D. Villiers, *Closed Borders, Closed Ports: The Plight of Haitians Seeking Political Asylum in the United States*, 60 BROOK. L. REV. 841, 904-15 (1994); *see also* Peter Margulies, *Difference and Distrust in Asylum Law: Haitian and Holocaust Refugee Narratives*, 6 ST. THOMAS L. REV. 135 (1993) (analyzing difficulties faced by Haitian refugees and comparing their plight to that of Jews who fled Nazi Germany).

205. *See generally* READING RODNEY KING, READING URBAN UPRISING, *supra* note 35 (compiling essays analyzing issues surrounding the Los Angeles rebellion).

206. *See* James H. Johnson, Jr. & Walter C. Farrell, Jr., *The Fire This Time: The Genesis of the Los Angeles Rebellion of 1992*, 71 N.C. L. REV. 1403, 1418-20 (1993) (summarizing various initiatives to foster economic development and ease social tensions in south central Los Angeles).

207. For analysis of the campaign culminating in the passage of Proposition 187, see Johnson, *supra* note 34, at 650-72, and for analysis of its impacts, see Johnson, *supra* note 142, at 1568-75. *See also* Linda S. Bosniak, *Opposing Prop. 187: Undocumented Immigrants and the National Imagination*, 28 CONN. L. REV. 555 (1996) (analyzing complexity of nonracial fairness arguments in opposition to Proposition 187).

208. *See* John Marelius, *Wilson Ad Out to Ease Prop. 187 Drumbeat*, SAN DIEGO UNION-TRIB., Oct. 25, 1994, at A3.

likely attributable to drastic reductions in federal defense spending required by the end of the Cold War and the demise of the Soviet Union.[209]

Nativist and racist themes inflamed the bitter Proposition 187 campaign. One initiative sponsor, in a textbook example of nativist sentiment, boldly asserted that "'[i]llegal aliens are killing us in California. . . . Those who support illegal immigration are, in effect, anti-American.'"[210] An argument favoring the measure in a pamphlet distributed to registered voters proclaimed that "Proposition 187 will be the first giant stride in ultimately ending the ILLEGAL ALIEN invasion."[211] One leader in the pro-187 campaign even played on fears that, unless citizens took steps like the initiative, Mexico might ultimately annex California.[212]

The public statements of the drafters of Proposition 187 left the unmistakable imprint of racial animus. One initiative leader conjured up disturbing imagery of lynching, a device historically used to terrorize African Americans in the United States: "'[y]ou are the posse . . . and [Proposition 187] is the rope.'"[213] Harold Ezell, a high-ranking INS official during the Reagan presidency who was loathed by Latino activists because of his derogatory comments about illegal aliens,[214] attributed Proposition 187's widespread support to the fact that "'[t]he people are tired of watching their state run wild and become *a third world country*.'"[215] Barbara Kiley, mayor of an Orange County town, reportedly described the children of undocumented immigrants as "'those little f--kers.'"[216] Her husband

---

209. *See, e.g.*, TONY MILLER, CALIFORNIA BALLOT PAMPHLET: GENERAL ELECTION NOVEMBER 8, 1994, at 54 (1994) [hereinafter CALIFORNIA BALLOT PAMPHLET] ("It has been estimated that ILLEGAL ALIENS are costing taxpayers in excess of 5 billion dollars a year. While our own citizens and legal residents go wanting, those who choose to enter our country ILLEGALLY get royal treatment at the expense of the California taxpayer. IT IS TIME THIS STOPS!") (capitals in original) (Argument in Favor of Proposition 187). The fact that Proposition 187 placed in jeopardy federal funding of $15 billion, which greatly outweighed any cost savings, was virtually ignored in the campaign, *see id.* at 53, a fact suggesting that other factors besides fiscal ones were at work.

210. Patrick J. McDonnell, *Prop. 187 Turns Up Heat in U.S. Immigration Debate*, L.A. TIMES, Aug. 10, 1994, at A1 (alteration and omission added) (quoting Ronald Prince, head of the Proposition 187 campaign).

211. CALIFORNIA BALLOT PAMPHLET, *supra* note 209, at 54 (capitals in original).

212. *See* Linda R. Hayes, *Letter to the Editor*, N.Y. TIMES, Oct. 15, 1994, § 1, at 18 (expressing concern that "a Mexico-controlled California could vote to establish Spanish as the sole language of California, 10 million more English-speaking Californians could flee, and there could be a statewide vote to leave the Union and annex California to Mexico"). Hayes was the Proposition 187 media director for southern California. *See id.*

213. McDonnell, *supra* note 210, at A1 (alteration and omission added) (quoting "initiative co-founder").

214. *See* Olga Briseno, *Mister Migra Harold Ezell*, SAN DIEGO UNION-TRIB., Aug. 23, 1989, at F1 (recounting Ezell's "most famous quote" in which "he said illegal aliens should be 'caught, skinned and fried'").

215. Daniel B. Wood, *Ballot Vote on Illegal Immigrants Set for Fall in California*, CHRISTIAN SCI. MONITOR, June 1, 1994, at 1, 18 (alteration and emphasis added) (quoting Harold Ezell).

216. Elizabeth Kadetsky, *"Save Our State" Initiative: Bashing Illegals in California*, 259 NATION 416, 418 (1994) (quoting Barbara Kiley).

and the initiative campaign's political consultant, Richard Kiley, observed that the public protests of Proposition 187 were counterproductive because "'[o]n TV there was nothing but Mexican flags and brown faces.'"[217] Barbara Coe, a Proposition 187 supporter, expressed fear of the "'militant arm of the pro-illegal activists, who have vowed to take over first California, then the Western states and then the rest of the nation.'"[218]

Election results were polarized along racial lines. White voters supported Proposition 187 by two-to-one and Latinos opposed it by a three-to-one margin.[219] As the racially tinged campaign and racially polarized vote suggest, Proposition 187, though facially neutral, at its core focused on race. Although undocumented persons in the United States come from many nations other than Mexico,[220] this never figured prominently in the debate over the initiative. Moreover, the measure, if implemented, will disparately impact certain minority communities. Undocumented Mexicans, Mexican American citizens, and citizens of other minority groups viewed as foreign, including Asian Americans, are the groups most likely to feel the enforcement sting of Proposition 187.[221]

To this point, the courts have enjoined the implementation of most of Proposition 187, with the final disposition of the legal challenges unknown.[222] Nonetheless, the law triggered national action. In 1996, Congress enacted welfare reform restricting benefits to lawful, as well as unlawful, immigrants.[223] As with the Chinese exclusion laws,[224] California blazed a trail for the nation.

---

217. Margot Hornblower Lamont, *Making and Breaking Law*, TIME, Nov. 21, 1994, at 68, 73 (alteration added) (quoting Richard Kiley).

218. Carol Byrne, *Proposition 187's Uproar*, STAR TRIB. (Minneapolis), Oct. 20, 1994, at 7A (quoting Barbara Coe).

219. *See Times Poll: A Look at the Electorate*, L.A. TIMES, Nov. 10, 1994, at B2 (describing exit poll results). Polls taken immediately before the election suggested that the vote would be much closer than the results proved to be (59% to 41%). The inaccuracy may have resulted from the fear of some white supporters of being classified as "racists" if truthful to the pollsters. *See, e.g.*, Ed Mendel, *'The Door Is Open' if Voters Kill 187, Co-Author Warns*, SAN DIEGO UNION-TRIB., Nov. 4, 1994, at A1 (reporting that polls showed that Proposition 187 vote was dead heat). Racially polarized elections commonly produce a disjunction between polls and election results. *See* Lynn A. Baker, *Direct Democracy and Discrimination: A Public Choice Perspective*, 67 CHI.-KENT L. REV. 707, 734 & n.98 (1991).

220. *See supra* note 157 (citing statistical data on undocumented population in United States).

221. *See* Johnson, *supra* note 142, at 1571-72.

222. *See* League of United Latin Am. Citizens v. Wilson, 1998 U.S. Dist. LEXIS 3418 (C.D. Cal. Mar. 13, 1998); League of United Latin Am. Citizens v. Wilson, 908 F. Supp. 755 (C.D. Cal. 1995).

223. *See supra* note 26 (citing welfare reform bill). For a sketch of possible constitutional infirmities with the elimination of benefits to lawful immigrants, see Michael Scaperlanda, *Who Is My Neighbor?: An Essay on Immigrants, Welfare Reform, and the Constitution*, 29 CONN. L. REV. 1587, 1612-25 (1997). *See also* Berta Esperanza Hernández-Truyol & Kimberly A. Johns, *Global Rights, Local Wrongs, and Legal Fixes: An International Human Rights Critique of Immigration and Welfare "Reform"*, 71 S. CAL. L. REV. 547 (1998) (analyzing how immigration and welfare restrictions violate various international human rights norms).

224. *See supra* text accompanying notes 47-82.

Proposition 187 was about much more than immigration. The initiative represented the electorate's general frustration with changing racial demographics. While an effort to attack domestic racial minorities with full force is unsavory politically,[225] an all-out war against noncitizens, with the attack being focused on their immigration status rather than their race, could be pursued. Proposition 187 thus reflects racial tensions in a way similar to the ever-popular English-only laws,[226] which have racial impacts because of the link between language and national origin. Designation of English as the official language, though facially neutral, directly affects the Latino community.[227] It therefore should not be surprising that the national origins quota system of 1924 came on the heels of the addition of the English literacy requirement to the immigration laws in 1917.[228] Both constituted parts of an overall package to limit the immigration of minorities.

Two years after the voters passed Proposition 187, the electorate approved the California Civil Rights Initiative, which was designed to eliminate affirmative action by the State of California.[229] This followed a University of California Board of Regents' decision to eliminate affirmative action in student admissions.[230] Consequently, attacks on racial minorities followed attacks on immigrants of color.

---

225. *See, e.g.*, DINESH D'SOUZA, ILLIBERAL EDUCATION 194-228 (1991) (contending that vocal minority on university campuses frequently charge "racism" against professors and pressure campus administrators to side against professors).

226. *See generally* RAYMOND TATALOVICH, NATIVISM REBORN? THE OFFICIAL ENGLISH LANGUAGE MOVEMENT AND THE AMERICAN STATES (1995) (analyzing English-only movement in United States).

227. *See, e.g.*, Hernandez v. New York, 500 U.S. 352 (1991) (holding that prosecutors may lawfully base peremptory challenges against Latinos on ground that they speak Spanish); Yniguez v. Arizonans for Official English, 69 F.3d 920, 947 (9th Cir. 1995) (en banc) ("[T]he adverse impact of . . . the overbreadth [of Arizona's English-only law] is especially egregious because it is not uniformly spread over the population, but falls almost entirely upon Hispanics and other national origin minorities.") (citation omitted), *vacated as moot*, 117 S. Ct. 1055 (1997); *see also* Stephen W. Bender, *Direct Democracy and Distrust: The Relationship Between Language Law Rhetoric and the Language Vigilantism Experience*, 2 HARV. LATINO L. REV. 145, 149-53 (1997) (analyzing instances of "language vigilantism" directed at Spanish-speaking Latinos). *See generally* BILL PIATT, ¿ONLY ENGLISH? LAW AND LANGUAGE POLICY IN THE UNITED STATES (1990) (advocating language rights). For analysis of the law analyzing the speak-English-only rules in the workplace, showing how they reveal Latino invisibility, legal indeterminacy, and racial dualism, see Christopher David Ruiz Cameron, *How the Garcia Cousins Lost Their Accents: Understanding the Language of Title VII Decisions Approving Speak-English-Only Rules as the Product of Racial Dualism, Latino Invisibility, and Legal Indeterminacy*, 85 CAL. L. REV. 1347 (1997).

228. *See supra* text accompanying notes 97-101.

229. *See generally* Coalition for Econ. Equity v. Wilson, 110 F.3d 1431 (9th Cir.) (holding that the California Civil Rights Initiative did not violate the Equal Protection Clause), *cert. denied*, 118 S. Ct. 397 (1997).

230. *See* Jeffrey B. Wolff, Comment, *Affirmative Action in College and Graduate School Admissions—The Effects of* Hopwood *and the Actions of the U.C. Board of Regents on Its Continued Existence*, 50 SMU L. REV. 627, 654-57 (1997) (summarizing events surrounding the University of California Board of Regents' abolition of affirmative action).

II. LESSONS FROM THE IMMIGRATION LAWS FOR DOMESTIC MINORITIES

Immigration law offers a helpful gauge for measuring this nation's racial sensibilities. Long a fixture of immigration law, the plenary power doctrine, a judicially created immunity for substantive immigration decisions, emphasizes that the legislative and executive branches of the U.S. Government enjoy "plenary power" over immigration matters and that little, if any, room exists for judicial review. Though consistently criticized, and arguably narrowed by the Supreme Court, the doctrine continues to represent the law of the land.[231] In this important way, immigration law has been, and remains to some extent, estranged from traditional public law, where the Constitution operates in full force.[232]

At the tail end of the twentieth century, immigration law and policy have increasingly become a visible hotbed of racial conflict. This section analyzes the teachings of the plenary power doctrine for domestic race relations.

A. Racial Exclusions in the Immigration Laws Reinforce the Subordinated Status of Minority Citizens in the United States

Academic attacks on the plenary power doctrine are legion, coming from many different angles.[233] Some, for example, challenge the fundamental idea

---

231. *See, e.g.*, Fiallo v. Bell, 430 U.S. 787, 792 (1977) (upholding gender and legitimacy classifications in immigration laws and recognizing the "limited scope of judicial inquiry into immigration legislation"); Kleindienst v. Mandel, 408 U.S. 753, 770 (1972) (holding "that when Executive exercises . . . power . . . on the basis of a facially neutral and bona fide reason, the courts will neither look behind the exercise of that discretion, nor test it by balancing its justification against the First Amendment interests of those who seek personal communication with the applicant").

232. *See* Peter H. Schuck, *The Transformation of Immigration Law*, 84 COLUM. L. REV. 1, 1 (1984):

> Immigration has long been a maverick, a wild card, in our public law. Probably no other area of American law has been so radically insulated and divergent from those fundamental norms of constitutional right, administrative procedure, and judicial role that animate the rest of our legal system. . . . [I]mmigration law remains the realm in which government authority is at the zenith, and individual entitlement is at the nadir.

233. *See, e.g.*, Louis Henkin, *The Constitution and United States Sovereignty: A Century of Chinese Exclusion and Its Progeny*, 100 HARV. L. REV. 853 (1987) (challenging the *Chinese Exclusion Case* from an international law perspective); Linda Kelly, *Preserving the Fundamental Right to Family Unity: Championing Notions of Social Contract and Community Ties in the Battle of Plenary Power Versus Aliens' Rights*, 41 VILL. L. REV. 725, 771-82 (1996) (advocating that all persons subject to U.S. laws should have constitutional rights and applying theory to family reunification under immigration laws); Stephen H. Legomsky, *Immigration Law and the Principle of Plenary Congressional Power*, 1984 SUP. CT. REV. 255 (criticizing various theories for judicial deference); Stephen H. Legomsky, *Ten More Years of Plenary Power: Immigration, Congress, and the Courts*, 22 HASTINGS CONST. L.Q. 925 (1995) (analyzing recent plenary power case law and predicting future inroads in doctrine); Victor C.

underlying the doctrine—that nations have unfettered sovereign power to seal their borders.[234] Few, if any, modern defenders of the plenary power doctrine can be found in the legal academy.

Federal plenary power over immigration contrasts sharply with the Supreme Court's occasional strict scrutiny of *state* alienage classifications. In *Graham v. Richardson*, which invalidated a state welfare regulation, the Court recognized that "[a]liens as a class are a prime example of a 'discrete and insular' minority . . . for whom heightened judicial solicitude is appropriate."[235] This reasoning would seem to apply with full force to federal regulation.[236] However, the Supreme Court consistently has been deferential to federal alienage

---

Romero, *The Congruence Principle Applied: Rethinking Equal Protection Review of Federal Alienage Classifications After* Adarand Constructors, Inc. v. Peña, 76 OR. L. REV. 425 (1997) (arguing for more scrutinizing judicial review of federal alienage classifications and immigration law classifications that affect fundamental rights); Michael Scaperlanda, *Partial Membership and the Constitutional Community*, 81 IOWA L. REV. 707 (1996) (rejecting ideas of inherent and unlimited sovereign power over immigration and calling for constitutional dialogue on place of noncitizens in national community); Margaret H. Taylor, *Detained Aliens Challenging Conditions of Confinement and the Porous Border of the Plenary Power Doctrine*, 22 HASTINGS CONST. L.Q. 1087, 1155-56 (1995) (examining case law involving detention of aliens and observing that the "focus on an eroding plenary power doctrine, which until recently has dominated immigration law scholarship, overlooks the polluting effect of the plenary power doctrine *outside* the immigration law realm") (emphasis added) (footnote omitted); Wu, *supra* note 52, at 43-50 (arguing for abrogation of plenary power doctrine); Gabriel J. Chin, Segregation's Last Stronghold: Race Discrimination and the Constitutional Law of Immigration (unpublished manuscript, on file with author) (contending that racial classifications in immigration laws should be subject to judicial scrutiny).

234. For a sampling of this sort of challenge, see NEUMAN, *supra* note 48, at 119-22, James A.R. Nafziger, *The General Admission of Aliens Under International Law*, 77 AM. J. INT'L L. 804 (1983), and Michael Scaperlanda, *Polishing the Tarnished Golden Door*, 1993 WIS. L. REV. 965. *See also* Ibrahim J. Wani, *Truth, Strangers, and Fiction: The Illegitimate Uses of Legal Fiction in Immigration Law*, 11 CARDOZO L. REV. 51, 59-89 (1989) (analyzing the importance, and weaknesses, of sovereignty fiction in immigration law).

235. 403 U.S. 365, 372 (1971) (quoting United States v. Carolene Prods. Co., 304 U.S. 144, 153 n.4 (1938)); *see* Sugarman v. Dougall, 413 U.S. 634 (1973) (invalidating prohibition of noncitizens from state civil service system); *see also* ELY, *supra* note 16, at 161-62 (suggesting that, because aliens are a discrete and insular minority, alienage classifications deserve strict scrutiny). In contrast to *Graham*, the Court at times has declined to opt for strict scrutiny review of state alienage classifications. *See* Ambach v. Norwick, 441 U.S. 68 (1979) (upholding state law barring aliens from jobs as public school teachers); Foley v. Connelie, 435 U.S. 291 (1978) (refusing to apply strict scrutiny and upholding state law requiring police officer to be a U.S. citizen). Nonetheless, courts occasionally have been willing to find that state laws in effect regulate immigration and usurp national power in the field and therefore are preempted by federal law. *See, e.g.*, Toll v. Moreno, 458 U.S. 1 (1982) (holding that federal law preempted state policy discriminating against lawful permanent residents); League of United Latin Am. Citizens v. Wilson, 908 F. Supp. 755 (C.D. Cal. 1995) (holding that federal law preempted core provisions of Proposition 187 because they attempted to regulate immigration).

236. *See* Gerald M. Rosberg, *The Protection of Aliens from Discriminatory Treatment by the National Government*, 1977 SUP. CT. REV. 275, 294 ("[I]f alienage is a suspect classification when made the basis of state regulation, should it not remain suspect when it is used by the federal government?").

classifications, just like it has been with respect to Congress's judgments about substantive immigration admissions criteria. For example, in *Mathews v. Diaz*,[237] the Court invoked the plenary power doctrine and upheld limits on lawful immigrants' eligibility for a federal benefits program.

The plenary power doctrine fortunately has not been invoked in recent years to shield any laws as contrary to this nation's modern constitutional sensibilities as the infamous Chinese exclusion laws.[238] Express racial and national origin exclusions, which would squarely contradict such icons of the law as *Brown v. Board of Education*,[239] rarely arise in modern immigration law and policy.[240] As we have seen, however, the facially neutral immigration laws of the modern era have distinctively racial impacts.[241]

Assuming that under the plenary power doctrine *noncitizens* possess few, if any, constitutional protections with respect to entering the country, the implications of racial and national origin exclusions on *citizens* must be considered. Because the Constitution unquestionably protects the rights of citizens, citizens claiming injury have a better chance at successfully challenging the immigration laws than noncitizens directly affected by their operation. Courts have recognized that citizens in certain circumstances may challenge the lawfulness of immigration laws because of the impact on their rights.[242]

Gerald Rosberg focuses on the damage to U.S. citizens sharing the race or national origin of groups barred from joining the national community:

> *[A racial or national origin] classification would . . . require strict scrutiny, not because of the injury to the aliens denied admission, but rather because of the injury to American citizens of the same race or national origin who are stigmatized by the classification.* When Congress declares that aliens of Chinese or Irish or Polish origin are excludable on the grounds of ancestry

---

237. 426 U.S. 67 (1976).

238. *See supra* text accompanying notes 47-54.

239. 347 U.S. 483 (1954).

240. However, such situations arise occasionally. *See, e.g.*, Narenji v. Civiletti, 617 F.2d 745 (D.C. Cir. 1979) (holding that national origin discrimination against noncitizens from Iran did not violate the Constitution); *supra* text accompanying notes 179-206 (analyzing Haitian interdiction and repatriation). In addition, one could envision a scenario in which Congress might pass an immigration law that expressly discriminates on the basis of race. *See* LEGOMSKY, *supra* note 130, at 94-96 (setting out hypothetical exercise in which Congress enacts law limiting immigration from Latin America into the United States because of domestic racial tensions attributed to growing Latino population).

241. *See supra* text accompanying notes 121-49.

242. *See, e.g.*, Kleindienst v. Mandel, 408 U.S. 753, 762-65 (1972) (refusing, because Attorney General offered legitimate and bona fide reason not to waive exclusion grounds, to consider First Amendment interests of those citizens who would have communicated with noncitizen in United States); Adams v. Baker, 909 F.2d 643, 647 n.1 (1st Cir. 1990) ("[I]t is important to recognize that the only issue that may be addressed by this court is the possibility of *impairment of United States citizens' First Amendment rights* through the exclusion of the alien.") (emphasis added) (citing *Mandel*, 408 U.S. at 762); Allende v. Schultz, 605 F. Supp. 1220, 1224 (D. Mass. 1985) ("The lower federal courts have interpreted *Mandel* to require the Government to provide a justification for an alien's exclusion when that exclusion is challenged *by United States citizens asserting constitutional claims*.") (emphasis added), *aff'd*, 845 F.2d 1111 (1st Cir. 1988).

> alone, it fixes a badge of opprobrium on citizens of the same ancestry. . . . *Except when necessary to protect a compelling interest, Congress cannot implement a policy that has the effect of labeling some group of citizens as inferior to others because of their race or national origin.*[243]

Others also have observed the impacts of racial and national origin exclusions on citizens. In vetoing the INA,[244] President Truman observed that the national origins quota system was founded on the idea

> that Americans with English or Irish names were better people and better citizens than Americans with Italian or Greek or Polish names. It was thought that people of West European origin made better citizens than Rumanians or Yugoslavs or Ukrainians or Hungarians or Balts or Austrians. Such a concept . . . violates the great political doctrine of the Declaration of Independence that "all men are created equal."[245]

Similarly, in arguing for the abolition of the quota system, Secretary of State Dean Rusk recognized that excluding certain noncitizens suggested that "'we think . . . less well of our own citizens of those national origins, than of other citizens.'"[246]

Brown v. Board of Education[247] suggests that racial and national origin exclusions in the immigration laws adversely affect domestic minorities. In that case, the Supreme Court relied on social science studies documenting the fact that segregation of African Americans "generates a feeling of inferiority as to their status in the community that may affect their hearts and minds in a way unlikely to be undone."[248] Similarly, exclusion from the country of immigrants

---

243. Rosberg, *supra* note 236, at 327 (emphasis added); *see also* Chang, *supra* note 102, at 1213 ("[X]enophobia . . . is inconsistent with equal concern and respect for citizens who may share the cultural traits that the xenophobe finds disagreeable.") (footnote omitted); Motomura, *supra* note 99, at 1947 ("[I]mmigration law that excludes members of a particular race or ethnicity may cast stigma on that group. Unless the government can show a compelling interest, any such provable stigma violates the bedrock equal protection prohibition against treating any person as inferior to another by virtue of race or ethnicity.") (footnotes omitted). Such an approach is consistent with theories of equal protection law that link the level of judicial review to the stigma created by the challenged legislative classification. *See* Daniel Farber & Suzanna Sherry, *The Pariah Principle*, 13 CONST. COMMENTARY 257, 271-75 (1996) (comparing stigma approach to equal protection to other theories).

244. *See supra* text accompanying notes 114-15 (noting that Congress overrode presidential veto).

245. TRUMAN PAPERS, *supra* note 115, at 443.

246. Chin, *supra* note 88, at 302 (omission added) (quoting *Immigration: Hearings Before Subcomm. No. 1 of the House Comm. on the Judiciary on H.R. 7700 and 55 Identical Bills*, 88th Cong. 390 (1964)); *see also* Louis L. Jaffe, *The Philosophy of Our Immigration Law*, 21 LAW & CONTEMP. PROBS. 358, 358 (1956) ("[National origin] quota provisions were born in racial prejudice. They give needless offense to many of our citizens and to the people of other countries; they bedevil the conduct of our foreign relations and add nothing to our public welfare.").

247. 347 U.S. 483 (1954).

248. *Id.* at 494. The Court cited various social science sources for this proposition. *See id.* at 494 n.11. Though the use of social science in constitutional interpretation, and particularly in *Brown*, has been much discussed, often critically, social science influenced the Court's decisions long before *Brown*. *See* Herbert Hovenkamp, *Social Science and Segregation Before* Brown, 1985 DUKE L.J. 624, 664 n.226.

of color may well "generate[] a feeling of inferiority as to the[] status in the community"[249] of domestic minorities who share a similar racial and national origin background.

Racial exclusion of noncitizens under the immigration laws, be they express or covert, reveals to domestic minorities how they are viewed by society. The unprecedented efforts to seal the U.S.-Mexico border combined with the increased efforts to deport undocumented Mexicans, for example, tell much about how a majority of society views Mexican Americans and suggests to what lengths society might go, if permitted under color of law, to rid itself of domestic Mexican Americans.[250] In fact, during the New Deal, Mexican American *citizens*, as well as Mexican *immigrants*, were "repatriated" to Mexico.[251] It therefore is no surprise that the organized Mexican American community consistently resists the harsh attacks on immigration and immigrants.[252] This is true despite sentiment among some Mexican Americans to restrict immigration because of perceived competition with immigrants in the job market.[253]

For similar reasons, African American activist organizations protested when the U.S. Government acted ruthlessly toward poor Haitian refugees facing death from the political violence gripping Haiti.[254] Asian activist groups criticized the treatment of Chinese immigrants in the 1990s,[255] as well as anti-immigrant sentiment and welfare reforms that adversely affected the Asian immigrant community.[256] These minority groups implicitly understand the link between racial exclusions and their place in the racial hierarchy in the United States. It is not just that they share a common ancestry, though that no doubt plays some role in the formulation of political support. These communities instead understand that animosity toward members of immigrant minority communities is not just

---

249. *Brown*, 347 U.S. at 494.

250. *See supra* text accompanying notes 150-78.

251. *See supra* text accompanying note 152. Today, the "deportation" of citizens occurs most frequently when Mexican citizens with U.S.-citizen children (due to their birth in this country) are deported; the citizen children, especially younger ones, almost inevitably accompany their deported parents. *See* Bill Piatt, *Born as Second Class Citizens in the U.S.A.: Children of Undocumented Parents*, 63 NOTRE DAME L. REV. 35, 40-41 (1988).

252. *See* PETER SKERRY, MEXICAN AMERICANS 304-08 (1993) (criticizing Mexican American leaders' liberal stance on immigration as out of step with rank-and-file).

253. *See generally* DAVID G. GUTIÉRREZ, WALLS AND MIRRORS (1995) (analyzing restrictionist sentiment in Mexican American community because of, among other things, fear of job loss to low wage labor provided by Mexican immigrants).

254. *See supra* text accompanying note 199 (discussing amicus brief filed with the Supreme Court by NAACP and other African American groups in Haitian interdiction case); *see also* Hing, *supra* note 111 (contending that U.S. immigration law's exclusion of immigrants from Africa sent "messages of exclusion" to African American community).

255. *See, e.g.*, Pamela Burdman, *Human-Smuggling Crackdown Reported in Chinese Press*, S.F. CHRON., Aug. 20, 1993, at A2 (reporting that Asian Law Caucus attorney questioned U.S. Government's treatment of Chinese asylum-seekers); Gregory Gross & Angela Lau, *Mexico Refuses to Let Chinese Land*, SAN DIEGO UNION-TRIB., July 10, 1993, at A1 (same).

256. *See* Steve A. Holmes, *Anti-Immigrant Mood Moves Asians to Organize*, N.Y. TIMES, Jan. 3, 1996, at A1; Lena Sun, *Ethnic Groups Unite Against Benefit Cuts*, WASH. POST, July 10, 1995, at C1.

limited to immigrants. In this way, immigration has proven to be a battlefield for status among Anglos and people of color in the United States.[257]

The concerns of minority activists find support in psychological theory, which suggests that people generally view persons of national origin ancestries other than their own as fungible. Put differently, in-groups tend to define out-groups as homogeneous.[258] The out-group homogeneity theory helps explain the persistence of racial stereotypes.[259] Many have experienced the homogenizing of racial minorities in crude and obviously false statements about how all certain racial minorities "look alike."[260] The theory supports the idea that society generally classifies all persons of Mexican ancestry, for example, as the same and fails to make fine legal distinctions between them based on such things as immigration status.

In the end, we must understand that the impact of racially exclusionary immigration laws does more than just stigmatize domestic minorities. Such laws reinforce domestic subordination of the same racial minority groups who are excluded. By barring admission of the outsider group that is subordinated domestically, society rationalizes the disparate treatment of the domestic racial minority group in question and reinforces that group's inferiority. Exclusion in the immigration laws must be viewed as an integral part of a larger mosaic of racial discrimination in American society.

---

257. *See supra* text accompanying notes 167-69 (citing authority analyzing status conflict).

258. *See* Patricia W. Linville et al., *Stereotyping and Perceived Distributions of Social Characteristics: An Application to Ingroup-Outgroup Perception, in* PREJUDICE, DISCRIMINATION, AND RACISM 165 (John F. Dovidio & Samuel L. Gaertner eds., 1986) (summarizing studies on cultural homogeneity theory and elaborating on them in empirical study); *see also* Linda Hamilton Krieger, *The Content of Our Categories: A Cognitive Bias Approach to Discrimination and Equal Employment Opportunity*, 47 STAN. L. REV. 1161, 1192 (1995) ("While ingroup members perceive similarities between themselves and others in their group, they perceive outgroup members as being even more homogeneous. In other words, subjects tend to perceive outgroup members as an undifferentiated mass, while ingroup members are more highly differentiated."); *id.* at 1192 n.133 (citing studies). Krieger offers as an example a reference by a white supervisor to her Salvadoran client in an employment dispute as "Mexican," which "tended to show that he perceived Latinos as an undifferentiated outgroup." *Id.* at 1192.

259. *See* Henri Tajfel, *Cognitive Aspects of Prejudice*, 25 J. SOC. ISSUES 79, 82 (1969).

260. *See* Harry H.L. Kitano, *Asian-Americans: The Chinese, Japanese, Koreans, Pilipinos, and Southeast Asians*, 454 ANNALS AM. ACAD. POL. & SOC. SCI. 125, 126 (1981) (stating that people "presume[] homogeneity among Asian groups, not only on the physiological level, as typified by the phrase, 'They all look alike,' but on a cultural level"); *see also* Charles R. Lawrence III, *The Id, the Ego, and Equal Protection: Reckoning with Unconscious Racism*, 39 STAN. L. REV. 317, 341 n.100 (1987) (discussing common experience of African or Asian American "being mistaken for another black or Asian who looks nothing like you (the 'they all look alike' syndrome)") (citation omitted).

B. Lessons from Psychological Theory: Why Immigrants of Color Are Society's Scapegoats

The historical dynamic identified here cannot be marginalized as simply an "immigration" issue, which is how legal academia often has treated immigration law. Indeed, immigration law sounds the alarm for racial minorities in the United States. Efforts to exclude noncitizen minorities from the country under the immigration laws threaten citizen minorities. An obvious threat is that, if for whatever reason—narrow interpretation by the Supreme Court, for example—the protections of the Constitution are limited or eviscerated, domestic minorities have much to fear.[261] The punishment of noncitizens of color suggests just how society might zealously attack domestic minorities of color absent legal protections. *Korematsu*, in which the Supreme Court sanctioned the internment of citizens as well as noncitizens of Japanese ancestry in the name of national security, is a stark example.[262]

Moreover, a relationship exists between society's treatment of domestic minorities and noncitizens of color. Congress passed the Chinese exclusion laws not long after ratification of the revolutionary Reconstruction Amendments designed to protect the rights of African Americans.[263] *Korematsu* and "Operation Wetback" came close in time to *Brown v. Board of Education*.[264] Haitian repatriation continued at roughly the same time as the "Rebuild L.A." campaign in the wake of the Rodney King violence.[265] Because of the recurring nature of such events, it cannot be viewed as a coincidence that they occurred at the same time but should be considered to be part and parcel of a complex pattern of racial subordination in the United States.

Psychological theory at times has served as a tool for analyzing the legal implications of racial discrimination.[266] In some ways, the reaction to immigrants

---

261. Indeed, they have much to fear even with legal protections. Legal constraints can only do so much to constrain anti-minority sentiment. *See supra* note 16 (noting limits on legal remedies in facilitating meaningful social change).

262. Korematsu v. United States, 323 U.S. 214 (1944); *see supra* text accompanying notes 83-89.

263. *See supra* text accompanying notes 47-96.

264. 347 U.S. 483 (1954); *see supra* text accompanying notes 174-78.

265. *See supra* text accompanying notes 205-06.

266. *See, e.g.*, Jody D. Armour, *Race Ipsa Loquitur: Of Reasonable Racists, Intelligent Bayesians, and Involuntary Negrophobes*, 46 STAN. L. REV. 781, 811-14 (1994) (analyzing psychological theory on unconscious nature of racism in rejecting claim that assailant's race should be considered in evaluating self-defense claim); Peggy C. Davis, *Law as Microaggression*, 98 YALE L.J. 1559 (1989) (analyzing psychological impacts of microaggressions, subtle put-downs, and slights of minorities); Richard Delgado, *Words that Wound: A Tort Action for Racial Insults, Epithets, and Name-Calling*, 17 HARV. C.R.-C.L. L. REV. 133, 135-49 (1982) (analyzing psychological harms of racial insults to racial minorities); Lawrence, *supra* note 260 (analyzing how unconscious racism undermines effectiveness of modern equal protection law, which requires proof of discriminatory intent). For examination of social psychology literature on anti-immigrant sentiment, see Victor C. Romero, Expanding the Circle of Membership by Reconstructing the "Alien": Lessons from Social Psychology and

of color can be explained by the psychological construct known as transference "in which feelings toward one person are refocused on another."[267] Transference ordinarily occurs unconsciously in the individual.[268] The general public, in light of modern sensibilities, often is foreclosed from directly attacking minority citizens, at least publicly. Society can, however, lash out with full force at noncitizens of color. In so doing, they contend that the attacks are not racially motivated but that other facially neutral factors animate restrictionist goals.[269] Such attacks amount to transference of frustration from domestic minorities to immigrants of color.

The related psychological construct of displacement also helps understand the phenomenon.[270] "Displacement" is "[a] defense mechanism in which a drive or feeling is shifted upon a substitute object, one that is psychologically more available. For example, aggressive impulses may be displaced, as in 'scapegoating,' upon people (or even inanimate objects) *who are not sources of frustration but are safer to attack.*"[271]

Psychological studies show how displaced frustration may unconsciously result in the development of racial prejudice.[272] For example, one famous study of displaced aggression found that negative attitudes toward persons of Japanese and Mexican ancestry increased after a tedious testing session that caused children to miss a trip to the movies. Animosity was displaced from the test-givers, immune from attack because of their positions of authority, to defenseless racial minorities.[273]

---

the "Promise Enforcement" Cases 49-59 (Mar. 3, 1998) (unpublished manuscript, on file with author).

267. Thomas L. Shaffer, *Undue Influence, Confidential Relationship, and the Psychology of Transference*, 45 NOTRE DAME LAW. 197, 205 (1970). In psychoanalytic theory, transference refers to the patient's transference of feelings toward a particular individual to the therapist. *See generally* C.G. JUNG, THE PSYCHOLOGY OF THE TRANSFERENCE (R.F.C. Hull trans., 2d ed. 1966).

268. *See* Elizabeth F. Loftus, *Unconscious Transference in Eyewitness Identification*, 2 L. & PSYCHOL. REV. 93 (1976); *see also* Francis A. Gilligan et al., *The Theory of "Unconscious Transference": The Latest Threat to the Shield Laws Protecting the Privacy of Sex Offenses*, 38 B.C. L. REV. 107, 111-17 (1996) (discussing psychological theory of unconscious transference in witness identification and distinguishing it from psychological use of the term "transference").

269. *See, e.g.*, *supra* text accompanying notes 207-30 (discussing how supporters of Proposition 187 claimed that the measure was not racist or anti-immigrant).

270. I readily concede, as Gordon Allport observed in a different context, that "[n]o single theory of prejudice is adequate." GORDON W. ALLPORT, THE NATURE OF PREJUDICE 352 (1954). The psychological literature makes clear that a complex interplay of factors contributes to the development of anti-immigrant sentiment. *See, e.g.*, Gregory R. Maio et al., *Ambivalence and Persuasion: The Processing of Messages About Immigrant Groups*, 32 J. EXPERIMENTAL SOC. PSYCHOL. 513 (1996); Gregory R. Maio et al., *The Formation of Attitudes Toward New Immigrant Groups*, 24 J. APPLIED SOC. PSYCHOL. 1762 (1994).

271. DAVID KRECH ET AL., ELEMENTS OF PSYCHOLOGY 768 (2d ed. 1969) (emphasis added).

272. *See* ALLPORT, *supra* note 270, at 343-53.

273. *See* Neal E. Miller & Richard Bugelski, *Minor Studies of Aggression: II. The Influence of Frustrations Imposed by the In-Group on Attitudes Expressed Toward Out-Groups*, 25 J. PSYCHOL. 437 (1948).

Such examples square with the history of scapegoating immigrants for the social problems of the day.[274] For example, the U.S. economy went south in the late 1800s and the frustration was displaced from diffuse economic causes to Chinese immigrants.[275] Gordon Allport offered a most apt example: "Most Germans did not see the connection between their humiliating defeat in World War I and their subsequent anti-Semitism."[276] Frustration was displaced from complex real-world causes to a simple—and defenseless—solution.

Transference and displacement serve to hide racial animosity toward all people of color, not just immigrants of color. Unfortunately, however, an unsatisfied appetite for homogeneity knows no border between immigrants and citizens.[277] Minority citizens as well as minority noncitizens remain a distinct racial minority whatever the fine legal distinctions made with respect to immigration status. The popular perception that Latinos[278] and Asian Americans[279] are "foreigners" in the United States, supports this idea.

Transference and displacement also help us better understand interethnic conflict in the United States.[280] Racial minorities all too often fight each other because their frustration is displaced from white society, too powerful to attack successfully. Latinos and African Americans, for example, have blamed each other for their social and economic woes.[281] African Americans and Asian Americans have done the same.[282] Though understandable, this displaced animosity obscures the fact that dominant society, which is fighting to maintain

---

274. *See* ALLPORT, *supra* note 270, at 243-59; *see also id.* at 346-47 ("[I]t is not economic advice that rules immigration policy, but rather the *felt frustrations* of citizens who rightly or wrongly think an immigration iron curtain will protect them in their search for status.") (emphasis in original) (footnote omitted).

275. *See supra* text accompanying notes 69-82.

276. ALLPORT, *supra* note 270, at 352.

277. *See supra* text accompanying notes 258-60 (discussing out-group homogeneity thesis). Along similar lines, Alex Aleinikoff has expressed fear about the difficulties of ensuring that the United States include lawful immigrants in the national community when efforts are made to exclude undocumented immigrants. *See* T. Alexander Aleinikoff, *The Tightening Circle of Membership*, 22 HASTINGS CONST. L.Q. 915 (1995). The difficulty of cabining such sentiment is demonstrated by the fact that, not long after the California voters passed Proposition 187 to limit the availability of public benefits to undocumented persons, *see supra* text accompanying notes 207-30 (discussing Proposition 187), Congress enacted welfare "reform" denying public benefits to lawful immigrants, *see supra* note 26 (citing legislation).

278. *See supra* text accompanying note 170.

279. *See supra* text accompanying note 92.

280. *See* Johnson, *supra* note 35, at 57-63 (analyzing how interethnic conflict is symptomatic of larger racial and social problems).

281. *See generally* BILL PIATT, BLACK AND BROWN IN AMERICA (1997) (analyzing African American/Latino conflict and advocating cooperation).

282. *See* Lisa C. Ikemoto, *Traces of the Master Narrative in the Story of African American/Korean American Conflict: How We Constructed "Los Angeles"*, 66 S. CAL. L. REV. 1581, 1584-85 (1993) (analyzing how media and other portrayals of African American and Korean American conflict in Los Angeles reflected dominant society's racial views); Reginald Leamon Robinson, *"The Other Against Itself": Deconstructing the* Violent Discourse *Between Korean and African Americans*, 67 S. CAL. L. REV. 15 (1993) (analyzing conflict along class as well as racial lines).

the racial status quo, is the true culprit. This insight suggests the importance of efforts to resolve interethnic conflict and build constructive coalitions between communities of color to challenge discrimination.[283]

Cognitive dissonance theory, under which the human mind attempts to reconcile conflicting ideas,[284] also helps explain how dominant society pits subordinated peoples against one another. Being generous to one racial minority allows one to rationalize the harsh treatment of other minorities and offer a facially neutral explanation, such as the group's failure to assimilate, its deficient work ethic, that its members speak a foreign language, or that members of the group entered the country in violation of the immigration laws. As Cass Sunstein observed,

> [t]he beneficiaries of the status quo tend to . . . conclud[e] that the victims deserve their fate, that they are responsible for it, or that the current situation is part of the intractable, given, or natural order. . . . [P]eople who behave cruelly change their attitudes toward the objects of their cruelty and thus devalue them. Observers of cruelty and violence tend to do the same. The phenomenon of blaming the victim has clear cognitive and motivational foundations. The notion that the world is just, and that existing inequalities are deserved or desired, plays a large role in forming preferences and beliefs. All these phenomena played an enormous part in the history of racial and sexual discrimination.[285]

A number of other psychological and sociological theories offer some explanatory role for the relationship between domestic and foreign subordination.[286] The theory of status conflict focuses on conflicting groups fighting for status in the country.[287] Competition theory sees various ethnic groups, including whites, Asian Americans, and African Americans, competing for scarce economic and social resources.[288] Though these and many other theories of race relations differ in important ways, each considers the whole of social relations as opposed to focusing on the particular misfortune of one

---

283. *See* Charles R. Lawrence III, *Foreword: Race, Multiculturalism, and the Jurisprudence of Transformation*, 47 STAN. L. REV. 819, 828-47 (1995) (analyzing benefits and impediments to multiracial coalition building); Francisco Valdes, *Foreword: Latina/o Ethnicities, Critical Race Theory, and Post-Identity Politics in Postmodern Legal Culture: From Practices to Possibilities*, 9 LA RAZA L.J. 1, 30 n.118 (1996) (advocating "sophisticated approach to coalitional efforts").

284. *See generally* LEON FESTINGER, A THEORY OF COGNITIVE DISSONANCE (1957) (hypothesizing that when confronted with internally inconsistent ideas, a person will try to reduce cognitive dissonance by avoiding situations and information that would likely increase the inconsistency).

285. Cass R. Sunstein, *Three Civil Rights Fallacies*, 79 CAL. L. REV. 751, 759-60 (1991) (footnote omitted).

286. For a discussion of various psychological theories that help explain racial conflict, see Sylvia R. Lazos, *Deconstructing Homo[geneous] Americanus: The White Ethnic Immigrant Narrative and Its Exclusionary Effect*, 72 TUL. L. REV. (forthcoming May 1998).

287. *See supra* text accompanying notes 167-69 (explaining concept of status conflict in connection with the English-only movement in the United States).

288. *See generally* OLZAK, *supra* note 75 (applying theory to explain an empirical study considering conflict between various groups and noting rise in conflict and violence with increases in immigration).

minority group at a time. This lesson should not be lost on those analyzing anti-immigrant sentiment and domestic race relations.

CONCLUSION

This Article traces the historical relationship between subordination of domestic minorities and noncitizen minorities. Those serious about social change must engage and contend with these complex interrelationships for a better understanding of the operation of subordination in the United States. Because racial subordination is part of a cohesive whole, it cannot be fully appreciated by focusing on one aspect as separate and apart from the dynamic social context.

As seen in the instance of interethnic conflict, the complex interrelationship suggests the need to build coalitions between subordinated communities seeking to end subordination.[289] In the past, conflict between different minority groups—be it between Black and Latino, Black and Asian, or some other—has contributed to the maintenance of the status quo. Conflict has hindered the building of coalitions necessary to dismantle the entrenched racial hierarchy.

But, if change is not forthcoming, what is one to extrapolate from the past in predicting the future? We can expect crackdowns on immigrant minorities at times when minimal improvements are seen by domestic racial minorities. Foreigners, like sacrifices to the gods, are the price for domestic minorities to achieve marginal improvements in their plight. The psychological dynamics work together to buttress the status quo and ensure maintenance of the racial hierarchy in the United States.

For better or worse, the history of national origin and racial exclusion in U.S. immigration laws serves as a lens into this nation's soul. By considering the nationalities and racial minorities that a society seeks to exclude from the national community, we better understand how that society views citizens who share common characteristics with the excluded group. This phenomenon is not limited to racial minorities, but applies with equal force to other groups who have been excluded from our shores under the immigration laws, including political minorities, the poor, women, lesbians, and gay men.[290] Disadvantaged in the United States means multiply disadvantaged under the immigration laws.[291]

Transference of hate and displacement of frustration from one racial minority to another explain much in the heated racial dynamics of the twentieth century. Cognitive dissonance theory also teaches us how the nation can be so harsh to noncitizens of color while claiming that racism is dead in America. As immigration continues to change the complexion of U.S. society, we unfortunately can expect more of the same. One can only wonder what the

---

289. *See supra* text accompanying note 283 (discussing building of multiracial coalitions).

290. For analysis of different subordinated groups' attempts to achieve full citizenship rights in this country, see KENNETH L. KARST, BELONGING TO AMERICA (1989).

291. *Cf.* Kimberle Crenshaw, *Mapping the Margins: Intersectionality, Identity Politics, and Violence Against Women of Color*, 43 STAN. L. REV. 1241 (1991) (analyzing intersection of race and gender in subordination of women of color).

constant striving for homogeneity[292] means for the future, as racial diversity in the United States increases and the Anglo-Saxon ideal becomes less a possibility and more a distant, perhaps nostalgic, memory. Indeed, we are left with a terrifying vision into the heart of darkness. Are we robots? Insects?[293] In pondering the future, the question posed by Richard Delgado—"The Coming Race War?"—becomes all the more ominous.[294]

---

292. For critique of the Anglo-Saxon homogeneity assumption underlying U.S. law generally, see Lazos, *supra* note 286. *See also* Kenneth B. Nunn, *Law as a Eurocentric Enterprise*, 15 LAW & INEQ. J. 323 (1997) (analyzing Eurocentric nature of law and its use as instrument of cultural domination in the United States).

293. *See* George A. Martínez, Latinos, Assimilation, and the Law: A Philosophical Perspective (unpublished manuscript, on file with author).

294. RICHARD DELGADO, THE COMING RACE WAR? (1996).

LEGAL ASSISTANCE FOR VIETNAMESE ASYLUM SEEKERS; Thua Van Le; Em Van Vo; Thu Hoa Thi Dang; Truc Hoa Thi Vo, Appellants

v.

DEPARTMENT OF STATE, BUREAU OF CONSULAR AFFAIRS, et al., Appellees.

No. 94–5104.

United States Court of Appeals, District of Columbia Circuit.

Argued Nov. 4, 1994.

Decided Feb. 3, 1995.

As Amended Feb. 3, 1995.

Citizens' group, detained Vietnamese immigrants in Hong Kong, and American citizen sponsors brought action for declaratory and injunctive relief against United States Department of State on behalf of class of Vietnamese nationals in Hong Kong who were being instructed to return to Vietnam for visa processing. The United States District Court for the District of Columbia, Harold H. Greene, J., granted State Department's motion for summary judgment, and appeal was taken. The Court of Appeals, Sentelle, Circuit Judge, held that: (1) sponsors suffered requisite injury in fact and were within zone of interest protected by Immigration and Nationality Act for standing to bring action, and (2) State Department's refusal to process visas violated statutory prohibition on nationality-based discrimination in visa processing.

Reversed and remanded.

Randolph, Circuit Judge, filed dissenting opinion.

1. Administrative Law and Procedure ⚡668

Administrative Procedure Act grants standing to any party who is adversely affected or aggrieved by agency action within meaning of relevant statute. 5 U.S.C.A. § 702.

2. Administrative Law and Procedure ⚡668

Party must suffer injury in fact and interest sought to be protected must arguably be within zone of interests protected by statute in question for standing to bring action under Administrative Procedure Act. 5 U.S.C.A. § 702.

3. Administrative Law and Procedure ⚡668

Aliens ⚡54.3(1)

American citizens and permanent resident aliens in United States who were close relatives and were sponsoring Vietnamese boat people in Hong Kong suffered requisite injury in fact and were within zone of interest protected by Immigration and Nationality Act for standing to challenge State Department's change in policy requiring boat people to return to Vietnam for visa processing. 5 U.S.C.A. § 702; Immigration and Nationality Act, §§ 201–206, 8 U.S.C.A. §§ 1151–1156.

4. Federal Civil Procedure ⚡103.2

If one party to action has standing, court need not decide standing issue as to other parties when it makes no difference to merits of case.

5. Aliens ⚡18

Visa applicants have no vested right in issuance of visa.

6. Aliens ⚡44

State Department's refusal to process visas of detained Vietnamese boat people in Hong Kong violated statute prohibiting nationality-based discrimination in issuing immigrant visas. Immigration and Nationality Act, § 202(a), 8 U.S.C.A. § 1152(a).

7. Constitutional Law ⚡70.1(2)

Court may not rewrite statutory provision which by its own terms provides no exceptions or qualifications simply on preferred rational basis.

Appeal from the United States District Court for the District of Columbia, No. 94cv00361.

Daniel Wolf, Washington, DC, argued the cause for appellants. With him on the briefs were William R. Stein and Robert B. Jobe, Washington, DC.

Bernadette C. Sargeant, Asst. U.S. Atty., Washington, DC, argued the cause for appellees. With her on the brief were Eric H. Holder, Jr., U.S. Atty., John D. Bates and R. Craig Lawrence, Asst. U.S. Attys., Washington, DC.

Before EDWARDS, Chief Judge, and SENTELLE and RANDOLPH, Circuit Judges.

Opinion for the Court filed by Circuit Judge SENTELLE.

Dissenting opinion filed by Circuit Judge RANDOLPH.

SENTELLE, Circuit Judge:

This is an appeal from a grant of summary judgment by a not-for-profit corporation, Legal Assistance for Vietnamese Asylum Seekers, Inc. ("LAVAS"); two detained Vietnamese immigrants in Hong Kong; and their American citizen sponsors, against the United States Department of State and various government officials in their official capacities (collectively "the State Department" or "Department"). Appellants allege the State Department violated its own regulations as well as the Immigration and Nationality Act when refusing to process the visa applications of Vietnamese immigrants, who had not been screened in as political refugees, at the United States Consulate in Hong Kong. Because we find the district court erred in granting summary judgment in favor of appellees, we reverse and remand.

I. BACKGROUND

Since April 1975, when the North Vietnamese captured Saigon, large numbers of refugees have fled Vietnam to Hong Kong. Between June 1979 and June 1988, the treatment of these persons was guided by an informal agreement under which Hong Kong and other nations in the region committed themselves to granting temporary refuge in exchange for a commitment from the United States and other western countries to resettle these immigrants. As part of this agreement, the Hong Kong Government accorded these immigrants presumptive refugee status.

However, due to an increase in the number of persons fleeing Vietnam in the late 1980s, the Hong Kong Government announced it was revoking the presumptive refugee status of the Vietnamese immigrants as of June 15, 1988. Thereafter, all new arrivals would be detained and screened by local immigration authorities to determine whether they individually qualified for refugee status. In June 1989, this approach was adopted throughout the region in the form of a Comprehensive Plan of Action ("CPA"), a joint statement of policy also adopted by the United States. The CPA provides that asylum seekers who are screened out, that is those who do not qualify as refugees under the criteria established in the Refugee Convention, should return to Vietnam. Once returned, those eligible for immigrant visas may apply through the Orderly Departure Program, established to provide for the departure of Vietnamese directly from Vietnam to their resettlement destinations.

The United States permits Vietnamese immigrants, who have as sponsors close relatives who are United States citizens or permanent resident aliens in the United States, to enter as beneficiaries of immigrant visas under the criteria set forth in the Immigration and Nationality Act ("INA"), 8 U.S.C. §§ 1151–1156 (1988). To obtain a visa, eligible Vietnamese immigrants and their sponsors must complete several steps. First, the sponsor must file a petition with the Immigration and Naturalization Service ("INS"). 8 C.F.R. § 204.1(a) (1994). If the INS approves the petition, the Vietnamese applicant must complete and submit to the United States State Department an application for an immigrant visa. 22 C.F.R. § 42.63(a) (1994). Third, the applicant must provide various documents to a United States consulate, and appear at the consulate for final processing of the visa application. 22 C.F.R. § 42.62(a) (1994).

From June 1979 to April 1993, the State Department processed applications for Vietnamese boat people in Hong Kong at the

United States consulate. Although the Department directed its posts in November 1991 to advise screened out applicants to return to Vietnam, the United States consulate in Hong Kong ignored this change in policy. The consulate continued to process the visa applications from screened out Vietnamese. To facilitate this processing, the Consulate General issued letters to the Hong Kong Government requesting that Vietnamese be made available for interviews at the consulate.

In April 1993, however, after an exchange of cables in which the United States consulate in Hong Kong argued it should be permitted to continue processing those immigrants who had been screened out, the Department specifically instructed the consulate to cease such activity. Applicants who had been screened out were thus required to return to Vietnam for visa processing. The United States consulate officially informed the Hong Kong Government of the policy change on September 24, 1993.

On February 25, 1994, appellants brought this action against the State Department and various officials. Appellants sought declaratory and injunctive relief on behalf of a class of Vietnamese nationals desiring to be processed at the United States consulate in Hong Kong, yet who were instructed they would have to return to Vietnam for processing. Appellants also sought such relief on behalf of a class of sponsoring United States citizens and permanent residents who were related to the detained plaintiffs.

Appellants alleged that the State Department's change in policy was in violation of the INA and the regulations promulgated thereunder, the Administrative Procedure Act ("APA"), and the United States Constitution. Following a hearing consolidating appellants' application for a preliminary injunction with the trial of the action on its merits, the district court issued a final order on April 28, 1994, granting the State Department's motion for summary judgment and denying appellants' cross motion for summary judgment.

II. DISCUSSION

[1-3] As a threshold issue, appellees contend all of the appellants lack standing to bring this action. The APA grants standing to any party who is "adversely affected or aggrieved by agency action within the meaning of a relevant statute." 5 U.S.C. § 702 (1988). *See National Fed'n of Fed. Employees v. Cheney,* 883 F.2d 1038, 1042 (D.C.Cir. 1989). The party must suffer injury in fact, and the interest sought to be protected must arguably be within the zone of interests protected by the statute in question. *Clarke v. Securities Indus. Ass'n,* 479 U.S. 388, 395–96, 107 S.Ct. 750, 754–55, 93 L.Ed.2d 757 (1987). We first address the issue of whether the sponsoring resident appellants possess standing. Appellants argue these plaintiffs suffer the requisite injury in fact and are within the zone of interest protected by the INA.

We agree. First, as to injury in fact, the State Department's conduct prolongs the separation of immediate family members. The detained appellants must either remain in Hong Kong, where they are denied the opportunity to be processed, or, if they are required first to return to Vietnam, their processing will be further delayed. We have previously found injury in fact where the plaintiffs were far less aggrieved than in the case at bar. *See, e.g., Abourezk v. Reagan,* 785 F.2d 1043, 1050–51 (D.C.Cir.1986) (holding American plaintiffs possess standing where the State Department denied visas to aliens wishing to visit the United States to attend meetings at the behest of these plaintiffs).

Second, the resident appellants are within the zone of interest protected by the INA. As the Supreme Court held in *Clarke,* the zone of interest test does not necessarily require a specific congressional purpose to benefit the would-be plaintiff. It is sufficient if the plaintiffs " 'establish that their *particular* interest[ ]' " falls within the area of interests Congress intended to protect. *National Fed'n of Fed. Employees,* 883 F.2d at 1047 (quoting *Haitian Refugee Ctr. v. Gracey,* 809 F.2d 794, 812 (D.C.Cir.1987)). The INA authorizes the immigration of family members of United States citizens and permanent resident aliens. 8 U.S.C. §§ 1151–1156. In originally enacting the INA, Congress "implement[ed] the underlying intention of our immigration laws regarding the preservation of the family unit." H.R.Rep. No. 1365, 82d Cong., 2d Sess. (1952), *reprinted in* 1952 U.S.C.C.A.N. 1653, 1680. Given the nature and purpose of the statute, the resident appellants fall well within the zone of interest Congress intended to protect.

[4] Appellees also contend that neither LAVAS nor the detained appellants in Hong Kong have standing. We need not reach this issue. If one party to an action has standing, a court need not decide the standing issue as to other parties when it makes no difference to the merits of the case. *See Railway Labor Executives' Ass'n v. United States*, 987 F.2d 806, 810 (D.C.Cir.1993) (per curiam).[1]

[5] We now turn to the merits of the appeal. Appellants allege the State Department's refusal to process the visas of the detained appellants in Hong Kong violates 22 C.F.R. § 42.61(a) of the Department's visa regulations. The regulation concerns the circumstances under which an immigrant seeking a visa can have his case processed in a given consular district. The parties dispute the proper interpretation of this regulation, but we need not construe the version of the regulation in effect at the time the dispute arose because it has been rendered moot by 1994 amendments to 22 C.F.R. § 42.61(a). Visa applicants have no vested right in the issuance of a visa. *De Avilia v. Civiletti*, 643 F.2d 471, 477 (7th Cir.1981). They are certainly not entitled to prospective relief based on a no longer effective version of a later amended regulation. It is the amended version which will now govern the admission of the detained Vietnamese, and it is that version we must construe:

> (a) *Alien to apply in consular district of residence.* Unless otherwise directed by the Department, an alien applying for an immigrant visa shall make application at the consular office having jurisdiction over the alien's place of residence; except that, unless otherwise directed by the Department, an alien physically present in an area but having no residence therein may make application at the consular office having jurisdiction over that area if the alien can establish that he or she will be able to remain in the area for the period required to process the application....

59 Fed.Reg. 39,955 (1994) (to be codified at 22 C.F.R. § 42.61).

Under this regulation, an alien desiring a visa shall apply at the consular office where he resides. Alternatively, an alien physically present in an area has the option of applying at the consular office having jurisdiction over that area if he satisfies a precondition.[2] However, asserting its authority under the regulation to "direct otherwise," the Department has ceased processing Vietnamese immigrants in Hong Kong at the consular office. Nationals of other countries not subject to the CPA are still processed at the consular office.

[6] Although appellees' regulation permits this differing treatment, appellants claim the discrimination violates 8 U.S.C. § 1152(a) of the INA. This section provides "no person shall ... be discriminated against in the issuance of an immigrant visa because

1. We do not address the additional threshold question of mootness raised by the dissent because we do not view it as being properly in the case. No party has suggested that the case is moot on the basis asserted by the dissent nor do we understand the dissent to be asserting that the case is moot. The dissent from a reading of the facts determines that the case might possibly be moot and therefore, in the view of the dissent, should have been remanded. Unlike the dissent we find no authority for the proposition that we should remand a case upon our discovery of grounds that might possibly render the case moot. *Johnson v. New York State Education Department*, 409 U.S. 75, 76, 93 S.Ct. 259, 259, 34 L.Ed.2d 290 (1972) (per curiam), did not involve a suggestion that the case *might be* moot. The suggestion in *Johnson* was that the facts were such that the case had in fact become moot. The Supreme Court unremarkably remanded for a determination as to whether the facts were as represented. The suggestion by the dissent in the present case is that the facts *may* have changed so as to make the case moot after the hearing below. Such a speculative possibility not raised by any party to the case could be asserted in a wide array of cases but has never been the basis of a remand to our knowledge.

2. We need not distinguish the terms "reside" and "physically present" for purposes of this appeal.

of the person's ... nationality ... or place of residence." Appellants argue that the Department violated the statute in drawing an explicit distinction between Vietnamese nationals and nationals of other countries when refusing to process the visas of the screened out Vietnamese immigrants. Appellants assert this statute compels this court to invalidate any attempt to draw a distinction based on nationality in the issuance of visas. In contrast, appellees urge us to adopt the position that so long as they possess a rational basis for making the distinction, they are not in violation of the statute. Appellees maintain the goal of encouraging voluntary repatriation and the aims of the CPA certainly provide a rational basis for the practices and policies in question.

[7] We agree with appellants' interpretation of the statute. Congress could hardly have chosen more explicit language. While we need not decide in the case before us whether the State Department could never justify an exception under the provision, such a justification, if possible at all, must be most compelling—perhaps a national emergency. We cannot rewrite a statutory provision which by its own terms provides no exceptions or qualifications simply on a preferred "rational basis." *Cf. Haitian Refugee Ctr. v. Civiletti*, 503 F.Supp. 442, 453 (S.D.Fla.1980) (under 8 U.S.C. § 1152(a), INS has no authority to discriminate on the basis of national origin, except perhaps by promulgating regulations in a time of national emergency).

Appellees rely on *Narenji v. Civiletti*, 617 F.2d 745 (D.C.Cir.1979), for the proposition that their nationality-based discrimination passes muster under section 1152(a) as long as they possess a rational justification. In *Narenji*, we upheld an INS regulation requiring nonimmigrant alien students in the United States who were natives or citizens of Iran to report to an INS office to provide information concerning their nonimmigrant status. *Id.* at 746–47. The INA delegated to the Attorney General the authority to prescribe conditions of admission to the United States for nonimmigrant aliens. 8 U.S.C. § 1184(a). The INA also authorized the Attorney General to order the deportation of any nonimmigrant alien who failed to comply with the conditions of his status. 8 U.S.C. § 1251(a)(9). We held that a broad mandate of the INA delegating to the Attorney General the authority to prescribe conditions of admission to the United States on the part of nonimmigrant aliens authorized the Attorney General to draw distinctions among nonimmigrant aliens on the basis of nationality. *Narenji*, 617 F.2d at 747. We then examined whether the regulation violated the Constitution. In finding no violation, we stated that we would sustain classifications on the basis of nationality drawn by the Congress or the Executive in the immigration field, so long as they were not wholly irrational. *Id.* Appellants argue that *Narenji* compels us to sustain the distinctions drawn in the present regulations.

Appellees' reliance on *Narenji* is misplaced. In that case the court was considering the power of the Immigration and Naturalization Service to promulgate nationality-based regulations and the constitutionality of such regulations if otherwise properly promulgated. Under constitutional standards we found no equal protection violation. *Id.* at 748. The *Narenji* court did not consider the effect on the agency regulatory authority to make distinctions of a statute flatly forbidding nationality-based discrimination. Here the agency's nationality-based regulation runs athwart such a statute. The appellees' proffered statutory interpretation, leaving it fully possessed of all its constitutional power to make nationality-based distinctions, would render 8 U.S.C. § 1152(a) a virtual nullity.

Section 1152 is a part of the Immigration and Nationality Act. This is an act committed to the administration of the Immigration and Naturalization Service and we review its interpretations deferentially under the standard of *Chevron U.S.A., Inc. v. Natural Resources Defense Council, Inc.*, 467 U.S. 837, 842–43, 104 S.Ct. 2778, 2781–82, 81 L.Ed.2d 694 (1984). Even under that standard the Service's present interpretation fails. Where Congress has unambiguously expressed its intent, we need go no further. Here, Congress has unambiguously directed that no nationality-based discrimination shall occur. There is no room for the Service's interpretation proffered by the Department.

Under the APA, this court is obligated to hold unlawful and set aside agency action found to be not in accordance with law. 5 U.S.C. 706(2)(A) (1988). The interpretation and application of the regulation so as to discriminate against Vietnamese on the basis of their nationality is in violation of the Act, and therefore not in accordance with law.

The dissent's contention that the distinction drawn by the Department is the permissible line between legal and illegal immigrants as opposed to the impermissible nationality-based line between Vietnamese and non-Vietnamese illegal immigrants is simply not supported by the record. The case reaches us on appeal from summary judgment. At the summary judgment stage in the district court, the defendants expressly stated in their "Statement in Response to Plaintiffs' Statement of Material Facts as to which there is no Genuine Dispute," that "in approximately April, 1993, the Department changed its practice or policy relating to the processing of immigrant visa petitions of *Vietnamese nationals* residing illegally in Hong Kong." (Joint Appendix 353) (emphasis added). The Department has never contended here or in the district court that this change was made as to any other nationals than Vietnamese nationals nor that illegally present nationals of other countries would be treated the same as illegally present Vietnamese nationals. We neither hold nor imply that any statute requires that the same treatment be afforded legal and illegal status.

III. CONCLUSION

Accordingly, we reverse the district court's grant of summary judgment in favor of appellees and remand the case for a disposition consistent with this opinion.

It is so ordered.

RANDOLPH, Circuit Judge, dissenting:

My objections to the majority opinion are, first, that the decision on the merits is in error, and second, that the prospect of mootness should have precluded any decision on the merits. I realize that discussing the issues in this sequence inverts the usual order. But the majority's mistake on the merits is the more serious in terms of lasting consequences and I shall therefore begin with it.

The British crown colony of Hong Kong is one of the most densely populated regions in the world. Within its tiny area, nearly six million people reside. Because of Hong Kong's proximity to Vietnam it has become one of the prime destinations for Vietnamese "boat people," more than 750,000 of whom have fled to the countries of Southeast Asia during the past nineteen years. After the fall of Saigon in 1975, the United States pressed "first asylum" countries such as Hong Kong to provide a safe haven for these people until they could be resettled elsewhere or returned to Vietnam. But as the years passed, the influx of boat people continued. Since June 1988, more than 71,000 individuals from Vietnam have arrived on Hong Kong's shores and wound up in its detention camps. In an effort to stem the tide and to relieve itself of the burdens imposed by this mass exodus, Hong Kong entered into a Comprehensive Plan of Action with fifty other nations, including the United States. Developed in 1989, the Plan governs the screening of asylum seekers and provides that those persons not recognized as "refugees" pursuant to international criteria—those who have been "screened out"—must return to Vietnam in order to seek resettlement in a third country.

For the moment, Hong Kong and the other "first asylum" countries are exercising forbearance. They are following a program of voluntary repatriation for those who have been "screened out." Hong Kong is, in other words, asking these people to depart voluntarily rather than forcibly expelling them, as it presumably has every right to do since they are there illegally. The head of the State Department's Bureau of Refugee Programs believes that it is "fundamentally important to the success" of the Comprehensive Plan that "Vietnamese in the camps have the clear perception that there is no alternative for the screened out but to return to Vietnam." "[A]nything that clouds that perception or gives birth to rumors that resettlement of the screened out is possible will reduce voluntary repatriation and create a situation in which resort to mandatory repatriation by first asylum governments is made more likely."

The potential repercussions of the majority's decision are, to say the least, disquieting. The flight of illegal aliens to Hong Kong and elsewhere has created an international crisis. Fifty nations have sought to avert the flood by stopping the flow. Not processing their visas in Hong Kong removes one of the reasons so many of these people are leaving their homeland and embarking on the dangerous journey across the South China Sea. Now the majority holds that it is illegal for the United States consular office in Hong Kong to abide by the Comprehensive Plan and refuse to process immigrant visas for Vietnamese boat people detained in the camps. Why? Because this is discrimination on the basis of nationality and 8 U.S.C. § 1152 provides, with certain exceptions, that "no person shall ... be discriminated against in the issuance of an immigrant visa because of the person's race, sex, nationality, place of birth, or place of residence."

But it is not nationality that precludes visa processing. The so-called "discrimination" the majority detects stems from the illegal status of the screened out boat people, rather than from the fact (if it is a fact) that they are all Vietnamese nationals. Compare two Vietnamese nationals in Hong Kong, one there illegally and currently living in a detention camp and the other there legally, perhaps working or on holiday. As implemented, the current regulation allows processing of the legal Vietnamese but not the illegal one. That is not discrimination on the basis of nationality, but discrimination on the basis of legality. And the statute does not forbid it. Still less is the State Department's current regulation a "nationality based regulation," as the majority supposes. The regulation reads:

> (a) *Alien to apply in consular district of residence.* Unless otherwise directed by the Department, an alien applying for an immigrant visa shall make application at the consular office having jurisdiction over the alien's place of residence; except that, unless otherwise directed by the Department, an alien physically present in an area but having no residence therein may make application at the consular office having jurisdiction over that area if the alien can establish that he or she will be able to remain in the area for the period required to process the application....

59 Fed.Reg. 39,955 (1994) (to be codified at 22 C.F.R. § 42.61). There is not a word here relating to an alien's nationality. Within the United States illegal aliens are treated far differently than those who are legally here. It is beyond belief that distinguishing—that is, discriminating—among visa applicants on the same ground is forbidden. The regulation, through the words "unless otherwise directed," permits the State Department to make this distinction and section 1152 does not forbid it.

To show that the State Department was discriminating against the detainees because they were Vietnamese, the majority quotes a statement of the defendants and italicizes two words: "in approximately April, 1993, the Department changed its practice or policy relating to the processing of immigrant visa petitions of *Vietnamese nationals* residing illegally in Hong Kong." Consider the quotation again, this time without the distracting italics. It indicates that the State Department's policy dealt only with those Vietnamese "residing illegally in Hong Kong." That makes my point, not the majority's. Other Vietnamese in Hong Kong may be processed. What causes the difference in treatment? Not nationality, but the common sense international distinction between aliens who enter a country illegally and those who enter legally.

There may be room for an argument that the State Department will process other illegal immigrants—that is, other than the Hong Kong detainees—in foreign countries despite their illegal status, and therefore the Vietnamese boat people are being singled out because they are Vietnamese. But there is no evidence that this sort of thing is going on; and the regulation is so new that I doubt whether any world-wide customary practice under it can yet be discerned.

Given the profound consequences of judicial intervention and the danger that a decision might dismantle this carefully wrought international program designed to bring a humane and swift end to the continuing problem of illegal immigration, it is critical that we decide only what we have to decide. The majority has followed another course, which brings me to my second objection. Of the five plaintiffs, two are—or were—screened out Vietnamese residing in one of the Hong Kong camps. The oral argument in this case revealed that these alien-plaintiffs may have already been processed. Their preference numbers came up nearly a year ago. *See Kooritzky v. Reich*, 17 F.3d 1509, 1510–11 (D.C.Cir.1994). At the time of the district court's decision—April 1994—the State Department was still processing detainees whose visa applications were current, that is, those whose preference numbers had been reached. It therefore appears quite likely that the alien-plaintiffs are now in the United States. If they are, their two sponsors, who are also plaintiffs, have no further interest in the case. The case was never certified as a class action. The district court made no findings regarding the status of the alien-plaintiffs and neither the plaintiffs' nor the government's counsel at oral argument could say whether a live controversy still exists.

If the alien-plaintiffs have already received relief, the case could not be saved by qualifying as one capable of repetition but evading review. The capable of repetition part of the formulation means the complaining party is likely to be subjected to the same challenged activity in the future. We so held in *Christian Knights of the Ku Klux Klan v. District of Columbia*, 972 F.2d 365, 370 (D.C.Cir. 1992), citing several Supreme Court decisions on the point. If the individual Hong Kong plaintiffs already had their applications processed, they will not suffer the same fate in the future.

Without the aliens or their sponsors in the case, our deciding the merits would be warranted only if the remaining plaintiff, LAVAS, had standing, which it does not. The harm it alleges—a possible future strain on its resources—is general and speculative, *see Allen v. Wright*, 468 U.S. 737, 751, 104 S.Ct. 3315, 82 L.Ed.2d 556 (1984); and the organization is not within the zone of interest the statute was meant to protect, *cf. INS v. Legalization Assistance Project of the Los Angeles County Fed'n of Labor*, — U.S. —, —, 114 S.Ct. 422, 424, 126 L.Ed.2d 410 (1993) (Circuit Justice O'Connor).

The proper course therefore should have been to remand the case to the district court to make a finding whether the case is moot. We do not have to be entirely certain the case has become moot; if there is cause to believe it has met that fate, a remand is warranted. That is what the Supreme Court does when it encounters this sort of situation. *See, e.g., White v. Regester*, 422 U.S. 935, 936, 95 S.Ct. 2670, 2671, 45 L.Ed.2d 662 (1975) (per curiam); *Hill v. Printing Indus. of the Gulf Coast*, 422 U.S. 937, 938, 95 S.Ct. 2670, 2670, 45 L.Ed.2d 664 (1975) (per curiam); *Indiana Employment Security Div. v. Burney*, 409 U.S. 540, 541–42, 93 S.Ct. 883, 883–85, 35 L.Ed.2d 62 (1973) (per curiam); *Johnson v. New York State Educ. Dep't*, 409 U.S. 75, 76, 93 S.Ct. 259, 259, 34 L.Ed.2d 290 (1972) (per curiam) ("[G]iven the suggestion at oral argument ... the case is remanded to the [district court] to determine whether this case has become moot."). And that is what we should have done rather than rushing into the merits.

LEGAL ASSISTANCE FOR VIETNAMESE ASYLUM SEEKERS, et al., Appellants,

v.

DEPARTMENT OF STATE, BUREAU OF CONSULAR AFFAIRS, et al., Appellees.

Nos. 94–5104, 95–5425 and 96–5058.

United States Court of Appeals, District of Columbia Circuit.

Argued Nov. 26, 1996.

Decided Jan. 7, 1997.

Actions were brought challenging Department of State's consular venue policy with regard to Vietnamese and Laotian migrants seeking immigrant visas. Challenges were asserted under nondiscrimination provision of Immigration and Nationality Act (INA), Administrative Procedure Act (APA), and equal protection clause. The United States District Court for the District of Columbia granted Department's motion for summary judgment, but the Court of Appeals, 45 F.3d 469, reversed and remanded. On remand, the District Court, Stanley S. Harris, J., 909 F.Supp. 1, dismissed case as moot, and plaintiffs appealed. The Court of Appeals, 74 F.3d 1308, reversed and remanded, but the Supreme Court remanded for further consideration, — U.S. —, 117 S.Ct. 378, — L.Ed.2d —. On remand, the Court of Appeals, Sentelle, Circuit Judge, held that: (1) recent amendment to INA did not raise retroactivity concerns and applied to render statutory and APA claims unreviewable, and (2) venue policy did not violate equal protection.

Remanded.

1. Aliens ⚷40

In context of pending suit challenging State Department's consular venue policy with regard to Vietnamese and Laotian migrants seeking immigrant visas, no retroactivity concerns were raised by application of amendment to Immigration and Nationality Act effected by the Illegal Immigration Reform and Immigrant Responsibility Act of 1996 and providing that pertinent provision of INA was not to be construed to limit authority of Secretary of State to determine procedures for processing of immigrant visa applications or locations where such applications would be processed; right involved was procedural right rather than substantive right, and plaintiffs were seeking only prospective relief. Immigration and Nationality Act, § 202(a)(1)(B), as amended, 8 U.S.C.A. § 1152(a)(1)(B).

2. Administrative Law and Procedure ⚷701

Aliens ⚷44

Amendment to Immigration and Nationality Act (INA) effected by the Illegal Immigration Reform and Immigrant Responsibility Act of 1996 and providing that pertinent provision of INA was not to be construed to limit authority of Secretary of State to determine procedures for processing of immigrant visa applications or locations where such applications would be processed rendered unreviewable claims under INA and Administrative Procedure Act (APA) challenging consular venue policy with regard to Vietnamese and Laotian migrants seeking immigrant visas; venue determinations were entrusted to the discretion of the State Department. 5 U.S.C.A. § 701(a); Immigration and Nationality Act, § 202(a)(1)(B), as amended, 8 U.S.C.A. § 1152(a)(1)(B).

3. Administrative Law and Procedure ⚷701

Although there is a strong presumption of reviewability under the Administrative Procedure Act (APA), agency action is deemed to be committed to agency discretion when statutes are drawn in such broad terms that in a given case there is no law to apply or there is no meaningful standard against which to judge the agency's exercise of discretion. 5 U.S.C.A. § 701(a).

4. Constitutional Law ⚷252

As aliens, Vietnamese and Laotian migrants could not assert a Fifth Amendment right in challenging the procedures for granting immigrant visas. U.S.C.A. Const.Amend. 5.

5. Aliens ⚷51.5

Constitutional Law ⚷250.5, 274.3

State Department's consular venue policy with regard to Vietnamese and Laotian migrants seeking immigrant visas did not violate equal protection component of Fifth Amendment's Due Process Clause; policy did not depend on national origin of migrants' sponsors, who could be either United States citizens or permanent resident aliens, even though sponsor asserting familial relationship would more often than not be of Vietnamese or Laotian origin. U.S.C.A. Const. Amend. 5; Immigration and Nationality Act, § 204(a), as amended, 8 U.S.C.A. § 1154(a).

Appeals from the United States District Court for the District of Columbia (Nos. 94cv00361, 95cv00989).

Daniel Wolf, argued the cause, for appellants, with whom William R. Stein, Washington, DC, M. Kathleen O'Connor, Dallas, TX, and Robert B. Jobe, San Francisco, CA, were on the briefs.

Edwin S. Kneedler, Deputy Solicitor General, argued the cause, for appellees pro hac vice, with whom Frank W. Hunger, Assistant Attorney General, Eric H. Holder, Jr., United States Attorney, Michael J. Singer, Assistant Director, United States Department of Justice, and Robert M. Loeb, Attorney, were on the brief. Catherine W. Brown, Attorney, Washington, DC, United States Department of State, entered an appearance.

Before: EDWARDS, Chief Judge, and SENTELLE and RANDOLPH, Circuit Judges.

Opinion for the court filed by Circuit Judge SENTELLE.

SENTELLE, Circuit Judge:

These consolidated cases present challenges to the Department of State's consular venue policy. Plaintiffs assert that the policy discriminates on the basis of nationality in violation of Section 202 of the Immigration and Nationality Act ("INA"), 8 U.S.C. § 1152(a)(1). Plaintiffs also claim that the policy is arbitrary and capricious within the meaning of the Administrative Procedure Act, 5 U.S.C. § 706(2)(a), and that it violates the equal protection component of the Fifth Amendment's Due Process Clause. We conclude that under a recent amendment to the INA, plaintiffs' statutory and APA claims are unreviewable. We also hold that the constitutional claim has no merit.

I.

Because we discuss the background of the State Department policy at issue and this litigation in some detail in our opinion in *Legal Assistance for Vietnamese Asylum Seekers v. Department of State, Bureau of Consular Affairs*, 45 F.3d 469 (D.C.Cir.1995), *reh'g denied*, 74 F.3d 1308 (D.C.Cir.), *vacated*, — U.S. —, 117 S.Ct. 378, — L.Ed.2d — (1996) [hereinafter *LAVAS*], we present an abbreviated version here. During the 1980s an overwhelming number of migrants from Vietnam and Laos fled their home countries seeking refuge in other countries in Southeast Asia. To deal with the migration crisis some 50 countries, including the United States, entered into an international agreement known as the Comprehensive Plan of Action ("CPA"). Under the CPA, Vietnamese and Laotian migrants who land in other countries are screened by local officials to determine refugee status. Those migrants who are "screened-out," that is determined not to be refugees, are repatriated. A repatriated migrant may then apply for an immigrant visa from his home country. Until 1993, the United States Consulate General in Hong Kong processed the visa applications of migrants before, and sometimes after, they were screened-out as nonrefugees. Other nations party to the CPA objected that this practice encouraged further migration, so the State Department adopted a policy against processing visa applications of "screened-out" Vietnamese or Laotian migrants in Hong Kong. Under current State Department policy, the migrant is repatriated and his visa application is processed in his home country.

In 1994, two Vietnamese migrants, the migrants' sponsors in the United States, and a nonprofit legal-rights organization challenged the State Department policy under Section 202 of the INA, 8 U.S.C. § 1152(a), which prohibits United States consular officials from discriminating on the basis of nationality in the issuance of immigrant visas. The plaintiffs also claimed that the policy was arbitrary and capricious within the meaning of the Administrative Procedure Act ("APA"), 5 U.S.C. § 706(2)(a), and that it violated the equal protection component of the Fifth Amendment's Due Process Clause. The district court granted the State Department's motion for summary judgment. In *LAVAS*, a divided panel of this Court reversed, holding that the consular venue policy violated 8 U.S.C. § 1152(a)(1) because the State Department had drawn a distinction between Vietnamese and Laotian nationals and nationals of other countries. 45 F.3d at 473. We did not reach plaintiffs' remaining APA or constitutional claims. The government filed a petition for rehearing and suggestion of rehearing *en banc*. In the meantime, on remand, the district court held that the case had become moot. 909 F.Supp. 1 (D.D.C.1995). The panel reversed as to mootness and held that rehearing was unwarranted. 74 F.3d 1308 (D.C.Cir.1996).

While the government's rehearing petition in *LAVAS* was pending, a separate action, *Le v. United States Dept. of State*, was filed in United States District Court. The district court, relying on this Court's opinion in *LAVAS*, granted summary judgment for plaintiffs and enjoined the Government from implementing its policy of declining to process the applications of screened-out migrants in Hong Kong. 919 F.Supp. 27 (D.D.C.1996). The Government appealed the injunction, and this Court granted initial hearing *en banc*. In the meantime, the Supreme Court granted certiorari in *LAVAS*. — U.S. —, 116 S.Ct. 2521, 135 L.Ed.2d 1046 (1996). We then suspended *en banc* proceedings in *Le* pending the Supreme Court's decision.

On September 30, 1996, shortly before the Supreme Court was to hear oral argument in *LAVAS*, the President signed into law the Illegal Immigration Reform and Immigrant Responsibility Act of 1996 ("IIRA") (enacted as Division C of the Department of Defense Appropriations Act, 1997, Pub.L. No. 104–208, 110 Stat. 3009 (1996)). Section 633 of the IIRA amends the Immigration and Nationality Act (INA) by adding the following to 8 U.S.C. § 1152(a)(1): "(B) Nothing in this paragraph shall be construed to limit the authority of the Secretary of State to determine the procedures for the processing of immigrant visa applications or the locations where such applications will be processed." After requesting supplemental briefing on the effects of section 633, the Supreme Court vacated our judgment in *LAVAS* and remanded the case to us for "further consideration in light of Section 633." — U.S. —, 117 S.Ct. 378 (1996) (per curiam). We then consolidated *LAVAS* and *Le*.

The State Department argues that section 633 applies to plaintiffs' claim. Although section 633 was not in effect at the time the State Department enacted the new policy, the State Department asserts that Congress intended section 633 to be retroactive from its enactment. The State Department further argues that section 633 applies because the plaintiffs are seeking only prospective relief.

We need not determine whether Congress intended section 633 to apply retroactively because we hold that application of the amendment does not raise retroactivity concerns. Plaintiffs' claim raises a procedural right and is governed by the INA as amended by section 633. We also hold that this case concerns prospective relief and so does not raise problems of retroactivity. Applying section 633, we hold that the Secretary's actions are unreviewable because there is "no law to apply." We therefore reject plaintiffs' claims under the statute and the APA. Finally, we hold that plaintiffs' constitutional claim is without merit.

II.

Plaintiffs' statutory claim raises the question of whether the case is governed by the law in effect at the time the Secretary enacted the new consular venue policy or the law as amended by section 633. The Supreme Court set out the principles for determining whether a newly enacted provision is applicable to a pending case in *Landgraf v. USI Film Products*, 511 U.S. 244, 114 S.Ct. 1483, 128 L.Ed.2d 229 (1994). In *Landgraf*, the Court considered whether provisions of the

1991 Civil Rights Act permitting compensatory and punitive damages in a Title VII case would apply to a case that was pending on appeal when the statute was enacted. *Id.* at 247, 114 S.Ct. at 1488. In concluding that the provisions would not govern retroactively, the Court noted that application of a statute is not retroactive "merely because it is applied in a case arising from conduct antedating the statute's enactment or upsets expectations based in prior law." *Id.* at 269, 114 S.Ct. at 1499 (citation omitted). Rather, the statute has a retroactive effect if it "would impair rights a party possessed when he acted, increase a party's liability for past conduct, or impose new duties with respect to transactions already completed." *Id.* at 280, 114 S.Ct. at 1505. It is therefore necessary for the Court to examine the temporal relationship between the statute and the activity the statute is meant to govern.

In *Landgraf,* the Supreme Court observed that changes in procedural rules will often not raise problems of retroactivity. *Id.* at 275, 114 S.Ct. at 1502. The Court stated that "[b]ecause rules of procedure regulate secondary rather than primary conduct, the fact that a new procedural rule was instituted after the conduct giving rise to the suit does not make application of the rule ... retroactive." *Id.* The Court also noted that an intervening statute conferring or ousting jurisdiction may apply without operating retroactively. *Id.* at 274, 114 S.Ct. at 1502. The Court stated that "[a]pplication of a new jurisdictional rule usually 'takes away no substantive right but simply changes the tribunal that is to hear the case.'" *Id.* (quoting *Hallowell v. Commons,* 239 U.S. 506, 508, 36 S.Ct. 202, 203, 60 L.Ed. 409 (1916)). Finally, the Court stated that, because "'relief by injunction operates *in futuro,*'" a case seeking only prospective relief is governed by the law in effect at the time of decision. *Id.* at 273–74, 114 S.Ct. at 1501 (quoting *American Steel Foundries v. Tri-City Central Trades Council,* 257 U.S. 184, 201, 42 S.Ct. 72, 75, 66 L.Ed. 189 (1921)).

[1] Applying the principles of *Landgraf* to this case, we conclude that application of section 633 would not raise retroactivity concerns. First, plaintiffs are asserting a procedural right. The challenged State Department action merely enacts a change in the procedure by which plaintiffs' visa applications are considered. This policy does not upset any substantive right. As we held in our earlier consideration of this case, plaintiffs do not have a substantive right to any particular process for having their applications considered. *See LAVAS,* 45 F.3d at 472. The Supreme Court has stated that such procedural claims do not raise retroactivity concerns. *Landgraf,* 511 U.S. at 275, 114 S.Ct. at ——.

Moreover, plaintiffs are seeking only prospective relief. Plaintiffs characterize the remedy sought as a "reparative injunction," *i.e.,* an injunction to compel the State Department to process the application of plaintiffs in a way that would remedy the effects of the Department's past illegal conduct. However, the sole purpose and effect of the injunction would be to direct the Secretary of State not to apply the consular venue policy in the future. It is true that an injunction may be considered retroactive relief when the injunction is "tantamount to an award for damages." *Cf. Papasan v. Allain,* 478 U.S. 265, 278, 106 S.Ct. 2932, 2940, 92 L.Ed.2d 209 (1986) (distinguishing between prospective and retrospective relief in the context of the Eleventh Amendment). In *Beverly Hosp. v. Bowen,* 872 F.2d 483 (D.C.Cir.1989) (per curiam), for instance, we overturned a district court's refusal to consider granting an order that would require a hospital to consider claims for reimbursement of photocopying costs. We characterized the claim as a "matter of retrospective relief." *Id.* at 485. However, in this case the injunction would not serve as a remedy commensurate with damages for past wrongs. Instead, the injunction would serve to prevent what would allegedly be a continuing violation of the statute. The Supreme Court has made clear that in such cases the law in effect at the time of decision is to govern the availability of the relief. *Landgraf,* 511 U.S. at 273–74, 114 S.Ct. at ——.

[2, 3] Having concluded that section 633 applies, we agree with the State Department that plaintiffs' statutory and APA claims are unreviewable because consular venue deter-

minations are entrusted to the discretion of the State Department. Under the APA, a person "adversely affected or aggrieved by agency action within the meaning of a relevant statute" is entitled to judicial review. 5 U.S.C. § 702. Judicial review is not available, however, if the statute precludes judicial review or the agency action is "committed to agency discretion by law." 5 U.S.C. § 701(a). Although there is a strong presumption of reviewability under the APA, *Abbott Labs. v. Gardner*, 387 U.S. 136, 140, 87 S.Ct. 1507, 1510–11, 18 L.Ed.2d 681 (1967), agency action is deemed to be committed to agency discretion when "statutes are drawn in such broad terms that in a given case there is no law to apply," *Citizens to Preserve Overton Park, Inc. v. Volpe*, 401 U.S. 402, 410, 91 S.Ct. 814, 821, 28 L.Ed.2d 136 (1971) (internal quotations omitted), or there is "no meaningful standard against which to judge the agency's exercise of discretion," *Heckler v. Chaney*, 470 U.S. 821, 830, 105 S.Ct. 1649, 1655, 84 L.Ed.2d 714 (1985). As the Supreme Court has stated, "if no judicially manageable standards are available for judging how and when an agency should exercise its discretion, then it is impossible to evaluate agency action." *Id.* After reviewing the text of the statute and the nature of the agency action at issue we conclude that the consular venue policy falls within this category of unreviewable agency discretion.

First, the broad language of the statute suggests that the State Department policy is unreviewable. Congress has determined that "[e]very alien applying for an immigrant visa and for alien registration shall make application therefor in such form and manner *and at such place as shall be by regulations prescribed.*" 8 U.S.C. § 1202(a) (emphasis added). This section grants to the Secretary discretion to prescribe the place at which aliens apply for immigrant visas without providing substantive standards against which the Secretary's determination could be measured. Plaintiffs argue that there is a standard against which to measure the Secretary's decision in the prohibition against nationality discrimination contained in 8 U.S.C. § 1152. That argument is untenable after the adoption of section 633. That enactment made clear that the prohibition against nationality discrimination does not apply to decisions of where to process visa applications. These determinations are left entirely to the discretion of the Secretary of State

In addition, the nature of the administrative action counsels against review of plaintiffs' claim. By way of comparison, the Supreme Court has held that the Food and Drug Administration's refusal to take enforcement action is unreviewable because it "involves a complicated balancing of a number of factors which are peculiarly within [the agency's] expertise." *Heckler*, 470 U.S. at 831, 105 S.Ct. at 1655–56. Similarly, in this case the agency is entrusted by a broadly worded statute with balancing complex concerns involving security and diplomacy, State Department resources and the relative demand for visa applications. However, in this case the argument for executive branch discretion is even stronger. By long-standing tradition, courts have been wary of second-guessing executive branch decision involving complicated foreign policy matters. *See, e.g, Williams v. Suffolk Ins. Co.*, 38 U.S. 415, 420, 13 Pet. 415, 10 L.Ed. 226 (1839); *Garcia v. Lee*, 37 U.S. 511, 517–18, 520–21, 12 Pet. 511, 9 L.Ed. 1176 (1838); *Foster v. Neilson*, 27 U.S. 253, 307–310, 2 Pet. 253, 7 L.Ed. 415 (1829). As we noted in another context, "where the President acted under a congressional grant of discretion as broadly worded as any we are likely to see, and where the exercise of that discretion occurs in the area of foreign affairs, we cannot disturb his decision simply because some might find it unwise or because it differs from the policies pursued by previous administrations." *DKT Memorial Fund Ltd. v. Agency for Int'l Dev.*, 887 F.2d 275, 282 (D.C.Cir.1989). In light of the lack of guidance provided by the statute and the complicated factors involved in consular venue determinations, we hold that plaintiffs' claims under both the statute and the APA are unreviewable because there is "no law to apply."

[4, 5] We likewise reject plaintiffs' claim that the State Department's consular venue policy violates the equal protection compo-

nent of the Fifth Amendment's Due Process Clause. Plaintiffs concede that the migrants, as aliens, may not assert a Fifth Amendment right in challenging the procedures for granting immigrant visas. *See United States. v. Verdugo–Urquidez*, 494 U.S. 259, 269, 110 S.Ct. 1056, 1062–63, 108 L.Ed.2d 222 (1990). The equal protection claim must be asserted, if at all, by the citizen sponsors of the migrants. However, the State Department's policy does not depend on the national origin of the sponsor. Under the INA, a United States citizen or a permanent resident alien may sponsor an alien by filing a petition stating that the alien is an immediate relative and is eligible for an immigration preference. 8 U.S.C. § 1154(a). Employment-based immigration preferences are also available when a citizen desiring to employ an alien files a petition.. 8 U.S.C. § 1154(a)(1)(D). While we can assume that a sponsor who is asserting a familial relationship to the migrant will more often than not be of Vietnamese or Laotian origins, the State Department does not require this to be the case. We have no reason to think that the nationality of an employer-sponsor at all corresponds to that of the migrant. Moreover, the substantive rights of the citizen-sponsor to a particular process cannot be greater than the right of the applicant himself, and we have concluded that the applicants have no substantive right to have their visa applications processed in any particular venue.

For the foregoing reasons, we remand to the district court for proceedings consistent with this opinion.

So ordered.

THE GENDER DIMENSION OF U.S. IMMIGRATION POLICY

Joan Fitzpatrick†

I. INTRODUCTION

The United States is widely regarded as the premier country of immigration, with current levels of lawful immigration approaching historic peaks.[1] The place of migrants in the national community figures to a surprising degree in public policy debates over crime, employment, social services and even campaign-finance reform.[2] Yet, in this swirl of discourse over migration[3] it is often

---

† Professor of Law and Foundation Scholar, University of Washington School of Law; B.A. Rice University; J.D. Harvard Law School; Diploma in Law, Oxford University. I express my thanks for financial support to the University of Washington Law School Foundation and for research assistance to Dorothy Liu and Kimbrely Holtom. I deeply appreciate the comments given on earlier drafts by Patty Blum, Christine Chinkin, Daniel Foote, Paul Hoffman, Kevin Johnson, Deborah Maranville, Frances Olsen, Andrew Shacknove, and Ralph Steinhardt.

1. For the ten years between 1984 and 1993, legal immigration totaled 9.3 million. This approaches the peak decade of 1905-1914 during which 10.1 million persons immigrated to the United States. *See* U.S. IMMIGRATION & NATURALIZATION SERVICE, STATISTICAL YEARBOOK OF THE IMMIGRATION AND NATURALIZATION SERVICE 1994, 16 tbl.1 (1996).

2. Debate over immigration policy in the past several years has sometimes reflected the resurgence of virulent forms of nativism, including elements of racism. *See generally* IMMIGRANTS OUT! THE NEW NATIVISM AND THE ANTI-IMMIGRANT IMPULSE IN THE UNITED STATES (Juan F. Perea ed., 1996); Kevin R. Johnson, *An Essay on Immigration Politics, Popular Democracy, and California's Proposition 187: The Political Relevance and Legal Irrelevance of Race*, 70 WASH. L. REV. 629 (1995); Gerald L. Neuman, *Aliens as Outlaws: Government Services, Proposition 187, and the Structure of Equal Protection Doctrine*, 42 UCLA L. REV. 1425 (1995); Peter H. Schuck, *Alien Rumination*, 105 YALE L.J. 1963 (1996) (reviewing PETER BRIMELOW, ALIEN NATION: COMMON SENSE ABOUT AMERICA'S IMMIGRATION DISASTER (1995)). The fund-raising efforts of naturalized U.S. citizen John Huang, including his fundraising appeals to lawful permanent residents of Asian origin, received extensive media coverage in the waning days of the 1996 presidential election. *See, e.g.*, Alison Mitchell, *Democrats to Return More Money Received from 'Improper' Sources*, N.Y. TIMES, Feb. 22, 1997, at A1.

3. The current level of concern over the direction of U.S. immigration policy is reflected in the creation of an expert commission to make wide-ranging recommendations to Congress on revision of the immigration laws. *See* U.S. COMM'N ON IMMIGRATION REFORM, LEGAL IMMIGRATION: SETTING PRIORITIES 39-200 (1995) [hereinafter LEGAL IMMIGRATION]. Without awaiting the completion of the Commission's work, however,

overlooked that lawful immigration to the United States has been predominantly female for much of the past half-century.[4]

This pattern is explained largely by the favored position of family-based immigration under U.S. law[5] and the fact that men are more likely to choose a foreign spouse[6] or to immigrate to the United States and subsequently marry a foreign spouse.[7] Equally noteworthy, though of less impact on overall rates of immigration, is sustained female dominance in the family-based immigrant categories for parents of U.S. citizens[8] and adopted orphans.[9]

Gender is an organizing principle, not a simple variable, in migration, and the experience of the United States as a receiving state is no exception to this

---

Congress enacted three bills in 1996 that effect major alterations in immigration policy, especially with regard to aliens convicted of crimes, immigrants dependent on public benefits, and undocumented migrants. *See* Antiterrorism and Effective Death Penalty Act of 1996, 18 U.S.C.A. § 1 et seq. (1996); Personal Responsibility and Work Opportunities Reconciliation Act of 1996, Pub. L. No. 104-193, 110 Stat. 2105 (1996); Illegal Immigration Reform and Immigrant Responsibility Act of 1996, Pub. L. No. 104-208, 110 Stat. 3009 (1996), *amended by* Pub. L. No. 104-302, 110 Stat. 3656 (1996).

4. *See* Marion F. Houstoun et al., *Female Predominance in Immigration to the United States Since 1930: A First Look*, 18 INT'L MIGRATION REV. 908, 909 (1984).

5. Both U.S. citizens and lawful permanent residents may petition for the admission of foreign-born spouses and children. However, citizens may petition for the admission of their parents and siblings. *See* Immigration and Nationality Act (INA) § 203(a), 8 U.S.C.A. § 1153(a) (West Supp. 1997). Moreover, while no numerical limits are placed on the entry of immediate family members (spouses, unmarried children under age 21, and parents) of U.S. citizens, numerical ceilings are placed on entry of immediate family members of lawful permanent residents, and on the entry of adult or married children and siblings of U.S. citizens, resulting in backlogs and lengthy delays. *See* U.S. IMMIGRATION & NATURALIZATION SERVICE, STATISTICAL YEARBOOK OF THE IMMIGRATION AND NATURALIZATION SERVICE 1993, 18 (1995) [hereinafter 1993 STATISTICAL YEARBOOK]; LEGAL IMMIGRATION, *supra* note 3, at 65 (reporting that backlogs in family-based second preference for spouses and children of lawful permanent residents had increased to 1,138,544 by January 1995, that waiting times had increased to more than three years, and that growth in backlog might mean waits as long as ten years except where petitioning spouse naturalizes and escapes numerical limits).

6. This is especially true for members of the armed forces. The popular title of the "War Brides Act" of 1945 is evocative. From 1946 to 1948 "war brides" (who included only 0.3% husbands) constituted 25% of all lawful immigrants to the United States. *See* Houstoun et al., *supra* note 4, at 920.

7. Between 1972 and 1979, 366,691 foreign-born wives of U.S. citizens entered the United States as immigrants, compared to 224,691 foreign-born husbands. *See id.* at 924. In fiscal year 1994, 60% of the admitted spouses of U.S. citizens were female. LEGAL IMMIGRATION, *supra* note 3, at 51. The same gender disparity characterizes spouses of lawful permanent residents, with wives constituting two-thirds of the entrants in this category between 1972 and 1979, *see* Houstoun et al., *supra* note 4, at 925, as well as in fiscal year 1994, *see* LEGAL IMMIGRATION, *supra* note 3, at 64.

8. Mothers constituted 66.9% of admitted parents of U.S. citizens between 1972 and 1979, *see* Houstoun et al., *supra* note 4, at 924, and nearly 65% in fiscal year 1994, *see* LEGAL IMMIGRATION, *supra* note 3, at 55. Admissions of parents totalled 65,000 in fiscal 1992, declining to 62,000 in fiscal 1993, *see* 1993 STATISTICAL YEARBOOK, *supra* note 5, at 17 tbl.B, and to 48,382 in fiscal 1995. *See* Immigration & Naturalization Serv., *Immigration to the United States in Fiscal Year 1995* (last modified Oct. 17, 1996) <http://www.usdoj.gov/ins/public/stats.htm> [hereinafter *Immigration to the United States in Fiscal Year 1995*]. Female dominance in this immigration category may be attributed to higher female rates of longevity and economic dependency. *See* LEGAL IMMIGRATION, *supra* note 3, at 55. Only U.S. citizens who are at least 21 years of age may petition for the admission of their parents. For a discussion of the gendered impact of recently-enacted restrictions on public benefits for immigrant parents, see *infra* notes 81-120 and accompanying text.

9. Sixty-one percent of the foreign orphans adopted between 1972 to 1979 were female, *see* Houstoun et al., *supra* note 4, at 924; as were 54% in fiscal year 1993, *see* 1993 STATISTICAL YEARBOOK, *supra* note 5, at 57 tbl.15; and 62% in fiscal year 1995. *See Immigration to the United States in Fiscal Year 1995*, *supra* note 8. In contrast, slightly more male than female children of citizens and lawful permanent residents are admitted. *See* LEGAL IMMIGRATION, *supra* note 3, at 64. The difference may reflect both preferences of adoptive parents and higher rates of abandonment of foreign female children.

pattern. Being female, like being male, strongly shapes the direction and consequences of many migrations. Women's greater responsibility for family and household (often referred to as the tasks of social reproduction) affects their labor-force participation and consequently exerts a strong influence on their migratory patterns.

A striking difference exists in the bases for male and female admission, largely because female dominance of lawful immigration derives disproportionately from family ties. Female primary beneficiaries consume only a paltry number of employment-based immigrant visas to the United States.[10] While a substantial number of women immigrate in the employment-based categories, they do so largely by means of derivative status based on a family relationship with a male primary beneficiary.[11] Employment-based immigration increasingly favors those with advanced education, scientific or technical renown, prominent managerial position, or wealth,[12] a shift in valued attributes that is likely to impede rather than to enhance the ability of women to qualify independently for employment-based immigration.

This does not mean that female immigrants to the United States do not work outside the home.[13] Once lawfully admitted on the basis of a family relationship, immigrants receive unrestricted work authorization. While workforce participation rates among immigrant women are comparable to those among female U.S. citizens, they fall short of male rates, reflecting the disparate allocation of household responsibilities.[14] The fact that immigrant women are

10. For example, women were the primary beneficiaries of only 3% of the employment-based immigrant visas in 1979. *See* Andrea Tyree & Katharine Donato, *A Demographic Overview of the International Migration of Women*, *in* INTERNATIONAL MIGRATION: THE FEMALE EXPERIENCE 21, 34 (Rita James Simon & Caroline B. Brettell eds., 1986).

11. In fiscal year 1995, for example, admissions under the first employment-based preference category totalled 17,339, including 6,733 priority workers and 10,606 of their family members. *See Immigration to the United States in Fiscal Year 1995*, *supra* note 8.

12. Congress adopted substantial alterations in the criteria for employment-based immigration in 1990, to favor such qualifications. *See generally* William V. Roebuck, Jr., *The Move to Employment-Based Immigration in the Immigration Act of 1990: Towards a New Definition of 'Immigrant*,' 16 N.C. J. INT'L L. & COM. REG. 523 (1991) (discussing effects of Immigration Act of 1990); Robert S. Groban, Jr., *The Immigration Act of 1990: An Employer's Primer of Its New Provisions*, 17 EMPLOYEE REL. 357 (1991-92) (describing reconfigured employment-based immigrant categories in Immigration Act of 1990).

13. As Mirjana Morokvašic observes: "Women always work. They are not in and out of economic activity, but at various stages in their life cycle they are either paid for their work or not and their work is either recognized as economic activity or not." Mirjana Morokvašic, *Birds of Passage are Also Women*, 18 INT'L MIGRATION REV. 886, 888 (1984). It is thus misleading to say that immigrant women outside the formal labor market do not work. However, Congress has recently chosen to impose new disadvantages on those immigrants, largely female, who lack a lengthy formal work history. *See infra* notes 93, 97, and 100.

14. According to the 1970 census, 46.5% of recent immigrant women 16 years and older who have lived in the United States for less than five years were employed, whereas 41.6% of the general population of all women 16 years and older were employed. Tyree & Donato, *supra* note 10, at 34. A Labor Department report, based on 1989 data, found that labor-force participation rates for recent female immigrants tended to be lower than those of native women, but that the disparity lessened with the length of the immigrants' residence. *See* Joseph R. Meisenheimer II, *How Do Immigrants Fare in the U.S. Labor Market?*, MONTHLY LABOR REV., Dec. 1992, at 3. Meisenheimer reports that among women aged 35 to 44, 78% of natives and 68% of immigrants participated in the labor force; the rate for immigrant women who have lived in the United States for less than three years was only 49% while those who have lived in the United States thirty or more years ago had a participation rate of 77%, nearly the same as the rate for natives. *Id.* at 5. Meisenheimer also reports that

disproportionately unable to secure lawful entry based upon their employability forces them either to depend on family-based immigration as the key to access to the U.S. labor market or enter unlawfully. Immigrant women therefore disproportionately face disadvantages, including uncertainty with respect to their right to remain in the United States,[15] diminished economic leverage in the labor market, and threats to their physical security due to their inability to turn to governmental authorities for protection.[16]

Enhancing the visibility of female migration to the United States promotes but does not ensure that women migrants' particular needs and risks are addressed in immigration policy. Even after rectification of the long-standing scholarly neglect of the gendered aspects of migration,[17] policy neglect persists. Gender-specific constraints on women's social and spatial mobility continue to be overlooked or discounted by policy-makers, except when their attention is seized by carefully organized, sustained pressure by advocates for women migrants. Such pressure has produced some advancements for battered immigrant women[18] and for female asylum-seekers.[19] Recent U.S. legislation, however, reflects continued complacency toward differential harm to women, especially where the gendered nature of the harm is not immediately obvious. Exposing policy bias and its roots in the gendered allocation of burdens of social reproduction is a first step toward ameliorating harsh, if hidden, adverse effects on women migrants.

---

immigrant men experience lower rates of labor-force participation during their first three years of residence: 85% of new entrants entered into the workforce as compared to 97% of those entered three to eight years previously. *Id.* at 4.

A study of 698 Mexican women in the United States found that 467 of the 562 undocumented women and 110 of the 136 lawful female immigrants were employed, primarily in factory work. Rita J. Simon & Margo Corona DeLey, *Undocumented Mexican Women: Their Work and Personal Experiences*, *in* INTERNATIONAL MIGRATION: THE FEMALE EXPERIENCE 113, 115, 130 (Rita James Simon & Caroline B. Brettell eds., 1986).

15. *See infra* notes 48-64 and accompanying text.

16. Some undocumented female migrants experience slave-like conditions as a result of their indebtedness to smugglers and fear of seeking assistance from authorities. *See* Laura Ho et. al, *(Dis)Assembling Rights of Women Workers Along the Global Assembly Line: Human Rights and the Garment Industry*, 31 HARV. C.R.-C.L. L. REV. 383, 383 (1996) (describing conditions for undocumented Thai women working in garment factory in El Monte, California).

17. *See* Richard E. Bilsborrow & Hania Zlotnik, *Preliminary Report of the United Nations Expert Group Meeting on the Feminization of Internal Migration*, 26 INT'L MIGRATION REV. 138, 140 (1992) ("The problem of viewing women who moved mostly as associational migrants (i.e., moving as passive companions of other family members), while assuming that males were generally autonomous migrants or active decision-makers was recognized as a serious obstacle in advancing the understanding of the causes and consequences of female migration."); Houstoun et al., *supra* note 4, at 908 ("[T]he concept of the international migrant as a young economically motivated male has become so pervasive that it has overshadowed migration streams that are, in fact, dominated by females."); *see also* INTERNATIONAL MIGRATION: THE FEMALE EXPERIENCE (Rita James Simon & Caroline B. Brettell eds., 1986) (discussing women's migration patterns); Silvia Pedraza, *Women and Migration: The Social Consequences of Gender*, 17 INT'L REV. SOC. 303, 304-05 (1991) (discussing transformation of migration studies in recent years by addition of a gendered perspective).

18. *See infra* note 64.

19. *See infra* notes 120-125 and accompanying text.

II. GENDER-"BLIND" IMMIGRATION POLICY—THE U.S. EXPERIENCE

Women ordinarily constitute a majority of each year's legal immigrants.[20] One might conclude that women are favorites of U.S. immigration law, since an immigrant visa is "one of the scarcest, and most highly sought after, public benefits" that the U.S. Government confers.[21] In reality, however, immigration statutes adopted for apparently gender-neutral objectives can disrupt female-migration patterns or disadvantage immigrant women because of their gendered social roles.

A. *Gender Impact of the 1986 Amnesty Programs*

A striking example of facially neutral legislation with an unanticipated gender impact is the 1986 Immigration Reform and Control Act (IRCA),[22] which granted legal status to large numbers of undocumented migrants. Inadvertently, the IRCA resulted in a dramatic, if temporary, shift toward male dominance of lawful migration. More troubling, and possibly more enduring, is the IRCA's contribution toward the feminization of undocumented migration.

The 1986 Immigration Reform and Control Act effected a marked, and presumably unintended, shift in gender ratios among immigrants from 1988 to 1992 through two "amnesty" programs for undocumented migrants: one permitting legalization for long-time undocumented residents[23] and one permitting legalization for persons who had engaged in agricultural labor ("Special Agricultural Workers" or "SAWs").[24] Unlike other provisions for lawful immigration, the amnesty programs did not confer derivative benefits upon immediate family members of eligible applicants.

Men were overwhelmingly the beneficiaries of the IRCA's amnesty programs: fifty-seven percent of the long-time undocumented resident applicants and eighty-two percent of the SAW applicants were male.[25] The effect of the IRCA admissions was so great as to reverse the ordinary female domination of U.S. immigration—lawful immigration in fiscal year 1991, the height of the IRCA's impact, was sixty-six percent male.[26] By 1993, after the last immigration

---

20. *See supra* notes 4, 7-9 and accompanying text.

21. Kevin R. Johnson, *Public Benefits and Immigration: The Intersection of Immigration Status, Ethnicity, Gender and Class*, 42 UCLA L. REV. 1509, 1512 (1995).

22. Immigration Reform and Control Act of 1986, 8 U.S.C.A. § 1101 et seq. (1986).

23. The 1986 Immigration Reform and Control Act provided a process for persons unlawfully present in the United States who had entered prior to 1982 to adjust to lawful immigrant status. As of 1991, 82.3% of legalization applicants reported that they had entered without inspection while 17.7% had entered in lawful non-immigrant status but overstayed or otherwise had violated the terms of their admission. U.S. IMMIGRATION & NATURALIZATION SERVICE, STATISTICAL YEARBOOK OF THE IMMIGRATION AND NATURALIZATION SERVICE 1991, 70 (1993) [hereinafter 1991 STATISTICAL YEARBOOK].

24. Special Agricultural Workers were eligible for the program if they had engaged in seasonal agricultural work for a minimum of 90 days in the year preceding May, 1986. *See id.*

25. *See id.* at 70-71.

26. *See* 1993 STATISTICAL YEARBOOK, *supra* note 5, at 52 tbl.13 (1,213,767 male immigrants and 613,166 female immigrants).

applicants under the IRCA had been granted legal status, gender ratios quickly shifted back to the familiar pattern of female predominance.[27]

Certain of the gender disparities encountered under the IRCA can be traced to earlier, distinctively gendered immigration patterns to the United States. Although undocumented immigration to the United States is multifaceted and by no means restricted to surreptitious Mexican entrants,[28] a strikingly high percentage of beneficiaries of both the IRCA legalization program and the SAW program came from Mexico.[29] Thus, patterns of Mexico-U.S. migration exerted a strong influence on the overall amnesty experience, including its gender imbalance.

Undocumented Mexican migration to the United States has until recently been male-dominated.[30] The Bracero Program of 1940-1964, though long since terminated, established enduring patterns of labor migration from Mexico:

> Virtually all bracero contracts went to men. This gender-discriminatory labor policy mandated an elastic supply of labor, one that could be synchronized with seasonal agricultural fluctuations and that would externalize labor reproduction costs to Mexico. . . . What the designers of the program had not anticipated, however, was the extent to which the bracero program would stimulate more Mexican immigration, both legal and undocumented. Many of the braceros acquired permanent legal status through labor certification, while others repeatedly migrated without documents or contracts; many of them started social networks that facilitated the future migration of their friends and family. And importantly, the bracero program ultimately germinated large-scale permanent settlement of Mexican immigrants.[31]

---

27. *See id.* at 22, 52 tbl.13 (women constituted 53.1% of total immigrants).

28. A generally accepted study by Robert Warren of the INS estimated that 31% of undocumented migrants residing in the United States in October, 1992 (after the IRCA's amnesty programs had been implemented) were Mexican. *See* MICHAEL FIX & JEFFREY S. PASSEL, IMMIGRATION AND IMMIGRANTS: SETTING THE RECORD STRAIGHT 24 tbl.2, 86 n.13 (1994). Europe and Canada contributed 13% of the undocumented immigrants in the United States in 1992. *Id.* at 24 tbl.2. While 40% of these immigrants had entered without inspection, 60% entered legally and later violated the terms of their non-immigrant admission. *Id.* at 25. An INS study released on February 7, 1997, however, estimates that 54% of the five million undocumented immigrants are Mexican nationals. The study also assesses the proportion of current visa overstays at 41% of the total, with illegal entrants comprising 59% of the total. *See* OFFICE OF POLICY & PLANNING, U.S. DEP'T OF JUSTICE, ESTIMATES OF THE UNAUTHORIZED IMMIGRANT POPULATION RESIDING IN THE UNITED STATES: OCTOBER 1996, at 4, 3 (1997); Eric Schmitt, *Illegal Immigrants Rose to 5 Million in '96*, N.Y. TIMES, Feb. 8, 1997, at A7.

29. *See* 1991 STATISTICAL YEARBOOK, *supra* note 23, at 70 (69.8% of the legalization applicants and 81.6% of the SAW applicants were Mexican).

30. *See* Katharine M. Donato, *Current Trends and Patterns of Female Migration: Evidence from Mexico*, 27 INT'L MIGRATION REV. 748, 749, 761 (1993).

31. *See* PIERRETTE HONDAGNEU-SOTELO, GENDERED TRANSITIONS: MEXICAN EXPERIENCES OF IMMIGRATION 20-23 (1994) (citation omitted); *see also* KITTY CALAVITA, INSIDE THE STATE: THE BRACERO PROGRAM, IMMIGRATION AND THE I.N.S. (1992). Scholars of Mexico-U.S. migration long discounted its female component because of this perception of male dominance. *See* Sherrie A. Kossoudji & Susan I. Ranney, *The Labor Market Experience of Female Migrants: The Case of Temporary Mexican Migration to the U.S.*, 18 INT'L MIGRATION REV. 1120, 1120-21 (1984).

Men's experiences under the Bracero program help to explain their disproportionate application for legalization under the IRCA.

In addition to the influence of traditional migration patterns from Mexico, the gendered impact of the IRCA amnesty programs may be traceable, at least in part, to role divisions within migrant families. It is plausible that Congress had a male paradigm in view when it decided to legalize the status of long-time undocumented residents. Given patterns of serial migration by family members, with male earners frequently taking the lead,[32] it is possible that among migrant families husbands were more likely to have accrued the necessary years of sustained residence to qualify for legalization. Moreover, even among families where both spouses had accrued the necessary residence, the household economy may have dictated that application for legalization, which required a substantial fee, be restricted to the primary earner. Gendered evaluations of the relative importance of securing legal access to the labor market and lawful residence for the male "head of household," as compared to female and minor family members, could thus have contributed to male numerical dominance among amnesty applicants.

The even more highly gendered SAW program was added to the IRCA under pressure from large agricultural interests who feared the loss of a low-wage workforce as a consequence of the introduction into federal law of sanctions against employers of undocumented migrants.[33] Congress' primary concern in denying derivative status to family members of SAWs may have been to avoid a multiplier or magnet effect. The denial of derivative status may also reflect policy-makers' attitudes toward the relative social desirability of persons whose work sustains a major industry at low cost, compared to those workers' low-income spouses and children. A more charitable view of denial of derivative status to SAW families is that Congress might have assumed that legalized agricultural workers would maintain their traditional pattern of seasonal presence in the United States, broken by periods of reunion with wives and children in the country of origin. The migration pattern, however, has shifted from temporary stays toward long-term settlement of Mexican laborers in the United States.[34]

The Immigration Reform and Control Act continues to exert a substantial, and significantly gendered, influence on U.S. immigration patterns. After the IRCA beneficiaries gained lawful permanent residence, their spouses and children became eligible to immigrate lawfully in the second family-based

32. *See generally* HONDAGNEU-SOTELO, *supra* note 31 (describing evolution of Mexico-U.S. migration from earlier patterns of solo migration by male heads-of-households and elder sons).

33. *See* THOMAS ALEXANDER ALEINIKOFF ET AL., IMMIGRATION PROCESS AND POLICY 295-96 (3d ed. 1995).

34. *See* Wayne A. Cornelius, *From Sojourners to Settlers: The Changing Profile of Mexican Immigration to the United States*, *in* U.S.-MEXICO RELATIONS: LABOR MARKET INTERDEPENDENCE 155, 155 (Jorge A. Bustamante et al. eds., 1992).

preference category and many chose to pursue this option.[35] They encountered substantial delays in entry because of numerical limits on second-preference visas and per-country limits on immigration.[36] Congress reacted to this serious impediment to family unity by establishing temporary additional visa allocations and special dispensation from deportation for immediate relatives of legalization beneficiaries,[37] but the backlog continued to grow.[38] As the IRCA beneficiaries became naturalized,[39] surges in the rate of entry of immediate family members of U.S. citizens were expected to occur.[40] This trend should have reinforced female dominance of lawful immigration since "[h]igh proportions of young adult legalized aliens were men, many of whom already have petitioned for their wives and children."[41]

However, severe restrictions on the ability of lower-income U.S. citizens to petition for their alien relatives, enacted as part of the Illegal Immigration Reform and Responsibility Act of 1996, impede lawful immigration by spouses of some naturalized IRCA beneficiaries.[42] No data yet exist on the impact of the restrictions on family members of IRCA beneficiaries, but it is reasonable to assume that especially among the SAW population the new financial demands will pose a high barrier to successful family-based immigrant petitions.[43] The result may be the accelerated feminization of undocumented migration, as couples who have lost the possibility of lawful reunion determine to reunite unlawfully.

35. *See* Cornelius Scully, *Immigrant Visa Waiting List in the Family-Sponsored and Employment-Based Preferences: January 1995*, 18 IN DEFENSE OF THE ALIEN 21, 22 (1996).

36. *See* LEGAL IMMIGRATION, *supra* note 3, at 65.

37. Congress allocated 55,000 immigrant visas per year for fiscal years 1992, 1993, and 1994 for dependents seeking legalization. *See* 1993 STATISTICAL YEARBOOK, *supra* note 5, at 16. In fiscal year 1993, 39,243 of the recipients of these visas were Mexican. *See id.* at 18. Congress also exempted up to 75% of the entrants in the second family-based preference category from the per country limits and the INS instituted "family unity" policies that spared many undocumented family members from being deported while they awaited immigrant visas. *See* Immigration Act of 1990, 8 U.S.C.A. § 1152(a)(4)(A) (West Supp. 1997).

38. *See* LEGAL IMMIGRATION, *supra* note 3, at 65 (reporting backlog in January 1995 of 1,138,544 spouses and children in the second family-based preference). Second-preference entries in fiscal year 1995 totalled 144,535. *See Immigration to the United States in Fiscal Year 1995*, *supra* note 8.

39. Naturalization generally requires five years as a lawful permanent resident. *See* 8 U.S.C. § 1427(a) (1997).

40. Entry by immediate relatives of U.S. citizens is not subject to numerical limits. *See* LEGAL IMMIGRATION, *supra* note 3, at 69-70 (predicting that backlog in second-preference category would be eroded by rapid naturalization of beneficiaries of IRCA and SAW programs because of their ability to secure entry of family members as immediate relatives of U.S. citizens).

41. *Id.* at 15.

42. *See* Illegal Immigration Reform and Immigrant Responsibility Act of 1996 (IIRIRA), Pub. L. No. 104-208, 110 Stat. 3009 (1996), which restricted family visa petitions to persons earning 125% of federal poverty guidelines. Although the specific effects of this measure on spouses of naturalized IRCA beneficiaries are unpredictable, a recent study by the INS found that one half of the lawful permanent residents and 30% of the citizens who successfully petitioned for entry of alien relatives in 1994 would have been unable to do so under the IIRIRA's new income limits. *See* Celia Dugger, *Immigrant Study Finds Many Below New Income Limit*, N.Y. TIMES, Mar. 16, 1997, at A1. The study, based on a sample of 2,160 statements by sponsors filed in 1994, found that Mexicans and Salvadorans, whose incomes tend to be lower than those of other immigrant groups, are likely to be particularly affected by the income requirements. *See id.*

43. *See* Dugger, *supra* note 42.

The failure to provide automatic derivative immigration benefits to immediate family members of legalization and SAW beneficiaries had already contributed to an increased flow of undocumented female migrants. Many wives (especially those from Mexico) entered unlawfully to join their legalized husbands while awaiting approval of immigrant visas.[44] The greatest predictor of undocumented migration is a previous migration experience;[45] nearly as predictive and valuable is access to a migration network of family members or other acquaintances.[46] Women are increasingly joining these migration networks, and may even be forming specifically female networks.[47]

Unfortunately, the feminization of undocumented migration occurs at a particularly inopportune time. The prospect of another amnesty could not be more remote. As Congress manifests increasing hostility toward lawful and unlawful migrants, little hope exists that the female identity of the new migrants, or their links to family members already resident in the United States, will preserve them from draconian measures of inadmissibility and removal.

B. *The 1986 Immigration Marriage Fraud Amendments*

Policies that restructure family-based immigration to the United States tend to have a profound impact on the fate of migrating women. Petitioning relatives, not the mostly female beneficiaries, control the family-based immigration process. Especially following the 1986 enactment of the Immigration Marriage Fraud Amendments (IMFA),[48] the leverage U.S. immigration law confers on petitioners over their alien spouses became in many cases "a license to abuse."[49] Advocates for immigrant women and domestic violence victims lobbied successfully for a series of ameliorative changes to the IMFA,[50] establishing a model for reversing other unintended gender-specific consequences of immigration policies.

The Immigration Marriage Fraud Amendments altered the system for marriage-based immigration by restricting most immigrant spouses to conditional residency for a two-year period following entry.[51] Previously, alien spouses of U.S. citizens and lawful permanent residents immediately became

44. *See* HONDAGNEU-SOTELO, *supra* note 31, at 26 ("Demographic analyses suggest that after IRCA, women may even compose a majority of the Mexican undocumented immigrant population.").

45. *See* Donato, *supra* note 30, at 748, 761.

46. *See* Kossoudji & Ranney, *supra* note 31, at 1130.

47. HONDAGNEU-SOTELO, *supra* note 31, at 92-97.

48. Immigration Marriage Fraud Amendments of 1986, Pub. L. No. 99-639, 100 Stat. 3537 (codified as amended in scattered sections of 8 U.S.C.). The main provisions of the IMFA are codified at 8 U.S.C. § 1186a.

49. Michelle J. Anderson, Note, *A License to Abuse: The Impact of Conditional Status on Female Immigrants*, 102 YALE L.J. 1401 (1993).

50. *See infra* note 64.

51. Spouses married for more than two years prior to entry and those entering in derivative status with an immigrant spouse are exempted from the IMFA. Those affected by the IMFA are alien spouses of U.S. citizens and "after-acquired" (i.e., married after the petitioning spouse has immigrated) alien spouses of lawful permanent residents. *See* 8 U.S.C.A. § 1251(a)(1)(G) (West Supp. 1996).

lawful permanent residents upon entry with a marriage-based immigrant visa.[52] Under the IMFA both spouses must cooperate in a second petition, two years after entry, to remove conditional status and to confer legal permanent resident status on the alien spouse, permitting her to remain indefinitely in the United States. To remove conditional status the spouses were required to prove that the marriage was not a sham contracted to gain immigration benefits and that the spouses' union remained intact.[53]

The Immigration Marriage Fraud Amendments aggravated power disparities in marriages between petitioning husbands and their alien wives.[54] The leverage that the immigration system confers on the petitioning spouse can be misused in a relationship in which domination and control are sought.[55] Even severely-abused wives may feel compelled to remain in their marriages in order to avoid deportation,[56] which could mean permanent separation from their children and a marginal existence. The migration experience itself aggravates the plight of the battered spouse through isolation from family and friends, language barriers, and unfamiliarity with legal and social services.[57]

---

52. The idea that entering spouses have ties to the national community, formerly expressed by the immediate grant of lawful permanent resident status to entering alien spouses, is still reflected in the unusually short period of lawful residency (three years) for naturalization by persons who immigrate on the basis of marriage (the normal minimum residency for naturalization being five years). *See* 8 U.S.C.A. §§ 1427(a) & 1430(a) (West Supp. 1997).

53. 8 U.S.C.A. § 1186a(d)(1)(A) (West Supp. 1996). The statute reads:

> Each petition. . . shall contain the following facts and information: (A) Statement of proper marriage and petitioning process—The facts are that (i) the qualifying marriage—(I) was entered into in accordance with the laws of the place where the marriage took place, (II) has not been judicially annulled or terminated, other than through the death of the spouse, and (III) was not entered into for the purpose of procuring an alien's entry as an immigrant; and (ii) no fee or other consideration was given. . . for filing of a petition.

Id.

54. *See* Anderson, *supra* note 49, at 1416-17. Janet Calvo observes:

> The 1986 Marriage Fraud Amendments thus gave the citizen or resident spouse enormous power over the alien spouse. He controls whether she and her children can stay, live, and work in the United States. He can make his spouse and her children illegal aliens by refusing to initially file a petition for her, by refusing to file a petition to remove her conditional status, or by refusal to appear at an interview.

Janet M. Calvo, *Spouse-Based Immigration Laws: The Legacies of Coverture*, 28 SAN DIEGO L. REV. 593, 608 (1991).

55. Abusive and controlling men may seek relationships with foreign women, in the belief that the wife's cultural background conditions her to submissiveness. The "mail-order bride" business exploits the cultural stereotype of subservient Asian women and appears to attract American men with character flaws, including a tendency toward gender-based violence. *See* Anderson, *supra* note 49, at 1407-11. One Filipina woman advertised by a mail-order catalogue was murdered by her abusive husband in a Seattle courthouse in 1995, along with her unborn child and two friends. *See* Vicky Stifter, *The Vulnerability of Immigrant Women*, SEATTLE TIMES, Mar. 16, 1995, at B5; Alex Tizon, *The World of The Mail-Order Matchmaker*, SEATTLE TIMES, Mar. 12, 1995, at A1. Another Filipina woman advertised by a mail-order catalogue was murdered by her husband, a retired Army master sergeant who had been convicted of murdering a previous wife. *Man is Convicted, Again, of Killing a Wife*, N.Y. TIMES, Aug. 20, 1996, at A12. Even partners who contract marriages across cultural divides with the best initial intentions risk severe stress and misunderstanding, sometimes fueling domestic violence.

56. *See* Anderson, *supra* note 49, at 1401-02.

57. *See* Sandra D. Pressman, *The Legal Issues Confronting Conditional Resident Aliens Who Are Victims of Domestic Violence: Past, Present, and Future Perspectives*, 6 MD. J. CONTEMP. LEGAL ISSUES 129, 134-35 (1995).

None of these observations would surprise anyone attuned to American gender relations, yet Congress seems to have been impervious to them in enacting the IMFA. The obsession with "fraud" that animated the legislation is traceable to a since-debunked Immigration and Naturalization Service (INS) estimate that 30% of the marriages bringing immigrant spouses to the United States were fraudulent.[58] Even though immigrant spouses are predominantly female, the testimony on marriage fraud presented to Congress was oddly restricted to women recounting their manipulation by scheming, insincere immigrant husbands.[59] Congress failed to consider the needs and concerns of immigrant women when legislating on marriage-based immigration, despite the fact that nearly twice as many women as men immigrate as spouses.[60] While the rate of petitioning for male spouses was on the rise immediately prior to enactment of the IMFA,[61] the rate declined after the IMFA was enacted,[62] possibly because of the indirect effects of male dominance among beneficiaries of the IRCA legalization.[63]

Congress responded to sustained pressure from groups active in combatting violence against women by liberalizing the eligibility of battered spouses for waivers of the IMFA's joint petition requirements, establishing a new form of relief from deportation for domestic violence victims, and making certain immigrants eligible to self-petition for immigration benefits.[64] Together, these measures significantly diminish the potential for manipulation of the immigration system by spouse batterers. The domestic violence lobby has been particularly effective because it combines the efforts of immigrant advocates with those of feminist, public health, and criminal justice organizations. At a time when the political mood is largely anti-immigrant, such coalition-building is of special value.

---

58. *See* Anderson, *supra* note 49, at 1411-12 n.60 (citing revised INS estimates placing figure closer to 8%); *see also* Calvo, *supra* note 54, at 606-07.

59. *See* Calvo, *supra* note 54, at 615-16.

60. *See id.* (noting failure to consider gender composition of immigrant spouse population in enacting the IMFA and inaccurate prediction by Senate Judiciary Committee in context of major revision of immigration laws in early 1950s that "the present preponderance of female immigration will not continue") (citing S. REP. NO. 1515, 81st Cong., 2d Sess. 161 (1950)).

61. *See id.* at 615 n.155 (citing General Accounting Office figures on male spouse-based immigration between 1982 and 1984).

62. LEGAL IMMIGRATION, *supra* note 3, at 51.

63. *See supra* notes 22-44 and accompanying text.

64. *See generally* Calvo, *supra* note 54, at 612-13, 622-41 (discussing 1990 amendments to IMFA and suggesting further ameliorative measures); Pressman, *supra* note 57 at 137-53 (discussing 1990 amendments to IMFA and further amelioration through the Violence Against Women Act); Janet Calvo, *The Violence Against Women Act: An Opportunity for the Justice Department to Confront Domestic Violence*, 72 INTERP. RELEASES 485 (1995) (describing 1994 amendments liberalizing IMFA waivers, establishing abuse-related eligibility for suspension of deportation, and authorizing process by which battered immigrant spouses may self-petition for immigration benefits). Regulations to implement the self-petitioning process, arguably the most significant of the 1994 measures, were issued on April 16, 1996. *See* IMMIGRATION & NATURALIZATION SERV., U.S. DEP'T OF JUSTICE, IMPLEMENTATION OF CRIME BILL SELF-PETITIONING FOR ABUSED OR BATTERED SPOUSES OR CHILDREN OF U.S. CITIZENS OR LAWFUL PERMANENT RESIDENTS (Apr. 16, 1996), *reprinted in* 73 INTERP. RELEASES 737 (1996).

C. *Limits on Immigration by Household Workers*

Despite the lessons that should have been learned from the IMFA, Congress continued to legislate without gender sensitivity and with an attitude of tolerance toward disproportionate damage to women's interests. For example, a strict limitation imposed in 1990 on lawful immigration by unskilled workers was adopted without careful consideration of its impact on the availability of childcare workers and the ensuing impact on employed mothers.

Even as Congress in 1990 was undoing some of the damage caused to women by the IMFA, it created another, possibly unintended, gendered impact by imposing severe limits on the entry of unskilled workers with employment-based visas. The 1990 Immigration Act (IMMACT) restructured legal immigration to shift the balance between family-based and employment-based immigration and, within the latter category, to favor highly-skilled or wealthy immigrants.[65] One of the more obscure provisions of the IMMACT limited the number of "unskilled" workers (those whose occupations require fewer than two years of experience) to 10,000 entries per year.[66] Within the category of unskilled workers are the immigrant housekeepers and nannies upon whom American professional women, entering the work force in an unprecedented wave, have increasingly come to rely.

The extent of this reliance was inadvertently thrust upon American consciousness by the "nannygate" scandals of the Clinton Administration in 1993.[67] There were important differences in the situations of the two principals in the scandal, unsuccessful Attorney General nominees Kimba Wood and Zoë Baird, though these differences seemed lost on the President, Senate, and public at large.[68] Commentary was muted on the fact that male politicians with egregious histories of violating the immigration and tax laws with regard to

65. U.S. COMM'N ON IMMIGRATION REFORM, U.S. IMMIGRATION POLICY: RESTORING CREDIBILITY 189, 202-06 (1994) ("One of the major goals of IMMACT was to increase the number of highly-skilled workers entering the United States") [hereinafter RESTORING CREDIBILITY].

66. 8 U.S.C.A. § 1153(b)(3)(B) (1994 & West Supp. 1996).

67. *See, e.g.*, Kathleen A. DeLaney, *A Response to "Nannygate": Untangling U.S. Immigration Law to Enable American Parents to Hire Foreign Child Care Providers*, 70 IND. L.J. 305 (1994); Rochelle L. Stanfield, *Child Care Quagmire*, NAT'L J., Feb. 27, 1993, at 512 (1993).

68. Kimba Wood and her husband had employed her nanny prior to the enactment of the employer sanctions in the 1986 IRCA, and thus benefitted from the IRCA's "grandfather" clause which permits employees to remain in pre-existing employment without exposing their employers to penalty. *Wood Outlines Legality of Sitter's Employment*, L.A. TIMES, Feb. 6, 1993, at A20. Wood not only regularly paid Social Security taxes for her nanny, even prior to the IRCA, she also filed an appropriate and successful petition to enable her household employee to immigrate. *Id.* Zoë Baird and her husband, in sharp contrast, knowingly hired an undocumented immigrant couple following enactment of the IRCA, failed to pay Social Security taxes on their employees' wages, and did not regularize their employees' immigration status. *Confirmation Hearing for Zoë Baird, Attorney General-Designate, Before the Senate Comm. on the Judiciary*, 103d Cong. 1st Sess. (1993), *available in* LEXIS, News Library. Both nominees were rapidly jettisoned by the Clinton Administration following adverse media coverage, without any effort to explain to the public the significant legal distinctions between the two cases.

household workers managed to weather the storm with few ill effects.[69] It almost appeared as if the need to employ a full-time nanny to provide primary care to young children, a need disproportionately felt by women, was itself a black mark against Baird and Wood.

Since the imposition of the IMMACT's numerical restrictions on the entry of immigrant household workers, the backlog has so increased that an employer filing a immigrant visa petition for an infant's nanny might find the visa becoming available around the time the "infant" leaves primary school.[70] The categorization of child care as unskilled work has not been entirely uncontested, but efforts to shift trained childcare workers into the skilled category have generally been stymied.[71] The lawful entry of childcare workers, since 1990, has largely been restricted to non-immigrant participants in the disingenuous, time-limited, and troubled *au pair* program administered by the United States Information Agency.[72]

Other nations that value labor-force participation by educated women have created specialized programs for the entry of childcare and household workers,[73] recognizing that women in all income brackets remain burdened with primary responsibility for the tasks of social reproduction. While East Asian states have limited entry to short-term migrants,[74] Canada has offered the prospect of

69. Governor Pete Wilson of California, renowned for his vitriolic attacks on undocumented immigrants, not only employed an unauthorized housekeeper following the enactment of the IRCA, but failed to pay Social Security taxes on her behalf. While Governor Wilson initially blamed his first wife for these transgressions of the immigration and tax laws, later revelations disclosed that he had employed a succession of three housekeepers, both before and after his divorce and the enactment of the IRCA, without seeking employment authorization or making any attempt to pay Social Security taxes on their behalf. In October, 1995, Wilson paid $15,000 in back Social Security taxes due to the accounts of the three housekeepers for the years between 1971 and 1990. *California's Pete Wilson Admits That He Didn't Pay Taxes on Maids*, DES MOINES REG., Oct. 28, 1995, at 4.

70. *See* Helene Pepe, *Making Nannies Legal Can Be Done With Ease*, ARIZONA REPUBLIC, Feb. 22, 1993, at A11. The U.S. Commission on Immigration Reform reported in 1994 that the backlog for unskilled workers had grown to 94,000, extending the wait from four years to at least six years. The slow rate of new admissions of unskilled workers extended delays to at least nine years. However, drop-out by discouraged applicants began to slow the lengthening of the delay as of 1994. RESTORING CREDIBILITY, *supra* note 65, at 205-06.

71. *Labor Certification Applications Continue Downward Spiral*, 70 INTERP. RELEASES 1436, 1437 (1993).

72. The *au pair* program is a component of the non-immigrant category for foreign exchange visitors which is regulated by the United States Information Agency (USIA). *See* 8 U.S.C. § 1101(a)(15)(J). Technically, it is a cultural exchange program rather than a source of childcare workers. *See infra* note 77. Several participants in USIA-approved *au pair* programs have been prosecuted for the assault or murder of their young charges. These acts are sometimes blamed on the participants' isolation and lack of training. *See, e.g.*, James Langton, *Nanny Murder Case Feeds Parents' Paranoia*, SUNDAY TELEGRAPH, Feb. 16, 1997, at 25; *Nanny, Accused of Murdering Baby, Enters Not Guilty Plea*, N.Y. TIMES, Feb. 14, 1997, at A26.

73. *See, e.g.*, Nirmala Purushotam, *Caste: Women, Occupation: Domestic Maid; Exploring the Realm of Foreign Full-Time Domestic Workers in Singapore*, *in* PROCEEDINGS OF THE INTERNATIONAL COLLOQUIUM "MIGRATION, DEVELOPMENT AND GENDER IN THE ASEAN REGION" 164, 168 (Jamilah Ariffin ed., 1993) (discussing introduction of foreign domestic maid program by Singapore government).

74. *Id.*

permanent resettlement in exchange for several years' service as a live-in domestic.[75]

The difficulty in assessing the desirability of these specialized migration programs arises from the conflicting interests of three groups of women: the "foreign domestics," who seek economic and personal gain without exploitation; the employers, who seek effective surrogates to perform their social reproductive tasks at an affordable cost; and the "domestic domestics," citizen or lawful resident household workers who might enjoy better wages and working conditions if entry by additional foreign workers were restricted. Women's disproportionate responsibility for the family and the household makes sorting out these competing interests a highly feminized matter.

The fact that policy-makers act with complete indifference to this complex of women's interests is a sobering reminder of the gender-blind nature of contemporary immigration policy. The U.S. Commission on Immigration Reform recommended the complete abolition of entry by unskilled workers, with no mention of the potential impact on child-care availability.[76] Congressional discussion of the benefits and drawbacks of the *au pair* program is disconnected from the reality of employed mothers' needs.[77] In the debate over the IMMACT, Representative Constance Morella of Maryland seemed a voice crying in the wilderness about the decreased availability of laborers for those in dire need of home-care workers for children, the elderly, and the disabled.[78]

Congress' only response to the "nannygate" crisis was to raise the threshold of eligibility for Social Security coverage for domestic workers.[79] While this revision eased the tax and paperwork burdens on casual employers, it did nothing to address the needs of full-time employers and damaged the financial futures of both citizen and alien household workers. Exempting part-time domestic workers from Social Security will expose certain immigrant women to potentially dire consequences when they reach retirement age because they will

75. *See* Audrey Macklin, *Foreign Domestic Worker: Surrogate Housewife or Mail Order Servant?*, 37 McGILL L.J. 681, 684-85, 757-60 (1992).

76. *See* LEGAL IMMIGRATION, *supra* note 3, at 102-04. Attorney Helen Pepe, who represented Zoë Baird's undocumented chauffeur, pointed out that Congress could reallocate some of the many (up to 87,000) unused visas in the employment-based immigrant categories of the Immigration Act of 1990 to home-care workers without major alterations in the structure of the immigration laws: "It doesn't require overhauling the whole immigration law, it just requires Congressional understanding of the child care crisis." Nicole Wise, *Immigrants, Home Care and the Law*, N.Y. TIMES, June 20, 1993, at 3.

77. Critics of the *au pair* program have argued that it should be abolished because it is an unsuitable cultural exchange program. In 1990, the House Committee on the Judiciary concluded that program should not be abolished, but should be geared to providing "unique cultural and educational experience, through travel to U.S. points of interest, national monuments, institutions, and participation in certain courses of academic study," and should retain its limitation of 40 hours of child care per week. H.R. REP. NO. 101-723, at 68-69 (1990), *reprinted in* 1990 U.S.C.C.A.N. 6710, 6748-49. Clearly, a program with such restrictions is unsatisfactory as a source of adequate child care for most mothers employed full-time.

78. *See* 136 CONG. REC. H12364 (daily ed. Oct. 27, 1990).

79. *See* 20 C.F.R. § 404.1057 (1996) (Social Security Administration does not count cash wages for domestic service toward qualifying quarters, unless employer pays wages in excess of an applicable dollar threshold; wages paid by different household employers may not be aggregated).

lack a pension but find that their alienage disqualifies them from safety-net programs for the elderly poor.[80]

It is unlikely that the problems created by the IMMACT will be resolved any time soon. Effective advocacy to increase rates of lawful immigration by household workers is impeded by the conflict of economic interests among the three groups of women most directly affected: foreign domestics, employers, and domestic domestics. During periods of anti-immigrant sentiment, asking Congress to expand entry of working-class aliens is extraordinarily difficult. Moreover, the household worker issue is feminized by its relation to women's social reproductive role, and is thus easily ignored in policy debate. Childcare in the United States remains a private matter, a problem that women must generally solve without active assistance by policy-makers.

D. *Disqualification of Lawful Immigrants From Eligibility for Public Benefits*

Congress's impulse to deprive lawful immigrants of public benefits was expressed most recently in the Personal Responsibility and Work Opportunities Reconciliation Act of 1996 ("1996 Welfare Act" or the "Act").[81] With little or no regard for the gender dimension of the policy change, Congress enacted harsh measures that primarily affected a largely female and vulnerable segment of society. The 1996 Welfare Act proclaims the virtue of self-sufficiency as the justification for denying public benefits to immigrants.[82] As a result of this reasoning, many female immigrants who have devoted their lives to the care of their families will suffer harsh consequences. As is often the case, the disadvantages of women's social reproductive roles are heightened under policies crafted to suit a male paradigm.

While the public debate on the Act focused on the termination of the sixty-one-year old entitlement of poor women and children to federal financial assistance,[83] much of the Act's budget savings are projected to flow from cuts in benefits to lawful immigrants.[84] Despite popular misconceptions, undocumented immigrants have long been excluded from most federal-benefit programs, including cash assistance to families with dependent children, food stamps,

80. *See infra* notes 81-121.

81. *See supra* note 3.

82. The "national policy" expressed in the immigration provisions of the Personal Responsibility and Work Opportunities Reconciliation Act of 1996 is that "[s]elf-sufficiency . . . continues to be the immigration policy of the United States." Pub. L. No. 104-193, 110 Stat. 2105, § 400 (1996).

83. *See Clinton Still Expected to Sign Welfare Overhaul Bill*, 73 INTERP. RELEASES 1069, 1070 (1996). Under the 1996 Welfare Act, the Aid to Families with Dependent Children entitlement program was replaced by Temporary Assistance to Needy Families and was made subject to severe time limits and further restrictions at the state level. *See Impact of Welfare Reform on Immigrants and Refugees Assessed*, 17 REFUGEE REPTS. 1, 3 (1996) [hereinafter *Impact of Welfare Reform*].

84. *See Clinton to Sign Welfare Legislation with Significant Immigration Consequences*, 73 INTERP. RELEASES 1029, 1029 (1996) (calculating savings from cuts to legal immigrants at 40% of total savings expected to be extracted by the 1996 Welfare Act); *Impact of Welfare Reform*, *supra* note 83, at 2 (National Immigration Law Center estimates 44% of savings from the Act will come from reduction in benefits for legal immigrants).

Supplemental Security Income, Medicare and most Medicaid.[85] Reliance on public benefits occurs disproportionately among refugees and elderly family-based immigrants who enter legally,[86] though other lawful immigrants may experience reversals of fortune and turn to programs such as food stamps.[87]

There was no serious examination of the factors explaining increasing rates of reliance by immigrants on public benefits, especially from a gendered perspective, prior to the passage of the 1996 Welfare Act, nor were the likely effects on needy immigrant women carefully measured.[88] A preoccupation with abuse and fraud emerged in the arguments of the Act's supporters.[89] More fundamentally, however, the Act's sponsors seemed intent on imposing a new vision of moral worthiness and national community, with severe consequences for certain female immigrants.

Lawful immigrants failing the Act's definition of "self-sufficiency"[90] will be deprived of taxpayer support, notwithstanding long residence and close community ties. They may re-enter the community fold and regain their

---

85. *See* Johnson, *supra* note 21, at 1528-29. Under the 1996 Welfare Act, undocumented aliens will be eligible only for emergency medical assistance; short-term, in-kind, non-cash disaster relief; immunizations for communicable diseases; and in-kind, non-means-tested programs, such as soup kitchens, designated by the Attorney General. Personal Responsibility and Work Opportunities Reconciliation Act of 1996, Pub. L. No. 104-193, § 401, 110 Stat. 2105 (1996).

86. *See Use of SSI and Other Welfare Programs by Immigrants*, Senate Subcomm. on Immigration and Refugee Affairs, Testimony of Michael Fix, Jeffrey S. Passel & Wendy Zimmermann, Feb. 6, 1996, *available in* LEXIS, Legis Library, Cngtst file; *see also* FIX & PASSEL, *supra* note 28, at 6 ("Welfare use among working-age (15 to 64 years), non-refugee immigrants is very low. Most transfer payments going to immigrants consist of Supplemental Security Income (SSI) for elderly immigrants.").

87. Immigrants are excludable if they are "likely to become a public charge." 8 U.S.C.A. § 1182(a)(4) (West Supp. 1997). Immigrants are deportable if they become a public charge within five years of admission for causes not affirmatively shown to have arisen after admission. *See* 8 U.S.C.A. § 1227(a)(5) (West Supp. 1997). Thus, lawful immigrants who unexpectedly fall on hard times after admission have traditionally not been cast out from the community. The House of Representatives in the 104th Congress attempted a significant reversal of this policy by approving an amendment to Section 237(a)(5) of the Immigration and Nationality Act, which would have made deportable those immigrants who had depended on federal means-tested benefits for more than twelve months in the seven-year period following admission as a lawful permanent resident—even for causes arising after entry. *See* H.R. CONF. REP. NO. 104-828, § 532, 142 CONG. REC. H10876-77 *et seq.* (Sept. 24, 1996).

88. *See* UNITED STATES GENERAL ACCOUNTING OFFICE, WELFARE REFORM: IMPLICATIONS OF PROPOSALS ON LEGAL IMMIGRANTS' BENEFITS 12-13 (1995) [hereinafter GAO WELFARE REFORM REPORT] (stating data limitations prevented GAO from either fully describing the characteristics of immigrants receiving benefits or assessing their sponsors' ability to support them).

89. *See Impact of Welfare Reform*, *supra* note 83, at 2 (quoting Senator Richard Shelby as stating, "The generous package of welfare benefits available in America is a magnet for literally hundreds of thousands of legal and illegal immigrants," and Representative Lamar Smith as stating, "Rather than promoting hard work, welfare tempts immigrants to come to America to live off the American taxpayer."). The rate of welfare dependency among working age, lawful, non-refugee immigrants is lower than that for citizens (2% of lawful non-refugee immigrants between the ages of 15 and 64 who entered in the 1980s depended on public assistance, compared to 3.2% of pre-1980 lawful immigrants and 3.7% of natives, as measured at the time of the 1990 census). *See* FIX & PASSEL, *supra* note 28, at 65 fig. 21. Dependency rates among refugees are much higher (over 13% of working-age immigrants from refugee countries, and over 15% of immigrants over 15 years old from refugee countries received public assistance at the time of the 1990 census). *See id.* Welfare dependency among elderly lawful immigrants is higher than the national average (25.7% of elderly immigrants from non-refugee countries who immigrated in the 1980s received welfare in 1990, as compared to 6.9% of elderly native citizens). *See id.*

90. Personal Responsibility and Work Opportunities Reconciliation Act of 1996, Pub. L. No. 104-193, 110 Stat. 2105 (1996).

eligibility for public assistance only through three avenues: naturalization, formal sector employment for forty qualifying quarters, or service in the armed forces.[91] The first option is more problematic than it might appear, especially for elderly women,[92] while the latter two criteria are revealing of substantial male bias. Elderly immigrant mothers and divorced immigrant housewives, non-productive from a market point of view, will be among those most disadvantaged.

Supplemental Security Income (SSI) dependency, especially dependency on the SSI aged program, is high among immigrants who are both elderly and poor.[93] Immigrating parents of U.S. citizens are disproportionately older and female.[94] Supplemental Security Income benefits have special importance for elderly people who have a limited history of contribution to the Social Security system as wage-earners.[95] Previous "deeming" requirements delayed the eligibility of immigrant parents for SSI for up to five years by attributing the income of their sponsoring citizen children to them.[96] The 1996 Welfare Act

---

91. *Id.* at § 412(b)(1)-(3). The definition of qualifying quarters of coverage is set forth at 20 C.F.R. § 404.140 (1996). Under Section 435 of the 1996 Welfare Act, immigrant spouses are eligible for public benefits derivatively through marriage to a person who has been credited with quarters worked during the marriage. This eligibility survives the death of the qualifying spouse but terminates with divorce. The Illegal Immigration Reform and Immigrant Responsibility Act of 1996 extends eligibility for public benefits to certain immigrants who are battered spouses or parents of battered children, where "there is a substantial connection between such battery or cruelty and the need for the benefits to be provided" and where the immigrant no longer resides with the batterer. Pub. L. No. 104-208, § 501(c)(2), 110 Stat. 3009 (1996). *See infra* note 98.

92. *See generally* Marketa Lindt, *The 1996 Immigration Act: Public Benefits Restrictions, the Elderly and Citizenship*, 74 INTERP. RELEASES 101 (1997) (discussing barriers to naturalization faced by elderly immigrants).

93. According to a recent study,

> [a]pproximately 12 percent of the 5.9 million SSI recipients in 1993 were legal immigrants. However, about 29 percent of the over 1.4 million of those recipients in the program for the aged were noncitizens .... [L]egal immigrants made up only about 10 percent of the SSI recipients in the program for the aged who were receiving Social Security benefits, but they constituted 63 percent of the aged SSI recipients who did not qualify for Social Security.

Daniel Mont, *Welfare and Immigrants: Restricting the Eligibility of Legal Immigrants for Welfare Programs*, 24 MIGRATIONWORLD 20, 22 (1996).

94. The categories of immigrants with the highest percentage of women include parents of U.S. citizens (61%) and spouses and children of legal permanent residents (57%). U.S. DEPARTMENT OF JUSTICE, IMMIGRATION AND NATURALIZATION SERVICE, IMMIGRATION TO THE UNITED STATES IN FISCAL YEAR 1995, at 9 (Mar. 1996). The oldest entering immigrants were parents of U.S. citizens, who had a median age of 62 years in fiscal year 1995. *Id.*

95. Paying Social Security taxes for at least 40 quarters of earnings is necessary to establish eligibility to receive Social Security benefits as an earner. *See* 42 U.S.C.A. § 414(a)(2) (West 1994).

> Legal immigrants applying for SSI tend to arrive in this country when they are beyond or near the end of their working years, which is why in many cases they do not qualify for Social Security benefits. Among those nondisabled immigrants who arrived after January 1974 who were receiving SSI from the aged program, about 79 percent were age 60 or over when they entered the United States.

Mont, *supra* note 93, at 23.

96. *See id.* at 21-22. The extension (from three to five years) became effective with the passage of the Unemployment Compensation Amendments of 1993, 42 U.S.C. § 1382j(a) (1994). The deeming provision did not apply if an immigrant became blind or disabled after admission to the United States as a permanent resident. *See* GAO WELFARE REFORM REPORT, *supra* note 88, at 4. Though Medicaid technically had no deeming period, a similar restriction applied to many Medicaid recipients. The income or resources of spouses and parents (for recipients under age 21), but not the income or resources of any other sponsors, were used in calculating the eligibility of potential recipients of Medicaid. *See* Mont, *supra* note 93, at 22.

extends the deeming provisions up to the time of the alien's naturalization.[97] Moreover, under the 1996 Welfare Act elderly immigrants lose eligibility for SSI and other public benefits even if their sponsors have fallen on hard times.[98]

By these measures, Congress unmistakably intends to deter U.S. citizens with elderly dependent foreign parents from filing immigrant visa petitions on their behalf. These parents (disproportionately mothers) will be unlikely to qualify for public benefits through ten years of sustained employment, service in the armed forces, or naturalization. In this renegotiation of the social contract, Congress has signaled that filial piety to the foreign-born is a private rather than public matter, despite the unrealism of expecting that even affluent offspring of aged immigrants could assume the full lifetime cost of their physical and medical care. Women generally accrue fewer financial reserves to survive a period of extended dependency in their dotage, and often turn to the community or to their offspring for survival. The 1996 Welfare Act eliminates public support and erects substantial barriers between impoverished foreign parents and their U.S.-resident children.

Immigrants already in the United States will be also be profoundly affected by the Act. After a recertification process,[99] immigrants presently dependent on SSI, Medicaid, food stamps and other vital benefits will be terminated.[100] Immigrant women will be penalized for having dedicated their lives to the unpaid care of their families. Even those who have labored in domestic service for other families may be unable to qualify for the work exception, given extensive noncompliance with Social Security obligations for domestic workers.[101]

---

97. *See* Personal Responsibility and Work Opportunities Reconciliation Act of 1996, Pub. L. No. 104-193, § 421, 110 Stat. 2105 (1996).

98. Section 401 of the 1996 Welfare Act broadly excludes immigrants from "federal public benefits." Personal Responsibility and Work Opportunities Reconciliation Act of 1996, Pub. L. No. 104-193, § 401, 110 Stat. 2105 (1996). Section 402 establishes "limited eligibility" for certain federal benefits (including SSI and food stamps) for refugees and asylees (for the five-year period following acquisition of that status) and for lawful permanent residents who fit within one of two exceptions: employment for forty qualifying quarters after admission (or relation to a qualifying spouse or parent) or honorable discharge from the armed services. Personal Responsibility and Work Opportunities Reconciliation Act of 1996, Pub. L. No. 104-193, § 402, 110 Stat. 2105 (1996).

99. *See* Personal Responsibility and Work Opportunities Reconciliation Act of 1996, Pub. L. No. 104-193, § 402, 110 Stat. 2105, (1996); Lindt, *supra* note 92, at 104 (discussing notices being sent to SSI recipients during February and March 1997, notifying immigrants of a 90-day deadline to prove their continued eligibility).

100. Food stamp eligibility was terminated as of April 1, 1997, affecting an estimated 900,000 legal immigrants. Supplemental Security Income will cease upon recertification, affecting an estimated 500,000 immigrants, including refugees. States have been given the option to extend non-emergency Medicaid to legal immigrants, but up to 665,000 legal immigrants could potentially be affected after the effective date of January 1, 1997. *See Impact of Welfare Reform*, *supra* note 83, at 4-5.

101. There is a process by which employees whose employers have illegally failed to report earnings and pay FICA taxes may reconstruct their earnings history upon reaching retirement age. *See* 20 C.F.R. § 404.822 (1997) (requiring "satisfactory evidence"). The standards governing relevant evidence of earnings are flexible. *See* 20 C.F.R. §§ 404.708-.709 (1997) (referring to "convincing evidence"). Impoverished immigrants who have worked in the informal economy for multiple employers are likely to experience acute difficulty providing documentary proof of their earnings even under relaxed evidentiary rules.

Naturalization provides a potential for escape from termination of benefits under the 1996 Welfare Act. The Congressional Budget Office estimates that approximately eighty percent of the legal immigrants receiving SSI benefits who would be affected by the 1996 Welfare Act have been in the United States for at least five years and are thus potentially eligible to apply for naturalization.[102] However, elderly immigrants have much lower rates of naturalization than younger immigrants.[103] Among the obstacles to becoming a citizen are a lack of knowledge of U.S. civics and English,[104] a reluctance to adjust to a new culture,[105] emotional problems stemming from redefined roles within the family,[106] increased difficulty in acquiring a second language at an advanced age,[107] and age-related impediments to access to language or civics classes.[108] These problems may be especially aggravated for those elderly female immigrants who are illiterate in their first language and have little or no formal education.[109] Efforts were underway even prior to passage of the 1996 Welfare Act to provide a disability exemption from the naturalization requirements, but some critics characterize such relief as an impediment to the Welfare Act's cost-saving objectives.[110] The Clinton Administration has proposed a broad restoration of eligibility for SSI and Medicaid, without regard to naturalization, for those lawful immigrants who become disabled following admission.[111] However, the $14-15 billion cost of this restoration is a serious obstacle to its enactment.[112] Unless state and local authorities fill the gap created by the loss of federal benefits for elderly immigrants who do not or cannot naturalize, some

102. *See* Mont, *supra* note 93, at 24.

103. "Only 11 percent of legal immigrants who entered the United States in 1982 and were age 60 or over had become citizens by 1992." *Id.* By comparison, the naturalization rate was 37% for legal immigrants who entered in 1982 and were between the ages of 18 and 50. *See id.*

104. Federal law establishes as prerequisites to naturalization a demonstration of both English language proficiency and an understanding of the fundamentals of the history, principles, and form of government of the United States. *See* 8 U.S.C. § 1423 (1997). Immigrants over the age of 55 who have resided in the United States for 15 years after admission as a lawful permanent resident are exempted from this requirement, as are immigrants over the age of 50 who have resided as lawful permanent residents for 20 years. *See* 8 U.S.C. § 1423(1). In 1994, Congress added a further exemption for immigrants who are unable because of physical or developmental disability or mental impairment to meet the English language and civics requirements. *See* 8 U.S.C. § 1423; *see also* DONALD E. GELFAND, AGING AND ETHNICITY 39, 44-46, 153-55 (1994).

105. *See* GELFAND, *supra* note 104, at 39, 44-46.

106. *See id.* at 44-46.

107. *See* Bert Hayslip, Jr. & Kevin J. Kennelly, *Cognitive and Noncognitive Factors Affecting Learning Among Older Adults*, *in* THE OLDER ADULT AS LEARNER 76-79 (D. Barry Lumsden ed. 1985).

108. *See* GELFAND, *supra* note 104, at 153-55.

109. Tara Shioya, *Desperately Seeking Citizenship: With the Advent of New Federal Welfare Rules for Elderly Immigrants, S.F.'s Oldest and Poorest Are Running Out of Time*, S.F. WEEKLY, Feb. 12, 1997, *available in* LEXIS, News Library, Curnws File.

110. *See* Lindt, *supra* note 92, at 105-11; Celia W. Dugger, *U.S. Says Mental Impairment Might Be a Bar to Citizenship*, N.Y. TIMES, Mar. 19, 1997, at A1 (quoting Representative Clay Shaw expressing concern about costs of easing naturalization requirements for elderly disabled immigrants facing benefit termination); Patrick J. McDonnell, *Easy Citizenship for Disabled?* SEATTLE TIMES, Feb. 17, 1997, at A1; *see also* 8 U.S.C. § 1423(1).

111. *Prepared Testimony of Donna E. Shalala, Secretary U.S. Department of Health and Human Services, Before the Senate Fin. Comm.*, (Feb. 13, 1997), *available in* LEXIS, News Library, Curnws File.

112. *See* Patrick J. McDonnell, *Wilson Assails U.S. Plan to Restore Aid to Legal Immigrants*, L.A. TIMES, Feb. 13, 1997, *available in* LEXIS, News Library, Curnws File.

analysts fear that the official response to their plight will be to "put grandma out in the parking lot."[113]

The gendered impact of the 1996 Welfare Act does not stop with benefit cut-offs. Elderly immigrants who lose benefits will turn to relatives, if possible, to meet their basic needs. Because elder-care, like childcare, remains predominantly assigned to women, these changes will have a predictably disparate impact on the lives of their female relations.[114] The 1996 Welfare Act's notion of "self-sufficiency"[115] appears to rest, in part, on an expectation that families can provide physical care to their dependent immigrant members.[116] But that assumption may reflect a gendered disregard for unpaid female labor within the family setting:

> Although caregiving work underpins the economy, it is peripheral to the marketplace norms of competition and financial gain as defined by men. Nonmonetized and nontechnological, caregiving has been unrecognized and devalued in a society that defines work in terms of measurable output and wages rather than nurturance and maintenance . . . . What this means for women's roles and status is that women are expected to perform unpaid work in the home that is regarded as nonwork. As a result, assumptions underlying current public policies arise from a social system in which women as a class are at an economic disadvantage.[117]

---

113. *Welfare Fix Needs Fixing, Say Leavitt, Colleagues*, SALT LAKE TRIB., Feb. 1, 1997, *available in* LEXIS, News Library, Curnws File (quoting Elaine Ryan, Director of Government Affairs for the American Public Welfare Association). Representative Shaw observes that "natural attrition" may solve the narrower problem of mentally-disabled elderly immigrants who face a loss of benefits but are unable to naturalize even under liberalized regulations, indicating that he is optimistic that such persons will not be "pushed out of nursing homes onto the sidewalk." Dugger, *supra* note 110.

114. *See* Raymond T. Coward et al., *Demographic Perspectives on Gender & Family Caregiving*, *in* GENDER, FAMILIES, AND ELDER CARE 18, 25 (Jeffrey W. Dwyer & Raymond T. Coward, eds. 1992); *see also* EMILY K. ABEL, WHO CARES FOR THE ELDERLY? 4 (1991) (stating women represent 72% of all caregivers for the elderly).

115. *See* Personal Responsibility and Work Opportunities Reconciliation Act of 1996, Pub. L. No. 104-193, § 400, 110 Stat. 2105 (1996) ("[A]liens within the nation's borders [should] not depend on public resources to meet their needs, but rather rely on their own capabilities and the resources of their families, their sponsors, and private organizations.").

116. Congress has provided that affidavits of support, which sponsoring relatives provide to overcome the exclusion ground for aliens likely to become a public charge, be enforceable against the sponsor. *See* Personal Responsibility and Work Opportunities Reconciliation Act of 1996, Pub. L. No. 104-193, § 423, 110 Stat. 2105, 2271 (1996). The public charge ground is set forth at 8 U.S.C. § 1182(a)(4) (Supp. 1996) ("Any alien who, in the opinion of the consular officer at the time of application for a visa, or in the opinion of the Attorney General at the time of application for admission or adjustment of status, is likely at any time to become a public charge is excludable."). The Illegal Immigration Reform and Immigrant Responsibility Act of 1996 adds a set of criteria on which officials may base their prediction whether the alien applicant for admission is likely to become a public charge. Illegal Immigration Reform and Immigrant Responsibility Act of 1996 (IIRIRA), Pub. L. No. 104-208, § 531(a),110 Stat. 3009 (1996).

117. Nancy R. Hooyman, *Social Policy and Gender Inequities in Caregiving*, *in* GENDER, FAMILIES, AND ELDER CARE 181, 186 (Jeffrey W. Dwyer & Raymond T. Coward eds., 1992).

These general observations aptly describe attitudes implicit in the 1996 Welfare Act's immigration-related provisions.

Elderly men in the United States have less to fear from public policies constructed on an assumption that unpaid family members will meet their basic caregiving needs. While 67.8% of impaired older males receive help from their wives, only 21.6% of impaired older females receive similar assistance from their husbands.[118] Among the very old (those aged eighty-five or over) this disparity widens to 42.6% for men relying upon their wives, as compared to a mere 4.3% of women with helping husbands.[119] Since immigrant parents are disproportionately female and elderly,[120] they are unlikely to have spouses who can insulate them from the loss of public benefits.

Building a coalition to amend to the immigration-related provisions of the 1996 Welfare Act will be extraordinarily difficult, despite the dire circumstances facing those affected. The Act reflects a confluence of hostile attitudes both toward immigrants and toward the welfare-dependent. To an unusual degree, the support of governmental officials at the state and local level is crucial to securing a reversal of policies that have harsh effects on immigrants. These officials fear that the federal cutbacks will shift costs to states and counties. But given the pivotal importance of immigrant-benefit reductions to the overall federal cost-savings objectives of the 1996 Welfare Act, it cannot be safely predicted that immigrant women will receive the dispensation now proposed by the Clinton Administration.

III. FORCED MIGRATION OF WOMEN AND TREATMENT OF ASYLUM-SEEKERS

Significant, if belated, strides have been taken in recent years to recognize the dangers faced by women refugees.[121] Women and children constitute 80% of refugees.[122] Yet only in recent years have the specific risks faced by women refugees been given any serious attention by policy-makers. The United Nations

---

118. *See* Coward et al., *supra* note 114, at 26.

119. *See id.* at 28.

120. *See supra* notes 93-94.

121. *See* UNITED NATIONS HIGH COMMISSIONER FOR REFUGEES, EXECUTIVE COMMITTEE OF THE HIGH COMMISSIONER'S PROGRAMME, CONCLUSION NO. 64 (XLI) ON REFUGEE WOMEN AND INTERNATIONAL PROTECTION (1990); UNITED NATIONS HIGH COMMISSIONER FOR REFUGEES, EXECUTIVE COMMITTEE OF THE HIGH COMMISSIONER'S PROGRAMME CONCLUSION NO. 73 (XLIV) ON REFUGEE PROTECTION AND SEXUAL VIOLENCE (1993); UNITED NATIONS HIGH COMMISSIONER FOR REFUGEES, SEXUAL VIOLENCE AGAINST REFUGEES: GUIDELINES ON PREVENTION AND RESPONSE (1995) [hereinafter UNHCR GUIDELINES]; IMMIGRATION AND REFUGEE BOARD (CANADA), GUIDELINES ISSUED BY THE CHAIRPERSON PURSUANT TO SECTION 65(3) OF THE IMMIGRATION ACT, WOMEN REFUGEE CLAIMANTS FEARING GENDER-RELATED PERSECUTION (1993), *reprinted in* 5 INT'L J. REFUGEE L. 278 (1993) [hereinafter CANADA GUIDELINES]; Immigration and Naturalization Service, U.S. Dep't of Justice, *Considerations for Asylum Officers Adjudicating Asylum Claims from Women* (May 26, 1995), *reprinted in* 7 INT'L J. REFUGEE L. 700 (1995) [hereinafter INS *Considerations*].

122. Refugees in this context are defined as persons who have crossed an international border in flight from man-made disaster, whether persecution or armed conflict. *See* Elizabeth Hull, *At Long Last: Asylum Law Is Beginning to Address Violence Against Women*, 18 IN DEFENSE OF THE ALIEN 186, 186 (1995).

High Commissioner for Refugees has adopted a series of guidelines and programmatic improvements to deal sensitively and effectively with gender-specific risks and barriers.[123] Important asylum states, including Canada and the United States, have adopted guidelines[124] and announced precedent-setting decisions accepting the cognizability of gender-based asylum claims and improving adjudication processes so as to draw out rather than suppress the stories of female claimants.[125] Yet even now, adjudicators are more receptive to arguments premised on the physical vulnerability of women (for example, to the risk of female genital mutilation) than to the enhanced dangers women face as a result of prescribed social roles or gender-based constraints on mobility.

Because the developments favoring gender-based persecution claims have received much scholarly attention they do not require thorough treatment here.[126] The important point is to recognize that, without sustained and extraordinary efforts by refugee advocates, these advances would have been unlikely.[127] Moreover, it must be acknowledged that these developments will bring material improvement to few women.[128] In an ironic coincidence, just as the theoretical legitimacy of gender-based persecution claims is being accepted, reception states are erecting onerous barriers to access to their systems for asylum adjudication.[129]

---

123. *See* UNHCR GUIDELINES *supra* note 121.

124. *See* CANADA GUIDELINES *supra* note 121.

125. Pamela Goldberg, *U.S. Law and Women Asylum Seekers: Where Are They and Where Are They Going?*, 73 INTERP. RELEASES 889 (1996); Stephanie Kaye Pell, Comment, *Adjudication of Gender Persecution Cases Under the Canada Guidelines*, 20 N.C. J. INT'L L. & COM. REG. 655 (1995). This advance is "as incongruous as it is welcome," Hull, *supra* note 122, at 186, because recent trends in refugee law largely have taken a negative, restrictionist tack. *See* Joan Fitzpatrick, *Flight from Asylum: Trends Toward Temporary "Refuge" and Local Responses to Forced Migrations*, 35 VA. J. INT'L L. 13 (1994).

126. *See, e.g.*, Pamela Goldberg, *Anyplace But Home: Asylum in the United States for Women Fleeing Intimate Violence*, 26 CORNELL INT'L L.J. 565 (1993); Jacqueline Greatbatch, *The Gender Difference: Feminist Critiques of Refugee Discourse*, 1 INT'L J. REFUGEE L. 518 (1989); Nancy Kelly, *Gender-Related Persecution: Assessing the Asylum Claims of Women*, 26 CORNELL INT'L L.J. 625 (1993); Rebecca M. M. Wallace, *Making the Refugee Convention Gender Sensitive: The Canadian Guidelines*, 45 INT'L & COMP. L. Q. 702 (1996); Pamela Goldberg, *Asylum Law and Gender-Based Persecution Claims*, IMMIGR. BRIEFINGS, Sept. 1994.

127. *See, e.g.*, Deborah E. Anker, *Women Refugees: Forgotten No Longer?*, 32 SAN DIEGO L. REV. 771 (1995) (describing efforts by refugee advocates for adoption of 1995 INS Considerations).

128. *See* Deborah Anker et al., *The BIA's New Asylum Jurisprudence and Its Relevance for Women's Claims*, 73 INTERP. RELEASES 1173, 1173-74 (1996). Three of the leading gender-based persecution cases that have been reviewed by United States Courts of Appeals ended in denial of asylum to the claimant. *See* Fisher v. INS, 79 F.3d 955 (9th Cir. 1996); Safaie v. INS, 25 F.3d 636 (8th Cir. 1994); Fatin v. INS, 12 F.3d 1233 (3d Cir. 1993).

129. For example, Fauziya Kasinga would probably never have received full consideration of her claim of gender-based persecution had the summary removal provisions imposed by the Antiterrorism and Effective Death Penalty Act of 1996 (AEDPA) been in effect at the time she entered without proper documents. Karen Musalo, *In re Kasinga: A Big Step Forward for Gender-Based Asylum Claims*, 73 INTERP. RELEASES 853, 993-96 (1996) [hereinafter Musalo] (discussing provisions of the AEDPA that could have the effect of sending deserving refugees back to countries where they face prosecution); *see also* Michele R. Pistone, *Asylum and Exclusion Provisions in New and Pending Legislation: A Summary and Practice Guide*, 73 INTERP. RELEASES 993, 993-96 (1996) (discussing provisions of the AEDPA that could have the effect of sending deserving refugees back to countries where they face persecution).

Within the European Union, for example, the impulse to harmonize standards for asylum eligibility produced a definition of "refugee" that severely limits the possibility of persecution by non-state actors.[130] Intended to placate member states that adhere strictly to a state-focused theory of human rights, the measure was animated in part by French fears of a wave of Algerians fleeing attacks by militant Islamist groups.[131] Not so widely recognized is the fact that feminists are prime targets of Islamist violence in Algeria.[132] Gender-based persecution frequently involves a state's failure to protect women from private violence such as female genital mutilation, rape by insurgent forces, and domestic violence.[133] In these instances, it is improbable that a claimant could meet the European Union definition by proving that the harm inflicted on her was "encouraged or permitted by the [state] authorities" or that the state's failure to prevent the harm was "deliberate."[134]

Even where the legal cognizability of gender-based asylum claims involving non-state actors is conceded, various grounds for denying the claims of individual women are advanced. The growing significance of the internal flight alternative as a basis for denial of asylum, for example, requires that it be seriously reconsidered from a gendered perspective. Too heavy reliance on an internal flight alternative as a basis for denying asylum masks women's continued lack of social, economic, and spatial mobility within many countries. In some cases, the unavailability of internal safe havens is obvious. For example, following the end of its civil war, Yemen reverted to traditions of seclusion and subordination of women.[135] Recognizing the potential impact of the change on educated women, the U.S. ambassador asked how his country could assist those

---

130. The European Union's definition of "refugee" is as follows:

> Persecution by third parties will be considered to fall within the scope of the Geneva Convention where it is based on one of the grounds in Article 1A, is individual in nature and is encouraged or permitted by the authorities. Where the official authorities fail to act, such persecution should give rise to individual examination of each application for refugee status, in accordance with national judicial practice, in the light in particular of whether or not the failure to act was deliberate. The persons concerned may be eligible in any event for appropriate forms of protection under national law.

Council of the European Union, Joint Position Defined by the Council on the Basis of Article K.3 of the Treaty on European Union on the Harmonized Application of the Definition of the Term "Refugee" in Article 1 of the Geneva Convention of 28 July 1951 Relating to the Status of Refugees, EUR. UNION DOC. NO. 12105/95, § 5.2 (Dec. 19, 1995) [hereinafter EU JOINT POSITION].

131. *See* Janet McEvoy, *Some in EU Share Criticism of Its Refugee Policy*, REUTER N. AM. WIRE, Nov. 24, 1995, *available in* LEXIS, World Library, Txtlne File; *EU: Definition of Refugees Adopted by Justice Council a First Step*, AGENCE EUROPE, Nov. 28, 1995, *available in* LEXIS, World Library, Txtlne File.

132. *See* Abdelaziz Barrouhi, *Widowed and Raped, Algeria's Women "Try" Islamists*, REUTERS WORLD SERVICE, Mar. 8, 1995, *available in* LEXIS, News Library, Curnws File; Robert Fisk, *Forget Feminism, Talk About Survival*, INDEPENDENT, Mar. 9, 1995, *available in* LEXIS, News Library, Curnws File; Heba Saleh, *Pawns in a Political War*, GUARDIAN, May 24, 1995, *available in* LEXIS, News Library, Curnws File.

133. *See, e.g.*, *In re* Kasinga, Interim Decision 3278, 1996 WL 379826 (Board of Immigration Appeals June 13, 1996).

134. EU JOINT POSITION, *supra* note 130, § 5.2.

135. In 1994, the more traditional North won a victory over the secular and modern South, to the detriment of women who became subject to shari'a law. *See* Maxine Molyneux, *Women's Rights and Political Contingency: The Case of Yemen, 1990-1994*, 49 MIDDLE EAST J. 418, 430 (1995).

whose freedom would be constrained by the new restrictions. The answer reportedly was "10,000 green cards,"[136] signalling despair that internal solutions could be found.

In other cases, government officials seem unaware of the fact that internal safe havens may not be available to women. In the brief filed by the Immigration and Naturalization Service (INS) in *In re Kasinga*,[137] the "internal flight alternative" was raised as a possible ground for denial.[138] Yet in Togo, rebellious teenage girls fleeing forced marriage and mutilation have few if any opportunities for autonomous existence. Police and other officials are more likely to facilitate the persecution than to protect against it.[139] Even the prospect of a female rebel finding shelter with her natal family is unrealistic in a highly patriarchal society.[140] The INS urged that a risk of "ostracism or economic pressures" for refusing to submit to genital mutilation should not suffice to justify a grant of asylum.[141] Yet the fundamental premise of refugee law is that some persons must rely upon the international community for a safe place to exist, given their own state's failure to provide it. Asylum applicants such as Kasinga pose an acute example of this need for external safety. Similarly, the German Administrative Court recently ruled that Bosnian Muslim asylum-seekers, including rape victims who fled in 1992, are ineligible for asylum under German law because, at the present time, they may find refuge within non-Serb

---

136. *See id.* at 430 n.50.

137. *See* Government's Brief in Response to Applicant's Appeal from Decision of Immigration Judge, *In re* Kasinga, Interim Decision 3278 (Board of Immigration Appeals) (Feb. 28, 1996) (on file with the *Yale Journal of Law and Feminism*) [hereinafter Government's Brief].

138. *Id.* at 19. Asylum claims may be denied where the asylum-seeker is believed to have had an opportunity to find safety in another part of his or her own country. Deportation may be ordered even though the claimant suffered past persecution and cannot in safety return to his or her home or town. The United Nations High Commissioner for Refugees cautions against using the internal flight alternative too rigidly to deny claims:

> The fear of being persecuted need not always extend to the *whole* territory of the refugee's country of nationality. . . . [A] person will not be excluded from refugee status merely because he could have sought refuge in another part of the same country, if under all the circumstances it would not have been reasonable to expect him to do so.

OFFICE OF THE UNITED NATIONS HIGH COMM'R FOR REFUGEES, HANDBOOK ON PROCEDURES AND CRITERIA FOR DETERMINING REFUGEE STATUS, ¶ 91, U.N. Doc. HCR/PRO/4 (1979).

139. *See* Musalo, *supra* note 129, at 858 (stating husband whom Kasinga was forced to marry was friendly with Togolese police).

140. The INS suggested at oral argument that Kasinga could have been sheltered by her married sisters, without proof of their ability to make a decision independent of their husbands concerning the resident-members of the household. Interview with Karen Musalo, counsel to Fauziya Kasinga, in Boulder, Colo. (June 1, 1996). Kasinga's (her actual surname is Kassindja) mother was required to humiliate herself in a family ceremony, at which she was not permitted to speak on her own behalf, to atone for providing the funds from her meager inheritance for her daughter's escape from mutilation, and to secure the family patriarch's permission to live in the family compound. *Id.*; *see also* Celia W. Dugger, *A Refugee's Body Is Intact But Her Family Is Torn*, N.Y. TIMES, Sept. 11, 1996, at A1. The sister who assisted Kasinga's flight to Ghana briefly separated from her disapproving husband; he thereafter took another wife without her consent. *Id.* Having female relatives is thus not necessarily a girl's salvation. It was Kasinga's paternal aunt who originally sold her as the fourth wife of an older man and arranged her planned mutilation. *Id.*

141. Government's Brief, *supra* note 137, at 19.

controlled portions of Bosnia-Herzegovina.[142] The Court denied their claims even while acknowledging that they had been victims of persecution within the meaning of German asylum law.[143]

Afghanistan presents an extreme example of women's relative lack of spatial, social, and economic mobility and their subjection to domination by male household members or self-appointed guardians of female social morés. The recent advances by the Taliban, a fundamentalist Islamist insurgent group presently in occupation of nearly all of Afghanistan, pose a severe threat to women.[144] Taliban adherents are predominantly young, poorly educated men empowered by their access to sophisticated weapons and adherence to a set of values that exalts their moral superiority. In Taliban-controlled areas, strict rules of seclusion are imposed on women and girls, who are forbidden to work outside the home or to attend school,[145] making autonomous existence simply impossible.[146] Taliban rules on female seclusion in the city of Herat are so severe that war widows without male protectors are forbidden to leave their homes in order to obtain food for their children.[147]

Emerging, though unevenly,[148] in the evolving jurisprudence of gender-based asylum is a recognition that familiar forms of harm to women, such as domestic violence, can support a claim to refugee status under international standards.[149] Asylum law in the United States may begin to provide a haven from gender-based dangers faced by women, examining the structural inequalities

---

142. > [T]he applicants have no right to asylum, because the Republic of Bosnia and Hercegovina, whose citizens the applicants are, still effectively controls part of its territory. Inside that territory the applicants are not persecuted. Also, persecution by the "Republika Srpska" cannot be expected to take place inside that territory. Those who can obtain protection from their own State do not need asylum in Germany.

Press statement from the German Federal Administrative Court (Aug. 6, 1996) (translation on file with the *Yale Journal of Law and Feminism*).

143. *See id.* (noting that Administrative Appeals Court reasoned that "Republika Srpska" was capable of inflicting persecution on claimants as a "quasi-State").

144. *See Final Report on the Situation of Human Rights in Afghanistan Submitted by Mr. Choong-Hyun Paik, Special Rapporteur, in Accordance with Commission on Human Rights Resolution 1995/74*, U.N. Economic and Social Council, 52nd Sess., Agenda Item 10, ¶ 6, 11-20, 29-30, U.N. Doc. E/CN.4/1996/64 (1996) [hereinafter REPORT ON AFGHANISTAN]; Barbara Crossette, *Kabul Falls to Islamic Militia; Afghans Accuse Pakistan*, N.Y. TIMES, Sept. 26, 1996, at A3.

145. *See* REPORT ON AFGHANISTAN, *supra* note 144, ¶ 69-76. UNICEF suspended its operations in Taliban-controlled areas where women and girls had been denied access to education and other services funded by the agency. *See id.* ¶ 76.

146. In Kabul, where educated Afghan women have been concentrated during the lengthy war, one of the Taliban's first "governmental" decrees ordered women to abandon their employment and not to appear in public unless shrouded completely, with one small netted slit for their eyes. *See Guerrillas Take Afghan Capital as Troops Flee*, N.Y. TIMES, Sept. 28, 1996, at A1.

147. *See* REPORT ON AFGHANISTAN, *supra* note 144, ¶ 70.

148. The Court of Appeals for the Third Circuit refused to adopt a rationale that potentially would have brought all Iranian women within the refugee definition, despite the severe gender-discriminatory laws to which they are subjected. *See* Fatin v. INS, 12 F.3d 1233, 1238-42 (3d Cir. 1993).

149. One well-reasoned recent decision granted asylum to a Bangladeshi woman who was fleeing severe abuse by her husband. The Immigration Judge specifically rejected as "highly unrealistic and almost fanciful" the INS argument that the applicant could have found protection in Bangladesh by, for example, moving out and establishing an independent life. *See IJ Grants Asylum to Battered Bangladeshi Woman*, 74 INTERP. RELEASES 174, 176 (1997).

constraining women's lives and moving beyond a focus on particularly aggravated forms of gender-based violence.

While refugee advocates rightly celebrate regulatory and litigation successes, it is significant that a legislative strategy has not been a central component of their efforts. Instead, advances in gender-based asylum doctrine have come from approaching a presidential administration that is sensitive to "gender-gap" politics and adjudicators who can reasonably be expected to respond favorably to evolving international refugee standards. The only recent legislative expansion of the refugee definition is the product primarily of anti-abortion politics, redefining coercive family-planning measures as persecutory.[150] While forced abortion is clearly a form of gender-specific violence, forced sterilization is not and men are likely to predominate among asylum claimants relying upon this expanded definition.[151]

IV. Conclusion

The migration experience is deeply gendered. Women have lately emerged from the shadows of migration studies to a position of some prominence as research subjects, with complex and varied migration stories. While the experiences and hopes of female migrants have been illuminated by recent scholarship, legal policies have lagged in responding to these realities.

In the United States, a country with a strong immigration history and with female-dominant migration patterns for much of this century, laws are framed, sometimes with tragic consequences, in disregard of adverse gender-specific effects. Both the legalization programs of the Immigration Reform and Control Act of 1986 (IRCA) and the Immigration Marriage Fraud Amendments (IMFA) unexpectedly operated to the disadvantage of women. Congress adopted some ameliorative steps regarding the primarily female spouses of IRCA beneficiaries, but not consistently enough to stem the trend toward the feminization of undocumented migration. Responding to sustained pressure from groups concerned with the IMFA's aggravation of domestic violence against immigrant women, Congress gradually softened the IMFA's impact and introduced into the immigration laws a substantial amount of flexibility for the benefit of battered immigrant spouses.

Despite moderating the unintentionally gendered consequences of these two measures, Congress continues to evince indifference to the compelling needs of immigrant women. Even in the aftermath of the "nannygate" scandals of 1993, policy-makers treat immigration of household workers as a non-issue. Recently-enacted restrictions on the availability of public benefits to lawful immigrants

150. *See* Illegal Immigration Reform and Immigrant Responsibility Act of 1996, Pub. L. No. 104-208, § 601, 110 Stat. 3009 (1996); Immigration and Nationality Act, 8 U.S.C.A. § 1101(a)(42) (West Supp. 1997).

151. For example, many of the Chinese passengers on the grounded smuggling ship Golden Venture, who will now be permitted to renew their asylum claims under the amended law, are men. *See* Celia W. Dugger, *Chinese Immigrants From Stranded Ship Are to Be Released*, N.Y. TIMES, Feb. 15, 1997, at A1.

will have devastating consequences for female immigrants, particularly elderly mothers of U.S. citizens and divorced immigrant housewives. In designating the deserving lawful immigrants who will be spared the budget axe, Congress chose astoundingly male-biased criteria: service in the armed forces and lengthy employment in the formal labor market. These criteria denigrate the contributions of those, mostly female, whose lives have been devoted to the unpaid tasks of social reproduction.

While the international community is increasingly aware of gender-based violence and some advances have been made in the conceptual realm relating to gender-based persecution, few female refugees are likely to enjoy the benefits of these doctrinal advances because of onerous barriers to asylum. One of these obstacles is the presumed availability of an internal flight alternative, which may be misjudged due to ignorance concerning the severe constraints upon women's mobility. Whether evolving asylum jurisprudence will offer meaningful protection to a substantial number of women depends on whether law-makers and adjudicators bring within the scope of the refugee definition the more common forms of violence and social restrictions faced by women. The ordinariness of this violence and discrimination has, until recently, prevented its recognition as a form of persecution. Yet the tolerance of gender-specific harm by foreign authorities provides the rationale for applying refugee law in this context.

Women are more mobile and more active agents of migration than had previously been assumed. Individual women experience migration differently. Some women migrate in hope of a better life and others migrate out of necessity; some significantly improve their lives through migration while others are reduced to virtual slavery. Legal policy remains largely impervious to the rich tapestry of female migration, and law-makers continue to enact laws that have differential adverse effects on migrating women. This Article seeks to take a step toward gender-sensitive immigration laws by illuminating certain gendered aspects of migration. Bringing the concerns of immigrant women into policy-making depends upon their advocates' success either in building coalitions in the legislative arena or in convincing either executive officials or the judiciary that women migrants' claims are valid.

Lorelyn Penero MILLER, Petitioner,

v.

Madeleine K. ALBRIGHT, Secretary of State.

No. 96–1060.

Argued Nov. 4, 1997.

Decided April 22, 1998.

Illegitimate daughter of citizen father brought action against Secretary of State, after her application for citizenship was denied, challenging constitutionality, on equal protection grounds, of statute governing citizenship of illegitimate child born abroad of American father and alien mother. The United States District Court for the District of Columbia, Royce C. Lamberth, J., 870 F.Supp. 1, granted Secretary of State's motion to dismiss, and daughter appealed. The Court of Appeals, Buckley, Senior Circuit Judge, 96 F.3d 1467, affirmed and remanded. On certiorari, the Supreme Court, Justice

Stevens, held that: (1) daughter had standing to bring constitutional challenge, but (2) additional proof-of-paternity requirement imposed for citizenship by birth whenever the citizen parent of child who is born out of wedlock and abroad is child's father, as opposed to the mother, did not represent unconstitutional denial of equal protection based on sex of citizen parent.

Affirmed.

Justice O'Connor concurred in judgment and filed opinion, in which Justice Kennedy joined.

Justice Scalia concurred in judgment and filed opinion, in which Justice Thomas joined.

Justice Ginsburg dissented and filed opinion, in which Justice Souter and Justice Breyer joined.

Justice Breyer dissented and filed opinion, in which Justice Souter and Justice Ginsburg joined.

1. Aliens ⚷60.2

Citizens ⚷2

There are two sources of citizenship, and two sources only, birth and naturalization.

2. Aliens ⚷60.2

Citizens ⚷3

Fourteenth Amendment guarantees that every person born in the United States, and subject to jurisdiction thereof, becomes at once a citizen of the United States, and needs no naturalization. U.S.C.A. Const.Amend. 14, § 1.

3. Citizens ⚷2

Persons not born in the United States acquire citizenship by birth only as provided by Acts of Congress.

4. Declaratory Judgment ⚷299.1

Child who was allegedly born out of wedlock to alien mother and citizen father had standing to invoke jurisdiction of the federal courts in order to challenge constitutionality of statute governing the citizenship of children who were born abroad and out of wedlock to parents such as hers, where child did not request that court grant her citizenship, but instead sought a declaration that statute was unconstitutional and a finding by court that she was a citizen from birth. (Per Justice Stevens, with the Chief Justice concurring, and four Justices concurring in judgment.) U.S.C.A. Const.Amend. 5; Immigration and Nationality Act, § 309(a)(4), as amended, 8 U.S.C.A. § 1409(a)(4).

5. Citizens ⚷9

Constitutional Law ⚷224(2)

Additional proof-of-paternity requirement imposed for citizenship by birth whenever the citizen parent of child who is born out of wedlock and abroad is child's father, as opposed to the mother, did not represent unconstitutional denial of equal protection based on sex of citizen parent; desire to promote early ties to United States citizen relatives and recognition that mothers and fathers of out-of-wedlock children are not similarly situated supported requirement, whenever the citizen parent is the father, that child be legitimated, that father formally acknowledge his paternity, or that father's paternity be established by competent court prior to child's majority. (Per Justice Stevens, with the Chief Justice concurring, and four Justices concurring in judgment.) U.S.C.A. Const.Amend. 5; Immigration and Nationality Act, § 309(a)(4), as amended, 8 U.S.C.A. § 1409(a)(4).

Syllabus *

Petitioner was born out of wedlock in 1970 in the Philippines. Her mother is a Filipino national. Her father, Charlie Miller, is an American citizen residing in Texas who served in the United States military in the Philippines at the time of petitioner's conception. He never married petitioner's mother, and there is no evidence that he was in the Philippines at the time of her birth or that he ever returned there after completing his tour of duty. In 1992, the State Department

* The syllabus constitutes no part of the opinion of the Court but has been prepared by the Reporter of Decisions for the convenience of the reader. See *United States v. Detroit Timber & Lumber Co.*, 200 U.S. 321, 337, 26 S.Ct. 282, 287, 50 L.Ed. 499.

denied petitioner's application for registration as a United States citizen. After a Texas court granted Mr. Miller's petition for a paternity decree finding him to be her father, petitioner reapplied for citizenship status, which was again denied on the ground that the Texas decree did not satisfy 8 U.S.C. § 1409(a)(4)'s requirement that a child born out of wedlock and outside the United States to an alien mother and an American father be legitimated before age 18 in order to acquire citizenship. Petitioner and Mr. Miller then sued the Secretary of State in Federal District Court in Texas, seeking a judgment declaring her to be a United States citizen. They emphasized that the citizenship of an out-of-wedlock, foreign-born child of an alien father and an American mother is established at birth under § 1409(c), and alleged that § 1409's different treatment of citizen fathers and citizen mothers violated Mr. Miller's Fifth Amendment equal protection right by utilizing the suspect classification of gender without justification. Concluding that Mr. Miller did not have standing, the court dismissed him as a party and transferred venue to the District Court for the District of Columbia. That court dismissed the suit on the ground that federal courts do not have power to grant citizenship. The Court of Appeals affirmed, holding that petitioner had standing to sue, but concluding that the § 1409 requirements imposed on a child like her, but not on the foreign-born, out-of-wedlock child of an American mother, were justified by governmental interests in fostering the child's ties with this country and with her citizen parent.

Held: The judgment is affirmed.

96 F.3d 1467, affirmed.

Justice STEVENS, joined by THE CHIEF JUSTICE, concluded that § 1409(a)(4)'s requirement that children born abroad and out of wedlock to citizen fathers, but not to citizen mothers, obtain formal proof of paternity by age 18 does not violate the Fifth Amendment. Pp. 1434–1442.

(a) The foregoing is the only issue presented by this case's facts. Certain other issues need not be resolved: Whether *Fiallo v. Bell*, 430 U.S. 787, 97 S.Ct. 1473, 52 L.Ed.2d 50, dictates the outcome here; the validity of the distinction drawn by §§ 1401(g) and 1409(c) between residency requirements for unmarried citizen fathers and unmarried citizen mothers wishing to transmit citizenship at birth to their foreign-born, out-of-wedlock children; and the validity of §§ 1409(a)(1) and (a)(3), which impose additional requirements on citizen fathers wishing to transmit such citizenship. Because petitioner is contesting the Government's refusal to register and treat her as a citizen, a judgment in her favor would confirm her preexisting citizenship rather than grant her rights that she does not now possess. The Court of Appeals was therefore correct that she has standing to invoke the federal courts' jurisdiction. Moreover, because her claim relies heavily on the proposition that her citizen father should have the same right to transmit citizenship as would a citizen mother, the Court should evaluate the alleged discrimination against him, as well as its impact on her. See, *e.g.*, *Craig v. Boren*, 429 U.S. 190, 193–197, 97 S.Ct. 451, 454–457, 50 L.Ed.2d 397. Pp. 1434–1436.

(b) The § 1409(a)(4) rule applicable to each class of out-of-wedlock children born abroad is eminently reasonable and justified by important Government interests: ensuring reliable proof that a person born out of wedlock who claims citizenship by birth actually shares a blood relationship with an American citizen; encouraging the development of a healthy relationship between the citizen parent and the child while the child is a minor; and fostering ties between the child and the United States. Male and female parents of foreign-born, out-of-wedlock children are differently situated in several pertinent respects. The child's blood relationship to its birth mother is immediately obvious and is typically established by hospital records and birth certificates, but the relationship to the unmarried father may often be undisclosed and unrecorded in any contemporary public record. Similarly, the child's birth mother certainly knows of the child's existence and typically will have immediate custody, whereas, due to the normal interval of nine months between conception and birth, an unmarried father may not even know that his child exists, and the child may not know the father's identity. Section 1409(a)(4)'s requirement—that children born out of wedlock to citizen fathers obtain formal proof of paternity by age 18, either through legitimation, written acknowledgment by the father under oath, or adjudication by a competent court—is well tailored to address these concerns. The conclusion that Congress may require an affirmative act by unmarried fathers and their children, but not mothers and their children, is directly supported by *Lehr v. Robertson*, 463 U.S. 248, 103 S.Ct. 2985, 77 L.Ed.2d 614. Pp. 1436–1440.

(c) The argument that § 1409(a)(4) is unconstitutional because it is a stereotypical "gender-based classification" must be rejected. None of the governmental interests underlying § 1409(a)(4) can be fairly characterized as an accidental byproduct of a traditional way of thinking about the members of either sex. The biological differences between single men and single women provide a relevant basis for differing rules governing their ability to confer citizenship on children born out of wedlock in foreign lands, and an impartial analysis of those differences rebuts the strong presumption that gender-based legal distinctions are suspect. Pp. 1440–1442.

Justice O'CONNOR, joined by Justice KENNEDY, concluded that petitioner should not be accorded standing to raise her father's gender discrimination claim. This Court applies a presumption against third-party standing as a prudential limitation on the exercise of federal jurisdiction, see, *e.g.*, *Singleton v. Wulff*, 428 U.S. 106, 113, 96 S.Ct. 2868, 2873–2874, 49 L.Ed.2d 826, and that presumption may only be rebutted in particular circumstances: where a litigant has suffered injury in fact and has a close relation to a third party, and where some hindrance to the third party's ability to protect his or her own interests exists, see *Powers v. Ohio*, 499 U.S. 400, 411, 111 S.Ct. 1364, 1370–1371, 113 L.Ed.2d 411. Petitioner has not demonstrated a genuine obstacle to her father's ability to assert his own rights that rises to the level of a hindrance. Accordingly, she is precluded from raising his equal protection claims in this case. Although petitioner may still assert her own rights, she cannot invoke a gender discrimination claim that would trigger heightened scrutiny. Section 1409 draws a distinction based on the gender of the parent, not the child, and any claim of discrimination based on differential treatment of illegitimate versus legitimate children is not presented in the question on which certiorari was granted. Thus, petitioner's own constitutional challenge is subject only to rational basis scrutiny. Even though § 1409 could not withstand heightened scrutiny, it is sustainable under the lower standard. Pp. 1442–1446.

Justice SCALIA, joined by Justice THOMAS, agreed with the outcome of this case on the ground that the complaint must be dismissed because the Court has no power to provide the relief requested: conferral of citizenship on a basis other than that prescribed by Congress. Petitioner, having been born outside United States territory, can only become a citizen by naturalization under congressional authority. See, *e.g.*, *United States v. Wong Kim Ark*, 169 U.S. 649, 702–703, 18 S.Ct. 456, 477–478, 42 L.Ed. 890. If there is no congressional enactment granting her citizenship, she remains an alien. By its plain language, 8 U.S.C. § 1409 sets forth a precondition to the acquisition of citizenship that petitioner admittedly has not met. Thus, even if the Court were to agree that the difference in treatment between the illegitimate children of citizen-fathers and citizen-mothers is unconstitutional, it could not, consistent with the extremely limited judicial power in this area, see, *e.g.*, *Fiallo v. Bell*, 430 U.S. 787, 792, 97 S.Ct. 1473, 1477–1478, 52 L.Ed.2d 50, remedy that constitutional infirmity by declaring petitioner to be a citizen or ordering the State Department to approve her application for citizenship, see *INS v. Pangilinan*, 486 U.S. 875, 884, 108 S.Ct. 2210, 2216–2217, 100 L.Ed.2d 882. This is not a case in which the Court may remedy an alleged equal-protection violation by either expanding or limiting the benefits conferred so as to deny or grant them equally to all. Pp. 1446–1455.

STEVENS, J., announced the judgment of the Court and delivered an opinion, in which REHNQUIST, C. J., joined. O'CONNOR, J., filed an opinion concurring in the judgment, in which KENNEDY, J., joined. SCALIA, J., filed an opinion concurring in the judgment, in which THOMAS, J., joined. GINSBURG, J., filed a dissenting opinion, in which SOUTER and BREYER, JJ., joined. BREYER, J., filed a dissenting opinion, in which SOUTER and GINSBURG, JJ., joined.

Donald R. Patterson, Tyler, TX, for petitioner.

Edwin S. Kneedler, Washington, DC, for respondent.

For U.S. Supreme Court briefs, see:

1997 WL 325338 (Pet.Brief)

1997 WL 433315 (Resp.Brief)

1997 WL 583469 (Reply.Brief)

Justice STEVENS announced the judgment of the Court and delivered an opinion, in which THE CHIEF JUSTICE joined.

[1–3] There are "two sources of citizenship, and two only: birth and naturalization." *United States v. Wong Kim Ark*, 169 U.S. 649, 702, 18 S.Ct. 456, 477, 42 L.Ed. 890 (1898). Within the former category, the Fourteenth Amendment of the Constitution guarantees that every person "born in the United States, and subject to the jurisdiction thereof, becomes at once a citizen of the United States, and needs no naturalization." 169 U.S., at 702, 18 S.Ct., at 477. Persons not born in the United States acquire citizenship by birth only as provided by Acts of Congress. *Id.*, at 703, 18 S.Ct., at 477–478.

The petitioner in this case challenges the constitutionality of the statutory provisions governing the acquisition of citizenship at birth by children born out of wedlock and outside of the United States. The specific challenge is to the distinction drawn by § 309 of the Immigration and Nationality Act (INA), 66 Stat. 238, as amended, 8 U.S.C. § 1409, between the child of an alien father and a citizen mother, on the one hand, and the child of an alien mother and a citizen father, on the other. Subject to residence requirements for the citizen parent, the citizenship of the former is established at birth; the citizenship of the latter is not established unless and until either the father or his child takes certain affirmative steps to create or confirm their relationship. Petitioner contends that the statutory requirement that those steps be taken while the child is a minor violates the Fifth Amendment because the statute contains no limitation on the time within which the child of a citizen mother may prove that she became a citizen at birth.

We find no merit in the challenge because the statute does not impose any limitation on the time within which the members of either class of children may prove that they qualify for citizenship. It does establish different qualifications for citizenship for the two classes of children, but we are persuaded that the qualifications for the members of each of those classes, so far as they are implicated by the facts of this case, are well supported by valid governmental interests. We therefore conclude that the statutory distinction is neither arbitrary nor invidious.

I

Petitioner was born on June 20, 1970, in Angeles City, Republic of the Philippines. The records of the Local Civil Registrar disclose that her birth was registered 10 days later, that she was named Lorena Penero, that her mother was Luz Penero, a Filipino national, and that her birth was "illegitimate." Spaces on the form referring to the name and the nationality of the father are blank.

Petitioner grew up and received her high school and college education in the Philippines. At least until after her 21st birthday, she never lived in the United States. App. 19. There is no evidence that either she or her mother ever resided outside of the Philippines.[1]

Petitioner's father, Charlie Miller, is an American citizen residing in Texas.[2] He ap-

1. Her mother was born in Leyte. Several years after petitioner's birth, her mother married a man named Frank Raspotnik and raised a family in Angeles City. App. 22.

2. Although there is no formal finding that his paternity has been established by clear and convincing evidence, it is undisputed. In a letter to petitioner's attorney, the State Department ac-

parently served in the United States Air Force and was stationed in the Philippines at the time of petitioner's conception. *Id.*, at 21. He never married petitioner's mother, and there is no evidence that he was in the Philippines at the time of petitioner's birth or that he ever returned there after completing his tour of duty. In 1992, Miller filed a petition in a Texas court to establish his relationship with petitioner. The petition was unopposed and the court entered a "Voluntary Paternity Decree" finding him "to be the biological and legal father of Lorelyn Penero Miller." The decree provided that "[t]he parent-child relationship is created between the father and the child as if the child were born to the father and mother during marriage." App. to Pet. for Cert. 38.

In November 1991, petitioner filed an application for registration as a United States citizen with the State Department. The application was denied in March 1992, and petitioner reapplied after her father obtained the paternity decree in Texas in July 1992. The reapplication was also denied on the ground that the Texas decree did not satisfy "the requirements of Section 309(a)(4) INA, which requires that a child born out of wedlock be legitimated before age eighteen in order to acquire U.S. citizenship under Section 301(g) INA (formerly Section 301(a)(7) INA)." *Id.*, at 33. In further explanation of its reliance on § 309(a)(4), the denial letter added: "Without such legitimation before age eighteen, there is no legally recognized relationship under the INA and the child acquires no rights of citizenship through an American citizen parent."[3] *Ibid.*

II

In 1993, petitioner and her father filed an amended complaint against the Secretary of State in the United States District Court for the Eastern District of Texas, seeking a judgment declaring that petitioner is a citizen of the United States and that she therefore has the right to possess an American passport. They alleged that the INA's different treatment of citizen mothers and citizen fathers violated Mr. Miller's "right to equal protection under the laws by utilizing the suspect classification of gender without justification." App. 11. In response to a motion to dismiss filed by the Government, the District Court concluded that Mr. Miller did not have standing and dismissed him as a party. Because venue in Texas was therefore improper, see 28 U.S.C. § 1391(e), the court transferred the case to the District Court for the District of Columbia, the site of the Secretary's residence. The Government renewed its motion in that forum, and that court concluded that even though petitioner had suffered an injury caused by the Secretary's refusal to register her as a citizen, the injury was not "redressable" because federal courts do not have the power to "grant citizenship." 870 F.Supp. 1, 3 (1994) (citing *INS v. Pangilinan*, 486 U.S. 875, 884, 108 S.Ct. 2210, 2216–2217, 100 L.Ed.2d 882 (1988)).

The Court of Appeals for the District of Columbia Circuit affirmed, but on different grounds. It first held that petitioner does have standing to challenge the constitutionality of 8 U.S.C. § 1409(a). If her challenge should succeed, the court could enter a judgment declaring that she was already a citizen pursuant to other provisions of the INA. 96 F.3d 1467, 1470 (C.A.D.C.1996). On the merits, however, the court concluded that the requirements imposed on the "illegitimate"

knowledged that it was "satisfied that Mr. Charlie R. Miller, the putative father, is a U.S. citizen, that he possesses sufficient physical presence in the United States to transmit citizenship, and that there is sufficient evidence that he had access to the applicant's mother at the probable time of conception." App. to Pet. for Cert. 32–33.

3. The comment, of course, related only to cases in which the child born out of wedlock claims citizenship through her father. Moreover, the reference to age 18 was inaccurate; petitioner was born prior to 1986, when § 309(a) was amended to change the relevant age from 21 to 18, see Pub.L. 99–653, § 13, 100 Stat. 3657, and she falls within a narrow age bracket whose members may elect to have the pre-amendment law apply, see note following 8 U.S.C. § 1409 (Effective Date of 1986 Amendment) (quoting § 23(e), as added, Pub L. 100–525, § 8(r), 102 Stat. 2619). This oversight does not affect her case, however, because she was over 21 when the Texas decree was entered.

child of an American citizen father, but not on the child of a citizen mother, were justified by the interest in fostering the child's ties with this country. It explained:

> "[W]e conclude, as did the Ninth Circuit, that 'a desire to promote early ties to this country and to those relatives who are citizens of this country is not a[n ir]rational basis for the requirements made by' sections 1409(a)(3) and (4). *Ablang* [*v. Reno*], 52 F.3d [801] at 806 [(9th Cir.1995)]. Furthermore, we find it entirely reasonable for Congress to require special evidence of such ties between an illegitimate child and its father. A mother is far less likely to ignore the child she has carried in her womb than is the natural father, who may not even be aware of its existence. As the Court has recognized, 'mothers and fathers of illegitimate children are not similarly situated.' *Parham v. Hughes*, 441 U.S. 347, 355, 99 S.Ct. 1742, 1747, 60 L.Ed.2d 269 (1979). 'The putative father often goes his way unconscious of the birth of the child. Even if conscious, he is very often totally unconcerned because of the absence of any ties to the mother.' *Id.* at 355, n. 7, 99 S.Ct. at 1748, n. 7 (internal quotation marks and citation omitted). This sex-based distinction seems especially warranted where, as here, the applicant for citizenship was fathered by a U.S. serviceman while serving a tour of duty overseas." *Id.*, at 1472.

Judge Wald concurred in the judgment despite her opinion that there is "no rational basis for a law that requires a U.S. citizen father, but not a U.S. citizen mother, to formally legitimate a child before she reaches majority as well as agree in writing to provide financial support until that date or forever forfeit the right to transmit citizenship." *Id.*, at 1473. While she agreed that "requiring some sort of minimal 'family ties' between parent and child, as well as fostering an early connection between child and country, is rational government policy," she did not agree that those goals justify "a set of procedural hurdles for men—and only men—who wish to confer citizenship on their children." *Id.*, at 1474. She nevertheless regretfully concurred in the judgment because she believed that our decision in *Fiallo v. Bell*, 430 U.S. 787, 97 S.Ct. 1473, 52 L.Ed.2d 50 (1977), required the court to uphold the constitutionality of § 1409. 96 F.3d, at 1473.

We granted certiorari to address the following question:

> "Is the distinction in 8 U.S.C. § 1409 between 'illegitimate' children of United States citizen mothers and 'illegitimate' children of United States citizen fathers a violation of the Fifth Amendment to the United States Constitution?" 520 U.S. ——, 117 S.Ct. 1551, 137 L.Ed.2d 700 (1997).

III

Before explaining our answer to the single question that we agreed to address, it is useful to put to one side certain issues that need not be resolved. First, we need not decide whether *Fiallo v. Bell* dictates the outcome of this case, because that case involved the claims of several aliens to a special immigration preference, whereas here the petitioner claims that she is, and for years has been, an American citizen.[4] Additionally, *Fiallo* involved challenges to the

4. The sections of the INA challenged in *Fiallo* defined the terms "child" and "parent," which determine eligibility for the special preference immigration status accorded to the "children" and "parents" of United States citizens and lawful permanent residents. *Fiallo v. Bell*, 430 U.S. 787, 788–789, 97 S.Ct. 1473, 1476, 52 L.Ed.2d 50 (1977). "Child" was defined to include "an illegitimate child, by, through whom, or on whose behalf a status, privilege, or benefit is sought by virtue of the relationship of the child to its natural mother." *Id.*, at 788–789, n. 1, 97 S.Ct. at 1476, n. 1 (quoting 8 U.S.C. § 1101(b)(1)(D) (1976 ed.)). Thus, the statute did not permit an illegitimate child to seek preference by virtue of relationship with its citizen or resident father, nor could an alien father seek preference based on his illegitimate child's citizenship or residence. 430 U.S., at 789, 97 S.Ct., at 1476. Following this Court's decision in *Fiallo* upholding those provisions, in 1986 Congress amended the INA to recognize "child" and "parent" status where the preference is sought based on the relationship of a child born out of wedlock to its natural father "if the father has or had a bona fide parent-child relationship with the person." Pub.L. 99–603, § 315(a), 100 Stat. 3439, as amended, 8 U.S.C. § 1101(b)(1)(D) (1982 ed., Supp. IV).

statutory distinctions between "illegitimate" and "legitimate" children, which are not encompassed in the question presented in this case and which we therefore do not consider.

The statutory provision at issue in this case, 8 U.S.C. § 1409, draws two types of distinctions between citizen fathers and citizen mothers of children born out of wedlock. The first relates to the class of unmarried persons who may transmit citizenship at birth to their offspring, and the second defines the affirmative steps that are required to transmit such citizenship.

With respect to the eligible class of parents, an unmarried father may not transmit his citizenship to a child born abroad to an alien mother unless he satisfies the residency requirement in § 1401(g) that applies to a citizen parent who is married to an alien.[5] Under that provision, the citizen parent must have resided in the United States for a total of at least five years, at least two of which were after attaining the age of 14 years.[6] If the citizen parent is an unmarried mother, however, § 1409(c) rather than § 1401(g) applies; under that subsection she need only have had one year of continuous residence in the United States in order to confer citizenship on her offspring.[7] Since petitioner's father satisfied the residency requirement in § 1401(g), the validity of the distinction between that requirement and the unusually generous provision in § 1409(c) is not at issue.[8]

As for affirmative steps, § 1409(a), as amended in 1986, imposes four requirements concerning unmarried citizen fathers that must be satisfied to confer citizenship "as of the date of birth" on a person born out of wedlock to an alien mother in another country. Citizenship for such persons is established if:

"(1) a blood relationship between the person and the father is established by clear and convincing evidence,

"(2) the father had the nationality of the United States at the time of the person's birth,

"(3) the father (unless deceased) has agreed in writing to provide financial support for the person until the person reaches the age of 18 years, and

"(4) while the person is under the age of 18 years—

"(A) the person is legitimated under the law of the person's residence or domicile,

"(B) the father acknowledges paternity of the person in writing under oath, or

"(C) the paternity of the person is established by adjudication of a competent court." 8 U.S.C. § 1409(a).

Only the second of these four requirements is expressly included in § 1409(c), the

5. See 8 U.S.C. § 1409(a) (directing that §§ 1401(c), (d), (e), (g) and 1408(2) "shall apply" if the specified conditions of § 1409(a) are met).

6. Title 8 U.S.C. § 1401 provides:
"The following shall be nationals and citizens of the United States at birth:

. . . . .

"(g) a person born outside the geographical limits of the United States and its outlying possessions of parents one of whom is an alien, and the other a citizen of the United States who, prior to the birth of such person, was physically present in the United States or its outlying possessions for a period or periods totaling not less than five years, at least two of which were after attaining the age of fourteen years. . . ."
Prior to its amendment in 1986, the section had required residence of 10 total years, at least 5 of which were after attaining the age of 14. See § 301(a)(7), 66 Stat. 236.

7. Section 309(c) of the INA, codified in 8 U.S.C. § 1409(c), provides: "(c) Notwithstanding the provision of subsection (a) of this section, a person born, after December 23, 1952, outside the United States and out of wedlock shall be held to have acquired at birth the nationality status of his mother, if the mother had the nationality of the United States at the time of such person's birth, and if the mother had previously been physically present in the United States or one of its outlying possessions for a continuous period of one year."

8. The Government has offered two explanations for the special rule applicable to unmarried citizen mothers who give birth abroad: first, an assumption that the citizen mother would probably have custody, and second, that in most foreign countries the nationality of an illegitimate child is that of the mother unless paternity has been established. The Government submits that the special rule would minimize the risk that such a child might otherwise be stateless. See Brief for Respondent 32–34.

provision applicable to unwed citizen mothers. See n. 7, *supra*. Petitioner, relying heavily on Judge Wald's separate opinion below, argues that there is no rational basis for imposing the other three requirements on children of citizen fathers but not citizen mothers. The first requirement is not at issue here, however, because the Government does not question Mr. Miller's blood relationship with petitioner.

Moreover, even though the parties have disputed the validity of the third condition [9] —and even though that condition is repeatedly targeted in Justice BREYER's dissent—we need not resolve that debate because it is unclear whether the requirement even applies in petitioner's case; it was added in 1986, after her birth, and she falls within a special interim provision that allows her to elect application of the pre-amendment § 1409(a), which required only legitimation before age 21. See n. 3, *supra*. And even if the condition did apply to her claim of citizenship, the State Department's refusal to register petitioner as a citizen was expressly based on § 1409(a)(4). Indeed, since that subsection is written in the disjunctive, it is only necessary to uphold the least onerous of the three alternative methods of compliance to sustain the Government's position. Thus, the only issue presented by the facts of this case is whether the requirement in § 1409(a)(4)—that children born out of wedlock to citizen fathers, but not citizen mothers, obtain formal proof of paternity by age 18, either through legitimation, written acknowledgment by the father under oath, or adjudication by a competent court—violates the Fifth Amendment.

[4] It is of significance that the petitioner in this case, unlike the petitioners in *Fiallo*, see 430 U.S., at 790, n. 3, 97 S.Ct., at 1473, n. 3 is not challenging the denial of an application for special status. She is contesting the Government's refusal to register and treat her as a citizen. If she were to prevail, the judgment in her favor would confirm her pre-existing citizenship rather than grant her rights that she does not now possess. We therefore agree with the Court of Appeals that she has standing to invoke the jurisdiction of the federal courts. See 96 F.3d, at 1469–1470 (distinguishing *INS v. Pangilinan*, 486 U.S. 875, 108 S.Ct. 2210, 100 L.Ed.2d 882 (1988)). Moreover, because her claim relies heavily on the proposition that her citizen father should have the same right to transmit citizenship as would a citizen mother, we shall evaluate the alleged discrimination against him as well as its impact on her. See, *e.g.*, *Craig v. Boren*, 429 U.S. 190, 193–197, 97 S.Ct. 451, 454–457, 50 L.Ed.2d 397 (1976).[10]

IV

[5] Under the terms of the INA, the joint conduct of a citizen and an alien that results in conception is not sufficient to produce an American citizen, regardless of whether the citizen parent is the male or the female partner. If the two parties engage in a second joint act—if they agree to marry one another—citizenship will follow. The provision at issue in this case, however, deals only with cases in which no relevant joint conduct occurs after conception; it determines the ability of each of those parties, acting separately,

9. The Government asserts that the purpose of § 1409(a)(3) is " 'to facilitate the enforcement of a child support order and, thus, lessen the chance that the child could become a financial burden to the states.' " Brief for Respondent 25–26, n. 13 (quoting Hearings on H.R. 4823 et al. before the Subcommittee on Immigration, Refugees, and International Law of the House Committee on the Judiciary, 99th Cong., 2d Sess., 150 (1986) (statement of Joan M. Clark, Assistant Secretary of State for Consular Affairs) (hereinafter Hearings)).

10. As a threshold matter, the Government now argues—though it never asserted this position below or in opposition to certiorari—that an alien outside the territory of the United States "has no substantive rights cognizable under the Fifth Amendment." Brief for Respondent 11–12. Even if that is so, the question to be decided is whether petitioner is such an alien or whether, as she claims, she is a citizen. Thus, we must address the merits to determine whether the predicate for this argument is accurate. In the cases on which the Government relies, *Johnson v. Eisentrager*, 339 U.S. 763, 70 S.Ct. 936, 94 L.Ed. 1255 (1950), and *United States v. Verdugo-Urquidez*, 494 U.S. 259, 110 S.Ct. 1056, 108 L.Ed.2d 222 (1990), it was perfectly clear that the complaining aliens were not citizens or nationals of the United States.

to confer citizenship on a child born outside of the United States.

If the citizen is the unmarried female, she must first choose to carry the pregnancy to term and reject the alternative of abortion—an alternative that is available by law to many, and in reality to most, women around the world. She must then actually give birth to the child. Section 1409(c) rewards that choice and that labor by conferring citizenship on her child.

If the citizen is the unmarried male, he need not participate in the decision to give birth rather than to choose an abortion; he need not be present at the birth; and for at least 17 years thereafter he need not provide any parental support, either moral or financial, to either the mother or the child, in order to preserve his right to confer citizenship on the child pursuant to § 1409(a). In order retroactively to transmit his citizenship to the child as of the date of the child's birth, all that § 1409(a)(4) requires is that he be willing and able to acknowledge his paternity in writing under oath while the child is still a minor. 8 U.S.C. § 1409(a)(4)(B). In fact, § 1409(a)(4) requires even less of the unmarried father—that provision is alternatively satisfied if, before the child turns 18, its paternity "is established by adjudication of a competent court." § 1409(a)(4)(C). It would appear that the child could obtain such an adjudication absent any affirmative act by the father, and perhaps even over his express objection.

There is thus a vast difference between the burdens imposed on the respective parents of potential citizens born out of wedlock in a foreign land. It seems obvious that the burdens imposed on the female citizen are more severe than those imposed on the male citizen by § 1409(a)(4), the only provision at issue in this case. It is nevertheless argued that the male citizen and his offspring are the victims of irrational discrimination because § 1409(a)(4) is the product of " 'overbroad stereotypes about the relative abilities of men and women.' " Brief for Petitioner 8. We find the argument singularly unpersuasive.[11]

Insofar as the argument rests on the fact that the male citizen parent will "forever forfeit the right to transmit citizenship" if he does not come forward while the child is a minor, whereas there is no limit on the time within which the citizen mother may prove her blood relationship, the argument overlooks the difference between a substantive condition and a procedural limitation. The substantive conduct of the unmarried citizen mother that qualifies her child for citizenship is completed at the moment of birth; the relevant conduct of the unmarried citizen father or his child may occur at any time within 18 years thereafter. There is, however, no procedural hurdle that limits the time or the method by which either parent (or the child) may provide the State Department with evidence that the necessary steps were taken to transmit citizenship to the child.

The substantive requirement embodied in § 1409(a)(4) serves, at least in part, to ensure that a person born out of wedlock who claims citizenship by birth actually shares a blood relationship with an American citizen. As originally enacted in 1952, § 1409(a) required simply that "the paternity of such child [born out of wedlock] is established while such child is under the age of twenty-one years by legitimation." 66 Stat. 238. The section offered no other means of proving a biological relationship. In 1986, at the same time that it modified the INA provi-

11. Though petitioner claims to be a citizen from birth, rather than claiming an immigration preference, citizenship does not pass by descent. *Rogers v. Bellei*, 401 U.S. 815, 830, 91 S.Ct. 1060, 1068–1069, 28 L.Ed.2d 499 (1971). Thus she must still meet the statutory requirements set by Congress for citizenship. *Id.*, at 828–830, 91 S.Ct., at 1067–1069; *United States v. Ginsberg*, 243 U.S. 472, 474, 37 S.Ct. 422, 425, 61 L.Ed. 853 (1917). Deference to the political branches dictates "a narrow standard of review of decisions made by the Congress or the President in the area of immigration and naturalization." *Mathews v. Diaz*, 426 U.S. 67, 82, 96 S.Ct. 1883, 1892, 48 L.Ed.2d 478 (1976). Even if, as petitioner and her *amici* argue, the heightened scrutiny that normally governs gender discrimination claims applied in this context, see *United States v. Virginia*, 518 U.S. 515, ——— - ———, 116 S.Ct. 2264, 2275–2276, 135 L.Ed.2d 735 (1996), we are persuaded that the requirement imposed by § 1409(a)(4) on children of unmarried male, but not female, citizens is substantially related to important governmental objectives.

sions at issue in *Fiallo* in favor of unmarried fathers and their out-of-wedlock children, see n. 4, *supra*, Congress expanded § 1409(a) to allow the two other alternatives now found in subsections (4)(B) and (4)(C). Pub.L. 99–653, § 13, 100 Stat. 3657. The purpose of the amendment was to "simplify and facilitate determinations of acquisition of citizenship by children born out of wedlock to an American citizen father, by eliminating the necessity of determining the father's residence or domicile and establishing satisfaction of the legitimation provisions of the jurisdiction." Hearings, at 150. The 1986 amendment also added § 1409(a)(1), which requires paternity to be established by clear and convincing evidence, in order to deter fraudulent claims; but that standard of proof was viewed as an ancillary measure, not a replacement for proof of paternity by legitimation or a formal alternative. See *id.*, at 150, 155.

There is no doubt that ensuring reliable proof of a biological relationship between the potential citizen and its citizen parent is an important governmental objective. See *Trimble v. Gordon*, 430 U.S. 762, 770–771, 97 S.Ct. 1459, 1465, 52 L.Ed.2d 31 (1977); *Fiallo*, 430 U.S., at 799, n. 8, 97 S.Ct., at 1482, n. 8. Nor can it be denied that the male and female parents are differently situated in this respect. The blood relationship to the birth mother is immediately obvious and is typically established by hospital records and birth certificates; the relationship to the unmarried father may often be undisclosed and unrecorded in any contemporary public record. Thus, the requirement that the father make a timely written acknowledgment under oath, or that the child obtain a court adjudication of paternity, produces the rough equivalent of the documentation that is already available to evidence the blood relationship between the mother and the child. If the statute had required the citizen parent, whether male or female, to obtain appropriate formal documentation within 30 days after birth, it would have been "gender-neutral" on its face, even though in practical operation it would disfavor unmarried males because in virtually every case such a requirement would be superfluous for the mother. Surely the fact that the statute allows 18 years in which to provide evidence that is comparable to what the mother provides immediately after birth cannot be viewed as discriminating against the father or his child.

Nevertheless, petitioner reiterates the suggestion that it is irrational to require a formal act such as a written acknowledgment or a court adjudication because the advent of reliable genetic testing fully addresses the problem of proving paternity, and subsection (a)(1) already requires proof of paternity by clear and convincing evidence. See 96 F.3d, at 1474. We respectfully disagree. Nothing in subsection (a)(1) requires the citizen father or his child to obtain a genetic paternity test. It is difficult, moreover, to understand why signing a paternity acknowledgment under oath prior to the child's 18th birthday is more burdensome than obtaining a genetic test, which is relatively expensive,[12] normally requires physical intrusion for both the putative father and child,[13] and often is not available in foreign countries.[14] Congress could fairly conclude that despite recent scientific advances, it still remains preferable to re-

12. See 7 U.S. Dept. of State, Foreign Affairs Manual § 1131.5–4(c) (1996) (hereinafter Foreign Affairs Manual). Commercially available testing in the United States presently appears to cost between about $450 to $600 per test. See Hotaling, Is He or Isn't He?, Los Angeles Times Magazine, Sept. 7, 1997, pp. 36, 54 (hereinafter Hotaling); Mirabella, Lab's Tests Give Answers to Genetic Questions, Baltimore Sun, Nov. 25, 1997, pp. 1C, 8C, cols. 2, 4 (hereinafter Mirabella).

13. Laboratories that conduct genetic paternity testing typically use either blood samples or cells scraped from the inside of the cheek of the putative father, the child, and often the mother as well. See, *e.g.*, 1 D Faigman, D. Kaye, M. Saks, & J. Sanders, Modern Scientific Evidence §§ 19–2.2, 19–2.7.1, pp. 761, 763, 775 (1997); Hotaling, pp. 36, 54; Mirabella, p. 8C, cols. 2, 4.

14. The State Department has observed that "the competence, integrity, and availability of blood testing physicians and facilities vary around the world." 7 Foreign Affairs Manual § 1131.5–4(c). There are presently about 75 DNA testing laboratories in the United States, 51 of which are accredited by the American Association of Blood Banks. Hotaling, p. 36.

quire some formal legal act to establish paternity, coupled with a clear-and-convincing evidence standard to deter fraud. The time limitation, in turn, provides assurance that the formal act is based upon reliable evidence, and also deters fraud.[15] Congress is of course free to revise its collective judgment and permit genetic proof of paternity rather than requiring some formal legal act by the father or a court,[16] but the Constitution does not now require any such change.

Section 1409 also serves two other important purposes that are unrelated to the determination of paternity: the interest in encouraging the development of a healthy relationship between the citizen parent and the child while the child is a minor; and the related interest in fostering ties between the foreign-born child and the United States. When a child is born out of wedlock outside of the United States, the citizen mother, unlike the citizen father, certainly knows of her child's existence and typically will have custody of the child immediately after the birth. Such a child thus has the opportunity to develop ties with its citizen mother at an early age, and may even grow up in the United States if the mother returns. By contrast, due to the normal interval of nine months between conception and birth, the unmarried father may not even know that his child exists, and the child may not know the father's identity. Section 1409(a)(4) requires a relatively easy, formal step by either the citizen father or his child that shows beyond doubt that at least one of the two knows of their blood relationship, thus assuring at least the opportunity for them to develop a personal relationship.

The facts of this very case provide a ready example of the concern. Mr. Miller and petitioner both failed to take any steps to establish a legal relationship with each other before petitioner's 21st birthday, and there is no indication in the record that they had any contact whatsoever before she applied for a United States passport. Given the size of the American military establishment that has been stationed in various parts of the world for the past half century, it is reasonable to assume that this case is not unusual. In 1970, when petitioner was born, about 683,000 service personnel were stationed in the Far East, 24,000 of whom were in the Philippines. U.S. Dept. of Commerce, Statistical Abstract of the United States 381 (99th ed.1978). Of all Americans in the military at that time, only one percent were female.[17] These figures, coupled with the interval between conception and birth and the fact that military personnel regularly return to the United States when a tour of duty ends, suggest that Congress had legitimate concerns about a class of children born abroad out of wedlock to alien mothers and to American servicemen who would not necessarily know about, or be known by, their children. It was surely reasonable when the INA was enacted in 1952, and remains equally reasonable today, for Congress to condition the award of citizenship to such children on an act that demonstrates, at a minimum, the possibility that those who become citizens will develop ties with this country—a requirement that performs a meaningful purpose for citizen fathers but normally would be superfluous for citizen mothers.

It is of course possible that any child born in a foreign country may ultimately fail to establish ties with its citizen parent and with this country, even though the child's citizen parent has engaged in the conduct that qualifies the child for citizenship. A citizen mother may abandon her child before returning to the States, and a citizen father, even after acknowledging paternity, may die or abscond

15. Once a child reaches the legal age of majority, a male citizen could make a fraudulent claim of paternity on the person's behalf without any risk of liability for child support.

16. In a different context Congress has already recognized the value of genetic paternity testing. See 96 F.3d 1467, 1474–1475 (C.A.D.C.1996) (discussing Child Support Enforcement Amendments of 1984).

17. Office of the Assistant Secretary of Defense, Background Study, Use of Women in the Military 5 (2d ed.1978). The proportion of military personnel who were female in 1970 had dropped from a high of 2.2% in 1945. *Id.*, at 3. Since 1970, the proportion has steadily increased to its present level of about 13 percent. See Dept. of Defense, Selected Manpower Statistics 23 (1996).

before his child has an opportunity to bond with him or visit this country. The fact that the interest in fostering ties with this country may not be fully achieved for either class of children does not qualify the legitimacy or the importance of that interest. If, as Congress reasonably may have assumed, the formal requirements in § 1409(a)(4) tend to make it just as likely that fathers will have the opportunity to develop a meaningful relationship with their children as does the fact that the mother knows of her baby's existence and often has custody at birth, the statute's effect will reduce, rather than aggravate, the disparity between the two classes of children.

We are convinced not only that strong governmental interests justify the additional requirement imposed on children of citizen fathers, but also that the particular means used in § 1409(a)(4) are well tailored to serve those interests. It is perfectly appropriate to require some formal act, not just any evidence that the father or his child know of the other's existence. Such a formal act, whether legitimation, written acknowledgment by the father, or a court adjudication, lessens the risk of fraudulent claims made years after the relevant conduct was required. As for the requirement that the formal act take place while the child is a minor, Congress obviously has a powerful interest in fostering ties with the child's citizen parent and the United States during his or her formative years. If there is no reliable, contemporaneous proof that the child and the citizen father had the opportunity to form familial bonds before the child turned 18, Congress reasonably may demand that the child show sufficient ties to this country on its own rather than through its citizen parent in order to be a citizen.[18]

Our conclusion that Congress may require an affirmative act by unmarried fathers and their children, but not mothers and their children, is directly supported by our decision in *Lehr v. Robertson*, 463 U.S. 248, 103 S.Ct. 2985, 77 L.Ed.2d 614 (1983). That case involved a New York law that automatically provided mothers of "illegitimate" children with prior notice of an adoption proceeding and the right to veto an adoption, but only extended those rights to unmarried fathers whose claim of paternity was supported by some formal public act, such as a court adjudication, the filing of a notice of intent to claim paternity, or written acknowledgment by the mother. *Id.*, at 251–252, n. 5, 266, 103 S.Ct., at 2988, n. 5, 2996. The petitioner in *Lehr*, an unmarried putative father, need only have mailed a postcard to the State's "putative father registry" to enjoy the same rights as the child's undisputed mother, *id.*, at 264, 103 S.Ct., at 2995, yet he argued that this gender-based requirement violated the Equal Protection Clause. We rejected that argument, and we find the comparable claim in this case, if anything, even less persuasive. Whereas the putative father in *Lehr* was deprived of certain rights because he failed to take some affirmative step within about two years of the child's birth (when the adoption proceeding took place), here the unfavorable gender-based treatment was attributable to Mr. Miller's failure to take appropriate action within 21 years of petitioner's birth *and* petitioner's own failure to obtain a paternity adjudication by a "competent court" before she turned 18.[19]

Even though the rule applicable to each class of children born abroad is eminently reasonable and justified by important Government policies, petitioner and her *amici* argue that § 1409 is unconstitutional because it is a "gender-based classification." We shall comment briefly on that argument.

V

The words "stereotype," "stereotyping," and "stereotypical" are used repeatedly in

18. The same policy presently applies to foreign-born persons not eligible for citizenship at birth: A child may obtain special immigration preference and the immediate issuance of a visa based on a parent's citizenship or lawful residence, but only until age 21. 8 U.S.C. §§ 1101(b)(1), 1153(d).

19. Justice BREYER questions the relevance of *Lehr* because it was decided before advances in genetic testing, see *post*, at 1463; there was, however, no question about the paternity of the father in that case. As in this case, the father there failed to act promptly to establish a relationship with his child.

petitioner's and her *amici's* briefs. They note that we have condemned statutory classifications that rest on the assumption that gender may serve as a proxy for relevant qualifications to serve as the administrator of an estate, *Reed v. Reed*, 404 U.S. 71, 92 S.Ct. 251, 30 L.Ed.2d 225 (1971), to engage in professional nursing, *Mississippi Univ. for Women v. Hogan*, 458 U.S. 718, 102 S.Ct. 3331, 73 L.Ed.2d 1090 (1982), or to train for military service, *United States v. Virginia*, 518 U.S. 515, 116 S.Ct. 2264, 135 L.Ed.2d 735 (1996), to name a few examples. Moreover, we have expressly repudiated cases that rested on the assumption that only the members of one sex could suitably practice law or tend bar. See *Hogan*, 458 U.S., at 725, n. 10, 102 S.Ct., at 3336, n. 10 (commenting on *Bradwell v. State*, 16 Wall. 130, 83 U.S. 130, 21 L.Ed. 442 (1872) and *Goesaert v. Cleary*, 335 U.S. 464, 69 S.Ct. 198, 93 L.Ed. 163 (1948)). Discrimination that "is merely the accidental byproduct of a traditional way of thinking about females" is unacceptable. *Califano v. Goldfarb*, 430 U.S. 199, 223, 97 S.Ct. 1021, 1035, 51 L.Ed.2d 270 (1977) (STEVENS, J., concurring in judgment).

The gender equality principle that was implicated in those cases is only indirectly involved in this case for two reasons.[20] First, the conclusion that petitioner is not a citizen rests on several coinciding factors, not just the gender of her citizen parent. On the facts of this case, even if petitioner's mother had been a citizen[21] and her father had been the alien, petitioner would not qualify for citizenship because her mother has never been to the United States. Alternatively, if her citizen parent had been a female member of the Air Force and, like Mr. Miller, had returned to the States at the end of her tour of duty, § 1409 quite probably would have been irrelevant and petitioner would have become a citizen at birth by force of the Constitution itself.[22] Second, it is not merely the sex of the citizen parent that determines whether the child is a citizen under the terms of the statute; rather, it is an event creating a legal relationship between parent and child—the birth itself for citizen mothers, but post-birth conduct for citizen fathers and their offspring. Nevertheless, we may assume that if the classification in § 1409 were merely the product of an outmoded stereotype, it would be invalid.

The "gender stereotypes" on which § 1409 is supposedly premised are (1) "that the American father is never anything more than the proverbial breadwinner who remains aloof from day-to-day child rearing duties,"[23] and (2) "that a mother will be closer to her child born out of wedlock than a father will be to his."[24] Even disregarding the statute's separate, non-stereotypical purpose of ensuring reliable proof of a blood relationship, neither of those propositions fairly reflects the justifications for the classification actually at issue.

Section 1409(a)(4) is not concerned with either the average father or even the average father of a child born out of wedlock. It is concerned with a father (a) whose child was born in a foreign country, and (b) who is unwilling or unable to acknowledge his paternity, and whose child is unable or unwilling to obtain a court paternity adjudication. A congressional assumption that such a father and his child are especially unlikely to develop a relationship, and thus to foster the child's ties with this country, has a solid basis even if we assume that all fathers who have made some effort to become acquainted with their children are as good, if not better, parents than members of the opposite sex.

20. Of course, the sex of the person claiming citizenship is irrelevant; if she were a male, petitioner's case would be no stronger.

21. Theoretically she might have been the child of an American soldier stationed in the Philippines during World War II. See *Ablang v. Reno*, 52 F.3d 801, 802 (C.A.9 1995), cert. denied, 516 U.S. 1043, 116 S.Ct. 701, 133 L.Ed.2d 658 (1996).

22. "All persons born or naturalized in the United States and subject to the jurisdiction thereof, are citizens of the United States and of the State wherein they reside." U.S. Const., Amdt. 14, § 1.

23. Brief for American Civil Liberties Union et al. as *Amici Curiae* 8.

24. 96 F.3d, at 1473 (Wald, J., concurring in judgment).

Nor does the statute assume that all mothers of illegitimate children will necessarily have a closer relationship with their children than will fathers. It does assume that all of them will be present at the event that transmits their citizenship to the child, that hospital records and birth certificates will normally make a further acknowledgment and formal proof of parentage unnecessary, and that their initial custody will at least give them the opportunity to develop a caring relationship with the child. Section 1409(a)(4)—the only provision that we need consider—is therefore supported by the undisputed assumption that fathers are less likely than mothers to have the *opportunity* to develop relationships, not simply, as Justice BREYER contends, *post,* at 1461, that they are less likely to take advantage of that opportunity when it exists.[25] These assumptions are firmly grounded and adequately explain why Congress found it unnecessary to impose requirements on the mother that were entirely appropriate for the father.

None of the premises on which the statutory classification is grounded can be fairly characterized as an accidental byproduct of a traditional way of thinking about the members of either sex. The biological differences between single men and single women provide a relevant basis for differing rules governing their ability to confer citizenship on children born in foreign lands. Indeed, it is the suggestion that simply because Congress has authorized citizenship at birth for children born abroad to unmarried mothers, it cannot impose any post-birth conditions upon the granting of citizenship to the foreign-born children of citizen fathers, that might be characterized as merely a byproduct of the strong presumption that gender-based legal distinctions are suspect. An impartial analysis of the relevant differences between citizen mothers and citizen fathers plainly rebuts that presumption.[26]

The judgment of the Court of Appeals is affirmed.

It is so ordered.

Justice O'CONNOR, with whom Justice KENNEDY joins, concurring in the judgment.

This Court has long applied a presumption against third-party standing as a prudential limitation on the exercise of federal jurisdiction. Federal courts, we have held, "must hesitate before resolving a controversy, even one within their constitutional power to resolve, on the basis of the rights of third persons not parties to the litigation." *Singleton v. Wulff,* 428 U.S. 106, 113, 96 S.Ct. 2868, 2874, 49 L.Ed.2d 826 (1976); see also *Warth v. Seldin,* 422 U.S. 490, 499, 95 S.Ct. 2197, 2205, 45 L.Ed.2d 343 (1975). Contrary to this prudential rule, the Court recognizes that petitioner has standing to raise an equal protection challenge to 8 U.S.C. § 1409. The statute, however, accords differential treatment to fathers and mothers, not to sons and daughters. Thus, although petitioner is clearly injured by the fact that she has been denied citizenship, the *discriminatory* impact of the provision falls on petitioner's father, Charlie Miller, who is no longer a party to

25. Justice BREYER does not dispute the fact that the unmarried father of a child born abroad is less likely than the unmarried mother to have the opportunity to develop a relationship with the child. He nevertheless would replace the gender-based distinction with either a "knowledge-of-birth" requirement or a distinction between "caretaker and non-caretaker parents." *Post,* at 1463. Neither substitute seems a likely candidate for serious congressional consideration. The former in practice would be just as gender-based as the present requirement, for surely every mother has knowledge of the birth when it occurs; nor would that option eliminate the need for formal steps and time limits to ensure that the parent truly had knowledge during the child's youth. The latter would be confusing at best, for Justice BREYER does not tell us how he would decide whether a father like Mr. Miller would qualify as a "caretaker" or a "non-caretaker"; and it would also be far less protective of families than the present statute, for it would deny citizenship to out-of-wedlock children who have relationships with their citizen parents but are not in the primary care or custody of those parents.

26. See *Michael M. v. Superior Court, Sonoma Cty.,* 450 U.S. 464, 497–498, n. 4, 101 S.Ct. 1200, 1218–1219, n. 4, 67 L.Ed.2d 437 (1981) (STEVENS, J., dissenting). Justice SCALIA argues that petitioner's suit must be dismissed because the courts have "no power to provide the relief requested." *Post,* at 1446. Because we conclude that there is no constitutional violation to remedy, we express no opinion on this question.

this suit. Consequently, I do not believe that we should consider petitioner's gender discrimination claim.

The Court recognizes that petitioner's claim turns on "the proposition that her citizen father should have the same right to transmit citizenship as would a citizen mother" and resolves to "evaluate the alleged discrimination against [petitioner's father] as well as its impact on [petitioner]." *Ante,* at 1436. But even when "the very same allegedly illegal act that affects the litigant also affects a third party," a plaintiff "cannot rest his claim to relief on the legal rights or interests of [the] third part[y]." *U.S. Department of Labor v. Triplett,* 494 U.S. 715, 720, 110 S.Ct. 1428, 1431, 108 L.Ed.2d 701 (1990) (internal quotation marks omitted). A party raising a constitutional challenge to a statute must demonstrate not only "that the alleged unconstitutional feature [of the statute] injures him" but also that "he is within the class of persons with respect to whom the act is unconstitutional." *Heald v. District of Columbia,* 259 U.S. 114, 123, 42 S.Ct. 434, 435, 66 L.Ed. 852 (1922). This requirement arises from the understanding that the third-party rightholder may not, in fact, wish to assert the claim in question, as well as from the belief that "third parties themselves usually will be the best proponents of their rights." *Singleton, supra,* at 113–114, 96 S.Ct., at 2874; see also *Holden v. Hardy,* 169 U.S. 366, 397, 18 S.Ct. 383, 390, 42 L.Ed. 780 (1898).

In support of the decision to consider Charlie Miller's claim, both Justice STEVENS, writing for the Court, and Justice BREYER, in dissent, cite *Craig v. Boren,* 429 U.S. 190, 97 S.Ct. 451, 50 L.Ed.2d 397 (1976). In that case, we allowed a vendor to challenge a state law that permitted sales of 3.2% beer to females who had reached the age of 18 but prohibited such sales to males until they turned 21. Because the law proscribed the sale rather than the consumption of beer, the Court determined that a vendor was the "least awkward challenger" to the gender-based distinction. *Id.,* at 197, 97 S.Ct., at 456. We reasoned that prudential objectives would not be served by rejecting third-party standing because "the lower court already ha[d] entertained the relevant constitutional challenge." *Id.,* at 193, 97 S.Ct., at 455. Here, however, the court below expressly did *not* take account of Charlie Miller's equal protection rights, instead reviewing petitioner's challenge as a first-party claim of gender discrimination against the children of citizen fathers as opposed to the children of citizen mothers. See 96 F.3d 1467, 1470 (C.A.D.C.1996).

More importantly, since this Court decided *Craig,* we have articulated the contours of the third-party standing inquiry in greater detail. In *Powers v. Ohio,* 499 U.S. 400, 111 S.Ct. 1364, 113 L.Ed.2d 411 (1991), we stated that a litigant seeking to assert the rights of another party must satisfy three interrelated criteria: "The litigant must have suffered an injury in fact, thus giving him or her a sufficiently concrete interest in the outcome of the issue in dispute; the litigant must have a close relation to the third party; and there must exist some hindrance to the third party's ability to protect his or her own interests." *Id.,* at 411, 111 S.Ct., at 1370–71 (internal quotation marks and citations omitted); see also *Campbell v. Louisiana,* — U.S. ——, ——, 118 S.Ct. 1419, 1423, — L.Ed.2d —— (1998). While it seems clear that petitioner has a significant stake in challenging the statute and a close relationship with her father, she has not demonstrated a substantial hindrance to her father's ability to assert his own rights. *Powers* and our earlier precedents suggest that the absence of such an obstacle precludes third-party standing. See 499 U.S., at 411, 111 S.Ct., at 1370 (explaining that "[all] three important criteria [must be] satisfied," *i.e.,* that there "must exist some hindrance to the third party's ability to protect his or her own interests" before the presumption is rebutted); see also *Singleton, supra,* at 116, 96 S.Ct., at 2875 ("Even where the relationship is close, the reasons for requiring persons to assert their own rights will generally still apply").

Petitioner has not demonstrated that Charlie Miller confronted a "genuine obstacle" to the assertion of his own rights that rises to the level of a hindrance. 428 U.S., at 116, 96 S.Ct., at 2875; see also *Barrows v.*

Jackson, 346 U.S. 249, 257, 73 S.Ct. 1031, 1035, 97 L.Ed. 1586 (1953) (third-party standing accorded because it "would be difficult if not impossible for the persons whose rights are asserted to present their grievance before any court"). In fact, Charlie Miller originally filed suit and asserted his own rights but then opted not to pursue his claim throughout this litigation. It is true that he was wrongly dismissed from the action by the Eastern District of Texas, and that the Government made the misguided argument before that court that "[t]he rights, if any, which have been injured are those of Lorelyn Penero Miller, the true plaintiff in this action." See Motion to Dismiss Plaintiff's First Amended Complaint or, in the Alternative, Transfer Venue 4. But because he failed to appeal the erroneous dismissal of his claim, any hindrance to the vindication of Charlie Miller's constitutional rights is ultimately self imposed.

I am reluctant to accept that the Government's litigation strategy, or an unfavorable ruling in the lower courts, could be a sufficiently severe obstacle to the assertion of a litigant's own rights to warrant an exception to our prudential standing requirements. Those requirements were adopted to serve the institutional interests of the federal courts, not the convenience of the litigants. See *FW/PBS, Inc. v. Dallas*, 493 U.S. 215, 231, 110 S.Ct. 596, 607–608, 107 L.Ed.2d 603 (1990); *Bender v. Williamsport Area School Dist.*, 475 U.S. 534, 541, 106 S.Ct. 1326, 1331, 89 L.Ed.2d 501 (1986). Justice BREYER asserts that appeals take time and money, and that a change of venue left Charlie Miller uncertain where to appeal. See *post*, at 1456. But the only obstacle was the inconvenience caused by the normal course of litigation, which often involves a transfer of venue. Charlie Miller never indicated any intent to challenge his dismissal from the suit, and there is no suggestion that he faced any unusual practical or legal barriers to filing a notice of appeal. Instituting a suit is itself burdensome—arguably as burdensome as filing an appeal from the denial of a claim—and to conclude that the course of events that transpired in this case constituted a hindrance to Charlie Miller's ability to assert his rights would be a step toward eliminating the hindrance prong altogether.

Thus far, we have permitted third-party standing only where more "daunting" barriers deterred the rightholder. *Powers, supra*, at 414, 111 S.Ct., at 1372–1373. To take an extreme example, in *Hodel v. Irving*, 481 U.S. 704, 107 S.Ct. 2076, 95 L.Ed.2d 668 (1987), we concluded that plaintiffs had third-party standing to assert the rights of their deceased parents. *Id.*, at 711–712, 107 S.Ct., at 2080–2081. And in *Powers*, we noted that potential jurors are not parties to the proceeding, cannot easily obtain declaratory or injunctive relief from a prosecutor's exercise of peremptory challenges, would find it difficult to demonstrate a likelihood that discrimination against them would recur, and have economic disincentives to filing suit. 499 U.S., at 414–415, 111 S.Ct., at 1372–1373. Privacy concerns may also provide a compelling explanation for a third party's absence from the litigation. In *Carey v. Population Services Int'l*, 431 U.S. 678, 97 S.Ct. 2010, 52 L.Ed.2d 675 (1977), we determined that a vendor could challenge the law prohibiting the distribution of contraceptives to minors because the desire to avoid publicity would deter potential purchasers from defending their own rights. *Id.*, at 684, n. 4, 97 S.Ct., at 2015 n. 4; see also *Eisenstadt v. Baird*, 405 U.S. 438, 446, 92 S.Ct. 1029, 1034–1035, 31 L.Ed.2d 349 (1972). Likewise, in *NAACP v. Alabama ex rel. Patterson*, 357 U.S. 449, 78 S.Ct. 1163, 2 L.Ed.2d 1488 (1958), the Court held that an organization could raise the privacy rights of its members because litigation initiated by those members would disclose their identity and destroy the very privacy they sought to protect. *Id.*, at 459, 78 S.Ct., at 1170. Where insurmountable procedural obstacles preclude a rightholder's own suit, the Court has also accorded third-party standing. In *Singleton*, we concluded that physicians could assert the rights of indigent women denied funding for abortion because imminent mootness prevented the women from bringing their claims. See 428 U.S., at 108, 96 S.Ct., at 2871. Similarly, *Barrows* involved the constitutional rights of the prospective victims of a racially restrictive real estate covenant, who were unidentified and thus not before the Court. See 346 U.S., at 254, 73 S.Ct., at 1033–1034. And in *Craig*, the case from which the Court garners its sole support for according third-party standing here, the named plaintiff turned 21 during the course of the litigation, which mooted his challenge to the beer-sale restriction. See 429 U.S., at 192, 97 S.Ct., at 454.

Where legitimate obstacles such as these exist, which lie beyond the control of the rightholder, that party's absence from a suit more likely stems from disability than from disinterest. A hindrance signals that the rightholder did not simply decline to bring the claim on his own behalf, but could not in fact do so. See *Singleton, supra*, at 116, 96 S.Ct., at 2875 ("If there is some genuine obstacle ... the third party's absence from court loses its tendency to suggest that his right is not truly at stake, or truly important to him, and the party who is in court becomes by default the right's best available proponent"). Furthermore, where a hindrance impedes the assertion of a claim, the right likely will not be asserted—and thus the relevant law will not be enforced—unless the Court recognizes third-party standing. In *Barrows*, for example, the Court permitted third-party standing because "the reasons which underlie [the] rule denying standing to raise another's rights" were "outweighed by the need to protect the fundamental rights" which would otherwise have been denied. 346 U.S., at 257, 73 S.Ct., at 1035.

Moreover, in contrast to this case, the white property owner contesting the racially restrictive covenant in *Barrows* was its "only effective adversary" because she was "the one in whose charge and keeping repose[d] the power to continue to use her property to discriminate or to discontinue such use." *Id.*, at 259, 73 S.Ct., at 1036. Here, although we have an injured party before us, the party actually discriminated against is both best suited to challenging the statute and available to undertake that task. See *Gladstone, Realtors v. Village of Bellwood*, 441 U.S. 91, 100, 99 S.Ct. 1601, 1608, 60 L.Ed.2d 66 (1979) (prudential barriers seek "to limit access to the federal courts to those litigants best suited to assert a particular claim"). In light of petitioner's uncertain constitutional status and the potential problems with fashioning a remedy for her injury, see *post*, at 1446–1448 (SCALIA, J., concurring in judgment), allowing her to assert Charlie Miller's claim will likely dilute rather than protect his constitutional rights.

Although petitioner cannot raise her father's rights, she may raise her own. While it is unclear whether an alien may assert constitutional objections when he or she is outside the territory of the United States, see *Johnson v. Eisentrager*, 339 U.S. 763, 70 S.Ct. 936, 94 L.Ed. 1255 (1950), and *United States v. Verdugo–Urquidez*, 494 U.S. 259, 110 S.Ct. 1056, 108 L.Ed.2d 222 (1990), I will assume that petitioner may challenge the constitutionality of § 1409. Her challenge, however, triggers only rational basis scrutiny. As pointed out above, see *supra*, at 1442, § 1409 does not draw a distinction based on the gender of the child, so petitioner cannot claim that she has been injured by gender discrimination. See *Allen v. Wright*, 468 U.S. 737, 755, 104 S.Ct. 3315, 3326, 82 L.Ed.2d 556 (1984) (an injury arising from discrimination "accords a basis for standing only to those persons who are personally denied equal treatment by the challenged discriminatory conduct") (internal quotation marks omitted). Moreover, the grant of certiorari was limited to the question whether § 1409 discriminates "between 'illegitimate' children of United States citizen mothers and 'illegitimate' children of United States citizen fathers," so any claim of discrimination based on differential treatment of illegitimate versus legitimate children is not presented. See 520 U.S. ——, 117 S.Ct. 1551, 137 L.Ed.2d 700 (1997).

Given that petitioner cannot raise a claim of discrimination triggering heightened scrutiny, she can argue only that § 1409 irrationally discriminates between illegitimate children of citizen fathers and citizen mothers. Although I do not share Justice STEVENS' assessment that the provision withstands heightened scrutiny, *ante*, at 1436–1442, I believe it passes rational scrutiny for the reasons he gives for sustaining it under the higher standard. It is unlikely, in my opinion, that any gender classifications based on stereotypes can survive heightened scrutiny, but under rational scrutiny, a statute may be defended based on generalized classifications unsupported by empirical evidence. See *Heller v. Doe,* 509 U.S. 312, 320, 113 S.Ct. 2637, 2462–2463, 125 L.Ed.2d 257 (1993) ("[A] classification must be upheld against equal protection challenge if there is any reasonably conceivable state of facts that could provide a rational basis for the classification. A State, moreover, has no obligation to produce evidence to sustain the rationality of a statutory classification") (internal quotation marks and citations omitted). This is particularly true when the classification is adopted with reference to immigration, an area where Congress frequently must base its decisions on generalizations about groups of people.

* * *

We adopted the presumption against third-party standing to preserve the court's "properly limited" role, *Warth,* 422 U.S., at 498, 95 S.Ct., at 2204–2205, and we have identified a particular set of circumstances that will rebut that presumption. I believe that we should treat those considerations, in particular the hindrance prong, as meaningful criteria. Consequently, I would not accord petitioner standing to raise her father's claim of gender discrimination. Petitioner's own constitutional challenge triggers only rational basis scrutiny, and § 1409 is sustainable under that standard. Accordingly, I concur in the judgment affirming the Court of Appeals' decision.

Justice SCALIA, with whom Justice THOMAS joins, concurring in the judgment.

I agree with the outcome in this case, but for a reason more fundamental than the one relied upon by Justice STEVENS. In my view it makes no difference whether or not § 1409(a) passes "heightened scrutiny" or any other test members of the Court might choose to apply. The complaint must be dismissed because the Court has no power to provide the relief requested: conferral of citizenship on a basis other than that prescribed by Congress.

The Constitution "contemplates two sources of citizenship, and two only: birth and naturalization." *United States v. Wong Kim Ark,* 169 U.S. 649, 702, 18 S.Ct. 456, 477, 42 L.Ed. 890 (1898). Under the Fourteenth Amendment, "[e]very person born in the United States, and subject to the jurisdiction thereof, becomes at once a citizen of the United States, and needs no naturalization." *Ibid.* Petitioner, having been born outside the territory of the United States, is an alien as far as the Constitution is concerned, and "can only become a citizen by being naturalized, either by treaty, as in the case of the annexation of foreign territory; or by authority of Congress." *Id.,* at 702–703, 18 S.Ct., at 477; see also *Rogers v. Bellei.* 401 U.S. 815, 827, 91 S.Ct. 1060, 1067, 28 L.Ed.2d 499 (1971). Here it is the "authority of Congress" that is appealed to—its power under Art. I, § 8, cl. 4, to "establish an uniform Rule of Naturalization." If there is no congressional enactment granting petitioner citizenship, she remains an alien.

The enactment on which petitioner relies is § 309 of the Immigration and Nationality Act (INA), 66 Stat. 238, as amended, 8 U.S.C. § 1409, which establishes the requirements for the acquisition of citizenship by a child born out of wedlock when the child's father is a United States citizen. Section 1409(a) provides, in relevant part, that § 1401(g), which confers citizenship on foreign-born children when one parent is an alien and the other a citizen of the United States, shall apply:

> "(a) ... as of the date of birth to a person born out of wedlock if—
>
> "(1) a blood relationship between the person and the father is established by clear and convincing evidence,
>
> "(2) the father had the nationality of the United States at the time of the person's birth,
>
> "(3) the father (unless deceased) has agreed in writing to provide financial support for the person until the person reaches the age of 18 years, and
>
> "(4) while the person is under the age of 18 years—
>
> "(A) the person is legitimated under the law of the person's residence or domicile,
>
> "(B) the father acknowledges paternity of the person in writing under oath, or

"(C) the paternity of the person is established by adjudication of a competent court."

By its plain language, § 1409(a) sets forth a precondition to the acquisition of citizenship under § 1401(g) by the illegitimate child of a citizen-father. Petitioner does not come into federal court claiming that she met that precondition, and that the State Department's conclusion to the contrary was factually in error. Rather, she acknowledges that she did not meet the last two requirements of that precondition, §§ 1409(a)(3) and (4). She nonetheless asks for a "declaratory judgment that [she] is a citizen of the United States" and an order to the Secretary of State requiring the State Department to grant her application for citizenship, App. 11–12, because the requirements she did not meet are not also imposed upon illegitimate children of citizen-mothers, and therefore violate the Equal Protection Clause.[1] Even if we were to agree that the difference in treatment between illegitimate children of citizen-fathers and citizen-mothers is unconstitutional, we could not, consistent with the limited judicial power in this area, remedy that constitutional infirmity by declaring petitioner to be a citizen or ordering the State Department to approve her application for citizenship. "Once it has been determined that a person does not qualify for citizenship, ... the district court has no discretion to ignore the defect and grant citizenship." *INS v. Pangilinan*, 486 U.S. 875, 884, 108 S.Ct. 2210, 2216, 100 L.Ed.2d 882 (1988) (internal quotation marks and citation omitted).

Judicial power over immigration and naturalization is extremely limited. "Our cases 'have long recognized the power to expel or exclude aliens as a fundamental sovereign attribute exercised by the Government's political departments largely immune from judicial control.'" *Fiallo v. Bell*, 430 U.S. 787, 792, 97 S.Ct. 1473, 1478, 52 L.Ed.2d 50 (1977) (quoting *Shaughnessy v. United States ex rel. Mezei*, 345 U.S. 206, 210, 73 S.Ct. 625, 628, 97 L.Ed. 956 (1953)). See also *Landon v. Plasencia*, 459 U.S. 21, 32, 103 S.Ct. 321, 329, 74 L.Ed.2d 21 (1982) ("[T]he power to admit or exclude aliens is a sovereign prerogative"); *Mathews v. Diaz*, 426 U.S. 67, 79–80, 96 S.Ct. 1883, 1891, 48 L.Ed.2d 478 (1976) ("In the exercise of its broad power over naturalization and immigration, Congress regularly makes rules that would be unacceptable if applied to citizens"); *Kleindienst v. Mandel*, 408 U.S. 753, 769–770, 92 S.Ct. 2576, 2585, 33 L.Ed.2d 683 (1972) ("[P]lenary congressional power to make policies and rules for exclusion of aliens has long been firmly established"); *Galvan v. Press*, 347 U.S. 522, 531, 74 S.Ct. 737, 743, 98 L.Ed. 911 (1954) ("That the formulation of [policies pertaining to the entry of aliens and their right to remain here] is entrusted exclusively to Congress has become about as firmly imbedded in the legislative and judicial tissues of our body politic as any aspect of our government"). Because only Congress has the power to set the requirements for acquisition of citizenship by persons not born within the territory of the United States, federal courts cannot exercise that power under the guise of their remedial authority. "Neither by ap-

1. Petitioner makes the equal-protection claim on behalf of her father, not on her own behalf. Justice BREYER finds that she has third-party standing to make the claim because "[s]he has a 'close' and relevant relationship" with her father, and "there was 'some hindrance' to her father's asserting his own rights." *Post*, at 1456 (quoting from *Powers v. Ohio*, 499 U.S. 400, 411, 111 S.Ct. 1364, 1370–1371, 113 L.Ed.2d 411 (1991)). As an original matter, I would agree with Justice O'CONNOR that this ground is inadequate, but I do not read our cases as demanding so significant an impairment of the rightholder's ability to sue as she does. For example, in *Craig v. Boren*, 429 U.S. 190, 197, 97 S.Ct. 451, 456–457, 50 L.Ed.2d 397 (1976), although the rightholder who was one of the named plaintiffs had indeed lost his ability to sue because he had turned 21, there was "no barrier whatever" to assertion of the constitutional claim by other Oklahoma males between 18 and 20. *Id.*, at 216, 97 S.Ct., at 466–467 (Burger, C. J., dissenting). Certainly here, as in *Craig*, petitioner is the "least awkward challenger," *id.*, at 197, 97 S.Ct., at 456–457, since it is her right to citizenship that is at stake. Our law on this subject is in need of what may charitably be called clarification, but I would leave it for another day. Since I accept petitioner's third-party standing, there is no need for me to reach the Government's claim (which it asserts for the first time in its brief on the merits in this Court) that petitioner cannot invoke the Equal Protection Clause on her own behalf because she is not within the jurisdiction of the United States. Brief for Respondent 11–12.

plication of the doctrine of estoppel, nor by invocation of equitable powers, nor by any other means does a court have the power to confer citizenship in violation of [statutory] limitations." *Pangilinan, supra,* at 885, 108 S.Ct., at 2217. "An alien who seeks political rights as a member of this Nation can rightfully obtain them *only upon terms and conditions specified by Congress. Courts are without authority to sanction changes or modifications.*" *United States v. Ginsberg,* 243 U.S. 472, 474, 37 S.Ct. 422, 425, 61 L.Ed. 853 (1917) (emphasis added).

Petitioner argues, and Justice BREYER's dissent seems to agree, see *post,* at 1463–1464 (BREYER, J., dissenting), that because she meets the requirements of § 1401(g), the Court may declare her a citizen "at birth" under that provision and ignore § 1409(a) entirely, which allegedly unconstitutionally takes away that citizenship. Brief for Petitioner 14–15. This argument adopts a fanciful view of the statute, whereby § 1409(a) takes away what § 1401(g) has unconditionally conferred—as though § 1409(a) were some sort of a condition subsequent to the conveyance of real estate in a will. If anything, of course, it would be a condition *precedent,* since it says that § 1401(g) "shall apply as of the date of birth to a person born out of wedlock *if*" the person meets the requirements there set forth. 8 U.S.C. § 1409(a) (emphasis added). But a unitary statute is not to be picked apart in this fashion. To be sure, § 1401(g), read in isolation, might refer to both married and unmarried parents. We do not, however, read statutory provisions in isolation, as if other provisions in the same Act do not exist, see *King v. St. Vincent's Hospital,* 502 U.S. 215, 221, 112 S.Ct. 570, 574, 116 L.Ed.2d 578 (1991). Section 1401(g) does *not* confer citizenship upon children born out of wedlock unless the requirements in § 1409 are satisfied.

It can be argued that in exempting an applicant from an unconstitutional requirement (either part or all of § 1409(a)) a court is not rewriting the law, but simply ignoring that portion of the law which is a nullity. See *post,* at 1463–1464 (BREYER, J., dissenting). That assumes, however, a judicial power to sever the unconstitutional portion from the remainder, and to apply the remainder unencumbered. Such a power exists in other cases—and is exercised on the basis of the Court's assessment as to whether Congress would have enacted the remainder of the law without the invalidated provision. See *New York v. United States,* 505 U.S. 144, 186, 112 S.Ct. 2408, 2433–2434, 120 L.Ed.2d 120 (1992). I know of no instance, however, in which this Court has severed an unconstitutional restriction upon the grant of immigration or citizenship. It is in my view incompatible with the plenary power of Congress over those fields for judges to speculate as to what Congress would have enacted if it had not enacted what it did—whether it would, for example, have preferred to extend the requirements of §§ 1409(a)(3) and (4) to mothers instead of eliminating them for fathers, or even to deny citizenship to illegitimate children entirely. ("[T]he Court has specifically recognized the power of Congress not to grant a United States citizen the right to transmit citizenship by descent." *Rogers,* 401 U.S., at 830, 91 S.Ct., at 1069.) Moreover, if the mere character of the naturalization power were not enough to render the severing of a limitation upon citizenship improper, the INA itself contains a clear statement of congressional intent: "A person may only be naturalized as a citizen of the United States in the manner and under the conditions prescribed in this subchapter *and not otherwise.*" 8 U.S.C. § 1421(d) (emphasis added). Justice BREYER's reliance upon the INA's general severability clause, 66 Stat. 281, § 406, is misplaced because the specific governs the general, see *Morales v. Trans World Airlines, Inc.,* 504 U.S. 374, 384–385, 112 S.Ct. 2031, 2037–2038, 119 L.Ed.2d 157 (1992). The question of severance ultimately turns on "whether the provisions are inseparable by virtue of inherent character," *Carter v. Carter Coal Co.,* 298 U.S. 238, 322, 56 S.Ct. 855, 877, 80 L.Ed. 1160 (1936), which must be gleaned from the structure and nature of the Act.

Another obstacle to judicial deletion of the challenged requirements is the fact that when a statutory violation of equal protection has occurred, it is not foreordained which particular statutory provision is invalid. The constitutional vice consists of unequal treatment, which may as logically be attributed to the disparately generous provision (here, supposedly, the provision governing citizenship of illegitimate children of citizen mothers) as to the disparately parsimonious one (the provision governing citizenship of illegitimate children of citizen fathers). "[W]e have noted that a court sustaining [an equal protection] claim faces 'two remedial alternatives: [it] may either declare [the statute] a nullity and order that its benefits not extend to the class that the legislature intended to benefit, or it may extend the coverage of the statute to include those who are aggrieved by the exclusion.'" *Heckler v. Mathews,* 465 U.S. 728, 738, 104 S.Ct. 1387, 1394–1395, 79 L.Ed.2d 646 (1984), quoting *Welsh v. United States,* 398 U.S. 333, 361, 90 S.Ct. 1792, 1807–1808, 26 L.Ed.2d 308 (1970) (Harlan, J., concurring in result). Given the nature of the law at issue here, and given the clear command of 8 U.S.C. § 1421(d) ("under the conditions prescribed in this subchapter and not otherwise") there is no doubt which of those alternatives the court must employ. It cannot confer citizenship where Congress has not done so.

In any event, this is not like the ordinary equal protection case, in which one class is subjected to a restriction from which the other class is exempt. See, *e. g., Craig v. Boren,* 429 U.S. 190, 191–192, 97 S.Ct. 451, 453–454, 50 L.Ed.2d 397 (1976) (men can be served alcoholic beverages only if over 21 years of age, whereas women need be only 18). Here *each* class is subjected to restrictions from which the other is exempt. While illegitimate children of citizen fathers must meet the requirements of § 1409(a) from which illegitimate children of citizen mothers are exempt, illegitimate children of citizen mothers must meet the quite different requirements of § 1409(c), from which illegitimate children of citizen fathers are exempt.[2] In this situation, eliminating the restrictions on fathers does not produce a law that complies with the Equal Protection Clause (assuming it is initially in violation), but rather produces a law that treats fathers *more* favorably than mothers. There is no way a court can "fix" the law by merely disregarding one provision or the other as unconstitutional. It would have to disregard them *both,* either leaving no restrictions whatever upon citizenship of illegitimate children or (what I think the more proper course) denying naturalization of illegitimate children entirely (since § 1401(g) was not meant to apply by its unqualified terms to illegitimate children). Even outside the particularly sensitive area of immigration and naturalization, I am aware of no case that has engaged in such radical statutory surgery, and it certainly cannot be engaged in here.

In sum, this is not a case in which we have the power to remedy the alleged equal protection violation by either expanding or limiting the benefits conferred so as to deny or grant them equally to all. "We are dealing here with an exercise of the Nation's sovereign power to admit or exclude foreigners in accordance with perceived national interests." *Fiallo,* 430 U.S., at 795, n. 6, 97 S.Ct., at 1479, n. 6. Federal judges may not decide what those national interests are, and what requirements for citizenship best serve them.

Because petitioner is not a citizen under any Act of Congress, we cannot give her the declaratory judgment or affirmative relief she requests. I therefore concur in the judgment.

Justice GINSBURG, with whom Justice SOUTER and Justice BREYER join, dissenting.

As Justice BREYER convincingly demonstrates, 8 U.S.C. § 1409 classifies unconstitutionally on the basis of gender in determining the capacity of a parent to qualify a child for citizenship. The section rests on familiar generalizations: mothers, as a rule, are responsible for a child born out of wedlock; fathers unmarried to the child's mother, ordinarily, are not. The law at issue might have made custody or support the relevant criterion. Instead, it treats mothers one way, fathers another, shaping government policy to

2. Title 8 U.S.C. § 1409(c) provides that an illegitimate child born to a citizen mother shall be a citizen "if the mother had previously been physically present in the United States or one of its outlying possessions for a continuous period of one year."

fit and reinforce the stereotype or historic pattern.

Characteristic of sex-based classifications, the stereotypes underlying this legislation may hold true for many, even most, individuals. But in prior decisions the Court has rejected official actions that classify unnecessarily and overbroadly by gender when more accurate and impartial functional lines can be drawn. While the Court is divided on Lorelyn Miller's standing to sue, a solid majority adheres to that vital understanding. As Justice O'CONNOR's opinion makes plain, distinctions based on gender trigger heightened scrutiny and "[i]t is unlikely ... that any gender classifications based on stereotypes can survive heightened scrutiny." *Ante*, at 1445–1446 (opinion concurring in judgment); *post*, at 1460–1463 (BREYER, J., dissenting).

On the surface, § 1409 treats females favorably. Indeed, it might be seen as a benign preference, an affirmative action of sorts. Compare *Mississippi Univ. for Women v. Hogan*, 458 U.S. 718, 731, and n. 17, 102 S.Ct. 3331, 3340 and n. 17, 73 L.Ed.2d 1090 (1982) with *id.*, at 740–744, 102 S.Ct., at 3344–3346 (Powell, J., dissenting). Two Justices today apparently take this view. Justice STEVENS' opinion, in which THE CHIEF JUSTICE joins, portrays § 1409 as helpfully recognizing the different situations of unmarried mothers and fathers during the pre-natal period and at birth, and fairly equalizing the "burdens" that each parent bears. See *ante*, at 1436–1437, 1439. But pages of history place the provision in real-world perspective. Section 1409 is one of the few provisions remaining in the United States Code that uses sex as a criterion in delineating citizens' rights. It is an innovation in this respect: During most of our Nation's past, laws on the transmission of citizenship from parent to child discriminated adversely against citizen mothers, not against citizen fathers.

I

The first statute on the citizenship of children born abroad, enacted in 1790, stated: "[T]he children of citizens of the United States, that may be born beyond sea, or out of the limits of the United States, shall be considered as natural born citizens: *Provided*, That the right of citizenship shall not descend to persons whose fathers have never been resident in the United States." Act of Mar. 26, 1790, ch. 3, 1 Stat. 104. Statutes passed in 1795 and 1802 similarly conditioned the citizenship of the child born abroad on the father's at least one-time residence in the United States. Act of Jan. 29, 1795, § 3, 1 Stat. 415; Act of Apr. 14, 1802, § 4, 2 Stat. 155. This father's residence requirement suggests that Congress intended a child born abroad to gain citizenship only when the father was a citizen. That, indeed, was the law of England at the time. See 2 J. Kent, Commentaries on American Law *50–*51 (hereinafter Kent's Commentaries); 4 Geo. 2, ch. 21 (1731). The statutory language Congress adopted, however, was ambiguous. One could read the words "children of citizens" to mean that the child of a United States citizen mother and a foreign father would qualify for citizenship if the father had at some point resided in the country. See Binney, The Alienigenae of the United States, 2 Am. L. Reg. 193, 203–205 (1854). Or, as Chancellor Kent observed, the words might mean that both parents had to be United States citizens for citizenship to pass. 2 Kent's Commentaries *53.

Under the 1802 legislation, children born abroad could not become citizens unless their parents were citizens in 1802, which meant that as the years passed few foreign-born persons could qualify. Daniel Webster, among others, proposed remedial legislation. His bill would have granted citizenship to children born abroad to United States-born citizen mothers as well as fathers. His effort was unsuccessful. See Cong. Globe, 30th Cong., 1st Sess., 827 (1848); F. Franklin, The Legislative History of Naturalization in the United States 271–276 (reprint ed.1971). Instead, in 1855, Congress clarified that citizenship would pass to children born abroad only when the father was a United States citizen. Act of Feb. 10, 1855, § 2, 10 Stat. 604. Codified as § 1993 of the Revised Statutes, the provision originating in 1855 read: "All children heretofore born or hereafter born out of the limits and jurisdiction of the United States, whose fathers were or may be at the time of their birth citizens thereof, are declared to be citizens of the United States; but the rights of citizenship shall not descend to children whose fathers never resided in the United States." Rev. Stat. § 1993.

In these early statutes, Congress did not differentiate between children born abroad to married parents and those born out of wedlock. Section 1993, as applied, allowed transmission of citizenship to children born out of wedlock if the father legitimated the child. See, *e.g.*, 32 Op. Atty. Gen. 162, 164–165 (1920); see also *Guyer v. Smith*, 22 Md. 239 (1864) (foreign born children who remain illegitimate do not qualify for citizenship). In several reported instances, children legitimated by their fathers gained citizenship even though the legitimation occurred, as it did in Lorelyn Miller's case, after the child reached majority. See *In re P*, 4 I. & N. Dec. 354 (C.O. 1951); 7 C. Gordon, S. Mailman, & S. Yale-Loehr, Immigration Law and Procedure § 93.04[2][d], pp. 93-43 to 93-44 (1992) (hereinafter Gordon). But see 3 G. Hackworth, Digest of International Law 29 (1942) (noting a case in which legitimation post-majority was deemed sufficient, but maintaining that "[n]ormally the legitimation must take place during the minority of the child").

In the early part of this century, the State Department permitted the transmission of citizenship from unwed mother to child reasoning that, for the child born out of wedlock, the mother "stands in the place of the father." House Committee on Immigration and Naturalization, A Report Proposing A Revision and Codification of the Nationality Laws of the United States, Part One: Proposed Code with Explanatory Comments, 76th Cong., 1st Sess., 18 (Comm. Print 1939) (hereinafter Proposed Code). Ultimately, however, the Attorney General rejected the Department's reasoning, finding it incompatible with § 1993's exclusive reference to fathers. See 39 Op. Atty. Gen. 397, 398 (1939).

Women's inability to transmit their United States citizenship to children born abroad was one among many gender-based distinctions drawn in our immigration and nationality laws. The woman who married a foreign citizen risked losing her United States nationality. In early days, "marriage with an alien, whether a friend or an enemy, produce[d] no dissolution of the native allegiance of the wife." *Shanks v. Dupont*, 3 Pet. 242, 246, 7 L.Ed. 666 (1830) (Story, J.). By the end of the nineteenth century, however, a few courts adopted the view that a woman's nationality followed her husband's, see, *e.g.*, *Pequignot v. Detroit*, 16 F. 211, 216 (C.C.E.D.Mich.1883), particularly when the woman resided abroad in her husband's country, see, *e.g.*, *Ruckgaber v. Moore*, 104 F. 947, 948–949 (C.C.E.D.N.Y.1900). See generally C. Bredbenner, Toward Independent Citizenship: Married Women's Nationality Rights in the United States: 1855–1937, 54–59 (Ph. D. dissertation, University of Virginia, 1990) (hereinafter Bredbenner); Sapiro, Women, Citizenship, and Nationality: Immigration and Naturalization Policies in the United States, 13 Politics & Soc. 1, 4–10 (1984). State Department officials inclined towards this view as well. See L. Gettys, The Law of Citizenship in the United States 118 (1934). In 1907, Congress settled the matter: It provided by statute that a female United States citizen automatically lost her citizenship upon marriage to an alien. Act of Mar. 2, 1907, § 3, 34 Stat. 1228. This Court upheld the statute, noting that "[t]he identity of husband and wife is an ancient principle of our jurisprudence." *Mackenzie v. Hare*, 239 U.S. 299, 311, 36 S.Ct. 106, 108, 60 L.Ed. 297 (1915).

The statutory rule that women relinquished their United States citizenship upon marriage to an alien encountered increasing opposition, fueled in large part by the women's suffrage movement and the enhanced importance of citizenship to women as they obtained the right to vote. See Bredbenner 81, 95–105; Sapiro, *supra*, at 12–13. In response, Congress provided a measure of relief. Under the 1922 Cable Act, marriage to an alien no longer stripped a woman of her citizenship automatically. Act of Sept. 22, 1922 (Cable Act), ch. 411, § 3, 42 Stat. 1022. But equal respect for a woman's nationality remained only partially realized. A woman still lost her United States citizenship if she married an alien ineligible for citizenship; she could not become a citizen by naturalization if her husband did not qualify for citizenship; she was presumed to have renounced her citizenship if she lived abroad in her husband's country for two years, or if she lived abroad elsewhere for five years. *Id.*, §§ 3, 5; see also Sapiro, *supra*, at 11–12. A woman who became a naturalized citizen was unable to transmit her citizenship to her children if her noncitizen husband remained alive and they were not separated. See *In re Citizenship Status of Minor Children*, 25 F.2d 210, 210 (D.N.J.1928) ("the status of the wife was dependent upon that of her husband, and therefore the children acquired their citizenship from the same source as had been theretofore existent under the common law"); see also Gettys, *supra*, at 56–57. No restrictions of like kind applied to male United States citizens.

Instead, Congress treated wives and children of male United States citizens or immigrants benevolently. The 1855 legislation automatically granted citizenship to women who married United States citizens. Act of Feb. 10, 1855, ch. 71, § 2, 10 Stat. 604; see also *Kelly v. Owen*, 7 Wall. 496, 498, 19 L.Ed. 283 (1868) (the 1855 Act "confers the privileges of citizenship upon women married to citizens of the United States" without further action). Under an 1804 statute, if a male alien died after completing the United States residence requirement but before actual naturalization, his widow and children would be "considered as citizens." Act of Mar. 26, 1804, § 2, 2 Stat. 292, 293. That 1804 measure granted no corresponding dispensation to the husband and children of an alien woman. In addition, Congress provided statutory exemptions to entry requirements for the wives and children of men but not for the husbands and children of women. See, *e.g.*, Act of Mar. 3, 1903, § 37, 32 Stat. 1213, 1221 (wives and children entering the country to join permanent resident aliens and found to have contracted contagious diseases during transit shall not be deported if the diseases were easily curable or did not present a danger to others); S.Rep. No. 1515, 81st Cong., 2d Sess., 415–417 (1950) (wives exempt from literacy and quota requirements).

In 1934, Congress moved in a new direction. It terminated the discrimination against United States citizen mothers in regard to children born abroad. Specifically, Congress amended § 1993 to read:

> "Any child hereafter born out of the limits and jurisdiction of the United States, whose father or mother or both at the time of the birth of such child is a citizen of the United States, is declared to be a citizen of the United States; but the rights of citizenship shall not descend to any such child unless the citizen father or citizen mother, as the case may be, has resided in the United States previous to the birth of such child." Act of May 24, 1934, § 1, 48 Stat. 797.[1]

Senate and House Reports on the Act stated that the change was made "to establish complete equality between American men and women in the matter of citizenship for themselves and for their children." S.Rep. No. 865, 73d Cong., 2d Sess., 1 (1934); accord, H.R.Rep. No. 131, 73d Cong., 2d Sess., 2 (1933); see generally Orfield, The Citizenship Act of 1934, 2 U. Chi. L.Rev. 99, 100–106 (1935). Congress again did not speak of children born out of wedlock, but the 1934 Act "was construed as authorizing transmission of American citizenship by descent by an American citizen mother to a child born abroad ... out of wedlock under the same conditions as a child born in wedlock." 7 Gordon § 93.04[2][b], p. 93–42; see also *id.*, § 93.04[2][d][iii], p. 93–46.

The 1934 Act's equal respect for the citizenship stature of mothers and fathers of children born abroad did not remain unmodified. Six years later, Congress passed the Nationality Act of 1940, which replaced the

1. A 1921 bill contained a similar provision allowing United States citizen women to transmit citizenship to their children born abroad. The bill provided: "A child born at any time without the United States, either parent being at the time of such birth a citizen of the United States, may, if not a citizen under section 1993 of the Revised Statutes, derive United States citizenship under this section." H.R.Rep. No. 15603, 66th Cong., 3d Sess., § 33(2), p. 26 (1921). This 1921 bill, a precursor to the Cable Act, passed the House Committee on Immigration and Naturalization but proceeded no further. See H.R.Rep. No. 1185, 66th Cong., 3d Sess., 1 (1921); Bredbenner 137.

Revised Statutes' single provision on citizenship of children born abroad with an array of provisions that turned on whether the child was born in an outlying possession of the United States, whether one or both of the child's parents were United States citizens, and whether the child was born in or out of wedlock. The 1940 Act preserved Congress' earlier recognition of parental equality in regard to children born in wedlock, but established a different regime for children born out of wedlock, one that disadvantaged United States citizen fathers and their children.

Under the 1940 Act, if the mother of the child born abroad out of wedlock held United States citizenship and previously had resided in the country or in a United States possession, the child gained the mother's nationality from birth, provided the child's paternity was not established by legitimation or a court order.[2] But if the father and not the mother held United States citizenship, then the child would qualify for United States citizenship only upon legitimation or adjudication of paternity during the child's minority. Furthermore, the child generally had to live in the United States for five years before the age of 21. The same residency requirement applied to children born abroad to married couples with only one United States citizen parent, whether that parent was the mother or the father. Nationality Act of 1940, §§ 201, 205, 54 Stat. 1138–1140.[3]

Subsequent legislation retained the gender lines drawn in the 1940 Act. The Immigration and Nationality Act of 1952 made only one significant change regarding the citizenship of children born abroad out of wedlock. It removed the provision that a mother could pass on her nationality to her child only if the paternity of the child had not been established.[4] Immigration and Nationality Act, § 309, 66 Stat. 238–239. In 1986, however, Congress added further gender-based differentials. The Legislature that year permitted substitution of a written acknowledgment under oath or adjudication of paternity prior to age 18 in place of formal legitimation. To that extent, Congress eased access to citizenship by a child born abroad out of wedlock to a United States citizen father. At the same time, however, Congress imposed on such a child two further requirements: production of clear and convincing evidence of paternity, also a written statement from the father promising support until the child turned 18. The requirements for a child of a United States citizen mother remained the same; such a child obtained the mother's nationality if the mother had resided in the United States or its territorial possessions for at least a year before the child's birth. Act of Nov. 14, 1986, § 13, 100 Stat. 3657, codified as amended at 8 U.S.C. § 1409. No substantive change has been made since 1986 in the law governing citizenship of children born abroad out of wedlock.

II

The history of the treatment of children born abroad to United States citizen parents

2. Nationality and citizenship are not entirely synonymous; one can be a national of the United States and yet not a citizen. 8 U.S.C. § 1101(a)(22). The distinction has little practical impact today, however, for the only remaining noncitizen nationals are residents of American Samoa and Swains Island. See T. Aleinikoff, D. Martin, & H. Motomura, Immigration: Process and Policy 974–975, n. 2 (3d ed.1995). The provision that a child born abroad out of wedlock to a United States citizen mother gains her nationality has been interpreted to mean that the child gains her citizenship as well; thus if the mother is not just a United States national but also a United States citizen, the child is a United States citizen. See 7 Gordon § 93.04[2][b], p. 93–42; *id.*, § 93.04[2][d][viii], p. 93–49.

3. The provision granting citizenship to children born abroad out of wedlock applied retroactively; the provision granting citizenship to children born in wedlock did not. The 1934 Act, too, was nonretroactive. The net result was that a child born abroad out of wedlock to a United States citizen mother in 1933 or earlier had United States citizenship after the 1940 Act, but a child born in wedlock did not until 1994 when Congress enacted legislation making the 1934 Act retroactive. Pub.L. 103–416, Tit. I, § 101(a)(2), 108 Stat. 4306, codified at 8 U.S.C. § 1401(h).

4. The 1952 Act also provided that periods of service in the Armed Forces abroad could count towards satisfying the parental residency requirement in regard to a child born after January 13, 1941. Immigration and Nationality Act of 1952, §§ 301(a)(7), 309(b), 66 Stat. 236, 238, codified as amended at 8 U.S.C. §§ 1401(g), 1409(b).

counsels skeptical examination of the Government's prime explanation for the gender line drawn by § 1409—the close connection of mother to child, in contrast to the distant or fleeting father-child link. Or, as Justice STEVENS puts it, a mother's presence at birth, identification on the birth certificate, and likely "initial custody" of the child give her an "opportunity to develop a caring relationship with the child," *ante*, at 1442, which Congress legitimately could assume a father lacks. For most of our Nation's past, Congress demonstrated no high regard or respect for the mother-child affiliation. It bears emphasis, too, that in 1934, when Congress allowed United States citizen mothers to transmit their citizenship to their foreign-born children, Congress simultaneously and for the first time required that such children (unless both parents were citizens) fulfill a residence requirement: "[T]he right of citizenship shall not descend unless the child comes to the United States and resides therein for at least five years continuously immediately previous to his eighteenth birthday." Act of May 24, 1934, § 1, 48 Stat. 797. Commentary underscores what the text conveys. Congress largely relied on a residence requirement, not the sex of the child's citizen parent, to assure an abiding affiliation with the United States. See Proposed Code 10–11, 14.

Even if one accepts at face value the Government's current rationale, it is surely based on generalizations (stereotypes) about the way women (or men) are. These generalizations pervade the opinion of Justice STEVENS, which constantly relates and relies on what "typically," or "normally," or "probably" happens "often." *E.g.*, *ante*, at 1438, 1439, 1441.

We have repeatedly cautioned, however, that when the Government controls "gates to opportunity," it "may not exclude qualified individuals based on 'fixed notions concerning the roles and abilities of males and females.'" *United States v. Virginia*, 518 U.S. 515, ——, 116 S.Ct. 2264, 2280, 135 L.Ed.2d 735 (1996) (quoting *Mississippi Univ. for Women v. Hogan*, 458 U.S. 718, 725, 102 S.Ct. 3331, 3336, 73 L.Ed.2d 1090 (1982)); see also *Orr v. Orr*, 440 U.S. 268, 283, 99 S.Ct. 1102, 1114, 59 L.Ed.2d 306 (1979) ("Where, as here, the State's ... purposes are as well served by a gender-neutral classification as one that gender classifies and therefore carries with it the baggage of sexual stereotypes, the State cannot be permitted to classify on the basis of sex."). Only an "'exceedingly persuasive justification,'" *Kirchberg v. Feenstra*, 450 U.S. 455, 461, 101 S.Ct. 1195, 1199, 67 L.Ed.2d 428 (1981) (quoting *Personnel Administrator of Mass. v. Feeney*, 442 U.S. 256, 273, 99 S.Ct. 2282, 2293, 60 L.Ed.2d 870 (1979)), one that does "not rely on overbroad generalizations about the different talents, capacities, or preferences of males and females," *United States v. Virginia*, 518 U.S., at ——, 116 S.Ct., at 2275, will support differential treatment of men and women. See *J.E.B. v. Alabama ex rel. T. B.*, 511 U.S. 127, 152, 114 S.Ct. 1419, 1433, 128 L.Ed.2d 89 (1994) (Kennedy, J., concurring in judgment) (noting that prevailing case law "reveal[s] a strong presumption that gender classifications are invalid").

One can demur to the Government's observation that more United States citizen mothers of children born abroad out of wedlock actually raise their children than do United States citizen fathers of such children. As Justice BREYER has elucidated, this observation does not justify distinctions between male and female United States citizens who take responsibility, or avoid responsibility, for raising their children. Nor does it justify reliance on gender distinctions when the alleged purpose—assuring close ties to the United States—can be achieved without reference to gender. As Judge Wald commented in discussing an analogous claim when this case was before the Court of Appeals,

> "Congress is free to promote close family ties by ensuring that citizenship is conferred only on children who have at least minimal contact with citizen parents during their early and formative years .... But this putative interest provides absolutely no basis for requiring fathers, and only fathers, to formally declare parentage and agree to provide financial support before a child reaches age 18." *Miller v.*

Christopher, 96 F.3d 1467, 1476 (C.A.D.C. 1996) (Wald, J., concurring in judgment).

* * *

In 1934, it was no doubt true that many female United States citizens who gave birth abroad had married foreigners and moved to their husbands' country, and that the children of such marriages were brought up as natives of a foreign land. And if a female United States citizen were married to a United States citizen, her children born abroad could obtain United States citizenship through their father. Thus, the historic restriction of citizenship to children born abroad of United States citizen fathers may not have affected many women. But, in the words of one woman who testified in favor of the 1934 Act (and later became the first woman to sit as a federal district court judge), "[w]hether there are a lot of people who suffer or whether there are a few who suffer, it seems to us that the principle of equal application of the law to men and women ought to receive recognition." Hearings on H.R. 3673 and H.R. 77 before the House Committee on Immigration and Naturalization, 73d Cong., 1st Sess., 36 (1933) (testimony of Burnita Shelton Matthews). Congress recognized this equality principle in 1934, and is positioned to restore that impartiality before the century is out.

Justice BREYER, with whom Justice SOUTER and Justice GINSBURG join, dissenting.

Since the founding of our Nation, American statutory law, reflecting a long-established legal tradition, has provided for the transmission of American citizenship from parent to child—even when the child is born abroad. Today's case focuses upon statutes that make those children, when born out of wedlock, "citizens of the United States at birth." 8 U.S.C. §§ 1401 and 1409. The statutes, as applied where only one parent is American, require the American parent—whether father or mother—to prove the child is his or hers and to meet a residency requirement. The statutes go on to require (1) that the American parent promise to provide financial support for the child until the child is 18, and (2) that the American parent (or a court) legitimate or formally acknowledge the child before the child turns 18—*if and only if the American parent is the father*, but not if the parent is the mother.

What sense does it make to apply these latter two conditions only to fathers and not to mothers in today's world—where paternity can readily be proved and where women and men both are likely to earn a living in the workplace? As Justice O'CONNOR has observed, and as a majority of the Court agrees, "[i]t is unlikely ... that any gender classifications based on stereotypes can survive heightened scrutiny." *Ante*, at 1445–1446. These two gender-based distinctions lack the "exceedingly persuasive" support that the Constitution requires. *United States v. Virginia*, 518 U.S. 515, 530, 116 S.Ct. 2264, 2281, 135 L.Ed.2d 735 (1996). Consequently, the statute that imposes them violates the Fifth Amendment's "equal protection" guarantee. See *Bolling v. Sharpe*, 347 U.S. 497, 500, 74 S.Ct. 693, 694–695, 98 L.Ed. 884 (1954).

I

The family whose rights are at issue here consists of Charlie Miller, an American citizen, Luz Penero, a citizen of the Philippines, and their daughter, Lorelyn. Lorelyn was born out of wedlock in 1970 in the Philippines. The relevant citizenship statutes state that a child born out of wedlock shall be a "citize[n] of the United States at birth," § 1401, if the child is born to a father who "had the nationality of the United States at the time of the person's birth," if the "blood relationship between the person and the father is established by clear and convincing evidence," if the father had been physically present in the United States for five years, and:

> "(3) the father (unless deceased) has agreed in writing to provide financial support for the person until the person reaches the age of 18 years, and
>
> "(4) while the person is under the age of 18 years—
>
> "(a) the person is legitimated under the law of the person's residence or domicile,

"(b) the father acknowledges paternity of the person in writing under oath, or

"(c) the paternity of the person is established by adjudication of a competent court." 8 U.S.C. §§ 1409(a) and 1401(g).

Charlie Miller did not meet the requirements set forth in (3) and (4) above on time. And the question before us is whether the Constitution forbids the application of those requirements for the reason that the statute imposed them only where the child's American parent is the child's father, not the mother. In my view the Constitution does forbid their application.

II

I agree with Justice STEVENS' resolution of the Government's three threshold claims. First, the Government takes issue with Lorelyn's argument that provisions (3) and (4) unconstitutionally infringe the rights of her father, Charlie, an American citizen. Brief for Respondent 11. It adds that Charlie, not Lorelyn, should assert those rights himself and that Lorelyn lacks legal "standing" to do so. *Id.*, at 11, and n. 2. This Court has made clear, however, that a party can "assert" the constitutional rights of another person, where (1) that party has "suffered an 'injury in fact' "; (2) the party and the other person have a "close relationship"; and (3) "there was some hindrance" to the other person's "asserting" his "own rights." *Campbell v. Louisiana*, — U.S. ——, ——, 118 S.Ct. 1419, 1423, — L.Ed.2d —— (1998); see also *Powers v. Ohio*, 499 U.S. 400, 411, 111 S.Ct. 1364, 1370–1371, 113 L.Ed.2d 411 (1991). And these three requirements are met here.

Lorelyn has suffered an "injury in fact." She has a "close" and relevant relationship with the other person, namely, her father. And there was "some hindrance" to her father's asserting his own rights. Charlie began this lawsuit (originally filed in Texas) as a party, raising his own Equal Protection claim. The Government originally moved to dismiss the complaint, contending that *Charlie* "should be dismissed from this suit because he lacked standing." Motion to Dismiss Plaintiff's First Amended Complaint, or, in the Alternative, Transfer Venue 6. The District Court agreed with the Government that Charlie lacked "standing," and he was dismissed from the suit. App. 11a. Lorelyn remained as the sole plaintiff, and for reasons of venue, see 28 U.S.C. § 1391(e)(1), the court then transferred the case to the District of Columbia pursuant to § 1406(a). App. 11a. The conclusion that the Government "hindered" Charlie's assertion of his own rights in this case is irresistible.

The Government points out that Charlie might have appealed the adverse Texas District Court ruling. Brief for Respondent 11, n. 2. But appeals take time and money; the transfer of venue left the plaintiffs uncertain about where to appeal; the case was being heard with Lorelyn as plaintiff in any event; and the resulting comparison of costs and benefits (viewed prospectively) likely would have discouraged Charlie's pursuit of the alternative appeal route. The Government's successful dismissal motion thus had practical consequences that "hindered" Charlie at least as much as those we have elsewhere said create "hindrances" sufficient to satisfy this portion of the "third party standing" test. See, *e.g.*, *Campbell*, *supra*, at ——, 118 S.Ct., at 1419 (criminal defendant can assert rights of racially-excluded petit jurors because of "arduous" process surrounding, and small benefits accruing to, juror effort to vindicate own rights); cf. *Craig v. Boren*, 429 U.S. 190, 193–194, 97 S.Ct. 451, 455, 50 L.Ed.2d 397 (1976) ("decision ... to forgo consideration of the constitutional merits ... to await" another party's identical claim would "foster repetitive and time-consuming litigation under the guise of caution and prudence").

Second, the Government, citing *United States v. Verdugo–Urquidez*, 494 U.S. 259, 110 S.Ct. 1056, 108 L.Ed.2d 222 (1990), and *Johnson v. Eisentrager*, 339 U.S. 763, 70 S.Ct. 936, 94 L.Ed. 1255 (1950), argues that the Fifth Amendment does not protect an alien, such as Lorelyn, living outside the United States. Brief for Respondent 11–12. The rights to be vindicated here, however, are Charlie's, not Lorelyn's. And, in any event, those cases, as Justice STEVENS points out, are irrelevant, for the matter at issue here is whether or not Lorelyn is a citizen. See *Rogers v. Bellei,* 401 U.S. 815, 91 S.Ct. 1060, 28 L.Ed.2d 499 (1971) (considering on the merits a putative citizen's claim that he was a citizen due to the operation of the Fifth Amendment, even though he apparently was living outside the United States at the time he filed suit).

Third, the Government argues that Lorelyn cannot succeed because a federal court lacks the power to grant her the relief she seeks, namely, a grant of citizenship. Brief for Respondent 43–50. As I shall later explain in more detail, however, this argument is beside the point, for, once the two unconstitutional clauses are excised from the statute, that statute operates automatically to confer citizenship upon Lorelyn "at birth." 8 U.S.C. § 1401; see Part V, *infra.*

Justice O'CONNOR, joined by Justice KENNEDY, says that Lorelyn cannot assert her father's rights because "she has not demonstrated a substantial hindrance to her father's ability to assert his own rights." *Ante,* at 1443. But the obstacles that the Government placed in her father's path substantially hindered his efforts to do so in practice. See *supra,* at 1456. Several of the cases mentioned in Justice O'CONNOR's opinion involved the denial of standing, but none of those cases involved any "hindrance," and Justice O'CONNOR does not claim that they do. See *FW/PBS, Inc. v. Dallas,* 493 U.S. 215, 234, 110 S.Ct. 596, 609, 107 L.Ed.2d 603 (1990) (husband lacks standing to assert wife's moot claim); *Bender v. Williamsport Area School Dist.,* 475 U.S. 534, 544–545, 106 S.Ct. 1326, 1332–1333, 89 L.Ed.2d 501 (1986) (school board member lacks standing to defend on board's behalf a claim that all other board members voted not to defend); *Gladstone, Realtors v. Village of Bellwood,* 441 U.S. 91, 112, n. 25, 99 S.Ct. 1601, 1614, n. 25, 60 L.Ed.2d 66 (1979) (nonresidents lack standing to challenge local real estate practices as discriminatory); *Heald v. District of Columbia,* 259 U.S. 114, 123, 42 S.Ct. 434, 435, 66 L.Ed. 852 (1922) (District resident lacks standing to claim local tax unconstitutional as applied to bonds held by nonresidents outside District). I have previously pointed to cases in which the Court has found third-party standing where the "hindrance" was of the same kind and approximate degree as that present here. *Supra,* at 1456. There are, of course, other cases finding standing that arguably involve even greater hindrance. See, *e.g., Hodel v. Irving,* 481 U.S. 704, 711–712, 107 S.Ct. 2076, 2080–2081, 95 L.Ed.2d 668 (1987); *Carey v. Population Services Int'l,* 431 U.S. 678, 684, n. 4, 97 S.Ct. 2010, 2015, n. 4, 52 L.Ed.2d 675 (1977); *Singleton v. Wulff,* 428 U.S. 106, 108, 96 S.Ct. 2868, 2871, 49 L.Ed.2d 826 (1976); *Craig, supra,* at 192, 97 S.Ct., at 454; *Eisenstadt v. Baird,* 405 U.S. 438, 446, 92 S.Ct. 1029, 1034–1035, 31 L.Ed.2d 349 (1972); *NAACP v. Alabama ex rel. Patterson,* 357 U.S. 449, 459, 78 S.Ct. 1163, 1170, 2 L.Ed.2d 1488 (1958); *Barrows v. Jackson,* 346 U.S. 249, 254, 73 S.Ct. 1031, 1033–1034, 97 L.Ed. 1586 (1953). But they set no inner limit.

Nor do I agree with Justice O'CONNOR's determination that "rational scrutiny" must apply to Lorelyn's assertion of her own rights. Lorelyn belongs to a class made up of children of citizen-fathers, whom the law distinguishes from the class of children of citizen-mothers, solely on grounds of the parent's gender. This Court, I assume, would use heightened scrutiny were it to review discriminatory laws based upon ancestry, say laws that denied voting rights or educational opportunity based upon the religion, or the racial make-up, of a parent or grandparent. And, if that is so, I am not certain that it makes a significant difference whether one calls the rights at issue those of Lorelyn or of her father. *Allen v. Wright,* 468 U.S. 737, 104 S.Ct. 3315, 82 L.Ed.2d 556 (1984), does not hold to the contrary. *Id.,* at 755, 104 S.Ct., at 3326–3327 (black schoolchildren's parents who claimed a "stigmatizing injury" due to Internal Revenue Service decision to grant tax exempt status to racially discriminatory private schools had not been "personally denied equal treatment," and thus had not been injured).

Regardless, like Justice O'CONNOR, I "do not share," and thus I believe a Court majority does not share, "Justice STEVENS' assessment that the provision withstands heightened scrutiny." *Ante,* at 1445. I also agree with Justice O'CONNOR that "[i]t is unlikely" that "gender classifications based on stereotypes can survive heightened scrutiny," *ante*, at 1445–1446, a view shared by at least five members of this Court. Indeed, for reasons to which I shall now turn, we must subject the provisions here at issue to "heightened scrutiny." And those provisions cannot survive.

III

This case is about American citizenship and its transmission from an American parent to his child. The right of citizenship, as this Court has said, is "a most precious right." *Kennedy v. Mendoza–Martinez*, 372 U.S. 144, 159, 83 S.Ct. 554, 562–563, 9 L.Ed.2d 644 (1963); see also *Fedorenko v. United States*, 449 U.S. 490, 507, 101 S.Ct. 737, 747–748, 66 L.Ed.2d 686 (1981) (citizenship is a "priceless treasure") (internal quotation marks omitted); *Luria v. United States*, 231 U.S. 9, 22, 34 S.Ct. 10, 13, 58 L.Ed. 101 (1913) ("Citizenship is membership in a political society"); *Afroyim v. Rusk*, 387 U.S. 253, 268, 87 S.Ct. 1660, 1668, 18 L.Ed.2d 757 (1967) ("[This Nation's] citizenry is the country and the country is its citizenry").

Further, the tie of parent to child is a special one, which in other circumstances by itself has warranted special constitutional protection. See, *e.g.*, *Wisconsin v. Yoder*, 406 U.S. 205, 92 S.Ct. 1526, 32 L.Ed.2d 15 (1972); *Pierce v. Society of Sisters*, 268 U.S. 510, 45 S.Ct. 571, 69 L.Ed. 1070 (1925); *Meyer v. Nebraska*, 262 U.S. 390, 43 S.Ct. 625, 67 L.Ed. 1042 (1923); see also *Skinner v. Oklahoma ex rel. Williamson*, 316 U.S. 535, 62 S.Ct. 1110, 86 L.Ed. 1655 (1942).

Moreover, American statutory law has consistently recognized the rights of American parents to transmit their citizenship to their children. See Act of Mar. 26, 1790, § 1 1 Stat. 103; Act of Jan. 29, 1795, § 3, 1 Stat. 415; Act of Apr. 14, 1802, § 4, 2 Stat. 155; Act of Feb. 10, 1855, § 1, 10 Stat. 604; Rev. Stat. § 1993; Act of Mar. 2, 1907, § 6, 34 Stat. 1229; Act of May 24, 1934, § 1, 48 Stat. 797; Nationality Act of 1940, § 201(g), 54 Stat. 1139; Immigration and Nationality Act of 1952, § 301(a)(7), (b), 66 Stat. 235, 236, as amended, 8 U.S.C. § 1401; cf., *e.g.*, 1 Oppenheim's International Law § 384 (R. Jennings & A. Watts 9th ed.1992) (noting that in many States, children born abroad of nationals become nationals); 43 A. Berger, Encyclopedic Dictionary of Roman Law 389 (1953) (Roman citizenship was acquired principally by parentage); Sandifer, A Comparative Study of Laws Relating to Nationality at Birth and to Loss of Nationality, 29 Am. J. Int'l L. 248, 248–261, 278 (1935) (discussing citizenship laws throughout the world and noting the "widespread extent of the rule of *jus sanguinis* "); E. de Vattel, The Law of Nations 101–102 (J. Chitty trans., 1883) (1758).

Finally, the classification at issue is gender-based, and we have held that, under the equal protection principle, such classifications may not rest on generalizations about the different capacities of males and females when neutral categories would serve the legislature's end. *United States v. Virginia*, 518 U.S., at 540–546, 116 S.Ct., at 2274–2279.

These circumstances mean that courts should not diminish the quality of review—that they should not apply specially lenient standards—when they review these statutes. The statutes focus upon two of the most serious of human relationships, that of parent to child and that of individual to the State. They tie each to the other, transforming both while strengthening the bonds of loyalty that connect family with Nation. Yet because they confer the status of citizenship "at birth," they do not involve the transfer of loyalties that underlies the naturalization of aliens, where precedent sets a more lenient standard of review. See *Fiallo v. Bell*, 430 U.S. 787, 97 S.Ct. 1473, 52 L.Ed.2d 50 (1977).

To the contrary, the same standard of review must apply when a married American couple travel abroad or temporarily work abroad and have a child as when a single American parent has a child born abroad out of wedlock. If the standard that the law applies is specially lenient, then statutes conferring citizenship upon these children could discriminate virtually free of independent judicial review. And as a result, many such children, lacking citizenship, would be placed outside the domain of basic constitutional protections. Nothing in the Constitution requires so anomalous a result.

I recognize that, ever since the Civil War, the transmission of American citizenship from parent to child, *jus sanguinis*, has played a role secondary to that of the transmission of citizenship by birthplace, *jus soli*. See *Rogers v. Bellei*, 401 U.S., at 828, 91 S.Ct., at 1067–1068; see also *Weedin v. Chin Bow*, 274 U.S. 657, 669–671, 47 S.Ct. 772, 775–777, 71 L.Ed. 1284 (1927) (citing *United States v. Wong Kim Ark*, 169 U.S. 649, 674, 18 S.Ct. 456, 466–467, 42 L.Ed. 890 (1898), and *id.*, at 714, 18 S.Ct., at 481–482 (Fuller, C. J., dissenting)). That lesser role reflects the fact that the Fourteenth Amendment's Citizenship Clause does not mention statutes that might confer citizenship "at birth" to children of Americans born abroad. U.S. Const., Amdt. 14, § 1 (stating that "[a]ll persons born or naturalized in the United States ... are citizens"). But that omission, though it may give Congress the power to decide whether or not to extend citizenship to children born outside the United States, see *Rogers v. Bellei*, *supra*, at 835, 91 S.Ct., at 1071, does not justify more lenient "equal protection" review of statutes that embody a congressional decision to do so.

Nothing in the language of the Citizenship Clause argues for less close scrutiny of those laws conferring citizenship at birth that Congress decides to enact. Nor have I found any support for a lesser standard in either the history of the Clause or its purpose. To the contrary, those who wrote the Citizenship Clause hoped thereby to assure that courts would not exclude newly freed slaves—born within the United States—from the protections the Fourteenth Amendment provided, including "equal protection of the laws." See, *e.g.*, *Afroyim v. Rusk*, 387 U.S., at 262, 87 S.Ct., at 1665; *id.*, at 283–284, 87 S.Ct., at 1675–1676 (Harlan, J., dissenting); H. Flack, Adoption of the Fourteenth Amendment 83–97 (1908). They took special care, lest deprivation of citizenship undermine the Amendment's guarantee of "equal protection of the laws." Care is no less necessary when statutes, transferring citizenship between American parent and child, make the child a citizen "at birth." How then could the Fourteenth Amendment itself provide support for a diminished standard of review?

Nor have I found any such support in the history of the *jus sanguinis* statutes. That history shows a virtually unbroken tradition of transmitting American citizenship from parent to child "at birth," under statutes that imposed certain residence requirements. *Supra*, at 1457; see also *Bellei*, *supra*, at 835, 91 S.Ct., at 1071. A single gap occurred when, for a brief period of time, the relevant statutes (perhaps inadvertently) failed to confer citizenship upon what must have been a small group of children born abroad between 1802 and 1855 whose citizen-fathers were also born between 1802 and 1855. See *Montana v. Kennedy*, 366 U.S. 308, 311–312, 81 S.Ct. 1336, 1338–1339, 6 L.Ed.2d 313 (1961); *Weedin*, *supra*, at 663–664, 47 S.Ct., at 773–774; *Wong Kim Ark*, *supra*, at 673–674, 18 S.Ct., at 466–467. But even then, some courts, recognizing the importance of the right, found common-law authority for the transmission to those children of their parent's American citizenship. See *Ludlam v. Ludlam*, 26 N.Y. 356, 362–372 (1863); see also *Lynch v. Clarke*, 1 Sand.Ch. 583, 659–663 (N.Y.1844).

The history of these statutes does reveal considerable discrimination against women, particularly from 1855 to 1934. See *ante*, at 1450–1451 (GINSBURG, J., dissenting). But that discrimination then cannot justify this discrimination now, when much discrimination that the law once tolerated, including "*de jure* segregation and the total exclusion of women from juries," is "now unconstitutional even though [it] once coexisted with the Equal Protection Clause." *J.E.B. v. Alabama ex rel. T.B.*, 511 U.S. 127, 142, n. 15, 114 S.Ct. 1419, 1428, n. 15, 128 L.Ed.2d 89 (1994).

Neither have I found case law that could justify use here of a more lenient standard of review. Justice STEVENS points out that this Court has said it will apply a more lenient standard in matters of " 'immigration and naturalization.' " *Ante*, at 1437, n. 11 (quoting *Mathews v. Diaz*, 426 U.S. 67, 82, 96 S.Ct. 1883, 1892–1893, 48 L.Ed.2d 478 (1976)). But that language arises in a case involving aliens. The Court did not say it intended that phrase to include statutes that confer citizenship "at birth." And Congress does not believe that this kind of citizenship involves "naturalization." 8 U.S.C. § 1101(a)(23) ("The term 'naturalization' means the conferring of nationality of a state upon a person *after* birth, by any means whatsoever") (emphasis added). The Court to my knowledge has never said, or held, or reasoned that statutes automatically conferring citizenship "at birth" upon the American child of American parents receive a more lenient standard of review.

The Court has applied a deferential standard of review in cases involving aliens, not in cases in which only citizens' rights were at issue. See *Mathews, supra* (rights of alien residents); *Kleindienst v. Mandel*, 408 U.S. 753, 92 S.Ct. 2576, 33 L.Ed.2d 683 (1972) (citizens' rights related to treatment of alien); *Fiallo v. Bell*, 430 U.S. 787, 97 S.Ct. 1473, 52 L.Ed.2d 50 (1977) (citizens' rights to obtain immigration preferences for relatives who are aliens). When the Court has considered the latter kind of case, it has not lowered the standard of review. See *Bellei, supra*, at 828–836, 91 S.Ct., at 1067–1072 (evaluating due process challenge to citizenship statute under generally applicable standard).

In sum, the statutes that automatically transfer American citizenship from parent to child "at birth" differ significantly from those that confer citizenship on those who originally owed loyalty to a different nation. To fail to recognize this difference, and consequently to apply an unusually lenient constitutional standard of review here, could deprive the children of millions of Americans, married and unmarried, working abroad, traveling, say, even temporarily to Canada or Mexico, of the most basic kind of constitutional protection. See U.S. Dept. of Commerce, Bureau of Census, Statistical Abstract of the United States 53 (1997) (table 54) (reporting that, as of 1990, 1.86 million United States citizens were born abroad or at sea to American parents); see also Hearing before the Subcommittee on International Operations of the House Committee on Foreign Affairs, 102d Cong., 1st Sess., 114 (1991) (testimony of Andrew P. Sundberg) ("According to the most recent survey carried out by the State Department, 40,000 children are born abroad each year to a U.S. citizen parent"). Thus, generally prevailing, not specially lenient, standards of review must apply.

IV

If we apply undiluted equal protection standards, we must hold the two statutory provisions at issue unconstitutional. The statutes discriminate on the basis of gender, making it significantly more difficult for American fathers than for American mothers to transmit American citizenship to their children born out of wedlock. If the citizen-parent is a man, the statute requires (1) a promise by the father to support the child until the child is 18, and (2) before the child turns 18, legitimation, written acknowledgment by the father under oath, or an adjudication of paternity. 8 U.S.C. § 1409(a). If the citizen-parent is a woman, she need not do either. § 1409(c).

Distinctions of this kind—based upon gender—are subject to a " 'strong presumption' " of constitutional invalidity. *Virginia*, 518 U.S., at 532, 116 S.Ct., at 2275 (quoting *J.E.B., supra*, at 152, 114 S.Ct., at 1433–1434 (KENNEDY, J., concurring in judgment)). The Equal Protection Clause permits them only if the Government meets the "demanding" burden of showing an " 'exceedingly persuasive' " justification for the distinction. *Virginia, supra*, at 533, 116 S.Ct., at 2276; see also *J.E.B., supra*, at 136, 114 S.Ct., at 1425; *Mississippi Univ. for Women v. Hogan*, 458 U.S. 718, 724, 102 S.Ct. 3331, 3336, 73 L.Ed.2d 1090 (1982); *Personnel Administrator of Mass. v. Feeney*, 442 U.S. 256, 273, 99 S.Ct. 2282, 2293, 60 L.Ed.2d 870 (1979); *Kirchberg v. Feenstra*, 450 U.S. 455, 461, 101 S.Ct. 1195, 1199, 67 L.Ed.2d 428 (1981). That distinction must further important governmental objectives, and the discriminatory means employed must be "substantially related" to the achievement of those objectives. *Virginia, supra*, at 533, 116 S.Ct., at 2271 (citing *Mississippi Univ. for Women, supra*, at 724, 102 S.Ct., at 3336). This justification "must be genuine, not hypothesized or invented *post hoc* in response to litigation." *Virginia*, 518 U.S., at 533, 116 S.Ct., at 2275. Further, "it must not rely on overbroad generalizations about the different talents, capacities, or preferences of males and females." *Ibid.*; see also *J.E.B.*, 511 U.S., at 139–140, and n. 11, 114 S.Ct., at 1427, and n. 11; *Craig*, 429 U.S., at 201, 97 S.Ct., at 458–459; *Califano v. Goldfarb*, 430 U.S. 199, 223–224, 97 S.Ct. 1021, 1035–1036, 51 L.Ed.2d 270 (1977) (STEVENS, J., concurring in judgment); *Weinberger v. Wiesenfeld*, 420 U.S. 636, 643, 95 S.Ct. 1225, 1230–1231, 43 L.Ed.2d 514 (1975). The fact that the statutes "discriminat[e] against males rather than against females" is beside the point. *Mississippi Univ. for Women*, 458 U.S., at 723, 102 S.Ct., at 3335.

The statutory distinctions here violate these standards. They depend for their validity upon the generalization that mothers are significantly more likely than fathers to care for their children, or to develop caring relationships with their children. But consider how the statutes work once one abandons that generalization as the illegitimate basis for legislative line-drawing we have held it to be. *Id.*, at 726, 730, 102 S.Ct., at 3337, 3339. First, assume that the American citizen is also the Caretaker Parent. The statute would then require a Male Caretaker Parent to acknowledge his child prior to the child's 18th birthday (or for the parent or child to obtain a court equivalent) and to provide financial support. It would not require a Female Caretaker Parent to do either. The gender-based distinction that would impose added burdens only upon the Male Caretaker Parent would serve no purpose at all. Second, assume that the American citizen is the Non–Caretaker Parent. In that circumstance, the statute would forgive a Female Non–Caretaker Parent from complying with the requirements (for formal acknowledgment and written promises to provide financial support) that it would impose upon a Male Non–Caretaker Parent. Again, the gender based distinction that would impose lesser burdens only upon the Female Non–Caretaker Parent would serve no purpose.

To illustrate the point, compare the family before us—Charlie, Lorelyn, and Luz—with an imagined family—Carlos, a Philippine citizen, Lucy, his daughter, and Lenora, Lucy's mother and an American citizen. Suppose that Lenora, Lucy's unmarried mother, returned to the United States soon after Lucy's birth, leaving Carlos to raise his daughter. Why, under those circumstances, should Lenora not be required to fulfill the same statutory requirements that here apply to Charlie? Alternatively, imagine that Charlie had taken his daughter Lorelyn back to the United States to raise. The statute would not make Lorelyn an American from birth unless Charlie satisfied its two conditions. But had our imaginary family mother, Lenora, taken her child Lucy back to the United States, the statute would have automatically made her an American from birth without anyone having satisfied the two conditions. The example suggests how arbitrary the statute's gender-based distinction is once one abandons the generalization that mothers, not fathers, will act as caretaker parents.

Let me now deal more specifically with the justifications that Justice STEVENS finds adequate. Justice STEVENS asserts that subsection (a)(4) serves two interests: first, "ensuring reliable proof of a biological relationship between the potential citizen and its citizen parent," *ante*, at 1438, and second, "encouraging" certain relationships or ties, namely "the development of a healthy relationship between the citizen parent and the child while the child is a minor," *ante*, at 1439, as well as "the related interest in fostering ties between the foreign-born child and the United States." *Ibid.* I have no doubt that these interests are important. But the relationship between the statutory requirements and those particular objectives is one of total misfit.

Subsection (a)(4) requires, for example, the American citizen father to "acknowledg[e]" paternity before the child reaches 18 years of age, or for the child or parent to obtain a court equivalent (legitimation or adjudication of paternity). Justice STEVENS suggests that this requirement "produces the rough equivalent of the documentation," such as a birth certificate memorialized in hospital records, "already available to evidence the blood relationship between the mother and the child." *Ante*, at 1438. But, even if I assume the "equivalency" (only for argument's sake, since birth certificates do not invariably carry a mother's true name or omit the father's), I still do not understand the need for the prior-to-18 legitimation-or-acknowledgment requirement. When the statute was written, one might have seen the requirement as offering some protection against false paternity claims. But that added protection is unnecessary in light of inexpensive DNA testing that will prove paternity with certainty. See Shapiro, Reifler, and Psome, The DNA Paternity Test: Legislating the Future Paternity Action, 7 J. Law & Health 1, 29 (1992–1993) (current testing methods can determine probability of paternity to 99.999999% accuracy); see also H.R.Rep. No. 98–527, p. 38 (1983).

Moreover, a different provision of the statute, subsection (a)(1), already requires proof of paternity by "clear and convincing evidence." No one contests the validity of that provision, and I believe that biological differences between men and women would justify its imposition where paternity is at issue. In light of that provision, subsection (a)(4)'s protection against false claims is not needed. Indeed, the Government concedes that, in light of the "clear and convincing evidence" requirement, the "time limit for meeting the legitimation-or-acknowledgement requirement of Section 309(a)(4) must . . . reflect, at least in part, some *other* congressional concern." Brief for Respondent 27 (emphasis added).

Justice STEVENS says that this "other concern" is a concern for the establishment of relationships and ties, to the father and to the United States, all before the child is 18. *Ante*, at 1439. According to Justice STEVENS, the way in which the requirement serves this purpose is by making certain the father knows of the child's existence—in the same way, it says, that a mother, by giving birth, automatically knows that the child exists. *Ibid.*

The distance between this knowledge and the claimed objectives, however, is far too great to satisfy any legal requirement of tailoring or proportionality. And the assumption that this knowledge-of-birth could make a significant gender-related difference rests upon a host of unproved gender-related hypotheses. Simple knowledge of a child's existence may, or may not, be followed by the kinds of relationships for which Justice STEVENS hopes. A mother or a father, knowing of a child's birth, may nonetheless fail to care for the child or even to acknowledge the child. A father with strong ties to the child may, simply by lack of knowledge, fail to comply with the statute's formal requirements. A father with weak ties might readily comply. Moreover, the statute does little to assure any tie for, as Justice STEVENS acknowledges, a child might obtain an adjudication of paternity "absent any affirmative act by the father, and perhaps even over his express objection." *Ante*, at 1437.

To make plausible the connection between the statute's requirement and the asserted "relationship" goals, Justice STEVENS must find a factual scenario where a father's knowledge—equivalent to the mother's knowledge that she has given birth—could lead to the establishment of a more meaningful parenting relationship or tie to America. It therefore points to what one might term the "war baby" problem—the problem created by American servicemen fathering children overseas and returning to America unaware of the related pregnancy or birth. The statutory remedy before us, however, is disproportionately broad even when considered in relation to that problem. Justice STEVENS refers to 683,000 service personnel stationed in the Far East in 1970 when Lorelyn was born. *Ante*, at 1439. The statute applies, however, to all Americans who live or travel abroad, including the 3.2 million private citizens, and the 925,000 Federal Government employees, who live, or who are stationed, abroad—of whom today only 240,000 are active duty military employees, many of whom are women. U.S. Dept. of State, Private American Citizens Residing Abroad (Nov. 21, 1997); U.S. Dept. of Commerce, Bureau of the Census, Americans Overseas in U.S. Censuses, Technical Paper 62, p. 62 (Nov.1993) (1990 census figures); U.S. Dept. of Defense, Selected Manpower Statistics 23, 44 (DIOR/MO1–96 1996). Nor does the statute seem to have been aimed at the "war baby" problem, for the precursor to the provisions at issue was first proposed in a 1938 report and was first adopted in the Nationality Act of 1940, which was enacted *before* the United States entered World War II. Nationality Laws of the United States: Message from the President of the United States, 76th Cong., 1st Sess., pt. 1, pp. 17–18 (Comm. Print submitted to House Comm. on Immigration and Naturalization, 1939); Nationality Act of 1940, § 205, 54 Stat. 1139.

Nor is there need for the gender-based discrimination at issue here, for, were Congress truly interested in achieving the goals Justice STEVENS posits in the way Justice STEVENS suggests, it could simply substitute a requirement of knowledge-of-birth for the present subsection (a)(4); or it could distinguish between caretaker and non-caretaker parents, rather than between men and women. A statute that does not do so, but instead relies upon gender-based distinctions, appears rational only, as I have said, *supra*, at 1463, if one accepts the legitimacy of gender-based generalizations that, for example, would equate gender and caretaking—generalizations of a kind that this Court has previously found constitutionally impermissible. See, *e.g., Virginia*, 518 U.S., at 542, 546, 116 S.Ct., at ——, —— (striking down men-only admissions policy at Virginia Military Institute even assuming that "most women would not choose VMI's adversative method"); *J.E.B.*, 511 U.S., at 139, n. 11, 114 S.Ct., at 1427, n. 11 (invalidating gender-based peremptory challenges "[e]ven if a measure of truth can be found in some of the gender stereotypes used to justify" them); *Craig*, 429 U.S., at 201, 97 S.Ct., at 459 (invalidating Oklahoma law that established different drinking ages for men and women, although the evidence supporting the age differential was "not trivial in a statistical sense"); *Wiesenfeld*, 420 U.S., at 645, 95 S.Ct., at 1231–1232 (holding unconstitutional statutory classification giving to widowed mothers benefits not available to widowed fathers even though "the notion that men are more likely than women to be the primary supporters of their spouses and children is not entirely without empirical support"). Although Justice STEVENS cites *Lehr v. Robertson*, 463 U.S. 248, 103 S.Ct. 2985, 77 L.Ed.2d 614 (1983), for support, *ante*, at 1440, that case was decided before the DNA advances described earlier.

For similar reasons, subsection (3) denies Charlie Miller "equal protection" of the laws. That subsection requires an American father to "agre[e] ... to provide financial support" for the child until the child "reaches the age of 18," but does not require the same of an American mother. I agree with the Government that this provision has as one objective helping to assure ties between father and child. Brief for Respondent 26. But I do not see why the same need does not exist with respect to a mother. And, where the American parent is the Non–Caretaker Parent, the need for such assurances would seem the same in respect to either sex. Where the American parent is the Caretaker Parent, there would seem no need for the assurance regardless of gender. Since either men or women may be caretakers, and since either men or women may be "breadwinners," one could justify the gender distinction only on the ground that more women are caretakers than men, and more men are "breadwinners" than women. This, again, is the kind of generalization that we have rejected as justifying a gender-based distinction in other cases. *Virginia, supra*, at 540–546, 116 S.Ct., at 2274–2279; *J.E.B., supra*, at 139, n. 11, 114 S.Ct., at 1427, n. 11; *Craig, supra*, at 201, 97 S.Ct., at 458–459; *Wiesenfeld, supra*, at 645, 95 S.Ct., at 1231–1232.

For these reasons, I can find no "exceedingly persuasive" justification for the gender-based distinctions that the statute draws.

V

Justice SCALIA argues that, if the provisions at issue violate the Constitution, we nonetheless are powerless to find a remedy. But that is not so. The remedy is simply that of striking from the statute the two subsections that offend the Constitution's equal protection requirement, namely (a)(3) and (a)(4). With those subsections omitted, the statute says that the daughter, Lorelyn, of one who, like Charlie, has proved paternity by "clear and convincing evidence," is an American citizen, and has lived in the United States for five years, is a "citize[n] of the United States at birth." 8 U.S.C. §§ 1409(a) and 1401. Whatever limitations there may be upon a Court's powers to grant citizenship, those limitations are not applicable here, for the Court need not grant citizenship. The statute itself grants citizenship automatically, and "at birth." And this Court need only declare that that is so. *INS v. Pangilinan*, 486 U.S. 875, 108 S.Ct. 2210, 100 L.Ed.2d 882 (1988), which Justice SCALIA cites in support, is beside the point, for the plaintiffs in that case, conceding that the statute at issue did not make them citizens, asked the courts to confer citizenship as a remedy in equity. Cf. *Bellei*, 401 U.S., at 828–836, 91 S.Ct., at 1067–1072 (assessing claim that statute conferred citizenship in the absence of a provision argued to be unconstitutional, without identifying any special remedial problems).

Of course, we can excise the two provisions only if Congress likely would prefer their excision, rather than imposing similar requirements upon mothers. *Califano v. Westcott*, 443 U.S. 76, 89–93, 99 S.Ct. 2655, 2663–2665, 61 L.Ed.2d 382 (1979); *Welsh v. United States*, 398 U.S. 333, 361, 90 S.Ct. 1792, 1807–1808, 26 L.Ed.2d 308 (1970) (Harlan, J., concurring in result). But, since the provisions at issue seem designed in significant part to address difficulties in proving paternity (along with providing encouragement for fathers to legitimate the child) and, since DNA advances have overcome the paternity-proof difficulties, I believe that Congress would have preferred severance.

Justice SCALIA is also wrong, I believe, when he says that "the INA itself contains a clear statement of congressional intent" not to sever, *ante*, at 1449, for the Act in fact contains the following explicit severability provision:

> "If any particular provision of this Act, or the application thereof to any person or circumstance, is held invalid, the remainder of the Act and the application of such provision to other persons or circumstances shall not be affected thereby." § 406, 66 Stat. 281; see note following 8 U.S.C. § 1101, p. 38, "Separability."

The provision cited by Justice SCALIA says:

> "A person may be naturalized as a citizen of the United States in the manner and under the conditions prescribed in this title and not otherwise." § 310(d), 66 Stat. 239, 8 U.S.C. § 1421(d).

As "naturalization" under this statute does not include the conferral of citizenship at birth, the provision does not apply here. See 8 U.S.C. § 1101(a)(23) ("The term 'naturalization' means the conferring of nationality of a state upon a person *after* birth") (emphasis added).

Justice SCALIA also says that the law, as excised, would favor fathers over mothers. *Ante*, at 1449. The law, however, would require both fathers and mothers to prove their parentage; it would require that one or the other be an American, it would impose residency requirements that, if anything, would disfavor fathers. I cannot find the reverse favoritism that Justice SCALIA fears.

For these reasons, I would reverse the judgment of the Court of Appeals.

LEADING CASES

I. Constitutional Law

D. *Equal Protection*

Gender Discrimination — Immigration and Nationality Act. — Courts and commentators generally agree that none of Congress's powers is more far-reaching than its power over immigration.[1]

[1] *See, e.g.*, Oceanic Steam Navigation Co. v. Stranahan, 214 U.S. 320, 339 (1909) ("[O]ver no conceivable subject is the legislative power of Congress more complete than it is over [immigration law]."); Louis Henkin, *The Constitution and United States Sovereignty: A Century of Chinese Exclusion and Its Progeny*, 100 HARV. L. REV. 853, 863 (1987) ("The Court has left only immigra-

Deferring to Congress's plenary power, courts have declined to extend many of the constitutional protections afforded citizens to noncitizen immigrants,[2] and have even applied deferential scrutiny to immigration laws that infringe upon the constitutional rights of citizens.[3] One commentator has gone so far as to call immigration law "the unwanted child of constitutional jurisprudence."[4] Last Term, in *Miller v. Albright*,[5] the Supreme Court further explored the role of traditional constitutional norms in immigration law. In a splintered decision, the Court rejected an equal protection challenge to provisions of the Immigration and Nationality Act (INA) that require illegitimate foreign-born children of citizen fathers to establish paternity before reaching majority in order to obtain citizenship, but have no analogous requirement for illegitimate foreign-born children of citizen mothers.[6] However, while the D.C. Circuit saw the case as squarely within the precedent established by *Fiallo v. Bell*,[7] in which the Court applied deferential scrutiny to uphold provisions of the INA that established similar gender-based requirements for immigration preferences,[8] no Justice viewed the result in *Fiallo* as directly applicable, and some explicitly rejected *Fiallo*'s deferential standard.[9] Those Justices who discussed the applicability of *Fiallo* distinguished it on the basis that while in *Fiallo* the rights of citizens and aliens were at stake, in *Miller* the plaintiff claimed to have been a citizen since birth,[10] and thus "only citizens' rights were at issue."[11] However, this narrow exception

tion and deportation outside the reach of fundamental constitutional protections."). *But cf.* Stephen H. Legomsky, *Ten More Years of Plenary Power: Immigration, Congress, and the Courts*, 22 HASTINGS CONST. L.Q. 925, 930 (1995) ("On the one hand, many lower courts continue to apply the [plenary power] doctrine in its more rigid form .... On the other hand, ... many other lower courts have reinforced and expanded the devices for circumventing at least the traditional version of the plenary power doctrine.").

[2] *See, e.g.*, Mathews v. Diaz, 426 U.S. 67, 79–80 (1976) ("In the exercise of its broad power over naturalization and immigration, Congress regularly makes rules that would be unacceptable if applied to citizens.").

[3] *See, e.g.*, Fiallo v. Bell, 430 U.S. 787, 799–800 (1977) (upholding against an equal protection challenge the sections of the Immigration and Nationality Act that gave an immigration preference to alien children by virtue of their relationship with their citizen mothers but not citizen fathers, and to alien mothers of citizens but not alien fathers); Kleindienst v. Mandel, 408 U.S. 753, 769–70 (1972) (applying the "facially legitimate and bona fide reason" standard to a citizen's First Amendment challenge to the Attorney General's decision to exclude a noncitizen Marxian theorist).

[4] Linda Kelly, *Preserving the Fundamental Right to Family Unity: Championing Notions of Social Contract and Community Ties in the Battle of Plenary Power Versus Aliens' Rights*, 41 VILL. L. REV. 725, 725 (1996).

[5] 118 S. Ct. 1428 (1998).

[6] *See id.* at 1442 (discussing 8 U.S.C. § 1409 (1994)).

[7] *See* Miller v. Christopher, 96 F.3d 1467, 1471 (D.C. Cir. 1996) (citing *Fiallo*, 430 U.S. 787).

[8] *See Fiallo*, 430 U.S. at 799–800 (discussing 8 U.S.C. §§ 1101(b)(1)(D)–(b)(2), 1151(a)–(b), 1182(a)(14) (1976) (amended 1986)).

[9] *See Miller*, 118 S. Ct. at 1460 (Breyer, J., dissenting).

[10] *See id.* at 1434.

[11] *Id.* at 1460 (Breyer, J., dissenting).

for statutes that confer citizenship at birth is untenable, and thus, the move in *Miller* away from *Fiallo* may demand a more general application of traditional constitutional principles in immigration law.

Lorelyn Penero Miller was born in the Philippines on June 20, 1970, to Luz Penero, a Filipino national, and Charlie Miller, an American citizen who had been stationed in the Philippines at the time of her conception.[12] In November 1991, Ms. Miller, who did not live in the United States until after her twenty-first birthday, applied for registration as a United States citizen.[13] The State Department denied Ms. Miller's initial application in March 1992, as well as her reapplication submitted after her father obtained a paternity decree, on the ground that the INA required that an illegitimate foreign-born child of a citizen father and alien mother be legitimated before the age of eighteen in order to acquire citizenship.[14]

In 1993, Ms. Miller and her father filed a complaint against the Secretary of State in the Eastern District of Texas requesting that she be declared a citizen, on the ground that the preferential treatment accorded to citizen mothers of illegitimate children under the INA violated the right of citizen fathers to equal protection.[15] Upon motion by the Government, the district court dismissed Mr. Miller as a plaintiff for lack of standing.[16] As a result, venue in Texas was no longer appropriate, and the court transferred the case to the District of Columbia.[17] The District of Columbia district court granted the Government's renewed motion to dismiss on the ground that Ms. Miller also

---

12 *See Miller*, 118 S. Ct. at 1432–33.

13 *See id.*

14 *See id.*

15 *See id.* at 1433. 8 U.S.C. § 1401(g) grants citizenship to children born outside the United States to married parents if at least one is a citizen. *See* 8 U.S.C. § 1401(g) (1994). 8 U.S.C. § 1409, the portion of the INA challenged in *Miller*, provides that § 1401(g) will also apply to illegitimate children on certain conditions. *See id.* § 1409. Illegitimate children born outside the United States to citizen fathers can establish citizenship if the following conditions are met:

> (1) [A] blood relationship between the person and the father is established by clear and convincing evidence,
> (2) the father had the nationality of the United States at the time of the person's birth,
> (3) the father (unless deceased) has agreed in writing to provide financial support for the person until the person reaches the age of 18 years, and
> (4) while the person is under the age of 18 years —
> (A) the person is legitimated under the law of the person's residence or domicile,
> (B) the father acknowledges paternity of the person in writing under oath, or
> (C) the paternity of the person is established by adjudication of a competent court.

Id. § 1409(a). However, the law relating to children of citizen mothers differs significantly:

> [A] person born, after December 23, 1952, outside the United States and out of wedlock shall be held to have acquired at birth the nationality status of his mother, if the mother had the nationality of the United States at the time of such person's birth, and if the mother had previously been physically present in the United States or one of its outlying possessions for a continuous period of one year.

Id. § 1409(c).

16 *See Miller*, 118 S. Ct. at 1433.

17 *See id.*

lacked standing, reasoning that her injury was not redressable because Supreme Court precedent dictates that "courts do not have the power to confer citizenship in the absence of statutory authority."[18]

The D.C. Circuit affirmed.[19] Unlike the lower court, the court of appeals held that Ms. Miller had standing.[20] The court noted that Ms. Miller did not seek a grant of citizenship from the court, because "if the district court had held section 1409(a) to be unconstitutional, it could have found that she was a U.S. citizen pursuant to section 1401(g)."[21] Relying on *Fiallo v. Bell*, the court then held that § 1409 did not violate equal protection.[22] Applying the highly deferential "facially legitimate and bona fide reason" standard of review employed in *Fiallo*,[23] the court reasoned that the more burdensome requirements imposed on citizen fathers in order to gain citizenship for their illegitimate children could be justified by Congress's "desire to promote early ties to this country and to those relatives who are citizens of this country."[24] Finally, in response to Ms. Miller's argument that the statute employs a distinction based on "overbroad and outdated stereotype[s]," the court recommended that such an argument "be addressed to the Congress rather than the courts."[25]

The Supreme Court granted certiorari to address whether § 1409's distinction between illegitimate children of citizen mothers and illegitimate children of citizen fathers violated the equal protection component of the Fifth Amendment.[26] In a fractured decision, the Court affirmed.[27]

In the opinion announcing the judgment of the Court, Justice Stevens[28] agreed with the court of appeals that Ms. Miller had standing,[29] but that there was no equal protection violation.[30] As a preliminary

---

[18] Miller v. Christopher, 870 F. Supp. 1, 3 (D.D.C. 1994) (citing INS v. Pangilinan, 486 U.S. 875, 884 (1988)).

[19] *See* Miller v. Christopher, 96 F.3d 1467, 1468 (D.C. Cir. 1996).

[20] *See id.* at 1470.

[21] *Id.*; *see also supra* note 15.

[22] *See Miller*, 96 F.3d at 1471.

[23] *Id.* at 1470 (quoting Kleindienst v. Mandel, 408 U.S. 753, 770 (1972)) (internal quotation marks omitted); *see also* Fiallo v. Bell, 430 U.S. 787, 795 (1977). Some commentators view this test as "roughly equivalent" to rational-basis scrutiny. Gerald L. Neuman, *The Lost Century of American Immigration Law (1776–1875)*, 93 COLUM. L. REV. 1833, 1839 n.31 (1993). However, others view it as even more deferential. *See, e.g.*, Hiroshi Motomura, *The Curious Evolution of Immigration Law: Procedural Surrogates for Substantive Constitutional Rights*, 92 COLUM L. REV. 1625, 1697–98 (1992).

[24] *Miller*, 96 F.3d at 1472 (quoting Ablang v. Reno, 52 F.3d 801, 806 (9th Cir. 1995)). The court based this judgment both on the perceived absence of family ties between illegitimate children and their natural fathers and on the inherent difficulty in proving paternity. *See id.*

[25] *Id.* (quoting *Fiallo*, 430 U.S. at 799 n.9).

[26] *See Miller*, 118 S. Ct. at 1434.

[27] *See id.* at 1442.

[28] Chief Justice Rehnquist joined Justice Stevens.

[29] *See Miller*, 118 S. Ct. at 1436.

[30] *See id.* at 1442.

matter, Justice Stevens found that it was unnecessary to "decide whether *Fiallo v. Bell* dictates the outcome of this case,"[31] because *Fiallo* involved the claim of aliens to an immigration preference, whereas Ms. Miller claimed that "she is, and for years has been, an American citizen."[32] Although Justice Stevens did not concede that intermediate scrutiny, which courts typically apply to instances of gender discrimination, necessarily applied here, he still argued that § 1409(a) would survive even this heightened standard.[33]

Justice Stevens first listed various important governmental objectives that § 1409(a) served, such as ensuring proof of paternity, encouraging family ties between the citizen parent and the minor child, and developing ties between the child and the United States.[34] Justice Stevens next insisted that the means relied upon in § 1409(a) were "well tailored to serve those interests."[35] Given Congress's intent to address the problem posed by children born to American servicemen stationed overseas, it was reasonable, Justice Stevens argued, for Congress to "condition the award of citizenship to such children on an act that demonstrates, at a minimum, the possibility that those who become citizens will develop ties with this country."[36] That the formal act of acknowledging parenthood "would be superfluous for citizen mothers,"[37] Justice Stevens maintained, was the result of "biological differences between single men and single women," rather than "a traditional way of thinking about the members of either sex."[38]

Justice O'Connor concurred in the judgment.[39] She reasoned that because Mr. Miller's earlier, yet still appealable, dismissal from the suit did not constitute "a substantial hindrance to [his] ability to assert his own rights," he remained the most appropriate party to bring this claim.[40] Therefore, Ms. Miller could not assert her father's equal protection claim, but could only argue that § 1409(a) irrationally discriminated against her.[41] Although Justice O'Connor argued that "[i]t is unlikely . . . that any gender classifications based on stereotypes can survive heightened scrutiny," such classifications could survive the rational basis scrutiny accorded Ms. Miller's claim.[42]

---

[31] *Id.* at 1434–35.

[32] *Id.* at 1434.

[33] *See id.* at 1437 n.11.

[34] *See id.* at 1438–39.

[35] *Id.* at 1440.

[36] *Id.*

[37] *Id.*

[38] *Id.* at 1442.

[39] *See id.* (O'Connor, J., concurring in the judgment). Justice Kennedy joined Justice O'Connor.

[40] *See id.* at 1443 (citing Powers v. Ohio, 499 U.S. 400, 411 (1991)).

[41] *See id.* at 1445.

[42] *Id.* at 1445–46.

Justice Scalia also concurred in the judgment.[43] Declining to reach the merits, he argued, echoing the trial court,[44] that the complaint should have been dismissed because "the Court has no power to . . . confer[] . . . citizenship on a basis other than that prescribed by Congress."[45] Justice Scalia rejected as a "fanciful view of the statute" Ms. Miller's contention that "the Court may declare her a citizen 'at birth'" under § 1401(g) and "ignore § 1409(a) entirely, which allegedly unconstitutionally takes away that citizenship."[46] Justice Scalia objected that "a unitary statute is not to be picked apart in this fashion,"[47] and that such "radical statutory surgery" would fail to respect Congress's plenary power.[48]

Justice Ginsburg dissented,[49] arguing that the Government's justifications for § 1409(a) were inconsistent with the statute's history.[50] For instance, Congress had never "demonstrated [a] high regard or respect for the mother-child affiliation," which the Government now put forth to justify the current disparate treatment.[51] Justice Ginsburg noted further that even if the Government's justifications were the motivating factors behind the statute, the statutory means used to achieve those ends are "based on generalizations (stereotypes) about the way women (or men) are," thus rendering the statute unconstitutional.[52]

Justice Breyer wrote a separate dissenting opinion.[53] After responding to Justice O'Connor's argument that Ms. Miller did not have third-party standing,[54] Justice Breyer contended that heightened scrutiny was the appropriate standard under which to review her third-party gender discrimination claim.[55] He distinguished *Fiallo v. Bell*, in which the Court applied deferential scrutiny to arguably similar provi-

---

43 *See id.* at 1446 (Scalia, J., concurring in the judgment). Justice Thomas joined Justice Scalia.

44 *See* Miller v. Christopher, 870 F. Supp. 1, 3 (D.D.C. 1994).

45 *Miller*, 118 S. Ct. at 1446 (Scalia, J., concurring in the judgment).

46 *Id.* at 1448.

47 *Id.* Moreover, Justice Scalia remarked that this particular construction is especially implausible: section 1401(g) is not generally applicable to children of a citizen parent; rather, it is applicable to such children if their parents are married, and § 1409(a) extends this provision to children born out of wedlock only in certain circumstances. *See id.*

48 *Id.* at 1449.

49 *See id.* (Ginsburg, J., dissenting). Justices Souter and Breyer joined Justice Ginsburg.

50 *See id.* at 1453–54.

51 *Id.* at 1454. Actually, Justice Ginsburg argued, the precursors to the current version of the INA traditionally discriminated against mothers in their ability to transmit citizenship. *See id.* at 1451–52.

52 *Id.* at 1454.

53 *See id.* at 1455 (Breyer, J., dissenting). Justices Souter and Ginsburg joined Justice Breyer.

54 Justice Breyer insisted that Mr. Miller was indeed hindered by the time and money that an appeal would cost him, as well as by uncertainty about the appropriate venue in which to appeal. *See id.* at 1456. Justice Breyer also pointed out that Mr. Miller knew that the case was "being heard with [Ms. Miller] as plaintiff in any event," thus giving him little incentive to assert his own claim separately. *Id.*

55 *See id.* at 1460.

sions, on the basis that in the instant case "only citizens' rights were at issue."[56] Statutes that confer citizenship at birth, Justice Breyer argued, do not fall within Congress's definition of "naturalization," and they do not "involve the transfer of loyalties that underlies the naturalization of aliens."[57] Therefore, the deferential review traditionally applied to immigration and naturalization was not appropriate.[58]

Justice Breyer concluded that the provisions at issue could not survive heightened scrutiny, arguing that an age restriction applied only to children of citizen fathers is not a well-tailored means of achieving the government's purported goal of encouraging ties between child and parent.[59] In response to Justice Scalia's redressability concern, Justice Breyer argued that the Court need not grant citizenship to provide Ms. Miller with a remedy; the statute itself, once the unconstitutional provisions were excised, would confer citizenship.[60]

Although the court of appeals saw *Miller* as squarely within the framework of *Fiallo v. Bell*,[61] strikingly absent from the Supreme Court's opinions in *Miller* was the argument that § 1409 should have been analyzed under the deferential standard applied in *Fiallo*. In a suit brought by citizens and their noncitizen relatives, the *Fiallo* Court upheld a section of the INA that excluded from the preferential immigration status bestowed upon a child or parent of a United States citizen the relationship between an illegitimate child and his father.[62] The dissenters in *Miller* argued that, unlike statutes involving aliens, statutes that confer citizenship at birth, "in which only citizens' rights are at issue," do not merit deferential treatment.[63] Even Justice Stevens, who reserved judgment as to the appropriate level of scrutiny, began his opinion by distinguishing *Fiallo* on the basis that it involved the claims of aliens, while Ms. Miller claimed that "she is, and for years has been, an American citizen."[64] Finally, Justice O'Connor implied that a challenge to this statute, if brought by the proper claimant, would receive heightened scrutiny and would fail under that test.[65]

---

56 *Id.*

57 *Id.* at 1458.

58 *See id.*

59 *See id.* at 1462. Rather than employing a gender distinction, Justice Breyer suggested that Congress could, for instance, have required the parent, mother or father, either to have knowledge of the child's birth or to be the child's caretaker. *See id.* at 1462–63.

60 *See id.* at 1464.

61 *See* Miller v. Christopher, 96 F.3d 1467, 1470–71 (D.C. Cir. 1996); *id.* at 1473 n.2 (Wald, J., concurring in the judgment).

62 *See* Fiallo v. Bell, 430 U.S. 787, 799–800 (1977).

63 *Miller*, 118 S. Ct. at 1460 (Breyer, J., dissenting).

64 *Miller*, 118 S. Ct. at 1434.

65 *See id.* at 1445 (O'Connor, J., concurring in the judgment). Although Justice O'Connor did not definitively state that Mr. Miller's claim would have received heightened scrutiny, the tenor and language of the opinion suggest it. *See id.* ("[P]etitioner cannot raise her father's rights .... [P]etitioner cannot make a claim of discrimination triggering heightened scrutiny ....").

Commentators might welcome a move away from the highly deferential stance of *Fiallo v. Bell*, because the statute in that case, as in *Miller*, implicated the constitutional rights of citizens.[66] However, there is no principled justification for limiting this expansion of constitutional protection to statutes that confer citizenship at birth. Moreover, such a limitation is inconsistent with the traditional justifications for Congress's plenary power over immigration.

Section 1409's conferral of citizenship at birth played two distinct roles in the Court's opinions. First, Justices Stevens and Breyer relied on this feature of the statute to argue that an appropriate remedy would not require the Court to grant citizenship, since the statute itself, once the unconstitutional provision was severed, would grant citizenship.[67] Although Justice Scalia found evidence of congressional intent against severability in the provision that allowed for naturalization "under the conditions prescribed in this title *and not otherwise*,"[68] Justice Breyer noted that congressional conferral of citizenship at birth is not included in the statutory definition of "naturalization."[69]

Second, Justices Stevens and Breyer saw § 1409's conferral of citizenship at birth as carrying constitutional significance. Justice Stevens distinguished *Fiallo* on the basis that Ms. Miller claimed that she had been a citizen since birth, although he did not decide whether *Fiallo*'s deferential standard was applicable.[70] Justice Breyer went further, as he saw the citizenship-conferring nature of the provisions as mandating heightened scrutiny in cases in which only the rights of citizens were involved.[71] Although the Court traditionally applies a deferential standard when reviewing "immigration and naturalization" requirements,[72] statutes that confer citizenship at birth do not fall within Congress's definition of "naturalization," and thus the Court has never held that such statutes "receive a more lenient standard of review."[73]

---

66 *See, e.g.*, Kelly, *supra* note 4, at 778 ("Congress should not be given unquestioning deference when the rights of U.S. citizens are at stake."); *cf. Miller*, 96 F.3d at 1473 n.2 (Wald, J., concurring in the judgment) ("*Fiallo*'s application of the 'facially legitimate and bona fide reason' standard to all immigration legislation, no matter how directly or severely that legislation interferes with fundamental rights of U.S. citizens, is . . . outdated."). Congress objected to the result in *Fiallo* as well, as evidenced by its later amendment to the relevant provision. *See* 8 U.S.C. § 1101 (1994) (extending the definition of "child" to include the relationship of illegitimate children with their natural fathers for the purpose of immigration preferences if the father and child had a "bona fide parent-child relationship").

67 *See Miller*, 118 S. Ct. at 1436; *id.* at 1463–64 (Breyer, J., dissenting).

68 *Id.* at 1448 (Scalia, J., concurring in the judgment) (quoting 8 U.S.C. § 1421(d) (1994) (emphasis added)).

69 *See id.* at 1464 (Breyer, J., dissenting) (citing 8 U.S.C. S 1101(a)(23) (1994) ("The term 'naturalization' means the conferring of nationality of a state upon a person after birth.").

70 *See Miller*, 118 S. Ct. at 1434, 1437 n.11.

71 *See id.* at 1460 (Breyer, J., dissenting).

72 *Miller*, 118 S. Ct. at 1437 n.11 (quoting Mathews v. Diaz, 426 U.S. 67, 82 (1976)).

73 *Id.* at 1460 (Breyer, J., dissenting).

Despite its relevance to the question of redressability, that § 1409 confers citizenship at birth is not a logical basis for failing to apply the deferential review of *Fiallo*, while maintaining its applicability generally. Although Congress has defined "naturalization" to refer only to grants of citizenship *after* birth,[74] when the Court has referred to the deferential standard commonly applied in the "immigration and naturalization" context, it might have used "naturalization" loosely, in keeping not with the narrow congressional definition but with the historical legacy of the concept as used in the Fourteenth Amendment.[75] It also seems an odd legal fiction that because Ms. Miller claimed citizenship retroactive to her date of birth, she should be treated as a citizen before acquiring that status. Ms. Miller's citizenship was not constitutionally mandated, and to consider her a citizen at the time of the suit runs counter to the accepted rule that "[n]o alien has the slightest right to naturalization unless all statutory requirements are complied with."[76]

Moreover, arguments for carving out a limited exception to the general rule of deferential review based solely on Ms. Miller's status as a putative citizen lack grounding in the traditional justifications for the Court's plenary power doctrine. One justification for different treatment based on the "status of those excluded"[77] has been that nonresident aliens have no ties to the United States and thus "lack any standing to complain that our Constitution has been violated."[78] However, despite Justice Breyer's argument that statutes that confer citizenship at birth "do not involve the transfer of loyalties that underlies the naturalization of aliens,"[79] children of citizens who claim their citizenship before majority do not necessarily have significantly stronger ties to the United States than do aliens who choose to become naturalized after birth. Nor is it the case that children like Ms. Miller necessarily have stronger ties to the United States than did the plaintiffs in *Fiallo*, who could only claim immigration preferences. Moreover, any justification for disparate treatment based on the status of the excluded will fail in this context because the constitutional right in the instant case belonged to Mr. Miller, a citizen, and the protection

[74] *See* 8 U.S.C. § 1101(a)(23) (1994).

[75] *See* Rogers v. Bellei, 401 U.S. 815, 841 (1971) (Black, J., dissenting) ("As shown in *Wong Kim Ark*, naturalization when used in its constitutional sense is a generic term describing and including within its meaning all those modes of acquiring American citizenship other than birth in this country."); *cf.* Anna Williams Shavers, *A Century of Developing Citizenship Law and the Nebraska Influence: A Centennial Essay*, 70 NEB. L. REV. 462, 512 (1991) ("We are thus left with two separate uses of the term naturalization — one by Congress and one by the Constitution.").

[76] United States v. Ginsberg, 243 U.S. 472, 475 (1917).

[77] Richard F. Hahn, Note, *Constitutional Limits on the Power to Exclude Aliens*, 82 COLUM. L. REV. 957, 966 (1982).

[78] Stephen H. Legomsky, *Immigration Law and The Principle of Plenary Congressional Power*, 1984 SUP. CT. REV. 255, 277 (citing Fiallo v. Bell, 430 U.S. 787 (1977)).

[79] *Miller*, 118 S. Ct. at 1458 (Breyer, J., dissenting).

accorded to that right should not depend on whether his daughter was an alien or a putative citizen.[80] Thus, a limited exception to *Fiallo* for statutes that confer citizenship at birth cannot be rooted in those justifications for Congress's plenary power that focus on the status of the excluded.

Moreover, it seems equally difficult to draw such an exception based on those justifications that rely on the "character of the exclusion power," and that "contend[] that it belongs to a special class of government powers not subject to constitutional limitations."[81] For instance, one commentator has characterized as "[p]erhaps the most popular theory in support of the plenary power doctrine" the theory that deferential scrutiny should be applied to immigration decisions that implicate foreign policy.[82] However, even if § 1409 falls outside this category in light of its domestic focus on reuniting families of citizens and noncitizens, the same could be said of a broader class of statutes than those that confer citizenship at birth.[83] Such statutes include those that regulate the right of alien spouses of citizens to reside in the United States,[84] as well as the statute in *Fiallo*, which bestowed immigration preferences on family members of citizens.

Similarly, another justification for Congress's plenary power, namely, that the power to exclude aliens is among a nation's sovereign powers,[85] cannot explain a narrow exception to *Fiallo*. The act of conferring citizenship on noncitizens, even if retroactive to the date of birth, is no less inherent in a nation's sovereignty than are other congressional powers over noncitizens. Even if one could argue that it were, there is still no basis, as some commentators have argued, for allowing the nation's sovereignty ever to trump with little justification the constitutional rights of citizens,[86] including, as was the case in

---

[80] *Cf.* T. Alexander Aleinikoff, *Federal Regulation of Aliens and the Constitution*, 83 AM. J. INT'L L. 862, 870 (1989) (arguing that "the mere fact that [a] policy burdens aliens should not be grounds for denying that Congress has an obligation" to offer "careful examination of the Government's justifications for such a policy").

[81] Hahn, *supra* note 77, at 965.

[82] Legomsky, *supra* note 78, at 261; *see also* Galvan v. Press, 347 U.S. 522, 530 (1954) ("The power of Congress over the admission of aliens and their right to remain is necessarily very broad, touching as it does basic aspects of national sovereignty, more particularly our foreign relations and the national security.").

[83] *See* Gerald M. Rosberg, *The Protection of Aliens From Discriminatory Treatment by the National Government*, 1977 SUP. CT. REV. 275, 318 ("Congress has placed so much emphasis on [the goal of family reunification] that our immigration scheme can reasonably be said to reflect a 'national policy of nepotism.'").

[84] *See, e.g.*, 8 U.S.C. § 1186a(a)(1), (b) (1994).

[85] *See* Shaughnessy v. United States *ex rel.* Mezei, 345 U.S. 206, 210 (1953) ("Courts have long recognized the power to expel or exclude aliens as a fundamental sovereign attribute exercised by the Government's political departments largely immune from judicial control.").

[86] *See, e.g.*, Kelly, *supra* note 4, at 778–80; David Moyce, *Petitioning on Behalf of an Alien Spouse: Due Process Under the Immigration Laws*, 74 CAL. L. REV. 1747, 1763–64 (1986).

Miller, the rights of citizens to be free from gender discrimination, as well as the fundamental right of a family to live together.[87]

Because there is no justification for carving out a narrow exception to *Fiallo* for statutes that confer citizenship at birth, *Miller v. Albright* may foreshadow a more general, and arguably desirable, move in immigration law toward increased protection of the constitutional rights of citizens. *Miller* may affect the resolution of a wide range of constitutional questions arising in immigration law, as the line between injury to citizen and injury to alien is often blurred. For instance, the Supreme Court's earlier decision in *Kleindienst v. Mandel*[88] illustrates that immigration statutes can implicate citizens' First Amendment right of association.[89] Similarly, current immigration laws arguably infringe on citizens' fundamental rights of marriage and marital privacy.[90] Thus, to the extent that it signals a move away from *Fiallo* even in cases that do not deal with statutes that confer citizenship at birth, *Miller v. Albright* may portend a significant extension of traditional constitutional norms into, and in turn a limitation on Congress's plenary power over, the area of immigration and naturalization.

---

[87] *See* Moore v. City of Cleveland, 431 U.S. 494, 504–06 (1977) (holding that the right of extended family members to live together is a fundamental right protected by substantive due process).

[88] 408 U.S. 753 (1972).

[89] *See id.* at 770.

[90] For example, one statute allows aliens who marry citizens to acquire permanent resident status after two years, conditional upon a subsequent showing that the marriage is bona fide. *See* 8 U.S.C. § 1186a(a)(1), (b) (1994). This statute has already drawn the critical attention of commentators for infringing upon the fundamental rights of citizens. *See, e.g.*, Kikuyo Matsumoto-Power, *Aliens, Resident Aliens, and U.S. Citizens in the Never-Never Land of the Immigration and Nationality Act*, 15 U. HAW. L. REV. 61, 76 (1993). However, courts, relying on *Fiallo*, have rejected challenges to related sections of the INA. *See, e.g.*, Azizi v. Thornburgh, 908 F.2d 1130, 1133 (2d Cir. 1990) (citing Fiallo v. Bell, 430 U.S. 787, 794 (1977)) (upholding 8 U.S.C. §§ 1154(h), 1255(e) (1994), which requires an alien who marries a U.S. citizen during the pendency of a deportation hearing to reside outside the country for two years).

UNITED STATES IMMIGRATION POLICY AND SEXUAL ORIENTATION: IS ASYLUM FOR HOMOSEXUALS A POSSIBILITY?

BRIAN J. MCGOLDRICK*

I. INTRODUCTION

Until very recently, the policy of the Immigration and Naturalization Service (INS) toward Homosexuals has been, not surprisingly, hostile. However, the passage of the Immigration Act of 1990 (1990 Act)[1] heralds a new era for Homosexuals coming to America. There is no longer a bar on Homosexuals entering the country. Today some Homosexuals are seeking refuge here because of persecution based on sexual orientation in their homelands.

The focus of this Article is to examine the current law on asylum claims based on persecution due to sexual orientation and to uncover hurdles practitioners must overcome to be successful in making such claims. Part two briefly examines the history of United States immigration policy towards Homosexuals and the impact of the 1990 Act on that policy. Part three looks at the current law regarding claims for asylum based on social group persecution in general. Part four is an analysis of two cases that demonstrate the concerns and prejudices courts will exhibit in asylum claims based on sexual orientation with some conclusions on what practitioners can do to assuage those concerns.

II. AMERICAN IMMIGRATION POLICY TOWARDS HOMOSEXUALS

A. *History Prior to the 1990 Act*

American policy towards Homosexuals has its roots, like most of our law, in the English common law.[2] The commonly held view of Homosexuals was that they were perpetrators of an "abominable crime against nature" whose penalty was death. This attitude toward Homosexuals

---

* Practitioner in Private Practice. B.A., University of California, Los Angeles, 1981; M.A., University of California, Berkeley, 1987; J.D., Southwestern University School of Law, 1993.

1. Immigration Act of 1990, Pub. L. No. 101-649, 104 Stat. 4978 (1990) (amending scattered sections of 8 U.S.C.) [hereinafter 1990 Act].

2. Jorge L. Carro, *From Constitutional Psychopathic Inferiority to AIDS: What is in the Future for Homosexual Aliens?*, 7 YALE L. & POL'Y REV. 201, 205 (1989).

came to America with the Pilgrims. To this day, some state statutes still address sodomy in those terms.[3]

However, for the first century of the nation's history, the ingress and egress of immigrants remained unfettered. America's open immigration policy changed as the numbers of immigrants began to rise exponentially and as citizens began to demand some curtailment.[4] Americans directed their xenophobia and bigotry against immigrants, leading to the enaction of numerous restrictive immigration laws.

The first immigration laws, beginning with the Chinese Exclusion Act of 1875,[5] targeted specific ethnic groups. The policy of excluding those deemed either inferior or undesirable subsequently received codification in the Immigration Act of 1917.[6] This act set out the provision and method for the exclusion of Homosexuals practiced until the passage of the 1990 Act. The Immigration Act of 1917 excluded any person that an examining physician certified as "mentally defective" or afflicted with a "constitutional inferiority."[7] Congress' requirement of a diagnosis by the Public Health System (PHS) became a crucial point in subsequent litigation. However, at the time of the act's passage, there were no problems with its provisions.

As Congress began to reexamine the immigration laws in the late 1940s and early 1950s, there was a determined interest by some members of Congress to make homosexuality a specific reason for exclusion from the United States.[8] Testimony from the PHS asserted that a specific clause was not necessary because, first, detecting Homosexuals was no easy task, and second, once detected, Homosexuals were clearly excludable as being afflicted with a psychopathic personality or a mental defect. Accordingly, the Immigration and Nationality Act of 1952 (INA)[9] did not specifically mention Homosexuals, but Congress' intention was clearly that they be excludable.[10]

The attempt to exclude a Lesbian from the United States challenged this notion in 1961. In *Quiroz v. Neelly*,[11] the plaintiff, a Lesbian, asserted that the term psychopathic personality did not necessarily refer to Homosexuals. The Fifth Circuit flatly rejected her argument stating that whatever psychiatrists may mean by psychopathic personality, Congress

---

3. *See, e.g.*, N.C. GEN. STAT § 14-177 (1992); R.I. GEN. LAWS § 11-10-1 (1992); S.C. CODE ANN. § 16-15-120 (1991) ("abominable crime of buggery" is punishable as a felony).
4. Carro, *supra* note 2, at 207-08.
5. Chinese Exclusion Act, ch. 141, 18 Stat. 477 (1875) (repealed 1974).
6. Peter N. Fowler & Leonard Graff, *Gay Aliens and Immigration*, 10 U. DAYTON L. REV. 621, 624 (1985).
7. *Id.* at 626.
8. *Id.* at 626 n.34 (citing S. REP. NO. 1515, 81st Cong., 2d Sess. 345 (1950)).
9. The McCarran-Walter Act is the popular name for the Immigration and Nationality Act. Immigration and Nationality Act of 1952, Pub. L. No. 82-412, 66 Stat. 163 (codified as amended in scattered sections of 8 U.S.C.) [hereinafter INA].
10. Fowler & Graff, *supra* note 6, at 627.
11. 291 F.2d 906 (5th Cir. 1961).

meant Homosexuals and perverts.[12] However, only one year later in *Fleuti v. Rosenberg*,[13] the Ninth Circuit ruled that the term was vague and therefore unconstitutional.[14] Congress acted swiftly in response to the Ninth Circuit's ruling and added "sexual deviation" to the list of reasons for exclusion.[15] In *Boutilier v. INS*,[16] the United States Supreme Court ruled that the term "sexual deviation" was not unconstitutionally vague. Further, the Court reaffirmed congressional dominance in the immigration field, recognizing that Congress has plenary power to exclude.[17]

After *Boutilier*, it seemed that only an act of Congress could bring relief to Homosexuals seeking admission to the United States. In fact, the decision led to a standard policy of aliens lying on their applications as to their mental capacity and sexual orientation.[18] However, this tactic was a two-edged sword, as deceiving the government as to admissibility was also grounds for exclusion.[19]

In 1973, the American Psychiatric Association removed homosexuality from its list of psychopathologies.[20] In 1979, the United States Surgeon General directed PHS employees to refrain from issuing certificates diagnosing homosexuality as a "psychopathic personality" or "sexual deviation."[21] Once removed from the list, Homosexuals began to assert that they were no longer excludable since the INA required that the INS receive a certificate of diagnosis from PHS.[22]

In 1983, the Ninth Circuit upheld a district court order staying the deportation of a Homosexual plaintiff.[23] The court further held that the statute clearly called for a determination by the PHS that a person be mentally defective.[24] Without such a certificate, the INS was not free to exclude Homosexuals simply on the basis of their homosexuality.[25]

The court spent considerable time reviewing the history of the relevant statute used to exclude Homosexuals and determined that Congress was clear in demanding the certificate from the PHS.[26] The court went on to note that the INS itself, the agency charged with interpreting and administering the statutes, had, until very recently,

---

12. *Id.* at 907.
13. 302 F.2d 652 (9th Cir. 1962), *vacated and remanded on other grounds*, 374 U.S. 449 (1963).
14. *Id.* at 658.
15. Fowler & Graff, *supra* note 6, at 629.
16. 387 U.S. 118 (1967).
17. *Id.*
18. *Id.*
19. Fowler & Graff, *supra* note 6, at 630.
20. Carro, *supra* note 2, at 213 n.80.
21. *Id.*
22. *Id.*
23. *In re Hill*, 714 F.2d 1470 (9th Cir. 1983).
24. *Id.*
25. *Id.*
26. *Id.* at 1477.

always demanded the certificate and without the certificate would not exclude an alien.[27] The court concluded:

> In sum, we find Congress' intent to require a medical examination and certification of all aliens excluded on medical grounds apparent on the face of the statute, corroborated by and legislated history, and supported by an unbroken string of administrative and judicial decisions. The judgment of the District court . . . is affirmed.[28]

However, that year the Fifth Circuit, in *In re Longstaff*,[29] held just the opposite. Longstaff, an alien seeking naturalization, revealed during the naturalization process that he was Homosexual. The INS determined that Longstaff was not eligible for naturalization because he was excludable as a Homosexual when he entered the United States, and admissibility is a requirement for naturalization.

In making its determination, although the Fifth Circuit also analyzed the history of the INA and its application, the court focused on congressional intent to exclude Homosexuals rather than on the procedures to be implemented. The court resolved the issue by holding that if someone admits he or she is Homosexual, a certificate is no longer necessary:[30]

> The procedural protection built into the exclusion process demonstrate Congress' intent that only competent evidence of medical excludability be adduced in exclusion proceedings. But there is no reason why an informed applicant's admission that he falls within an excludable class is not competent evidence on which to base an exclusion decision.[31]

Based on the conflicting decisions of the two circuits, the INS instituted a policy of excluding Homosexuals from entry everywhere except in the Ninth Circuit.[32]

B. *The 1990 Act: A Shift In Policy*

As enacted in 1952, section 212(a)(4) of the INA specifically excluded individuals with psychopathic personalities, sexual deviations, or mental defect.[33] As determined by the Supreme Court, Congress clearly in-

---

27. *Id.*
28. *Id.* at 1480 (footnote omitted).
29. 716 F.2d 1439 (5th Cir. 1983).
30. *Id.* at 1439.
31. *Id.*
32. Fowler & Graff, *supra* note 6, at 638.
33. *Id.* at 626; *see also* INA, § 212(a)(4), 8 U.S.C. § 1182(a)(4) (1988).

tended to exclude homosexuality even though it was not named as a grounds for exclusion.

As amended by the 1990 Act, section 212 revamps the former nineteen health-related categories into five new ones.[34] The pertinent section, 212(a)(1)(A)(ii), lists anyone with a "physical or mental disorder and behavior associated with the disorder that may pose, or has posed, a threat to the property, safety, or welfare of the alien or others" as excludable.[35] While the legislative history is clear that members of Congress wished to remove homosexuality as a ground for exclusion,[36] it is not so clear that they succeeded. It does not take much imagination to foresee a court ruling that allowing the entry of a Homosexual into a state that criminalizes sodomy is in fact a threat to the welfare of the citizens of that state. Again, most commentators agree that Homosexuals are no longer excludable, and Homosexuals are not being excluded at this time.[37] The courts have yet to test this theory. The 1990 Act does not affirmatively state that homosexuality is not a ground for exclusion. The only record of that is the legislative history and the removal of the previous language that was enacted specifically to exclude Homosexuals. It is certainly something to be wary of.

C. *The Current Effect of the 1990 Act: Asylum for Sexual Minorities*

Since the effective date of the 1990 Act, there have been no reports of exclusion on the basis of sexual orientation. On the contrary, the common perception of the 1990 Act is that it is a great step forward for the civil rights of Homosexuals.[38] Needless to say, the gay community has not been sitting on its hands since the 1990 Act's effective date, July 1991. The Lambda Legal Defense and Education Fund is sponsoring three cases for asylum for Homosexuals who fear persecution in their homelands.[39]

While the INA prior to amendment by the 1990 Act did not make asylum for Homosexuals impossible, it certainly discouraged anyone from trying. However, one Homosexual has successfully applied for asylum in the United States based on a well-founded fear of being

34. *See* 8 U.S.C. § 1182(a) (1990).
35. 8 U.S.C. § 1182(a)(1) (1990).
36. 136 CONG. REC. H12,358, H12,367 (daily ed. Oct. 27, 1990) (statement of Rep. Weiss).
37. 68 INTERPRETER RELEASES 288 n.10 (Mar. 11, 1991).
38. 136 CONG. REC. H12,358, H12,367 (daily ed. Oct. 27, 1990) (statement of Rep. Weiss).
39. Telephone Interview with Suzanne Goldberg, Staff Attorney, Lambda Legal Defense and Education Fund. *See also* J. Craig Fong, *Any Port in a Storm: Lambda's Lesbian & Gay Asylum Cases*, 10 THE LAMBDA UPDATE 4 (1993). Lambda co-sponsors suits with cooperating attorneys. Two of the three cases involve asylum based on sexual orientation, one alien is a Lesbian from Russia who has been incarcerated there for her orientation and one alien is a male from Iran who fears the death penalty should he be returned. The third case involves a gay Nicaraguan who is seropositive for HIV and fears deportation will mean substandard care. The Russian case was denied by the trial court and is on appeal. *Id.* at 4-5.

persecuted upon return to his homeland due to his membership in a particular social group, Homosexuals. Many more have been successful in other Western European countries.[40] The remainder of this Article focuses on the history of asylum based on membership in a social group and will evaluate the viability of this as a means for Homosexuals to flee persecution abroad.

III. REFUGEES IN INTERNATIONAL LAW

A. *International Standards for Determining Asylum*

The constitution of the International Refugee Organization (IRO) provides the original definition of a refugee.[41] This definition did not include membership in a social group as one of the categories describing refugees. During the Conference of Plenipotentiaries of the Convention on Refugees, the Swedish representative pointed out that the definition adopted by the Convention would be too restrictive if limited to those categories set out in the IRO.[42] The convention adopted a proposal to include membership in a social group as part of the definition.[43] The definition of a refugee in the Convention describes a person who:

> [a]s a result of events occurring before 1 January 1951 and owing to a well-founded fear of being persecuted for reasons of race, religion, nationality, membership of a particular social group or political opinion, is outside the country of his nationality and is unable or, owing to such fear, is unwilling to avail himself of the protection of that country; or who, not having a nationality and being outside the country of his former habitual residence as a result of such events, is unable or, owing to such fear, unwilling to return to it.[44]

The Protocol to the Convention of 1967 further amended the definition.[45] The Protocol omitted the words "[a]s a result of events occurring before 1 January 1951 . . ." and "as a result of such events."[46]

While the Convention and the Protocol both set out membership in a social group as a basis of refugee status, neither provides a clear definition of what constitutes a social group. This is not uncommon

---

40. *See, e.g.*, T. David Parish, *Membership in a Particular Social Group Under the Refugee Act of 1980: Social Identity and the Legal Concept of the Refugee*, 92 COLUM. L. REV. 923, 950 & n.154.

41. Arthur C. Helton, *Persecution on Account of Membership in a Social Group as a Basis for Refugee Status*, 15 COLUM. HUM. RTS. L. REV. 39, 40 (1983).

42. *Id.* at 41.

43. 189 U.N.T.S. 137, U.N. Doc A/CONF.2/108 (1951).

44. *Id.*, art. 1 § A(2).

45. 19 U.S.T. 6223, T.I.A.S. No. 6577, 606 U.N.T.S. 267 [hereinafter Protocol].

46. *Id.*, art. 1, para. 2.

since conventions are not the only source of international law.[47] Custom is also an established source of international law, and conventions that state general principles are usually an embodiment of customary law.[48] The practices of states establish custom in international law.[49] Thus to clearly understand the meaning of "social group" we must look to how members of the international community have interpreted the phrase.

The first source we may turn to is the Handbook on Procedures and Criteria for Determining Refugee Status (Handbook), adopted by the United Nations High Commissioner for Refugees.[50] This is the most current articulation of refugee status in international law. The Handbook sets out general parameters for defining a social group, including persecutor-based definitions.

The introduction to the Handbook states that it is a guide to assist contracting parties to the Convention and the Protocol in interpreting the Convention.[51] It also states that the basic elements of the Handbook are the practices of states from 1954 (the date the Convention went into force) until the drafting of the Handbook.[52] The Handbook goes on to define social group as one that "normally comprises persons of similar background, habits and social status."[53] This definition appears so broad as to be vague when taken by itself. While this may appear to be, when read in conjunction with the other provisions in the Handbook and the practice of states since the Convention went into force, some guidelines are evident.

The Handbook establishes that social groups are externally identifiable, rather than by some internal aspect of the group. The persecutor's perceptions are important:

> Membership in a particular social group may be at the root of persecution because there is no confidence in the group's loyalty to the Government or because the political outlook, antecedents or economic activity of its members or the very existence of the social group as such, is held to be an obstacle to the Government's policies.[54]

What this means is that while the members of a particular group may not voluntarily associate, or do not have some immutable characteristic,

---

47. MICHAEL AKEHURST, A MODERN INTRODUCTION TO INTERNATIONAL LAW 23 (4th ed. 1982).
48. *Id.*
49. *Id.* at 25.
50. Handbook on Procedures and Criteria for Determining Refugee Status, U.N. Doc. HCR/PRO/4 (1979) [hereinafter Handbook].
51. *Id.* at para. v-vi.
52. *Id.*
53. *Id.* at para. 77.
54. *Id.* at para. 78.

it is enough that the government nonetheless perceives them as a social group. This distinction may be important for some claims for asylum.

The Handbook is not so broad as to allow any member of any group to assert refugee status based solely on his or her membership without some further proof of persecution. In conjunction with membership in the group, the refugee must show "special circumstances" to be successful in his or her claim.[55] As shall be shown, American courts have tried to keep the doors shut to social group claims by narrowing the definition of a social group. However, the original intent was to keep the social group criteria flexible and to narrow the number of claimants by making them show these special circumstances. The circumstances are simply the facts that give rise to a well-founded fear.

It is not easy to decide what the special circumstances may be. For example, in retrospect, one would not deny that anyone of Jewish ancestry fleeing Germany during the early 1940s would have a valid claim for asylum. One would not expect applicants to demonstrate that they base their fears on specific actions against them. Based on the circumstances, a reasonable person would assume that any Jew would be afraid of persecution. On the other hand, a Jew seeking asylum from France today would have a heavy burden to show that his or her membership in the Jewish community was the basis of persecution.

Finally, the Handbook establishes that a well-founded fear:

> need not necessarily be based on the applicant's own personal experience. What, for example, happened to his friends and relatives and other members of the same racial or social group may well show that his fear that sooner or later he also will become a victim of persecution is well-founded.[56]

This goes even further in establishing that a court may grant asylum to an individual based on external criteria such as the persecutor's perception of the refugee and how the persecutor has treated others in the group.

The Handbook, with its liberal attitude toward asylum based on social group, is not the only source to consider. As already mentioned, the Swedish delegate to the commission preparing the Convention argued for this group because the others, sex, race, nationality, and political opinion, were too restrictive.[57] The social groups seeking asylum at the time were members of the business class who were under persecution by

---

55. *Id.* at para. 79.
56. *Id.* at para. 43.
57. Daniel Compton, *Asylum for Persecuted Social Groups: A Closed Door Left Slightly Ajar*—Sanchez-Trujillo v. INS, *801 F.2d 1571 (9th Cir. 1986)*, 62 WASH. L. REV. 913, 925 (1987).

communist regimes. The perception and political opinion of the oppressor, not the oppressed, formed the basis of these claims.[58]

During the preparation of the Protocol to the Convention,[59] a special consultant to the United Nations High Commissioner for Refugees wrote:

> The notion of "social group" is of broader application than the combined notions of racial, ethnic, and religious groups and in order to stop a possible gap, the conference felt that it would be as well to mention this reason for persecution explicitly. . . . Nobility, capitalists, landowners, civil servants, businessmen, professional people, farmers, workers, members of a linguistic or other minority, even members of certain associations, clubs, or societies, all constitute social groups of various kinds.[60]

International law may be established by the practice of states.[61] How other nations have treated claims for asylum must also receive consideration. For example, former members of the bourgeoisie in Hungary were successful in their claim for asylum based on their status as landowners.[62] They made no plea for refuge based on their political opinion, but instead argued that the new government was communist and they were the objects of persecution because they were landowners.[63] Other cases in Europe have recognized very broad parameters for social groups.[64] The critical point of analysis in these cases was the perceptions of the persecutors, and whether this led to a well-founded fear of the groups being persecuted, not the attributes.[65] This is a fact we must keep in mind when analyzing the current position of American courts and the Board of Immigration Appeals (BIA).

In relation to Homosexuals then, while it is safe to assume that the Convention did not have sexual minorities specifically in mind when the Convention was ratified, it is clear that the intent of the Convention was to accommodate groups that did not get specific enumeration. The Convention intended that individuals that are members of particular

---

58. *Id.* at 926.

59. Protocol, *supra* note 45. The United States is a party to the Protocol.

60. Maureen Graves, *From Definition to Exploration: Social Groups and Political Asylum Eligibility*, 26 SAN DIEGO L. REV. 739, 748 (1989) (citing UN Doc. A/CONF.2/SR.19, at 14 (1951)).

61. AKEHURST, *supra* note 47, at 25.

62. Compton, *supra* note 57, at 927.

63. *See* Case 2053 II/55 (Feb. 4, 1957) (Bayersches Verwaltungsgerict Ansbach, West Germany)

64. Case 3008 II/57 (Nov. 25, 1957) ("independent businessmen"); Case 2531 II/56 (Jan. 15, 1957) ("textile manufacturer"); Refugee Sur Place case, 57 I.L.R. 324, 326 (1966) (The German Supreme Court agreed that the capitalist class was a social group for consideration of asylum. The petition was not granted because the petitioner was the wife of a tailor, a group not subject to persecution).

65. Helton, *supra* note 42, at 47.

social groups who could show that they were under persecution due to their membership in that social group have a right to relief, regardless whether the groups were landowners, union members, or Homosexuals.

B. *The United States' Attempt To Conform With International Standards: Adoption of the Refugee Act of 1980*

Prior to the adoption of the Refugee Act of 1980 (Refugee Act), the Attorney General had the discretionary power to "withhold deportation of any alien . . . to any country in which in his opinion the alien would be subject to physical persecution" on account of race, religion, or political opinion.[66] Because the United States had become a party to the Protocol to the Convention Relating to the Status of Refugees,[67] Congress decided to update the INA. It was the intent of Congress to make United States law conform to the Protocol.[68] The Supreme Court recognized this and stated:

> If one thing is clear from the legislative history of the new definition of "refugee", and indeed the entire 1980 Act, it is that one of Congress' primary purposes was to bring the United States refugee law into conformance with the 1967 United Nations Protocol Relating to the Status of Refugees, to which the United States acceded in 1968.[69]

Under the INA, there are two remedies available for aliens subjected to persecution in their homelands. First, asylum is available to aliens who have a well-founded fear of persecution in their homelands due to race, religion, nationality, membership in a social group, or political opinion.[70] This is a discretionary grant reserved to the Attorney General. Second, withholding of deportation is a mandatory relief from the courts where a deportable alien shows a clear probability of persecution based on the same criteria.[71]

Both of these options now offered in the Act are an incorporation of the Protocol. The application of these sections should take into account the history and meaning of the terms in the Protocol. The United States Supreme Court has recognized that "where . . . Congress adopts a new law incorporating sections of a prior law, Congress normally can be presumed to have had knowledge of the interpretation given to the

66. Pub. L. No. 82-414, § 243(h), 66 Stat. 163 (codified as amended at 8 U.S.C. § 1253(h) (1993)).
67. 114 CONG. REC. 29,607 (1968).
68. Graves, *supra* note 60, at 743.
69. INS v. Cardoza-Fonseca, 480 U.S. 421, 436-37 (1987).
70. 8 U.S.C. § 1101(a)(42) (1982).
71. 8 U.S.C. § 1253(h) (1982).

incorporated law, at least insofar as it affects the new statute."[72] If Congress had intended to make the social group criterion more restrictive than it is in international law, certainly it would have done so. As we shall see, domestic decisions seem to be restricting this interpretation on their own.

IV. DOMESTIC LAW SINCE INCORPORATION OF THE ACT INTERPRETING MEMBERSHIP IN A SOCIAL GROUP

A. *Domestic Interpretations of Social Group*

In determining whether an alien is eligible for asylum due to persecution based on membership in a particular social group, the courts and the BIA have had to grapple with defining the term "social group." Irrespective of the history of the Refugee Act, it is appropriate to look to the language itself to make an initial determination. As Justice Powell noted, "[t]he starting point in every case involving construction of a statute is the language itself."[73]

Arthur C. Helton, in his analysis of the term, assigns four basic meanings to it.[74] First, a social group can be statistical, such as left-handed males. This statistical group, of itself, has no significance in terms of persecution and asylum. However, a state could turn such a group into a significant one. It was not so long ago that some people considered left-handed people "sinister" and untrustworthy.[75] The statistical group then may become the focus of persecution, if there is an imputation of a characteristic.

Second, a group may be societal.[76] These are people who share common immutable characteristics and are aware of themselves as a group. Examples are women, Blacks and Homosexuals.

The third group is the social group *per se*.[77] These are the voluntary groups such as acquaintance groups, congregations, etc. The common interests of the people involved are what form the group.

The fourth group identified by Helton is the associational form of social group.[78] This is different from the third group in that members join to actively pursue a common goal. This would include groups like the YWCA or trade unions.

72. Lorillard v. Pons, 434 U.S. 575, 581 (1981).
73. Blue Chip Stamps v. Manor Drug Stores, 421 U.S. 723, 756 (1975) (Powell, J., concurring).
74. Helton, *supra* note 42, at 51.
75. Sinistre-M.E. and O.F.; from Latin, meaning "left-hand." OXFORD ENGLISH DICTIONARY 87 (4th ed. 1978).
76. Helton, *supra* note 42, at 51.
77. *Id.* at 52.
78. *Id.*

Helton describes the groups as follows:

> To indicate how these groups grow out of one another, let us consider an example. Redheaded people do not ordinarily associate with one another simply because they are redheaded. All people who have red hair, nevertheless, do constitute a statistical group, and it is important for clothing manufacturers, dress designers, hairdressers, and various others to know roughly how many redheaded people there are. It is a fact that has statistical, but not yet much sociological, significance.
>
> Suppose, however, that the government, through some capricious legislation, should impose a tax upon redheaded people. They would then become a societal group, a group conscious of their kind. They would be united not only in their possession of red hair . . . but also in their opposition to the tax. They would then begin to greet each other as fellow-sufferers of discrimination. . . . If they would then formally organize and establish a Redheaded League in order to resist the legislation, the league would be the fourth kind of group, an association.[79]

When courts attempt to make sense of the term "social group" for asylum purposes they must take these common meanings into consideration.

The leading case considered by the BIA, the agency body that reviews decisions by immigration courts, is *In re Acosta*.[80] Gilberto Acosta-Solorzano was a native of El Salvador. In 1976, Acosta and several others formed a cooperative of taxis calling themselves COTAXI. At that time guerrillas in El Salvador were attempting to disrupt the government by organizing general work stoppages. When approached by the guerrillas, the board of COTAXI, Acosta included, refused to cooperate with the insurgents. Eventually, the directors of the co-op began to report being abducted by riders and threatened if they did not cooperate with the insurgents. Subsequently, some of the directors were murdered, evidently the work of the guerrillas. Acosta fled to the United States after he endured an abduction, beating, and received a death threat.[81] Upon capture in the United States, Acosta applied for political asylum.[82]

Acosta's general claim was persecution based on membership in a social group—namely, his membership in COTAXI. The INS issued a ruling against his petition, stating that he did not suffer persecution due to race, religion, nationality, membership in a particular social group, or

79. *Id.* (citing ROBERT BIERSTEDT, THE SOCIAL ORDER 258 (1957)).
80. 19 I. & N. Dec. 211 (BIA 1985).
81. *Id.* at 216-18.
82. *Id.*

political opinion.[83] At his hearing, the immigration judge (IJ) also denied his petition, finding that Acosta had not met the criteria set out in the Refugee Act.[84] As a result, Acosta appealed to the BIA.

A major question the BIA faced was reaching a workable definition of "social group" as used in the Refugee Act. In reaching a definition the BIA recognized the role of the Protocol in Congress enacting the Refugee Act and began its analysis with the Handbook:[85]

> Since Congress intended the definition of a refugee in section 101(a)(42)(A) of the [Refugee] Act to conform to the Protocol, it is appropriate for us to consider various international interpretations of that agreement. However, these interpretations are not binding upon us . . . for the determination of who should be considered a refugee is ultimately left by the Protocol to each state in whose territory a refugee finds himself.[86]

The BIA admitted that the Protocol suggests a broader definition than the other terms used to identify refugees.[87] However, the BIA simply dismissed the meaning in the Protocol as only suggestive and decided to adopt the doctrine *ejusdem generis,* literally "of the same kind," to determine the meaning Congress had in mind.[88] The BIA then focused on the other four criteria which would allow for asylum and reasoned that since they were narrow, restrictive terms, Congress must have meant that social group also be as restrictive.[89] The BIA ultimately determined that:

> the other grounds of persecution in the Act and the Protocol listed in association with "membership in a particular social group" are persecution on account of "race," "religion," "nationality," and "political opinion." Each of these grounds describes persecution aimed at an immutable characteristic: a characteristic that either is beyond the power of an individual to change or is so fundamental to individual identity or conscience that it ought not be required to be changed.[90]

83. *Id.*

84. *Id.* The immigration judge also ruled that while Acosta was a credible witness, his testimony would be stricken because it was self-serving without complete corroboration. The BIA found this part of the immigration judge's decision erroneous and stated that the petitioner's facts must be accepted if the witness is found to be credible. *Id.* This is extremely important in showing persecution based on sexual orientation. The dissenting judge in *In re Inaudi* decided against the applicant because the judge found his testimony regarding rape insupportable. Credibility is a major issue in asylum cases. *See infra* text accompanying note 109.

85. *In re Acosta*, 19 I. & N. Dec. at 231-32.

86. *Id.*

87. *Id.*

88. *Id.*

89. *Id.*

90. *Id.* at 233.

By construing the term in this fashion, the BIA easily dismissed Acosta's claim that his membership in COTAXI was a valid basis for asylum. His membership was not a fundamental or immutable characteristic. In a very facile way, the BIA suggested that all Acosta had to do was to change jobs to avoid persecution.[91] Evidently, the BIA did not feel that Acosta's freedom to choose his profession was so fundamental that he should receive protection from being threatened into a new profession. The question we must keep in mind is whether homosexuality is an immutable characteristic or so fundamental to a person's identity there should not be a requirement for he or she to change. As Graves notes:

> The BIA test permits the ready characterization of claims as definitionally inadequate—because the characteristics involved are apparently "mutable" or not self-evidently "fundamental"—without an examination of either the actual risk a person faces because of them, or the real feasibility of obtaining safety at home. Neither *In re Acosta* nor subsequent BIA decisions explain how "fundamental" characteristics are to be identified, or even whether the concept is a descriptive one aimed at identifying the actual centrality of given activities to applicants' lives, or a normative one aimed at protecting only traits the "we" judge fundamental.[92]

Several courts have recognized the broad scope of social group based claims and have not tried to define them. For example, in *Castaneda-Hernandez v. INS*,[93] a twenty-four-year-old Salvadoran male argued that he risked persecution because he was a single male, of military age, had not served and had fled the country. He argued that were he returned, others would consider him very suspicious and that he would be subject to persecution. He also presented testimony that supported the belief that the government targets males who have not served in the military for persecution. The Fourth Circuit remanded the case, and noted that the BIA had too easily dismissed the evidence and testimony produced by the alien.[94]

The Ninth Circuit, in *Sanchez-Trujillo v. INS*,[95] addressed the meaning of "social group" head-on and seems the clearest articulation in federal courts today. In that case the aliens, Sanchez and Escobar, conceded deportability at their joint hearing in 1982 but petitioned for asylum based on persecution due to membership in a particular social group. The two alleged that young, urban, working-class males who had

---

91. *Id.*
92. Graves, *supra* note 60, at 772-73.
93. 802 F.2d 1518 (4th Cir. 1986).
94. *Id.* at 1523.
95. 801 F.2d 1571 (9th Cir. 1986).

not served in the military or otherwise expressed support for the government of El Salvador constituted a social group, and that as members of that group they were subject to persecution by the government.[96]

The court began its analysis by recognizing that the Handbook was a valuable source to determine what Congress had in mind when it adopted the Refugee Act.[97] The court found that the definition in the Handbook was too broad and so, rather than look to other sources of international law to determine its meaning in international law, sought to create its own definition. After dismissing other relevant case law, the court announced a four-part test to determine social group status under the Refugee Act.[98] The court held:

> In determining whether the petitioners have established eligibility for relief premised upon group membership, four questions must be answered. First, we must decide whether the class of people identified by the petitioners is cognizable as a "particular social group" under the immigration statutes. Second, the petitioners must have established that they qualify as members of the group. Third, it must be determined whether the purported "social group" has in fact been targeted for persecution on account of the characteristics of the group members. Finally, we must consider whether such "special circumstances" are present to warrant us in regarding mere membership in that "social group" as constituting per se eligibility for asylum or prohibition of deportation.[99]

The key to this definition is, of course, the first criterion. The court left itself open to making the determination of whether the group is cognizable because it dismissed both national and international precedent. In trying to reach that definition, the court stated:

> The statutory words "particular" and "social" which modify "group," indicate that the term does not encompass every broadly defined segment of a population, even if a certain demographic division does have some statistical relevance. Instead the phrase "particular social group" implies a collection of people closely affiliated with each other, who are actuated by some common impulse or interest. Of central concern is the existence of a voluntary associational relationship among the purported members, which imparts some common characteristic that is fundamental to their identity as a member of that discrete social group.

96. *Id.* at 1573.
97. *Id.* at 1574.
98. *Id.*
99. *Id.* at 1574-75 (citation omitted).

> Perhaps a prototypical example of a "particular social group" would consist of the immediate members of a certain family, the family being a focus of fundamental affiliational concerns and common interests for most people.[100]

By insisting on this volitional association, the court ruled out the other three groups that Helton had established, narrowed its definitions far beyond what the international community had in mind, and also ruled out the perceptions of the persecutor in determining whether the group exists. Graves noted that this only makes sense if the court had an agenda, and she identified that agenda as a serious effort to limit the availability of social group based claims.[101] Regardless of its agenda, the court has left us with an odd definition of what constitutes a social group for asylum purposes.

IV. HOMOSEXUALS AS A SOCIAL GROUP

The next logical question seems to be whether Homosexuals meet the criteria for the test. Several foreign courts and one domestic court have ruled that Homosexuals do meet the requirements for social group based claims for asylum. We shall focus on two of those cases to analyze which test they comply with and what problems we can expect for Homosexuals trying to make asylum claims in the future.

A. In re Toboso

In *In re Toboso,*[102] the BIA upheld the IJ's order to withhold deportation. Fidel Toboso-Alfonso initially came to the United States as part of the Mariel Boatlift in 1980. Toboso testified that while he lived in Cuba it became known to the authorities that he was a Homosexual. The authorities subsequently subjected him to periodic "examinations." These "examinations" included physical examinations and interrogations about his sexual partners. He went on to say that frequently, he would be held by the police after the exams for three to four days, without being charged.

These exams did not occur because of any specific activity of Toboso but merely because he was on the list of Homosexuals. He further testified that, at the time of the boat lift, the government forced him to leave and threatened that if he did not leave, the government would send him to prisons for four years because he was a Homosexual. Toboso chose to leave the country.[103] While in the United States,

100. *Id.* at 1576 (citation omitted).
101. Graves, *supra* note 60, at 782.
102. No. A23 220 644 (BIA Mar. 12, 1990).
103. *Id.* slip op. at 1-4.

Toboso was convicted for drug-related crimes and the INS subsequently ordered him to show cause why he should not be deported. The IJ found it was more likely than not that Toboso would suffer persecution upon return to Cuba due to his membership in the social group of Homosexuals.[104] The INS appealed, arguing that Homosexuals did not constitute a social group as defined under the Refugee Act and that Toboso had not shown a well-founded fear of persecution. The BIA dismissed both of these contentions.[105]

The BIA held that Homosexuals did in fact constitute a social group eligible for asylum in the United States. The BIA initially focused on the INS' contention that because Homosexual activity is illegal in Cuba, Homosexuals could not constitute the requisite type of group. The BIA reasoned that this would mean any group of criminals who suffer prosecution would be eligible for a claim of asylum. The BIA was careful to note that Toboso did not suffer persecution because of any particular act, but because of his status as a Homosexual.[106] Recalling its previous ruling in *In re Acosta*, the BIA noted that there was no objection to the IJ's finding that homosexuality was an "immutable characteristic."[107]

Toboso had testified that he was a practicing Homosexual since he was nine and that his repeated interrogations were as a result of his status, not because of his activities.[108] The BIA seemed to think this was important in relation to his social group status, but did not elaborate. The dissent did not make any statements as to the status of homosexuality generally or whether Homosexuals could ever achieve the status necessary for asylum. Rather, the dissent insisted that the interrogations were a result of the criminality of Homosexual activity and so were valid criminal investigations.[109]

The BIA seemed to be implying that Homosexuals' status was a result of their activity and so they could never qualify for asylum. To successfully meet the BIA's immutable characteristics requirement, it will be important to show that the persecution suffered has to do with status and not activity, particularly where the activity is illegal. Citing *Bowers v. Hardwick*,[110] the dissent noted that prosecution under laws against homosexuality would not qualify one for asylum since our Supreme Court has recognized that governments may enact anti-sodomy laws.

In *In re Acosta*, the BIA found that social group status required an immutable characteristic or a characteristic so fundamental that there

104. *Id.* slip op. at 2.
105. *Id.* slip op. at 4.
106. *Id.*
107. *Id.*
108. *Id.* slip op. at 1 (dissenting opinion).
109. *Id.* slip op. at 2.
110. 478 U.S. 186 (1986).

should not be any requirement to change it.[111] The dissenting opinion in *In re Toboso* seemed to indicate that the decision in *Bowers* precluded a grant of asylum by legitimating state condemnation of homosexual activity. Therefore, the dissent appeared to reason, homosexual activity was not so fundamental that it deserved protection. However, because *Bowers* dealt with the legality of certain sexual acts, not the legal status of identifying oneself as Homosexual, it would appear that an alien might be able to make a successful asylum claim if he or she could show that the state responded to the individual's identity, rather than his or her actions.

In terms of persecution, the BIA saw the acts of the government, particularly the extended incarcerations without charge and the final threat of prison if Toboso did not leave, as acts against Toboso because of his homosexuality, not his activities:

> The applicant's testimony that simply because of his status as a homosexual he was advised by his government to leave the country or face incarceration for a period of four years is not contested. There is no evidence or allegation that this "choice" he was given resulted from any specific acts on his part or that the government did not intend to jail him if he failed to leave. The record indicates that rather than a penalty for misconduct, this action resulted from the government's desire that all homosexuals be forced to leave their homeland.[112]

The BIA concluded that Toboso's persecution was not the result of specific acts. Once again, the BIA distinguished between status and activity. This tactic seemed adequately to undermine the dissent's position.

The dissent based its argument on the illegality of homosexual activity in Cuba. The dissent characterized the examinations as legitimate health and crime-related investigations that did not amount to persecution. Again, citing *Bowers*, the dissent noted that Homosexuals did not enjoy fundamental rights as to sexual activity. Therefore, Cuba was free to enact sodomy laws, carry out investigations, and even incarcerate persons guilty of the crime.

The dissent failed, however, to answer the crucial question: does the use of sodomy laws to investigate someone who has not committed a crime amount to persecution? Toboso was not under continual interrogation because he was a criminal. He suffered these humiliations because of his status as a Homosexual. It is just this kind of governmen-

111. *In re Acosta*, 19 I. & N. Dec. at 233 (BIA 1985).
112. *In re Toboso*, No. A23 220 644, slip. op. at 5.

tal abuse of process that constitutes persecution rather than prosecution.

Unfortunately, the Attorney General did not publish the *In re Toboso* opinion as precedent. Regardless, it is instructive for future cases. The BIA seems willing to accept Homosexuals as an appropriate classification for social group claims. One should remember that each applicant must show not only group membership but persecution or a well-founded fear of persecution. The persecution must be on account of status, not activity, at least where the activity is illegal.

One must wonder whether the Ninth Circuit would have decided in Toboso's favor given its test as set out in *Sanchez-Trujillo*. As noted above, the crucial factor for the court is the "existence of a voluntary associational relationship among the purported members, which imparts some common characteristic that is fundamental to their identity as a member of the discrete social group."[113] What voluntary associational relationship exists among gay Cubans?

It is arguable that the common characteristic is the commission of illegal acts. What creates the voluntary association is the willingness to engage in criminal activity. It is cases such as these that manifest the inadequacy of the Ninth Circuit test of voluntary association. We have few facts about the social relationships of Toboso, but if his only voluntary associations with other Homosexuals were clandestine sexual encounters, that would seem to be the common characteristic fundamental to his identity. The INS' and the dissent's case against Toboso appears much stronger under this test. The definition of status under the test is activity and association.

The Ninth Circuit in *Sanchez-Trujillo* was responding to a claim based on statistical groupings rather than on social groups in the sense outlined by Helton. The court was trying to set outer limits to the claim. The court did recognize that previous decisions were instructive in particular cases. For instance, it recognized that "characteristics that are essentially beyond the petitioner's power to change" were adequate criteria for a First Circuit claim.[114] This indicates that certain circumstances may require different tests. For Toboso's claim to pass muster he must convince the court of the inadequacy of its test where the voluntary association is illegal. That is the very basis of the claim of persecution. It is not the illegal activity which defines the group. What brings the members secretly together is not the sexual activity but their basic identities as Homosexuals.

---

113. Sanchez-Trujillo v. INS, 801 F.2d 1571, 1576 (9th Cir. 1986).
114. *Id.* at 1575 (quoting Ananeh-Firempong v. INS, 766 F.2d 621, 626 (1st Cir. 1985)).

B. *Canada's Attempt To Define Social Group*

Early this year Canada granted asylum to a gay Argentine man named Jorge Alberto Inaudi. Canada is also party to the Protocol,[115] and uses identical language to define a refugee as is used in the Refugee Act.[116] Unlike American courts, in Canadian courts there are two judges who sit at a hearing for refugee status with only one vote necessary for asylum. Both the assenting and dissenting opinions in *In re Inaudi*[117] are useful because the court was grappling with similar issues regarding social group definition and refugee status for Homosexuals. Of particular interest is the dissent's attitude toward the witness' credibility and how the dissent supports that attitude. Anyone preparing a similar case should keep these in mind.

Jorge Alberto Inaudi was born in Argentina and claimed that he was aware of his sexual orientation from an early age and suffered for it in school.[118] As an adult his first painful experience came while serving in the military. The military learned about his romantic liaison with another soldier and incarcerated him for eight days.[119] He subsequently had to bribe his superior for the remainder of his service to avoid having his charges made public.[120]

Inaudi lived in Cordoba for several years from the time he finished his military service until several years later when he first encountered the police in 1985.[121] On that occasion, his landlady secured his release and then evicted him from his apartment.[122] There were several repetitions of this scenario. When the police caught Inaudi in a gay bar or at a gay area of town they forced him to pay a bribe for them to release him.[123] If he didn't have the bribe, the police would contact his landlord and his employer and reveal his sexual orientation. This would lead to Inaudi's dismissal from his job and eviction from his apartment. He also reported being beaten by the police on several occasions.[124]

As the violence and the repercussions increased, so did Inaudi's fear and he refrained from going to gay bars for a while. Eventually, he met someone and established a stable relationship. While at a party for a friend, someone suggested that everyone go to a gay bar. Inaudi and his lover accompanied the group. On the way, the police stopped the group and took the entire group to the station. Inaudi complained of his

---

115. Protocol, *supra* note 45. The Protocol entered into force for Canada on June 4, 1969.

116. In re Inaudi, T91-04459 (Can. Immigr. & Refugee Bd. 1992). All references to Canadian Law will be as cited in the decision.

117. *Id.*

118. *Id.*

119. *Id.*

120. *Id.* at 1.

121. *Id.*

122. *Id.* at 2.

123. *Id.*

124. *Id.*

treatment by the police and demanded that they stop mistreating Homosexuals without cause.[125] The police then took him and, according to Inaudi, severely tortured him. According to his testimony, the police stripped him, tied him to a wall, and repeatedly raped him. Although he pled for them to stop, they continued his torture by beating him and applying electrodes to his genitals:

> My hands were tied together over my head onto a clamp or something. I was on my tiptoes. Two people entered my cell. One of them said I was a rebellious faggot. I was told to get ready for the first session. I was beaten with billy clubs and fists. I was then stripped naked and sodomized. After the rape, I was left alone, naked and still tied up. From that time on, I was released. Later, I was taken to another room—a torture chamber. I was tied to the walls in a spread-eagle fashion and beaten and given electric shocks to sensitive parts of my body. I could hear the screams of others being tortured the same way.
>
> When I was taken back to my cell, I apologized for my behavior at the police station in Cordoba and asked for forgiveness. The police told me that I was on file. From my cell, I could hear the screams of other men and women who were being tortured. Later, I was returned to the torture chamber and tortured with electricity and threatened with death. I was verbally abused and raped. Then I was taken back to my cell and tied up. I begged for forgiveness and was told that was all for the day. Later someone came in and raped me and then left me alone. I lost all notion of time.[126]

After four days of torture, Inaudi woke up on the side of a road, found his way back to his home and began planning his trip to Canada.[127] Shortly after his arrival, he sought protection as a refugee.

The assenting judge had to determine whether Homosexuals constituted a social group within the meaning of the Protocol and Canada's statute. Echoing the standard set out in the American *Acosta* case, the court determined that homosexuality was an immutable characteristic. The court went on to claim that even if it found homosexuality only to be a voluntary condition, it was one "so fundamental to a person's identity that a claimant ought not to be compelled to change it."[128] Based on these qualities, both the assenting and dissenting judges agreed that Homosexuals do qualify as a social group for convention purposes.[129]

---

125. *Id.* at 8. The opinion reports that private homosexual activity among men over the age of 22 is not prohibited in Argentina.

126. Excerpt of Inaudi's testimony as reported in 3 TEMA INT'L 8 (Spring 1992).

127. *In re Inaudi*, at 4.

128. *Id.* at 5.

129. *Id.* at 11.

The court proceeded to determine whether Inaudi's treatment amounted to persecution. The standard was "persecution due to membership in a particular social group,"[130] not just membership alone. The court pointed out that homosexual activity was not illegal for males over the age of twenty-two and therefore, Inaudi was not suffering any legal prosecution by the police. The court cited several publications to support the claim that Homosexuals continued to suffer persecution in Argentina. In fact, when leaders of the Buenos Aires-based group, Comunidad Homosexual Argentina, went public with their attempt to have the organization given legal status, someone, presumably the police, published all their names and identity card numbers and they all lost their jobs.[131] These facts that corroborated the witness' testimony led the court to believe Inaudi's claims of persecution and ultimately to grant him asylum.

The dissent's reasoning is alarming and is as important for future claims as is the fact that asylum was granted. Most of the dissent's problems with the case stemmed from the judge's firm belief that macho, heterosexual men do not rape other men:

> I find implausible that a police force that allegedly hunts homosexuals would itself take part in sexual assaults that would involve the very activities it finds so disturbing including homosexual sexual contact. Would that not leave police open to blackmail by other officers—mirroring what happened to the claimant in the army?[132]

This opinion evidences a complete lack of understanding of both human sexuality and the motives behind torture and rape. Research has shown that rape is primarily an act of violence and domination, rather than a sexual act.[133] Part of the cult of *machismo* is dominating other men as well as women. What could be more degrading and emasculating in the eyes of these men than to make other men submit to them sexually? As long as the officers continue to view this as an act to dominate, rather than to be sexually fulfilled, their comrades are not going to extort them but extol them for their ability completely to dominate another male.[134] While this certainly is not the mindset of the

130. Protocol, *supra* note 45, Art. 1.2.
131. *In re Inaudi*, 19 I. & N. Dec. at 8.
132. *Id.* at 17 (dissenting opinion).
133. Toni M. Massaro, *Experts, Psychology, Credibility, and Rape: The Rape Trauma Syndrome Issue and Its Implications for Expert Psychological Testimony*, 69 MINN. L. REV. 395, 403 n.44 (1985).
134. A. Nicholas Groth, *Male Rape: Offenders and Victims*, 137 AM. J. PSYCHIATRY 806 (1980). The authors interviewed both male victims of rape and male perpetrators of male rape to investigate, *inter alia*, motives behind male rape. As with female rape, the driving concerns were violence and domination, not personal sexual gratification. Five motivational categories were established: 1) Conquest and control; 2) Revenge and retaliation; 3) Sadism and

average "macho" male, it is consistent with the mindset of those interested in torturing and degrading Homosexuals.

To support his thesis, Judge Colle set out to discredit the evidence of abuse reported in gay publications. He assumed that because the publications had a Homosexual focus, they have an inherent bias and were exaggerating the facts to suit their purposes.[135] Unfortunately, this is simply a sophisticated expression of homophobia. What Judge Colle was really saying is that not only was Inaudi unbelievable, but all Homosexuals are! Judge Colle also inferred that only the heterosexual press could discern an unbiased story. While it is true that gay publications focus on gay issues, they provide a different point of view. In further support of his conclusion that the abuse was fictitious, Judge Colle pointed out that none of the major human rights organizations, such as Amnesty International (AI), reported any persecution targeted toward Homosexuals.[136]

It is true that, at that time, AI had not reported human rights abuses perpetrated against Homosexuals. Until recently, it actively refused to do so. It was only in September 1991, that AI's Board agreed to add Homosexuals to their list of prisoners of conscience.[137] Human rights groups are not free from homophobia. It took seventeen years of debate to get the AI's Board to change its position.[138] For more conservative

---

degradation; 4) Conflict and counteraction; and 5) Status and affiliation (with peers in association with gang rape). *Id.* at 808. Only a minority of the rapists were identified as Homosexuals and for a majority of the rapists, the victim's gender was not pivotal. The authors wrote:

> Since rape is commonly misconstrued to be a sexually motivated crime, it is generally assumed that males are unlikely targets of such victimization, and that when it does occur, it reflects homosexual orientation on the part of the offender. However, the cases of male rape that we have had an opportunity to study do not lend much support to either assumption . . . The victim may symbolize what they want to control, punish and/or destroy, something they want to conquer and defeat. The assault is an act of retaliation, an expression of power, and an assertion of their strength or manhood.
>
> The selection of a male as a victim seemed even less significant than the choice of sex as the means of domination and retribution. Rape is a complex, multi-determined act prompted more by nonsexual than by sexual motives.
>
> As in the case of sexual assault of females, male rape (whether it occurs in the community or in an institutional setting) does not appear to be motivated primarily by the need for sexual gratification. Satisfaction and pleasure in male rape appear to be experienced in the sense of power, the discharge of anger, and the erotization of aggression more than in sexual acts. Offenders differ in their need for control. Some offenders wish to control, others to control and to degrade, still others to control, degrade, and destroy. Sex becomes an instrument of control, retaliation, degradation, and punishment.

Id. at 809. These observations clearly refute the naive assumption of Judge Colle that macho men would never rape other men.

135. *In re Inaudi*, 19 I. & N. Dec. at 13.

136. *Id.* at 18.

137. 2 TEMA INT'L 18 (1991).

138. However, since then Amnesty International has done considerable work in this field and has produced a document entitled BREAKING THE SILENCE: HUMAN RIGHTS VIOLATIONS BASED ON SEXUAL ORIENTATION. In that document AI explains why gay activists and anyone

groups, it would not even occur to them to ask the question. The real bias then is with the mainstream press that refuses to print anything on the abuse of Homosexuals.

I believe, however, that the basis of Judge Colle's confusion is the fact that Inaudi, after several terrorizing incidents with the police as a result of attending gay bars, still returned to gay bars. Judge Colle simply could not believe that anyone would go back if these acts continually occurred. "[I]t is inconceivable that the claimant would seek good times if in fact he would suffer ever increasing excruciating treatment with each eventful visit to a gay bar. He could be so worthwhile that he would put his life at risk."[139]

At first glance this seems like a reasonable question to ask. The problem is, again, the assumption that Inaudi was only going there for "good times." The society described by Inaudi and accepted by both judges is a terribly repressive, homophobic one. It is a society where even letting your landlord or employer know of your orientation will result in dire consequences. In situations such as this, gay bars are more than places to have "good times."

They are the only places where Homosexuals can meet, socialize, or dance. They are the places where Homosexuals can express themselves in a relatively safe environment—at least when they are not being raided. They are the places where Homosexuals can express themselves as a group or a community. Judge Colle apparently had no idea what it is like for someone to have to live almost every moment of their life covertly, always worrying about not being "found out." That type of life is terribly oppressive and most people trapped in that life desperately need a place like a gay bar where they can experience some level of acceptance. Even visiting one's friends and going to parties is done covertly. Going to a gay bar is much more than "good times." It is the basic human need for affirmation and acceptance that makes the risk worthwhile.

Finally, the dissent seemed to fault Inaudi for not going public with his abuse. Judge Colle suggested that Inaudi should have gone to the police or sought the help of the Canadian Health Association.[140] By this, Judge Colle was continuing to turn a blind eye to the repercussions of any of these activities. The one thing Inaudi never wanted to happen was to have his family find out about his sexual orientation. After his

---

prosecuted under sodomy laws now constitute prisoners of conscience and they review the history of persecution against Homosexuals. Several prisoners are also listed in the document as prisoners of conscience adopted by AI such as Mirel Ciprian Cucu and Milorad Mutascu of Romania who have been imprisoned for violating Romania's anti-sodomy law. AMNESTY INTERNATIONAL, BREAKING THE SILENCE: HUMAN RIGHTS VIOLATIONS BASED ON SEXUAL ORIENTATION (Feb. 1994).

139. *In re Inaudi*, 19 I. & N. Dec. at 16-17.

140. *Id.* at 15.

four days of torture, his family did find out and disowned him. By his own testimony, it was this final humiliation that drove him to leave Argentina.[141] Judge Colle seemed to be saying that this is just the price Inaudi had to pay for being a Homosexual.

V. CONCLUSION: CHARTING A COURSE FOR THE FUTURE

While this Canadian case is not precedential for the United States, it is possible to cite it as part of the emerging custom in international refugee law to recognize Homosexuals as refugees under the Convention, as have many recent cases in Europe.[142] I have included it here because of its value in charting the course for future asylum cases in the United States. I conclude that homophobia is at the root of the dissent in *In re Inaudi* and one will certainly encounter homophobia in domestic courts. In fact, overcoming the court's homophobia will probably be the biggest hurdle in proving persecution.

To be successful in a claim for refugee status, the alien must show first that Homosexuals constitute the requisite social group. Second, there must be documentation of the persecution by independent reports of similar abuse. Third, and most important, the alien must assume and then overcome the court's homophobia because of its effect on how the court views testimony.

In cases where homosexual activity is not illegal in the alien's country of origin, I believe the social group claim will be successful under either the *In re Acosta* standard or the *Sanchez-Trujillo* standard. For instance, in *In re Inaudi* there was no persecution for violating laws restricting homosexual conduct as the BIA argued in *In re Toboso*.[143] If there is an establishment of the social group then the claimant must show persecution.

The dissent in both *In re Toboso* and *In re Inaudi* found the claimants' testimonies regarding persecution unbelievable. Apart from a basic homophobia, both dissents found the supporting documentation of other cases of abuse too meager to support the claimants. Fortunately, as noted above, Amnesty International has begun to document abuses against Homosexuals, adopted prisoners of conscience, and published a document on abuses titled BREAKING THE SILENCE.[144] Judge Colle seemed to distrust publications by gay advocacy groups as biased and probably exaggerated.

---

141. *Id.* at 4.

142. *See* Parish, *supra* note 40, at 949-53. Time and space do not allow an exhaustive examination of other international cases.

143. *In re Toboso*, No. A23 220 664, at 2 (dissenting opinion). However, Judge Colle did try to argue that, once the torture and assault testimony was discredited, the treatment Inaudi received could only be described as the discriminatory application of laws banning public homosexual activity. *See In re Inaudi*, 19 I. & N. Dec. at 12-15 (dissenting opinion).

144. *See supra* note 138.

However, in many cases this will be the only source of corroboration that abuse occurs. It will be important to try to find as many different sources to document claims of abuse as possible. For example, the recently formed International Gay and Lesbian Human Rights Commission has been publishing country reports in its publication, TEMA INTERNATIONAL, along with names and addresses of contact groups in countries around the world. These groups may certainly be able to lend support.

However, it seems equally important to educate the bench regarding oppression in general, and how victims respond to it. It will be important in the future exhaustively to explain why closeted Homosexuals must risk going to gay bars even where the consequences can be catastrophic. Was Inaudi really going there just to have a good time? And what were his alternatives? Most likely the alternatives are cruising parks, bus stations and public bathrooms. The common view of these activities is that they are more egregious than attending gay bars, not less. Further, this activity is dangerous.

There have been recent reports that gay cruising areas of Griffith Park, in Los Angeles, are extremely dangerous, and there are reports of some deaths. Certainly gay bars appear safer than that. Not to mention that being forced to meet other Homosexuals under those conditions simply reinforces the public notion that homosexuality is bad and further degrades Homosexuals.

Homosexuals around the globe are struggling to create a safe, healthy place for themselves in their societies. This is a struggle for basic human rights. When they experience persecution for this struggle or just for being who they are, the Convention and the Refugee Act both invite them to seek refuge here in the United States. I have tried to show that our domestic law supports the claim of refugee status to Homosexuals based on persecution due to their membership in a particular social group. There is hope that we will see more and more success with this claim in our courts, as major international human rights organizations begin to document abuses abroad.[145]

---

145. Since this Article was first written, an immigration judge in the Ninth Circuit has granted asylum to a Brazilian man based solely on his persecution due to his sexual orientation. In re Tenorio, No. A72 093 558 (BIA July 26, 1993). The court focused on the *Sanchez-Trujillo* test and found that Homosexuals do constitute a social group under this test. *Id.* at 12. In making this determination, the court reviewed the findings of the Canadian court in *In re Inaudi*, finding both an immutable characteristic and voluntary association. *Id.* at 13. However, it has been reported that the INS is appealing this decision on the basis that 1) Homosexuals are not a persecuted group in Brazil; 2) the Brazilian government can protect Homosexuals from persecution; and 3) Homosexuals do not constitute a social group. 70 INTERPRETER RELEASES 1101 (Aug. 23, 1993). It will be important to follow this case through the BIA for its profound precedential value.

Richard Frank ADAMS and Anthony Corbett Sullivan, Plaintiffs-Appellants,

v.

Joseph D. HOWERTON, Acting District Director of the Immigration and Naturalization Service of the United States Department of Justice, Defendant-Appellee.

No. 80–5209.

United States Court of Appeals, Ninth Circuit.

Argued and Submitted Oct. 7, 1981.

Decided Feb. 25, 1982.

Certiorari Denied June 28, 1982. See 102 S.Ct. 3494.

Male American citizen and male alien who had been "married" by a minister in Colorado brought suit challenging decision of Board of Immigration Appeals affirming denial of petition for classification of alien as an immediate relative of an American citizen. The United States District Court for the Central District of California, Irving Hill, J., 486 F.Supp. 1119, held that homosexual marriage did not qualify alien as citizen's spouse pursuant to section of Immigration and Nationality Act, and plaintiffs appealed. The Court of Appeals, Wallace, Circuit Judge, held that: (1) a citizen's spouse within meaning of Act must be an individual of the opposite sex, and (2) statute, as so interpreted, was constitutional.

Affirmed.

Orvis v. Higgins, 180 F.2d 537, 539 (2d Cir.), *cert. denied*, 340 U.S. 810, 71 S.Ct. 37, 95 L.Ed. 595 (1950).

The view of this circuit, however, which is based on the history and purposes of Rule 52(a), is to the contrary. *See Lundgren v. Freeman*, 307 F.2d at 114. Moreover, deference to the judgment of the district court is warranted in this case, because the trial judge, with his special expertise in conducting trials, is in a better position to judge whether a defendant's behavior was outrageous or his motion for self-representation was made with the intent to delay the trial.

1. Aliens ⚿51½

Under Immigration and Nationality Act, two-step analysis is necessary to determine whether a marriage will be recognized for immigration purposes: first is whether marriage is valid under state law, and second is whether state-approved marriage qualifies under the Act; both steps are required. Immigration and Nationality Act, § 201(a, b) as amended 8 U.S.C.A. § 1151(a, b).

2. Aliens ⚿51½

Congress did not intend mere validity of marriage under state law to be controlling for immigration purposes under Immigration and Nationality Act. Immigration and Nationality Act, § 201(a, b) as amended 8 U.S.C.A. § 1151(a, b).

3. Aliens ⚿51½

Valid marriages entered into by parties not intending to live together as husband and wife are not recognized for immigration purposes, and thus even though two persons contract marriage, valid under state law, and even though they are recognized as spouses by that state, they are not necessarily spouses for purposes of Immigration and Nationality Act. Immigration and Nationality Act, §§ 101(a)(35), 201(b) as amended 8 U.S.C.A. §§ 1101(a)(35), 1151(b); C.R.S.1973, 14-2-104.

4. Aliens ⚿51½

Congress did not intend that homosexual marriages confer "spouse" status under section of Immigration and Nationality Act. Immigration and Nationality Act, § 201(b) as amended 8 U.S.C.A. § 1151(b).

See publication Words and Phrases for other judicial constructions and definitions.

5. Statutes ⚿219(1)

Where a statute has been interpreted by agency charged with its enforcement, courts are ordinarily required to accord substantial deference to that construction and should follow it unless there are compelling indications that it is wrong.

6. Marriage ⚿1

The term "marriage" ordinarily contemplates relationship between a man and a woman, and the term "spouse" commonly refers to one of the parties in a marital relationship so defined.

See publication Words and Phrases for other judicial constructions and definitions.

7. Statutes ⚿184, 205

Courts strive to interpret language in one section of a statute consistently with language of other sections and with the purposes of the entire statute considered as a whole.

8. Aliens ⚿40

Constitutional Law ⚿225.1, 274.3

Congress' decision to confer spouse status under Immigration and Nationality Act only upon parties to heterosexual marriages, has a rational basis and therefore comports with due process clause and its equal protection requirements. U.S.C.A. Const.Amends. 5, 14; Immigration and Nationality Act, § 201(b) as amended 8 U.S.C.A. § 1151(b).

9. Constitutional Law ⚿213(2)

Equal protection clause of Fourteenth Amendment applies only to the states and not to the federal government. U.S.C.A. Const.Amend. 14.

10. Aliens ⚿39

Congress has almost plenary power to admit or exclude aliens, and decisions of Congress are subject only to limited judicial review in this respect.

11. Aliens ⚿40

Where there is a rational basis for Congress' exercise of its power, whether articulated or not, court will uphold the immigration laws that Congress enacts.

David M. Brown, Robert A. DePiano, Brown, Weston & Sarno, Beverly Hills, Cal., for plaintiffs-appellants.

Dzintra I. Janavs, Asst. U. S. Atty., Los Angeles, Cal., argued, for defendant-appellee; Andrea Sheridan Ordin, U. S. Atty., Eva S. Halbreich, Asst. U. S. Atty., Los Angeles, Cal., on brief.

Appeal from the United States District Court for the Central District of California.

Before WALLACE and TANG, Circuit Judges, and TURRENTINE,* District Judge.

WALLACE, Circuit Judge:

Adams, a male American citizen, and Sullivan, a male alien, appeal from the district court's entry of summary judgment for Howerton, Acting District Director of the Immigration and Naturalization Service (INS). The district court held that their homosexual marriage did not qualify Sullivan as Adams's spouse pursuant to section 201(b) of the Immigration and Nationality Act of 1952, as amended (the Act), 8 U.S.C. § 1151(b). We affirm.

I

Following the expiration of Sullivan's visitor's visa, Adams and Sullivan obtained a marriage license from the county clerk in Boulder, Colorado, and were "married" by a minister. Adams then petitioned the INS for classification of Sullivan as an immediate relative of an American citizen, based upon Sullivan's alleged status as Adams's spouse. The petition was denied, and the denial was affirmed on appeal by the Board of Immigration Appeals. Adams and Sullivan then filed an action in district court challenging this final administrative decision on both statutory and constitutional grounds. The parties agreed that there was no genuine issue as to any material fact and that the only issues presented were issues of law. On cross-motions for summary judgment, the district court entered judgment for the INS. *Adams v. Howerton*, 486 F.Supp. 1119 (C.D.Cal.1980). This appeal followed.

II

Two questions are presented in this appeal: first, whether a citizen's spouse within the meaning of section 201(b) of the Act must be an individual of the opposite sex; and second, whether the statute, if so interpreted, is constitutional.

Section 201(a) of the Act establishes immigration quotas and a system of preferential admissions based upon the existence of close family relationships. The section excludes immediate relatives of United States citizens from the quota limitations, which have been periodically revised by Congress. 8 U.S.C. § 1151(a). Section 201(b) defines "immediate relatives" to include the spouses of United States citizens. 8 U.S.C. § 1151(b).[1] Section 201(b) was added to the Act in its present form by the Immigration and Nationality Act Amendments of 1965, Pub.L. No. 89-236, § 1, 79 Stat. 911. Neither that section nor any subsequent amendments further define the term "spouse" directly.

[1] Cases interpreting the Act indicate that a two-step analysis is necessary to determine whether a marriage will be recognized for immigration purposes. The first is whether the marriage is valid under state law. The second is whether that state-approved marriage qualifies under the Act. Both steps are required. *E.g., United States v. Sacco*, 428 F.2d 264, 270 (9th Cir.) (construing 8 U.S.C. §§ 1302, 1306(a), 1451(a), (e)), *cert. denied*, 400 U.S. 903, 91 S.Ct. 141, 27 L.Ed.2d 140 (1970). This same two-step analysis is appropriate under section 201(b). We first consider the validity of the marriage under state law.

In visa petition proceedings addressing this question, the Board of Immigration Appeals has held that the validity of a marriage is governed by the law of the

* Honorable Howard B. Turrentine, United States District Judge, Southern District of California, sitting by designation.

1. Section 201(b), 8 U.S.C. § 1151(b), provides: The 'immediate relatives' referred to in subsection (a) of this section shall mean the children, spouses, and parents of a citizen of the United States: *Provided*, That in the case of parents, such children must be at least twenty-one years of age. The immediate relatives specified in this subsection who are otherwise qualified for admission shall be admitted as such, without regard to the numerical limitations in this chapter.

place of celebration. *See In re Gamero*, 14 I. & N. Dec. 674 (B.I.A.1974). *See also Gee Chee On v. Brownell*, 253 F.2d 814, 817 (5th Cir. 1958). Because a valid marriage is necessary for spouse status under the immigration laws, *In re P.*, 4 I. & N. Dec. 610, 613 (B.I.A.1952), we look to Colorado law to determine whether the Adams-Sullivan marriage is valid.

Adams and Sullivan argue, in effect, that we need not reach this question because each is a putative spouse under Colorado law. They claim that they held a good faith belief that they were married. The district judge rejected this claim as without merit, observing that Adams and Sullivan could not have been without doubts concerning the validity of their marriage. 486 F.Supp. at 1123. We need not reach the issue. Even if Adams and Sullivan held a good faith belief that they were legally married, it is clear that the provisions of Colorado law they cite were enacted not to confer validity on the marriage of a putative spouse, but rather to protect property rights and insure support for children when the invalidity of such a marriage is discovered. *See* Colo.Rev.Stat. § 14-2-111 (1973).

It is not clear, however, whether Colorado would recognize a homosexual marriage. There are no reported Colorado cases on the subject. The Colorado Attorney General in an informal, unpublished opinion addressed to a member of the Colorado legislature three days after the alleged marriage in question occurred, stated that purported marriages between persons of the same sex are of no legal effect in Colorado. Colorado statutory law, however, neither expressly permits nor prohibits homosexual marriages. Some statutes appear to contemplate marriage only as a relationship between a male and a female. *See* Colo.Rev. Stat. § 14-2-104 (1973) ("Formalities. Marriage between a man and a woman, licensed, solemnized, and registered . . . is valid in this state.").

While we might well make an educated guess as to how the Colorado courts would decide this issue, it is unnecessary for us to do so.[2] We decide this case solely upon construction of section 201(b), the second step in our two-step analysis.

III

Even if the Adams-Sullivan marriage were valid under Colorado law, the marriage might still be insufficient to confer spouse status for purposes of federal immigration law. So long as Congress acts within constitutional constraints, it may determine the conditions under which immigration visas are issued. Therefore, the intent of Congress governs the conferral of spouse status under section 201(b), and a valid marriage is determinative only if Congress so intends.

[2, 3] It is clear to us that Congress did not intend the mere validity of a marriage under state law to be controlling. Although the 1965 amendments do not define the term "spouse," the Act itself limits the persons who may be deemed spouses. Section 101(a)(35) of the Act specifically provides that the term "spouse" does not include

> a spouse, wife, or husband by reason of any marriage ceremony where the contracting parties thereto are not physically present in the presence of each other, unless the marriage shall have been consummated.

2. Because we do not reach the question of whether Colorado law permits homosexual marriages, we need not examine the constitutionality of the statute. We observe, however, that an appeal challenging a Minnesota law which authorized heterosexual but not homosexual marriages was dismissed by the Supreme Court for want of a substantial federal question. *See Baker v. Nelson*, 291 Minn. 310, 191 N.W.2d 185 (1971), *appeal dismissed*, 409 U.S. 810, 93 S.Ct. 37, 34 L.Ed.2d 76 (1972), a case decided after *Loving v. Virginia*, 388 U.S. 1, 87 S.Ct. 1817, 18 L.Ed.2d 1010 (1967), but before *Zablocki v. Redhail*, 434 U.S. 374, 98 S.Ct. 673, 54 L.Ed.2d 618 (1978). "A summary dismissal by the Supreme Court of an appeal from a state court for want of a substantial federal question . . . operates as a decision on the merits." *Carpenters Pension Trust v. Kronschnabel*, 632 F.2d 745, 747 (9th Cir. 1980), *cert. denied*, 453 U.S. 922, 101 S.Ct. 3159, 69 L.Ed.2d 1004 (1981). *See Hicks v. Miranda*, 422 U.S. 332, 334, 95 S.Ct. 2281, 2284, 45 L.Ed.2d 223 (1975).

8 U.S.C. § 1101(a)(35). Furthermore, valid marriages entered into by parties not intending to live together as husband and wife are not recognized for immigration purposes. *Garcia-Jaramillo v. INS*, 604 F.2d 1236, 1238 (9th Cir. 1979), *cert. denied*, 449 U.S. 828, 101 S.Ct. 94, 66 L.Ed.2d 32 (1980); *Voliantis v. INS*, 352 F.2d 766 (9th Cir. 1965). *See also Lutwak v. United States*, 344 U.S. 604, 611, 73 S.Ct. 481, 486, 97 L.Ed. 593 (1953); *United States v. Sacco, supra*, 428 F.2d at 269–71. Therefore, even though two persons contract a marriage valid under state law and are recognized as spouses by that state, they are not necessarily spouses for purposes of section 201(b).

[4, 5] We thus turn to the question of whether Congress intended that homosexual marriages confer spouse status under section 201(b). Where a statute has been interpreted by the agency charged with its enforcement, we are ordinarily required to accord substantial deference to that construction, and should follow it "unless there are compelling indications that it is wrong." *New York Dept. of Social Services v. Dublino*, 413 U.S. 405, 421, 93 S.Ct. 2507, 2517, 37 L.Ed.2d 688 (1973); *Faulkner v. Watt*, 661 F.2d 809, 812 (9th Cir. 1981); *United States v. Standard Oil Co. of California*, 618 F.2d 511, 518 (9th Cir. 1980). Thus, we must be mindful that the INS, in carrying out its broad responsibilities, has interpreted the term "spouse" to exclude a person entering a homosexual marriage.

[6] While we do accord this construction proper weight, we base our decision primarily on the Act itself. *See Southeastern Community College v. Davis*, 442 U.S. 397, 411, 99 S.Ct. 2361, 2369, 60 L.Ed.2d 980 (1979); *Usery v. First Nat'l Bank of Arizona*, 586 F.2d 107, 111 (9th Cir. 1978). Nothing in the Act, the 1965 amendments or the legislative history suggests that the reference to "spouse" in section 201(b) was intended to include a person of the same sex as the citizen in question. It is "a fundamental canon of statutory construction" that, "unless otherwise defined, words will be interpreted as taking their ordinary, contemporary, common meaning." *Perrin v. United States*, 444 U.S. 37, 42, 100 S.Ct. 311, 314, 62 L.Ed.2d 199 (1979). *See Rhodes v. Republic Nat'l Life Ins. Co.*, 501 F.2d 1213, 1217 (9th Cir. 1974), *cert. denied*, 420 U.S. 928, 95 S.Ct. 1126, 43 L.Ed.2d 298 (1975). The term "marriage" ordinarily contemplates a relationship between a man and a woman. *See* Webster's Third New International Dictionary 1384 (1971); Black's Law Dictionary 876 (5th ed. 1979). The term "spouse" commonly refers to one of the parties in a marital relationship so defined. Congress has not indicated an intent to enlarge the ordinary meaning of those words. In the absence of such a congressional directive, it would be inappropriate for us to expand the meaning of the term "spouse" for immigration purposes. *Consumer Prods. Safety Comm'n v. GTE Sylvania, Inc.*, 447 U.S. 102, 108, 100 S.Ct. 2051, 2056, 64 L.Ed.2d 766 (1980). Our role is only to ascertain and apply the intent of Congress. *See, e.g., Lavin v. Marsh*, 644 F.2d 1378, 1381 (9th Cir. 1981); *Hughes Air Corp. v. Public Utilities Comm'n of California*, 644 F.2d 1334, 1337 (9th Cir. 1981).

[7] Our conclusion is supported by a further review of the 1965 amendments to the Act. These amendments not only added section 201(b) in its present form, but also amended the mandatory exclusion provisions of section 212(a) of the Act, 8 U.S.C. § 1182(a). Yet, both section 15(b) of the amendments, Pub.L. No. 89–236, § 15(b), 79 Stat. 911, 919 (codified at 8 U.S.C. § 1182(a)(4)), and the accompanying Senate Report, S.Rep. No. 748, 89th Cong., 1st Sess., *reprinted in*, [1965] U.S.Code Cong. & Ad.News 3328, 3343, clearly express an intent to exclude homosexuals. *See Boutilier v. INS*, 387 U.S. 118, 121, 87 S.Ct. 1563, 1565, 18 L.Ed.2d 661 (1967). As our duty is to ascertain and apply the intent of Congress, we strive to interpret language in one section of a statute consistently with the language of other sections and with the purposes of the entire statute considered as a whole. *Philbrook v. Glodgett*, 421 U.S. 707, 713, 95 S.Ct. 1893, 1898, 44 L.Ed.2d 525 (1975). We think it unlikely that Congress intended to give homosexual spouses preferential admission treatment under section 201(b) of the Act when, in the very same amendments adding that section, it mandated their exclusion. Reading these provisions together, we can only conclude that Congress intended that only partners in heterosexual marriages be considered spouses under section 201(b).

IV

[8-10] We next consider the constitutionality of the section 201(b) so interpreted. Adams and Sullivan contend that the law violates the equal protection clause[3] because it discriminates against them on the bases of sex and homosexuality. They also argue that review of this claimed violation must be pursuant to a strict standard because the federal law abridges their fundamental right to marry.[4] We need not and do not reach the question of the nature of the claimed right[5] or whether such a right is implicated in this case. Even if it were, we would not apply a strict scrutiny standard of review to the statute. Congress has almost plenary power to admit or exclude aliens, *see Fiallo v. Bell*, 430 U.S. 787, 792, 97 S.Ct. 1473, 1478, 52 L.Ed.2d 50 (1977); *Kleindienst v. Mandel*, 408 U.S. 753, 765–67, 92 S.Ct. 2576, 2583–84, 33 L.Ed.2d 683 (1972), and the decisions of Congress are subject only to limited judicial review. *Fiallo v. Bell, supra*, 430 U.S. at 792, 97 S.Ct. at 1478, *quoting Hampton v. Mow Sun Wong*, 426 U.S. 88, 101 n.21, 96 S.Ct. 1895, 1904 n.21, 48 L.Ed.2d 495 (1976).

In *Kleindienst v. Mandel*, the Supreme Court refused to balance the government's interest in excluding certain aliens against the first amendment interests of American citizens who sought to communicate with the excluded aliens. In reaching its decision, the Court stated:

> Recognition that First Amendment rights are implicated, however, is not dispositive of our inquiry here. In accord with ancient principles of the international law of nation-states, the Court in *The Chinese Exclusion Case*, 130 U.S. 581, 609 [9 S.Ct. 623, 631, 32 L.Ed. 1068] (1889), and in *Fong Yue Ting v. United States*, 149 U.S. 698 [13 S.Ct. 1016, 37 L.Ed. 905] (1893), held broadly . . . that the power to exclude aliens is 'inherent in sovereignty, necessary for maintaining normal international relations and defending the country against foreign encroachment and dangers—a power to be exercised exclusively by the political branches of government . . . .' Since that time, the Court's general reaffirmations of this principle have been legion. The Court without exception has sustained Congress' 'plenary power to make rules for the admission of aliens and to exclude those who possess those characteristics which Congress has forbidden.' *Boutilier v. Immigration and Naturalization Service*, 387 U.S. 118, 123 [87 S.Ct. 1563, 1567, 18 L.Ed.2d 661] (1967). '[O]ver no conceivable subject is the legislative power of Congress more complete than it is over' the admission of aliens. *Oceanic Navigation Co. v. Stranahan*, 214 U.S. 320, 339 [29 S.Ct. 671, 676, 53 L.Ed. 1013] (1909).

408 U.S. at 765–67, 92 S.Ct. 2583 (footnotes omitted). Thus, the Court has upheld the broad power of Congress to determine immigration policy in the face of challenges based upon the first amendment, *id.* (statu-

3. Technically, the challenge to this construction of section 201(b) is based upon the equal protection "component" of the fifth amendment's due process clause. *See Bolling v. Sharpe*, 347 U.S. 497, 74 S.Ct. 693, 98 L.Ed. 884 (1954). *See also Richardson v. Belcher*, 404 U.S. 78, 81, 92 S.Ct. 254, 257, 30 L.Ed.2d 231 (1971). The equal protection clause itself, a portion of the fourteenth amendment, applies only to the states, not the federal government.

4. Adams and Sullivan contend that the right to marry is an intrinsic part of a constellation of personal rights variously described as rights of privacy and as components of substantive due process.

5. In *Zablocki v. Redhail, supra*, a case involving a traditional heterosexual marriage, the Supreme Court stated that "the right to marry is of fundamental importance." 434 U.S. at 383, 98 S.Ct. at 679. *See also Loving v. Virginia, supra*, 388 U.S. at 12, 87 S.Ct. at 1824; *Skinner v. Oklahoma*, 316 U.S. 535, 541, 62 S.Ct. 1110, 1113, 86 L.Ed. 1655 (1942).

tory exclusion of individuals advocating world communism), the due process clause, *Boutilier v. INS, supra* (vague statutory language excluding homosexuals), as well as the equal protection component of fifth amendment due process and constitutionally-implied fundamental rights, *Fiallo v. Bell, supra*, 430 U.S. at 794, 97 S.Ct. at 1479 (discrimination based on sex and illegitimacy and denial of fundamental constitutional interests in family relationships). In *Fiallo v. Bell*, the Court observed "that in the exercise of its broad power over immigration and naturalization, 'Congress regularly makes rules that would be unacceptable if applied to citizens.'" *Id.* at 792, 97 S.Ct. at 1478, *quoting Mathews v. Diaz*, 426 U.S. 67, 80, 96 S.Ct. 1883, 1891, 48 L.Ed.2d 478 (1976). Explaining the "special judicial deference to congressional policy choices in the immigration context," *id.* at 793, 97 S.Ct. at 1479 (footnotes omitted), the Court stated:

> Policies pertaining to the entry of aliens and their right to remain here are peculiarly concerned with the political conduct of government. In the enforcement of these policies, the Executive Branch of the Government must respect the procedural safeguards of due process.... But that the formulation of these policies is entrusted exclusively to Congress has become about as firmly embedded in the legislative and judicial tissues of our body politic as any aspect of our government.

Id. at 792 n.4, 97 S.Ct. at 1478 n.4, *quoting Galvan v. Press*, 347 U.S. 522, 530–32, 74 S.Ct. 737, 743, 98 L.Ed. 911 (1954).

The scope of this very limited judicial review has not been further defined; the Supreme Court has not determined what limitations, if any, the Constitution imposes on Congress. Faced with numerous challenges to laws governing the exclusion of aliens and the expulsion of resident and non-resident aliens, the Court has consistently reaffirmed the power of Congress to legislate in this area.

[11] We do know that where there is a rational basis for Congress's exercise of its power, whether articulated or not, the Court will uphold the immigration laws that Congress enacts. *Hampton v. Mow Sun Wong, supra*, 426 U.S. at 103, 96 S.Ct. at 1905. *See also Fiallo v. Bell, supra*, 430 U.S. at 799, 97 S.Ct. at 1481. We do not know whether this test must be met to validate legislation such as section 201(b) of the Act because the Court teaches that we only have a limited judicial review. As observed earlier, in this area of the law, Congress has almost plenary power and may enact statutes which, if applied to citizens, would be unconstitutional. Thus, it is not clear what treatment a seemingly irrational statute should receive. It may well depend on the nature of the statute. The Court has suggested, in dicta, that a statute could be "so baseless as to be violative of due process and therefore beyond the power of Congress." *Galvan v. Press, supra*, 347 U.S. at 529, 74 S.Ct. at 742. On the other hand, the Court has not dismissed the possibility that "there may be actions of the Congress with respect to aliens that are so essentially political in character as to be nonjusticiable." *Fiallo v. Bell, supra*, 430 U.S. at 793 n.5, 97 S.Ct. at 1478 n.5.

We need not, however, delineate the exact outer boundaries of this limited judicial review. We hold that Congress's decision to confer spouse status under section 201(b) only upon the parties to heterosexual marriages has a rational basis and therefore comports with the due process clause and its equal protection requirements. There is no occasion to consider in this case whether some lesser standard of review should apply.

Congress manifested its concern for family integrity when it passed laws facilitating the immigration of the spouses of some valid heterosexual marriages. This distinction is one of many drawn by Congress pursuant to its determination to provide some—but not all—close relationships with relief from immigration restrictions that might otherwise hinder reunification in this country. *See Fiallo v. Bell, supra*, 430 U.S. at 787, 97 S.Ct. at 1473, 52 L.Ed.2d 50. In effect, Congress has determined that preferential status is not warranted for the spouses of homosexual marriages. Perhaps this is because homosexual marriages never produce offspring, because they are not recognized in most, if in any, of the states, or because they violate traditional and often prevailing societal mores. In any event, having found that Congress rationally intended to deny preferential status to the spouses of such marriages, we need not further "probe and test the justifications for the legislative decision." *Id.* at 799, 97 S.Ct. at 1481.

We hold that section 201(b) of the Act is not unconstitutional because it denies spouses of homosexual marriages the preferences accorded to spouses of heterosexual marriages.

AFFIRMED.

Acknowledgments

Kelly, Linda. "Preserving the Fundamental Right to Family Unity: Championing Notions of Social Contract and Community Ties in the Battle of Plenary Power Versus Aliens' Rights," *Villanova Law Review* 41 (1996): 725–83. Reprinted with the permission of the *Villanova Law Review.*

Wu, Frank H. "The Limits of Borders: A Moderate Proposal for Immigration Reform," *Stanford Law and Policy Review* 7 (1996): 35–74. Reprinted with the permission of the Stanford Law School.

Scaperlanda, Michael. "Partial Membership: Aliens and the Constitutional Community," *Iowa Law Review* 81 (1996): 707–73. Reprinted with the permission of the *Iowa Law Review.*

Romero, Victor C. "Expanding the Circle of Membership by Reconstructing the 'Alien': Lessons from Social Psychology and the 'Promise Enforcement' Cases," *University of Michigan Journal of Law Reform* 32 (1998): 1–47. Reprinted with the permission of the University of Michigan Law School.

Johnson, Kevin R. "Race, the Immigration Laws, and Domestic Race Relations: A 'Magic Mirror' into the Heart of Darkness," *Indiana Law Journal* 73 (1998): 1111–1159. Copyright 1998 by the Trustees of Indiana University. Reprinted by permission.

LAVAS v. *Dept. of State,* 45 F.3d 469 (D.C. Cir. 1995). Reprinted with the permission of the West Publishing Company.

LAVAS v. *Dept. of State,* 104 F.3d 1349 (D.C. Cir. 1997). Reprinted with the permission of the West Publishing Company.

Fitzpatrick, Joan. "The Gender Dimension of U.S. Immigration Policy," *Yale Journal of Law and Feminism* 9 (1997): 23–49. Reprinted with the permission of the *Yale Journal of Law and Feminism.*

Miller v. *Albright,* 118 S.Ct. 1428-64 (1998). Reprinted with the permission of the West Publishing Company.

Note, "Leading Cases: Constitutional Law: Equal Protection," *Harvard Law Review* 112 (1998): 202–12. Copyright 1998 by the Harvard Law Review Association.

McGoldrick, Brian J. "United States Immigration Policy and Sexual Orientation: Is Asylum for Homosexuals a Possibility?" *Georgetown Immigration Law* Journal 8 (1994): 201-26. Reprinted with the permission of the Georgetown

University Law Center.

Adams v. *Howerton,* 673 F.2d 1036–43 (9th Cir. 1982). Reprinted with the permission of the West Publishing Company.

For Product Safety Concerns and Information please contact our EU
representative GPSR@taylorandfrancis.com
Taylor & Francis Verlag GmbH, Kaufingerstraße 24, 80331 München, Germany

www.ingramcontent.com/pod-product-compliance
Ingram Content Group UK Ltd.
Pitfield, Milton Keynes, MK11 3LW, UK
UKHW040102200926
475702UK00001B/14
* 9 7 8 0 8 1 5 3 4 0 6 0 7 *